Documents of
American Prejudice

Documents of American Prejudice

An Anthology of Writings on Race from
Thomas Jefferson to David Duke

edited by
S. T. Joshi

Foreword by Derrick Bell

A Member of the Perseus Books Group

Published by Basic Books, A Member of the Perseus Books Group

Library of Congress Cataloging-in-Publication Data
Documents of American prejudice : an anthology of writings on race
from Thomas Jefferson to David Duke / [compiled by] S. T. Joshi.
    p. cm.
  Includes bibliographical references (p.) and index.
  ISBN 0-465-01624-3
1. United States—Race relations—Sources. 2. United States—
Ethnic relations—Sources. 3. Racism—United States—History—
Sources. I. Joshi, S. T., 1958–   .
E184.A1D64   1998
305.8'00973—dc21   98-31638
                                                                    CIP

Design by Heather Hutchison

10   9   8   7   6   5   4   3   2   1

To my mother
Padmini Tryambak Joshi

Contents

Foreword:
Healing
Branches on a
Tainted Tree

DERRICK BELL[1]

I AM NOT SURE MY HARD-WORKING PARENTS or family members knew about any of the racist tracts republished in *Documents of American Prejudice*, but then they didn't need to read about what they experienced every day. There were few, if any, Jim Crow signs when I grew up in Pittsburgh during the 1930s and 1940s, but every black person knew where they could not go to eat, or dance, or swim. They knew the neighborhoods where they had to reside, and they filled the low-paying, dead-end, "nigger work" jobs reserved for persons like themselves. Racial subordination with varying dollops of overt bias marked their lives in indelible ways that they could survive but never overcome.

Even back then, though, my mother was able to bring a measure of encouragement to despairing dinner discussions of racist practices with the reminder: "If there were no good white people, all we black folks would be dead." On the national scene, she could refer to Eleanor Roosevelt. Closer to home there was the friendly Jewish grocer who extended credit as needed, the wealthy white family who helped and encouraged my uncle in his desire to study medicine, and some few whites with whom our dealings were marked by courtesy and at least the outer trappings of respect.

As a youngster, my mother's words provided me with a libation of nurturing hope with which to face the utterly hostile world my family and their friends described with such bitter resignation. Now, as an adult with forty years of professional civil rights work behind me, I have a wealth of experience that supports my mother's belief that our survival as a people was due in part to the fact that not all whites feed their sense of superiority by actions intended to keep blacks and other vulnerable minorities in their subordinate place. I also have plenty of personal proof of just how pernicious and resilient racism is.

Because so many Americans either never learned or have easily suppressed much of the less praiseworthy aspects of our history, S. T. Joshi's compilation of historic and more contemporary documents about prejudice offers both a timely and convenient source for views on race, religion, and aliens once widely held and openly embraced. Significantly, his selections of prejudice from the blatant to the subtle are not the utterances of unlettered workers or unthinking bigots. Rather, this harvest of hate issued from the mouths and pens of leaders in science, politics, and law.

Yes, these statements were made. There can be no denying them. What may be more difficult to discern from the text is why they were made and what purposes they served. What, for example, prompted Thomas Jefferson (p. 3) to take his minuscule knowledge about both Africans and Native Americans and combine it with outlandish speculation so as to conclude that those persons of color Europeans found here were more human than the Africans kidnapped and forced here from their homeland? The Indians, even as Jefferson mused about them, were being wiped out in order to obtain their land. And the Africans, for whom he could find nothing positive to say, were a people who, having survived the dreaded Middle Passage, were condemned for life to a particularly brutal slavery. How, one wonders, does Jefferson reason that whites capable of such savagery issue from a higher breed?

In so many of the documents, the reader finds a similar assumption that white dominance is the result of a higher intelligence, a more advanced civilization that is, nevertheless, capable of the most brutal and bloody behavior. There is no acknowledgment that the peoples they oppress and now demean were subdued by force of superior arms, not by a more developed humanity. Self-righteousness of this character is particularly pernicious precisely because it blinds those in power to the enormity of their sins.

One thing is clear: in the times when they were expressed, the racist, anti-Semitic, nativist, and anti-immigration views contained in these documents affirmed rather than challenged the general view of white superiority. The expression of views that demeaned, distanced, and diminished people of color, Jews, and recent immigrants, reflected and reinforced what a clear majority of American whites believed, many fervently. Much of the populace welcomed the reaffirmation of their personal prejudices from sources readily deemed authoritative.

And why not? From colonial times, poor and working-class whites have identified with their more powerful brethren on the basis of racial connections. Historian Edmond Morgan in *American Slavery, American Freedom* (1975) explains that plantation owners convinced whites, most of whom were formerly indentured servants, to ignore their economic interests and support slavery even though without land or the wealth to purchase slaves, they could never compete with those who had both.

The rationale: because they were both white, the lower classes must stand with the rich against the threat of slave revolts or escapes. For reasons that defy logic and common sense, poor whites identified with the rich slave owners. They came to hate the slaves rather than their masters who held both black slave and free white in economic bondage. Advocates who urged the abolition of slavery ran into serious and sometimes deadly opposition, often from whites who would benefit economically if they did not have to compete with enslaved labor. Even when slavery ended, the willingness of poorer whites to identify on the basis of race with their better-off counterparts across a great class divide continued despite its clear economic and political costs.

During the latter half of the nineteenth century, this by now well-developed shared feeling of superiority to blacks was one of the few things that united a nation filled with immigrants, themselves horribly exploited by the mine and factory owners for whom they tolled long hours under brutal conditions for subsistence wages. Many of these immigrants were far more recent arrivals than the blacks they mocked. Even so, rather than uniting across racial lines to resist the exploitation and deprivation that both suffered, immigrants flocked to the blackface and racially derogatory minstrel shows of that period, an activity that not only entertained but helped them acculturate and assimilate by inculcating a nationalism whose common theme was the disparagement and disadvantaging of blacks.

The historic patterns, regrettably, tend to survive in the present. The ideology of whiteness continues to oppress whites as well as people of color. It is employed to make whites settle for despair in politics and anguish in the daily grind of life. Unfortunately, the attractions of whiteness afflict as well peoples of color, including some African Americans. All confuse their real interests with the sense that identification with those in power is the key to acceptance and success.

Today, of course, most white people reject the rabid positions contained in these documents. With much sincerity and no little pride, they deny any prejudice against minorities, Jews, or recent immigrants. Many

would point out that they work with, live near, and are friendly with minorities. What many do not recognize, however, is that as Professor
Beverly Daniel Tatum points out, racism is a system of advantage based
on race that benefits all whites whether or not they seek it.[2] In America,
whites are not simply in the majority, they hold most positions of power,
they own much of the wealth, and set most of the nation's policies. They
are for all of these reasons the norm.

As a result, many do not consider themselves as white, but simply normal. They do not recognize that their whiteness provides a wide range of
presumptions that people of color may earn, but simply cannot take for
granted. As Americans we want to believe that our country is a meritocracy where anyone who has talent and works hard can be successful.
Charges of racial discrimination threaten that image and, in all but the
most blatant cases, many whites find it difficult to take them seriously.
Thus, when blacks claim that racism is alive and flourishing, whites find
denial is the easier, the more comforting, route.

Inaccurate assertions like those by Dinesh D'Souza (p. 37), that racism
is no more, are welcomed, even hailed, because they serve as a connection across economic and other lines, with whites using as adhesive the
commonality of their resentment of blacks, a resentment that blinds
them to their class disadvantages. As it did during colonial time, racial
denial and resentment, particularly when fueled by economic anxiety, is a
combustible formula for the racial conflict that is the apparent goal of
those who currently use radio talk shows and the Internet to spout hate-
ful racial rhetoric as vicious as anything in these documents.

True to my mother's observation, the good white people have not remained silent during this turbulent time in our racial history. A crusade
to diminish race as a basis of privilege and priority is already under way.
There are many white, anti-racist groups who are meeting and taking action to reduce the dangers and disadvantages of using whiteness as a
measure of worth, a standard of normality. Consider, for example, the
publication, *Race Traitor*, a journal published in Cambridge, Massachusetts, whose editors utilize it as a source of information and encouragement for whites and others seeking to abolish the white race and
serve as advocates of the human race.[3]

There are an increasing number of college courses and conferences
studying the phenomenon of whiteness, its benefits, its costs, and its possible cures. At one such conference held at a University of California
campus, Professor Michael Omi, one of the conference's faculty spon-
sors, said in response to criticism of the event: "There's a growing interest in expanding the study of race to address whiteness, which was at

previous times transparent. We hope as a political consequence to bring to the forefront what white identity and politics are to make comprehensive links for groups that are trying to challenge racism."[4]

The chasm of difference in racial perspective discussed by Professor Alan Dershowitz (p. 349) in the context of the O. J. Simpson case remains, but there are more and more whites who because of their contacts with people of color in a wide variety of work and social situations are able to recognize the advantages of whiteness for those who have it and sense the difficulties faced by those who don't.

Sociologist Howard Winant observes that U.S. society was once a nearly monolithic racial hierarchy, and while white power and privilege continue, racial identity and status are no longer identical. Indeed, even the determination of race by blood no longer makes sense—if it ever did. Most blacks have "white blood" and tens of millions of whites have "black blood." When you consider the intermixture of Latinos, Native Americans, and Asian Americans both in this country and across the centuries, we are far more one people than our continuing racial conflicts would suggest.[5] The steady increase in interracial marriages and adoptions reflect the growing number of our citizens who are making the most sacred commitments across racial lines.

If we rely on history as a basis for prediction, then the seeming priority of whiteness will continue to play a key stabilizing role, and those whites working to eliminate prejudice against the disadvantaged in our society will fight a losing but no less necessary battle. Their primary goal, though, will not be the elimination of prejudice, an elusive victory that may never be attained, but rather the maintenance through word and deed of an opposition that will enable mothers like mine to retain a faith that their world is not all evil—that there are some good white folks out there.

Introduction

THE DOCUMENTS INCLUDED in this volume testify to the pervasiveness of racial prejudice existing in this country from its beginnings as a British colony in the seventeenth century to the present day. The central point this book seeks to make is not merely that individuals and entire groups have been prejudiced throughout this country's history, but that blatant prejudice—bolstered by "scientific" and "historical" theories—has been a dominant feature of *public discourse* in America. Historians, sociologists, philosophers, political scientists, literary figures, and businessmen have exhibited racial prejudice in a variety of ways, ranging from assertions of the superiority or inferiority of given races to the utterance of broad generalizations and stereotypes regarding a wide range of ethnic groups, including immigrants. Their views were supported and implemented by policymakers—including presidents, congressmen, governors, and judges—who codified their prejudices in laws and court decisions such as those restricting immigration and enforcing segregation.

To say that racial prejudice is as old as human civilization is neither to excuse its existence nor to assert that it is somehow endemic to society. Prejudice can be found in the writings of the Egyptians, Indians, Chinese, Jews, Greeks, Romans, and other ancient peoples; but its scope and direction appear to have been widely different from the prejudice exhibited in the European and American civilizations of the eighteenth through twentieth centuries. When Herodotus deemed all non-Greek-speaking people "barbarians," he was reflecting a belief common to the Greeks that the barbarians were linguistically incomprehensible (they uttered sounds that the Greeks could only interpret as "bar-bar-bar . . . ") and, secondarily, culturally incompatible. The notion of a *biological* difference between the barbarians and themselves seemed alien to their thinking. During the Renaissance, racial prejudice flowered sporadically during the "Age of Exploration," as explorers came upon people of widely differing types and brought back fantastic accounts of their appearance and behavior; but prejudice was largely submerged in simple curiosity, and the thirst for these travelers' narratives was consuming. Racial prejudice in its modern form first emerged during the Enlightenment and reached its height during the latter half of the nineteenth and the early decades of the twentieth centuries.

It is not my purpose, either in this brief introduction or in the introductory notes to the twelve sections of this book, to give a comprehensive account of racial prejudice in America, a vast subject that has produced an entire library of scholarly work.[1] Instead, I seek to present here a wide sampling of writings—mostly by Americans, but some by Europeans who had a significant influence on American thought—that address various facets of the conception of racial prejudice or focus specifically on those racial or ethnic groups who have historically suffered from prejudice in this country. Not every work contained in this book is necessarily racist; some selections clearly present arguments against racist beliefs, while others—especially among the more recent selections—have been accused of being racist and engendered considerable controversy thereby.

That such writings have largely disappeared from the mainstream press shows, at a minimum, that the prejudices espoused in earlier eras and reflected in many of the selections in this book are no longer given wide credence. Of course, it was not simply that the intelligentsia suddenly decided that expressing racial prejudice in print was no longer fashionable; instead, it required the gradual amassing of overwhelming evidence of the falsity of racial conceptions by a wide array of scientists and historians. The central intellectual figure in the downfall of racism was the anthropologist Franz Boas (1858–1942), whose relentless work over the first four decades of this century systematically demolished all the pseudo-scientific bases of racist thought. The Holocaust also revealed to many what would happen if racial or ethnic prejudice went beyond the mere bandying of words and was carried to its ultimate extreme.

To imagine, however, that there has been any kind of wholesale change of attitude on the part of those average citizens whose views never reach the public except in the form of isolated incidents or statistical surveys is more problematical. A recent news item reports that there are 474 hate groups functioning in the United States, ranging from paramilitary organizations to churches to rock groups.[2] The Internet has allowed anyone with minimal computer skills to establish his or her own website; and it is no surprise that racial hatred flourishes here. Racism may have gone "underground" in polite society, but it has resurfaced with a vengeance in the unfettered wilderness of the Internet.

There is always an advantage in exposing what Bertrand Russell called "intellectual rubbish," for, in the case of racial prejudice, it is remarkable to what degree this rubbish continues to be recycled in remarkably similar forms up to the present day. A systematic reading of this volume should reveal the long history of the use of code words that seem bland and unobjectionable on the surface but that are in fact highly inflammatory if their implications and ramifications are closely studied. When John O'Sullivan wrote in 1845 that it is "the common duty of Patriotism to the Country" to take Texas away from the Spaniards; when Theodore Roosevelt in 1889 spoke of the "winning of the West" as if the extermination of Native Americans were a kind of sporting event, we are perhaps not so far from the remarks of those politicians today who, having mastered the technique of doublespeak, speak of "our national heritage" or our "traditional values" in advocating measures against immigrants or minorities.

All this makes one more than skeptical of Dinesh D'Souza's claim regarding the "end of racism." Paradoxically, D'Souza appears to resurrect racial prejudice in another form by asserting the actual validity of prejudices and stereotypes:

> Prejudices and stereotypes merely reflect a human tendency to generalize from experience; they can only be refuted by showing that the group in question does not empirically possess the quality attributed to it. Since this is often difficult to show, we would do better to acknowledge the reality of group traits and ask how we should act on them.

D'Souza does not appear to be aware that the true injustice and falsity of stereotypes resides not merely in the many exceptions they yield, but in the unspoken assumption that what are termed "racial characteristics" are *intrinsic*—biologically, genetically hardwired into a given race or ethnic group. Stereotypes also relieve one from the burden of thinking—from the tedium of having to regard individuals as individuals, with their own distinctive traits of mind and character, rather than as part of a group whose purported characteristics can be casually summed up in a few offhand phrases.

I would like to end on a personal note. I was born in India but have lived in this country since the age of five. I have, accordingly, received my entire education here and as one who has devoted the bulk of his career to the criticism of English and American literature, I am as thoroughly assimilated an alien as any nativist could want. I have been, to my recollection, the victim of exactly one instance of prejudice—a seriocomic incident during the Iran hostage crisis of 1979 when I was mis-taken for an Arab. My interest in the phenomenon of racial prejudice is largely abstract and academic, and I am fascinated at the degree to which it has insinuated itself into the intellectual, social, and political history of this country. I would imagine that the overwhelming number of general readers are unfamiliar with the extent of racist writing (and this volume only reprints a fraction of it). Whether a careful reading of this book will persuade anyone to abandon racial prejudice is an open question; if it makes people more aware of racism's many forms, then its mission will have been served.

S. T. Joshi
New York City
April 1998

A Note on This Edition

THIS BOOK SEEKS TO PRESENT a wide-ranging selection of documents embodying or relating to racial prejudice in America from the seventeenth century to the present. The first six sections of the volume feature general overviews of the subject or significant branches of it; there follow five sections relating to prejudice directed against specific minority groups, followed by a concluding section on immigration. In each section, extracts are arranged chronologically by date of first publication. Both the size and the chronological scope of each section have been determined in accordance with the relative abundance of the material relating to it. As a result, some sections (for example, those on African Americans, Jews, and immigration) contain a great many selections and proceed down to the present day; in other cases, material is less abundant and ceases at a given chronological point (for example, the issue of manifest destiny, which became a moot point shortly after the turn of the century). I may note that I was refused permission to reprint certain recent works by the authors or copyright holders of the articles in question.

I have sought to present the documents with a minimum of intrusive editing. Accordingly, the original spelling, punctuation, and syntax of the documents have been generally preserved, even when these are now archaic, idiosyncratic, or in some cases actually erroneous. Most of the footnotes contained in the original texts, however, have been omitted, save those that are required for the identification of otherwise unattributed quotations. I have added a minimal number of my own notes when necessary; it would have been an endless task to correct all the scientific and other errors in these texts, so I have let them pass. I have attempted where possible to secure the first editions of the works in question. My introductory notes to the various sections and my headnotes to the individual extracts seek to provide some of the background information nec-

essary for the understanding of the selections; many of the issues, however, are of considerable complexity, and readers are referred to the bibliography at the rear of the volume for detailed discussions of the
subjects raised. That bibliography lists only a small fraction of the immense body of work on the overall issue of racial prejudice, focusing on
studies that specifically address the topics in question.

Most of my research was done at the New York Public Library (including the Jewish Division and the Schomburg Center for Research in
Black Culture), the New York University Library, and the Columbia
University Library. I am grateful to the staffs of these and other institutions for their courtesy and assistance. Mindi Rayner, Suzanne L. Stut-
tman, Scott D. Briggs, and others have aided me in numerous ways. My
editors, Richard Fumosa, Michelle Trader, and Tim Bartlett, deserve
special credit for the care and attention they have devoted in preparing
this book for publication.

PART ONE

Some Overviews

In this section will be found a variety of general discussions of the issue of racial prejudice in the United States, including such topics as the possibility of a "pure" race, the comparison of different races, and the validity of prejudices and stereotypes.

With the settlement of the North American continent, prejudices manifested themselves in a variety of ways. Each of the "civilized" colonizers (English, Dutch, Spanish) asserted their right to the "new" land on the strength of their intrinsic "superiority," whether in strength, intelligence, foresight, bravery, or some other fancied quality. Prejudice was more pronounced once the English had achieved military dominance and encountered the two "alien" races who would exercise the greatest fascination and contempt among the colonists over the coming decades and centuries—Native Americans and (with the introduction of slavery in Virginia in 1619) African Americans.

The contrasting views of the Native American and the African American found in Thomas Jefferson's *Notes on the State of Virginia* (1785) are illuminating. Jefferson detects in the former the rudiments of "civilization" that may one day parallel that of *Homo sapiens Europaeus*, but finds very little good to say of the latter ("I advance it, therefore, as a suspicion only, that the blacks, whether originally a distinct race, or made distinct by time and circumstances, are inferior to the whites in the endowments both of body and mind"). Jefferson may well have been led by national (or, should we say, continental?) pride to defend the native products of his adopted land; African slaves, as an "alien" importation, need not be encompassed within his North American patriotism. The

1

French traveler Alexis de Tocqueville had no such bias to nurture, and his poignant depiction of the two oppressed groups is encapsulated by his vignette of the little white girl with her unmistakable "consciousness of superiority" over her Native American and African American attendants. Contrast this again with Oliver Wendell Holmes's bland assertion in 1855 that the Native American is merely a "half-filled outline of humanity" who needs to be replaced by the white man, "a picture of manhood a little more like God's own image."

Later in the nineteenth century, racists were forced to come to terms with the issue of whether any "pure" race existed at all. The whole history of human migration, conquest, and intermixture would seem to militate against such a view, and as early as 1856 Emerson, in *English Traits*, was issuing a warning on the point ("though we flatter the self-love of men and nations by the legend of pure races, all our experience is of the gradation and resolution of races, and strange resemblances meet us everywhere"). But voices like this were drowned out by more strident tones from the other side. The most notorious work on this subject is Houston Stewart Chamberlain's *Foundations of the Nineteenth Century* (1899), written by an Englishman who migrated to Germany and wrote his treatise in German. To Chamberlain, every feature of human activity comes down to race, and he scoffs at those who would assert that the very word "race" has no meaning. The importance of race is so self-evident, Chamberlain seems to be saying, that we hardly need scientific evidence to justify it.

And yet, Chamberlain's comment that "race lifts a man above himself" is unwittingly on target, although scarcely in the way he intended: the consciousness of one's fancied racial "superiority" can be a crucial psychological shield against the gnawing sense of one's intrinsic unworth. Transferring this psychological crutch to the realm of politics, Madison Grant's best-selling *The Passing of the Great Race* (1916) condemns democracy as a political theory whereby the "lower types" gain ascendancy over "a picked minority" who ought to be the true rulers of society.

1

Notes on the State of Virginia

BY THOMAS JEFFERSON

The racial views of Thomas Jefferson (1743–1826), principal author of the Declaration of Independence, vice president under James Madison (1797–1801), and third president of the United States (1801–09), have long been a matter of debate. Here was a man who asserted that "all men are created equal" and who publicly opposed slavery and favored emancipation, but who also owned between one hundred and two hundred slaves on his own Virginia estate and in all likelihood had a long-term affair with one of them, Sally Hemings. Jefferson's most detailed exposition of his views is found in his celebrated monograph Notes on the State of Virginia, *written in 1781–82 as responses to queries sent to him by the Marquis de Barbé-Marbois and published in 1785, while Jefferson was in Paris as minister to France. The radically different way in which Native Americans and African Americans are discussed in the treatise is noteworthy; the relative praise of the former may (in the words of Jefferson's biographer Dumas Malone) have been intended to "demonstrate the excellence of what was native to America." For Jefferson's later modification of his views on African Americans see chapter 44.*

O F THE INDIAN OF SOUTH AMERICA I know nothing; for I would not honor with the appellation of knowledge, what I derive from the fables published of them. These I believe to be just as true as the fables of Æsop. This belief is founded on what I have seen of man, white, red, and black, and what has been written of him by authors, enlightened themselves, and writing among an enlightened people. The Indian of North America being more within our reach, I can speak of him somewhat from my own knowledge, but more from the information of others better acquainted with him, and on whose truth and judgment I can rely. From these sources I am able to say, in contradiction to this representation, that he is neither more defective in ardor, nor more impotent with his female, than the white reduced to the same diet and exercise; that he is brave, when an enterprise depends on bravery; education with him making the point of honor consist in the destruction of an enemy by stratagem, and in the preservation of his own person free from injury; or, perhaps, this is nature, while it is education which teaches us to honor force more than finesse; that he will defend himself against a host of enemies, always choosing to be killed, rather than to surrender, though it be to the whites, who he knows will treat him well; that in other situations, also, he meets death with more deliberation, and endures tortures with a firmness unknown almost to religious enthusiasm with us; that he is affectionate to his children, careful of them, and indulgent in the extreme; that his affections comprehend his other connections, weakening, as with us, from circle to circle, as they recede from the centre; that his friendships are strong and faithful to the uttermost extremity; that his sensibility is keen, even the warriors weeping most bitterly on the loss of their children, though in general they endeavor to appear superior to human events; that his vivacity and activity of mind is equal to ours in the same situation; hence his eagerness for hunting, and for games of chance. The women are submitted to unjust drudgery. This I believe is the case with every barbarous people. With such, force is law. The stronger sex imposes on the weaker. It is civilization alone which replaces women in the enjoyment of their natural equality. That first teaches us to subdue the selfish passions, and to respect those rights in others which we value in ourselves. Were we in equal barbarism, our females would be equal drudges. The man with them is less strong than with us, but their women stronger than ours; and both for the same obvious reason; because our man and their woman is habituated to labor, and formed by it. With both races the sex which is indulged with ease is the least athletic. An Indian man is small in the hand and wrist, for the same reason for which a sailor is large and strong in the arms and shoulders, and a porter in the legs and thighs. They raise fewer children than we do. The causes of this are to be found, not in a difference of nature, but of circumstance. The women very frequently attending the men in their parties of war and of hunting, child-bearing becomes extremely inconvenient to them. It is said, therefore, that they have learned the practice of procuring abortion by the use of some vegetable; and that it even extends to prevent conception for a considerable time after. During these parties they are exposed to numerous hazards, to excessive exertions, to the greatest extremities of hunger. Even at their homes the nation depends for food, through a certain part of every year, on the gleanings of the forest; that is, they experience a famine once in every year. With all animals, if the female be badly fed, or not fed at all, her young perish; and if both male and female be reduced to like want, generation becomes less active, less productive. To the obstacles, then, of want and hazard, which nature has opposed to the multiplication of wild animals, for the purpose of restraining their numbers within certain bounds, those of labor and of voluntary abortion are added with the Indian. No wonder, then, if they multiply less than we do. Where food is regularly supplied, a single farm will show more of cattle, than a whole country of forests can of buffaloes. The same Indian women, when married to white traders, who feed them and their children plentifully and regularly, who exempt them from excessive drudgery, who keep them stationary and unexposed to accident, produce and raise as many children as the white women. Instances are known, under these circumstances, of their rearing a dozen children. An inhuman practice once prevailed in this country, of making slaves of the Indians. It is a fact well known with us, that the Indian women so enslaved produced and raised as numerous families as either the whites or blacks among whom they lived. It has been said that Indians have less hair than the whites, except on the head. But this is a fact of which fair proof can scarcely be had. With them it is disgraceful to be hairy on the body. They say it likens them to hogs. They therefore pluck the hair as fast as it appears. But the traders who marry their women, and prevail on them to discontinue this practice, say, that nature is the same with them as with the whites. Nor, if the fact be true, is the consequence necessary which has been drawn from it. Negroes have notoriously less hair than the whites; yet they are more ardent. But if cold and moisture be the agents of nature for diminishing the races of animals, how comes she all at once to suspend their operation as to the physical man of the new world, whom the Count acknowledges to be "à peu près de même stature que l'homme de notre monde," and to let loose their influence on his moral faculties? How has this "combination of the elements and other physical causes, so contrary to the enlargement of animal nature in this new world, these obstacles to the development and formation of great germs,"[1] been arrested and suspended, so as to permit the human body to acquire its just dimensions, and by what inconceivable process has their action been directed on his mind alone? To judge of the truth of this, to form a just estimate of their genius and mental powers, more facts are wanting, and great allowance to be made for those circumstances of their situation which call for a display of particular talents only. This done, we shall probably find that they are formed in mind as well as in body, on the same module with the "Homo sapiens Europæus." The principles of their society forbidding all compulsion, they are to be led to duty and to enterprise by personal influence and persuasion. Hence eloquence in council, bravery and address in war, become the foundations of all consequence with them. To these acquirements all their faculties are directed. Of their bravery and address in war we have multiplied proofs, because we have been the subjects on which they were exercised. Of their eminence in oratory we have fewer examples, because it is displayed chiefly in their own councils. Some, however, we have, of very superior lustre. . . .

Before we condemn the Indians of this continent as wanting genius, we must consider that letters have not yet been introduced among them. Were we to compare them in their present state with the Europeans, north of the Alps, when the Roman arms and arts first crossed those mountains, the comparison would be unequal, because, at that time, those parts of Europe were swarming with numbers; because numbers produce emulation, and multiply the chances of improvement, and one improvement begets another. Yet I may safely ask, how many good poets, how many able mathematicians, how many great inventors in arts or sciences, had Europe, north of the Alps, then produced? And it was sixteen centuries after this before a Newton could be formed. I do not mean to deny that there are varieties in the race of man, distinguished by their powers both of body and mind. I believe there are, as I see to be the case in the races of other animals. I only mean to suggest a doubt, whether the bulk and faculties of animals depend on the side of the Atlantic on which their food happens to grow, or which furnishes the elements of which they are compounded? Whether nature has enlisted herself as a Cis or Trans-Atlantic partisan? I am induced to suspect there has been more eloquence than sound reasoning displayed in support of this theory. . . .

Whether the black of the negro resides in the reticular membrane between the skin and scarf-skin, or in the scarf-skin itself; whether it proceeds from the color of the blood, the color of the bile, or from that of some other secretion, the difference is fixed in nature, and is as real as if its seat and cause were better known to us. And is this difference of no importance? Is it not the foundation of a greater or less share of beauty in the two races? Are not the fine mixtures of red and white, the expressions of every passion by greater or less suffusions of color in the one, preferable to that eternal monotony, which reigns in the countenances, that immovable veil of black which covers the emotions of the other race? Add to these, flowing hair, a more elegant symmetry of form, their own judgment in favor of the whites, declared by their preference of them, as uniformly as is the preference of the Oran-ûtan for the black woman over those of his own species. The circumstance of superior beauty, is thought worthy attention in the propagation of our horses, dogs, and other domestic animals; why not in that of man? Besides those of color, figure, and hair, there are other physical distinctions proving a difference of race. They have less hair on the face and body. They secrete less by the kidneys, and more by the glands of the skin, which gives them a very strong and disagreeable odor. This greater degree of transpiration, renders them more tolerant of heat, and less so of cold than the whites. Perhaps, too, a difference of structure in the pulmonary apparatus, which a late ingenious experimentalist has discovered to be the principal regulator of animal heat, may have disabled them from extricating, in the act of inspiration, so much of that fluid from the outer air, or obliged them in expiration, to part with more of it. They seem to require less sleep. A black after hard labor through the day, will be induced by the slightest amusements to sit up till midnight, or later, though knowing he must be out with the first dawn of the morning. They are at least as brave, and more adventuresome. But this may perhaps proceed from a want of forethought, which prevents their seeing a danger till it be present. When present, they do not go through it with more coolness or steadiness than the whites. They are more ardent after their female; but love seems with them to be more an eager desire, than a tender delicate mixture of sentiment and sensation. Their griefs are transient. Those numberless afflictions, which render it doubtful whether heaven has given life to us in mercy or in wrath, are less felt, and sooner forgotten with them. In general, their existence appears to participate more of sensation than reflection. To this must be ascribed their disposition to sleep when abstracted from their diversions, and unemployed in labor. An animal whose body is at rest, and who does not reflect must be disposed to sleep of course. Comparing them by their faculties of memory, reason, and imagination, it appears to me that in memory they are equal to the whites; in reason much inferior, as I think one could scarcely be found capable of tracing and comprehending the investigations of Euclid; and that in imagination they are dull, tasteless, and anomalous. It would be unfair to follow them to Africa for this investigation. We will consider them here, on the same stage with the whites, and where the facts are not apocryphal on which a judgment is to be formed. It will be right to make great allowances for the difference of condition, of education, of conversation, of the sphere in which they move. Many millions of them have been brought to, and born in America. Most of them, indeed, have been confined to tillage, to their own homes, and their own society; yet many have been so situated, that they might have availed themselves of the conversation of their masters; many have been brought up to the handicraft arts, and from that circumstance have always been associated with the whites. Some have been liberally educated, and all have lived in countries where the arts and sciences are cultivated to a considerable degree, and all have had before their eyes samples of the best works from abroad. The Indians, with no advantages of this kind, will often carve figures on their pipes not destitute of design and merit. They will crayon out an animal, a plant, or a country, so as to prove the existence of a germ in their minds which only wants cultivation. They astonish you with strokes of the most sublime oratory; such as prove their reason and sentiment strong, their imagination glowing and elevated. But never yet could I find that a black had uttered a thought above the level of plain narration; never saw even an elementary trait of painting or sculpture. In music they are more generally gifted than the whites with accurate ears for tune and time, and they have been found capable of imagining a small catch. Whether they will be equal to the composition of a more extensive run of melody, or of complicated harmony, is yet to be proved. Misery is often the parent of the most affecting touches in poetry. Among the blacks is misery enough, God knows, but no poetry. Love is the peculiar œstrum of the poet. Their love is ardent, but it kindles the senses only, not the imagination. Religion, indeed, has produced a Phyllis Whately; but it could not produce a poet.[2] The compositions published under her name are below the dignity of criticism. The heroes of the Dunciad are, to her, as Hercules to the author of that poem. Ignatius Sancho has approached nearer to merit in composition; yet his letters do more honor to the heart than the head. They breathe the purest effusions of friendship and general philanthropy, and show how great a degree of the latter may be compounded with strong religious zeal. He is often happy in the turn of his compliments, and his style is easy and familiar, except when he affects a Shandean fabrication of words. But his imagination is wild and extravagant, escapes incessantly from every restraint of reason and taste, and, in the course of its vagaries, leaves a tract of thought as incoherent and eccentric, as is the course of a meteor through the sky. His subjects should often have led him to a process of sober reasoning; yet we find him always substituting sentiment for demonstration. Upon the whole, though we admit him to the first place among those of his own color who have presented themselves to the public judgment, yet when we compare him with the writers of the race among whom he lived and particularly with the epistolary class in which he has taken his own stand, we are compelled to enrol him at the bottom of the column. This criticism supposes the letters published under his name to be genuine, and to have received amendment from no other hand; points which would not be of easy investigation. The improvement of the blacks in body and mind, in the first instance of their mixture with the whites, has been observed by every one, and proves that their inferiority is not the effect merely of their condition of life. We know that among the Romans, about the Augustan age especially, the condition of their slaves was much more deplorable than that of the blacks on the continent of America. The two sexes were confined in separate apartments, because to raise a child cost the master more than to buy one. Cato, for a very restricted indulgence to his slaves in this particular, took from them a certain price. But in this country the slaves multiply as fast as the free inhabitants. Their situation and manners place the commerce between the two sexes almost without restraint. The same Cato, on a principle of economy, always sold his sick and superannuated slaves. He gives it as a standing precept to a master visiting his farm, to sell his old oxen, old wagons, old tools, old and diseased servants, and everything else become useless. "Vendat boves vetulos, plaustrum vetus, feramenta vetera, servum senem, servum morbosum, et si quid aliud supersit vendat." Cato de re rustica, c. 2. The American slaves cannot enumerate this among the injuries and insults they receive. It was the common practice to expose in the island Æsculapius, in the Tyber, diseased slaves whose cure was like to become tedious. The emperor Claudius, by an edict, gave freedom to such of them as should recover, and first declared that if any person chose to kill rather than to expose them, it should not be deemed homicide. The exposing them is a crime of which no instance has existed with us; and were it to be followed by death, it would be punished capitally. We are told of a certain Vedius Pollio, who, in the presence of Augustus, would have given a slave as food to his fish, for having broken a glass. With the Romans, the regular method of taking the evidence of their slaves was under torture. Here it has been thought better never to resort to their evidence. When a master was murdered, all his slaves, in the same house, or within hearing, were condemned to death. Here punishment falls on the guilty only, and as precise proof is required against him as against a freeman. Yet notwithstanding these and other discouraging circumstances among the

Romans, their slaves were often their rarest artists. They excelled too in science, insomuch as to be usually employed as tutors to their master's children. Epictetus, Terence, and Phædrus, were slaves. But they were of the race of whites. It is not their condition, then, but nature, which has produced the distinction. Whether further observation will or will not verify the conjecture, that nature has been less bountiful to them in the endowments of the head, I believe that in those of the heart she will be found to have done them justice. That disposition to theft with which they have been branded, must be ascribed to their situation, and not to any depravity of the moral sense. The man in whose favor no laws of property exist, probably feels himself less bound to respect those made in favor of others. When arguing for ourselves, we lay it down as a fundamental, that laws, to be just, must give a reciprocation of right; that, without this, they are mere arbitrary rules of conduct, founded in force, and not in conscience; and it is a problem which I give to the master to solve, whether the religious precepts against the violation of property were not framed for him as well as his slave? And whether the slave may not as justifiably take a little from one who has taken all from him, as he may slay one who would slay him? That a change in the relations in which a man is placed should change his ideas of moral right or wrong, is neither new, nor peculiar to the color of the blacks. Homer tells us it was so two thousand six hundred years ago.

'Emisu, ger t' aretes apoainutai euruopa Zeus
Haneros, eut' an min kata doulion ema elesin.

                                                        Odd. 17, 323.

Jove fix'd it certain, that whatever day
Makes man a slave, takes half his worth away.

But the slaves of which Homer speaks were whites. Notwithstanding these considerations which must weaken their respect for the laws of property, we find among them numerous instances of the most rigid integrity, and as many as among their better instructed masters, of benevolence, gratitude, and unshaken fidelity. The opinion that they are inferior in the faculties of reason and imagination, must be hazarded with great diffidence. To justify a general conclusion, requires many observations, even where the subject may be submitted to the anatomical knife, to optical glasses, to analysis by fire or by solvents. How much more then where it is a faculty, not a substance, we are examining; where it eludes the research of all the senses; where the conditions of its existence are various and variously combined; where the effects of those which are present or absent bid defiance to calculation; let me add too, as a circumstance of great tenderness, where our conclusion would degrade a whole race of men from the rank in the scale of beings which their Creator may perhaps have given them. To our reproach it must be said, that though for a century and a half we have had under our eyes the races of black and of red men, they have never yet been viewed by us as subjects of natural history. I advance it, therefore, as a suspicion only, that the blacks, whether originally a distinct race, or made distinct by time and circumstances, are inferior to the whites in the endowments both of body and mind. It is not against experience to suppose that different species of the same genus, or varieties of the same species, may possess different qualifications. Will not a lover of natural history then, one who views the gradations in all the races of animals with the eye of philosophy, excuse an effort to keep those in the department of man as distinct as nature has formed them? This unfortunate difference of color, and perhaps of faculty, is a powerful obstacle to the emancipation of these people. Many of their advocates, while they wish to vindicate the liberty of human nature, are anxious also to preserve its dignity and beauty. Some of these, embarrassed by the question, "What further is to be done with them?" join themselves in opposition with those who are actuated by sordid avarice only. Among the Romans emancipation required but one effort. The slave, when made free, might mix with, without staining the blood of his master. But with us a second is necessary, unknown to history. When freed, he is to be removed beyond the reach of mixture.

Source:
Thomas Jefferson, *Notes on the State of Virginia* (1785), in *The Writings of Thomas Jefferson,* edited by Albert Ellery Bergh (Washington, DC: Thomas Jefferson Memorial Association, 1905), vol. 2, pp. 81–87, 90–93, 192–201.

2

Democracy in America

BY ALEXIS DE TOCQUEVILLE

Alexis Charles Henri Maurice Clérel de Tocqueville (1805–1859) was a French historian and statesman who, with Gustave de Beaumont, traveled to America in 1831 to study the American prison system. Traversing the continent from Boston to New Orleans to Wisconsin, Tocqueville produced the monograph Du Système pénitentiare aux Etats-Unis et de son application en France *(1833); but he is now best known for what was originally a mere appendage to that work,* De la démocratie en Amérique, *published in two parts in 1835 and 1840.*

Democracy in America *was quickly translated into many languages. Because of the perspicacity of Tocqueville's observations on American political, social, and economic institutions, and because his account was written at so early a stage in the development of American democracy, his work has become a permanent classic of historical writing and remains an invaluable survey of American society of this period. In chapter 18 of part 1 of* Democracy in America, *Tocqueville offers a very different assessment of the relations between whites, African Americans, and Native Americans from that put forth by Jefferson.*

T HE TERRITORY NOW OCCUPIED or claimed by the American Union spreads from the shores of the Atlantic to those of the Pacific ocean. On the east and west its limits are those of the continent itself. On the south it advances nearly to the tropic, and it extends upward to the icy regions of the north.

The human beings who are scattered over this space do not form, as in Europe, so many branches of the same stock. Three races naturally distinct, and I might almost say hostile to each other, are discoverable among them at the first glance. Almost insurmountable barriers had been raised between them by education and by law, as well as by their origin and outward characteristics; but fortune has brought them together on the same soil, where, although they are mixed, they do not amalgamate, and each race fulfils its destiny apart.

Among these widely differing families of men, the first which attracts attention, the superior in intelligence, in power, and in enjoyment, is the white or European, the MAN pre-eminent; and in subordinate grades, the negro and the Indian. These two unhappy races have nothing in common; neither birth, nor features, nor language, nor habits. Their only resemblance lies in their misfortunes. Both of them occupy an inferior rank in the country they inhabit; both suffer from tyranny; and if their wrongs are not the same, they originate at any rate with the same authors.

If we reasoned from what passes in the world, we should almost say that the European is to the other races of mankind, what man is to the lower animals;—he makes them subservient to his use; and when he cannot subdue, he destroys them. Oppression has at one stroke deprived the descendants of the Africans of almost all the privileges of humanity. The negro of the United States has lost all remembrance of his country; the language which his forefathers spoke is never heard around him; he abjured their religion and forgot their customs when he ceased to belong to Africa, without acquiring any claim to European privileges. But he remains half-way between the two communities, sold by the one, repulsed by the other; finding not a spot in the universe to call by the name of country, except the faint image of a home which the shelter of his master's roof affords.

The negro has no family; woman is merely the temporary companion of his pleasures, and his children are upon an equality with himself from the moment of their birth. Am I to call it a proof of God's mercy, or a visitation of his wrath, that man in certain states appears to be insensible to his extreme wretchedness, and almost affects with a depraved taste the cause of his misfortunes? The negro, who is plunged in this abyss of evils, scarcely feels his own calamitous situation. Violence made him a slave, and the habit of servitude gives him the thoughts and desires of a slave; he admires his tyrants more than he hates them, and finds his joy and his pride in the servile imitation of those who oppress him: his understanding is degraded to the level of his soul.

The negro enters upon slavery as soon as he is born; nay, he may have been purchased in the womb, and have begun his slavery before he began his existence. Equally devoid of wants and of enjoyment, and useless to himself, he learns, with his first notions of existence, that he is the property of another who has an interest in preserving his life, and that the care of it does not devolve upon himself; even the power of thought appears to him a useless gift of Providence, and he quietly enjoys the privileges of his debasement.

If he becomes free, independence is often felt by him to be a heavier burden than slavery; for having learned, in the course of his life, to submit to everything except reason, he is too much unacquainted with her dictates to obey them. A thousand new desires beset him, and he is destitute of the knowledge and energy necessary to resist them: these are masters which it is necessary to contend with, and he has learned only to submit and obey. In short, he sinks to such a depth of wretchedness, that while servitude brutalizes, liberty destroys him.

Oppression has been no less fatal to the Indian than to the negro race, but its effects are different. Before the arrival of the white men in the New World, the inhabitants of North America lived quietly in their woods, enduring the vicissitudes, and practising the virtues and vices common to savage nations. The Europeans, having dispersed the Indian tribes and driven them into the deserts, condemned them to a wandering life full of inexpressible sufferings.

Savage nations are only controlled by opinion and by custom. When the North American Indians had lost their sentiment of attachment to their country; when their families were dispersed, their traditions obscured, and the chain of their recollections broken; when all their habits were changed, and their wants increased beyond measure, European tyranny rendered them more disorderly and less civilized than they were before. The moral and physical condition of these tribes continually grew worse, and they became more barbarous as they became more wretched. Nevertheless the Europeans have not been able to metamorphose the character of the Indians; and though they have had power to destroy them, they have never been able to make them submit to the rules of civilized society.

The lot of the negro is placed on the extreme limit of servitude, while that of the Indian lies on the uttermost verge of liberty; and slavery does not produce more fatal effects upon the first, than independence upon the second. The negro has lost all property in his own person, and he cannot dispose of his existence without committing a sort of fraud: but the savage is his own master as soon as he is able to act; parental authority is scarcely known to him; he has never bent his will to that of any of his kind, nor learned the difference between voluntary obedience and a shameful subjection; and the very name of law is unknown to him. To be free, with him, signifies to escape from all the shackles of society. As he delights in this barbarous independence, and would rather perish than sacrifice the least part of it, civilization has little power over him.

The negro makes a thousand fruitless efforts to insinuate himself among men who repulse him; he conforms to the taste of his oppressors, adopts their opinions, and hopes by imitating them to form a part of their community. Having been told from infancy that his race is naturally inferior to that of the whites, he assents to the proposition and is ashamed of his own nature. In each of his features he discovers a trace of slavery, and, if it were in his power, he would willingly rid himself of everything that makes him what he is.

The Indian, on the contrary, has his imagination inflated with the pretended nobility of his origin, and lives and dies in the midst of these dreams of pride. Far from desiring to conform his habits to ours, he loves his savage life as the distinguishing mark of his race, and he repels every advance to civilization, less perhaps from the hatred which he entertains for it, than from a dread of resembling the Europeans. While he has nothing to oppose to our perfection in the arts but the resources of the desert, to our tactics nothing but undisciplined courage; while our well-digested plans are met by the spontaneous instincts of savage life, who can wonder if he fails in this unequal contest?

The negro, who earnestly desires to mingle his race with that of the European, cannot effect it; while the Indian, who might succeed to a certain extent, disdains to make the attempt. The servility of the one dooms him to slavery, the pride of the other to death.

I remember that while I was travelling through the forests which still cover the state of Alabama, I arrived one day at the log-house of a pioneer. I did not wish to penetrate into the dwelling of the American, but retired to rest myself for a while on the margin of a spring, which was not far off, in the woods. While I was in this place (which was in the neighbourhood of the Creek territory), an Indian woman appeared, followed by a negress, and holding by the hand a little white girl of five or six years old, whom I took to be the daughter of the pioneer. A sort of barbarous luxury set off the costume of the Indian; rings of metal were hanging from her nostrils and ears; her hair, which was adorned with glass beads, fell loosely upon her shoulders; and I saw that she was not married, for she still wore the necklace of shells which the bride always deposits on the nuptial couch. The negress was clad in squalid European garments.

They all three came and seated themselves upon the banks of the fountain; and the young Indian, taking the child in her arms, lavished upon her such fond caresses as mothers give; while the negress endeavoured by various little artifices to attract the attention of the young creole. The child displayed in her slightest gestures a consciousness of superiority which formed a strange contrast with her infantine weakness; as if she received the attentions of her companions with a sort of condescension.

The negress was seated on the ground before her mistress, watching her smallest desires, and apparently divided between strong affection for the child and servile fear; while the savage displayed, in the midst of her tenderness, an air of freedom and of pride which was almost ferocious. I had approached the group, and I contemplated them in silence; but my curiosity was probably displeasing to the Indian woman, for she suddenly rose, pushed the child roughly from her, and giving me an angry look, plunged into the thicket.

I had often chanced to see individuals met together in the same place, who belonged to the three races of men which people North America. I had perceived from many different results the preponderance of the whites. But in the picture which I have just been describing there was something peculiarly touching; a bond of affection here united the oppressors with the oppressed, and the effort of Nature to bring them together rendered still more striking the immense distance placed between them by prejudice and by law.

Source:
Alexis de Tocqueville, *De la Démocratie en Amérique* (1835–40), translated by Henry Reeve (1835–40) as *Democracy in America*; reprinted as *The Republic of the United States of America* (New York: E. Walker & Co., 1849), vol. 1, pp. 362–66.

3

The Pilgrims of Plymouth

BY OLIVER WENDELL HOLMES

Oliver Wendell Holmes (1809–1894), one of the leading literary figures of his time, was instrumental in establishing the literary prominence of Boston during the later nineteenth century. He was renowned as an essayist (The Autocrat of the Breakfast Table, *1858), novelist (* Elsie Venner, *1861), and poet. Holmes was frequently praised for his liberal spirit and humanitarianism: he was an advocate of free speech and a critic of harsh religious dogma, expressed sympathy for the poor and underprivileged, and advocated the entry of women into Harvard Medical School. However, in 1855 Holmes delivered a lecture, "The Pilgrims of Plymouth," before the New England Society of New York that created a furor in its defense of southern slavery and its bland unconcern for the fate of the Native Americans wiped out by the territorial expansion of the American people.*

IT WOULD BE A MOCKERY to speak of the present moral aspect of New England, and not allude to her position with reference to the great question in which the destinies of the whole country are involved.

The same conscientiousness which alone could have rendered possible the passage of that extraordinary law just referred to,[1] shows itself in the deep feeling with which the whole subject of slavery is regarded. No sin of our own, not even intemperance, is so perpetually before the conscience of New England as this detested social arrangement of our neighbors. There is hardly need of saying that we all agree in saving every inch of American soil we fairly can for freedom, and reducing our involuntary

17

participation in slavery to the minimum consistent with our existence as a united people. The question is, whether New England, bound up with a group of confederate sovereignties, cherishes the right temper and uses the right language to her slaveholding sister States.

There is no denying that there is a manly logic in the extreme left of abolitionism. Tear the Constitution to tatters, empty the language of its opprobrious epithets on the men of the southern section of what has been foolishly called our common country, and take the consequences. The ultra melanophiles accept all the possibilities of such a course with a boldness that would be heroism if it were only action instead of talk; that is at any rate consistent and true to its premises. We always have a respect for a principle carried out without compromises or coalitions to round off its edges, so that it may be rolled by politicians, instead of being lifted and borne in the arms of true reformers. And this respect we have for the men of the extreme party; we cannot change the definitions of traitor and treason as the dictionaries insist on giving them; but we must concede to these confederates logical heads as well as daring and often eloquent lips. We feel for Othello, even in his murderous delusion; and these are our political Othellos, who proclaim that our boasted Liberty, with her fair face and matronly air, is a courtezan, and would treat her as Desdemona was treated, but for the machinery of retribution which is close at hand.

But from those who do not profess to repudiate the fundamental compact and the general laws of their country, we may be pardoned if we ask an equal degree of logical consistency. They must either annul the contract made by their fathers, or keep it, not according to any ingenious interpretations they may choose to put upon it, but with the same punctilious honesty and honor that high-minded men show in their private dealings. If it involves a sin, they are accomplices, and have no right to open their lips against it until they have washed their own hands clean from its stains. You may plead as a moralist with a Turk or a Mormon, to give up nine of his ten wives. But if you enter into a partnership with him, and agree to return the truant ladies of his household against their will, for a certain consideration, or if your fathers did, and you hold to the agreement, you have forfeited the right to declaim against polygamy.

It is, perhaps, owing to the violence of the extreme party, and the want of moral power that springs from the false position of many of the more moderate opponents of slavery, that so little impression has been made upon the feelings and opinions of slaveholders. We have labored for a whole generation, and they tell us we have not made out our case against them. We have convinced ourselves a hundred times over, and they lay their hands on their hearts and say, "We have listened to your arguments, and grant you nothing—nothing." Slavery, then, is amongst us exactly like any physical fact. It has proved of no more avail to reason against it than it would have been to launch a syllogism against the embattled crests of the Alleghanies. The question, therefore, comes plainly before us, shall we of New England, men of the front rank, standard-bearers by our position and antecedents; shall we of the North feel and act to these Southern men as equals and brothers; shall we treat them always in the spirit of Christian love; or shall we proscribe, excommunicate, anathematize, vituperate and irritate them until mutual hatred shall ripen into open warfare?

The question of interfering races is a very terrible one; it never was, and perhaps never will be, settled according to the abstract principles of justice. Look at the aboriginal inhabitants of the land we occupy. It pleased the Creator to call into existence this half-filled outline of humanity; this sketch in red crayons of a rudimental manhood; to keep the continent from being a blank until the true lord of creation should come to claim it. Civilization and Christianity have tried to humanize him, and he proves a dead failure. Theologians stand aghast at a whole race destined, according to their old formulæ, to destruction, temporal and eternal. Philanthropists mourn over them, and from time to time catch a red man and turn him into their colleges as they would turn a partridge in among the barn-door fowls. But instinct has its way sooner or later; the partridge makes but a troublesome chicken, and the Indian but a sorry Master of Arts, if he does not run for the woods, where all the *feræ naturæ* impulses are urging him. These instincts lead to his extermination; too often the sad solution of the problem of his relation to the white race. As soon as any conflict arises between them, his savage nature begins to show itself. He dashes the babes' heads against their fathers' hearthstones—as at our Oxford—a heap of stones still shows you where he did it; or flings them out of windows, as at Haverhill; he mutilates his prostrate enemy; he drives away the women like beasts of burden. Then the white man hates him, and hunts him down like the wild beasts of the forest, and so the red-crayon sketch is rubbed out, and the canvas is ready for a picture of manhood a little more like God's own image.

And so of the other question between the white and black races. We see no apparent solution of it except in the indefinite, we may hope not the perpetual continuance of the present relation between them. Here, as in the case of the Indians, or any other inferior natural tribe of men, our sympathies will go with our own color first. Far be it from us to palliate any act of injustice that a man of one complexion may be guilty of against a man of a different one. Whatever wrongs we can win the masters away from committing; whatever woes we can alleviate in the weaker people; we should remember and care for. But always in the last appeal it will come to this; if we must choose between the two races, alliance with the superior one, which we may hope to raise to our own level, if it is below it, or with the lower one which we never can, no abstract principle of benevolence can reverse the great family instinct that settles the question for us. The Creator has hung out the colors that form the two rallying points, so that they shall be unmistakable, eternal; nay, there is hardly a single sense that does not bear witness to the ineffaceable distinction of blood, only prevented from producing open opposition by the unchallenged supremacy of the higher of the two races. The white man must be the master in effect, whatever he is in name; and the only way to make him do right by the Indian, the African, the Chinese, is to make him better by example and loving counsel.

Source:
Oliver Wendell Holmes, "The Pilgrims of
Plymouth" (1855), in *The New England
Society Orations,* edited by Cephas Brainerd
and Eveline Warner Brainerd (New York:
Century Co., 1901), vol. 2, pp. 295–99.

4

Race

BY RALPH WALDO EMERSON

In a chapter entitled "Race" in English Traits *(1856), the American poet and essayist Ralph Waldo Emerson (1803–1882) studies English literary and political achievements and the extent to which they can be attributed to race. Emerson argues that a "pure" race is probably a myth and that societal and environmental factors have much to do with the accomplishments of an individual or of a nation.*

MEN HEAR GLADLY OF THE POWER of blood or race. Every body likes to know that his advantages cannot be attributed to air, soil, sea, or to local wealth, as mines and quarries, nor to laws and traditions, nor to fortune; but to superior brain, as it makes the praise more personal to him.

We anticipate in the doctrine of race something like that law of physiology that whatever bone, muscle, or essential organ is found in one healthy individual, the same part or organ may be found in or near the same place in its congener; and we look to find in the son every mental and moral property that existed in the ancestor. In race, it is not the broad shoulders, or litheness, or stature that give advantage, but a symmetry that reaches as far as to the wit. Then the miracle and renown begin. Then first we care to examine the pedigree, and copy heedfully the training,—what food they ate, what nursing, school, and exercises they had, which resulted in this mother-wit, delicacy of thought and robust wisdom. How came such men as King Alfred, and Roger Bacon, William of Wykeham, Walter Raleigh, Philip Sidney, Isaac Newton, William Shakspeare, George Chapman, Francis Bacon, George Herbert, Henry Vane, to exist here? What made these delicate natures? was it the air? was

it the sea? was it the parentage? For it is certain that these men are samples of their contemporaries. The hearing ear is always found close to the
speaking tongue, and no genius can long or often utter any thing which
is not invited and gladly entertained by men around him.

It is race, is it not, that puts the hundred millions of India under the
dominion of a remote island in the north of Europe? Race avails much,
if that be true which is alleged, that all Celts are Catholics and all Saxons
are Protestants; that Celts love unity of power, and Saxons the representative principle. Race is a controlling influence in the Jew, who, for two
millenniums, under every climate, has preserved the same character and
employments. Race in the negro is of appalling importance. The French
in Canada, cut off from all intercourse with the parent people, have held
their national traits. I chanced to read Tacitus[2] On the Manners of the
Germans, not long since, in Missouri and the heart of Illinois, and I
found abundant points of resemblance between the Germans of the
Hercynian forest, and our *Hoosiers, Suckers* and *Badgers* of the American
woods.

But whilst race works immortally to keep its own, it is resisted by other
forces. Civilization is a re-agent, and eats away the old traits. The Arabs
of to-day are the Arabs of Pharaoh; but the Briton of to-day is a very different person from Cassibelaunus or Ossian. Each religious sect has its
physiognomy. The Methodists have acquired a face; the Quakers, a face;
the nuns, a face. An Englishman will pick out a dissenter by his manners.
Trades and professions carve their own lines on face and form. Certain
circumstances of English life are not less effective; as personal liberty;
plenty of food; good ale and mutton; open market, or good wages for
every kind of labor; high bribes to talent and skill; the island life, or the
million opportunities and outlets for expanding and misplaced talent;
readiness of combination among themselves for politics or for business;
strikes; and sense of superiority founded on habit of victory in labor and
in war: and the appetite for superiority grows by feeding.

It is easy to add to the counteracting forces to race. Credence is a main
element. 'Tis said that the views of nature held by any people determine
all their institutions. Whatever influences add to mental or moral faculty,
take men out of nationality as out of other conditions, and make the national life a culpable compromise.

These limitations of the formidable doctrine of race suggest others
which threaten to undermine it, as not sufficiently based. The fixity or
inconvertibleness of races as we see them is a weak argument for the eter-
nity of these frail boundaries, since all our historical period is a point to
the duration in which nature has wrought. Any the least and solitariest

fact in our natural history, such as the melioration of fruits and of animal stocks, has the worth of a *power* in the opportunity of geologic periods. Moreover, though we flatter the self-love of men and nations by the legend of pure races, all our experience is of the gradation and resolution of races, and strange resemblances meet us everywhere. It need not puzzle us that Malay and Papuan, Celt and Roman, Saxon and Tartar should mix, when we see the rudiments of tiger and baboon in our human form, and know that the barriers of races are not so firm but that some spray sprinkles us from the antediluvian seas.

Source:
Ralph Waldo Emerson, *English Traits* (1856);
in *The Complete Works of Ralph Waldo
Emerson,* Centenary Edition (Boston:
Houghton Mifflin, 1903), pp. 46–50.

$\smallfrown$ *5* $\smallfrown$

Foundations of the Nineteenth Century

BY HOUSTON STEWART CHAMBERLAIN

Houston Stewart Chamberlain (1855–1927) was the son-in-law of composer Richard Wagner. Although born in England, Chamberlain spent much of his life in Germany, became a German citizen and a rabid England hater and anti-Semite, and produced a landmark in the history of racism, Die Grundlagen des neunzehnten Jahrhunderts *(1899). In this widely popular work, which had sold sixty thousand copies by 1910 (when it was translated into English as* Foundations of the Nineteenth Century*), Chamberlain sought to reconcile racism and German nationalism with the doctrines of Christianity. Chamberlain sees all the best facets of human personality, and indeed all history, as the triumph of "racial purity."*

IS NATION, IS RACE A MERE WORD? Is it the case, as the ethnographer Ratzel asserts, that the fusion of all mankind should be kept before us as our "aim and duty, hope and wish"? Or do we not rather deduce from the example of Hellas and Rome, on the one hand, and of the pseudo-Roman empire on the other, as well as from many other examples in history, that man can only attain his zenith within those limits in which sharply defined, individualistic national types are produced? Is the present condition of things in Europe with its many fully formed idioms, each with its own peculiar poetry and literature, each the expression of a definite, characteristic national soul—is this state of things really a retrograde step in comparison with the time, when Latin and Greek, as

24

a kind of twin Volapuk, formed a bond of union between all those Roman subjects who had no fatherland to call their own? Is community of blood nothing? Can community of memory and of faith be replaced by abstract ideals? Above all, is the question one to be settled by each as he pleases, is there no clearly distinguishable natural law, according to which we must fit our judgment? Do not the biological sciences teach us that in the whole animal and vegetable kingdoms pre-eminently noble races—that is, races endowed with exceptional strength and vitality—are produced only under definite conditions, which restrict the begetting of new individuals? Is it not possible, in view of all these human and non-human phenomena, to find a clear answer to the question, What is race? And shall we not be able, from the consciousness of what race is, to say at once what the absence of definite races must mean for history? When we look at those direct heirs of the great legacy, these questions force themselves upon us. Let us in the first place discuss races quite generally; then, and then only, shall we be able to discuss with advantage the conditions prevailing in this special case, their importance in the course of history, and consequently in the nineteenth century.

There is perhaps no question about which such absolute ignorance prevails among highly cultured, indeed learned, men, as the question of the essence and the significance of the idea of "race." What are pure races? Whence do they come? Have they any historical importance? Is the idea to be taken in a broad or a narrow sense? Do we know anything on the subject or not? What is the relation of the ideas of race and of nation to one another? I confess that all I have ever read or heard on this subject has been disconnected and contradictory: some specialists among the natural investigators form an exception, but even they very rarely apply their clear and detailed knowledge to the human race. Not a year passes without our being assured at international congresses, by authoritative national economists, ministers, bishops, natural scientists, that there is no difference and no inequality between nations. Teutons, who emphasise the importance of race-relationship, Jews, who do not feel at ease among us and long to get back to their Asiatic home, are by none so slightingly and scornfully spoken of as by men of science. Professor Virchow, for instance, says that the stirrings of consciousness of race among us are only to be explained by the "loss of sound common sense": moreover, that it is "all a riddle to us, and no one knows what it really means in this age of equal rights." Nevertheless, this learned man closes his address with the expression of a desire for "beautiful self-dependent personalities." As if all history were not there to show us how personality and race are most closely connected, how the nature of the personality is determined by the nature of its race, and the power of the personality dependent upon certain conditions of its blood! And as if the scientific rearing of animals and plants did not afford us an extremely rich and reliable material, whereby we may become acquainted not only with the conditions but with the importance of "race"! Are the so-called (and rightly so-called) "noble" animal races, the draught-horses of Limousin, the American trotter, the Irish hunter, the absolutely reliable sporting dogs, produced by chance and promiscuity? Do we get them by giving the animals equality of rights, by throwing the same food to them and whipping them with the same whip? No, they are produced by artificial selection and strict maintenance of the purity of the race. Horses and especially dogs give us every chance of observing that the intellectual gifts go hand in hand with the physical; this is specially true of the moral qualities: a mongrel is frequently very clever, but never reliable; morally he is always a weed. Continual promiscuity between two pre-eminent animal races leads without exception to the destruction of the pre-eminent characteristics of both. Why should the human race form an exception? A father of the Church might imagine that it does, but is it becoming in a renowned natural investigator to throw the weight of his great influence into the scale of mediæval ignorance and superstition? Truly one could wish that these scientific authorities of ours, who are so utterly lacking in philosophy, had followed a course of logic under Thomas Aquinas; it could only be beneficial to them. In spite of the broad common foundation, the human races are, in reality, as different from one another in character, qualities, and above all, in the degree of their individual capacities, as greyhound, bulldog, poodle and Newfoundland dog. Inequality is a state towards which nature inclines in all spheres; nothing extraordinary is produced without "specialisation"; in the case of men, as of animals, it is this specialisation that produces noble races; history and ethnology reveal this secret to the dullest eye. Has not every genuine race its own glorious, incomparable physiognomy? How could Hellenic art have arisen without Hellenes? How quickly has the jealous hostility between the different cities of the small country of Greece given each part its sharply defined individuality within its own family type! How quickly this was blurred again, when Macedonians and Romans with their levelling hand swept over the land! And how everything which had given an everlasting significance to the word "Hellenic" gradually disappeared when from North, East and West new bands of unrelated peoples kept flocking to the country and mingled with genuine Hellenes! The equality, before which Professor Virchow bows the knee, was now there, all walls were razed to the ground, all the boundaries became meaningless; the philosophy, too, with which Virchow in the same lecture breaks so keen a lance, was destroyed, and its place taken by the very soundest "common sense"; but the beautiful Hellenic personality, but for which all of us would to-day be merely more or less civilised barbarians, had disappeared, disappeared for ever. *"Crossing obliterates characters."* . . .

Nothing is so convincing as the consciousness of the possession of Race. The man who belongs to a distinct, pure race, never loses the sense of it. The guardian angel of his lineage is ever at his side, supporting him where he loses his foothold, warning him like the Socratic Daemon where he is in danger of going astray, compelling obedience, and forcing him to undertakings which, deeming them impossible, he would never have dared to attempt. Weak and erring like all that is human, a man of this stamp recognises himself, as others recognise him, by the sureness of his character, and by the fact that his actions are marked by a certain simple and peculiar greatness, which finds its explanation in his distinctly typical and super-personal qualities. Race lifts a man above himself: it endows him with extraordinary—I might almost say supernatural—powers, so entirely does it distinguish him from the individual who springs from the chaotic jumble of peoples drawn from all parts of the world: and should this man of pure origin be perchance gifted above his fellows, then the fact of Race strengthens and elevates him on every hand, and he becomes a genius towering over the rest of mankind, not because he has been thrown upon the earth like a flaming meteor by a freak of nature, but because he soars heavenward like some strong and stately tree, nourished by thousands and thousands of roots—no solitary individual, but the living sum of untold souls striving for the same goal. He who has eyes to see at once detects Race in animals. It shows itself in the whole habit of the beast, and proclaims itself in a hundred peculiarities which defy analysis: nay more, it proves itself by achievements, for its possession invariably leads to something excessive and out of the common—even to that which is exaggerated and not free from bias. Goethe's dictum, "only that which is extravagant (*überschwänglich*) makes greatness," is well known. That is the very quality which a thoroughbred race reared from superior materials bestows upon its individual descendants—something "extravagant"—and, indeed, what we learn from every race-horse, every thoroughbred fox-terrier, every Cochin China fowl, is the very lesson which the history of mankind so eloquently teaches us! Is not the Greek in the fulness of his glory an unparalleled example of this "extravagance"? And do we not see this "extravagance" first make its appearance when immigration from the North has ceased, and the various strong breeds of men, isolated on the peninsula once for all, begin to fuse into a new race, brighter and more brilliant, where, as in Athens, the racial blood flows from many sources—simpler and more resisting where, as in Lacedæmon, even this mixture of blood had been barred out. Is the race not as it were extinguished, as soon as fate wrests the land from its proud exclusiveness and incorporates it in a greater whole? Does not Rome teach us the same lesson? Has not in this case also a special mixture of blood produced an absolutely new race, similar in qualities and capacities to no later one, endowed with exuberant power? And does not victory in this case effect what disaster did in that, but only much more quickly? Like a cataract the stream of strange blood overflooded the almost de-populated Rome and at once the Romans ceased to be. Would one small tribe from among all the Semites have become a world-embracing power had it not made "purity of race" its inflexible fundamental law? In days when so much nonsense is talked concerning this question, let Disraeli teach us that the whole significance of Judaism lies in its purity of race, that this alone gives it power and duration, and just as it has outlived the people of antiquity, so, thanks to its knowledge of this law of nature, will it outlive the constantly mingling races of to-day.

What is the use of detailed scientific investigations as to whether there are distinguishable races? whether race has a worth? how this is possible? and so on. We turn the tables and say: it is evident that there are such races: it is a fact of direct experience that the quality of the race is of vital importance; your province is only to find out the how and the where-fore, not to deny the facts themselves in order to indulge your ignorance. One of the greatest ethnologists of the present day, Adolf Bastian, testi-fies that, "what we see in history is not a transformation, a passing of one race into another, but entirely new and perfect creations, which the ever-youthful productivity of nature sends forth from the invisible realm of Hades." Whoever travels the short distance between Calais and Dover, feels almost as if he had reached a different planet, so great is the differ-ence between the English and French, despite their many points of rela-tionship. The observer can also see from this instance the value of purer "inbreeding." England is practically cut off by its insular position: the last (not very extensive) invasion took place 800 years ago; since then only a few thousands from the Netherlands, and later a few thousand Huguenots have crossed over (all of the same origin), and thus has been reared that race which at the present moment is unquestionably the strongest in Europe.

Direct experience, however, offers us a series of quite different obser-vations on race, all of which may gradually contribute to the extension of our knowledge as well as to its definiteness. In contrast to the new, growing, Anglo-Saxon race, look, for instance, at the Sephardim, the so-called "Spanish Jews"; here we find how a genuine race can by purity keep itself noble for centuries and tens of centuries, but at the same time how very necessary it is to distinguish between the nobly reared portions of a nation and the rest. In England, Holland and Italy there are still genuine Sephardim but very few, since they can scarcely any longer avoid crossing with the Ashkenazim (the so-called "German Jews"). Thus, for example, the Montefiores of the present generation have all without exception married German Jewesses. But every one who has travelled in the East of Europe, where the genuine Sephardim still as far as possible avoid all intercourse with German Jews, for whom they have an almost comical repugnance, will agree with me when I say that it is only when one sees these men and has intercourse with them that one begins to comprehend the significance of Judaism in the history of the world. This is nobility in the fullest sense of the word, genuine nobility of race! Beautiful figures, noble heads, dignity in speech and bearing. The type is Semitic in the same sense as that of certain noble Syrians and Arabs. That out of the midst of such people Prophets and Psalmists could arise—that I understood at the first glance, which I honestly confess that I had never succeeded in doing when I gazed, however carefully, on the many hundred young Jews—"Bochers"—of the Friedrichstrasse in Berlin. When we study the Sacred Books of the Jews we see further that the conversion of this monopolytheistic people to the ever sublime (though according to our ideas mechanical and materialistic) conception of a true cosmic monotheism was not the work of the community, but of a mere fraction of the people; indeed, this minority had to wage a continuous warfare against the majority, and was compelled to enforce the acceptance of its more exalted view of life by means of the highest Power to which man is heir, the might of personality. As for the rest of the people, unless the Prophets were guilty of gross exaggeration, they convey the impression of a singularly vulgar crowd, devoid of every higher aim, the rich hard and unbelieving, the poor fickle and ever possessed by the longing to throw themselves into the arms of the wretchedest and filthiest idolatry. The course of Jewish history has provided for a peculiar artificial selection of the morally higher section: by banishments, by continual withdrawals to the Diaspora—a result of the poverty and oppressed condition of the land—only the most faithful (of the better classes) remained behind, and these abhorred every marriage contract—even with Jews!—in which both parties could not show an absolutely pure descent from one of the tribes of Israel and prove their strict orthodoxy beyond all doubt. There remained then no great choice; for the nearest neighbours, the

Samaritans, were heterodox, and in the remoter parts of the land, except in the case of the Levites who kept apart, the population was to a large extent much mixed. In this way race was here produced. And when at last the final dispersion of the Jews came, all or almost all of these sole genuine Jews were taken to Spain. The shrewd Romans in fact knew well how to draw distinctions, and so they removed these dangerous fanatics, these proud men, whose very glance made the masses obey, from their Eastern home to the farthest West, while, on the other hand, they did not disturb the Jewish people outside of the narrower Judea more than the Jews of the Diaspora.—Here, again, we have a most interesting object-lesson on the origin and worth of "race"! For of all the men whom we are wont to characterise as Jews, relatively few are descended from these great genuine Hebrews, they are rather the descendants of the Jews of the Diaspora, Jews who did not take part in the last great struggles, who, indeed, to some extent did not even live through the Maccabean age; these and the poor country people who were left behind in Palestine, and who later in Christian ages were banished or fled, are the ancestors of "our Jews" of to-day. Now whoever wishes to see with his own eyes what noble race is, and what it is not, should send for the poorest of the Sephardim from Salonici or Sarajevo (great wealth is very rare among them, for they are men of stainless honour) and put him side by side with any Ashkenazim financier; then will he perceive the difference between the nobility which race bestows and that conferred by a monarch.

Source:
Houston Stewart Chamberlain,
Die Grundlagen des neunzehnten Jahrhunderts
(1899); translated by John Lees as
Foundations of the Nineteenth Century
(London: The Bodley Head, 1910),
vol. 1, pp. 258–62, 269–75.

6

The Passing of the Great Race

BY MADISON GRANT

The Passing of the Great Race *(1916) was a best-selling treatise written by Madison Grant (1865–1937), an American lawyer who was president of the New York Zoological Society and vice president of the Immigration Restriction League. The first chapter of this work, titled "Race and Democracy," testifies to the close connection between racism and fascism. Grant also wrote* The Conquest of a Continent; or, The Expansion of Races in America *(1933) and coedited* The Alien in Our Midst *(1930).*

FAILURE TO RECOGNIZE the clear distinction between race and nationality and the still greater distinction between race and language and the easy assumption that the one is indicative of the other have been in the past serious impediments to an understanding of racial values. Historians and philologists have approached the subject from the viewpoint of linguistics and as a result we are to-day burdened with a group of mythical races, such as the Latin, the Aryan, the Indo-Germanic, the Caucasian and, perhaps, most inconsistent of all, the Celtic race.

Man is an animal differing from his fellow inhabitants of the globe not in kind but only in degree of development and an intelligent study of the human species must be preceded by an extended knowledge of other mammals, especially the primates. Instead of such essential training, anthropologists often seek to qualify by research in linguistics, religion or marriage customs or in designs of pottery or blanket weaving, all of which relate to ethnology alone. As a result the influence of envi-

31

ronment is often overestimated and overstated at the expense of heredity.

The question of race has been further complicated by the effort of old-
fashioned theologians to cramp all mankind into the scant six thousand
years of Hebrew chronology as expounded by Archbishop Ussher.
Religious teachers have also maintained the proposition not only that
man is something fundamentally distinct from other living creatures, but
that there are no inherited differences in humanity that cannot be obliterated by education and environment.

It is, therefore, necessary at the outset for the reader to appreciate
thoroughly that race, language and nationality are three separate and distinct things and that in Europe these three elements are found only occasionally persisting in combination, as in the Scandinavian nations.

To realize the transitory nature of political boundaries one has but to
consider the changes which have occurred during the past century and as
to language, here in America we hear daily the English language spoken
by many men who possess not one drop of English blood and who, a few
years since, knew not one word of Saxon speech.

As a result of certain religious and social doctrines, now happily becoming obsolete, race consciousness has been greatly impaired among
civilized nations but in the beginning all differences of class, of caste and
of color marked actual lines of race cleavage.

In many countries the existing classes represent races that were once
distinct. In the city of New York and elsewhere in the United States there
is a native American aristocracy resting upon layer after layer of immigrants of lower races and these native Americans, while, of course, dis-
claiming the distinction of a patrician class and lacking in class
consciousness and class dignity, have, nevertheless, up to this time supplied the leaders in thought and in the control of capital as well as of education and of the religious ideals and altruistic bias of the community.

In the democratic forms of government the operation of universal suffrage tends toward the selection of the average man for public office
rather than the man qualified by birth, education and integrity. How this
scheme of administration will ultimately work out remains to be seen but
from a racial point of view it will inevitably increase the preponderance of
the lower types and cause a corresponding loss of efficiency in the community as a whole.

The tendency in a democracy is toward a standardization of type and a
diminution of the influence of genius. A majority must of necessity be inferior to a picked minority and it always resents specializations in which
it cannot share. In the French Revolution the majority, calling itself "the

people," deliberately endeavored to destroy the higher type and something of the same sort was in a measure done after the American Revolution by the expulsion of the Loyalists and the confiscation of their lands, with a resultant loss to the growing nation of good race strains, which were in the next century replaced by immigrants of far lower type.

In America we have nearly succeeded in destroying the privilege of birth; that is, the intellectual and moral advantage a man of good stock brings into the world with him. We are now engaged in destroying the privilege of wealth; that is, the reward of successful intelligence and industry and in some quarters there is developing a tendency to attack the privilege of intellect and to deprive a man of the advantage gained from an early and thorough classical education. Simplified spelling is a step in this direction. Ignorance of English grammar or classic learning must not, forsooth, be held up as a reproach to the political or social aspirant.

Mankind emerged from savagery and barbarism under the leadership of selected individuals whose personal prowess, capacity or wisdom gave them the right to lead and the power to compel obedience. Such leaders have always been a minute fraction of the whole, but as long as the tradition of their predominance persisted they were able to use the brute strength of the unthinking herd as part of their own force and were able to direct at will the blind dynamic impulse of the slaves, peasants or lower classes. Such a despot had an enormous power at his disposal which, if he were benevolent or even intelligent, could be used and most frequently was used for the general uplift of the race. Even those rulers who most abused this power put down with merciless rigor the antisocial elements, such as pirates, brigands or anarchists, which impair the progress of a community, as disease or wounds cripple an individual.

True aristocracy or a true republic is government by the wisest and best, always a small minority in any population. Human society is like a serpent dragging its long body on the ground, but with the head always thrust a little in advance and a little elevated above the earth. The serpent's tail, in human society represented by the antisocial forces, was in the past dragged by sheer strength along the path of progress. Such has been the organization of mankind from the beginning, and such it still is in older communities than ours. What progress humanity can make under the control of universal suffrage, or the rule of the average, may find a further analogy in the habits of certain snakes which wiggle sideways and disregard the head with its brains and eyes. Such serpents, however, are not noted for their ability to make rapid progress.

A true republic, the function of which is administration in the interests of the whole community—in contrast to a pure democracy, which in last analysis is the rule of the demos or a majority in its own interests—should be, and often is, the medium of selection for the technical task of government of those best qualified by antecedents, character and education, in short, of experts.

To use another simile, in an aristocratic as distinguished from a plutocratic or democratic organization the intellectual and talented classes form the point of the lance while the massive shaft represents the body of the population and adds by its bulk and weight to the penetrative impact of the tip. In a democratic system this concentrated force is dispersed throughout the mass. It supplies, to be sure, a certain amount of leaven but in the long run the force and genius of the small minority is dissipated, and its efficiency lost. *Vox populi,* so far from being *Vox Dei,* thus becomes an unending wail for rights and never a chant of duty.

Where a conquering race is imposed on another race the institution of slavery often arises to compel the servient race to work and to introduce it forcibly to a higher form of civilization. As soon as men can be induced to labor to supply their own needs slavery becomes wasteful and tends to vanish. From a material point of view slaves are often more fortunate than freemen when treated with reasonable humanity and when their elemental wants of food, clothing and shelter are supplied.

The Indians around the fur posts in northern Canada were formerly the virtual bond slaves of the Hudson Bay Company, each Indian and his squaw and papoose being adequately supplied with simple food and equipment. He was protected as well against the white man's rum as the red man's scalping parties and in return gave the Company all his peltries—the whole product of his year's work. From an Indian's point of view this was nearly an ideal condition but was to all intents serfdom or slavery. When through the opening up of the country the continuance of such an archaic system became an impossibility, the Indian sold his furs to the highest bidder, received a large price in cash and then wasted the proceeds in trinkets instead of blankets and in rum instead of flour, with the result that he is now gloriously free but is on the highroad to becoming a diseased outcast. In this case of the Hudson Bay Indian the advantages of the upward step from serfdom to freedom are not altogether clear. A very similar condition of vassalage existed until recently among the peons of Mexico, but without the compensation of the control of an intelligent and provident ruling class.

In the same way serfdom in mediæval Europe apparently was a device through which the landowners repressed the nomadic instinct in their tenantry which became marked when the fertility of the land declined after the dissolution of the Roman Empire. Years are required to bring land to its highest productivity and agriculture cannot be successfully practised even in well-watered and fertile districts by farmers who continually drift from one locality to another. The serf or villein was, therefore, tied by law to the land and could not leave except with his master's consent. As soon as the nomadic instinct was eliminated serfdom vanished. One has but to read the severe laws against vagrancy in England just before the Reformation to realize how widespread and serious was this nomadic instinct. Here in America we have not yet forgotten the wandering instincts of our Western pioneers, which in that case proved beneficial to every one except the migrants.

While democracy is fatal to progress when two races of unequal value live side by side, an aristocracy may be equally injurious whenever, in order to purchase a few generations of ease and luxury, slaves or immigrants are imported to do the heavy work. It was a form of aristocracy that brought slaves to the American colonies and the West Indies and if there had been an aristocratic form of governmental control in California, Chinese coolies and Japanese laborers would now form the controlling element, so far as numbers are concerned, on the Pacific coast.

It was the upper classes who encouraged the introduction of immigrant labor to work American factories and mines and it is the native American gentleman who builds a palace on the country side and who introduces as servants all manner of foreigners into purely American districts. The farming and artisan classes of America did not take alarm until it was too late and they are now seriously threatened with extermination in many parts of the country. In Rome, also, it was the plebeian, who first went under in the competition with slaves but the patrician followed in his turn a few generations later.

The West Indian sugar planters flourished in the eighteenth century and produced some strong men; to-day from the same causes they have vanished from the scene.

During the last century the New England manufacturer imported the Irish and French Canadians and the resultant fall in the New England birth-rate at once became ominous. The refusal of the native American to work with his hands when he can hire or import serfs to do manual labor for him is the prelude to his extinction and the immigrant laborers are now breeding out their masters and killing by filth and by crowding as effectively as by the sword.

Thus the American sold his birthright in a continent to solve a labor problem. Instead of retaining political control and making citizenship an honorable and valued privilege, he intrusted the government of his country and the maintenance of his ideals to races who have never yet succeeded in governing themselves, much less any one else.

Associated with this advance of democracy and the transfer of power from the higher to the lower races, from the intellectual to the plebeian class, we find the spread of socialism and the recrudescence of obsolete religious forms. Although these phenomena appear to be contradictory, they are in reality closely related since both represent reactions from the intense individualism which a century ago was eminently characteristic of Americans.

Source:
Madison Grant, *The Passing of the Great Race;
or, The Racial Basis of European History*
(New York: Scribner's, 1916), pp. 3–12.

7

The End of Racism

BY DINESH D'SOUZA

Dinesh D'Souza (b. 1961), journalist and author, was born in India but has lived in the United States since 1978. His first book was a flattering biography of evangelist Jerry Falwell, Falwell: Before the Millennium *(1985). D'Souza gained notoriety with his book* Illiberal Education *(1991), in which he attacked "liberals" for what he believed to be their "politically correct" attitudes in dealing with the problems of race and sex. D'Souza continued the polemic in* The End of Racism *(1995), in which he seeks to "reconsider the meaning of . . . prejudice and stereotype."*

Prejudices and Conclusions

Prejudice engages the mind in a steady course of wisdom and virtue, and does not leave the man hesitating in the moment of decision. . . . Prejudice renders a man's virtue his habit.
——Edmund Burke

IT MAY NOW BE USEFUL TO RECONSIDER the meaning of familiar terms such as prejudice and stereotype, and examine the conventional liberal understanding of racism. This understanding is expressed by Henry Louis Gates, Jr., who writes: "Racism exists when one generalizes about attributes of an individual, and treats him or her accordingly." Gates offers some specific examples: "Skip, sing me one of those old Negro spirituals," "You people sure can dance," and "Black people play basketball so remarkably well." He concludes, "These are racist statements." Why are they viewed as racist? Because contemporary liberalism

37

is constructed on the scaffolding of cultural relativism, which posits that all groups are inherently equal. Since all groups are equal, adverse group judgments are presumed to constitute "prejudices" and "stereotypes" that are almost always regarded as wrongheaded and ignorant. The civil rights laws of the 1950s and 1960s were based on the assumption that as whites and blacks came into closer contact and learned more about each other, the similarity of all groups would become evident and white prejudices and stereotypes would dissipate.

Consider some definitions. The *Encyclopedia Britannica* identifies prejudice as "an attitude, usually emotional, acquired without or prior to adequate evidence or experience." For Thomas Pettigrew, a psychologist who studies race relations, prejudice is "irrationally based . . . an antipathy accompanied by a faulty generalization." Christine Bennett in *Comprehensive Multicultural Education* argues that "prejudice is an erroneous judgment, usually negative, which is based on incomplete or faulty information." Bennett adds that "a prejudice becomes a stereotype when it is used to label all or most members of a group." Another leading textbook defines a stereotype as "an overgeneralization associated with a racial or ethnic category that goes beyond existing evidence." *Webster's New World Dictionary* defines a stereotype as "a fixed or conventional notion or conception, as of a person or group . . . allowing no individuality and critical judgment."

In *The Nature of Prejudice,* Gordon Allport draws on modern social science theories to explicate the paradigm of liberal antiracism. Allport argues that prejudices and stereotypes reveal less about their objects than their subjects. Applying such concepts as displacement and frustration-aggression theory, Allport maintains that when whites feel hostility and anger which they have difficulty coping with or explaining, they project it onto others, who thus become sacrificial victims or "scapegoats." Allport conveys the assumption of many social scientists today: prejudices and stereotypes endure because of the principle of self-selection. From the distorted perspective of the racist, blacks who do not conform to preconceived notions simply do not exist; they are, in Ralph Ellison's term, invisible men. Thus prejudices and stereotypes are presumed to be impervious to correction.

For the better part of a generation, this liberal understanding of racism worked fairly well. The reason was that both whites and blacks had indeed developed many erroneous views about each other as a consequence of Southern segregation. During slavery the races stayed in regular, even intimate, contact, but after emancipation the forced separation of the races created a divided society in which dubious and even absurd generalizations could endure, unchecked by contrary experience.

Thus the intellectual assault on prejudice and stereotypes, as well as the experience of desegregation, both helped to topple many preconceived group generalizations that could not withstand empirical examination. In 1920, George Jean Nathan and H. L. Mencken listed a number of such popular prejudices and stereotypes about blacks.

- Negroes who are intelligent are always part white
- Negro parties always end up in bloody brawls
- Negroes who have money head straight for the dentist to have their front teeth filled with gold
- Illiterate Negroes labor hard but educated Negroes lose all interest in work
- Negro prize fighters marry white women and then beat them
- Negroes will sell their votes for a dollar

As the widespread popularity of African Americans such as Colin Powell, Bill Cosby, and Michael Jordan illustrates, none of these beliefs seems to be held today by any measurable segment of the population. We can speculate about the roots of some of these stereotypes. Undoubtedly the white prejudice about black intelligence did not begin with, but was strengthened by, the observed preponderance of light-skinned mulattoes in the black middle class. Perhaps the suspicion of vote-peddling among blacks was a legacy from the Reconstruction era when many blacks voted and many Southern whites were disenfranchised. The reputation of black boxers probably began with the flamboyant experience of Jack Johnson, who raised controversy in the early part of the century when he married a white woman.

These prejudices, loosely anchored in popular experience, proved easy to refute through the liberal remedy of increased education and exposure. Not only were whites in a more informed position to see what blacks were like, but the black community itself was changing, rendering crude generalizations from the past increasingly obsolete. The positive effect of the assault on prejudices and stereotypes, based on the liberal paradigm, has been a vastly more sophisticated perception of blacks on the part of whites. The problem with the paradigm is its premise that all group perceptions are misperceptions: that every negative generalization about blacks is automatically false and the product of distorted projections. Paradoxically it is desegregation and integration which have now called the liberal paradigm into question. One of the risks of increased exposure to blacks is that it has also placed whites in a position to discover which of their preconceived views about blacks are true. Education and integration can help to dispel erroneous judgments about groups but they are only likely to reinforce accurate ones.

In fact ethnic groups that have had little history of oppressing each other and in some cases very limited previous contact now seem to be formulating clear and often critical images of other groups. In one of the more remarkable surveys of recent years, the National Conference of Christians and Jews reports that many minority groups harbor much more hostile attitudes toward each other than do whites. For example, 49 percent of blacks and 68 percent of Asians said that Hispanics "tend to have bigger families than they can support." Forty-six percent of Hispanics and 42 percent of blacks agreed that Asian Americans are "unscrupulous, crafty and devious in business." And 53 percent of Asians and 51 percent of Hispanics affirmed that blacks "are more likely to commit crimes and violence."

It is, of course, possible that these minority perceptions reveal that, by a kind of social osmosis, everyone is learning their racism from whites. But if so why would minority perceptions be stronger than those of whites who are the alleged racists *par excellence*? More likely, these intergroup minority perceptions are the product of experience. Most people today have fairly regular contact with others of different races, and have many opportunities to verify their collective judgments about other groups. It is the possibility of accurate generalizations about blacks and other groups that gives rise to the problem of rational discrimination.

Are Stereotypes Generally Accurate?

Do blacks as a group have certain distinct characteristics? We read in Andrew Hacker's *Two Nations* that "the erotic abandon displayed in black dancing has no white counterpart." Thomas Kochman in *Black and White: Styles in Conflict* cites an African American source describing the black walk: "Rather than simply walk, we *move* . . . a strong rhythmic mode of walking. . . . *Where* the young black male is going is not as important as *how* he gets there." Kochman proceeds with some pretty strong generalizations:

Where whites use the relatively detached and unemotional *discussion* mode to engage an issue, blacks use the emotionally intense and involving mode of *argument*. Where whites tend to *understate* their exceptional talents and abilities, blacks tend to *boast* about theirs. Where white men, meeting women for the first time, *defuse* the potency of their sexual messages . . . black men make their sexual interest explicit and hope to *infuse* their presentations with sexual potency.

Although both Hacker and Kochman are white, neither can be accused of racism; indeed, their views are extremely popular in the black community. "My black students," Hacker says, "love what I have to say." During my speaking trips to college campuses, I decided, as a journalistic exercise, to test people's perception of group traits by raising the question of whether stereotypes may be true and prejudices based on them therefore legitimate. Inevitably I encounter strong emotional opposition. As a result of the deeply rooted assumptions of cultural relativism, educated people today have been taught to despise group generalizations. In a sense, we are all Boasians. We have been raised to be prejudiced against prejudice.

Recently on a West Coast campus, I raised the question of whether, as a group, "blacks have rhythm." A professor of Afro-American Studies insisted, "Absolutely not," and a number of white students readily agreed. Instinctively, they raised the familiar defenses, "I know a black man who can't dance," "How can you generalize about a group that is so diverse?" "What about Elvis? He had rhythm, and he wasn't black," and so on. I pointed out that these were poor refutations of a proposition that was being offered as true on average, or compared with the experience of other groups. One cannot rebut the statistically irrefutable statement that men are taller than women by producing a six-foot woman and a four-foot man. Those individuals would merely constitute exceptions to a general pattern that has persisted across cultures for most of recorded history.

Incidentally, the view that blacks tend to be more rhythmic than whites is no whimsical recent invention but is supported by observation and experience in several societies over two millennia. In ancient Greece and Rome, which held no negative view of black skin color, Ethiopians and other blacks were celebrated for a perceived natural inclination to music and dance. This is a central theme of that segment of Greek and Roman art which focuses on blacks. Moreover, the same perception of blacks is evident in many Arab descriptions of African blacks, written in the late Middle Ages. Ibn Butlan, for example, writes that if a black man was dropped from heaven "he would beat time as he goes down." In a ninth century Muslim travel account, blacks are praised for their rhythm and for being able to play music without instruction. . . . Ibn Khaldun, the greatest Arab historian of the Middle Ages, speculates that the black propensity for music and rhythmic dancing derives from the relaxing influence of the warm climate.

In a recent book on cultural diversity, Taylor Cox compiled the results of several surveys that sought to identify negative generalizations that many Americans believe about various groups. Here are some stereotypes about males from different backgrounds.

- *Japanese:* Studious, meticulous, workaholics, business-oriented, nationalistic, unemotional, sexist, productive, good at math and science, defer to authority, carry cameras.
- *Jews:* Rich, miserly, support Israel, well-educated, complainers, good at business, take care of their own, not rhythmic or coordinated, sensitive to criticism.
- *Blacks:* Athletes, good dancers, expressive in communication, poor, too concerned about what they wear, uneducated, oversexed, on welfare, funny.
- *French:* Romantic, unfaithful, egotistical, enjoy a drink of wine, dry-humored, do not shower often, dislike Americans, proud of their country.
- *Whites:* Insecure, domineering, wear Dockers, enjoy privileges handed to them, manipulative, insensitive, competitive, opportunistic, enjoy drinking beer.

The liberal paradigm holds that, since racial and ethnic generalizations are irrational, none of them can accurately reflect group differences. On one point the theory is sound: people's perceptions of others are always filtered through the lens of their own prior experience. But the liberal understanding cannot explain how particular traits come to be identified with particular groups. Only because group traits have an empirical basis in shared experience can we invoke them without fear of contradiction. Think of how people would react if someone said that "Koreans are lazy" or that "Hispanics are constantly trying to find ways to make money." Despite the prevalence of anti-Semitism, Jews are rarely accused of stupidity. Blacks are never accused of being tight with a dollar, or of conspiring to take over the world. By reversing stereotypes we can see how their persistence relies, not simply on the assumptions of the viewer, but also on the characteristics of the group being described.

This is no case for group traits having a biological foundation. Probably the vast majority of group traits are entirely cultural, the distilled product of many years of shared experience. Yet prejudices and stereotypes are not intended to explain the origins of group traits, only to take into account their undisputed existence. Nor is this an argument to emphasize negative traits. Stereotypes can be negative or positive. Indeed the same stereotype can be interpreted favorably or unfavorably. One can deplore Roman machismo or admire Roman manliness; deride traditional Spanish superstition or exalt Spanish piety; scorn Jewish avarice or praise Jewish entrepreneurship; ridicule English severity or cherish English self-control. In each of these interpretations, we see a single set of facts, a different set of values.

Not surprisingly, ethnic activists frequently offer a positive interpretation of their group's distinctive characteristics. Richard Gambino's *Blood of My Blood* is almost embarrassing in its corroboration of "Godfather" stereotypes about Italian Americans. Gambino elaborates the code of *la famiglia*, and proceeds to give a rich and sympathetic account of how it shapes something resembling an Italian American worldview. Thomas Sowell's *Ethnic America* and Nathan Glazer and Daniel Patrick Moynihan's *Beyond the Melting Pot* also acknowledge ethnic differences and relate them to group performance in America. Black stereotypes are frequently given a positive spin and celebrated by members of the African American community.

- Paul Robeson identified the "characteristic qualities" of blacks as including "a deep simplicity, a sense of mystery . . . great emotional depth and spiritual intuition."
- In *Shadow and Act* Ralph Ellison exulted in the fact that "Negro music and dances are frenzied and erotic, Negro religious ceremonies violently ecstatic, Negro speech strongly rhythmical and weighted with image and gesture."
- More recently, Ralph Wiley notes that "Creativity is at the root of all forms of music, which is why black people are so adept at it. Creativity is black people's middle name."
- A contemporary book on African culture remarks, "This culture is identified by jazz, blues, gospel and soul music, by modern dance and tap dance, by hip talking, pimp walking, and high-five passing."

William Helmreich in his book *The Things They Say Behind Your Back* takes up the controversial issue of whether there is a rational basis for group stereotypes. Helmreich finds some stereotypes that are clearly false. During the Middle Ages, for example, apparently many Christians took religious polemic literally and came to believe that Jews have horns. Clearly this was not a perception destined to last: one only has to encounter a few Jews to discover that they do not, in fact, possess horns. Helmreich takes up other stereotypes, however, such as the view that many Nobel laureates are Jewish, or that the Mafia is largely made up of Italians, or that the Japanese tend to be xenophobic and nationalistic, or that Latin Americans are typically macho and sexist, or that many Irishmen and American Indians drink enormous quantities of alcohol. Basically, Helmreich finds that these perceptions are confirmed by the data. Of all the stereotypes he considers—many of them now outdated and not widely held—Helmreich concludes that "almost half the stereotypes have a strong factual basis." This is a remarkable refutation of the a priori assumption that group generalizations are always erroneous and unwarranted.

It is obvious to most people that groups do differ. Therefore it is possible to make accurate generalizations. As the term suggests, generalizations hold true in general: they work best when, circumstances permitting, they take into account individual exceptions to the rule and overlapping traits between groups. Stated in this form, it is not clear that group generalizations constitute prejudice or stereotypes at all. They do not satisfy one crucial criterion, what Gordon Allport terms making critical judgments "without sufficient warrant." Allport offers as an exception to his theory of prejudice what he calls the "well-deserved reputation theory." It is no prejudice or stereotype to say that Indians eat curry or that Mexicans eat enchiladas: Indians and Mexicans really do these things.

Since groups do possess distinguishing traits, the liberal assumption that greater contact between groups can be expected to eliminate prejudices and stereotypes turns out to be illusory. It is possible to tell a young boy or girl who has never met Puerto Ricans that they have no recognizable group traits, but after that child has lived in New York for a few months, such an argument from a sensitivity counselor will come to sound comical. In fact, studies confirm that greater exposure often has the effect of reinforcing negative perceptions of distinguishing group traits: familiarity sometimes does breed contempt. One study showed that "teachers, nurses and physicians working in Alaska had much more negative stereotypes of Eskimos than those having little contact" and concluded, "Contact does generate prejudice." Another survey found that whites who live in areas with high concentrations of blacks exhibit greater hostility to them and oppose government race-based programs far more strongly than whites who live in areas with few if any blacks. Thus the relativist assumption that groups do not differ and that group generalizations are irrational turns out to be wrong. Indeed it generates a liberal antiracist paradigm which is at variance with most people's direct observation of the real world. Prejudices and stereotypes merely reflect a human tendency to generalize from experience; they can only be refuted by showing that the group in question does not empirically possess the quality attributed to it. Since this is often difficult to show, we would do better to acknowledge the reality of group traits and ask how we should act on them.

Source:
Dinesh D'Souza, *The End of Racism:*
Principles for a Multiracial Society
(New York: Free Press, 1995), pp. 268–76.

8

America at the Crossroads

BY DAVID DUKE

Few figures have embodied the racial polarization of contemporary American society more distinctly than David Duke (b. 1950). A former Grand Wizard of the Ku Klux Klan and avowed Nazi sympathizer who for a time denied the existence of the Holocaust, Duke was elected in 1989 to the Louisiana House of Representatives. He then won 40 percent of the vote in 1991 in a failed campaign for governor and 44 percent of the vote in 1992 in his attempt to unseat Senator J. Bennett Johnston. Duke also created the National Association for the Advancement of White People and once advocated resettling all African Americans to Africa and all American Jews to Long Island. He now declares himself a born-again Christian. Duke runs as a Republican, although he has been vehemently repudiated by many mainstream Republicans.

In "America at the Crossroads," the "mission statement" that can be found on Duke's homepage on the Internet, Duke sums up his manifold concerns regarding the "non-White birthrate," excessive immigration, the media's purported degradation of the nation's "heritage," and other matters.

AMERICA IS AT THE CROSSROADS. Americans have a simple yet very difficult decision to make. Are they willing to let this nation inevitably become a Third World society, or are they willing to stand up and fight, while they still can, for their heritage, traditions, and values?

Multi-Culturalism and "Diversity" are lies. The non-White birthrate, coupled with massive immigration (both legal and illegal) and racial intermarriage, will reduce the founding people of America into a minority in our own nation. As the racial composition of America changes, so will America. Our children and theirs will live in an America where alien cultures and values will not simply be present but will dominate us.

It may be politically-incorrect to state it, but this alien influx is a disaster for our country, our people, and our families. Crime will continue to escalate, as schools deteriorate, corruption increases, and quality of life plummets.

One can see clearly the change coming by observing America's capitol, where despite the federal flood of our tax money, brutal crimes of violence, drugs, illiteracy, and corruption flourish.

This transformation is personified in the mayor of Washington, Marion Barry. Barry was ousted in 1990 when, as DC's mayor, he was caught on videotape, smoking crack cocaine in the hotel room of a prostitute. He was convicted, but received very little jail time. Upon release, he ran for the DC City Council and was elected! And after "serving" without distinction on the DC City Council for one term, he ran for Mayor and was elected!

Many other cities are also becoming unlivable. My home city of New Orleans has a young mulatto mayor who has fathered at least one illegitimate child, and has been hospitalized for a drug abuse. He, too, was elected by the overwhelming Black bloc. His first three years in office correspond with a murder rate in New Orleans of more than one per day (city population just over 500,000).

Louis Farakhan (who is virulently anti-White) is the most popular Black leader in America. He attracts the largest Black turnouts of any "Afro-American" and although the "Million Man March" did not draw enough devotees to live up to its name, the Muslim minister had still orchestrated the largest Black demonstration in American history, a day long orgy of anti-White hatred.

When the American people saw the L.A. riots and crowds of Blacks cheering O. J. Simpson (who was acquitted by the almost all Black jury), they received a peek into their future.

Could a Marion Barry or Louis Farakhan–type eventually become President of the United States? Unthinkable? Remember that a Marion Barry as mayor of our country's capitol, L.A. riots, and Affirmative Action also would have been unthinkable just a few short years ago.

Most of the largest cities in America now have non-white mayors, councils, and judges. Many parts of the Southwest and sections of American cities more closely resemble Mexico than "Anglo" America.

Check out Dallas, San Antonio, Phoenix, Los Angeles, San Diego, El Paso, Houston, Miami, Midland-Odessa, Las Cruces, or Albuquerque.

Non-white majorities are now on the horizon in many states, with California and Texas acutely in danger. However, it will not take a numerical majority of aliens to bring us down, just a sizeable enough minority.

It is not necessary to dwell too long on the implications for America. The darkening of our nation mimics histories of many other nations. The nations of the Caribbean, Central, and South America, are predictive examples of the fate that awaits us. The Third World awaits our children. It is on our streets, in our taxpayer subsidized housing projects, in our jails, and in our mayors' chairs. Whites in Haiti once produced most of the world's sugar and their nation was called the "Jewel of the Caribbean." Most of them could not have imagined the Haiti of today. Are we so short-sighted that we cannot see where America is heading?

Great nations do fall. In history, every great nation which once graced this planet with high civilization and great achievement has fallen. America, though, is a young nation. We should be vibrant and entering our greatest age. Instead our children grow up in an alien society that our forefathers would not recognize.

The Government and the Mass Media Have Become Enemies of the Founding Heritage of This Nation.

- They support immigration quotas that are over 90 percent non-White. They have made sure that we do not adequately enforce our laws and protect our borders.
- They have supported and financed (with our own tax money) a massive non-White welfare birthrate that is producing chronic crime, degenerated schools and cities, huge costs in welfare, medical care, education, housing, policing, courts, and incarceration.
- They have fostered intense discrimination against White people in jobs, promotions, scholarships, college admissions and union hiring.
- They have destroyed the quality of many of our schools, the civilized quality of our major cities, and the safety of our neighborhoods with forced integration and HUD subsidized housing.
- They have attacked our heritage with an endless array of hate literature, movies, and television that vilifies our White history, character, values, and traditions.

- They have hurt American businesses and workers, and are reducing the overall standard of living and independence of the American people through New World Order inspired trade policies such as NAFTA and GATT.
- They have attacked our Christian values, heritage, and traditions.

We must strive to save our nation and its beseiged heritage. I will fight to stop the massive immigration and the welfare-financed, illegitimate birthrates that are reducing us to a minority in our own land. We must awaken our people of the disaster that looms before us, and inspire them to join the fight for our survival.

- I will fight to limit the power of the Federal Government that is taking more and more of our hard-earned money and more and more of our hard-won rights.
- I will fight for personal responsibility. The welfare system that proliferates the underclass and all its social ills must end as we know it.
- I will fight to limit overpopulation and protect our environment by stopping illegal immigration and almost all "legal immigration" into America.
- I will fight for a simple and fair national sales tax to abolish the income tax and the abusive IRS.
- I will fight for the constitutional right of Americans to Keep and Bear Arms.
- I will fight for reform in the Political process by ending all large political contributions and having free and open broadcast time and debates for all qualified candidates.
- I will fight for freedom of choice in education and in association by ending forced busing and integration.
- I will fight for an absolute end to the racial discrimination called "affirmative action."
- I will fight for fair trade and against agreements such as NAFTA and GATT that hurt the American people.
- I will fight for real freedom of speech for the American people not just for the politically correct by ending the control of a few conglomerates over the American media.
- I will fight for America First by putting an end to foreign aid and the New World Order.

Although the media has unfairly depicted me as a racist and a hater, I am neither. For although I recognize the important inherent distinctions between the races, I do not seek to oppress Blacks and other minorities, nor do I hate them.

I do, though, have an abiding love for our White race and the civilization and values that it created. I want my children and all my descendants to live in a free and healthy society, not a Third World hovel. I want to preserve the unique character and beauty of my people the same way that, as an ecology-minded individual, I desire the preservation of the Blue Whale or the great African Elephant.

I demand the same things for our progeny that all healthy people throughout history have sought: the right for us to live and go on generation after generation;

- for our heritage to be enriched rather than degraded;
- for us to be free and not constrained by tyranny;
- for us to be safe and secure in our homes and when about in society;
- for us to be happy and fulfilled, and not alienated in a culture foreign to us;
- for us to achieve all that our talents and abilities allow.

America is at the crossroads.

Now is the time for all real Americans to journey with me. Together we can secure the existence of our people, and a bright future for our children.

I am asking for you to join our efforts to save our heritage and our country.

Source:
David Duke, "America at the Crossroads,"
http://www.duke.org/mission.htm (1997).

PART TWO

Science and
Pseudo-Science

AMERICAN PREJUDICE BLOSSOMED in the eighteenth and nineteenth centuries, drawing upon the work of scientists—notably in the realms of biology, anthropology, and political science—who were debating the central issues of race that would dominate the intellectual world until the dawn of the twentieth century. Among these issues were the following: Are there any "pure" races, and, if so, what are they? Is any race superior or inferior to another? Are all human beings members of the same species? What *is* a "race," and how can it be properly defined? To say that much ink was spilled on futile and, as it now seems to us, absurdly erroneous discussions of these and other questions is only to say that scientists can exhibit the same prejudices as the rest of us.

The attempt to classify human races appears to have begun in 1684 with François Bernier, who focused largely on physical characteristics.[1] In the later eighteenth century the Swedish naturalist Linnaeus (Carl von Linné, 1707–1778) introduced his revolutionary classification of all plant and animal life. It was also Linnaeus who promoted the distinction between *species* (which were fixed and immutable) and *varieties* (members of a species that could undergo change through climate, geography, nutrition, and other factors). Linnaeus's fourfold division of humanity (Homo Europaeus, Homo Asiaticus, Homo Afer, and Homo Americanus [referring to Native Americans]) was immensely influential, but he maintained that the human species was one and that these classifications related to varieties within the species. Georges-Louis Leclerc, Comte de Buffon (1707–1788), and

Johann Friedrich Blumenbach (1752–1840) followed Linnaeus, although the former asserted that the white race was manifestly the "norm" from which other races deviated, and the latter maintained the existence of five varieties of mankind—Caucasian (a term he coined), Mongolian, Ethiopian, American, and Malay. Blumenbach, however, rejected the view that any race was superior to any other.

It was indeed not a prudent thing in the eighteenth century to assert that different human races did not belong to the same species, since this view was associated with blasphemy and atheism. This did not prevent the iconoclastic Voltaire from adopting the belief that Native Americans and Africans were a separate species, and in this he was followed by Henry Home, Lord Kames, in *Sketches of the History of Man* (1774), and Charles White in his *Account of the Regular Gradation in Man* (1799). Presbyterian minister Samuel Stanhope Smith wrote an appendix to a later edition of his *Essay on the Causes of the Variety of Complexion and Figure* (1787) as a direct refutation of White.

As the nineteenth century advanced, scientists became increasingly divided over the issue of whether there was a single or a multiple origin of the human species. On the polygenic side was Samuel George Morton, who developed Blumenbach's theories on cranial measurements as indicators of racial differences, and the Swiss-born Louis Agassiz, long the dean of American naturalists. Craniology incidentally led to the widespread popularity of phrenology (the purported analysis of character traits based on the shape and configuration of the cranium) in the nineteenth century. On the monogenic side were such individuals as John Bachman (*The Doctrine of the Unity of the Human Race,* 1850) and the Scottish publisher Robert Chambers, whose *Vestiges of the Natural History of Creation* (1844) exerted an influence on European thought far out of proportion to its value or originality as a scientific treatise. Chambers's assertion that "the human race is *one*" did not stop him from adopting Blumenbach's fivefold division of humanity; he did, however, introduce the novelty that each of the races was a stage in the development of the highest (that is, Caucasian) type. The whole monogenic/polygenic controversy was mercifully put to rest by the theory of evolution. And yet Darwin's contention that the features common to the various human "races" far outweigh the differences, and thereby establish the unity of the human race, paradoxically gave an additional impetus to racists to seek out those very differences as a means of establishing *biological* (as opposed to merely cultural) superiority.

It was at this time that what many identify as the single most significant work in the history of racism—Gobineau's *Inequality of Human Races* (1853–55)—emerged. There was precious little science in Gobineau's treatise; perhaps its mere size was meant to impress. Gobineau put forward three races—white, yellow, and black—and predictably asserted the incalculable superiority of the first. It seems not to have fazed racists of this period that they all came up with a different number of races or species, from Gobineau's three to as many as sixty-three, as put forward by the German biologist Ernst Haeckel, who with Thomas Henry Huxley was one of the chief promotors of the evolution theory. Even those who put forward the same number of races often classed humanity differently.

The theory of evolution gave an impetus to the search for racial distinctions, even if the majority of scientists were forced to abandon the polygenic theory of human origins. Mendel's discovery of the laws of heredity was similarly misused toward the end of the nineteenth century, being applied to cultural patterns that are manifestly a product of social conditioning. With the apparent triumph of nineteenth-century science in so many fields of inquiry, from biology to astrophysics, all racists wished to appear scientific. The anti-Semite Burton J. Hendrick went so far as to assert in 1922 that the "individualistic trading instinct of the Jew is . . . inherent in the very germ-plasm of the race."

Around the turn of the twentieth century "scientific" racists found a new tool in their quest to justify the superiority of their own race: the intelligence test. Such tests were first developed in the United States in the 1890s, and almost immediately scientists put them to use in attempts to gauge racial differences. The test results fed a growing belief that intelligence was hereditary, and monitors of the tests blithely ignored factors involving environment and differences in the quality of education in their assertions of the irremediable ignorance of the poor and underprivileged. With the refinement of the Stanford-Binet IQ test in 1916 many statisticians felt that they had obtained an infallible tool for distinguishing racial intelligence. A version of this test was used by the U.S. Army in 1917, upon the nation's entry into World War I, to "prove" that African Americans and other groups were unfit for military service. The absurdities occasioned by the careless use of these and other intelligence tests have now been widely demonstrated, but this did not stop Arthur R. Jensen from publishing a lengthy paper in 1969 on the differences between test scores by whites and African Americans—a paper that brought him death threats on the University of California campus and a torrent of rebuttals.[2] At about this time it began to dawn on people that many intelligence tests may be culturally biased; Jensen himself devoted much effort to refuting this idea in a massive volume, *Bias in Mental Testing* (1980), which similarly produced a mountain of criticism. Finally, Richard J. Herrnstein and Charles Murray resurrected the whole issue in *The Bell Curve* (1994), a volume that has also inspired tremendous controversy.

9

An Essay on the Causes of the Variety of Complexion and Figure in the Human Species

BY SAMUEL STANHOPE SMITH

Samuel Stanhope Smith (1750–1819) was a Presbyterian minister and professor of moral philosophy at the College of New Jersey, later to become Princeton University. The author of various works of philosophy and theology, Smith is chiefly remembered for An Essay on the Causes of the Variety of Complexion and Figure in the Human Species *(1787), originally an oration delivered before the American Philosophical Society in Philadelphia. Although intent on refuting the notion that African Americans are a separate human species, Smith is hampered by his religious view of creation and believes that humanity must have emerged in a civilized state; he accordingly takes a dim view of the "savages" who originally occupied the North American continent.*

T HE HYPOTHESIS THAT THE HUMAN KIND is divided into various species, radically different from one another, is commonly connected in the systems of philosophers with another opinion, which, however general the assent be which it has obtained, is equally contrary to true philosophy, and to the sacred history; I mean the primitive and absolute savagism of all the tribes of men. A few observations on this opinion calculated to demonstrate its utter improbability, if not its obvious falsehood, will not, I presume, be deemed impertinent to the object of the following essay; which is to confirm the doctrine of the unity of the human race, by pointing out the causes of its variety. As this argument, however, rests on an entirely different kind of proof, and is only incidentally related to my principal design, I shall present it to the reader with the greatest brevity. And I trust it will not be found to be an argument so trite, or so unimportant, as to render it, on either account, unworthy his serious attention.

The original, and absolute savagism of mankind, then, is a principle which appears to me to be contradicted equally by sound reason, and by the most authentic documents which remain to us of ancient history. All the earliest monuments of nations, as far as we can trace them, fix their origin about the middle regions of Asia, and present man to us in a state already civilized. From this centre we perceive the radiations of the race gradually shooting themselves towards every quarter of the globe. Savage life seems to have arisen only from idle, or restless spirits, who, shunning the fatigues of labor, or spurning the restraints and subordinations of civil society, sought, at once, liberty, and the pleasures of the chace, in wild, uncultivated regions remote from their original habitations. Here, forgetting the arts of civilized life, they, with their posterity, degenerated, in a course of time, into all the ignorance and rudeness of savagism, and furnished ample materials to the imagination of the poets for the pictures they have presented to us of the abject condition of the primitive men. But let us consult reason, as well as history, for the truth, or probability of their pictures.

Hardly is it possible that man, placed on the surface of the new world, in the midst of its forests and marshes, capable of reason, indeed, but without having formed principles to direct its exercise, should have been able to preserve his existence, unless he had received from his Creator, along with his being, some instructions concerning the use and employment of his faculties, for procuring his subsistence, and inventing the most necessary arts of life. Nature has furnished the inferior animals with many and powerful instincts to direct them in the choice of their food, and with natural instruments peculiarly adapted to enable them, either by climbing the forest tree for its fruits, or by digging in the earth for nutricious roots, to obtain it, in sufficient quantities for the sustenance of life. But man, destitute of the nice and accurate instincts of other animals, as well as of the effectual means which they possess of procuring their provision, must have been the most forlorn of all creatures, although destined to be lord of the creation; unless we can suppose him, like the primitive man of the sacred scriptures, to have been placed in a rich garden which offered him, at hand, its abundant and spontaneous fruits. Cast out, an orphan of nature, naked and helpless, into the savage forest, he must have perished before he could have learned how to supply his most immediate and urgent wants. Suppose him to have been created, or to have started into being, we know not how, in the full strength of his bodily powers, how long must it have been before he could have known the proper use of his limbs, or how to apply them to climb the tree, and run out upon its limbs to gather its fruit, or to grope in the earth for roots, to the choice of which he could not be led by his smell, and for the collection of which the human hand, especially in its soft, and original state, is most imperfectly adapted. Very inadequate must have been the supply obtained by these means, if a supply could have been obtained at all, for wants the most pressing and importunate in our nature, and for appetites the calls of which, in such a state, wherein its supplies must always be both scanty, and difficult to be procured, could never be intermitted. We are prone to judge of the mental powers of such a being, in the first moments of his existence, by the faculties which we perceive in ourselves, or observe among savages with whom we are acquainted, whose minds have been, in a degree, improved and strengthened by experience. The American savage, for example, has been taught from his infancy the necessary arts for supplying his wants. But the primitive man, if we suppose him to have received no communication of knowledge from his Creator, and to have been abandoned merely to his own powers, without the least aid from experience, or instruction, would have been nothing but a large infant. Reason, the supreme prerogative of our nature, and its chief distinction from that of the inferior animals, could have availed him little in that emergency. It would have required, in order to its exercise, a knowledge of principles, and of the nature of the objects around him, which could have been the result only of time, and a certain degree of experience. In the mean time, that recent mass of organized matter, called a man, would probably have perished.

But, if we believe that, in this deplorable condition, he could have found means to sustain life, man, originally a savage, and a savage in the most abject state in which it is possible for human nature to exist, must have remained a savage for ever. Urged by the most pressing wants of nature, for which all his exertions, undirected by skill, and unassisted by the natural arms which other creatures possess, could have furnished but a scanty supply, and which, therefore would have never ceased one moment to harass him, he would not have enjoyed leisure to invent any of those arts which enter into the first elements of civilized life. An importunate appetite, with brutal impulse, would have so continually precipitated him from object to object in order to gratify its cravings, that he could have redeemed no portion of his time for contemplating the powers of nature, or for combining his observations in such a manner as to apply those powers in ingenious inventions, for anticipating his wants, or for facilitating their supply. If he could indulge a moment's repose from the importunity of hunger, it would be to resign the next moment to absolute inaction, like a satiated beast in his den. The character of a savage is infinitely improvident. Nothing he abhors so much as labor, when he is not under the immediate impulse of some imperious appetite, or passion. The American savage, who possesses many advantages above the primitive man whom we are contemplating, as soon as he is released from the fatigues of the chace, generally gives himself up to listless and gloomy indolence. And, though he has derived from his ancestors, who probably emigrated from different regions in the old world, the rudiments of the arts of hunting and fishing, which might have been expected to lay a foundation for a further progress in improving the comforts of his condition; yet with these rude and scanty arts the indolent genius of savagism has been contented; and, during three centuries since America was first discovered by Europeans, he has not been known to advance a single step in the amelioration of his state. Even in those situations in which he has had the most favourable opportunities to observe the benefits resulting from agriculture and the mechanic arts, in augmenting the conveniences and comforts of living, he has never profited by the example. He regards the labors of the field, and the workshop, as an intolerable servitude to men who have it in their power to enjoy the range of the forest; and, after the sports of the chace, to recline themselves in indolent repose. To a few of the aboriginal tribes who would permit it, the government of the United States, with a laudable concern for the interests of humanity, has endeavoured to extend a benevolent patronage, with a view to raise them, if possible, above their present rude and savage condition. But it has found the greatest difficulty in introducing among them only two or three of the simplest arts of civilized society. And only two or three of those tribes have hitherto been induced to admit the smallest change in their habits of life. The love of complete personal independence, and the abhorrence of every species of restraint so natural to the savage, would for ever prevent him, when left to his own native impulses, and not encouraged, assisted, and directed, and, in some measure, controled, by extraneous and superior power, from making even the first advance in the career of civilization. But if any philosopher pretends that, in the natural progress of things, a savage tribe, cut off from all communication with more polished nations, will, by the efforts of their own genius, invent, and gradually perfect the arts of civilized life, let him point out the instance. Following the lights of history, we frequently see rude and barbarous people prompted and assisted in their progress to refinement by the example and influence of nations who have advanced far before them in this career. The Greeks were polished by the Asiatics, and Egyptians; the Italians by the Greeks, and by colonies from the Lesser Asia; and Italy extended her arts to Germany and Gaul. But history presents to us no tribe originally and perfectly savage who has voluntarily sought from abroad, and introduced among themselves the manners, and the arts of any civilized nation; much less has invented those arts, and cultivated those manners, from the operation of any causes arising solely within themselves, or any tendencies in human nature, while existing in such a state of society, towards further improvement. The unsuccessful efforts of the United States to introduce among the tribes of savages, who skirt along our western frontiers, only a few of our arts, most obviously tending to their own advantage, demonstrate that the genius of savagism is obstinately opposed to the labours, the restraints, and industrious habits required in civilized society. Hardly has any individual savage ever been induced to adopt our manners. Such, on the other hand, is the charm of their wandering and independent state, the pleasure of alternately pursuing their game, and reposing in indolence, that many of the citizens of the United States are found voluntarily to renounce all the conveniences of civilization to mingle with the savages in the wilderness, giving the preference to their idle and vagrant habits of life.—Two striking and practical examples which demonstrate, on one hand, with what facility civilized man sinks into the savage, especially in those circumstances which so frequently offered themselves to restless and idle spirits in the early periods of the world; and on the other hand, what difficulties, almost insurmountable, the savage state opposes to the ascent of human nature, in the contrary progression towards the cultivation of the arts of civilized life.

Source:
Samuel Stanhope Smith, *An Essay on the
Causes of the Variety of Complexion and Figure
in the Human Species* (Philadelphia: Robert
Aitken, 1787; reprinted New Brunswick, NJ:
J. Simpson & Co.; New York: Williams &
Whiting, 1810), pp. 15–25.

10

Vestiges of the Natural History of Creation

BY ROBERT CHAMBERS

Robert Chambers (1802–1871), a Scottish publisher and amateur scientist, wrote many historical and biographical works but is largely known for Vestiges of the Natural History of Creation *(1844), in which he attempts to refute the notion that different races of human beings belong to different species. He proposes instead a fivefold racial division of mankind, putting forth a pseudo-evolutionary theory that each of these races is one stage of development toward the highest (Caucasian) type.*

THE HUMAN RACE IS KNOWN TO CONSIST of numerous nations, displaying considerable differences of external form and colour, and speaking in general different languages. This has been the case since the commencement of written record. It is also ascertained that the external peculiarities of particular nations do not rapidly change. There is rather a tendency to a persistency of type in all lines of descent, insomuch that a subordinate admixture of various type is usually obliterated in a few generations. Numerous as the varieties are, they have all been found classifiable under five leading ones—1. The Caucasian, or Indo-European, which extends from India into Europe and Northern Africa; 2. The Mongolian, which occupies Northern and Eastern Asia; 3. The Malayan, which extends from the Ultra-Gangetic Peninsula into the numerous islands of the South Sea and Pacific; 4. The Negro, chiefly confined to

59

Africa; 5. The aboriginal American. Each of these is distinguished by certain general features of so marked a kind, as to give rise to a supposition that they have had distinct or independent origins. Of these peculiarities, colour is the most conspicuous: the Caucasians are generally white, the Mongolians yellow, the Negroes black, and the Americans red. The opposition of two of these in particular, white and black, is so striking, that of them, at least, it seems almost necessary to suppose separate origins. Of late years, however, the whole of this question has been subjected to a rigorous investigation, and it has been successfully shewn that the human race might have had one origin, for anything that can be inferred from external peculiarities. . . .

Assuming that the human race is *one,* we are next called upon to inquire in what part of the earth it may most probably be supposed to have originated. One obvious mode of approximating to a solution of this question is to trace backward the lines in which the principal tribes appear to have migrated, and to see if these converge nearly to a point. It is very remarkable that the lines do converge, and are concentrated about the region of Hindostan. The language, religion, modes of reckoning time, and some other peculiar ideas of the Americans, are now believed to refer their origin to North-Eastern Asia. Trace them farther back in the same direction, and we come to the north of India. The history of the Celts and Teutones represents them as coming from the east, the one after the other, successive waves of a tide of population flowing towards the north-west of Europe: this line being also traced back, rests finally at the same place. So does the line of Iranian population, which has peopled the east and south shores of the Mediterranean, Syria, Arabia, and Egypt. The Malay variety, again, rests its limit in one direction on the borders of India. Standing on that point, it is easy to see how the human family, originating there, might spread out in different directions, passing into varieties of aspect and of language as they spread, the Malay variety proceeding towards the Oceanic region, the Mongolians to the east and north, and sending off the red men as a sub-variety, the European population going off to the north-westward, and the Syrian, Arabian, and Egyptian, towards the countries which they are known to have so long occupied. The Negro alone is here unaccounted for; and of that race it may fairly be said, that it is the one most likely to have had an independent origin, seeing that it is a type so peculiar in an inveterate black colour, and so mean in development. But it is not necessary to presume such an origin for it, as much good argument might be employed to shew that it is only a deteriorated offshoot of the general stock. Our view of the probable original seat of man agrees with the ancient traditions of the race. There is one among the Hindoos which places the cradle of the human family in Thibet; another makes Ceylon the residence of the first man. Our view is also in harmony with the hypothesis detailed in the chapter before the last. According to that theory, we should expect man to have originated where the highest species of the quadrumana are to be found. Now these are unquestionably found in the Indian Archipelago.

After all, it may be regarded as still an open question, whether mankind is of one or many origins. The first human generation may have consisted of many pairs, though situated at one place, and these may have been considerably different from each other in external characters. And we are equally bound to admit, though this does not as yet seem to have occurred to any other speculator, that there may have been different lines and sources of origination, geographically apart, but which all resulted uniformly in the production of a being, one in species, although variously marked. . . .

The probability may now be assumed that the human race sprung from one stock, which was at first in a state of simplicity, if not barbarism. As yet we have not seen very distinctly how the various branches of the family, as they parted off, and took up separate ground, became marked by external features so peculiar. Why are the Africans black, and generally marked by coarse features and ungainly forms? Why are the Mongolians generally yellow, the Americans red, the Caucasians white? Why the flat features of the Chinese, the small stature of the Laps, the soft round forms of the English, the lank features of their descendants, the Americans? All of these phenomena appear, in a word, to be explicable on the ground of *development*. We have already seen that various leading animal forms represent stages in the embryotic progress of the highest— the human being. Our brain goes through the various stages of a fish's, a reptile's, and a mammifer's brain, and finally becomes human. There is more than this, for, after completing the animal transformations, it passes through the characters in which it appears, in the Negro, Malay, American, and Mongolian nations, and finally is Caucasian. The face partakes of these alterations. "One of the earliest points in which ossification commences is the lower jaw. This bone is consequently sooner completed than the other bones of the head, and acquires a predominance, which, as is well known, it never loses in the Negro. During the soft pliant state of the bones of the skull, the oblong form which they naturally assume, approaches nearly the permanent shape of the Americans. At birth, the flattened face, and broad smooth forehead of the infant, the position of the eyes rather towards the side of the head, and the widened space between, represent the Mongolian form; while it is only as the child advances to maturity, that the oval face, the arched forehead, and the marked features of the true Caucasian, become perfectly developed."* *The leading characters, in short, of the various races of mankind are simply representations of particular stages in the development of the highest or Caucasian type.* The Negro exhibits permanently the imperfect brain, projecting lower jaw, and slender bent limbs of a Caucasian child some considerable time before the period of its birth. The aboriginal American represents the same child nearer birth. The Mongolian is an arrested infant newly born. And so forth. All this is as respects form; but whence colour? This might be supposed to have depended on climatal agencies only; but it has been shewn by overpowering evidence to be independent of these. In further considering the matter, we are met by the very remarkable fact that colour is deepest in the least perfectly developed type, next in the Malay, next in the American, next in the Mongolian, the very order in which the degrees of development are ranged. *May not colour, then, depend upon development also?* We do not, indeed, see that a Caucasian fetus at the stage which the African represents is anything like black; neither is a Caucasian child yellow, like the Mongolian. There may, nevertheless, be a character of skin at a certain stage of development which is predisposed to a particular colour when it is presented as the envelope of a mature being. Development being arrested at so immature a stage in the case of the Negro, the skin may take on the colour as an unavoidable consequence of its imperfect organization. It is favourable to this view, that Negro infants are not deeply black at first, but only acquire the full colour tint after exposure for some time to the atmosphere. Another consideration in its favour is that there is a likelihood of peculiarities of form and colour, since they are so coincident, depending on one set of phenomena. If it be admitted as true, there can be no difficulty in accounting for all the varieties of mankind. They are simply the result of so many advances and retrogressions in the developing power of the human mothers, these advances and retrogressions being, as we have formerly seen, the immediate effect of external conditions in nutrition, hardship, &c., and also, perhaps, to some extent, of the suitableness and unsuitableness of marriages, for it is found that parents too nearly related tend to produce offspring of the Mongolian type,—that is, persons who in maturity still are a kind of children. According to this view, the greater part of the human race must be considered as having lapsed or declined from the original type. In the Caucasian or Indo-European family alone has the primitive organization

---

*Lord's Popular Physiology, explaining observations by M. Serres.

been improved upon. The Mongolian, Malay, American, and Negro, comprehending perhaps five-sixths of mankind, are degenerate. Strange that the great plan should admit of failures and aberrations of such portentous magnitude! But pause and reflect; take time into consideration: the past history of mankind may be, to what is to come, but as a day. Look at the progress even now making over the barbaric parts of the earth by the best examples of the Caucasian type, promising not only to fill up the waste places, but to supersede the imperfect nations already existing. Who can tell what progress may be made, even in a single century, towards reversing the proportions of the perfect and imperfect types? and who can tell but that the time during which the mean types have lasted, long as it appears, may yet be thrown entirely into the shade by the time during which the best types will remain predominant?

Source:
Robert Chambers, *Vestiges of the Natural
History of Creation* (London: John Churchill,
1844), pp. 277–78, 294–97, 305–10.

11

The Inequality of Human Races

BY JOSEPH ARTHUR, COMTE DE GOBINEAU

The Essai sur l'inégalité des races humaines *(1853–55) by Joseph Arthur, Comte de Gobineau (1816–1882), is perhaps the single most significant work in the literature of racism: it was the first work to attempt a systematic (albeit based largely upon mere assertion rather than scientific evidence) demonstration of the superiority or inferiority of the races of the world. Gobineau asserts that there are three fundamental races—white, yellow, and black—and that the first is clearly superior. Gobineau's work was widely read throughout Europe, especially in Germany, and did much to foster racist nationalism in the later nineteenth century; it was also used by American opponents of immigration during and after World War I. The work has never been fully translated into English; the 1915 volume,* The Inequality of Human Races, *is a translation of only part one of the original.*

I HAVE SHOWN THE UNIQUE PLACE in the organic world occupied by the human species, the profound physical, as well as moral, differences separating it from all other kinds of living creatures. Considering it by itself, I have been able to distinguish, on physiological grounds alone, three great and clearly marked types, the black, the yellow and the white. However uncertain the aims of physiology may be, however meagre its resources, however defective its methods, it can proceed thus far with absolute certainty.

The negroid variety is the lowest, and stands at the foot of the ladder. The animal character, that appears in the shape of the pelvis, is stamped on the Negro from birth and foreshadows his destiny. His intellect will always move within a very narrow circle. He is not however a mere brute, for behind his low receding brow, in the middle of his skull, we can see signs of a powerful energy, however crude its objects. If his mental faculties are dull or even non-existent, he often has an intensity of desire, and so of will, which may be called terrible. Many of his senses, especially taste and smell, are developed to an extent unknown to the other two races.

The very strength of his sensations is the most striking proof of his inferiority. All food is good in his eyes, nothing disgusts or repels him. What he desires is to eat, to eat furiously, and to excess; no carrion is too revolting to be swallowed by him. It is the same with odours; his inordinate desires are satisfied with all, however coarse or even horrible. To these qualities may be added an instability and capriciousness of feeling, that cannot be tied down to any single object, and which, so far as he is concerned, do away with all distinctions of good and evil. We might even say that the violence with which he pursues the object that has aroused his senses and inflamed his desires is a guarantee of the desires being soon satisfied and the object forgotten. Finally, he is equally careless of his own life and that of others: he kills willingly, for the sake of killing; and this human machine, in whom it is so easy to arouse emotion, shows, in face of suffering, either a monstrous indifference or a cowardice that seeks a voluntary refuge in death.

The yellow race is the exact opposite of this type. The skull points forward, not backward. The forehead is wide and bony, often high and projecting. The shape of the face is triangular, the nose and chin showing none of the coarse protuberances that mark the Negro. There is further a general proneness to obesity, which, though not confined to the yellow type, is found there more frequently than in the others. The yellow man has little physical energy, and is inclined to apathy; he commits none of the strange excesses so common among Negroes. His desires are feeble, his will-power rather obstinate than violent; his longing for material pleasures, though constant, is kept within bounds. A rare glutton by nature, he shows far more discrimination in his choice of food. He tends to mediocrity in everything; he understands easily enough anything not too deep or sublime. He has a love of utility and a respect for order, and knows the value of a certain amount of freedom. He is practical, in the narrowest sense of the word. He does not dream or theorize; he invents little, but can appreciate and take over what is useful to him. His whole desire is to live in the easiest and most comfortable way possible. The yellow races are thus clearly superior to the black. Every founder of a civilization would wish the backbone of his society, his middle class, to consist of such men. But no civilized society could be created by them; they could not supply its nerve force, or set in motion the springs of beauty and action.

We come now to the white peoples. These are gifted with reflective energy, or rather with an energetic intelligence. They have a feeling for utility, but in a sense far wider and higher, more courageous and ideal, than the yellow races; a perseverance that takes account of obstacles and ultimately finds a means of overcoming them; a greater physical power, an extraordinary instinct for order, not merely as a guarantee of peace and tranquillity, but as an indispensable means of self-preservation. At the same time, they have a remarkable, and even extreme, love of liberty, and are openly hostile to the formalism under which the Chinese are glad to vegetate, as well as to the strict despotism which is the only way of governing the Negro.

The white races are, further, distinguished by an extraordinary attachment to life. They know better how to use it, and so, as it would seem, set a greater price on it; both in their own persons and those of others, they are more sparing of life. When they are cruel, they are conscious of their cruelty; it is very doubtful whether such a consciousness exists in the Negro. At the same time, they have discovered reasons why they should surrender this busy life of theirs, that is so precious to them. The principal motive is honour, which under various names has played an enormous part in the ideas of the race from the beginning. I need hardly add that the word honour, together with all the civilizing influences connoted by it, is unknown to both the yellow and the black man.

On the other hand, the immense superiority of the white peoples in the whole field of the intellect is balanced by an inferiority in the intensity of their sensations. In the world of the senses, the white man is far less gifted than the others, and so is less tempted and less absorbed by considerations of the body, although in physical structure he is far the most vigorous.

Such are the three constituent elements of the human race. I call them secondary types, as I think myself obliged to omit all discussion of the Adamite man. From the combination, by intermarriage, of the varieties of these types come the tertiary groups. The quaternary formations are produced by the union of one of these tertiary types, or of a pure-blooded tribe, with another group taken from one of the two foreign species.

Below these categories others have appeared—and still appear. Some of these are very strongly characterized, and form new and distinct points of departure, coming as they do from races that have been completely fused. Others are incomplete, and ill-ordered, and, one might even say, anti-social, since their elements, being too numerous, too disparate, or too barbarous, have had neither the time nor the opportunity for combining to any fruitful purpose. No limits, except the horror excited by the possibility of infinite intermixture, can be assigned to the number of these hybrid and chequered races that make up the whole of mankind.

It would be unjust to assert that every mixture is bad and harmful. If the three great types had remained strictly separate, the supremacy would no doubt have always been in the hands of the finest of the white races, and the yellow and black varieties would have crawled for ever at the feet of the lowest of the whites. Such a state is so far ideal, since it has never been beheld in history; and we can imagine it only by recognizing the undisputed superiority of those groups of the white races which have remained the purest.

It would not have been all gain. The superiority of the white race would have been clearly shown, but it would have been bought at the price of certain advantages which have followed the mixture of blood. Although these are far from counter-balancing the defects they have brought in their train, yet they are sometimes to be commended. Artistic genius, which is equally foreign to each of the three great types, arose only after the intermarriage of white and black. Again, in the Malayan variety, a human family was produced from the yellow and black races that had more intelligence than either of its ancestors. Finally, from the union of white and yellow, certain intermediary peoples have sprung, who are superior to the purely Finnish tribes as well as to the Negroes.

I do not deny that these are good results. The world of art and great literature that comes from the mixture of blood, the improvement and ennoblement of inferior races—all these are wonders for which we must needs be thankful. The small have been raised. Unfortunately, the great have been lowered by the same process; and this is an evil that nothing can balance or repair. Since I am putting together the advantages of racial mixtures, I will also add that to them is due the refinement of manners and beliefs, and especially the tempering of passion and desire. But these are merely transitory benefits, and if I recognize that the mulatto, who may become a lawyer, a doctor or a business man, is worth more than his Negro grandfather, who was absolutely savage, and fit for nothing, I must also confess that the Brahmins of primitive India, the heroes of the Iliad and the Shahnameh, the warriors of Scandinavia—the glorious shades of noble races that have disappeared—give us a higher and more brilliant idea of humanity, and were more active, intelligent, and trusty instruments of civilization and grandeur than the peoples, hybrid a hundred times over, of the present day. And the blood even of these was no longer pure.

However it has come about, the human races, as we find them in history, are complex; and one of the chief consequences has been to throw into disorder most of the primitive characteristics of each type. The good as well as the bad qualities are seen to diminish in intensity with repeated intermixture of blood; but they also scatter and separate off from each other, and are often mutually opposed. The white race originally possessed the monopoly of beauty, intelligence and strength. By its union with other varieties, hybrids were created, which were beautiful without strength, strong without intelligence, or, if intelligent, both weak and ugly. Further, when the quantity of white blood was increased to an indefinite amount by successive infusions, and not by a single admixture, it no longer carried with it its natural advantages, and often merely increased the confusion already existing in the racial elements. Its strength, in fact, seemed to be its only remaining quality, and even its strength served only to promote disorder. The apparent anomaly is easily explained. Each stage of a perfect mixture produces a new type from diverse elements, and develops special faculties. As soon as further elements are added, the vast difficulty of harmonizing the whole creates a state of anarchy. The more this increases, the more do even the best and richest of the new contributions diminish in value, and by their mere presence add fuel to an evil which they cannot abate. If mixtures of blood are, to a certain extent, beneficial to the mass of mankind, if they raise and ennoble it, this is merely at the expense of mankind itself, which is stunted, abased, enervated and humiliated in the persons of its noblest sons. Even if we admit that it is better to turn a myriad of degraded beings into mediocre men than to preserve the race of princes whose blood is adulterated and impoverished by being made to suffer this dishonourable change, yet there is still the unfortunate fact that the change does not stop here; for when the mediocre men are once created at the expense of the greater, they combine with other mediocrities, and from such unions, which grow ever more and more degraded, is born a confusion which, like that of Babel, ends in utter impotence, and leads societies down to the abyss of nothingness whence no power on earth can rescue them.

Such is the lesson of history. It shows us that all civilizations derive from the white race, that none can exist without its help, and that a society is great and brilliant only so far as it preserves the blood of the noble group that created it, provided that this group itself belongs to the most illustrious branch of our species.

Of the multitude of peoples which live or have lived on the earth, ten alone have risen to the position of complete societies. The remainder have gravitated round these more or less independently, like planets round their suns. If there is any element of life in these ten civilizations that is not due to the impulse of the white races, any seed of death that does not come from the inferior stocks that mingled with them, then the whole theory on which this book rests is false. On the other hand, if the facts are as I say, then we have an irrefragable proof of the nobility of our own species. Only the actual details can set the final seal of truth on my system, and they alone can show with sufficient exactness the full implications of my main thesis, that peoples degenerate only in consequence of the various admixtures of blood which they undergo; that their degeneration corresponds exactly to the quantity and quality of the new blood, and that the rudest possible shock to the vitality of a civilization is given when the ruling elements in a society and those developed by racial change have become so numerous that they are clearly moving away from the homogeneity necessary to their life, and it therefore becomes impossible for them to be brought into harmony and so acquire the common instincts and interests, the common logic of existence, which is the sole justification for any social bond whatever. There is no greater curse than such disorder, for however bad it may have made the present state of things, it promises still worse for the future.

Source:
Joseph Arthur, Comte de Gobineau, *Essai sur
l'inégalité des races humaines* (1853–55);
abridged translation by Adrian Collins as *The
Inequality of Human Races* (London: William
Heinemann, 1915), pp. 205–11.

12

The Descent of Man

BY CHARLES DARWIN

*The British naturalist Charles Darwin (1809–1882) revolutionized biol-
ogy and all intellectual history with* On the Origin of Species *(1859),
which introduced the theory of evolution by natural selection. We have seen
how the misuse of the Darwin theory fostered the development of racism in
the latter nineteenth century. Darwin himself was circumspect on the issue
of the relative "superiority" or "inferiority" of races; more concerned with
the biology of the lower animals, he never directed serious attention to the
matter. In* The Descent of Man *(1871)—a volume designed to prove that
even the highest mental qualities of human beings have their analogues in
the animal world and can be shown to have developed through evolution—
Darwin includes a chapter entitled "On the Races of Man," which refutes
the hypothesis that different races belong to different species.*

IT IS NOT MY INTENTION HERE to describe the several so-called
races of men; but I am about to inquire what is the value of the differences between them under a classificatory point of view, and how they
have originated. In determining whether two or more allied forms ought
to be ranked as species or varieties, naturalists are practically guided by
the following considerations; namely, the amount of difference between
them, and whether such differences relate to few or many points of
structure, and whether they are of physiological importance; but more
especially whether they are constant. Constancy of character is what is
chiefly valued and sought for by naturalists. Whenever it can be shown,
or rendered probable, that the forms in question have remained distinct
for a long period, this becomes an argument of much weight in favor of

treating them as species. Even a slight degree of sterility between any two forms when first crossed, or in their offspring, is generally considered as a decisive test of their specific distinctness; and their continued persistence without blending within the same area, is usually accepted as sufficient evidence, either of some degree of mutual sterility, or in the case of animals of some mutual repugnance to pairing.

Independently of fusion from intercrossing, the complete absence, in a well-investigated region, of varieties linking together any two closely-allied forms, is probably the most important of all the criterions of their specific distinctness; and this is a somewhat different consideration from mere constancy of character, for two forms may be highly variable and yet not yield intermediate varieties. Geographical distribution is often brought into play unconsciously and sometimes consciously; so that forms living in two widely separated areas, in which most of the other inhabitants are specifically distinct, are themselves usually looked at as distinct; but in truth this affords no aid in distinguishing geographical races from so-called good or true species.

Now let us apply these generally-admitted principles to the races of man, viewing him in the same spirit as a naturalist would any other animal. In regard to the amount of difference between the races, we must make some allowance for our nice powers of discrimination gained by the long habit of observing ourselves. In India, as Elphinstone remarks, although a newly-arrived European cannot at first distinguish the various native races, yet they soon appear to him extremely dissimilar; and the Hindoo cannot at first perceive any difference between the several European nations. Even the most distinct races of man are much more like each other in form than would at first be supposed; certain negro tribes must be excepted, whilst others, as Dr. Rohlfs writes to me, and as I have myself seen, have Caucasian features. This general similarity is well shown by the French photographs in the Collection Anthropologique du Muséum de Paris of the men belonging to various races, the greater number of which might pass for Europeans, as many persons to whom I have shown them have remarked. Nevertheless, these men, if seen alive, would undoubtedly appear very distinct, so that we are clearly much influenced in our judgment by the mere color of the skin and hair, by slight differences in the features, and by expression.

There is, however, no doubt that the various races, when carefully compared and measured, differ much from each other,—as in the texture of the hair, the relative proportions of all parts of the body, the capacity of the lungs, the form and capacity of the skull, and even in the convolutions of the brain. But it would be an endless task to specify the numerous points of difference. The races differ also in constitution, in acclimatization and in liability to certain diseases. Their mental characteristics are likewise very distinct; chiefly as it would appear in their emotional, but partly in their intellectual faculties. Every one who has had the opportunity of comparison must have been struck with the contrast between the taciturn, even morose, aborigines of S. America and the light-hearted, talkative negroes. There is a nearly similar contrast between the Malays and the Papuans, who live under the same physical conditions, and are separated from each other only by a narrow space of sea. . . .

Although the existing races of man differ in many respects, as in color, hair, shape of skull, proportions of the body, &c., yet if their whole structure be taken into consideration they are found to resemble each other closely in a multitude of points. Many of these are so unimportant or of so singular a nature, that it is extremely improbable that they should have been independently acquired by aboriginally distinct species or races. The same remark holds good with equal or greater force with respect to the numerous points of mental similarity between the most distinct races of man. The American aborigines, Negroes and Europeans are as different from each other in mind as any three races that can be named; yet I was incessantly struck, whilst living with the Fuegians on board the "Beagle," with the many little traits of character, showing how similar their minds were to ours; and so it was with a full-blooded negro with whom I happened once to be intimate.

He who will read Mr. Tylor's and Sir J. Lubbock's interesting works can hardly fall to be deeply impressed with the close similarity between the men of all races in tastes, dispositions and habits. This is shown by the pleasure which they all take in dancing, rude music, acting, painting, tattooing, and otherwise decorating themselves; in their mutual comprehension of gesture-language, by the same expression in their features, and by the same inarticulate cries, when excited by the same emotions. This similarity, or rather identity, is striking when contrasted with the different expressions and cries made by distinct species of monkeys. There is good evidence that the art of shooting with bows and arrows has not been handed down from any common progenitor of mankind, yet as Westropp and Nilsson have remarked, the stone arrow-heads, brought from the most distant parts of the world, and manufactured at the most remote periods, are almost identical; and this fact can only be accounted for by the various races having similar inventive or mental powers. The same observation has been made by archæologists with respect to certain widely-prevalent ornaments, such as zigzags, &c.; and with respect to various simple beliefs and customs, such as the burying of the dead under megalithic structures. I remember observing in South America, that there, as in so many other parts of the world, men have generally chosen the summits of lofty hills, to throw up piles of stones, either as a record of some remarkable event, or for burying their dead.

Now when naturalists observe a close agreement in numerous small details of habits, tastes, and dispositions between two or more domestic races, or between nearly-allied natural forms, they use this fact as an argument that they are descended from a common progenitor who was thus endowed; and consequently that all should be classed under the same species. The same argument may be applied with much force to the races of man.

As it is improbable that the numerous and unimportant points of resemblance between the several races of man in bodily structure and mental faculties (I do not here refer to similar customs) should all have been independently acquired, they must have been inherited from progenitors who had these same characters. We thus gain some insight into the early state of man, before he had spread step by step over the face of the earth. The spreading of man to regions widely separated by the sea, no doubt, preceded any great amount of divergence of character in the several races; for otherwise we should sometimes meet with the same race in distinct continents; and this is never the case. Sir J. Lubbock, after comparing the arts now practiced by savages in all parts of the world, specifies those which man could not have known, when he first wandered from his original birthplace; for if once learnt they would never have been forgotten. He thus shows that "the spear, which is but a development of the knife-point, and the club, which is but a long hammer, are the only things left." He admits, however, that the art of making fire probably had been already discovered, for it is common to all the races now existing, and was known to the ancient cave-inhabitants of Europe. Perhaps the art of making rude canoes or rafts was likewise known; but as man existed at a remote epoch, when the land in many places stood at a very different level to what it does now, he would have been able, without the aid of canoes, to have spread widely. Sir J. Lubbock further remarks how improbable it is that our earliest ancestors could have "counted as high as ten, considering that so many races now in existence cannot get beyond four." Nevertheless, at this early period, the intellectual and social faculties of man could hardly have been inferior in any extreme degree to those possessed at present by the lowest savages; otherwise primeval man could not have been so eminently successful in the struggle for life, as proved by his early and wide diffusion.

From the fundamental differences between certain languages, some philologists have inferred that when man first became widely diffused, he was not a speaking animal; but it may be suspected that languages, far less perfect than any now spoken, aided by gestures, might have been used, and yet have left no traces on subsequent and more highly-developed tongues. Without the use of some language, however imperfect, it appears doubtful whether man's intellect could have risen to the standard implied by his dominant position at an early period.

Whether primeval man, when he possessed but few arts, and those of the rudest kind, and when his power of language was extremely imperfect, would have deserved to be called man, must depend on the definition which we employ. In a series of forms graduating insensibly from some ape-like creature to man as he now exists, it would be impossible to fix on any definite point when the term "man" ought to be used. But this is a matter of very little importance. So again, it is almost a matter of indifference whether the so-called races of man are thus designated, or are ranked as species or sub-species; but the latter term appears the more appropriate. Finally, we may conclude that when the principle of evolution is generally accepted, as it surely will be before long, the dispute between the monogenists and the polygenists will die a silent and unobserved death.

Source:
Charles Darwin, *The Descent of Man and
Selection in Relation to Sex* (London:
John Murray, 1871; 2nd ed. 1874),
pp. 257–60, 276–80.

13

Race Prejudice

BY JEAN FINOT

The French historian and social thinker Jean Finot (1858–1922), in La Préjugé des races *(1905; translated as* Race Prejudice*), did much to demolish the "scientific" foundations of racism, especially as propounded by Gobineau, Chamberlain, and others. Finot also wrote* Préjugé et problèmes des sexes *(1912), translated as* Problems of the Sexes *(1913).*

THE ANALYSIS OF ALL THE SUCCESSIVE THEORIES on inequality created in us before everything else a profound astonishment at the credulity and the inertness of our thought. Successive generations only added faith to the same error, and this faith which always favoured its growth also favoured its persistence. As all the appearances seemed to support the dogma of inequality, it was adopted with the first superficial sensations which affected us from without. This belief was thus as deeply rooted as was long ago the faith in the movement of the sun round the earth.

Some time will no doubt elapse before science, emancipated from the prejudices which have prevailed and multiplied for centuries, will succeed in making the truth triumph. All these measurements, with their imposing numbers and scientific pretensions, as also the theoretic observations and deductions, resolve themselves, as we have seen, into a nebulous doctrine which affirms many things and explains nothing.

The exact instruments which anthropologists and especially "craniometrists" use, offer us fantastical data. The results of their operations are deposited in thousands of volumes; and yet what is their real bearing? In examining them closely one can hardly attribute to them even a descriptive value, so much do they contradict and destroy each other.

We have seen, for example, how precarious are the affirmations of craniometry, which constitutes, however, the most developed section of anthropometry. Although the instruments which it places at the disposal of *savants* are very numerous, yet the ways of using them are still more varied. The lack of unity in the observations and the contradictory ends which those who use them seem to pursue, cause numerous misunderstandings, which end in chaotic affirmations. In bringing forward the most indisputable data and in proceeding to a kind of cross-examination, we arrive at a conclusion quite different from that which the adherents of the dogmas of races are anxious to impose on us, and which so many learned demographs, politicians, novelists, and statesmen blindly accept.

When we go through the list of external differences which appear to divide men, we find literally nothing which can authorise their division into superior and inferior beings, into masters and pariahs. If this division exists in our thought, it only came there as the result of inexact observations and false opinions drawn from them.

The science of inequality is emphatically a science of white people. It is they who have invented it and set it going, who have maintained, cherished, and propagated it, thanks to *their* observations and *their* deductions. Deeming themselves greater than men of other colours, they have elevated into superior qualities all the traits which are peculiar to themselves, commencing with the whiteness of the skin and the pliancy of the hair. But nothing proves that these vaunted traits are traits of real superiority.

"If the Chinese and the Egyptians had judged our ancestors as we too often judge foreign races," says Quatrefages, "they would have found in them many traits of inferiority such as this white skin in which we take so much pride, and which they might have regarded as showing an irremediable etiolation." This is what dogmatic anthropologists seem at all times to have forgotten. Human varieties have not been studied like those of animals and plants, that is to say, without conventional prejudices as to their respective values and as to those which are superior and inferior. Facts have often yielded to sentiments. We have been persuaded, with the help of our feelings, to accept our own preferences rather than impartial observations, and our own prejudices rather than scientific laws.

In pursuing this course the elementary commandments of experimental science are transgressed. The majority of the anthropologists, faithful in this respect to the scholastic teachings, have begun by assuming the inequality of human beings as an axiom. On this preliminary basis they have built an imposing edifice, but really one of fictitious solidity.

A radical condemnation of principle weighs on anthropology each time that it exceeds its descriptive limits in order to affect the attitude of a dogmatic science. It becomes teleological, and in that way is deprived of all value. If "*anthropo-sociology*," this too much vaunted branch of anthropology, had adopted this indispensable maxim of the experimental method, that every theory is only true till facts are discovered which are opposed to it, or which coming within its limits burst its barriers, this quasi-science would have had a short career! With what justice could not one apply to dogmatic anthropology and to the phalanx of its disciples what Claude Bernard says of the "scholastic" method, so severely judged by positive science? "Scholasticism never doubts its starting-point, to which it wishes to attribute everything. It has a proud and intolerant mind, and never accepts contradiction, since it does not admit that its starting-point can change." It is thus that all the main data which hurl themselves against the theory of races are empty in its sight. Deaf to the appeal of hostile facts, its adepts are specially distinguished for their intrepidity in maintaining their theory against evidence itself.

Commenting out of sight on the doubtful facts, and rejecting with scorn as worthless the observations of its adversaries, anthropo-sociology continues to live in its romantic hiding-place. It builds there, it is true, impassable walls between men with wide and narrow skulls, yellows and whites, tall and short men, those with thick and thin joints, those with small and large nostrils, those with straight and curved foreheads. But life passes above all these artificial partitions, and marches on their ruins towards unity.

Hypnotised by their primordial idea, they thus bring together without examination everything which seems propitious to their theory, a theory by the way which is political rather than scientific. In their comparisons of the cerebral index, what does it matter to them to know the age or the sex of the subject, his occupations, his intellectuality, or the state of his health? Naturally, if they wish to take all these points into consideration, they must reject nine-tenths of the constituent elements of their pretended truth.

We know, for example, that the weight of the brain varies in man, increasing up to the age of forty-five, and diminishing after that period; that the brain grows under the influence of occupation; that sex also plays a considerable part in it; that the subject's state of health reacts on his cerebral structure; that the form of the human head is often influenced by the pelvis of the mother; and still with what lightness do they not lay hold of their rough measures, leaving on one side the causes of the effects observed? They proceed with no less unconcern in distributing certificates of superiority among the ranks of human beings. After having stated that superior races are furthest removed from the anthropoid apes, whilst the inferior ones are nearer to them, they bring together all the facts which in this respect favour the Whites, and entirely forget those in which Negroes are shown to be more favoured. For example, we are told of the angle of the condyles that the Whites are in this respect nearer the monkeys than the Negroes. When dolichocephaly is regarded as a trait of incontestable superiority, they seem to forget that the majority of Europeans are to be classed in the miserable category of brachycephals, whereas the Negroes belong to the dolichocephalic aristocracy!

If you wish to take as element of comparison the facial angle of Jacquart, you will be forced to arrive at the conclusion that the French and Spanish Basques, a nobly pure race, approach the Esquimaux and the Chinese.

If we keep to the length of the forearm, or to that of the tibia, we fall into a number of eccentricities, where Oceanians accompany Europeans and Bushmen cut no sorry figure. The more we study the many variations which distinguish human beings, the more we perceive that these are in no way intended. They are due to accidents of climate, occupations—in one word, of the surrounding *milieu,* the almost exclusive creator of the phenomena which vex certain obstinate anthropologists, who deny its incessant activity.

It must not be forgotten that the different parts of the body among races called inferior do not vary simultaneously and in every respect from the ideal type which is adopted as basis for comparison. Whereas certain limbs in a Negro or an Australian seem to approach the simian type, other traits preserve their nobility (?) of form, and all this according to no preconceived plan, and especially with no respect for the colour of the skin or the relative beauty of civilisation. Thus are explained the supposed anomalies of races called inferior which are superior to us in many respects, and also those of superior races which so often deserve to be styled inferior. The beast and the angel are mixed in all human beings. All peoples seem equally good and bad, perfectible or susceptible to moral and physical degradation. A kind of enchanted dome covers humanity. It is in vain that it exerts itself, for it never succeeds in surpassing certain limits. Humanity has its boundaries, like the earth which holds it. . . .

The truths concerning man are confirmed when they find their application and their confirmation in his everyday life. The conception of human races in a "conventional" or "conditional" sense prevents us before everything else from regarding them as fatally divergent. On the ruins, therefore, of the belief in superior and inferior races, the possible development and amelioration of all human beings arise. Their evolution, having become of universal application, makes their extermination criminal.

The principle of human equality takes away the right of killing so-called inferior people, just as it destroys the right claimed by some of dominating others. If all peoples are equal, if their different appearances are only the result of changing circumstances, in virtue of what principle is it allowable to destroy their happiness and to compromise their right to independence?

Humanity, looked at from this point of view, becomes a concrete conception. Its solidarity is seen to be its real good. Regarded apart from the equality of races, or rather varieties, integral humanity becomes an expression devoid of meaning.

Once the "prejudice of races" has disappeared, we must acknowledge the beneficial reaction of this belief on the "inner" life of peoples. As we have shown, modern nations have been formed outside and very often in spite of the conceptions of races. When once amalgamated, ethnical principles regarded as most hostile have contributed towards creating the national principle. There are no longer "pure" peoples, if ever there were any.

The more advanced a people and the greater its vitality, so much the more intermixed with others is it found to be. Those which march at the van of civilisation, like the French, English, German, Italian, or those of the United States, all possess blood which is richest in heterogeneous elements. What Paul Broca said of the inhabitants of France—namely, that they exhibit every known type of cephalic index—is applicable to all civilised peoples. All those whose origins have been studied show the same richness of ethnical elements, which, intercrossed, have contributed towards forming their national unities.

Purity of blood is thus only a myth, and its talismanic virtue is found to be irremediably compromised. Unity of blood retreats to the background. What constitutes modern peoples is the solidarity of their moral and material interests. Switzerland, officially known as the union of four different races (really we find some dozens here as elsewhere), constitutes, for all that, a people united in an ideal way, owing to the moral cohesion of all its inhabitants. The same applies to other peoples. Between a Frenchman of the Pas-de-Calais and a Frenchman of the Alpes-Maritimes there is without doubt more divergence than between a Dane and a Norwegian. Yet the two former have one common country and the latter two diverse countries.

Once the nightmare of races is dissipated, we easily understand what Fatherland in the *human sense* of the word means.

How miserable seem to us to-day all the political and sociological doctrines founded on the principle of blood!

Of all the vulgar methods of sparing oneself the trouble of studying profoundly the moral and social factors which influence the human mind, the grossest, according to John Stuart Mill, is that which consists in attributing diversities of conduct and of character to those *natural differences* which are as proper to peoples as to individuals.

In the light of the facts brought together in this volume, we see the immense amount of nonsense connected with the racial theories of peoples. If patriotism was bound to our conceptions of races, what incessant metamorphoses would it not have to undergo? France, believed for centuries to be Gallic, is suddenly revealed to be Germanic! Must we under these circumstances embrace our German brothers, and at the same time espouse German hatreds and sympathies? Through such historic discoveries as to races, we should logically have to modify our loves, hopes, ideals, and sentiments!

The true conception of humanity, far from destroying the sentiment of patriotism, only fortifies and enhances it. It is no longer a brutal instinct of blood, but a high expression of community of ideals and of moral and material interests. With the erroneous principles of pure and irreducible races, and with the false theory of organic inequalities, we arrive, fatally and inevitably, at internal strifes and inextricable misunderstandings. Once, however, these principles are abolished, we understand the obvious and absolute fraternity of the inhabitants of the same country, together with the possibility and the necessity of advancing towards its political and social realisation.

As the differences among men are thus only individual, there will theoretically be no more room for internal and external hatreds, as there will be no more for the social and political inferiorities of classes.

On the ruins, therefore, of the falsehood of races, solidarity and true equality arise, both founded on a rational sentiment of respect for human dignity.

Source:
Jean Finot, *Le Préjugé des races* (1905);
translated by Florence Wade-Evans as
Race Prejudice (London: Constable, 1906),
pp. 309–13, 318–20.

14

The Effects of
Race Intermingling

BY C. B. DAVENPORT

*Charles Benedict Davenport (1866–1944) was the director of the Eugenics
Record Office at Cold Spring Harbor, New York. He received his Ph.D.
from Harvard and taught at Harvard and the University of Chicago.
Throughout his work Davenport warned against racial intermixture; he
even attributed the fall of civilizations to miscegenation.*

THE PROBLEM OF THE EFFECTS of race intermingling may well interest us of America, when a single state, like New York, of 9,000,000 inhabitants contains 840,000 Russians and Finns, 720,000 Italians,
1,000,000 Germans, 880,000 Irish, 470,000 Austro-Hungarians,
310,000 of Great Britain, 125,000 Canadians (largely French), and
90,000 Scandinavians. All figures include those born abroad or born of
two foreign-born parents. Nearly two thirds of the population of New
York State is foreign-born or of foreign or mixed parentage. Even in a state
like Connecticut it is doubtful if 2 per cent of the population are of pure
Anglo-Saxon stock for six generations of ancestors in all lines. Clearly a
mixture of European races is going on in America on a colossal scale.

Before proceeding further let us inquire into the meaning of "race."
The modern geneticists' definition differs from that of the systematist or
old fashioned breeder. A race is a more or less pure bred "group" of individuals that differs from other groups by at least one character, or,
strictly, a genetically connected group whose germ plasm is characterized
by a difference, in one or more genes, from other groups. Thus a blue-

eyed Scotchman belongs to a different race from some of the dark Scotch. Strictly, as the term is employed by geneticists they may be said to belong to different elementary species.

Defining race in this sense of elementary species we have to consider our problem: What are the results of race intermingling, or miscegenation? To this question no general answer can be given. A specific answer can, however, be given to questions involving specific characters. For example, if the question be framed: what are the results of hybridization between a blue-eyed race (say Swede) and a brown-eyed race (say South Italian)? The answer is that, since brown eye is dominant over blue eye, all the children will have brown eyes; and if two such children inter marry brown and blue eyes will appear among their children in the ratio of 3 to 1.

Again, if one parent be white and the other a full-blooded negro, then the skin color of the children will be about half as dark as that of the darker parent; and the progeny of two such mulattoes will be white, $\frac{1}{4}$, $\frac{1}{2}$, $\frac{3}{4}$ and full black in the ratio of 1:4:6:4:1.

Again, if one parent belong to a tall race—like the Scotch or some Irish—and the other to a short race, like the South Italians, then all the progeny will tend to be intermediate in stature. If two such intermediates intermarry then very short, short, medium, tall and very tall offspring may result in proportions that can not be precisely given, but about which one can say that the mediums are the commonest and the more extreme classes are less frequented, the more they depart from mediocrity. In this case of stature we do not have to do with merely one factor as in eye color, or two as in negro skin color, but probably many. That is why all statures seem to form a continuous curve of frequency with only one modal point, that of the median class.

What is true of physical traits is no less true of mental. The offspring of an intellectually well developed man of good stock and a mentally somewhat inferior woman will tend to show a fair to good mentality; but the progeny of the intermarriage of two such will be normal and feeble-minded in the proportion of about 3 to 1. If one parent be of a strain that is highly excitable and liable to outbursts of temper while the other is calm then probably all the children will be excitable, or half of them, if the excitable parent is not of pure excitable stock. Thus, in the intellectual and emotional spheres the traits are no less "inherited" than in the physical sphere.

But I am aware that I have not yet considered the main problem of the consequence of race intermixture, considering races as differing by a number of characters. First, I have to say that this subject has not been sufficiently investigated; but we may, by inference from studies that have been made, draw certain conclusions. Any well-established abundant race is probably well adjusted to its conditions and its parts and functions are harmoniously adjusted. Take the case of the Leghorn hen. Its function is to lay eggs all the year through and never to waste time in becoming broody. The brooding instinct is, indeed, absent; and for egg farms and those in which incubators are used such birds are the best type. The Brahma fowl, on the other hand, is only a fair layer; it becomes broody two or three times a year and makes an excellent mother. It is well adapted for farms which have no incubators or artificial brooders. Now I have crossed these two races; the progeny were intermediate in size. The hens laid fairly well for a time and then became broody and in time hatched some chicks. For a day or two they mothered the chicks, and then began to roost at night in the trees and in a few days began to lay again, while the chicks perished at night of cold and neglect. The hybrid was a failure both as egg layer and as a brooder of chicks. The instincts and functions of the hybrids were not harmoniously adjusted to each other.

Turning to man, we have races of large tall men, like the Scotch, which are long-lived and whose internal organs are well adapted to care for the large frames. In the South Italians, on the other hand, we have small short bodies, but these, too, have well adjusted viscera. But the hybrids of these or similar two races may be expected to yield, in the second generation, besides the parental types also children with large frame and inadequate viscera—children of whom it is said every inch over 5' 10" is an inch of danger; children of insufficient circulation. On the other hand, there may appear children of short stature with too large circulatory apparatus. Despite the great capacity that the body has for self adjustment it fails to overcome the bad hereditary combinations.

Again it seems probable, as dentists with whom I have spoken on the subject agree, that many cases of overcrowding or wide separation of teeth are due to a lack of harmony between size of jaw and size of teeth—probably due to a union of a large-jawed, large-toothed race and a small-jawed, small-toothed race. Nothing is more striking than the regular dental arcades commonly seen in the skulls of inbred native races and the irregular dentations of many children of the tremendously hybridized American.

Not only physical but also mental and temperamental incompatibilities may be a consequence of hybridization. For example, one often sees in mulattoes an ambition and push combined with intellectual inadequacy which makes the unhappy hybrid dissatisfied with his lot and a nuisance to others.

To sum up, then, miscegenation commonly spells disharmony—disharmony of physical, mental and temperamental qualities and this means also disharmony with environment. A hybridized people are a badly put together people and a dissatisfied, restless, ineffective people. One wonders how much of the exceptionally high death rate in middle life in this country is due to such bodily maladjustments; and how much of our crime and insanity is due to mental and temperamental friction.

This country is in for hybridization on the greatest scale that the world has ever seen.

May we predict its consequences? At least we may hazard a prediction and suggest a way of diminishing the evil. Professor Flinders-Petrie in his essay on "Revolutions of Civilization" suggests that the rise and fall of nations is to be accounted for in this fashion. He observes that the countries that developed the highest type of civilization occur on peninsulas—Egypt surrounded on two sides by water and on two sides by the desert and by tropical heat, Greece, and Rome on the Italian peninsula. It is conceded that such peninsulas are centers of inbreeding. Flinders-Petrie concluded that a period of prolonged inbreeding leads to social stratification. In such a period a social harmony is developed, the arts and sciences flourish but certain consequences of inbreeding follow, particularly, the spread of feeble-mindedness, epilepsy, melancholia and sterility. These weaken the nation, which then succumbs to the pressure of stronger, but less civilized, neighbors. Foreign hordes sweep in; miscegenation takes place, disharmonies appear, the arts and sciences languish, physical and mental vigor are increased in one part of the population and diminished in another part and finally after selection has done its beneficent work a hardier, more vigorous people results. In them social stratification in time follows and a high culture reappears; and so on in cycles. The suggestion is an interesting one and there is no evident biological objection to it. Indeed the result of hybridization after two or three generations is great variability. This means that some new combinations will be formed that are better than the old ones; also others that are worse. If selective annihilation is permitted to do its beneficent work, then the worse combinations will tend to die off early. If now new inter mixing is stopped and eugenical mating ensues, consciously or unconsciously, especially in the presence of inbreeding, strains may arise that are superior to any that existed in the unhybridized race. This, then, is the hope for our country; if immigration is restricted, if selective elimination is permitted, if the principle of the inequality of generating strains be accepted and if eugenical ideals prevail in mating, then strains with new and better combinations of traits may arise and our nation take front rank in culture among the nations of ancient and modern times.

Source:
C. B. Davenport, "The Effects of Race
Intermingling," *Proceedings of the American
Philosophical Society* 56, no. 4 (1917):
364–68.

15

How Much Can
We Boost IQ and
Scholastic Achievement?

BY ARTHUR R. JENSEN

Arthur R. Jensen (b. 1923) published the long article "How Much Can We Boost IQ and Scholastic Achievement?" in 1969; it created a furor in academic circles, especially at the University of California at Berkeley where Jensen was a professor of educational psychology. Anticipating the authors of The Bell Curve, *Jensen maintains that differences in test scores between whites and African Americans are attributable largely to genetic differences and that environmental factors are of little importance. Jensen elaborated his theories in an immense treatise,* Bias in Mental Testing *(1980), which was equally controversial.*

Genetic Aspects of Racial Differences

No ONE, TO MY KNOWLEDGE, questions the role of environmental factors, including influences from past history, in determining at least some of the variance between racial groups in standard measures of intelligence, school performance, and occupational status. The current literature on the culturally disadvantaged abounds with discussion—some of it factual, some of it fanciful—of how a host of environmental factors depresses cognitive development and performance. I recently coedited a book which is largely concerned with the environmental aspects of disadvantaged minorities. But the possible importance of genetic factors in racial behavioral differences has been greatly ignored, almost to the point of being a tabooed subject, just as were the topics of venereal disease and birth control a generation or so ago.

My discussions with a number of geneticists concerning the question of a genetic basis of differences among races in mental abilities have revealed to me a number of rather consistently agreed-upon points which can be summarized in general terms as follows: Any groups which have been geographically or socially isolated from one another for many generations are practically certain to differ in their gene pools, and consequently are likely to show differences in any phenotypic characteristics having high heritability. This is practically axiomatic, according to the geneticists with whom I have spoken. Races are said to be "breeding populations," which is to say that matings within the group have a much higher probability than matings outside the group. Races are more technically viewed by geneticists as populations having different distributions of gene frequencies. These genetic differences are manifested in virtually every anatomical, physiological, and biochemical comparison one can make between representative samples of identifiable racial groups. There is no reason to suppose that the brain should be exempt from this generalization. (Racial differences in the relative frequencies of various blood constituents have probably been the most thoroughly studied so far.)

But what about behavior? If it can be measured and shown to have a genetic component, it would be regarded, from a genetic standpoint, as no different from other human characteristics. There seems to be little question that racial differences in genetically conditioned behavioral characteristics, such as mental abilities, should exist, just as physical differences. The real questions, geneticists tell me, are not whether there are or are not genetic racial differences that affect behavior, because there undoubtedly are. The proper questions to ask, from a scientific standpoint are: What is the direction of the difference? What is the magnitude of the difference? And what is the significance of the difference—medically, socially, educationally, or from whatever standpoint that may be relevant to the characteristic in question? A difference is important only within a specific context. For example, one's blood type in the ABO system is unimportant until one needs a transfusion. And some genetic differences are apparently of no importance with respect to any context as far as anyone has been able to discover—for example, differences in the size and shape of ear lobes. The idea that all genetic differences have arisen or persisted only as a result of natural selection, by conferring some survival or adaptive benefit on their possessors, is no longer generally held. There appear to be many genetic differences, or polymorphisms, which confer no discernible advantages to survival.

Negro Intelligence and
Scholastic Performance

Negroes in the United States are disproportionately represented among groups identified as culturally or educationally disadvantaged. This, plus that fact that Negroes constitute by far the largest racial minority in the United States, has for many years focused attention on Negro intelligence. It is a subject with a now vast literature which has been quite recently reviewed by Dreger and Miller and by Shuey, whose 578-page review is the most comprehensive, covering 382 studies. The basic data are well known: on the average, Negroes test about 1 standard deviation (15 IQ points) below the average of the white population in IQ, and this finding is fairly uniform across the 81 different tests of intellectual ability used in the studies reviewed by Shuey. This magnitude of difference gives a median overlap of 15 percent, meaning that 15 percent of the Negro population exceeds the white average. In terms of proportions of variance, if the numbers of Negroes and whites were equal, the differences *between* racial groups would account for 23 percent of the total variance, but—an important point—the differences *within* groups would account for 77 percent of the total variance. When gross socioeconomic level is controlled, the average difference reduces to about 11 IQ points, which, it should be recalled, is about the same spread as the average difference between siblings in the same family. So-called "culture-free" or "culture-fair" tests tend to give Negroes slightly lower scores, on the average, than more conventional IQ tests such as the Stanford-Binet and Wechsler scales. Also, as a group, Negroes perform somewhat more poorly on those subtests which tap abstract abilities. The majority of studies show that Negroes perform relatively better on verbal than on nonverbal intelligence tests.

In tests of scholastic achievement, also, judging from the massive data of the Coleman study, Negroes score about 1 standard deviation (SD) below the average for whites and Orientals and considerably less than 1 SD below other disadvantaged minorities tested in the Coleman study— Puerto Rican, Mexican-American, and American Indian. The 1 SD decrement in Negro performance is fairly constant throughout the period from grades 1 through 12.

Another aspect of the distribution of IQs in the Negro population is their lesser variance in comparison to the white distribution. This shows up in most of the studies reviewed by Shuey. The best single estimate is probably the estimate based on a large normative study of Stanford-Binet IQs of Negro school children in five South-eastern states, by Kennedy, Van De Riet, and White. They found the SD of Negro children's IQs to be 12.4, as compared with 16.4 in the white normative sample. The Negro distribution thus has only about 60 percent as much variance (i.e., SD^2) as the white distribution.

There is an increasing realization among students of the psychology of the disadvantaged that the discrepancy in their average performance cannot be completely or directly attributed to discrimination or inequalities in education. It seems not unreasonable, in view of the fact that intelligence variation has a large genetic component, to hypothesize that genetic factors may play a part in this picture. But such an hypothesis is anathema to many social scientists. The idea that the lower average intelligence and scholastic performance of Negroes could involve, not only environmental, but also genetic, factors has indeed been strongly denounced. But it has been neither contradicted nor discredited by evidence.

The fact that a reasonable hypothesis has not been rigorously proved does not mean that it should be summarily dismissed. It only means that we need more appropriate research for putting it to the test. I believe such definitive research is entirely possible but has not yet been done. So all we are left with are various lines of evidence, no one of which is definitive alone, but which, viewed all together, make it a not unreasonable hypothesis that genetic factors are strongly implicated in the average Negro-white intelligence difference. The preponderance of the evidence is, in my opinion, less consistent with a strictly environmental hypothesis than with a genetic hypothesis, which, of course, does not exclude the influence of environment or its interaction with genetic factors. . . .

Inadequacies of
Purely Environmental Explanations

Strictly environmental explanations of group differences tend to have an *ad hoc* quality. They are usually plausible for the situation they are devised to explain, but often they have little generality across situations, and new *ad hoc* hypotheses have to be continually devised. Pointing to environmental differences between groups is never sufficient in itself to infer a causal relationship to group differences in intelligence. To take just one example of this tendency of social scientists to attribute lower intelligence and scholastic ability to almost any environmental difference that seems handy, we can look at the evidence regarding the effects of "father absence." Since the father is absent in a significantly larger proportion of Negro than of white families, the factor of "father absence" has been frequently pointed to in the literature on the disadvantaged as one of the causes of Negroes' lower performance on IQ tests and in scholastic achievement. Yet the two largest studies directed at obtaining evidence on this very point—the only studies I have seen that are methodologically adequate—both conclude that the factor of "father absence" *versus* "father presence" makes no independent contribution to variance in intelligence or scholastic achievement. The sample sizes were so large in both of these studies that even a very slight degree of correlation between father absence and the measures of cognitive performance would have shown up as statistically significant. Coleman concluded: "Absence of a father in the home did not have the anticipated effect on ability scores. Overall, pupils without fathers performed at approximately the same level as those with fathers—although there was some variation between groups" (groups referring to geographical regions of the U.S.). And Wilson concluded from his survey of a California school district: "Neither our own data nor the preponderance of evidence from other research studies indicate that father presence or absence, *per se,* is related to school achievement. While broken homes reflect the existence of social and personal problems, and have some consequence for the development of personality, broken homes do not have any systematic effect on the overall level of school success."

The nationwide Coleman study included assessments of a dozen environmental variables and socioeconomic indices which are generally thought to be major sources of environmental influence in determining individual and group differences in scholastic performance—such factors as: reading material in the home, cultural amenities in the home, structural integrity of the home, foreign language in the home, pre-school attendance, parents' education, parents' educational desires for child, parents' interest in child's school work, time spent on homework, child's self-concept (self-esteem), and so on. These factors are all correlated—in the expected direction—with scholastic performance within each of the racial or ethnic groups studied by Coleman. Yet, interestingly enough, they are not systematically correlated with differences *between* groups. For example, by far the most environmentally disadvantaged groups in the Coleman study are the American Indians. On every environmental index they average *lower* than the Negro samples, and overall their environmental rating is about as far below the Negro average as the Negro rating is below the white average. (As pointed out by Kuttner, American Indians are much more disadvantaged than Negroes, or any other minority groups in the United States, on a host of other factors not assessed by Coleman, such as income, unemployment, standards of health care, life expectancy, and infant mortality.) Yet the American Indian ability and achievement test scores average about half a standard deviation higher than the scores of Negroes. The differences were in favor of the Indian children on each of the four tests used by Coleman: nonverbal intelligence, verbal intelligence, reading comprehension, and math achievement. If the environmental factors assessed by Coleman are the major determinants of Negro-white differences that many social scientists have claimed they are, it is hard to see why such factors should act in reverse fashion in determining differences between Negroes and Indians, especially in view of the fact that *within* each group the factors are significantly correlated in the expected direction with achievement.

Early Developmental Differences

A number of students of child development have noted the developmental precocity of Negro infants, particularly in motoric behavior. Geber (1958) and Geber and Dean (1957) have reported this precocity also in African infants. It hardly appears to be environmental, since it is evident in 9-hour-old infants. Cravioto has noted that the Gesell tests of infant behavioral development, which are usually considered suitable only for children over 4 weeks of age, "can be used with younger African, Mexican, and Guatemalan infants, since their development at two or three weeks is similar to that of Western European infants two or three times as old." Bayley's study of a representative sample of 600 American Negro infants up to 15 months of age, using the Bayley Infant Scales of Mental and Motor Development, also found Negro infants to have significantly higher scores than white infants in their first year. The difference is largely attributable to the motor items in the Bayley test. For example, about 30 percent of white infants as compared with about 60 percent of Negro infants between 9 and 12 months were able to "pass" such tests as "pat-a-cake" muscular coordination, and ability to walk with help, to stand alone, and to walk alone. The highest scores for any group on the Bayley scales that I have found in my search of the literature were obtained by Negro infants in the poorest sections of Durham, North Carolina. The older siblings of these infants have an average IQ of about 80. The infants up to 6 months of age, however, have a Developmental Motor Quotient (DMQ) nearly one standard deviation above white norms and a Developmental IQ (i.e., the non-motor items of the Bayley scale) of about half a standard deviation above white norms.

The DMQ, as pointed out previously, correlates negatively in the white population with socioeconomic status and with later IQ. Since lower SES Negro and white school children are more alike in IQ than are upper SES children of the two groups, one might expect greater DMQ differences in favor of Negro infants in high socioeconomic Negro and white samples than in low socioeconomic samples. This is just what Walters found. High SES Negro infants significantly exceeded whites in total score on the Gesell developmental schedules at 12 weeks of age, while low SES Negro and white infants did not differ significantly overall. (The only difference, on a single subscale, favored the white infants.)

It should also be noted that developmental quotients are usually depressed by adverse prenatal, perinatal, and postnatal complications such as lack of oxygen, prematurity, and nutritional deficiency.

Another relationship of interest is the finding that the negative correlation between DMQ and later IQ is higher in boys than in girls. Bronfenbrenner cites evidence which shows that Negro boys perform relatively less well in school than Negro girls; the sex difference is much greater than is found in the white population. Bronfenbrenner says, "It is noteworthy that these sex differences in achievement are observed among Southern as well as Northern Negroes, are present at every socioeconomic level, and tend to increase with age."

Physiological Indices

The behavioral precocity of Negro infants is also paralleled by certain physiological indices of development. For example, X-rays show that bone development, as indicated by the rate of ossification of cartilage, is more advanced in Negro as compared with white babies of about the same socioeconomic background, and Negro babies mature at a lower birth-weight than white babies.

It has also been noted that brain wave patterns in African newborn infants show greater maturity than is usually found in the European newborn child. This finding especially merits further study, since there is evidence that brain waves have some relationship to IQ, and since at least one aspect of brain waves—the visually evoked potential—has a very significant genetic component, showing a heritability of about 0.80 (uncorrected for attenuation).

Magnitude of
Adult Negro-White Differences

The largest sampling of Negro and white intelligence test scores resulted from the administration of the Armed Forces Qualification Test (AFQT) to a national sample of over 10 million men between the ages of 18 and 26. As of 1966, the overall failure rate for Negroes was 68 percent as compared with 19 percent for whites. (The failure cut-off score that yields these percentages is roughly equivalent to a Stanford-Binet IQ of 86.) Moynihan has estimated that during the same period in which the AFQT was administered to these large representative samples of Negro and white male youths, approximately one-half of Negro families could be considered as middle-class or above by the usual socioeconomic criteria. So even if we assumed that all of the lower 50 percent of Negroes on the SES scale failed the AFQT, it would still mean that at least 36 percent of the middle SES Negroes failed the test, a failure rate almost twice as high as that of the white population for all levels of SES.

Do such findings raise any question as to the plausibility of theories that postulate exclusively environmental factors as sufficient causes for the observed differences?

Source:
Arthur R. Jensen, "How Much Can We Boost
IQ and Scholastic Achievement?" (1969), in
Jensen's *Genetics and Education* (New York:
Harper & Row, 1972), pp. 159–63, 165–69.

16

The Bell Curve

BY RICHARD J. HERRNSTEIN
AND CHARLES MURRAY

Richard J. Herrnstein (1930–1994) was a professor of psychology at Harvard and the author of many books, including I.Q. in the Meritocracy *(1973) and* Crime and Human Nature *(1985; with James Q. Wilson). Charles Murray (b. 1943) has been a program evaluator for the American Institutes of Research and a Bradley Fellow at the Manhattan Institute for Policy Research; he is currently a Bradley Fellow at the American Enterprise Institute, a conservative think tank. He has written several books, including* Losing Ground: American Social Policy 1950–1980 *(1984). In* The Bell Curve *(1994) Herrnstein and Murray follow up the work of Arthur R. Jensen and others in stressing the genetic role in intelligence. The book caused tremendous controversy and impelled many attempts at refutation of its fundamental assertions. For extensive discussion of it see* The Bell Curve *Debate, edited by Russell Jacoby and Naomi Glauberman (1995), and* The Bell Curve *Wars, edited by Steven Fraser (1995).*

A GOOD PLACE TO START IS BY CORRECTING a common confusion about the role of genes in individuals and in groups. . . . Scholars accept that IQ is substantially heritable, somewhere between 40 and 80 percent, meaning that much of the observed variation in IQ is genetic. And yet this information tells us nothing for sure about the origin of the differences between races in measured intelligence. This point is so basic, and so commonly misunderstood, that it deserves emphasis: *That a trait is genetically transmitted in individuals does not mean that group differences in that trait are also genetic in origin.* Anyone who doubts this assertion may take two handfuls of genetically identical seed corn and plant one handful in Iowa, the other in the Mojave Desert, and let nature (i.e., the environment) take its course. The seeds will grow in Iowa, not in the Mojave, and the result will have nothing to do with genetic differences.

The environment for American blacks has been closer to the Mojave and the environment for American whites has been closer to Iowa. We may apply this general observation to the available data and see where the results lead. Suppose that all the observed ethnic differences in tested intelligence originate in some mysterious environmental differences— mysterious, because we know from material already presented that socioeconomic factors cannot be much of the explanation. We further stipulate that one standard deviation (fifteen IQ points) separates American blacks and whites and that a fifth of a standard deviation (three IQ points) separates East Asians and whites. Finally, we assume that IQ is 60 percent heritable (a middle-ground estimate). Given these parameters, how different would the environments for the three groups have to be in order to explain the observed difference in these scores?

The observed ethnic differences in IQ could be explained solely by the environment if the mean environment of whites is 1.58 standard deviations better than the mean environment of blacks and .32 standard deviation worse than the mean environment for East Asians, when environments are measured along the continuum of their capacity to nurture intelligence. Let's state these conclusions in percentile terms: The *average* environment of blacks would have to be at the 6th percentile of the distribution of environments among whites, and the *average* environment of East Asians would have to be at the 63rd percentile of environments among whites, for the racial differences to be entirely environmental.

Environmental differences of this magnitude and pattern are implausible. Recall further that the B/W difference (in standardized units) is smallest at the lowest socioeconomic levels. Why, if the B/W difference is entirely environmental, should the advantage of the "white" environment compared to the "black" be greater among the better-off and better-educated blacks and whites? We have not been able to think of a plausible reason. An appeal to the effects of racism to explain ethnic differences also requires explaining why environments poisoned by discrimination and racism for some other groups—against the Chinese or the Jews in some regions of America, for example—have left them with higher scores than the national average.

Environmental explanations may successfully circumvent these problems, but the explanations have to be formulated rather than simply assumed. Our initial objective is to warn readers who come to the discussion with firmly held opinions on either side. The heritability of individual differences in IQ does not necessarily mean that ethnic differences are also heritable. But those who think that ethnic differences are readily explained by environmental differences haven't been tough-minded enough about their own argument. At this complex intersection of complex factors, the easy answers are unsatisfactory ones. . . .

If the reader is now convinced that either the genetic or environmental explanation has won out to the exclusion of the other, we have not done a sufficiently good job of presenting one side or the other. It seems highly likely to us that both genes and the environment have something to do with racial differences. What might the mix be? We are resolutely agnostic on that issue; as far as we can determine, the evidence does not yet justify an estimate.

We are not so naive to think that making such statements will do much good. People find it next to impossible to treat ethnic differences with detachment. That there are understandable reasons for this only increases the need for thinking clearly and with precision about what is and is not important. In particular, we have found that the genetic aspect of ethnic differences has assumed an overwhelming importance. One symptom of this is that while this book was in preparation and regardless of how we described it to anyone who asked, it was assumed that the book's real subject had to be not only ethnic differences in cognitive ability but the genetic source of those differences. It is as if people assumed that we are faced with two alternatives: either (1) the cognitive difference between blacks and whites is genetic, which entails unspoken but dreadful consequences, or (2) the cognitive difference between blacks and whites is environmental, fuzzily equated with some sort of cultural bias in IQ tests, and the difference is therefore temporary and unimportant.

But those are not the only alternatives. They are not even alternatives at all. The major ethnic differences in the United States are not the result of biased tests in the ordinary sense of the term. They may well include some (as yet unknown) genetic component, but nothing suggests that they are entirely genetic. And, most important, it matters little whether the genes are involved at all.

We have already explained why the bias argument does not readily explain the ethnic differences and also why we say that genes may be part of the story. To show why we believe that it makes next to no difference whether genes are part of the reason for the observed differences, a thought experiment may help. Imagine that tomorrow it is discovered that the B/W difference in measured intelligence is entirely genetic in origin. The worst case has come to pass. What difference would this news make in the way that you approach the question of ethnic differences in intelligence? Not someone else but *you*. What has changed for the worse in knowing that the difference is genetic? Here are some hypothetical possibilities.

If it were known that the B/W difference is genetic, would I treat individual blacks differently from the way I would treat them if the differences were environmental? Probably, human nature being what it is, some people would interpret the news as a license for treating all whites as intellectually superior to all blacks. But we hope that putting this possibility down in words makes it obvious how illogical—besides utterly unfounded—such reactions would be. Many blacks would continue to be smarter than many whites. Ethnic differences would continue to be differences in means and distributions; they would continue to be useless, for all practical purposes, when assessing individuals. If you were an employer looking for intellectual talent, an IQ of 120 is an IQ of 120, whether the face is black or white, let alone whether the mean difference in ethnic groups were genetic or environmental. If you were a teacher looking at a classroom of black and white faces, you would have exactly the same information you have now about the probabilities that they would do well or poorly.

If you were a government official in charge of educational expenditures and programs, you would continue to try to improve the education of inner-city blacks, partly out of a belief that everyone should be educated to the limits of his ability, partly out of fairness to the individuals of every degree of ability within that population—but also, let it be emphasized, out of a hardheaded calculation that the net social and economic return of a dollar spent on the elementary and secondary education of a student does not depend on the heritability of a group difference in IQ. More generally: *We cannot think of a legitimate argument why any encounter between individual whites and blacks need be affected by the knowledge that an aggregate ethnic difference in measured intelligence is genetic instead of environmental.*

It is true that employers might under some circumstances find it economically advantageous to use ethnicity as a crude but inexpensive screen to cut down hiring costs (assuming it were not illegal to do so). But this incentive exists already, by virtue of the existence of a difference in observed intelligence regardless of whether the difference is genetic. The *existence* of the difference has many intersections with policy issues. The *source* of the difference has none that we can think of, at least in the short term. Whether it does or not in the long term, we discuss below.

If the differences are genetic, aren't they harder to change than if they are environmental? Another common reaction, this one relies on false assumptions about intelligence. The underlying error is to assume that an environmentally caused deficit is somehow less hard-wired, that it has less impact on "real" capabilities, than does a genetically caused deficit. We have made this point before, but it bears repeating. Some kinds of environmentally induced conditions can be changed (lack of familiarity with television shows for a person without a television set will probably be reduced by purchasing him a television set), but there is no reason to think that intelligence is one of them. . . . An individual's realized intelligence, no matter whether realized through genes or the environment, is not very malleable.

Changing cognitive ability through environmental interventions has proved to be extraordinarily difficult. At best, the examples of special programs that have permanently raised cognitive ability are rare. Perhaps as time goes on we will learn so much about the environment, or so much about how intelligence develops, that effective interventions can be designed. But this is only a hope. Until such advances in social interventions come about, which is unlikely to happen any time soon, it is essential to grasp the point made earlier in the book: A short person who could have been taller had he eaten better as a child is nonetheless really short. The corn planted in the Mojave Desert that could have flourished if it had been planted in Iowa, wasn't planted in Iowa, and there's no way to rescue it when it reaches maturity. Saying that a difference is caused by the environment says nothing about how real it is.

Aren't genetic differences passed down through the generations, while environmental differences are not? Yes and no. Environmentally caused characteristics are by definition not heritable in the narrow technical sense that they do not involve genetic transmission. But nongenetic characteristics can nonetheless run in families. For practical purposes, environments are heritable too. The child who grows up in a punishing environment and thereby is intellectually stunted takes that deficit to the parenting of his children. The learning environment he encountered and the learning environment he provides for his children tend to be similar. The correlation between parents and children is just that: a statistical tendency for these things to be passed down, despite society's attempts to change them, without any necessary genetic component. In trying to break these intergenerational links, even adoption at birth has its limits. Poor prenatal nutrition can stunt cognitive potential in ways that cannot be remedied after birth. Prenatal drug and alcohol abuse can stunt cognitive potential. These traits also run in families and communities and persist for generations, for reasons that have proved difficult to affect.

In sum: If tomorrow you knew beyond a shadow of a doubt that all the cognitive differences between races were 100 percent genetic in origin, nothing of any significance should change. The knowledge would give you no reason to treat individuals differently than if ethnic differences were 100 percent environmental. By the same token, knowing that the differences are 100 percent environmental in origin would not suggest a single program or policy that is not already being tried. It would justify no optimism about the time it will take to narrow the existing gaps. It would not even justify confidence that genetically based differences will not be upon us within a few generations. The impulse to think that environmental sources of difference are less threatening than genetic ones is natural but illusory.

Source:
Richard J. Herrnstein and Charles Murray,
The Bell Curve: Intelligence and Class
Structure in American Life (New York: Free
Press, 1994), pp. 298–99, 311–15.

PART THREE

Aryans, Anglo-Saxons, and Teutons

T HE CONFUSION OF BIOLOGICAL with cultural traits is perhaps the most fundamental error in racist thought. The notion that certain features of character, certain intellectual proclivities, and even the nature and form of a given group's political and social organization are somehow as transmissible through heredity and intermixture as physical characteristics has been strangely persistent in spite of overwhelming scientific evidence to the contrary. This conception is exhibited in a particularly brazen form in the assertion of the political supremacy of the Teuton (or Anglo-Saxon or Aryan).

To such eighteenth-century classicists as David Hume and Edward Gibbon, the "barbarian invasions" of ancient Rome were a disaster for civilization, introducing a millennium of intellectual darkness relieved only by the rediscovery of ancient literature and thought in the Renaissance. This view gradually yielded in the nineteenth century to the assertion by English historians that English political and social institutions were uniquely the inheritance of the Anglo-Saxon tribes that settled England after the fall of Rome. Sir Francis Palgrave was the first to put forward a version of this theory in *The Rise and Progress of the English Commonwealth* (1832), and he was followed by a number of other historians, including John Mitchell Kemble (*The Saxons in England*, 1849) and Edward A. Freeman. The Scottish scientist Robert Knox gave the

99

most exhaustive early treatment of the theory in *The Races of Men* (1850). Admitting the Anglo-Saxon's many supposed faults (he is "plodding"; his "genius is wholly applicative, for he invents nothing"; he has poor taste in music and art), Knox nonetheless maintains that "no race perhaps exceeds them in an abstract sense of justice, and a love of fair play"—but, he adds with italics whose significance he fails to grasp, *"only to Saxons."* Knox is reduced to this expedient because he knows that his Anglo-Saxons have not displayed "fair play" toward other races, and so he is compelled to assert arbitrarily that these other races are of no relevance in determining the Anglo-Saxon's "sense of justice."

American historians were not slow in picking up on their English colleagues' views; for if English institutions could be established as racially inevitable, so, too, could the republican institutions of the United States. George Bancroft (*History of the United States,* 1834) gave a mild endorsement to the view, and the strain can be found throughout the work of the other leading American historians of the period—John Lothrop Motley, William H. Prescott, Francis Parkman, and others. As time went on, however, a confusion of terms began to set in—or, rather, an imprecision in their definition. Who exactly were the "Teutons" or the "Anglo-Saxons"? No satisfactory or self-consistent answers were ever given to this question. William F. Allen, a classicist who drew inspiration from the depiction of the primitive Teutons in Tacitus' *Germania,* could go so far as to refer in 1889 to "the English race." Several American thinkers, indulging in a scorn for things English, managed to find ways to determine that only the Americans exhibited true "Anglo-Saxon" traits and that the English had been so corrupted by admixture of other strains (notably the Normans) that they could not be thought of as proper inheritors of Teutonic greatness.

A new element entered into the mix in the later nineteenth century with the emergence of Aryanism. The Aryans were identified as the tall, blond people mentioned as conquerors in ancient Sanskrit literature; they were thought to have emerged from Persia, and it was assumed that these people were the progenitors of the white race and the ancestors of the Teutons. The linguist Max Müller (1823–1900) initially lent the great weight of his influence to this view, but he later abandoned it, stating that the term "Aryan" should only be used in a strictly linguistic and not racial sense, since the language of any given group bore no meaningful or systematic relationship to its racial characteristics. But his caveat went for naught as political scientists of all stripes began trumpeting the uniquely "Aryan" qualities of American civilization. Those who wished to retain the cultural inheritance of Greco-Roman civilization, such as political scientist John W. Burgess, could have their cake and eat it too by asserting that the Greeks, Romans, and Teutons were the three branches of the Aryan race. The Aryan theory even infected literary criticism: such American literary historians as Barrett Wendell and Charles F. Richardson asserted that the vigor of American literature was a direct product of the racial composition of the original (English) settlers.

John L. Brandt, a disciple of the "Social Gospel" advocate Josiah Strong, unites religion and imperialism in *Anglo-Saxon Supremacy* (1915) as he looks forward to the simultaneous political and religious domination of the West over China and Japan. To be sure, Brandt claims that "all races of men are capable of the highest development regardless of their present condition or the color of their skin"; nevertheless, it is the Anglo-Saxon who "holds in his hands the destinies of the world and has a commission from on high to civilize the world."

The Aryan supremacy myth was largely abandoned by American thinkers well before Hitler—inspired by the anti-Semitism of Houston Stewart Chamberlain and Richard Wagner, misreadings of Nietzsche,[1] and many other sources—lent it a renewed and baleful life. Its pathetic residue in the American Nazi Party, paramilitary organizations like the Aryan Brotherhood, and other fringe groups now spouting their venom on the Internet is a sad testimonial to its lasting strength.

17

The Races of Men

BY ROBERT KNOX

Robert Knox (1791–1862) was a professor of anatomy at the Edinburgh College of Surgeons and the author of several books on anatomy and physiology. In The Races of Men: A Fragment *(1850) Knox becomes one of the earliest to vaunt the supremacy of the Anglo-Saxon "race," especially for its contributions to English and American civilization.*

OF THE ORIGIN OF THE SAXON RACE we know just as much as we do of the origin of man; that is, nothing. History, such as it is, shows us that in remote times a race of men, differing from all others physically and mentally, dwelt in Scandinavia—say, in Norway, Denmark, Sweden, Holstein—on the shores of the Baltic, in fact; by the mouths of the Rhine, and on its northern and eastern bank. Cæsar met Ariovistus at the head of a German army on the Rhine. The Germans, as the Scandinavian and other transrhenal races were then called, had crossed the river, making excursions into the territories of their Celtic neighbours, inhabiting Old Gaul. The dictator defeated them, compelling them to recross the Rhine into their own territories. But he did not follow them into their native woods: the Romans never had any real power beyond the Rhine. At no period did they conquer the Saxon or true German, that is, Scandinavian, race.

What had induced the ancient Scandinavians to cross the Rhine in Cæsar's time? What had led them long before into Italy, where they encountered Marius? Ask the South-African Saxon Boor what induces him to spread himself over a land, one twentieth part of which could easily maintain him in comfort and affluence. What urges him against Caffraria—against Natal? It has been said, that the Scandinavian or Saxon tribes were pressed for space; that more numerous barbarous tribes pushed them on. The over-populousness of their woods and their retiring before another force do not well agree; there is some contradiction here. But the Cape Boor of Saxon origin has no such excuse for spreading himself in a few years over a vast region, which he leaves uncultivated; neither has the Anglo-Saxon American. To me it seems referable simply to the qualities of the race; to their inordinate self-esteem; to their love of independence, which makes them dislike the proximity of a neighbour; to their hatred for dynasties and governments; democrats by their nature, the only democrats on the earth, the only race which truly comprehends the meaning of the word liberty.

The Scandinavian or Saxon (I avoid the words German and Teuton, as liable to equivoque) was early in Greece, say 3500 years ago. This race still exists in Switzerland, forming its protestant portion; whilst in Greece, it contributed mainly, no doubt, to the formation of the noblest of all men— the statesmen, poets, sculptors, mathematicians, metaphysicians, historians of ancient Greece. But from that land nearly all traces of it have disappeared; so also from Italy. It is gradually becoming extinct in France and Spain, returning and confined once more to those countries in which it was originally found—namely, Holland, West Prussia, Holstein, the northern states of the ancient Rhenish Confederation, Saxony Proper, Norway, Sweden, and Denmark. The Saxon of England is deemed a colonist from Jutland, Holstein, and Denmark. I feel disposed to view the question differently. He must have occupied eastern Scotland and eastern England as far south as the Humber, long prior to the historic period, when the German Ocean was scarcely a sea. The Saxons of these northern coasts of Scotland and England, resemble very closely the natives of the opposite shores; but the Danes and Angles who attacked South England, already occupied by a Flemish race, did not make the same impression on the population. They merely mingled with it; the country, that is, South England, remains in the hands of the original inhabitants to this day. South England is mainly occupied by a Belgian race, and were it not for the centralization of London, it is by no means improbable that much of the true Saxon blood would have disappeared from south Britain, by that physiological law which extinguishes mixed races (a people composed of two or more races) and causes the originally more numerous one to predominate, unless supplies be continually drawn from the primitive pure breeds. This important law we shall consider presently. Following out the geographical position of the Saxon race, we find him in Europe, intersected but not amalgamated with the Sarmatian and Slavonian, in eastern Europe; with the Celtic in Switzerland; deeply with the Slavonian and Fleming in Austria and on the Rhine; thinly spread throughout Wales; in possession, as occupants of the soil, of northern and eastern Ireland; lastly, carrying out the destinies of his race, obeying his physical and moral nature, the Anglo-Saxon, aided by his insular position, takes possession of the ocean, becomes the great tyrant at sea; ships, colonies, commerce—these are his wealth, therefore his strength. A nation of shopkeepers grasps at universal power; founds a colony (the States of America) such as the world never saw before; loses it, as a result of the principle of race. Nothing daunted, founds others, to lose them all in succession, and for the same reasons—race: a handful of large-handed spatula-fingered Saxon traders holds military possession of India. Meantime, though divided by nationalities into different groups, as English, Dutch, German, United States man, cordially hating each other, the race still hopes ultimately to be masters of the world.

But I have not yet spoken of the physical and mental qualities of the Saxon race; these words include all, for "the Chronicle of Events" which have happened to them, whether in England or elsewhere, is a mere chapter of accidents, influenced deeply by the qualities of the average men of the race. So soon as I shall briefly have described these, it will be proper to consider the import of two great physiological laws already mooted—namely, Can a mixed race be produced and supported by the intermingling of two races? Can any race occupy, colonize, and people a region of the earth to which they are *not* indigenous?

In all climes, and under all circumstances, the Saxons are a tall, powerful, athletic race of men; the strongest, as a race, on the face of the earth. They have fair hair, with blue eyes, and so fine a complexion, that they may almost be considered the only absolutely fair race on the face of the globe. Generally speaking, they are not a well-made or proportioned race, falling off most in the limbs; the torso being large, vast, and disproportioned. They are so described by Livy, and have never altered; the mistake of Prichard, and the difficulty experienced by the illustrious Niebuhr, the greatest of all historians, respecting the complexion of the *modern German* differing from the ancient, arises simply from this, that the middle and south German belong to another race of men. They are not Scandinavians or Saxons at all, and never were. The mistake centres in the abuse of the word German; it has been applied to two or three different races: so also has the word Teuton; hence my objections to these terms. The true Germans or Saxons of modern times resemble, or rather are identical, with those of antiquity; they follow the law of hereditary descent; climate exercises no influence over them. Two hundred years of Java, three hundred years of southern Africa, affect them not. Alter their health it may, and does, withering up the frame; rendering the body thin and juiceless; wasting the adipose cellular tissue; relaxing the muscles and injuring the complexion, by altering the condition of the blood and secretions; all this may be admitted, but they produce no permanent results.

Under the influence of climate, the Saxon decays in northern America and in Australia, and he rears his offspring with difficulty. He has changed his continental locality; a physiological law, I shall shortly explain, is against his naturalization there. Were the supplies from Europe not incessant, he could not stand his ground in these new continents. A *real native* permanent American, or Australian race of pure Saxon blood, is a dream which can never be realized.

The Saxon is fair, not because he lives in a temperate or cold climate, but because he is a Saxon. The Esquimaux are nearly black, yet they live amidst eternal snows; the Tasmanian is, if possible, darker than the negro, under a climate as mild as England. Climate has no influence in permanently altering the varieties or races of men; destroy them it may and does, but it cannot convert them into any other race; nor can this be done even by act of parliament, which, to a thorough-going Englishman, with all his amusing nationalities, will appear as something amazing. It has been tried in Wales, in Ireland, in Caledonia—and failed. Explain it, ye Utopians, as you choose; I merely mention the fact. When I lectured in Liverpool, a gentleman, of the name of Martineau, put forth a discourse, in which he maintained, that we had forced Saxon laws upon the Irish too hurriedly; that we had not given them time enough to become good Saxons, into which they would be metamorphosed at last. In what time, Mr. Martineau, do you expect this notable change? The experiment has been going on already for 700 years; I will concede you seven times 700 more, but this will not alter the Celt: no more will it change the Saxon, to whom I return.

Thoughtful, plodding, industrious beyond all other races, a lover of labour for labour's sake; he cares not its amount if it be but profitable; large handed, mechanical, a lover of order, of punctuality in business, of neatness and cleanliness. In these qualities no race approaches him; the wealthy with him is the sole respectable, the respectable the sole good; the word comfort is never out of his mouth—it is the beau ideal of the Saxon.

His genius is wholly applicative, for he invents nothing. In the fine arts, and in music, taste cannot go lower. The race in general has no musical ear, and they mistake noise for music. The marrow-bones and cleaver belong to them. Prize fights, bull-baiting with dogs; sparring matches; rowing, horse racing, gymnastics: the Boor is peculiar to the Saxon race. When young they cannot sit still an instant, so powerful is the desire for work, labour, excitement, muscular exertion. The self-esteem is so great, the self-confidence so matchless, that they cannot possibly imagine any man or set of men to be superior to themselves. Accumulative beyond all others, the wealth of the world collects in their hands.

Our good qualities when in excess become foibles and even vices. I need not dwell on this: my notes to this lecture will supply the deficiency. The social condition of the Saxon can only be seen in the free States of America, which I have not yet visited. In Britain he was enslaved by a Norman dynasty, antagonistic of his race. His efforts to throw it off have not yet succeeded, though oft repeated. On the Continent, the Saxon race, broken up into petty monarchies, without wealth or power; miserably enslaved and crushed down by the dynasties of Hapsburgh, Brandenburgh, and a host of others, presents a condition seemingly hopeless. In their last struggle for liberty, or in other words for institutions suited to their race, they were not joined by the Scandinavian nations, the very best of their blood. Holland, too, would have risen, but she remembered the Celtic treachery; the betrayal of the cause of liberty by the French Celt in '92; the plunder of Europe by a body of disciplined savages under Napoleon; so she responded not to the Celt. The cap of liberty was raised in vain in Paris; the cautious Hollander was not again to be deceived. He knew also that England, commercial England, was sure to betray him into the hands of the brutal Pruss and Russ. Thus, the noblest blood of the race is in abeyance: sunk into political insignificance. Sweden, Denmark, Norway, Holstein, Holland, commercial England, have overshadowed you. A colony of your own (England), your first, your greatest colony, has exercised over your fortunes that fatal influence which England's first and greatest colony may some day exercise over hers: we are to you, what America seems destined to be to us. Of the same race, commercial, naval, the only really good sailors in the world, our American colony disputes with us the empire of the seas; a future Paul Jones may yet repay Britain the affair of Copenhagen; but it must come from a Saxon race, for the Saxons alone are sailors.

The results of the physical and mental qualities of a race are naturally manifested in its civilization, for every race has its own form of civilization. The historian, the talented statesman, Guizot, for example, who failed in forty years to learn the character of the race amongst whom he lived and ruled, he of all others (always excepting the Prince of Bunglers, Metternich), the most outrageously mistaken, has written a work about European civilization; about an abstraction which does not exist. Each race has its own form of civilization, as it has its own language and arts; I would almost venture to say, science; for although exact science, as being based on eternal and indisputable truths, must ever be the same under all circumstances and under all climes, it does not follow that its truths should even be formuled after the same fashion. Civilization, or the social condition of man, is the result and test of the qualities of every race; but it would be unfair to judge the European Saxon by this standard, seeing that the entire race, insular and continental, is crushed down by dynasties antagonistic of their race. What is effected at Berlin and Vienna by the bayonet, is usually accomplished in London by the law. Hence, notwithstanding the wealth of the Anglo-Saxon, no nation presents such a frightful mass of squalid poverty and wretchedness, rendering it doubtful whether such a form of civilization be a blessing or curse to humanity. I lean with Tacitus to the latter opinion.

No race perhaps—(for I must make allowances for my Saxon descent,)—no race perhaps exceeds them in an abstract sense of justice, and a love of fair play; *but only to Saxons.* This of course they do not extend to other races. Aware of his strength of chest and arms, he uses them in self-defence: the Celt flies uniformly to the sword. To-day and to-morrow is all the Saxon looks to; yesterday he cares not for; it is past and gone. He is the man of circumstances, of expediency without method; "try all things, but do not theorize." Give me "constants," a book of constants; this is his cry. Hence his contempt for men of science: his hatred for genius arises from another cause; he cannot endure the idea that any man is really superior in anything to himself. The absence of genius in his race he feels; he dislikes to be told it: he attempts to crush it wherever it appears. Men of genius he calls humbugs, impostors. His literature is peculiar to himself, and must not be confounded with modern German literature: this latter is chiefly of Slavonian origin, mingled with the race occupying central Europe and stretching into Flanders. Uncertain as to their nature, I have called this race Flemish or Belgian; but the modern Belgians do not well represent them. I believe them peculiar; an off-set perhaps of the Slavonian race; at all events not Saxon or Scandinavian. The word German, and the equivoque it admits of, has greatly confused a very simple matter. It misled Arnold; it misled Niebuhr, and a host of others: my countrymen have confounded the literature of the middle, south German, and Slavonian races, with the Scandinavian or north German; nothing was ever more distinct.

All that is free in Saxon countries they, the Saxons, owe to themselves; their laws, manners, institutions, they brought with them from the woods of Germany, and they have transferred them to the woods of America. They owe nothing to any kings or princes or chiefs: originally, they had neither chief nor king; a general in war was *elected* when required. In their ideas of "property in land" they differ also from other races; they do not admit that any class or family, dynasty or individual, can appropriate to himself and to his hereditary heirs, any portion of the earth's surface. Hence their abhorrence for feudality, tenures, hereditary rights, and laws of primogeniture. Soldiers and soldiering they despise as being unworthy of free men: the difficulty of teaching them military discipline and tactics, arises from the awkwardness of their forms and slowness of movement, and from their inordinate self-esteem. But when disciplined, their infantry, owing to the strength of the men, becomes the first in the world. . . . The failure of the Continental Saxon during the late struggle for liberty, I ventured to foretel at the commencement. They desired to be united, free; disenthralled from the hideous iron despotism which crushes them down: in a German unity, a race mustering at least sixty millions, they hoped to find a counterpoise to Celtic France, and Swinish Russia; that is, to the two *dominant races* of Europe, the Celt and the Sarmatian. But true to their selfish nature, they had not the soul to offer the same freedom to the Slavonian, whom they neglected and despised. They fought with the Slavonians in Posen; they resisted them in Bohemia; they contended with them in Austria; liberty for the German was the war-cry; slavery for all the rest. They now reap the fruits of their selfish nature; hopeless slavery for centuries: the dynasties are in the ascendant: they have alarmed the holders of *property*, always timid, always cowardly: as a class, the property men are sure to back any dynasty if well supported by the bayonet. No sympathies can be extended to a selfish grasping race, without feelings for others. To their eternal dishonour, they suffered an infamous coward, the first who fled from Potsdam to Windsor, to return and butcher their brethren in Baden and Saxony. When the imbecile House of Hapsburgh fled from Vienna, then was the time to have said to the Slavonian race,—"Arise, and form a nation." But *self* prevailed with the Saxon, and ruin followed. The words of Napoleon have now been verified; Europe is "all Cossaque." All fear of a *Celtic Republic* has vanished: the character of the Celt is now fully understood. Rome has settled the question for a time. Celtic liberty is now well comprehended by all Europe. The world thought Celtic France a great and free people; but the world was wrong if they did, for the world forgot the element of race in its calculation on the probable destinies of the French Celt; that element, duly weighed, would have shown them, that a race being composed of individuals resembling each other must, even in its greatest efforts, merely shadow forth the character of the individual. When the French Celt drove out the insupportable and paltry Orleans dynasty, they were merely a fighting clan without a chief; having no self-esteem, how could they act without a leader? That leader had not then, and has not yet, appeared.

The introduction of the Saxon element of mind into civilized Europe is, no doubt, a remarkable event in history: the literature and arts of the Roman world had been already influenced by the Celtic mind; the Gothic or Slavonian followed next; then came the Saxon. Its first result was to produce the dark ages. What the race had been doing since the beginning of time it is impossible to say, but being without inventive genius, I see not how they could originate any but the lowest forms of civilization, such as

I have seen in Southern Africa amongst the Dutch, that is, Saxon, Boors, and such as I have heard prevails in "the far west." Man sinks rapidly in the scale of civilization when removed from the great stream. They are wrong who fancy otherwise. At the third generation the Saxon Boor, in a remote land, sinks nearly to the barbarian; active and energetic, no doubt: still a Saxon, but not the less a boor and a vulgar barbarian.

The remarkable, and almost prophetic, saying of Gibbon, seems about to be verified. As a statesman and a historian, a chronicler of the social and political histories of nations, he applies his remark to England; but it is strictly applicable to the European Saxon, wherever found; insular or continental; applicable to the descendants of those free and bold men who originally brought with them, in all their migrations from Scandinavia, those free institutions under which freemen alone can live, namely, that of trial by jury, and equality before the law, protection of life and property; a race who obeyed no king nor chief; who resisted oppression in every shape, and to whom the most abhorred of all despotisms, a feudal nobility with laws of primogeniture, were unknown: amongst whom all were equal; all noble alike. Such were the ancient Scandinavian or Saxon, called Germans occasionally by some Roman writers—and confounded in later times, even by the immortal Niebuhr, with the middle German or Upper Danubian race: occasionally, even with the Slavonians.

To all this race, now crushed down by the Sarmatian and Celtic races of Europe: broken up, dispersed, enslaved: their lives and properties placed at the mercy of some five or six brutal families or dynasties: the very best blood of all the race, the Jutlander, the Saxon, the free man of Baden and of Wirtemberg, lorded it over by a few paltry families, unknown to fortune or renown; to all this race Gibbon's remarks apply; to Celtic republican (!) France they now know they need not look for aid in their next struggle for liberty; let Rome be a lesson to them; to all this race, and not to England alone, does this prophetic passage in Gibbon's works apply.

"Should it ever happen," says the immortal historian, whom I quote from recollection, "that in Europe brutal military despots should succeed in extinguishing the liberties of men, threatening with the same unhappy fate the inhabitants of this island (England), they, mindful of their Saxon origin, would doubtless escape across the ocean, carrying to a new world their institutions, religion, and laws."

Source:
Robert Knox, *The Races of Men: A Fragment*
(Philadelphia: Lea & Blanchard, 1850),
pp. 40–51.

18

The Place of the Northwest in General History

BY WILLIAM F. ALLEN

William F. Allen (1830–1889) was the author of many books on ancient history and literature. He was a professor of classics at the University of Wisconsin and had studied extensively in Germany. Fascinated by Tacitus' account of the Teutons in the Germania, *Allen came to believe that many features of the colonization of New England duplicated those found in Tacitus' account.*

It is not my practice to insist overmuch upon inherent differences in race—a theory upon which a great deal of nonsense has been talked and written. But that different races have independent and well defined traditions and environment, and a disparity of capacities and powers as the outgrowth of these, no person can question. In accordance with this we readily recognize that from some cause lying too far back for us to comprehend, the Germanic race has been distinguished at all ages for its political capacity, and the possession of vigorous institutions of self-government; that there grew up among the nations of this race a well-ordered system of government based upon the rights of the individual; and that all the Germanic nations of the North have preserved these institutions in a more or less complete degree of vigor and efficiency.

The nations of this race were never brought under the authority of the Roman Empire, and made to exchange their native system of government for that of Rome; the victory of Arminius in the Teutoburgensian

Forest preserved our ancestors from this fate. I would not be understood to deprecate the great services to humanity rendered by the Roman Empire. It was without question a great good fortune for Gaul to be conquered by Cæsar, because the tribal institutions, by which the nations of Gaul were still governed, appear to have received all the development of which they were capable, and to have consisted at this time in the un-restricted rule of an imperious aristocracy, indifferent to the welfare of its subjects and incapable of progress. Vercingetorix was perhaps a nobler and more heroic man than Arminius; and at any rate the uprising led by him inspires the heartiest human interest and sympathy. But when it failed we cannot feel that humanity or even Gaul was worse off for it; his success would have been a disaster. So with most of the other nations conquered by Rome. They had passed their prime, and were stagnating in an effete civilization, or trembling under cruel despotism. But with the Germans it was different. It would have been a great calamity if they, with their uncorrupted social life, and their vigorous, though undevel-oped, political institutions, had been forced to become subjects to the Roman system. Those German nations which pushed across the bounds, and established themselves upon the soil of the empire, were obliged to submit to this fate. The Goths and Franks lost all memory of their orig-inal liberties, and entered into the traditions of the Roman Empire. But free Germany and Scandinavia retained their institutions essentially unimpaired, and with the triumph of England, in the eighteenth century, the Germanic principles of self-government triumphed for all Europe.

For five hundred years the leadership in Europe had been held by na-tions which dwelt within the bounds of the Roman Empire, and had in-herited its principles of unlimited authority and despotic rule. Italy had first exercised this influence, not so much by superiority of material or political force, as by her intellectual maturity, the splendor of her civi-lization, and the spiritual authority possessed by her ecclesiastical head. With the Renaissance of the fifteenth century the nations beyond the Alps entered into the intellectual life of Italy, which country now lost its intellectual leadership, while the spiritual power of the Pope, with a cer-tain authority growing out of it, as arbiter in international controversies, was destroyed by the religious revolution of the century following. Spain and France, which enjoyed undisputed precedence among nations dur-ing the sixteenth and seventeenth centuries, inherited in the fullest de-gree the traditions and practices of the Roman domination. It was only slowly and feebly that the free institutions of the North asserted them-selves successively in England, Holland, Sweden, and Prussia, and wrested a tardy recognition from the autocratic states of the South.

It is not an accident that the moment of the advance of England to the leading place among nations was also a turning-point in the *constitutional* and the *international* relations of these nations. For a hundred years, since the close of the period of religious wars by the treaty of Westphalia in 1648, and of the English civil war the next year, by the execution of Charles I.; during these hundred years the sovereigns of Europe had been engaged in unintermitted efforts to enlarge their territories and increase their power. In all this period it is hard to discern any issue in the wars or the diplomatic relations, except pure greed, or the desire to place a check to this greed, and preserve the balance of power. And in internal affairs the only principle of government was the absolute authority of the sovereign. This principle held sway everywhere except in England, and even in England the more liberal principle of government was to a great extent neutralized by despotic practice. No country in Europe at this epoch was governed more arbitrarily, with a more complete disregard of popular rights, than Catholic Ireland under the rule of the Whig, or Constitutional party of Protestant England.

After the Seven Years' War, and the Peace of Paris (1763), we meet no more wars of an exclusively dynastic character. Always the rights of the people or of the nationality form an element, and more and more the controlling element, in public relations. Even the Partition of Poland, the grossest and most wanton abuse of absolute power, is a significant event, as for the first time bringing the principle of nationality actively and conspicuously into notice. Then followed the American Revolution, and the revolutionary period was fairly opened, which has lasted to the present day. In the tremendous struggles of the intervening century there have been many moments of reaction and depression, in which popular liberties have seemed hopelessly lost; but the result of it all is that nearly every country of Europe has, first or last, had its constitution remodelled on the plan of that of England, and constitutional liberty of the English type has everywhere, except in Russia and Turkey, superseded the absolute system of government which prevailed universally upon the Continent a century ago. I do not assert that these parliamentary institutions have always been well planned and successful in their workings. I do not overlook a certain reaction against them at the present time, not only in the nations of the Continent, but in England itself. The fact itself of their dissemination is none the less noteworthy and significant.

Along with parliamentary institutions and local self-government, equally with these an outgrowth of the democratic temper, the English race stands for the dignity of labor. No more fundamental contrast exists between ancient and modern society than in the absolute denial in the one, and the hearty recognition in the other, of the claims of industry in the organization of society. Industry in the ancient world was left to slaves and dependants; a freeman was disgraced by labor. Now, in those countries of the Continent which have derived their institutions and civilization by an unbroken succession from the Roman Empire, industry has continued to be held in the same contempt; and as even the countries of the North have been exposed to this influence in some degree, this aristocratic principle of contempt for labor has had control of society through all modern times. But least of all in England and the countries of Scandinavia. In these the democratic spirit was never extinct; and when England assumed the leadership among European nations, she ushered in the dawn of an industrial epoch, when the arts and avocations of peace shall take precedence of those of war. Even in the present age of enormous and costly armaments, it is noticeable how every one of these military nations is reorganizing its social system on an industrial basis. Railroads, manufactures, the technical arts, scientific agriculture, control society in France and Italy as truly as in England and America.

It cannot be said of this industrial revolution, as it can be said of the introduction of parliamentary institutions, that it is directly and entirely the work of England. It is the modern spirit, the spirit of the age, closely connected with that Christian civilization which forms the chief difference between modern society and ancient. But the English, having come less directly under the influence of Roman traditions than any other of the leading nations of Europe, and having, therefore, preserved more completely their primitive free institutions and the democratic spirit of which these were the outgrowth, are the foremost representatives and the pioneers of this movement. When Napoleon called the English "a race of shopkeepers," he spoke in a spirit of pagan antiquity, in high contempt of any but military interests. The industrial age has its faults and dangers. The shop-keeping spirit is prone to become mean-spirited, sordid, gross. But the nation of shop-keepers manifested a military energy and efficiency which humbled the great Napoleon himself, and it is a significant fact that Prussia did not lend her hand to the work until her social institutions had been reorganized in the modern spirit by the reforms of Stein.

Another point may be noted in passing. It is not in the nations thoroughly imbued with the modern industrial spirit, but in those which are ruled by the traditions of the Roman Empire, that social weakness exists, and those social agitations have originated, which threaten to subvert our social organization. Germany, the home of Socialism, forms no exception to this assertion. It is, it is true, a Teutonic country, and possessed originally the same free institutions as England; but it was brought at a very early date by the conquest of Charles the Great, into close connection with the Romance nations; was thoroughly feudalized, and, while never losing entirely its primitive local liberties, was reduced under the rule of absolutism as completely as its southern neighbors. But it is not too much to claim that in the nations of English race, along with inequalities of condition and inadequacy of law, such as are incident to human nature, there is nevertheless a fundamentally democratic spirit in social relations, which affords no hold to anti-social theories. Labor contests there may no doubt be; but schemes to destroy society itself could never have originated in an Anglo-Saxon community.

The leadership among European nations, secured to England by the Seven Years' War, meant for Europe free institutions and the advent of an industrial age: for America its significance was truly incalculable. Until now the English colonies had ranked third in extent and importance; now they divided the continent with those of Spain. However magnificent the claims of the English colonies, their actual occupation had been only a narrow strip along the coast; and, what is more, they were incapable of expansion, so long as Spain held Florida, and France the Mississippi valley. Now their territories seemed sufficient for an unlimited growth of population. The first great step had been taken toward the realization of the manifest destiny of the Anglo-Saxon race to control the continent of North America. The acquisition of Louisiana, the treaty of Guadaloupé Hidalgo, the Gadsden purchase—all followed almost by an uncontrollable necessity; and if some of these steps were marked with insolence and bad faith on our part, the injustice cannot now be undone; and to the lands themselves it is an almost unmixed benefit that they have been brought under the sway of the English race.

The establishment of the British empire in America brought with it English civilization, English law, English political ideas. The practices of local self-government, parliamentary institutions, the supremacy of law over the will of the sovereign, the place of precedence assumed by industrial interests—all these, which we have found to be the distinctive characteristics of the Germanic political ideals as opposed to those of the Romance nations, were by this event made dominant in the continent of North America.

Source:
William F. Allen, "The Place of the Northwest
in General History," *Papers of the American
Historical Association* 3, no. 2 (1889): 93–99.

19

The Ideal of
the American
Commonwealth

BY JOHN W. BURGESS

John W. Burgess (1844–1931) was a lawyer and professor who taught at Columbia and wrote many works of American history and law. Burgess had studied in Germany and then served in the Civil War on the Union side, at which time he gained a distaste for England because of its support of the Confederacy. In various writings he asserted that only Germans and Americans, not the English, were proper Teutons. In the following article Burgess asserts that the "prime mission of the ideal American commonwealth [is] the perfection of the Aryan genius for political civilization."

IF WE REGARD FOR A MOMENT the history of the world from the point of view of the production of political institutions, we cannot fail to discern that all the great states of the world, in the modern sense, have been founded and developed by three branches of the Aryan race—the Greeks, the Romans and the Teutons; that these three branches are territorially European; and that, upon the European soil, they have become distinct nations. Indian America has left no legacies to modern civilization; Africa has as yet made no contributions; and Asia, while producing all of our great religions, has done nothing, except in imitation of Europe, for political civilization. We must conclude from these facts that American Indians, Asiatics and Africans cannot properly form any active, directive part of the political population which shall be able to produce

115

modern political institutions and ideals. They have no element of political civilization to contribute. They can only receive, learn, follow Aryan example. Hence my proposition that the ideal American commonwealth is not to be *of* the world, but *for* the world—is to be national in its origin, but cosmopolitan in its application.

But if national, what shall be the nationality? The merest glance at the census tables will show us that it *is* Aryan, and predominantly Teutonic. The historic facts which I have already adduced demonstrate that it *must be* Aryan. And the historic facts which I shall now present will explain that if Aryan, it must be Teutonic. These facts are (1) the loss, in large degree, of the Aryan genius on the part of the Greeks, by their amalgamation with the Turks and other Asiatic populations, and (2) the same loss on the part of the Romans, in nearly equal degree, by their amalgamation with the Saracens in Europe and Africa, and with the Indians in South and Middle America. Only the race-proud Teutons have resisted amalgamation with non-Aryan branches, while they have suffered but in small measure the mixture of other Aryan blood. Only the race-proud Teutons, thus, have preserved the Aryan genius for political civilization; and, while guarding jealously their own type of that genius, they have supplemented it with those elements of permanent value that belong more specifically to the Greek and Roman types.

I consider, therefore, the prime mission of the ideal American commonwealth to be the perfection of the Aryan genius for political civilization, upon the basis of a predominantly Teutonic nationality,—emancipated, however, from the remaining prejudices of European Teutonism against the other branches of the Aryan family and against the genuine products of their exertions. And I conceive that the political system evolved through such a development will be the model for the political organization of the world.

If such, in truth, be the transcendent mission of the American commonwealth,—and I cannot see how any student of history can read it otherwise,—what folly, on the part of the ignorant, what wickedness, on the part of the intelligent, are involved in the attempts, on the one side to sectionalize the nation, or on the other, to pollute it with non-Aryan elements. Both have been tried, and both, thanks to an all-wise Providence, have failed; for both were sins against American civilization, and both were sins of the highest order. We must preserve our Aryan nationality in the state, and admit to its membership only such non-Aryan race-elements as shall have become Aryanized in spirit and in genius by contact with it, if we would build the superstructure of the ideal American commonwealth.

If this proposition should be met with the objection that it contemplates an aristocratic instead of a democratic state, I would answer, that there is not now, and that there never has been, a non-Aryan democratic state; that Aryan nationalities alone have created democratic states; that no other peoples or populations have ever given the slightest evidence of the ability to create democratic states; and that Aryan history is ever moving toward the realization of genuine democracy and the impartation of its example to the world. I cannot arbitrarily turn from that direction which must be followed in treading the path of the world's history, and pursue the baseless speculation of a fanatical humanitarianism.

Source:
John W. Burgess, "The Ideal of the American
Commonwealth," *Political Science Quarterly*
10, no. 3 (September 1895): 405–7.

20

Anglo-Saxon Supremacy

BY JOHN L. BRANDT

John L. Brandt (1860–1946) was a minister of the Disciples of Christ, an American religious group formed in the 1830s by Presbyterians and Baptists who sought to return to the original teachings of the Scriptures. Brandt wrote several books on theology, including America or Rome, Christ or the Pope *(1895). In* Anglo-Saxon Supremacy *(1915) he unites racism and religion in looking forward to Anglo-Saxon domination of China and Japan.*

THE QUESTION OFTEN ARISES, will our civilization continue? Doubtless there will be many changes and marked improvement in the years to come. Many nations have risen to glory only to fade away into everlasting night. Many nations have come to their culmination and their death. The ancient ruins, uncovered cities and monuments bespeak of mighty nations and populous cities of the past that are now no more. What shall be our destiny? Shall we in turn take our place with the races of men that have appeared on the earth and disappeared never to rise again—shall these world civilizers be supplanted by a more powerful people, and forced to pass from the stage of action? I think not, because they possess the essential principles of civilization to give them permanency. Principles that the civilizations of the past did not possess. They have entrenched on the Lord's side. They have the truth and so long as they let it shine they will never outgrow it. They have founded their civilization on the principles of righteousness and brotherly love as taught in the Bible, and the heavens may pass away but the word of God shall abide, and if these people continue on the firm foundation they shall never be moved. With these principles embodied in the very heart and soul of the people their destiny is determined and their mission is evident.

Their history is a record of progress in all the arts of civilization. Their motto has been "Onward." They have passed from generation to generation doubling their inherited treasures and multiplying their victories. The nineteenth century recorded their progress that is beyond all precedent; their territory and population were quadrupled; their wealth multiplied many fold and their people made a remarkable advance in knowledge and wisdom. In religion their liberality has made ample provision for the religious instruction of the people. Never before in the history of the world has there been such a call for the Anglo-Saxon nations to advance to their true position as there is to-day. The principles of their civilization are so much to be desired that as they became known to Asiatic people the gates of those nations were opened to bid the Anglo-Saxons welcome to enter and disseminate the principles and plant the institutions for which they stand. This suggests that the gigantic struggle in Europe is for supremacy and influence in Asia as well as in Europe and other parts of the world. Lord Rosebery says, "It is a war for supremacy of liberty and all that we hold sacred." The European question is only one issue; a new world has come to view, another century may witness the human activities and ambitions of the West transferred to the East. The Pacific as well as the Atlantic is destined to become the theater of great commercial activity.

The greatest interest of humanity once encircled the Mediterranean Sea; it may now be said to encircle the Atlantic; it will soon be transferred to the Pacific. This peaceful ocean with its shores, islands and vast regions so well located for men's greatest achievements and surrounded by three fifths of the population of the globe, with the opening of the Panama Canal may be destined to become the chief theatre of events in the world's history. The Pacific with its nations and islands is bound to be dominated by Western politics, thoughts, forces and civilization; it is already demanding a reconstruction of the diplomacy and program of the great powers of the world. Every opportunity is being embraced by the great nations of the earth to gain a vantage ground in the Pacific and on its shores for their commerce and their civilization. These are tremendous movements of nations in sweeping forward in the greatness of their power, preparing for their future when boundary lines will be drawn and unalterably established. It is the all absorbing question among the great rulers of the world. More and more European and American statesmen are addressing themselves to conditions in Asia and Africa. Within the past decade or two the European statesmen have awakened like magic to the importance of possessing colonies and establishing foreign stations for their people and their commerce. There has been a scramble for the unappropriated corners of the earth. We have witnessed Africa divided between the rival claimants and again and again we have seen Asia threatened with a like partition.

Of the lands that border on the Pacific, Old Glory floats over the United States, Alaska, Hawaii and the Philippines, and the Union Jack proudly waves over New Zealand, Australia, Canada, Hong-Kong, and parts of New Guinea and Borneo.

The United States has played an important part in this drama of the world. By conquest, by purchase, by diplomacy, by education, by commerce and by missionaries we have planted ourselves squarely face to face with the Asiatic civilization. For years the United States looked upon a future of political isolation but the conflict with Spain made short work of this tradition and revolutionized our place in the world. It closed the period of selfish isolation and opened to view and enlarged the destiny which divine Providence seemed to mark for us as a nation. It brought us into intimate relations with sections of the globe with which we had but little communication, save in a commercial way and through missionaries, and it brought a sudden moral demand upon us to make our voice heard and our power felt in the interests of humanity throughout the world. It presents problems, the solution of which have been vexing and trying to the great reformers, philanthropists, and statesmen of the world; the Asiatic problems. The missionary heroes of the Anglo-Saxon race have long been the foremost in mission work in Japan, China, India and the Islands of the Sea, and the U.S. now stands in the political and commercial world in close relation with these countries. The statesmen of these nations consider the presence of England and the United States as friendly and unselfish and as the harbinger of a brighter day for those who are seeking the light and advantage of Western civilization. The earth is belted with the nations, islands, fortresses, harbors and coaling stations that the Anglo-Saxons hold for the good of the world. Without the Anglo-Saxon program being prepared by any set of men, it doth seem that some unseen hand has been directing the movements of these world conquerors and civilizers. More important than the discovery of the New World, or the organization of society on the basis of the sovereignty of the people, is this belting the world by the Anglo-Saxon people and clasping hands in Asia. It is a reunion of the two civilizations that separated more than four thousand years ago and traveling in opposite directions are now meeting again in the nations and islands of the Pacific. This meeting required years of preparation, it required waiting for navigation by steam and electricity, the development of mechanical inventions and scientific discoveries, the liberation of the human intellect, the freedom of individual enterprise enjoyed by the Anglo-Saxons and their abundance of gold. All of these elements entered into the preparation of this great movement in bringing about this great union of the human family by the will of God through Anglo-Saxon instrumentality.

Why this world wide influence and power? It must be not only to furnish liberty and opportunity for their industrial enterprises but it must be on the ground of a high trust to civilization, on the ground of indebtedness to humanity, and on the ground of a duty placed by the hand of almighty God. This being true the Anglo-Saxons must not turn a deaf ear to the voice of Providence but must shoulder the responsibility with all of its trials and all of its perplexing situations. If they have outstripped the other races of men in the conflicts for mastery, it is because they have more liberty, more Christianity, a better conception of duty and a civilization that gives a more complete development to the individual and a better organization of society. It is because they have the principles of civilization that make them permanent and paramount; again, if this be true the Anglo-Saxon holds in his hands the destinies of the world and has a commission from on high to civilize the world, therefore, we need not wonder at some nations being absorbed by us, at others being quick to accept our civilization by adopting of their own choice our heaven given principles. Think of it, the twentieth century and the march and call of the Anglo-Saxon civilization. What an inspiration to our people! What an incentive to authors, statesmen, teachers, editors and ministers to discuss these subjects and educate and prepare the people for the conquest of the world. Behold the magnitude of the enterprise. Anglo-Saxon liberties enlightening the world, Anglo-Saxon Christianity saving the world, Anglo-Saxon blending the great families of the world into one great brotherhood. The crisis has come and with other Anglo-Saxon nations we are now facing a great turning point in our history and questions are now being decided that will involve us for all time to come. The influences and outcome of the great war of 1914 will have a tremendous effect upon history. The Asiatic people are rapidly being civilized and Christianized by the Anglo-Saxons. Shall this blessed work so auspiciously begun come to an end?

The leaven of the Anglo-Saxon civilization is at work in Japan. Japan's great awakening dates from the visit of Commodore Perry to the Island Empire. When he entered the harbor of Yeddo and unfurled Old Glory, it was the dawn of a new era for Japan. Having himself selected his presents he gave these people on the strand of Yokohama an object lesson, showing the forces of the West—the railway, locomotive and train, the telegraph, electric batteries, ploughs, sewing machines, and other tools especially the inventions of Americans. Corn crackers, rice hullers and Colt's revolvers, were the most popular and some of the former are still in use in Japan. Following Perry came merchants, teachers and missionaries.

Since the days of Perry Japan has been an ardent student of Anglo-Saxon civilization. From the appearance of Perry's peaceful armada, Anglo-Saxon influence in law, theology, medicine, agriculture, engineering, science, journalism, education, religion has been manifest and present in overwhelming force.

American and English enterprise have done much to develop and exploit the mines and industries of Japan. The new industrial Japan is one creation of the Anglo-Saxons. Their entire educational system is chiefly the work of a handful of Americans. Whole series of our educational text books, from Webster's speller and dictionary up through all the lines of science, history and theology have been bought, read, used, translated and adopted by tens of thousands of copies.

Likewise our political productions,—the Declaration of Independence, the Constitution of the United States, Washington's farewell address, the lives of our great statesmen and other writings,—have been widely read and their virtues and examples oft quoted.

The English language is studied in her colleges and universities and no man of Japan is considered educated who is not able to converse in English. I have traveled from one end of the Empire to the other and have delivered addresses in some of their institutions of learning and I was both surprised and pleased at the large number of students who understood English.

The missionaries have introduced Christianity and exemplified it in their daily lives. It has taken a deep hold upon the Japanese. My departed friend Dr. De Forest in "Sunrise in the Sunrise Kingdom" has forecasted the religion of Christ to become the prevailing religion of Japan in the near future.

I might here add that while Japan seeks to have her people respected she has no thought or plan of a future conflict with the United States. Such I know to be the sentiment of her educators and statesmen, yellow journalism, and subtle and secret diplomacy of envious powers to the contrary.

The leaven of the Anglo-Saxon civilization is also at work in China. The wonderful transformation that has taken place in China has been largely due to American and English influence. Through these channels the light of Western civilization pierced the heart of the Celestial Empire and the demands for reform were heard on all hands. Missionaries and educators were kept busy translating their best books on Western civilization, ideals and government into Chinese. The great nation awoke as if by magic. The intellect awakened to Western thought. Steamships are plying along the coasts and along the rivers; railroads are already crossing the country, telegraph and telephone wires are threading the land;

American and English engineers and machinists are found everywhere stimulating China's commerce.

Factories are being built and the printing press is at work. Mathematical, scientific, governmental and economic books are in demand. Millions of copies of the Bible are circulated in China. Confucius, who invented nothing but taught the people to worship their ancestors with reverence for the past and fear for the future, is losing his grasp upon China.

The leaven of the Anglo-Saxon is at work throughout the whole nation. He is active in commerce, in schools, colleges and universities, in scientific and professional pursuits, in Christian missions, hospitals, dispensaries and asylums. He is active stimulating the people to thought, molding public opinion and by his life and object lessons turning China upside down.

What is true of China and Japan is also true of Korea. Her first railway with iron bridges, her first street railways with modern equipments, her first electric lights and the development and exploitation of her mines, were begun and executed by Americans. The renovation of her capital city from filth and stench to cleanliness and purity, is the work of native officers who had experience in Washington. Her grammars and dictionaries and educational system; her material enterprises, and commercial prosperity, her converts to Christianity, with her schools, missions and churches, demonstrate the power and quality of Anglo-Saxon mind and character to turn people from darkness to light. And what is true of China, Japan and Korea is also true of India. . . .

In conclusion: It is important that the Anglo-Saxons know the programs of other nations and consider their right to a place in the world and their mission to humanity. They should generously appreciate all that is fine, good and worthy in character and culture of other races, study their needs and seek to maintain that friendly relation to them that will secure a hearing and perhaps an opportunity that may help to overcome any deficiencies, remove any jealousies and to attain the loftier ideals. President Wilson has well said, "No man is a true Christian who does not think of how he can help his brothers, how he can uplift mankind, and who does not labor unselfishly for others."

Anglo-Saxons must steadfastly adhere to the view that both science and religion have affirmed that the human family had a common origin, belong to a common brotherhood, with a common Fatherhood and that while some races have had better climatic conditions and other advantages that gave to them a better start, yet all races of men are capable of the highest development regardless of their present condition or the color of their skin.

Anglo-Saxon people must not be content to rest on victories gained on land and sea, in commerce and in industry, in education and in religion. They must remain true to their ideals and strive to keep the body and soul of the race healthy, must prevent decline in religion and morals and must teach the youth of the race that the best citizen is he who gives the best manhood to the nation.

Anglo-Saxons must make progress in spiritual as well as mental culture; must seek, not by force, to impose Anglo-Saxon ideals on other races and nations but by fair dealings and righteous living they must let their ideals so shine that others may see and know their value and adopt them for their own good, happiness and progress.

As regards war, surely no war is justifiable unless it is in defense of ideals and institutions, defense of national existence and honor; better than preparation for war is the effort to maintain peace, to arrange for disarmament, to establish courts of international arbitration, to seek in every possible way to bring all men to the Christian conception of brotherhood so that war will never be a necessity. And while these ideals are to be the ultimate aim of the Anglo-Saxons, yet they cannot afford, so long as any great nation maintains a heavy armament and has no regard for Christ and His church and no respect for the rights of weak nations and international treaties, to beat their swords into plowshares and their spears into pruning hooks.

My faith leads me to believe divine Providence placed the Anglo-Saxon in every zone from the tropics to the Arctic for a purpose. He is there not only to build railways, lighthouses, telegraphs, telephones and warehouses for the introduction and distribution of products for the good of the whole people, but he is there to open dark places and let in the light; he is there to annihilate slavery, lessen poverty, drive out plague, pestilence and famine; he is there to promote the happiness and increase the comfort of the people; he is there to supplant the heavy and oppressive institutions of the old world with those of light and love of the new world; he is there to introduce the principles of liberty enjoyed by a sovereign people; he is there to tell the story of the Fatherhood of God and the brotherhood of man; he is there for the salvation of the human race and the glory of God. And furthermore, and perhaps best of all, to encourage and work for the reconstruction and reorganization of the relationship of all the nations of the world, to secure and maintain a permanent peace for the general welfare of all.

Source:
John L. Brandt, *Anglo-Saxon Supremacy; or,
Race Contributions to Civilization* (Boston:
Richard G. Badger, 1915), pp. 231–40.

PART FOUR

Manifest Destiny and Imperialism

THE ENORMITY OF AMERICAN SETTLEMENT of the North American continent naturally led to the development of the theory of "manifest destiny"—the belief that white Americans were destined by Fate or God to conquer and settle the New World, destroying or subjugating all other peoples in the region—and its overtones of racism and imperialism. Imperialist or expansionist thought flared up chiefly on two occasions in American history—first during the Mexican War of 1846–48 and second during the Spanish-American War of 1898. The political turmoil into which Mexico was plunged upon its independence from Spain in 1821 created the ideal setting for racial conflict. In March 1836, after years of enduring what its people considered intolerable restrictions of its rights as settlers, Texas declared its independence from Mexico. However, the debate over whether to extend slavery into the region if it were to join the union prevented American annexation for years. Annexation finally occurred by a joint resolution of the U.S. Congress on February 28, 1845, and some months later the Texas Congress ratified it. Texas was admitted as a state on December 29, 1845. The immediate cause of the war with Mexico was a boundary dispute over the demarcation of the western border of Mexico; but the end product was an immense addition to American territory, encompassing the present states of Texas, California, Nevada, Arizona, New Mexico, Utah, and part of Colorado.

The debates over the annexation of Texas and California resounded both in Congress and in the periodical press for years before the war commenced. John O'Sullivan, the reputed coiner of the term "manifest destiny," writing a year before the outbreak of the Mexican War, was already convinced that "Texas is now ours" and that, as far as California was concerned, "the advance guard of the irresistible army of Anglo-Saxon emigration has begun to pour down upon it." Once the whole of the continent fell into American hands, the imperialistic tumult of the 1840s subsided. In the 1880s, however, Theodore Roosevelt, writing in *The Winning of the West*, took considerable pride in the inexorable march of Anglo-Saxon might from sea to sea, filling in the "waste spaces" of the entire world (specifically Australia and America) whose aboriginal inhabitants were only obstacles to be overcome.

Many American thinkers were vexed over Henry Clay's resounding utterance: "I contend, that it is to arraign the disposition of Providence himself, to suppose that he has created beings incapable of governing themselves."[1] For it was the bland assumption of many imperialists that Anglo-American domination of foreign colonies was a political and even a moral necessity in light of the native people's manifest, and perhaps biological, incapacity to govern themselves. The Spanish-American War—which ultimately resulted in the freeing of Cuba from Spanish control and its brief occupation by the United States, along with the annexation of Puerto Rico, Guam, and the Philippines—represented the most virulent outbreak of American imperialism, and racism was rarely far from the surface. Of course there was also ferocious opposition to imperialist expansion—William Jennings Bryan made it the centerpiece of his presidential campaign in 1900, but he was defeated by the Republican ticket of McKinley and Theodore Roosevelt, the latter fresh from his invasion of Cuba with the Rough Riders; but this opposition only caused the imperialists to redouble their arguments. Kipling's poem "The White Man's Burden"—which circulated around the globe in a few days after its appearance in *McClure's Magazine* of February 1899—seemed to supply the poetic imprimatur for the imperialist cause.

21

Annexation

BY JOHN O'SULLIVAN

The term "manifest destiny" was reportedly coined in the following essay by John O'Sullivan (1813–1895). O'Sullivan, the author of Union, Disunion, and Reunion *(1862) and other political writings, was the founder and editor of the* United States Magazine and Democratic Review, *where this essay appeared. Its impetus was the debate over the annexation of Texas, which led to the Mexican War. The essay is here reprinted in its entirety.*

I T IS TIME NOW FOR OPPOSITION to the Annexation of Texas to cease, all further agitation of the waters of bitterness and strife, at least in connexion with this question,—even though it may perhaps be required of us as a necessary condition of the freedom of our institutions, that we must live on for ever in a state of unpausing struggle and excitement upon some subject of party division or other. But, in regard to Texas, enough has now been given to party. It is time for the common duty of Patriotism to the Country to succeed;—or if this claim will not be recognized, it is at least time for common sense to acquiesce with decent grace in the inevitable and the irrevocable.

Texas is now ours. Already, before these words are written, her Convention has undoubtedly ratified the acceptance, by her Congress, of our proffered invitation into the Union; and made the requisite changes in her already republican form of constitution to adapt it to its future federal relations. Her star and her stripe may already be said to have taken their place in the glorious blazon of our common nationality; and the sweep of our eagle's wing already includes within its circuit the wide extent of her fair and fertile land. She is no longer to us a mere geographical space—a certain combination of coast, plain, mountain, valley, forest and stream. She is no longer to us a mere country on the map. She comes within the dear and sacred designation of Our Country; no longer a *"pays,"* she is a part of *"la patrie;"* and that which is at once a sentiment and a virtue, Patriotism, already begins to thrill for her too within the national heart. It is time then that all should cease to treat her as alien, and even adverse—cease to denounce and vilify all and everything connected with her accession—cease to thwart and oppose the remaining steps for its consummation; or where such efforts are felt to be unavailing, at least to embitter the hour of reception by all the most ungracious frowns of aversion and words of unwelcome. There has been enough of all this. It has had its fitting day during the period when, in common with every other possible question of practical policy that can arise, it unfortunately became one of the leading topics of party division, of presidential electioneering. But that period has passed, and with it let its prejudices and its passions, its discords and its denunciations, pass away too. The next session of Congress will see the representatives of the new young State in their places in both our halls of national legislation, side by side with those of the old Thirteen. Let their reception into "the family" be frank, kindly, and cheerful, as befits such an occasion, as comports not less with our own self-respect than patriotic duty towards them. Ill betide those foul birds that delight to file their own nest, and disgust the ear with perpetual discord of ill-omened croak.

Why, were other reasoning wanting, in favor of now elevating this question of the reception of Texas into the Union, out of the lower region of our past party dissensions, up to its proper level of a high and broad nationality, it surely is to be found, found abundantly, in the manner in which other nations have undertaken to intrude themselves into it, between us and the proper parties to the case, in a spirit of hostile interference against us, for the avowed object of thwarting our policy and hampering our power, limiting our greatness and checking the fulfilment of our manifest destiny to overspread the continent allotted by Providence for the free development of our yearly multiplying millions. This we have seen done by England, our old rival and enemy; and by France, strangely coupled with her against us, under the influence of the Anglicism strongly tinging the policy of her present prime minister, Guizot. The zealous activity with which this effort to defeat us was pushed by the representatives of those governments, together with the character of intrigue accompanying it, fully constituted that case of foreign interference, which Mr. Clay himself declared should, and would unite us all in maintaining the common cause of our country against the foreigner and the foe. We are only astonished that this effect has not been more fully and strongly produced, and that the burst of indignation against this unauthorized, insolent and hostile interference against us, has not been more general even among the party before opposed to Annexation, and has not rallied the national spirit and national pride unanimously upon that policy. We are very sure that if Mr. Clay himself were now to add another letter to his former Texas correspondence, he would express this sentiment, and carry out the idea already strongly stated in one of them, in a manner which would tax all the powers of blushing belonging to some of his party adherents.

It is wholly untrue, and unjust to ourselves, the pretence that the Annexation has been a measure of spoliation, unrightful and unrighteous—of military conquest under forms of peace and law—of territorial aggrandizement at the expense of justice, and justice due by a double sanctity to the weak. This view of the question is wholly unfounded, and has been before so amply refuted in these pages, as well as in a thousand other modes, that we shall not again dwell upon it. The independence of Texas was complete and absolute. It was an independence, not only in fact, but of right. No obligation of duty towards Mexico tended in the least degree to restrain our right to effect the desired recovery of the fair province once our own—whatever motives of policy might have prompted a more deferential consideration of her feelings and her pride, as involved in the question. If Texas became peopled with an American population; it was by no contrivance of our government, but on the express invitation of that of Mexico herself; accompanied with such guaranties of State independence, and the maintenance of a federal system analogous to our own, as constituted a compact fully justifying the strongest measures of redress on the part of those afterwards deceived in this guaranty, and sought to be enslaved under the yoke imposed by its violation. She was released, rightfully and absolutely released, from all Mexican allegiance, or duty of cohesion to the Mexican political body, by the acts and fault of Mexico herself, and Mexico alone. There never was a clearer case. It was not revolution; it was resistance to revolution: and resistance under such circumstances as left independence the necessary resulting state, caused by the abandonment of those with whom her former federal association had existed. What then can be more preposterous than all this clamor by Mexico and the Mexican interest, against Annexation, as a violation of any rights of hers, any duties of ours?

We would not be understood as approving in all its features the expediency or propriety of the mode in which the measure, rightful and wise as it is in itself, has been carried into effect. Its history has been a sad tis-

sue of diplomatic blundering. How much better it might have been managed—how much more smoothly, satisfactorily, and successfully! Instead
of our present relations with Mexico—instead of the serious risks which
have been run, and those plausibilities of opprobrium which we have had
to combat, not without great difficulty, nor with entire success—instead
of the difficulties which now throng the path to a satisfactory settlement
of all our unsettled questions with Mexico—Texas might, by a more judicious and conciliatory diplomacy, have been as securely in the Union as
she is now—her boundaries defined—California probably ours—and
Mexico and ourselves united by closer ties than ever; of mutual friendship and mutual support in resistance to the intrusion of European interference in the affairs of the American republics. All this might have
been, we little doubt, already secured, had counsels less violent, less
rude, less one-sided, less eager in precipitation from motives widely foreign to the national question, presided over the earlier stages of its history. We cannot too deeply regret the mismanagement which has
disfigured the history of this question; and especially the neglect of the
means which would have been so easy of satisfying even the unreasonable
pretensions and the excited pride and passion of Mexico. The singular
result has been produced, that while our neighbor has, in truth, no real
right to blame or complain—when all the wrong is on her side, and there
has been on ours a degree of delay and forbearance, in deference to her
pretensions, which is to be paralleled by few precedents in the history of
other nations—we have yet laid ourselves open to a great deal of denunciation hard to repel, and impossible to silence; and all history will carry
it down as a certain fact, that Mexico would have declared war against us,
and would have waged it seriously, if she had not been prevented by that
very weakness which should have constituted her best defence.

We plead guilty to a degree of sensitive annoyance—for the sake of the
honor of our country, and its estimation in the public opinion of the
world—which does not find even in satisfied conscience full consolation
for the very necessity of seeking consolation there. And it is for this state
of things that we hold responsible that gratuitous mismanagement—
wholly apart from the main substantial rights and merits of the question,
to which alone it is to be ascribed; and which had its origin in its earlier
stages, before the accession of Mr. Calhoun to the department of State.

Nor is there any just foundation for the charge that Annexation is a
great pro-slavery measure—calculated to increase and perpetuate that institution. Slavery had nothing to do with it. Opinions were and are
greatly divided, both at the North and South, as to the influence to be
exerted by it on Slavery and the Slave States. That it will tend to facili-

tate and hasten the disappearance of Slavery from all the northern tier of the present Slave States, cannot surely admit of serious question. The greater value in Texas of the slave labor now employed in those States, must soon produce the effect of draining off that labor southwardly, by the same unvarying law that bids water descend the slope that invites it. Every new Slave State in Texas will make at least one Free State from among those in which that institution now exists—to say nothing of those portions of Texas on which slavery cannot spring and grow—to say nothing of the far more rapid growth of new States in the free West and North-west, as these fine regions are overspread by the emigration fast flowing over them from Europe, as well as from the Northern and Eastern States of the Union as it exists. On the other hand, it is undeniably much gained for the cause of the eventual voluntary abolition of slavery, that it should have been thus drained off towards the only outlet which appeared to furnish much probability of the ultimate disappearance of the negro race from our borders. The Spanish-Indian-American populations of Mexico, Central America and South America, afford the only receptacle capable of absorbing that race whenever we shall be prepared to slough it off—to emancipate it from slavery, and (simultaneously necessary) to remove it from the midst of our own. Themselves already of mixed and confused blood, and free from the "prejudices" which among us so insuperably forbid the social amalgamation which can alone elevate the Negro race out of a virtually servile degradation, even though legally free, the regions occupied by those populations must strongly attract the black race in that direction; and as soon as the destined hour of emancipation shall arrive, will relieve the question of one of its worst difficulties, if not absolutely the greatest.

No—Mr. Clay was right when he declared that Annexation was a question with which slavery had nothing to do. The country which was the subject of Annexation in this case, from its geographical position and relations, happens to be—or rather the portion of it now actually settled, happens to be—a slave country. But a similar process might have taken place in proximity to a different section of our Union; and indeed there is a great deal of Annexation yet to take place, within the life of the present generation, along the whole line of our northern border. Texas has been absorbed into the Union in the inevitable fulfilment of the general law which is rolling our population westward; the connexion of which with that ratio of growth in population which is destined within a hundred years to swell our numbers to the enormous population of *two hundred and fifty millions* (if not more), is too evident to leave us in doubt of the manifest design of Providence in regard to the occupation of this continent. It was disintegrated from Mexico in the natural course of events, by a process perfectly legitimate on its own part, blameless on ours; and in which all the censures due to wrong, perfidy and folly, rest on Mexico alone. And possessed as it was by a population which was in truth but a colonial detachment from our own, and which was still bound by myriad ties of the very heart-strings to its old relations, domestic and political, their incorporation into the Union was not only inevitable, but the most natural, right and proper thing in the world—and it is only astonishing that there should be any among ourselves to say it nay.

In respect to the institution of slavery itself, we have not designed, in what has been said above, to express any judgment of its merits or demerits, *pro* or *con*. National in its character and aims, this Review abstains from the discussion of a topic pregnant with embarrassment and danger—intricate and double-sided—exciting and embittering—and necessarily excluded from a work circulating equally in the South as in the North. It is unquestionably one of the most difficult of the various social problems which at the present day so deeply agitate the thoughts of the civilized world. Is the negro race, or is it not, of equal attributes and capacities with our own? Can they, on a large scale, co-exist side by side in the same country on a footing of civil and social equality with the white race? In a free competition of labor with the latter, will they or will they not be ground down to a degradation and misery worse than slavery? When we view the condition of the operative masses of the population in England and other European countries, and feel all the difficulties of the great problem, of the distribution of the fruits of production between capital, skill, and labor, can our confidence be undoubting that in the present condition of society, the conferring of sudden freedom upon our negro race would be a boon to be grateful for? Is it certain that competitive wages are very much better, for a race so situated, than guaranteed support and protection? Until a still deeper problem shall have been solved than that of slavery, the slavery of an inferior to a superior race— a relation reciprocal in certain important duties and obligations—is it certain that the cause of true wisdom and philanthropy is not rather, for the present, to aim to meliorate that institution as it exists, to guard against its abuses, to mitigate its evils, to modify it when it may contravene sacred principles and rights of humanity, by prohibiting the separation of families, excessive severities, subjection to the licentiousness of mastership, &c.? Great as may be its present evils, is it certain that we would not plunge the unhappy Helot race which has been entailed upon us, into still greater ones, by surrendering their fate into the rash hands of those fanatic zealots of a single idea, who claim to be their special friends and champions? Many of the most ardent social reformers of the present day are looking towards the idea of *Associated Industry* as containing the germ of such a regeneration of society as will relieve its masses from the hideous weight of evil which now depresses and degrades them to a condition which these reformers often describe as no improvement upon any form of legal slavery—is it certain, then, that the institution in question, as a mode of society, as a relation between the two races, and between capital and labor,—does not contain some dim undeveloped germ of that very principle of reform thus aimed at, out of which proceeds some compensation at least for its other evils, making it the duty of true reform to cultivate and develope the good, and remove the evils?

To all these, and the similar questions which spring out of any intelligent reflection on the subject, we attempt no answer. Strong as are our sympathies in behalf of liberty, universal liberty, in all applications of the principle not forbidden by great and manifest evils, we confess ourselves not prepared with any satisfactory solution to the great problem of which these questions present various aspects. Far from us to say that either of the antagonist fanaticisms to be found on either side of the Potomac is right. Profoundly embarrassed amidst the conflicting elements entering into the question, much and anxious reflection upon it brings us as yet to no other conclusion than to the duty of a liberal tolerance of the honest differences of both sides; together with the certainty that whatever good is to be done in the case is to be done only by the adoption of very different modes of action, prompted by a very different spirit, from those which have thus far, among us, characterized the labors of most of those who claim the peculiar title of "friends of the slave" and "champions of the rights of man." With no friendship for slavery, though unprepared to excommunicate to eternal damnation, with bell, book, and candle, those who are, we see nothing in the bearing of the Annexation of Texas on that institution to awaken a doubt of the wisdom of that measure, or a compunction for the humble part contributed by us towards its consummation.

California will, probably, next fall away from the loose adhesion which, in such a country as Mexico, holds a remote province in a slight equivocal kind of dependence on the metropolis. Imbecile and distracted, Mexico never can exert any real governmental authority over such a country. The impotence of the one and the distance of the other, must make the relation one of virtual independence; unless, by stunting the province of all natural growth, and forbidding that immigration which can alone develope its capabilities and fulfil the purposes of its creation, tyranny may retain a military dominion, which is no government in the legitimate sense of the term. In the case of California this is now impossible. The Anglo-Saxon foot is already on its borders. Already the advance guard of the irresistible army of Anglo-Saxon emigration has begun to pour down upon it, armed with the plough and the rifle, and marking its trail with schools and colleges, courts and representative halls, mills and meeting-houses. A population will soon be in actual occupation of California, over which it will be idle for Mexico to dream of dominion. They will necessarily become independent. All this without agency of our government, without responsibility of our people—in the natural flow of events, the spontaneous working of principles, and the adaptation of the tendencies and wants of the human race to the elemental circumstances in the midst of which they find themselves placed. And they will have a right to independence—to self-government—to the possession of the homes conquered from the wilderness by their own labors and dangers, sufferings and sacrifices—a better and a truer right than the artificial title of sovereignty in Mexico, a thousand miles distant, inheriting from Spain a title good only against those who have none better. Their right to independence will be the natural right of self-government belonging to any community strong enough to maintain it—distinct in position, origin and character, and free from any mutual obligations of membership of a common political body, binding it to others by the duty of loyalty and compact of public faith. This will be their title to independence; and by this title, there can be no doubt that the population now fast streaming down upon California will both assert and maintain that independence. Whether they will then attach themselves to our Union or not, is not to be predicted with any certainty. Unless the projected railroad across the continent to the Pacific be carried into effect, perhaps they may not; though even in that case, the day is not distant when the Empires of the Atlantic and Pacific would again flow together into one, as soon as their inland border should approach each other. But that great work, colossal as appears the plan on its first suggestion, cannot remain long unbuilt. Its necessity for this very purpose of binding and holding together in its iron clasp our fast-settling Pacific region with that of the Mississippi valley—the natural facility of the route—the ease with which any amount of labor for the construction can be drawn in from the overcrowded populations of Europe, to be paid in the lands made valuable by the progress of the work itself—and its immense utility to the commerce of the world with the whole eastern coast of Asia, alone almost sufficient for the support of such a road— these considerations give assurance that the day cannot be distant which shall witness the conveyance of the representatives from Oregon and California to Washington within less time than a few years ago was devoted to a similar journey by those from Ohio; while the magnetic telegraph will enable the editors of the "San Francisco Union," the "Astoria Evening Post," or the "Nootka Morning News," to set up in type the first half of the President's Inaugural before the echoes of the latter half shall have died away beneath the lofty porch of the Capitol, as spoken from his lips.

Away, then, with all idle French talk of *balances of power* on the American Continent. There is no growth in Spanish America! Whatever progress of population there may be in the British Canadas, is only for their own early severance of their present colonial relation to the little island three thousand miles across the Atlantic; soon to be followed by Annexation, and destined to swell the still accumulating momentum of our progress. And whosoever may hold the balance, though they should cast into the opposite scale all the bayonets and cannon, not only of France and England, but of Europe entire, how would it kick the beam against the simple, solid weight of the two hundred and fifty, or three hundred millions—and American millions—destined to gather beneath the flutter of the stripes and stars, in the fast hastening year of the Lord 1945!

Source:
John O'Sullivan, "Annexation," *United States
Magazine and Democratic Review* 17, no. 1
(July–August 1845): 5–10.

22

The Winning of
the West

BY THEODORE ROOSEVELT

*The racial views of Theodore Roosevelt (1858–1919), twenty-sixth president
of the United States (1901–09), are, as with so many other writers, thinkers,
and political figures, full of apparent contradictions. As president Roosevelt
provoked outrage in the South by inviting the African-American leader
Booker T. Washington to dinner at the White House in 1901; but earlier in
his career he expressed pride at the relentless expansion of the English in
Australia and the Americans in the western parts of the North American
continent. These views are embodied in one of his major historical works,*
The Winning of the West, *published in four volumes between 1889 and
1896. Roosevelt was influenced in his views by Thomas Hart Benton, a
United States senator who vigorously advocated the settlement of the west.*

D URING THE PAST THREE CENTURIES the spread of the English-
speaking peoples over the world's waste spaces has been not only the
most striking feature in the world's history, but also the event of all others most far-reaching in its effects and its importance.

The tongue which Bacon feared to use in his writings, lest they should
remain forever unknown to all but the inhabitants of a relatively unimportant insular kingdom, is now the speech of two continents. The
Common Law which Coke jealously upheld in the southern half of a single European island, is now the law of the land throughout the vast regions of Australasia, and of America north of the Rio Grande. The names
of the plays that Shakespeare wrote are household words in the mouths

136

of mighty nations, whose wide domains were to him more unreal than the realm of Prester John. Over half the descendants of their fellow countrymen of that day now dwell in lands which, when these three Englishmen were born, held not a single white inhabitant; the race which, when they were in their prime, was hemmed in between the North and the Irish seas, to-day holds sway over worlds, whose endless coasts are washed by the waves of the three great oceans.

There have been many other races that at one time or another had their great periods of race expansion—as distinguished from mere conquest,—but there has never been another whose expansion has been either so broad or so rapid. . . .

The settlement of the United States and Canada, throughout most of their extent, bears much resemblance to the latter settlement of Australia and New Zealand. The English conquest of India and even the English conquest of South Africa come in an entirely different category. The first was a mere political conquest, like the Dutch conquest of Java or the extension of the Roman Empire over parts of Asia. South Africa in some respects stands by itself, because there the English are confronted by another white race which it is as yet uncertain whether they can assimilate, and, what is infinitely more important, because they are there confronted by a very large native population with which they cannot mingle, and which neither dies out nor recedes before their advance. It is not likely, but it is at least within the bounds of possibility, that in the course of centuries the whites of South Africa will suffer a fate akin to that which befell the Greek colonists in the Tauric Chersonese, and be swallowed up in the overwhelming mass of black barbarism.

On the other hand, it may fairly be said that in America and Australia the English race has already entered into and begun the enjoyment of its great inheritance. When these continents were settled they contained the largest tracts of fertile, temperate, thinly peopled country on the face of the globe. We cannot rate too highly the importance of their acquisition. Their successful settlement was a feat which by comparison utterly dwarfs all the European wars of the last two centuries; just as the importance of the issues at stake in the wars of Rome and Carthage completely overshadowed the interests for which the various contemporary Greek kingdoms were at the same time striving.

Australia, which was much less important than America, was also won and settled with far less difficulty. The natives were so few in number and of such a low type, that they practically offered no resistance at all, being but little more hindrance than an equal number of ferocious beasts. There was no rivalry whatever by any European power, because the actual settlement—not the mere expatriation of convicts—only began when England as a result of her struggle with Republican and Imperial France, had won the absolute control of the seas. Unknown to themselves, Nelson and his fellow admirals settled the fate of Australia, upon which they probably never wasted a thought. Trafalgar decided much more than the mere question whether Great Britain should temporarily share the fate that so soon befell Prussia; for in all probability it decided the destiny of the island-continent that lay in the South Seas.

The history of the English-speaking race in America has been widely different. In Australia there was no fighting whatever, whether with natives or with other foreigners. In America for the past two centuries and a half there has been a constant succession of contests with powerful and warlike native tribes, with rival European nations, and with American nations of European origin. But even in America there have been wide differences in the way the work has had to be done in different parts of the country, since the close of the great colonial contests between England, France, and Spain.

The extension of the English westward through Canada since the war of the Revolution has been in its essential features merely a less important repetition of what has gone on in the northern United States. The gold miner, the trans-continental railway, and the soldier have been the pioneers of civilization. The chief point of difference, which was but small, arose from the fact that the whole of western Canada was for a long time under the control of the most powerful of all the fur companies, in whose employ were very many French voyageurs and coureurs des bois. From these there sprang up in the valleys of the Red River and the Saskatchewan a singular race of half-breeds, with a unique semi-civilization of their own. It was with these half-breeds, and not, as in the United States, with the Indians, that the settlers of northwestern Canada had their main difficulties.

In what now forms the United States, taking the country as a whole, the foes who had to be met and overcome were very much more formidable. The ground had to be not only settled but conquered, sometimes at the expense of the natives, often at the expense of rival European races. As already pointed out the Indians themselves formed one of the main factors in deciding the fate of the continent. They were never able in the end to avert the white conquest, but they could often delay its advance for a long spell of years. The Iroquois, for instance, held their own against all comers for two centuries. Many other tribes stayed for a time the oncoming white flood, or even drove it back; in Maine the settlers were for a hundred years confined to a narrow strip of sea-coast. Against the Spaniards, there were even here and there Indian nations who definitely recovered the ground they had lost.

When the whites first landed, the superiority and, above all, the novelty of their arms gave them a very great advantage. But the Indians soon became accustomed to the new-comers' weapons and style of warfare. By the time the English had consolidated the Atlantic colonies under their rule, the Indians had become what they have remained ever since, the most formidable savage foes ever encountered by colonists of European stock. Relatively to their numbers, they have shown themselves far more to be dreaded than the Zulus or even the Maoris.

Their presence has caused the process of settlement to go on at unequal rates of speed in different places; the flood has been hemmed in at one point, or has been forced to flow round an island of native population at another. Had the Indians been as helpless as the native Australians were, the continent of North America would have had an altogether different history. It would not only have been settled far more rapidly, but also on very different lines. Not only have the red men themselves kept back the settlements, but they have also had a very great effect upon the outcome of the struggles between the different intrusive European peoples. Had the original inhabitants of the Mississippi valley been as numerous and unwarlike as the Aztecs, de Soto would have repeated the work of Cortes, and we would very possibly have been barred out of the greater portion of our present domain. Had it not been for their Indian allies, it would have been impossible for the French to prolong, as they did, their struggle with their much more numerous English neighbors.

The Indians have shrunk back before our advance only after fierce and dogged resistance. They were never numerous in the land, but exactly what their numbers were when the whites first appeared is impossible to tell. Probably an estimate of half a million for those within the limits of the present United States is not far wrong; but in any such calculation there is of necessity a large element of mere rough guess-work. Formerly writers greatly over-estimated their original numbers, counting them by millions. Now it is the fashion to go to the other extreme, and even to maintain that they have not decreased at all. This last is a theory that can only be upheld on the supposition that the whole does not consist of the sum of the parts; for whereas we can check off on our fingers the tribes that have slightly increased, we can enumerate scores that have died out almost before our eyes. Speaking broadly, they have mixed but little with the English (as distinguished from the French and Spanish) invaders. They are driven back, or die out, or retire to their own reservations; but they are not often assimilated. Still, on every frontier, there is always a certain amount of assimilation going on, much more than is commonly admitted; and whenever a French or Spanish community has been absorbed by the energetic Americans, a certain amount of Indian blood has been absorbed also. There seems to be a chance that in one part of our country, the Indian territory, the Indians, who are continually advancing in civilization, will remain as the ground element of the population, like the Creoles in Louisiana, or the Mexicans in New Mexico.

The Americans when they became a nation continued even more successfully the work which they had begun as citizens of the several English colonies. At the outbreak of the Revolution they still all dwelt on the seaboard, either on the coast itself or along the banks of the streams flowing into the Atlantic. When the fight at Lexington took place they had no settlements beyond the mountain chain on our western border. It had taken them over a century and a half to spread from the Atlantic to the Alleghenies. In the next three quarters of a century they spread from the Alleghenies to the Pacific. In doing this they not only dispossessed the Indian tribes, but they also won the land from its European owners. Britain had to yield the territory between the Ohio and the Great Lakes. By a purchase, of which we frankly announced that the alternative would be war, we acquired from France the vast, ill-defined region known as Louisiana. From the Spaniards, or from their descendants, we won the lands of Florida, Texas, New Mexico, and California.

All these lands were conquered after we had become a power, independent of every other, and one within our own borders; when we were no longer a loose assemblage of petty seaboard communities, each with only such relationship to its neighbor as was implied in their common subjection to a foreign king and a foreign people. Moreover, it is well always to remember that at the day when we began our career as a nation we already differed from our kinsmen of Britain in blood as well as in name; the word American already had more than a merely geographical signification. Americans belong to the English race only in the sense in which Englishmen belong to the German. The fact that no change of language has accompanied the second wandering of our people, from Britain to America, as it accompanied their first, from Germany to Britain, is due to the further fact that when the second wandering took place the race possessed a fixed literary language, and, thanks to the ease of communication, was kept in touch with the parent stock. The change of blood was probably as great in one case as in the other. The modern Englishman is descended from a Low-Dutch stock, which, when it went to Britain, received into itself an enormous infusion of Celtic, a much smaller infusion of Norse and Danish, and also a certain infusion of Norman-French blood. When this new English stock came to America it mingled with and absorbed into itself immigrants from many European lands, and the process has gone on ever since. It is to be noted that, of the new blood thus acquired, the greatest proportion has come from Dutch and German sources, and the next greatest from Irish, while the Scandinavian element comes third, and the only other of much consequence is French Huguenot. Thus it appears that no new element of importance has been added to the blood. Additions have been made to the elemental race-strains in much the same proportion as these were originally combined.

Some latter-day writers deplore the enormous immigration to our shores as making us a heterogeneous instead of a homogeneous people; but as a matter of fact we are less heterogeneous at the present day than we were at the outbreak of the Revolution. Our blood was as much mixed a century ago as it is now. No State now has a smaller proportion of English blood than New York or Pennsylvania had in 1775. Even in New England, where the English stock was purest, there was a certain French and Irish mixture; in Virginia there were Germans in addition. In the other colonies, taken as a whole, it is not probable that much over half of the blood was English; Dutch, French, German, and Gaelic communities abounded.

But all were being rapidly fused into one people. As the Celt of Cornwall and the Saxon of Wessex are now alike Englishmen, so in 1775 Hollander and Huguenot, whether in New York or South Carolina, had become Americans, undistinguishable from the New Englanders and Virginians, the descendants of the men who followed Cromwell or charged behind Rupert. When the great western movement began we were already a people by ourselves. Moreover, the immense immigration from Europe that has taken place since, had little or no effect on the way in which we extended our boundaries; it only began to be important about the time that we acquired our present limits. These limits would in all probability be what they now are even if we had not received a single European colonist since the Revolution.

Source:
Theodore Roosevelt, *The Winning of the West*
(1889–96; reprinted New York: Current
Literature Publishing Co., 1905), vol. 1,
pp. 17–18, 31–40.

23

The War as a Suggestion of Manifest Destiny

BY H. H. POWERS

The Spanish-American War of 1898 and the resultant debates over the annexation of Cuba and the Philippines led many thinkers to ponder America's role as an imperialist nation. In an essay published only a few months after the invasion of Cuba in 1898, H. H. Powers (1859–1936), professor of economics and sociology at Oberlin, Smith, Stanford, and Cornell, and the author of several books on politics, history, art, and travel, engages in offhand stereotypes about the governing capacity of various nations in an attempt to show that the "Anglo-Saxon world" is alone in having "mastered the problem of industrial order."

THE WORLD IS ROUGHLY DIVIDED into two parts distinguished by different capacities for development. They are usually known as civilized and uncivilized, but such a classification is justly offensive to the sensibilities of nations like those of South America which must unquestionably fall into the less favored class. The difference is rather one of independence, the weaker nations being unable to exist as such save by the sufferance or the disagreements of the more powerful ones. The first result of the great struggle must necessarily be the subjection of the dependent to the independent world. The most of this is already accomplished. In the old world everything is appropriated except China, whose face is apparently soon to be determined. South America and Mexico are still nominally independent, but it is incredible that they should remain so. The Monroe Doctrine is an incipient protectorate which must become more definite and positive if it is to prevent their subjection to other powers. It is the belief of intelligent Germans everywhere that their government confidently expects to secure in South America not only an outlet for the overflowing German population, but an extension of the German state. That purpose will find its pretext in the inability of these governments to maintain order and guarantee security, and American sagacity will forestall it by increasing its influence over them and its responsibility for their action. It is probable that a generation more will see the entire world under the jurisdiction or within the "sphere of influence" of half a dozen powers who will continue the struggle for race supremacy with increasing definiteness and determination.

These powers again fall into groups, the Romance, the Germanic, and the Slavic, united by kinship and likely to be consolidated by similarity of circumstance.

The Romance peoples are emotional and imaginative, the proud possessors of a culture that has ripened into the æsthetic stage. But they are self-centred and self-complacent, with little aptitude for those pursuits which are the source of modern progress and power. Their slackened advance has everywhere changed to a halt or passed into avowed retreat. The status of Spain will not be questioned. Despite the rapacity of her officials and the persistence of her beggars, Spanish appreciation of wealth has never begotten a genius for its creation. The nation is primarily influenced by the spectacular side of life. In a moment of supreme crisis she devotes to the prosecution of the war the proceeds of a patriotic bull-fight. A Berlin paper prints the following apropos of the sinking of the "*Merrimac*" in Santiago harbor:

> Both capitals are celebrating the defeat of the enemy; New York in Yankee fashion, by a confident stock exchange; Madrid in southern emotional style, by shouting and enthusiastic jubilation.

The contrast is significant of far-reaching differences of character. There is much that is attractive in the light and gay temperament, with its incapacity for seriousness, but with characteristic ruthlessness nature sacrifices the picturesqueness to the practical in civilization.

If Italy is better off than Spain it is because she is farther away from her former greatness and has no remnants of empire to lose. Her position, too, has brought her under the tutelage of more virile nations and given her some infusion of their vigor. But those who know Italy intimately will doubt if she is better off. Caught by the glamor of the Triple

Alliance, she has readily sacrificed the substance of power for its appearance. Within a generation, without having met a serious emergency or acquired a substantial advantage, she has increased her debt from $625,000,000 to $2,500,000,000. A hundred thousand of her people are said to go mad from hunger every year. And all for what? For that same intangible "national honor," that instinct of stage decorum which infallibly betrays a spectacular people, a people that can not distinguish between shadows and facts.

Despite all contradictions, the same is also true of France. She is a dwindling power because she is an emotional and appearance-loving power. Said a shrewd critic of European politics in reference to a certain complication: "It will be said that France has no interests here. True, but she has susceptibilities." It is the same story. It needs no prophet to foretell the end of the man or nation whose susceptibilities are not the servants of his interests. But prophecy is already passing into fulfillment. Her people, alone among the great nations of Europe, neither emigrate nor multiply at home. Her industry is timid and unprogressive. Her merchant marine has declined in two years 14 per cent in the number of ships and 28 per cent in tonnage, while that of foreign nations entering her ports, already vastly superior to her own, has increased 18 and 117 per cent respectively. It helps the matter but little that in 1898 she was at work upon ninety-one warships with a tonnage almost equal to that of her entire merchant marine. Her colonial empire, a monument to her susceptibilities, burdens rather than enriches her, despite her monopoly of its markets. Her desperate attack upon the Jews becomes intelligible when we are told that a people constituting one five-hundredth of her population owns one-fourth of her active capital, and an anti-Semite leader openly defends the attack on the ground that Frenchmen cannot compete with Jews. Even the physique of the race as revealed by the careful annual measurements of her recruits is said to be slightly but continually deteriorating. I only quote the opinion of competent and sympathetic critics when I say that the Romance civilization, the ripest product of human development, is slowly but surely losing ground, and that no human power can arrest its dissolution.

In the Germanic group there is much of crudity, more than we are willing to confess, but there is virility, energy and growth. There is much that needs changing, but there is much power of change. I need not particularize on a point which is incontestable and of which we are sufficiently conscious. These nations are gaining as certainly as the others are losing. The surplus of their population is establishing itself in every unoccupied part of the habitable globe. In this group is to be found the only nation which owes the world nothing and the world is said to owe her thirty thousand millions of dollars. If there is any doubt, too, as to where industrial leadership has its headquarters it is at least somewhere in this group. Of the Slavic group we can say little because as yet there is little to say. The Slavs are an unknown quantity, but capable apparently of prodigious but slow expansion. As yet they have not demonstrated their capacity to meet the Germanic peoples on the basis of industrial competition where the question of supremacy must eventually be decided, but they may be able to do so.

Within two centuries, perhaps in one, the Romance peoples will be in vassalage, and Germany, without a foot of foreign territory on which white men can thrive, will have been reduced to insignificance by the increase of peoples who have room in which to grow. Slav and Saxon, it narrows down to these, each of them with room for five hundred millions. Which will rule the world? The Slav is as yet far below the Saxon in industrial efficiency, in everything that can make for success in the struggle, unless it be in his willingness to devote all his energies to national aggrandizement. His territory is compact and unified, but one in which development must be slow and which is ill-adapted to the production of a varied civilization. The Saxon has an ideal territory for the development of a world civilization, but one having little natural unity. Are the *psychic* bonds, the consciousness of kinship and the intellectual perception of interest strong enough to hold the race together? If so, its supremacy is assured by the nature and distribution of its territory, the character of its people and their enormous start in economic and intellectual development. If not, their fate, too, is vassalage, and America is not exempt.

The present crisis derives its chief significance, therefore, from its bearing on the problem of race cohesion, a bearing which is far greater than is ordinarily understood. The outburst of sympathy which has suddenly thrown England and America into each other's arms is in itself of small account. What will be the drift of our national interest in the near future?

It may be safely assumed that the irrepressible expansion of American energy and enterprise will continue for a long time to come. But for obvious reasons it cannot continue to assume the form of territorial extension. We have tackled about the only nation in the world from which we can obtain territory in the Eastern hemisphere. Whether we annex the Philippines or not we shall do very little more annexing, for the world is substantially appropriated. Our expansion must be a commercial expansion, and as a late comer we must trade by sufferance in other people's preserves. The whole expanding energy of our national life will assert itself in a demand for the two conditions necessary to its farther growth, access and order. Political and military control of the dependent part of the world will more and more be subordinated to these ends which alone can justify them to the exacting arbiter of life.

If we turn again to the three groups of powers with whom we have to do we find the sharpest line drawn between them in regard to this point, which is of supreme importance to us. The Romance nations, with a consciousness of their economic weakness, deny the world free access to their possessions. Their colonies languish under their inaptitude and are largely lost to the world with no corresponding gain to them. In the weaker members of the group there is not even the capacity to maintain order, the most fundamental condition of economic prosperity.

For different reasons the third group adopts a similar policy. Its economic weakness may be that of undevelopment rather than that of decadence, but for the present the result is the same. It will be apparent, too, that this condition must long continue. Political, geographical, physical and ethnic conditions all point to a slow development. Indeed if the Anglo-Saxon does not exhaust his own inner capacity for growth, it is difficult to see how the Slav is ever to catch up with him. And so long as he is industrially the weaker he will not welcome equal competition. To stake everything on an unqualified industrial struggle will not be good strategy. He will instinctively resort to those grosser weapons to which a highly organized industrial state becomes increasingly sensitive, and which tend to perpetuate that lower culture with which they are more compatible.

In broad contrast with these policies stands that of the Anglo-Saxon world. To this group of nations alone belongs the honor of having mastered the problem of industrial order. There is order in Russia, but it is not industrial. It is repressive and negative, one that substitutes deterrent certainties for deterrent risks. Ordered liberty is an Anglo-Saxon achievement. If England gets rich out of her colonies it is because she makes them rich enough to be good customers. Subordinating all else to her industrial interests, her expansion has been everywhere constructive, creative, a triumph of cosmos over chaos. Were this her only service to the world it would interest all those whose vitality makes them heirs of the future in the maintenance of her policy.

But this is not all. She alone among these nations has adopted the policy of the open door. This is a proof, not of her generosity but of her power. She welcomes all because she fears none. Perhaps this will not always continue. There is reason to apprehend that if American development seriously outstrips that of important parts of the British Empire the instinct of self-protection will conspire with the need of internal unification to close the British Empire against the new rival. But until this happens every blow at this order-creating power is a blow at the most vital American interests. And if the door should be closed those same interests will demand that we be on the inside. The Anglo-Saxon world is worth more than all the rest. The pressure of interest, but slightly felt as yet, but now rapidly increasing, is wholly unequivocal. Those who imagine that the American people will find their chief amusement in the future in "twisting the lion's tail" must have a poor opinion of their business sagacity.

I have said nothing of sentiment as affecting this relation, because it is a characteristic of these peoples and the secret of their success that they subordinate sentiment to interest. But when sentiment coincides with interest it is a force not to be despised. The unity of race, which is closer than that of any other people, is reinforced by unity of religion, language, social and political ideals. The burst of patriotic enthusiasm which followed the Venezuelan proclamation was met at the very outset by a revolt of our deeper sympathies as unmistakable as it was unprecedented, while England's moderation in dealing with what she regarded as an unwarrantable and outrageous interference has not been without effect on the most incorrigible American chauvinists. The spontaneous outburst of sympathy in the present crisis is as widespread and sincere as was ever witnessed between two independent states. The profound feeling that the two nations are joint guardians of a common civilization will not be without influence in uniting them against the advance of the Russian Macedon.

It may be said, and with truth, that these dangers are too remote to be urgent questions in present politics. I will not insist here upon the fact that the race that first shapes its action with reference to the great issue will occupy a position of advantage, or dwell upon the admitted fact that Russia is already so doing. I am not sounding the tocsin, but analyzing actual forces. My point is that considerations like these are already impressing the American imagination and are destined to do so increasingly. While race consciousness is disintegrating polyglot empires like Austria-Hungary it is uniting the Anglo-Saxon peoples. The nation that can give hundreds of millions of dollars and thousands of lives in what it believes to be a humane effort to free an insignificant and inferior people, will not stand unmoved and see the one people to which it is bound by ties of interest and speech and kinship, of religious and political and social ideals, menaced by an alien race.

That the ideal of national isolation is a Utopia is due to no accident of mood or circumstance, but to laws as fundamental as the constitution of protoplasm. We may deprecate the petty politics, the short-sighted sentiment and the unbridled passions which carried us with indecorous haste into a war whose costs we had not counted and whose results we could not foresee. But whence have come this pettiness and indecorum, these bickerings and feuds, this lawlessness and irresponsibility which are the repellent characteristics of American political and private life? From this same isolation and immunity from danger and responsibility. It is a fundamental law of social evolution that pressure from without is necessary to the unification and organization of societies. It was that that united Germany; it was that that first united us. With our growing power there has come a dangerous weakening of this sobering sense of danger and outside responsibility. The centrifugal forces have become dangerously strong, and pent-up energies riot in an alarming fermentation. Already a trifling diversion of attention from inner interests that divide us to outer interests that unite us has obliterated old antipathies between North and South and moderated the jealousies between East and West. We are justly distrustful of our present ability to govern dependencies with wisdom and to conduct with discretion the subtle diplomacy which the newer relations require, but how about our potential ability? If there are no resources in our character we have no future, either of growth or maintenance, for in the end the two are synonymous. If we have those resources the coming of new responsibilities will mean the development of character.

The annexation of the Spanish colonies will bring us serious embarrassments and may not be wise. I venture to suggest, however, that its wisdom will not be determined by the simple question of present convenience, but by its reaction upon our national character and our preparation for the serious responsibilities which are in store for us. These I apprehend to consist primarily in an ever stronger and more constructive influence over American affairs, and more generally in increasingly intimate co-operation with Great Britain in the extension of the higher industrial and social order over the world. No nation or combination of nations ever before had the power to do this, but it looks as if the Anglo-Saxon race by concerted action might accomplish it.

It is possible that the proposed annexations would contribute to both these ends. The West Indies are a natural stepping-stone to South America, not simply as a base for improbable military operations, but as a meeting place of the two civilizations which cannot remain distinct. We can not refuse to let England order and organize South America without becoming responsible for the task ourselves. The interest of the civilized world in industrial order is too great to permit any large concession to our jealousy and our neglect.

The Philippines would hasten that co-operation which Great Britain already desires by revealing the identity of interests which already exists and which would thereby be increased.

It would be a mistake, however, to assume that our decision on either of these points will seriously affect the ultimate result. The forces that make our destiny come from deep down in the constitution of things and care little for our yea or nay. The progress of mankind toward aggregation and order and peace is fortunately but little dependent upon our inclination or understanding. Our wisdom must consist in an intelligent adaptation of ourselves to conditions which transcend our power and our intelligence.

Source:
H. H. Powers, "The War as a Suggestion of Manifest Destiny," *Annals of the American Academy of Political and Social Science* 12, no. 2 (September 1898): 183–92.

24

Our New Duties: Their Later Aspects

BY WHITELAW REID

Whitelaw Reid (1837–1912) was a prominent journalist and longtime managing editor of the New York Tribune. *He was ambassador to France under Benjamin Harrison and also served in the McKinley and Roosevelt administrations. Reid wrote a number of essays at the turn of the century defending imperialism, most of them collected in* Problems of Expansion *(1900). In "Our New Duties: Their Later Aspects," an address delivered at Princeton University on October 21, 1899, Reid approves of the gradual American takeover of the Philippines from Spanish control, defending the policy against those who maintained that the United States was depriving the natives of their freedom.*

AGAINST SUCH A CONSCIENTIOUS and painstaking course in dealing with the grave responsibilities that are upon us in the East, two lines of evasion are sure to threaten. The one is the policy of the upright but short sighted and strictly Continental Patriot,—the same which an illustrious statesman of another country followed in the Soudan: "Scuttle as quick as you can." The other is the policy of the exuberant patriot, who believes in the universal adaptability and immediate extension of American institutions. He thinks all men everywhere as fit to vote as himself, and wants them for partners. He is eager to have them prepare at once, in our new possessions, first in the West Indies, then in the East, to send Senators and Representatives to Congress,—and his policy is: "Make Territories of them now and States in the American Union as

150

soon as possible." I wish to speak with the utmost respect of the sincere advocates of both theories, but must say that the one seems to me to fall short of a proper regard for either our duty or our interest, and the other to be National suicide.

Gentlemen in whose ability and patriotism we all have confidence have lately put the first of these policies for evading our duty in the form of a protest "against the expansion and establishment of the dominion of the United States, by conquest or otherwise, over unwilling peoples in any part of the globe." Of this it may be said, first, that any application of it to the Philippines probably assumes a factional and temporary outbreak to represent a settled unwillingness. Aaron Burr came near making New-Orleans as "unwilling" as Aguinaldo has made Manila. Mr. Lincoln, you remember, always believed the people of North Carolina not unwilling to remain in the Union, yet we know what they did. But next this protest contemplates evading the present responsibility by a reversal of our settled policy any way. Mr. Lincoln probably never doubted the unwillingness of South Carolina to remain in the Union, but that did not change his course. Mr. Seward never inquired whether the Alaskans were unwilling or not. The historic position of the United States, from the day when Jefferson braved the envenomed anti-expansion sentiment of his time and bought the territory west of the Mississippi, on down, has been to consider, not the willingness or unwillingness of any inhabitants, whether aboriginal or colonists, but solely our National opportunity, our own duty and our own interests.

Is it said that this is imperialism? That implies usurpation of power, and there is absolutely no ground for such a charge against this Administration, at any one stage in these whole transactions. If any complaint on this score is to lie, it must relate to the critical period when we were accepting responsibility for order at Manila, and must be for the exercise of too little power, not too much. It is not imperialism to take up honestly the responsibility for order we incurred before the world, and continue under it, even if that should lead us to extend the civil rights of the American Constitution over new regions and strange peoples. It is not imperialism when duty keeps us among these chaotic, warring, distracted tribes, civilized, semi-civilized and barbarous, to help them, as far as their several capacities will permit, toward self-government on the basis of those civil rights.

A terser and more taking statement of opposition has been recently attributed to a gentleman highly honored by this university, and by his townsmen here. I gladly seize this opportunity, as a consistent opponent during his whole political life, to add that his words carry great weight throughout the country by reason of the unquestioned ability, courage and patriotic devotion he has brought to the public service. He is reported as protesting simply against "the use of power in the extension of American institutions." But does not this, if applied to the present situation, seem also to miss an important distinction? What planted us in the Philippines was the use of our power in the most efficient naval and military defence then available for our own institutions where they already exist, against the attack of Spain. If the responsibility entailed by the result of these acts in our own defence does involve some extension of our institutions, shall we therefore run away from it? If a guarantee to chaotic tribes of the civil rights secured by the American Constitution does prove to be an incident springing from the discharge of the duty that has rested upon us from the moment we drove Spain out, is that a result so objectionable as to warrant us in abandoning our duty?

There is, it is true, one other alternative—the one which Aguinaldo himself is said to have suggested, and which has certainly been put forth in his behalf with the utmost simplicity and sincerity by a conspicuous statesman at Chicago. We might at once solicit peace from Aguinaldo. We might then encourage him to extend his rule over the whole country, Catholic, Pagan and Mahometan, willing and unwilling alike, and promise him whatever aid might be necessary for that task. Meantime, we should undertake to protect him against outside interference from any European or Asiatic nation whose interests on that oceanic highway and in those commercial capitals might be imperilled! I do not desire to discuss that proposition. And I submit to candid men that there are just those three courses and no more, now open to us—to run away, to protect Aguinaldo, or to back up our own Army and firmly hold on!

If this fact be clearly perceived, if the choice between these three courses be once recognized as the only choice the present situation permits, our minds will be less disturbed by the confused cries of perplexity and discontent that still fill the air. Thus, men often say, "If you believe in liberty for yourself, why refuse it to the Tagals?" That is right;—they should have, in the degree of their capacity, the only kind of liberty worth having in the world, the only kind that is not a curse to its possessors and to all in contact with them;—ordered liberty, under law, for which the wisdom of man has not yet found a better safeguard than the guarantees of civil rights in the Constitution of the United States. Who supposes that to be the liberty for which Aguinaldo is fighting? What his people want, and what the statesman at Chicago wishes us to use the Army and Navy of the United States to help him get, is the liberty to rule others;—the liberty first to turn our own troops out of the city and harbor we had in our own self-defense captured from their enemies; the liberty next to rule that great commercial city, and the tribes of the interior, instead of leaving us to exercise the rule over them that events have forced upon us, till it is fairly shown that they can rule themselves.

Again, it is said: "You are depriving them of freedom." But they never had freedom, and could not have it now. Even if they could subdue the other tribes in Luzon, they could not establish such order on the other islands and in the waters of the archipelago as to deprive foreign Powers of an immediate excuse for interference. What we are doing is in the double line of preventing otherwise inevitable foreign seizure and putting a stop to domestic war.

"But you cannot fit people for freedom—they must fit themselves, just as we must do our own crawling and stumbling in order to learn to walk." The illustration is unfortunate. Must the crawling baby, then, be abandoned by its natural or accidental guardian, and left to itself to grow strong by struggling, or to perish, as may happen? Must we turn the Tagals loose on the foreigners in Manila and on their enemies in the other tribes, that by following their instincts they may fit themselves for freedom?

Again, "It will injure us to exert power over an unwilling people—just as slavery injured the slave holders themselves." Then a community is injured by maintaining a police. Then a court is injured by rendering a just decree, and an officer by executing it. Then it is a greater injury, for instance, to stop piracy than to suffer from it. Then the manly exercise of a just responsibility enfeebles instead of developing and strengthening a nation.

"Governments derive their just powers from the consent of the governed." "No man is good enough to govern another against his will." Great truths, from men whose greatness and moral elevation the world admires. But there is a higher authority than Jefferson or Lincoln, who said: "If a man smite thee on thy right cheek, turn to him the other also." Yet he who acted literally on even that divine injunction toward the Malays that attacked our army in Manila would be a congenital idiot to begin with, and his corpse, while it lasted, would remain an object lesson of how not to deal with the present stage of Malay civilization and Christianity.

Why mourn over our present course as a departure from the policy of the Fathers? For a hundred years the uniform policy which they began and their sons continued has been acquisition, expansion, annexation, reaching out to remote wildernesses far more distant and inaccessible then than the Philippines are now,—to disconnected regions like Alaska,—to island regions like Midway, the Guano Islands, the Aleutians, the Sandwich Islands,—and even to quasi-protectorates like Liberia and

Samoa. Why mourn because of the precedent we are establishing? The precedent was established before we were born. Why distress ourselves with the thought that this is only the beginning, that it opens the door to unlimited expansion? The door is wide open now, and has been ever since Livingston in Paris jumped at Talleyrand's offer to sell him the wilderness west of the Mississippi instead of the settlements eastward to Florida, which we had been trying to get; and Jefferson eagerly sustained him. For the rest, the task that is laid upon us now is not proving so easy as to warrant this fear that we shall soon be seeking unlimited repetitions of it.

Source:
Whitelaw Reid, *Our New Duties: Their Later Aspects* (New York: H. Hall, 1899), pp. 17–25.

PART FIVE

Social Darwinism and Eugenics

WE HAVE SEEN HOW THE THEORY of evolution served as an impetus to racist thought. Although most naturalists were forced to abandon the polygenic theory of human origins, a countervailing tendency emphasized racial distinctions and bluntly asserted superiority depending upon the existence of traits suggesting intellectual, political, or social preeminence. Darwin himself was circumspect about the superiority or inferiority of individual races—it was simply a matter that failed to interest him—but his cousin Francis Galton was not so shy. In *Hereditary Genius* (1869), published only ten years after *On the Origin of Species,* Galton wrote the work that would later give birth to the eugenics movement. Herbert Spencer added the catchphrase "the survival of the fittest" to contemporary thought, thereby introducing the perversion of the theory of evolution known as Social Darwinism. The notion that some individuals are more "fit" to live and reproduce than others was vitiated throughout its history in the later nineteenth and early twentieth centuries by an imprecision as to who the "fit" and the "unfit" were and how they were to be constituted. Did "fitness" denote purely physical strength? intellectual superiority? "good genes"? artistic excellence? acceptable social or political views? It was impossible to pin down any of the eugenicists and Social Darwininists on this critical issue, since they (like the race classifiers) assumed the answer was so self-evident that it hardly required elucidation.

The danger that these movements represented, beyond their misuse of science, was most evident in the social and political realms. It became

155

easy to believe that "survival of the fittest" was a regrettable but iron law of nature that would be controverted if too much (or, indeed, anything) was done to rescue the "unfit" from their inevitable doom. (But if it was an iron law of nature, how could any human activity curtail or deflect it?) Hence the violent opposition of Social Darwinists to social amelioration, ranging from laws to protect labor from capitalist exploitation to attempts to cure the mentally ill. The political scientist William Graham Sumner was perhaps the chief American representative of Social Darwinism. If, as Sumner noted, "Competition . . . is a law of nature," then it is criminal folly to restrict people's "liberty" to work as hard as they wish "for the acquisition of material goods." Sumner here enunciates a principle still beloved by many conservatives, interpreting "liberty" narrowly as freedom from governmental interference in economic enterprise. It is predictable that Sumner would see in labor protection laws the baleful encroachment of a "socialism" that would undermine the entire political, social, and racial fabric of the nation.

The eugenicists cared less about social conditions than about controlling the human reproductive faculty. Who was "fit" to breed? How could the "fit" be persuaded to breed more bountifully, so that they could counteract the masses of "unfit" breeders? It was widely observed that "savages," poor people (many of them immigrants), and other undesirables propagated far more than the privileged, so that there was danger that all civilization would collapse if the birthrate of the latter could not be stimulated. Theodore Roosevelt addressed himself to the issue on one occasion, although not in an explicitly racist context.[1] But, in truth, the racial overtones of the eugenics movement were always evident, as Albert Edward Wiggam's *New Decalogue of Science* (1923) attests: "Eugenics means that nothing is true social progress that does not minister to race progress and that race progress must be seized and capitalized at every point to minister to social progress."

If many of the racist undercurrents of the eugenics movement have now dissipated, what are we to make of William Shockley? This Nobel Prize–winning physicist, abandoning his landmark work on the transistor, chose to devote much of the last three decades of his life to propounding eugenicist theories specifically relating to the biological inferiority of African Americans. But Shockley's views go beyond mere racial prejudice and extend to social and economic prejudice: "Many of the large improvident families with social problems simply have constitutional deficiencies in those parts of the brain which enable a person to plan and carry out plans."

25

Hereditary Genius

BY FRANCIS GALTON

Francis Galton (1822–1911), English statistician and the cousin of Charles Darwin, was the founder of the eugenics movement (he coined the word in 1883). Galton was a believer in the inheritance of talent, basing his views on the frequency of distinguished families in art, intellect, and athletics. In his landmark work Hereditary Genius *(1869), Galton makes blunt pronouncements on the relative intellectual capacities of various races, maintaining that the future of humanity is dependent on the rule of "civilized" races as opposed to nomadic "savages."*

EVERY LONG-ESTABLISHED RACE has necessarily its peculiar fitness for the conditions under which it has lived, owing to the sure operation of Darwin's law of natural selection. However, I am not much concerned, for the present, with the greater part of those aptitudes, but only with such as are available in some form or other of high civilization. We may reckon upon the advent of a time when civilization, which is now sparse and feeble and far more superficial than it is vaunted to be, shall overspread the globe. Ultimately it is sure to do so, because civilization is the necessary fruit of high intelligence when found in a social animal, and there is no plainer lesson to be read off the face of Nature than that the result of the operation of her laws is to evoke intelligence in connexion with sociability. Intelligence is as much an advantage to an animal as physical strength or any other natural gift, and therefore, out of two varieties of any race of animal who are equally endowed in other respects, the most intelligent variety is sure to prevail in the battle of life. Similarly, among intelligent animals, the most social race is sure to prevail, other qualities being equal.

Under even a very moderate form of material civilization a vast number of aptitudes acquired through the "survivorship of the fittest" and the unsparing destruction of the unfit, for hundreds of generations, have become as obsolete as the old mail-coach habits and customs, since the establishment of railroads, and there is not the slightest use in attempting to preserve them; they are hindrances, and not gains, to civilization. I shall refer to some of these a little further on, but I will first speak of the qualities needed in civilized society. They are, speaking generally, such as will enable a race to supply a large contingent to the various groups of eminent men, of whom I have treated in my several chapters. Without going so far as to say that this very convenient test is perfectly fair, we are at all events justified in making considerable use of it, as I will do, in the estimates I am about to give.

In comparing the worth of different races, I shall make frequent use of the law of deviation from an average, to which I have already been much beholden; and, to save the reader's time and patience, I propose to act upon an assumption that would require a good deal of discussion to limit, and to which the reader may at first demur, but which cannot lead to any error of importance in a rough provisional inquiry. I shall assume that the *intervals* between the grades of ability are the *same* in all the races—that is, if the ability of class A of one race be equal to the ability of class C in another, then the ability of class B of the former shall be supposed equal to that of class D of the latter, and so on. I know this cannot be strictly true, for it would be in defiance of analogy if the variability of all races were precisely the same; but, on the other hand, there is good reason to expect that the error introduced by the assumption cannot sensibly affect the offhand results for which alone I propose to employ it; moreover, the rough data I shall adduce will go far to show the justice of this expectation.

Let us, then, compare the Negro race with the Anglo-Saxon, with respect to those qualities alone which are capable of producing judges, statesmen, commanders, men of literature and science, poets, artists, and divines. If the negro race in America had been affected by no social disabilities, a comparison of their achievements with those of the whites in their several branches of intellectual effort, having regard to the total number of their respective populations, would give the necessary information. As matters stand, we must be content with much rougher data.

First, the negro race has occasionally, but very rarely, produced such men as Toussaint l'Ouverture, who are of our class F; that is to say, its X, or its total classes above G, appear to correspond with our F, showing a difference of not less than two grades between the black and white races, and it may be more.

Secondly, the negro race is by no means wholly deficient in men capable of becoming good factors, thriving merchants, and otherwise considerably raised above the average of whites—that is to say, it cannot unfrequently supply men corresponding to our class C, or even D. It will be recollected that C implies a selection of 1 in 16, or somewhat more than the natural abilities possessed by average foremen of common juries, and that D is as 1 in 64—a degree of ability that is sure to make a man successful in life. In short, classes E and F of the negro may roughly be considered as the equivalent of our C and D—a result which again points to the conclusion, that the average intellectual standard of the negro race is some two grades below our own.

Thirdly, we may compare, but with much caution, the relative position of negroes in their native country with that of the travellers who visit them. The latter, no doubt, bring with them the knowledge current in civilized lands, but that is an advantage of less importance than we are apt to suppose. A native chief has as good an education in the art of ruling men as can be desired; he is continually exercised in personal government, and usually maintains his place by the ascendancy of his character, shown every day over his subjects and rivals. A traveller in wild countries also fills, to a certain degree, the position of a commander, and has to confront native chiefs at every inhabited place. The result is familiar enough—the white traveller almost invariably holds his own in their presence. It is seldom that we hear of a white traveller meeting with a black chief whom he feels to be the better man. I have often discussed this subject with competent persons, and can only recall a few cases of the inferiority of the white man,—certainly not more than might be ascribed to an average actual difference of three grades, of which one may be due to the relative demerits of native education, and the remaining two to a difference in natural gifts.

Fourthly, the number among the negroes of those whom we should call half-witted men is very large. Every book alluding to negro servants in America is full of instances. I was myself much impressed by this fact during my travels in Africa. The mistakes the negroes made in their own matters were so childish, stupid, and simpleton-like, as frequently to make me ashamed of my own species. I do not think it any exaggeration to say, that their C is as low as our E, which would be a difference of two grades, as before. I have no information as to actual idiocy among the negroes—I mean, of course, of that class of idiocy which is not due to disease.

The Australian type is at least one grade below the African negro. I possess a few serviceable data about the natural capacity of the Australian, but not sufficient to induce me to invite the reader to consider them. . . .

It seems to me most essential to the well-being of future generations, that the average standard of ability of the present time should be raised. Civilization is a new condition imposed upon man by the course of events, just as in the history of geological changes new conditions have continually been imposed on different races of animals. They have had the effect either of modifying the nature of the races through the process of natural selection whenever the changes were sufficiently slow and the race sufficiently pliant, or of destroying them altogether when the changes were too abrupt or the race unyielding. The number of the races of mankind that have been entirely destroyed under the pressure of the requirements of an incoming civilization, reads us a terrible lesson. Probably in no former period of the world has the destruction of the races of any animal whatever been effected over such wide areas and with such startling rapidity as in the case of savage man. In the North American Continent, in the West Indian Islands, in the Cape of Good Hope, in Australia, New Zealand, and Van Diemen's Land, the human denizens of vast regions have been entirely swept away in the short space of three centuries, less by the pressure of a stronger race than through the influence of a civilization they were incapable of supporting. And we too, the foremost labourers in creating this civilization, are beginning to show ourselves incapable of keeping pace with our own work. The needs of centralization, communication, and culture, call for more brains and mental stamina than the average of our race possess. We are in crying want for a greater fund of ability in all stations of life; for neither the classes of statesmen, philosophers, artisans, nor labourers are up to the modern complexity of their several professions. An extended civilization like ours comprises more interests than the ordinary statesmen or philosophers of our present race are capable of dealing with, and it exacts more intelligent work than our ordinary artisans and labourers are capable of performing. Our race is overweighted, and appears likely to be drudged into degeneracy by demands that exceed its powers. If its average ability were raised a grade or two, our new classes F and G would conduct the complex affairs of the state at home and abroad as easily as our present F and G, when in the position of country squires, are able to manage the affairs of their establishments and tenantry. All other classes of the community would be similarly promoted to the level of the work required by the nineteenth century, if the average standard of the race were raised.

When the severity of the struggle for existence is not too great for the powers of the race, its action is healthy and conservative, otherwise it is deadly, just as we may see exemplified in the scanty, wretched vegetation that leads a precarious existence near the summer snow line of the Alps, and disappears altogether a little higher up. We want as much backbone as we can get, to bear the racket to which we are henceforth to be exposed, and as good brains as possible to contrive machinery, for modern life to work more smoothly than at present. We can, in some degree, raise the nature of a man to a level with the new conditions imposed upon his existence, and we can also, in some degree, modify the conditions to suit his nature. It is clearly right that both these powers should be exerted, with the view of bringing his nature and the conditions of his existence into as close harmony as possible.

In proportion as the world becomes filled with mankind, the relations of society necessarily increase in complexity, and the nomadic disposition found in most barbarians becomes unsuitable to the novel conditions. There is a most unusual unanimity in respect to the causes of incapacity of savages for civilization, among writers on those hunting and migratory nations who are brought into contact with advancing colonization, and perish, as they invariably do, by the contact. They tell us that the labour of such men is neither constant nor steady; that the love of a wandering, independent life prevents their settling anywhere to work, except for a short time, when urged by want and encouraged by kind treatment. Meadows says that the Chinese call the barbarous races on their borders by a phrase which means "hither and thither, not fixed." And any amount of evidence might be adduced to show how deeply Bohemian habits of one kind or another were ingrained in the nature of the men who inhabited most parts of the earth now overspread by the Anglo-Saxon and other civilized races. Luckily there is still room for adventure, and a man who feels the cravings of a roving adventurous spirit to be too strong for resistance, may yet find a legitimate outlet for it in the colonies, in the army, or on board ship. But such a spirit is, on the whole, an heirloom that brings more impatient restlessness and beating of the wings against cage-bars than persons of more civilized characters can readily comprehend, and it is directly at war with the more modern portion of our moral natures. If a man be purely a nomad, he has only to be nomadic, and his instinct is satisfied; but no Englishmen of the nineteenth century are purely nomadic. The most so among them have also inherited many civilized cravings that are necessarily starved when they become wanderers, in the same way as the wandering instincts are starved when they are settled at home. Consequently their nature has opposite wants, which can never be satisfied except by chance, through some very exceptional turn of circumstances. This is a serious calamity, and as the Bohemianism in the nature of our race is destined to perish, the sooner it goes the happier for mankind. The social requirements of English life are steadily destroying it. No man who only works by fits and starts is able to obtain his living nowadays; for he has not a chance of thriving in competition with steady workmen. If his nature revolts against the monotony of daily labour, he is tempted to the public-house, to intemperance, and, it may be, to poaching, and to much more serious crime; otherwise he banishes himself from our shores. In the first case, he is unlikely to leave as many children as men of more domestic and marrying habits, and, in the second ease, his breed is wholly lost to England. By this steady riddance of the Bohemian spirit of our race, the artisan part of our population is slowly becoming bred to its duties, and the primary qualities of the typical modern British workman are already the very opposite of those of the nomad. What they are now, was well described by Mr. Chadwick as consisting of "great bodily strength, applied under the command of a steady, persevering will, mental self-contentedness, impassibility to external irrelevant impressions, which carries them through the continued repetition of toilsome labour, 'steady as time.'"

It is curious to remark how unimportant to modern civilization has become the once famous and thoroughbred looking Norman. The type of his features, which is, probably, in some degree correlated with his peculiar form of adventurous disposition, is no longer characteristic of our rulers, and is rarely found among celebrities of the present day; it is more often met with among the undistinguished members of highly-born families, and especially among the less conspicuous officers of the army. Modern leading men in all paths of eminence, as may easily be seen in a collection of photographs, are of a coarser and more robust breed; less excitable and dashing, but endowed with far more ruggedness and real vigour. Such also is the case as regards the German portion of the Austrian nation; they are far more high-caste in appearance than the Prussians, who are so plain that it is disagreeable to travel northwards from Vienna and watch the change; yet the Prussians appear possessed of the greater moral and physical stamina.

Much more alien to the genius of an enlightened civilization than the nomadic habit, is the impulsive and uncontrolled nature of the savage. A civilized man must bear and forbear, he must keep before his mind the claims of the morrow as clearly as those of the passing minute; of the absent, as well as of the present. This is the most trying of the new conditions imposed on man by civilization, and the one that makes it hopeless for any but exceptional natures among savages, to live under them. The instinct of a savage is admirably consonant with the needs of savage life; every day he is in danger through transient causes; he lives from hand to mouth, in the hour and for the hour, without care for the past or forethought for the future: but such an instinct is utterly at fault in civilized life. The half-reclaimed savage, being unable to deal with more subjects of consideration than are directly before him, is continually doing acts through mere maladroitness and incapacity, at which he is afterwards deeply grieved and annoyed. The nearer inducements always seem to him, through his uncorrected sense of moral perspective, to be incomparably larger than others of the same actual size, but more remote; consequently, when the temptation of the moment has been yielded to and passed away, and its bitter result comes in its turn before the man, he is amazed and remorseful at his past weakness. It seems incredible that he should have done that yesterday which to-day seems so silly, so unjust, and so unkindly. The newly-reclaimed barbarian, with the impulsive, unstable nature of the savage, when he also chances to be gifted with a peculiarly generous and affectionate disposition, is of all others the man most oppressed with the sense of sin.

Now it is a just assertion, and a common theme of moralists of many creeds, that man, such as we find him, is born with an imperfect nature. He has lofty aspirations, but there is a weakness in his disposition, which incapacitates him from carrying his nobler purposes into effect. He sees that some particular course of action is his duty and should be his delight; but his inclinations are fickle and base, and do not conform to his better judgment. The whole moral nature of man is tainted with sin, which prevents him from doing the things he knows to be right.

The explanation I offer of this apparent anomaly, seems perfectly satisfactory from a scientific point of view. It is neither more nor less than that the development of our nature, whether under Darwin's law of natural selection, or through the effects of changed ancestral habits, has not kept pace with the development of our moral civilization. Man was barbarous but yesterday, and therefore it is not to be expected that the natural aptitudes of his race should already have become moulded into accordance with his very recent advance. We, men of the present centuries, are like animals suddenly transplanted among new conditions of climate and of food: our instincts fail us under the altered circumstances.

My theory is confirmed by the fact that the members of old civilizations are far less sensible than recent converts from barbarism, of their nature being inadequate to their moral needs. The conscience of a negro is aghast at his own wild, impulsive nature, and is easily stirred by a preacher, but it is scarcely possible to ruffle the self-complacency of a steady-going Chinaman.

The sense of original sin would show, according to my theory, not that man was fallen from a high estate, but that he was rising in moral culture with more rapidity than the nature of his race could follow. My view is corroborated by the conclusion reached at the end of each of the many independent lines of ethnological research—that the human race were utter savages in the beginning; and that, after myriads of years of barbarism, man has but very recently found his way into the paths of morality and civilization.

Source:
Francis Galton, *Hereditary Genius: An Inquiry into Its Laws and Consequences* (London: Macmillan, 1869; rev. ed. 1892), pp. 325–28, 332–37.

26

The Blood of
the Nation

BY DAVID STARR JORDAN

David Starr Jordan (1851–1931) taught biology at various universities be-
fore serving as president of Stanford University (1891–1913). He wrote
books on biology as well as Footnotes to Evolution *(1898),* Imperial
Democracy *(1899), and other volumes. In a long essay entitled* The Blood
of the Nation *(1902), Jordan laments the unwillingness of most societies to*
practice selective breeding so that the "best" are perpetuated.

SEND FORTH THE BEST YE BREED." This is Kipling's cynical ad-
vice to a nation which happily can never follow it. But could it be accepted literally and completely, the nation in time would breed only
second-rate men. By the sacrifice of their best or the emigration of the
best, and by such influences alone, have races fallen from first-rate to second-rate in the march of history.

For a race of men or a herd of cattle are governed by the same laws of
selection. Those who survive inherit the traits of their own actual ancestry. In the herd of cattle, to destroy the strongest bulls, the fairest cows,
the most promising calves, is to allow those not strong nor fair nor
promising to become the parents of the coming herd. Under this influence the herd will deteriorate, although the individuals of the inferior
herd are no worse than their own actual parents. Such a process is called
race-degeneration, and it is the only race-degeneration known in the history of cattle or men. The scrawny, lean, infertile herd is the natural offspring of the same type of parents. On the other hand, if we sell or

destroy the rough, lean, or feeble calves, we shall have a herd descended from the best. It is said that when the short-horned Durham cattle first attracted attention in England, the long-horns which preceded them, inferior for beef or milk, vanished "as if smitten by a pestilence." The fact was that, being less valuable, their owners chose to destroy them rather than the finer Durhams. Thus the new stock came from the better Durham parentage. If conditions should ever be reversed and the Durhams were chosen for destruction, then the long-horns might again appear, swelling in numbers as if by magic, unless all traces of the breed had in the meantime been annihilated.

In selective breeding with any domesticated animal or plant, it is possible, with a little attention, to produce wonderful changes for the better. Almost anything may be accomplished with time and patience. To select for posterity those individuals which best meet our needs or please our fancy, and to destroy those with unfavorable qualities, is the function of artificial selection. Add to this the occasional crossing of unlike forms to promote new and desirable variations, and we have the whole secret of selective breeding. This process Youatt calls the "magician's wand" by which man may summon up and bring into existence any form of animal or plant useful to him or pleasing to his fancy. . . .

The evolution of a race is selective only, never collective. Collective evolution, the movement upward or downward of a people as a whole, irrespective of education or of selection, is, as Lepouge has pointed out, a thing unknown. "It exists in rhetoric, not in truth nor in history."

No race as a whole can be made up of "degenerate sons of noble sires." Where decadence exists, the noble sires have perished, either through evil influences, as in the slums of great cities, or else through the movements of history or the growth of institutions. If a nation sends forth the best it breeds to destruction, the second best will take their vacant places. The weak, the vicious, the unthrifty will propagate, and in default of better will have the land to themselves.

We may now see the true significance of the "Man of the Hoe," as painted by Millet and as pictured in Edwin Markham's verse. This is the Norman peasant, low-browed, heavy-jawed, "the brother of the ox," gazing with lacklustre eye on the things about him. To a certain extent, he is typical of the French peasantry. Every one who has travelled in France knows well his kind. If it should be that his kind is increasing, it is because his betters are not. It is not that his back is bent by centuries of toil. He was not born oppressed. Heredity carries over not oppression, but those qualities of mind and heart which invite or which defy oppression. The tyrant harms those only that he can reach. The new generation is free-born, and slips from his hands, unless its traits be of the kind which demand new tyrants.

Millet's "Man of the Hoe" is not the product of oppression. He is primitive, aboriginal. His lineage has always been that of the clown and swineherd. The heavy jaw and slanting forehead can be found in the oldest mounds and tombs of France. The skulls of Engis and Neanderthal were typical men of the hoe, and through the days of the Gauls and Romans the race was not extinct. The "lords and masters of the earth" can prove an *alibi* when accused of the fashioning of the terrible shape of this primitive man. And men of this shape persist to-day in regions never invaded by our social or political tyranny, and their kind is older than any existing social order.

That he is "chained to the wheel of labor" is the result, not the cause, of his impotence. In dealing with him, therefore, we are far from the "labor problem" of to-day, far from the workman brutalized by machinery, and from all the wrongs of the poor set forth in the conventional literature of sympathy. . . .

The effect of alcoholic drink on race-progress should be considered in this connection. Authorities do not agree as to the final result of alcohol in race-selection. Doubtless, in the long run, the drunkard will be eliminated; and perhaps certain authors are right in regarding this as a gain to the race. On the other hand, there is great force in Dr. Amos G. Warner's remark, that of all caustics gangrene is the most expensive. The people of southern Europe are relatively temperate. They have used wine for centuries, and it is thought by Archdall Reid and others that the cause of their temperance is to be found in this long use of alcoholic beverages. All those with vitiated or uncontrollable appetites have been destroyed in the long experience with wine, leaving only those with normal tastes and normal ability of resistance. The free use of wine is, therefore, in this view, a cause of final temperance, while intemperance rages only among those races which have not long known alcohol, and have not become by selection resistant to it. The savage races which have never known alcohol are even less resistant, and are soonest destroyed by it.

In all this there must be a certain element of truth. The view, however, ignores the evil effect on the nervous system of long-continued poisoning, even if the poison be only in moderate amounts. The temperate Italian, with his daily semi-saturation, is no more a normal man than the Scotch farmer with his occasional sprees. The nerve disturbance which wine effects is an evil, whether carried to excess in regularity or irregularity. We know too little of its final result on the race to give certainty to our speculations. It is, moreover, true that most excess in the use of alcohol is not due to primitive appetite. It is drink which causes appetite, and not appetite which seeks for drink. In a given number of drunkards but a very few become such through inborn appetite. It is influence of bad example, lack of courage, false idea of manliness, or some defect in character or misfortune in environment which leads to the first steps in drunkenness. The taste once established takes care of itself. In earlier times, when the nature of alcohol was unknown and total abstinence was undreamed of, it was the strong, the boisterous, the energetic, the apostle of "the strenuous life," who carried all these things to excess. The wassail bowl, the bumper of ale, the flagon of wine,—all these were the attribute of the strong. We cannot say that those who sank in alcoholism thereby illustrated the survival of the fittest. Who can say that, as the Latin races became temperate, they did not also become docile and weak? In other words, considering the influence of alcohol alone, unchecked by an educated conscience, we must admit that it is the strong and vigorous, not the weak and perverted, that are destroyed by it. At the best, we can only say that alcoholic selection is a complex force, which makes for temperance—if at all, at a fearful cost of life which without alcoholic temptation would be well worth saving. We cannot easily, with Mr. Reid, regard alcohol as an instrument of race-purification, nor believe that the growth of abstinence and prohibition only prepares the race for a future deeper plunge into dissipation. If France, through wine, has grown temperate, she has grown tame. "New Mirabeaus," Carlyle tells us, "one hears not of; the wild kindred has gone out with this, its greatest." This fact, whatever the cause, is typical of great, strong, turbulent men who led the wild life of Mirabeau because they knew nothing better.

Source:
David Starr Jordan, *The Blood of the Nation:
A Study of the Decay of Races Through the
Survival of the Unfit* (Boston: American
Unitarian Association, 1902), pp. 11–14,
21–24, 36–40.

27

The Challenge of Facts

BY WILLIAM GRAHAM SUMNER

William Graham Sumner (1840–1910) began his career as a priest in the Episcopal church, then taught political and social science at Yale. He incorporated the theory of evolution into his religious worldview and thereby became a believer in the survival of the fittest and an opponent of state interference in the economic sphere. The author of many historical and biographical works, Sumner summed up his views in "The Challenge of Facts," published posthumously in 1914.

THE STRUGGLE FOR EXISTENCE IS AIMED against nature. It is from her niggardly hand that we have to wrest the satisfactions for our needs, but our fellow-men are our competitors for the meager supply. Competition, therefore, is a law of nature. Nature is entirely neutral; she submits to him who most energetically and resolutely assails her. She grants her rewards to the fittest, therefore, without regard to other considerations of any kind. If, then, there be liberty, men get from her just in proportion to their works, and their having and enjoying are just in proportion to their being and their doing. Such is the system of nature. If we do not like it, and if we try to amend it, there is only one way in which we can do it. We can take from the better and give to the worse. We can deflect the penalties of those who have done ill and throw them on those who have done better. We can take the rewards from those who have done better and give them to those who have done worse. We shall thus lessen the inequalities. We shall favor the survival of the unfittest, and we shall accomplish this by destroying liberty. Let it be understood that we cannot go outside of this alternative: liberty, inequality, survival of the fittest; not-liberty, equality, survival of the unfittest. The former carries society forward and favors all its best members; the latter carries society downwards and favors all its worst members.

For three hundred years now men have been trying to understand and realize liberty. Liberty is not the right or chance to do what we choose; there is no such liberty as that on earth. No man can do as he chooses: the autocrat of Russia or the King of Dahomey has limits to his arbitrary will; the savage in the wilderness, whom some people think free, is the slave of routine, tradition, and superstitious fears; the civilized man must earn his living, or take care of his property, or concede his own will to the rights and claims of his parents, his wife, his children, and all the persons with whom he is connected by the ties and contracts of civilized life.

What we mean by liberty is civil liberty, or liberty under law; and this means the guarantees of law that a man shall not be interfered with while using his own powers for his own welfare. It is, therefore, a civil and political status; and that nation has the freest institutions in which the guarantees of peace for the laborer and security for the capitalist are the highest. Liberty, therefore, does not by any means do away with the struggle for existence. We might as well try to do away with the need of eating, for that would, in effect, be the same thing. What civil liberty does is to turn the competition of man with man from violence and brute force into an industrial competition under which men vie with one another for the acquisition of material goods by industry, energy, skill, frugality, prudence, temperance, and other industrial virtues. Under this changed order of things the inequalities are not done away with. Nature still grants her rewards of having and enjoying, according to our being and doing, but it is now the man of the highest training and not the man of the heaviest fist who gains the highest reward. It is impossible that the man with capital and the man without capital should be equal. To affirm that they are equal would be to say that a man who has no tool can get as much food out of the ground as the man who has a spade or a plough; or that the man who has no weapon can defend himself as well against hostile beasts or hostile men as the man who has a weapon. If that were so, none of us would work any more. We work and deny ourselves to get capital just because, other things being equal, the man who has it is superior, for attaining all the ends of life, to the man who has it not. Considering the eagerness with which we all seek capital and the estimate we put upon it, either in cherishing it if we have it, or envying others who have it while we have it not, it is very strange what platitudes pass current about it in our society so soon as we begin to generalize about it. If our young people really believed some of the teachings they hear, it would not be amiss to preach them a sermon once in a while to reassure them, setting forth that it is not wicked to be rich, nay even, that it is not wicked to be richer than your neighbor.

It follows from what we have observed that it is the utmost folly to denounce capital. To do so is to undermine civilization, for capital is the first requisite of every social gain, educational, ecclesiastical, political, æsthetic, or other. . . .

We have now before us the facts of human life out of which the social problem springs. These facts are in many respects hard and stern. It is by strenuous exertion only that each one of us can sustain himself against the destructive forces and the ever recurring needs of life; and the higher the degree to which we seek to carry our development the greater is the proportionate cost of every step. For help in the struggle we can only look back to those in the previous generation who are responsible for our existence. In the competition of life the son of wise and prudent ancestors has immense advantages over the son of vicious and imprudent ones. The man who has capital possesses immeasurable advantages for the struggle of life over him who has none. The more we break down privileges of class, or industry, and establish liberty, the greater will be the inequalities and the more exclusively will the vicious bear the penalties. Poverty and misery will exist in society just so long as vice exists in human nature.

I now go on to notice some modes of trying to deal with this problem. There is a modern philosophy which has never been taught systematically, but which has won the faith of vast masses of people in the modern civilized world. For want of a better name it may be called the sentimental philosophy. It has colored all modern ideas and institutions in politics, religion, education, charity, and industry, and is widely taught in popular literature, novels, and poetry, and in the pulpit. The first proposition of this sentimental philosophy is that nothing is true which is disagreeable. If, therefore, any facts of observation show that life is grim or hard, the sentimental philosophy steps over such facts with a genial platitude, a consoling commonplace, or a gratifying dogma. The effect is to spread an easy optimism, under the influence of which people spare themselves labor and trouble, reflection and forethought, pains and caution—all of which are hard things, and to admit the necessity for which would be to admit that the world is not all made smooth and easy, for us to pass through it surrounded by love, music, and flowers.

Under this philosophy, "progress" has been represented as a steadily increasing and unmixed good; as if the good steadily encroached on the evil without involving any new and other forms of evil; and as if we could plan great steps in progress in our academies and lyceums, and then realize them by resolution. To minds trained to this way of looking at things, any evil which exists is a reproach. We have only to consider it, hold some discussions about it, pass resolutions, and have done with it. Every moment of delay is, therefore, a social crime. It is monstrous to say that misery and poverty are as constant as vice and evil passions of men! People suffer so under misery and poverty! Assuming, therefore, that we can solve all these problems and eradicate all these evils by expending our ingenuity upon them, of course we cannot hasten too soon to do it.

A social philosophy, consonant with this, has also been taught for a century. It could not fail to be popular, for it teaches that ignorance is as good as knowledge, vulgarity as good as refinement, shiftlessness as good as painstaking, shirking as good as faithful striving, poverty as good as wealth, filth as good as cleanliness—in short, that quality goes for nothing in the measurement of men, but only numbers. Culture, knowledge, refinement, skill, and taste cost labor, but we have been taught that they have only individual, not social value, and that socially they are rather drawbacks than otherwise. In public life we are taught to admire roughness, illiteracy, and rowdyism. The ignorant, idle, and shiftless have been taught that they are "the people," that the generalities inculcated at the same time about the dignity, wisdom, and virtue of "the people" are true of them, that they have nothing to learn to be wise, but that, as they stand, they possess a kind of infallibility, and that to their "opinion" the wise must bow. It is not cause for wonder if whole sections of these classes have begun to use the powers and wisdom attributed to them for their interests, as they construe them, and to trample on all the excellence which marks civilization as on obsolete superstition.

Another development of the same philosophy is the doctrine that men come into the world endowed with "natural rights," or as joint inheritors of the "rights of man," which have been "declared" times without number during the last century. The divine rights of man have succeeded to the obsolete divine right of kings. If it is true, then, that a man is born with rights, he comes into the world with claims on somebody besides his parents. Against whom does he hold such rights? There can be no rights against nature or against God. A man may curse his fate because he is born of an inferior race, or with an hereditary disease, or blind, or, as some members of the race seem to do, because they are born females; but they get no answer to their imprecations. But, now, if men have rights by birth, these rights must hold against their fellow-men and must mean that somebody else is to spend his energy to sustain the existence of the persons so born. What then becomes of the natural rights of the one whose energies are to be diverted from his own interests? If it be said that we should all help each other, that means simply that the race as a whole should advance and expand as much and as fast as it can in its career on earth; and the experience on which we are now acting has shown that we shall do this best under liberty and under the organization which we are now developing, by leaving each to exert his energies for his own success. The notion of natural rights is destitute of sense, but it is captivating, and it is the more available on account of its vagueness. It lends itself to the most vicious kind of social dogmatism, for if a man has natural rights, then the reasoning is clear up to the finished socialistic doctrine that a man has a natural right to whatever he needs, and that the measure of his claims is the wishes which he wants fulfilled. If, then, he has a need, who is bound to satisfy it for him? Who holds the obligation corresponding to his right? It must be the one who possesses what will satisfy that need, or else the state which can take the possession from those who have earned and saved it, and give it to him who needs it and who, by the hypothesis, has not earned and saved it.

It is with the next step, however, that we come to the complete and ruinous absurdity of this view. If a man may demand from those who have a share of what he needs and has not, may he demand the same also for his wife and for his children, and for how many children? The industrious and prudent man who takes the course of labor and self-denial to secure capital, finds that he must defer marriage, both in order to save and to devote his life to the education of fewer children. The man who can claim a share in another's product has no such restraint. The consequence would be that the industrious and prudent would labor and save, without families, to support the idle and improvident who would increase and multiply, until universal destitution forced a return to the principles of liberty and property; and the man who started with the notion that the world owed him a living would once more find, as he does now, that the world pays him its debt in the state prison.

The most specious application of the dogma of rights is to labor. It is said that every man has a right to work. The world is full of work to be done. Those who are willing to work find that they have three days' work to do in every day that comes. Work is the necessity to which we are born. It is not a right, but an irksome necessity, and men escape it whenever they can get the fruits of labor without it. What they want is the fruits, or wages, not work. But wages are capital which some one has earned and saved. If he and the workman can agree on the terms on which he will part with his capital, there is no more to be said. If not, then the right must be set up in a new form. It is now not a right to work, nor even a right to wages, but a right to a certain rate of wages, and we have simply returned to the old doctrine of spoliation again. It is immaterial whether the demand for wages be addressed to an individual capitalist or to a civil body, for the latter can give no wages which it does not collect by taxes out of the capital of those who have labored and saved.

Another application is in the attempt to fix the hours of labor *per diem* by law. If a man is forbidden to labor over eight hours per day (and the law has no sense or utility for the purposes of those who want it until it takes this form), he is forbidden to exercise so much industry as he may be willing to expend in order to accumulate capital for the improvement of his circumstances.

A century ago there were very few wealthy men except owners of land. The extension of commerce, manufactures, and mining, the introduction of the factory system and machinery, the opening of new countries, and the great discoveries and inventions have created a new middle class, based on wealth, and developed out of the peasants, artisans, unskilled laborers, and small shop-keepers of a century ago. The consequence has been that the chance of acquiring capital and all which depends on capital has opened before classes which formerly passed their lives in a dull round of ignorance and drudgery. This chance has brought with it the same alternative which accompanies every other opportunity offered to mortals. Those who were wise and able to profit by the chance succeeded grandly; those who were negligent or unable to profit by it suffered proportionately. The result has been wide inequalities of wealth within the industrial classes. The net result, however, for all, has been the cheapening of luxuries and a vast extension of physical enjoyment. The appetite for enjoyment has been awakened and nourished in classes which formerly never missed what they never thought of, and it has produced eagerness for material good, discontent, and impatient ambition. This is the reverse side of that eager uprising of the industrial classes which is such a great force in modern life. The chance is opened to advance, by industry, prudence, economy, and emigration, to the possession of capital; but the way is long and tedious. The impatience for enjoyment and the thirst for luxury which we have mentioned are the greatest foes to the accumulation of capital; and there is a still darker side to the picture when we come to notice that those who yield to the impatience to enjoy, but who see others outstrip them, are led to malice and envy. Mobs arise which manifest the most savage and senseless disposition to burn and destroy what they cannot enjoy. We have already had evidence, in more than one country, that such a wild disposition exists and needs only opportunity to burst into activity.

The origin of socialism, which is the extreme development of the sentimental philosophy, lies in the undisputed facts which I described at the outset. The socialist regards this misery as the fault of society. He thinks that we can organize society as we like and that an organization can be devised in which poverty and misery shall disappear. He goes further even than this. He assumes that men have artificially organized society as it now exists. Hence if anything is disagreeable or hard in the present state of society it follows, on that view, that the task of organizing society has been imperfectly and badly performed, and that it needs to be done over again. These are the assumptions with which the socialist starts, and many socialists seem also to believe that if they can destroy belief in an Almighty God who is supposed to have made the world such as it is, they will then have overthrown the belief that there is a fixed order in human nature and human life which man can scarcely alter at all, and, if at all, only infinitesimally.

The truth is that the social order is fixed by laws of nature precisely analogous to those of the physical order. The most that man can do is by ignorance and self-conceit to mar the operation of social laws. The evils of society are to a great extent the result of the dogmatism and self-interest of statesmen, philosophers, and ecclesiastics who in past time have done just what the socialists now want to do. Instead of studying the natural laws of the social order, they assumed that they could organize society as they chose, they made up their minds what kind of a society they wanted to make, and they planned their little measures for the ends they had resolved upon. It will take centuries of scientific study of the facts of nature to eliminate from human society the mischievous institutions and traditions which the said statesmen, philosophers, and ecclesiastics have introduced into it. Let us not, however, even then delude ourselves with any impossible hopes. The hardships of life would not be eliminated if the laws of nature acted directly and without interference. The task of right living forever changes its form, but let us not imagine that that task will ever reach a final solution or that any race of men on this earth can ever be emancipated from the necessity of industry, prudence, continence, and temperance if they are to pass their lives prosperously. If you believe the contrary you must suppose that some men can come to exist who shall know nothing of old age, disease, and death.

Source: William Graham Sumner, "The Challenge of Facts," in Sumner's *The Challenge of Facts and Other Essays,* edited by Albert Galloway Sumner (New Haven: Yale University Press, 1914), pp. 25–27, 30–38.

28

The New Decalogue of Science

BY ALBERT EDWARD WIGGAM

Albert Edward Wiggam (1871–1957), a lecturer and writer, was the author of many books on psychology and eugenics. The New Decalogue of Science *(1923) is a collection of essays that embodies his views on eugenics. Wiggam asserts that social progress is dependent on "race progress" and that "eugenics is simply evolution taken out of the hands of brute nature."*

THE FIRST COMMANDMENT OF SCIENCE to statesmanship is the duty of eugenics.

Three thousand years after the Hebrew statesmen incorporated eugenics into their civil and cannon law; twenty-four hundred years after Plato gave the science of eugenics its formulation in political philosophy; two thousand years after Jesus reinforced its moral and religious sanctions; sixty years after Darwin discovered its organizing principle in natural law; fifty years after Sir Francis Galton placed it clearly and finally among the analytical sciences; thirty years after Weismann proved that it was the only secure hope of human improvement; twenty years after Mendel gave it its biological mechanics and experimental method, I seem still to hear you inquiring in vague, mystified wonder, "What is eugenics?"

After all, your question is a very just one, because the eugenicists have probably been too cautious about taking you into their confidence. Perhaps I can, therefore, best answer your question by pointing out first what eugenics is not.

175

Eugenics is:
Not free love.
Not sex-hygiene.
Not public health.
Not trial marriage.
Not a vice crusade.
Not prenatal culture.
Not physical culture.
Not enforced marriage.
Not killing off the weaklings.
Not a scheme for breeding super-men.
Not a plan for producing genius to order.
Not a plan for taking the romance out of love.
Not a scheme "for breeding human beings like animals."
Not a departure from the soundest ideals of sex morals, love, marriage, home and parenthood.

Eugenics is none of these things. Nearly all of these would be anti-eugenical or "dysgenic." Some of them, such as prenatal culture and physical culture, may be pleasant personal exercises, but since they have no appreciable influence in making the next generation healthier, saner or more energetic, they do not belong to eugenics. Sex-hygiene or sex-education is an excellent program for improving health and morals, but since it, too, can have no inherited influence upon the offspring it belongs strictly in the field of education.

Turning to the positive side, however, eugenics is a method ordained of God and seated in natural law for securing better parents for our children, in order that they may be born more richly endowed, mentally, morally and physically for the human struggle. Modernizing the definition of its great founder, Sir Francis Galton, eugenics is the study and guidance of all those agencies that are within social control which will improve or impair the inborn qualities of future generations, mentally, morally and physically. These agencies can readily be divided into three categories, all interdependent, mutually harmonious and supporting. They are:

1. Biological, psychological, chemical and physical.
2. Economic, social and political.
3. Educational, moral and religious.

Through the control of all these great agencies, which if wrongly directed will impair man, and if rightly directed will automatically improve him, eugenics, in the words of the Department of Eugenics of the Carnegie Institution, is that science which "seeks to improve the natural physical, mental and temperamental qualities of the human family."

It passes belief that you should have managed the human family for ten or twenty thousand years without having seen all this yourself. Because it was only when man left the jungle and you took charge of his affairs that he began to deteriorate, and stood in need of eugenics. Had you only learned the lesson of the jungle at the beginning, instead of having defied it as you always have done, man would have continued to progress. But, up to the time you took charge of things and instituted "civilization" it is highly probable that no fool had ever lived to be ten years old. As F. C. S. Shiller, the British philosopher, has said, "The savage simply can not afford to be a fool or to breed fools; the fool-killing agencies in his life are much too potent." Yet up until mental measurements were recently devised, you were actually giving fools college diplomas. Animal trainers inform me that among domesticated—that is "civilized"—birds and animals they find an enormous number of idiots. No wild animal or bird society could afford idiots. As the direct result of your management of human society, man has progressed organically very little except in stupidity. The Cro-Magnon, and even the prior Mousterian man probably had as much or more brains than we have.

If you accept with me the simple, common sense explanation as to how man was first "created," namely the theory of evolution, it is perfectly evident that at one time man had scarcely more brains than his anthropoid cousins, the apes. But by kicking, biting, fighting, outmaneuvering and outwitting his enemies and by the fact that the ones who had not sense and strength enough to do this were killed off, man's brain became enormous and he waxed both in wisdom and agility if not in size and morals. Most of our morals to-day are jungle products. It would be safer biologically if they were more so now. But civilization instituted a new ethics.

The only reason why man's deterioration has not been more marked is because he started with such an enormous biological capital. For ten or twenty thousand years you have been drawing on that capital without the slightest effort to increase it, and have shaped practically every human institution and ideal to decrease it. You have tried to bribe evolution into giving man a biological reprieve. Your marriage customs, social taboos, family mores and institutions such as hereditary rank, wealth and democracy, which confer power upon mediocrity, also your philanthropic institutions, are all in the main devices for sheltering vast masses of inefficiency. As the philosopher, Shiller, further remarks, if man is really to progress, if these great processes of deterioration are to be stemmed and turned upward instead of being as they are now accelerated, "*every* institution and nearly every idea now current will have to be transformed and redirected."

Now just what is it that you have done and what must you do? You have substituted in the place of the jungle agencies which nature controlled, those agencies which you can control, but which so far have been managed only to your own hurt. Nature largely controlled the first four agencies which I have named, the biological, psychological, chemical and physical. Because you let her alone she lifted this tiny, thin-skinned creature from the jungle to the Kingdom of Man. You then took the other six agencies—the economic, social, political, educational, moral and religious—all largely of your own manufacture, and have reversed the whole process. By means of the last six agencies of your making you have tried to control the first four agencies of nature's making. Under your guidance man has turned his face backward toward the jungle from which he so painfully emerged.

Now the science of eugenics means just this and nothing else—that all these agencies be turned about again and civilization be made to minister to man's organic progress—the increase of his brain power instead of its decrease, and the improvement of his body resistance instead of its deterioration. Eugenics means that nothing is true social progress that does not minister to race progress and that race progress must be seized and capitalized at every point to minister to social progress. In short, upon a grand scale eugenics is simply evolution taken out of the hands of brute nature and managed at least as well as, and if possible better than, nature managed it. If you can not do this, then permanent civilization is utterly impossible. If man can not live eugenically he can not live at all, except for brief periods, above the state of savagery.

Source:
Albert Edward Wiggam,
The New Decalogue of Science (Indianapolis:
Bobbs-Merrill, 1923), pp. 99–104.

29

The Biology of the Race Problem

BY WESLEY CRITZ GEORGE

Wesley Critz George (1888–?) taught zoology, histology, and embryology at the University of North Carolina and was former head of the department of anatomy at the University of North Carolina Medical School. He was the author of Race Heredity and Civilization *(1961) and* Race Problems and Human Progress *(1967). In a monograph,* The Biology of the Race Problem *(1962), George recommends a variety of programs that he believes will raise the quality of the nation's gene pool, among them strict segregation of whites and blacks.*

Looking towards the end of raising the inherent possibilities of human life, our opportunity and clear duty, in the light of the best and most complete knowledge and understanding that we can command, is to:

1. Avoid those actions and programs that seem destined to bring about deterioration in the quality of our genetic pool. More specifically, it means the avoidance of any compulsory programs that would tend to bring about the mating of well-endowed, potentially creative people with poorly endowed, uncreative people. This avoidance does not involve the denial of any genuine rights to any group or individual. It does involve recognition of the differing natures of peoples and the taking of those differences into consideration in determining policies.

2. Adopt programs that have good promise of raising the quality of our pool of genes and so increasing the number of able and wise people in our population, since the production of the maximum number of able and wise men seems the surest way to national greatness. Here let me quote Julian Huxley again: ". . . where intelligence is . . . a major factor in progressive change, a quite small excess of individuals of very high intelligence will have disproportionately large effect." And again, "Further, in human evolution . . . the exceptional individual can play a much more important role than in any animal species, and the genetically gifted minority will of necessity be the most important agency of any change deserving the name of progress."

3. Insofar as our knowledge, wisdom, and resources permit, improve the quality of our environment so as to permit and stimulate the fruition of all our good genetic potentialities in order to further increase the chances for the production of wise leaders and able people at all levels. In engineering this good environment, it is desirable for the social planners and politicians to remember that it is apparently more difficult to tell what is a good environment than it is to tell what is good heredity. For example, Benjamin Franklin, Abraham Lincoln and Thomas A. Edison, representing different generations in our history, all arrived at their state of greatness with virtually no schooling and in types of environment not approved by social planners of our generation. Cultural privation in their youths did not make failures of these men nor keep them from the heights of competence and eminence. This is not to belittle the potential value of schools.

4. White people should assist Negroes in providing as good an environment for their children as they are capable of creating; but for the federal government to compel White parents to send their children to school in as bad an environment as Negroes can and do create is neither social justice nor wise national policy.

I am sorry that the need to protect the White race and our civilization against the evil results of false and insistent propaganda has made it necessary to present data that may hurt the feelings of some fine and able Negroes, but the alternative is greater tragedy. Well-meaning humanitarians forget that an overlap of 10–20% does not eliminate the existence of an 80–90% underlap. One swallow does not make a summer, and a few intelligent Negroes do not make a race. The integration of our White and Negro children in schools, and other forms of social integration, involve race masses, and race masses involve averages, not exceptions. The full impact of such integration may not be felt in the first generation, but in the second and third generations the trend to intermarriage moves with increasing momentum as the equalitarian ideology seduces young minds and the standards of society decline. In this we have the universal and invariable experience of history to instruct us. Our survey of the evidence in these pages shows that the process must surely result in evil, not good. Doing evil is not Christian.

It is difficult to find any real factual support for racial integration in statements coming from the organized forces behind it, but those forces are prolific in verbal devices for confusing the minds of those who do not know or do not think. During recent months we have often heard the appealing argument that we should treat every one according to his worth as an individual regardless of his race. To be sure, we should value every man according to his merit—within his own race. It does not follow that virtue would be served by admitting every man or woman that we value, regardless of his race, into those areas of Caucasian social life where mates are chosen. If we open those doors to select Negroes of high merit, we also open them in the end to millions of inferior individuals. If we allow ourselves to be deceived by that Trojan horse, we may expect a fate similar to that of ancient Troy that accepted the original trick and in consequence was overrun and destroyed.

Source:
Wesley Critz George, *The Biology of the Race Problem* (Birmingham, AL, 1962), pp. 75–78.

30

Is Quality of U.S. Population Declining?

BY WILLIAM SHOCKLEY

*William Shockley (1910–1989), a British-American physicist largely re-
sponsible for the development of the transistor (he, along with John Bardeen
and Walter Brattain, was awarded the Nobel Prize for physics in 1970),
created much controversy when, in the 1960s, he turned his attention to the
problems of race. Shockley came to regard his work on race as more important than that on transistors. At one point he offered financial awards for
"genetically disadvantaged" individuals to undergo voluntary sterilization. An interview published in* U.S. News & World Report *for November
22, 1965, displays most fully his views on racial degeneration.*

Q: Dr. Shockley, is the quality of the human race declining in this country, or elsewhere in the world?

A: We have reasons to worry about that possibility, and I have found
that many other thinking people are worrying seriously about it.

In fact, I understand there are people in our Government who feel
that this whole question should be studied extensively and vigorously
to get at the facts. But it's also my conviction that nothing of adequate vigor is being done now.

Q: Why do you say that this whole subject needs more study?

A: Last year Secretary of Labor Willard Wirtz made a statement to the
effect that there were strong indications that a disproportionate number of our unemployed come from exceptionally large families, Now,
I interpret this to suggest that a child of an exceptionally large family
is less likely to be able to hold a job.

Then Secretary Wirtz went on to say:

"But we"—meaning the Government and the nation—"do not pursue evidence that would permit establishing this as a fact or evaluating its significance."

Secretary Wirtz wrote me that he hoped his statement would encourage others to ferret out the facts.

In other words, we're not finding out *if* this is true. We're not finding out what it means if it *is* true. But my great worry is that, if adequate research along this line were carried out, we might find that there is a strong genetic factor at work, and that heredity very much limits the improvement we can expect in such cases.

What I am suggesting is that, even if we overcome currently limiting factors—like accidental brain damage during pregnancy or at birth, and unfavorable environments—we may find that a dismal possibility turns out to be a fact: Many of the large improvident families with social problems simply have constitutional deficiencies in those parts of the brain which enable a person to plan and carry out plans. And I also suggest that this characteristic, especially if found in both parents, can be passed from one generation to another.

But when I try to pin professional geneticists down on this point, the reaction is often: "We don't really know anything about this, and you shouldn't raise these possibilities." This withdrawn attitude does not fit my idea that progress is made by open-minded exploration.

Q: Isn't it now the tendency to blame such attributes on environment—to say that a boy becomes delinquent because he lives in the slums?

A: This is an assumption which many persons prefer to believe, and no doubt has some justification. On the other hand, there are some very definite things we know about the great variety of human brain cells and the enormous complexity of their organization. These things give us no reason to think that the distribution of these cells is not genetically determined.

It is my conjecture that people could have an inherited deficiency in frontal-lobe organization or other brain structure so that they act somewhat like patients with frontal lobotomies [in which nerve fibers in the brain are cut]. I would expect people like this to find difficulties in planning for careers or families. This is another area in which more-active research could be stimulated.

Q: Do such people tend to produce more children than persons of average or superior ability?

A: That is my basic worry, and it was driven home to me by a specific instance in San Francisco where the proprietor of a delicatessen was blinded by a hired acid-thrower. Who was the acid-thrower? He was a teenager, one of 17 illegitimate children of an improvident, irresponsible woman with an I.Q. of 55 who could remember the names of only nine of her children.

The probable father died in prison, sentenced for murder. If that woman can produce 17 children in our society, none of whom will be eliminated by survival of the fittest, she and others like her will be multiplying at an enormously faster rate than more intelligent people do.

Is she an isolated statistic? Who knows? For myself, I fear it is not an isolated statistic.

I can see how, if this sort of thing can occur at all in our society, it could snowball so that the fraction of our population composed of such people could double in less than 20 years and outnumber all the others in a few centuries.

Obviously, any substantial percentage of people like this could produce enormous social instability. There are some who deny these dangers on genetic and statistical grounds. But I have little confidence in the objectivity of their reasoning or the reliability of their optimism.

Q: Just what is known about the relative importance of heredity and environment in such cases?

A: Not nearly enough, but let me mention one item that seems to me quite telling. It comes from an article in "Science" not quite two years ago, collating the data on studies of intelligence quotients of identical twins, who, as you may know, are genetically identical.

Now, broadly, the conclusions were these:

If you had identical twins who were separated at birth and raised in different places, and you measured their I.Q.'s when they grew up, you would find much less difference between them than you would find between ordinary brothers and sisters who are genetically different but who are raised in the same environment. This small sample, about 100 individuals, impresses me enormously with the dominant importance of heredity on the individual's intelligence.

Really reliable facts along these lines could be obtained if the Government or some foundation sponsored a "controlled" program of adoption of abandoned infants to study the effect of differing environments on them.

Q: A few moments ago you mentioned "survival of the fittest." Has that been pretty well removed as a controlling factor in the quality of the human race?

A: I think so, at least in America. We live in such an abundant welfare state that the forces which, in the past, led to the evolution and development of man are playing a little role.

Maybe in some of the worst slums of great cities of the world, survival of the fittest is present. I don't know. If so, it may well be that some of the most effective improvements in the human race are occurring in the most dismal, unattractive areas of the world.

Q: Does it follow that an affluent society like that in America may be most in danger of producing deteriorating human beings?

A: I fear this is likely to be true. Proof, of course, does not exist, but the fact remains that our competitive system has brought us the highest standard of living of any place in the world.

We're living in a society in which the achievements of the human mind have made it possible for people to survive with the help of machines and technology and welfare. Therefore, adverse things may take place genetically, and the unfit may increase faster in our population than ever was true in the past.

Q: Just how much faster are people of inferior ability breeding than those of higher ability?

A: As far as substantially retarded persons are concerned, there have been studies showing very little breeding. They simply don't succeed in finding mates. Furthermore, many of the cases are not hereditary but result from lack of proper prenatal care.

The real cause of worry is people of somewhat higher ability but still, say, near the bottom of the population in ability to learn to reason and to plan ahead—vigorous, capable of mingling with the general population, and not considered "defective" on casual appraisal. Not only are they dull but they need help to survive. Most cannot advance and some are a threat to other people.

One frightening possibility is that our humanitarian relief programs may be exerting a negative influence. These fears are supported by views like those quoted recently by the Associated Press: "I know a 16-year-old girl who was raised on relief. Now she has three illegitimate children and they are all being raised on relief." So far as I can find out, no government agency is looking into the genetic aspects of this sort of thing.

Nor, of course, is there any discussion of what all-around benefits could come from more democratic contraceptive and abortion practices. Our present abortion customs insure the birth of the unwanted child of a poor girl who has made a sexual blunder, while permitting the rich—who at least could provide a better environment—to cancel a mistake. This makes no sense to me.

And we know about the families that are mired down in all kinds of problems they can't solve—crime, poverty, delinquency, disease—from one generation to the next. Census Bureau studies have shown a high degree of inheritance in educational poor performance. Will all of these misfortunes be eliminated with increasing standards of living, or do we have a situation that is being perpetuated genetically and growing out of proportion? That is a very nasty question, indeed, and it is not getting an objective study.

Q: To what extent may heredity be responsible for the high incidence of Negroes on crime and relief rolls?

A: This is a difficult question to answer. Crime seems to be mildly hereditary, but there is a strong environmental factor. Economic incompetence and lack of motivation are due to complex causes. We lack proper scientific investigations, possibly because nobody wants to raise the question for fear of being called a racist. I know of one man who is writing a book in this area, and I'm not sure he'll finish it because the subject is so touchy.

But let me say what I find in my own reading:

If you take the distribution of I.Q.'s of Negroes, and compare it with that of whites, you are going to find plenty of Negroes who are superior to plenty of whites.

But, if you look at the median Negro I.Q., it almost always turns out not to be as good as that of the median white I.Q. At least, this is so in the U.S. How much of this is genetic in origin? How much is environmental? And which precise environmental factors are to blame? Again, a "controlled" program of adoptions might give answers.

Actually, what I worry about with whites and Negroes alike is this: Is there an imbalance in the reproduction of inferior and superior strains? Does the reproduction tend to be most heavy among those we would least like to employ—the ones who would do least well in school? There are eminent Negroes whom we are proud of in every way, but are they the ones who come from and have large families? What is happening to the total numbers? This we do not know.

Q: Is the possibility of genetic decline a new kind of worry for the human race?

A: Not as an idea—the idea is old—but as a coming reality, yes. You see, with improvements of technology—especially in nations of the West—you have had declining death rates, so that inferior strains have increased chances for survival and reproduction at the same time that birth control has tended to reduce family size among the superior elements. Warnings about this were heard 100 years ago, but it is still as touchy a subject today as it was then.

Q: Why is that?

A: Oh, a deep, psychological reason, I think. People hate to feel that they are subject to the same laws of nature as "things" or "animals." It is unnerving to them. Furthermore, it runs counter to so much of our social doctrine—the belief that the poor are victims of hard luck and poor environment, and that all can be changed by giving them a helping hand and a change of environment.

Q: There are laws for sterilization of the unfit—

A: Various States have these laws, but the degree to which they are effective is not well known, and they may not be well formulated in terms of what might be known about human genetics.

In California, I did learn from a very humanitarian and well-informed physician that the rate of such sterilization had been quite significant when he was a young doctor. I did some telephoning and found the rate had dropped by something like 10 times during the last decade.

But the whole subject is being swept under the rug, so we have no real facts on the situation.

I am told Denmark has a sterilization system and there are reports and evaluations. I have not checked into this, but I know that this is a serious undertaking.

Q: Would there be a strong feeling against strengthening laws of this kind?

A: Well, I would hope that a great deal could be done through education and persuasion, and I think that the steps that are being taken in some of our cities to liberalize the dissemination of information on birth control, or liberalize abortion laws, are a great thing.

Q: What about the majority of uneducated people? Would they cooperate?

A: I once argued with Gregory Pincus, the father of the birth-control "pill," that improvident people would not avail themselves of birth-control methods nearly as much as they should. Pincus told me that, in fact, uneducated and impoverished women were the most assiduous users of the pill. They had less unexpected pregnancies than college graduates.

I can't remember being more encouraged by losing an argument! Still, in this area of human affairs, no universal and sweeping answers are likely to be available, so we're going to have to try many things that might add up to worthwhile results.

Q: Mightn't restrictions in breeding by the poor deprive us of an Abraham Lincoln in the future? Didn't he come out of an unpromising background?

A: Poor people can be quite gifted. Restrictions should be placed on the basis of sound genetics without regard to income, class, race, religion or national origin. The breeding of good genetic material, whether the people are rich or poor, is desirable. We want more Lincolns, not fewer.

Q: How sure can we be that this is going to happen?

A: If a man is exceptionally superior to his family background, a lucky combination of genes passed on by his parents is responsible. How much of this luck he will pass on is uncertain. Where both parents are of superior quality the element of luck is reduced.

Luck in genetics can't be eliminated entirely, of course—which is why, even in a family of exceptional children, you will find the average or even retarded child occasionally—just as in a family of average or dull children you will find the brilliant exception.

Much of this is a matter of statistics and probabilities. But we also need research to gain better insight into the various genetic mechanisms. The more we all know, the wiser our population policies can become.

Q: Don't children of superior ability sometimes turn out badly?

A: There is a common misconception that brilliant youngsters are likely to make a mess of their lives. Well, it happens that many years ago there was a study at Stanford University of gifted children, and a follow-up on what happened to them afterward. This study showed that these children, on any basis of comparison with the rest of the population, did very well. Fewer became alcoholics, they earned more money than the average person, fewer entered mental hospitals, fewer had divorces, fewer went to jail.

Q: How long do you think it will be before steps to improve the quality of the human race will become accepted on a wide scale?

A: General acceptance may be quite a way off, but maybe not so far off as we now think. I suspect that, if a study were made and we found out that the acid-throwing teenager represented a hereditary class which is now doubling its members in less than half the time of the rest of the population, we would soon start looking for solutions. Why? Because it would clearly be a matter of life or death for our nation.

Q: What do you think could be done in this country as a start on this whole problem?

A: First of all, we must have more study, and more objective study, of all the questions you've raised: Are the less able people really multiplying faster? Are there significant genetic differences in the ability of various human groups? To what degree is environment responsible for our "problem" families, and what environmental factors are involved, and how? How successful are the programs we have in advancing such problem families? Are we developing methods of evaluating the significance of their effects?

That's No. 1: a national research effort, thorough and open-minded—an objective, fact-finding approach.

Then I think we need to improve our science education—with emphasis on the existence of objective reality and the power of rational reasoning. Our science teaching in public schools doesn't seem to be driving home adequately the point that reasoning can sometimes be applied to deal with very difficult and nebulous problems and, when it can, it is man's most powerful tool for thinking.

Q: Is it education, broadly, that is going to be our likeliest solution to the problem—if there is a problem?

A: I would say so. Certainly the public needs to be stirred up to think about this whole question objectively. That's what I'm trying to do in this interview. It is ridiculous that some States have laws against teaching evolution.

Several eminent intellectuals have discouraged me from publicly expressing the ideas we have talked about. They feel the uninformed and prejudiced might react badly. But I have faith in the long-term values of open discussion.

Q: As more and more youngsters go to college and marry fellow students, will that have some effect on the genetic balance?

A: Yes, I would think that things will tend to move in that direction. In a modern society with high mobility, inbreeding is reduced to the minimum.

Q: Could some incentive be offered to such couples to have more children?

A: I know of no really good answer to this important problem, but let me discuss one provocative possibility:

Ernst Mayr, a zoologist at Harvard, has proposed making tax exemptions for children proportionate to total income of parents, rather than setting a fixed sum of $600 as at present. In other words, a family with an income of $15,000 a year would get a much larger exemption than a family making $5,000 a year.

Along the same lines, he proposes that allowances be given for educational costs that tend to be higher for parents of superior ability who want to give their youngsters a superior education.

This might work out well on the average by encouraging families that have shown above-average accomplishment to have more children and offset the situation where a woman of low intelligence can raise her income with each illegitimate child. Ideas like Mayr's need more public discussion.

Q: Can a society becoming more and more technological afford to continue having large numbers of defective and dull people in its population?

A: Certainly not. There will be less and less work that such people can do, and less and less that they will be able to comprehend in the world around them.

Q: They can be looked after by public welfare—

A: It's perfectly true that an affluent society can look after such people through charity, but I don't like it, and I don't like the common and dangerous notion that we don't have to worry about defective people whom science can "patch up" somehow.

Perhaps you can find employment even for the low I.Q.'s. But how is our democracy going to work if a large fraction of the electorate must be supported by the community and also lacks the brains and moral sense needed for good citizenship?

The more people we produce who are capable of higher education and are freer of defects, the more of our energy we can devote to the improvement of our environment. The more people we produce who are incapable of voting intelligently, the greater the risk of economic trouble and war.

But these are my personal reactions. What I worry about most is that there is so little discussion of these matters that no worthwhile consensus is having a chance to develop.

Q: How do you feel generally about the prospects of an improvement taking place in the quality of the human race?

A: On the whole, I'm hopeful. You remember that about 10 years ago people were saying that Malthus in his 1798 prediction had overplayed the dangers of population growth. President Eisenhower said that population control wasn't something the Government should concern itself with.

Now we find that Mr. Eisenhower changed his mind. And President Johnson is saying, in effect, that $5 spent on population control would be worth $100 spent on economic development.

In the broad field of population control, there has been an almost complete reversal in attitudes—and this, with the development of the intrauterine loop and other devices, suggests that the human race can solve the problem of growing populations.

This suggests to me that people will find sensible ways to solve the problem of the quality of the human race.

But there is another very grim possibility: A nuclear war might inflict so much genetic damage that it would become absolutely necessary to select from the survivors those persons with sufficiently undamaged genes to perpetuate a healthy human race. This would clearly require society to make complex eugenic decisions. I hope this task never will confront us, but this is one way in which the human race might be forced to resume its evolution.

I think our best chance for progress in human evolution without the eventual dismal detour of nuclear genetic damage is in more stress on research and public discussion.

My program for continued progress is: Let's ask the questions, do the necessary research, get the facts, discuss them widely—then either worries will evaporate, or plans for action will develop.

Source:
"Is Quality of U.S. Population Declining?"
U.S. News & World Report 59, no. 21
(November 22, 1965): 68–71.

PART SIX

Prejudice and Religion

THIS BOOK DOES NOT COVER instances of prejudice based purely on religion, although of course much of the prejudice against Jews and other ethnic groups involves a significant religious dimension. Moreover, although abolitionists were frequently inspired by religious sentiments in their opposition to slavery, the defenders of slavery also used a variety of religious arguments to defend the institution. It is uncanny, however, that so early a treatise as Ezra Stiles Ely's *The Duty of Christian Freemen to Elect Christian Rulers* echoes the views of modern fundamentalists that America is a "Christian nation" and is obligated to pursue its Christian heritage—by the suppression, if necessary, of other religions. Ely's scornful reference to "Turks [and] Jews" suggests a racial aspect to his religious intolerance, but race is not central to his argument.

Racism became united with religion when the "Social Gospel" movement emerged in the later nineteenth century. A variety of mainly Protestant religious leaders developed the notion that the evolution theory and other modern advances in science must be accepted and incorporated into a religious worldview; but—in direct contrast to the Social Darwinists—they maintained that these theories should not be used to justify the exploitation of the weak or the poor. For all the good that the promoters of the Social Gospel did in drawing attention to social injustice, many of them inexorably adopted theories of racial superiority and also united religion with imperialism in their desire to spread the Word to the heathen both in the United States (specifically the Native Americans and the African Americans) and throughout the world. Horace Bushnell in

Christian Nurture (1861) shows the potential ill effects, both on science and on religion, of misunderstandings of scientific fact. By asserting that "qualities of education, habit, feeling, and character have a tendency always to grow in, by long continuance, and become thoroughly inbred in the stock," Bushnell is able to maintain that Christianity can become inbred in successive generations and thereby result in "a general mitigation of the bad points of the stock, and a more and more completely inbred piety."

But the most vigorous proponent of the Social Gospel, and at the same time one of the most prominent racists of the time, was Josiah Strong. In *Our Country* (1885) Strong finds it evident that the Anglo-Saxon is preeminent both in "spiritual Christianity" and "civil liberty," and sees no paradox in asserting that "the marked superiority of this race is due, in large measure, to its highly mixed origin." This latter view diametrically contrasts with that of many others who saw a direct line of descent from the barbarian hordes of late antiquity to the Anglo-American stock of the present day. And if one of the Anglo-Saxon's chief characteristics is "an instinct or genius for colonizing," it is only logical to believe, as Strong does, that in the course of time the race will either destroy or rule over the other races of the world with its Christian might.

31

The Duty of Christian Freemen to Elect Christian Rulers

BY EZRA STILES ELY

Ezra Stiles Ely (1788–1861) was a Presbyterian minister and chaplain of the City Hospital in New York City and later a minister at Pine Street Church in Philadelphia. In a pamphlet, The Duty of Christian Freemen to Elect Christian Rulers *(1828), Ely foreshadows the views of modern fundamentalists in asserting that the United States is a Christian nation and that its people must not elect rulers of any other faith.*

ALL WHO PROFESS TO BE CHRISTIANS of any denomination ought to agree that they will support no man as a candidate for any office, who is not professedly friendly to Christianity, and a believer in divine Revelation. We do not say that true or even pretended Christianity shall be made a constitutional test of admission to office; but we do affirm that Christians may in their elections lawfully prefer the avowed friends of the Christian religion to Turks, Jews, and Infidels. Turks, indeed, might naturally prefer Turks, if they could elect them; and Infidels might prefer Infidels; and I should not wonder if a conscientious Jew should prefer a ruler of his own religious faith; but it would be passing strange if a Christian should not desire the election of one friendly to his own system of religion. While every religious system is tolerated in our country, and no one is established by law, it is still possible for me to think, that the friend of Christianity will make a much better governor of this commonwealth or President of the United States, than the advocate of Theism or Polytheism. We will not pretend to search the heart; but surely all sects of Christians may agree in opinion, that it is more desirable to have a Christian than a Jew, Mohammedan, or Pagan, in any civil office; and they may accordingly settle it in their minds, that they will never vote for any one to fill any office in the nation or state, who does not profess to receive the Bible as the rule of his faith. If three or four of the most numerous denominations of Christians in the United States, the Presbyterians, the Baptists, the Methodists and Congregationalists for instance, should act upon this principle, our country would never be dishonoured with an *avowed infidel* in her national cabinet or capitol. The Presbyterians alone could bring *half a million of electors* into the field, in opposition to any known advocate of Deism, Socinianism, or any species of avowed hostility to the truth of Christianity. If to the denominations above named we add the members of the Protestant Episcopal church in our country, the electors of these five classes of true Christians, united in the sole requisition of apparent friendship to Christianity in every candidate for office whom they will support, could govern every public election in our country, without infringing in the least upon the charter of our civil liberties. To these might be added, in this State and in Ohio, the numerous German Christians, and in New York and New Jersey the members of the Reformed Dutch Church, who are all zealous for the fundamental truths of Christianity. What should prevent us from co-operating in such a union as this? Let a man be of good moral character, and let him profess to believe in and advocate the Christian religion, and we can all support him. At one time he will be a Baptist, at another an Episcopalian, at another a Methodist, at another a Presbyterian of the American, Scotch, Irish, Dutch, or German stamp, and always a friend to our common Christianity. Why then should we ever suffer an enemy, an open and known enemy of the true religion of Christ, to enact our laws or fill the executive chair? Our Christian rulers will not oppress Jews or Infidels; they will *kiss the Son and serve the Lord;* while we have the best security for their fidelity to our republican, and I may say scriptural forms of government.

It deprives no man of his right for me to prefer a Christian to an Infidel. If Infidels were the most numerous electors, they would doubtless elect men of their own sentiments; and unhappily such men not unfrequently get into power in this country, in which ninety-nine hundredths of the people are believers in the divine origin and authority of the Christian religion. If hundreds of thousands of our fellow citizens should agree with us in an effort to elect men to public office who read the Bible, profess to believe it, reverence the Sabbath, attend public worship, and sustain a good moral character, who could complain? Have we not as much liberty to be the supporters of the Christian cause by our votes, as others have to support anti-christian men and measures?

Let us awake, then, fellow Christians, to our sacred duty to our Divine Master; and let us have no rulers, with our consent and co-operation, who are not known to be avowedly Christians.

It will here be objected, that frequently we must choose between two or more candidates who are in nomination, or must lose our votes; and that no one of the candidates may be of the right religious and moral character.

I must answer, that every freeman is bound to give his voice in such a manner as he judges will best conduce to the public good; and that it is not usually beneficial to give a suffrage for one whose election is wholly out of the question. If no good man is in nomination he must choose the least of two natural evils, and support the better man to exclude the worse. But I pray you, who make, or should make, our nominations? Are they not the people who select their own candidates? And are not the majority of the people in profession Christians? The influence of the friends of Christ ought to be exerted, known, and felt *in every stage* of our popular elections. If we intend to have our civil and religious liberty continued to us, and to transmit our institutions unimpaired to posterity, we must not suffer immoral, unprincipled, and irreligious men to nominate themselves to office, and then tell us, that we must elect them or have no rulers.

We have good men in abundance to fill all civil offices, from the highest to the lowest; and it is the fault of all the numerous Christians of our country if such are not elected.

It will be objected that my plan of a truly Christian party in politics will make hypocrites. We are not answerable for their hypocrisy if it does. There is no natural tendency in the scheme to make men deceivers; and if real enemies of the Christian religion conceal their enmity, that concealment is for the public good. We wish all iniquity, if not exterminated, may, as if ashamed, hide its head. It will be well for our country when all men who expect office are under the necessity of appearing honest, sober, pure, benevolent, and religious. It will be well for us when men cannot expect to retain, if they for a time occupy high places, by bribery, deception, coalition, and hypocrisy. It is most of all desirable that public officers SHOULD BE good men, friends of God, followers of Jesus Christ, and lovers of their country; but it is a matter of thankfulness if they are constrained TO SEEM such persons; for in this way vice, and the propagation of vice by evil example, is prevented. It will be objected, moreover, that my scheme of voting on political elections according to certain fixed religious principles, will create jealousies among the different denominations of Christians. But why should it? Our rulers which we have elected are of some, or of no religious sect. If they are of no religious denomination, they belong to the party of infidels. If they are of any one of the denominations of true Christians, it is better, in the judgment of all true Christians, that they should be of that one company than in the fellowship of infidels. Let a civil ruler, then, be a Christian *of some sort,* we will all say, rather than not a Christian of any denomination. If we fix this as a principle of our political morality, we shall all be gratified in turn, and in part, by having Christian rulers of our own description.

I am free to avow, that other things being equal, I would prefer for my chief magistrate, and judge, and ruler, a sound Presbyterian; and every candid religionist will make the same declaration concerning his own persuasion; but I would prefer a religious and moral man, of any one of the truly Christian sects, to any man destitute of religious principle and morality.

Suffer, my Christian fellow-citizens, a word of exhortation. Let us all be Christian politicians; and govern ourselves by supreme love to our blessed Master, whether we unite in prayers or in the election of our civil rulers. Let us be as conscientiously religious at the polls as in the pulpit, or house of worship. This course of conduct will promote good government and true religion in our country at the same time. Our public rulers then will prove a terror to them who do evil, and a praise to them who do well. Let us choose men who dare to be honest in their own religious creed, while they are too much of Christians and of republicans, to attempt to lord it over the faith of others. Let us never support by our votes any immoral man, or any known contemner of any of the fundamental doctrines of Christ, for any office: and least of all for the Presidency of these United States; for "blessed are they who put their trust in Christ." The people who with their rulers *kiss the Son,* shall experience special divine protection, and be a praise in the whole earth. Let us elect men who dare to acknowledge the Lord Jesus Christ for their Lord in their public documents. Which of our Presidents has ever done this? It would pick no infidel's pocket, and break no Jew's neck, if our President should be so singular as to let it be known, that he is a *Christian* by his Messages, and an advocate for the Deity of Christ by his personal preference of a Christian temple to a Socinian conventicle. It would be no violation of our national constitution, if our members of

Congress should quit reading of newspapers and writing letters on the Lord's day, at least during public worship in the Hall of Representatives.

If all our great men should set a holy example of reverence for the Sabbath and the worship of Almighty God, it would not convert them into tyrants; it would not make our national government a religious aristocracy; it would not violate our federal constitution.

We are a Christian nation: we have a right to demand that all our rulers in their conduct shall conform to Christian morality; and if they do not, it is the duty and privilege of Christian freemen to make a new and a better election.

May the Lord Jesus Christ for ever reign in and over these United States, and call them peculiarly his own. *Amen.*

Source:
Ezra Stiles Ely, *The Duty of Christian Freemen
to Elect Christian Rulers* (Philadelphia:
William F. Geddes, 1828), pp. 10–14.

32

The Progress and Prospects of Christianity in the United States of America

BY ROBERT BAIRD

Robert Baird (1798–1863), a Protestant minister who traveled widely throughout the American continent, was the author of numerous works of theology, including Religion in America *(1844). He also wrote an anti-slavery treatise,* A Letter to Lord Brougham, on the Subject of American Slavery *(1836). In a volume published in London,* The Progress and Prospects of Christianity in the United States of America *(1851),* Baird *ruminates on the effect of Christianity on Native Americans and also on the interplay between religion and slavery.*

The Aborigines

The first colonists found the whole country possessed, or rather occupied, if the word may be used, by many tribes of Aborigines, speaking different languages, and hostile to each other in many cases, and living by fishing and the chase. The number of these people was small in comparison with the extent of the country. Wars and pestilential dis-

200

eases were steadily diminishing them in some regions; in others they were perhaps slowly increasing. It was the desire and intention of the colonists, as expressed in the charters of most if not all of them, to christianize these people. Some attempts were made at the outset, but with very partial success. It was not long till wars began between them, as we have elsewhere stated, and with the exception of the efforts of Elliot, the Mayhews, and others in new England, in the seventeenth century, and of David Brainerd and his brother John in New Jersey and Pennsylvania, and of Zeisberger and others in Ohio, in the eighteenth, there was nothing done worthy of mention until the present century; nor even then till about the year 1816. Since that time missions and schools have been planted in many of the tribes, and civilization and religion have made much progress, especially among the Choctaws, and Cherokees, and some of the smaller tribes. The Gospel is also gaining a foothold among the Creeks, one of the largest of all the tribes. The General Government has for several years been collecting the tribes which were within the limits of the States, upon a large territory west of the States of Arkansas and Missouri, which may be their own as long as they choose to maintain a national or tribal existence, and so get clear of the conflicts which so often arose whilst they were within the limits of any of the States. This work has advanced very much, and the worst of the evils attendant on the removal of so many people, partially civilized, have, it is hoped, passed away.

The United States Government pays to these tribes large sums of money, in the shape of annuities, being either interest of the purchase-money for the lands which they sold to the Government at their removal, or instalments of that money, agreeably to treaties made. Out of these moneys, large sums are now appropriated by the governments of these tribes to the maintenance of schools and academies, and for the promotion of the useful arts. A large number of these Indians, especially among the Choctaws and Cherokees, can read, and some are well-educated men, and would do themselves credit in any legislative body. There are respectable newspapers in the Cherokee and Choctaw languages. Civilization is steadily advancing among them. There are several thousand members of the churches planted among the several tribes by Methodist, Presbyterian, Baptist, Moravian, and other missionaries. The Cherokees are about 18,000; the Choctaws, 15,000; the Creeks, 22,000: and there are several small tribes which have been removed to the same extensive territory. The entire population of that territory is quite large enough to make a respectable State; and it is sincerely to be desired that these tribes may one day unite and form a regular member of the American Union. Diversity of language and the influence of the chiefs, who now have the government of each tribe very much in their hands, are the great obstacles to this plan at present. The English language is, however, gaining ground, and will one day—though comparatively distant,—supplant all others. These tribes, now that civilization has gained so great an ascendancy among them, are, it is believed, increasing instead of diminishing.

A great deal has been said about the wasting away of the Aborigines of America before the European races. That this has been the case, to a considerable extent, is true; but not to the extent that is often supposed. The remains of former tribes have been greatly absorbed in other and larger ones. It is possible that Civilization and Christianity may save some of the tribes,—Cherokees, Choctaws, etc.,—for a long time from annihilation, or absorption in other tribes; but it is certain, I think, that all of them will, sooner or later, be absorbed in the Europeo-American population. To this destiny every thing infallibly points. And probably it will be seen to be the best arrangement in the long run. The United States seem to be destined to be the scene in which a more complete fusion of the races is to take place than the world has hitherto seen. I know an excellent man, born in Virginia, who represents the four continents, as it were; for in his veins is the blood of the European, African, Asiatic, and American (aboriginal) races!

Slavery

What has Christianity done for the African race? The first of these people that came to our shores were brought by a Dutch ship in the year 1620. The slave-trade soon commenced, and for a hundred and fifty-five years it was carried on by English ships, and exclusively so, so far as the English Colonies were concerned, and indeed so far as all the American Continent was concerned for many years, has England had a monopoly of the whole trade for a period. At the time of the declaration of Independence, there were more than 500,000 of these people in the country, almost all of them slaves, and chiefly in Southern states.

The colonists at first and for a long time, looked upon these people as heathen and aliens, that had been obtruded upon them, and spoke and acted in regard to them very much as they seem to have supposed that the Jews did about the Canaanites who remained in their country, after the conquest, and whom they were permitted to enslave. It was much the *fashion,* if I may so say, in those days, to speak in that way. For a long time the poor degraded people seem to have shared but little in the protection of the laws, and to have had but little sympathy from the churches. The laws appear scarcely to have contemplated them as coming within their scope. And the Church that was the dominant, and for a long time the exclusive one in the portions of the country where slavery most accumulated—that is, in Maryland, Virginia, the Carolinas—had not sufficient religious zeal and vitality, though it had many excellent people in it—to accomplish much in a work so eminently missionary, as the labour of converting these people. And let it be remembered that this Church was at that time established by law, as really so as that of England.

The Presbyterians and Baptists had no foothold there, until more than one hundred years after slavery had commenced its existence in Virginia, and the Methodists were fifty years later still in gaining an organization in any of the southern States. The evil was great before these three denominations began to exist in that part of the country. At present the Baptist and Methodist Churches are the great ecclesiastical bodies which exist in the South. The Presbyterians and Episcopalians combined are far less numerous than either of them.

What would have been the state of things at the present day, if the Churches had from the first taken the ground that no slave-holder should share in church-fellowship, I cannot say, for I do not know—it would require omniscience to answer that question. But that was not done; nor was it to be expected, considering what was the then state of opinion in the religious world, on the subject. Good men in England were engaged in the slave-trade till long after that day. The churches in the southern colonies could hardly be expected to be in advance of the world on that subject, situated as they were. All that they thought of doing,—all that they thought that Christianity required,—was, that they should inculcate on masters and slaves their correlative duties, and do as well as they could under laws which evidently regarded these people as aliens and property which might be transferred from hand to hand, and place to place. I simply state the facts of the case, and I think they will not be questioned.

And now the question returns: what has Christianity done for these people? And we are better prepared to answer it.—It has endeavoured, under laws unjust and barbarous, and in many respects unfavourable for the successful propagation of the Gospel, to inculcate humanity and kindness on the part of the master, and obedience and fidelity on the part of the Slave. It has secured the comfortable maintenance of the slaves, as to food and clothing and lodging,—I speak generally—for I know there are exceptions. It has secured the enforcement of the laws relating to the sabbath, and so given the slave a seventh part of his time as a day of rest. It is certainly a rare thing for a slave to be compelled to work on the Lord's day—especially in those portions of the South where Christianity is most prevalent. It has exerted a very great counteracting influence in regard to the loose and unjust position in which the laws have left the subject of marriage. Whatever those laws may permit in the shape of what often leads to polygamy, Christianity has done much to cause the marriage relation to be held sacred. It has done much to prevent the separation of families by sale; and its influence has been much felt in this respect by Christian masters. But so long as the laws remain as they are, death and even debt will often defeat the wishes of the best masters. It has brought tens of thousands of both masters and slaves to the knowledge of Christ. There are probably more than 300,000 slaves who profess Christ in the fifteen slave-holding States. It is reported that there are 50,000 in the single State of South Carolina. Christianity has induced many a master to liberate his slaves. There are more than 400,000 free people of African origin in the United States, who are the descendants of slaves, if they were not slaves themselves. These people or their fathers, were liberated through the influence of Christianity. Their present value, if the value of human beings can be estimated by money, far exceeds all that England gave to free her West India Slaves, and all this was the gift, as it were, of individuals. Christianity is steadily advancing in the Southern States, as is demonstrable in many ways. And this is our hope. As the Legislatures of the Southern States have exclusive control, by the Constitution, over the subject of slavery, each in its own sphere, it is only through the prevalence of Christianity in all those States, that we can hope for the peaceable overthrow of slavery in the United States—and of no other overthrow of it will we speak, or can we speak, as Christian men. It is this, in connexion with the operation of other causes—among which may be named its circumscription within its present limits, and the consequent diminution of the value of slave-labour, at no very distant day,—that will lead to its overthrow sooner or later. It will require time; but the great consummation will come. The Christian influence in the South, though considerable, is not sufficient to control legislation there. The proportion of the slave-holders,—I refer to men, men of influence,—who profess to be religious men,—is not great. Many of their wives and children, many poor white men, and many slaves and free negroes are pious; but the overwhelming preponderance of political influence is in the hands of unconverted masters.

But religion is gaining ground in the South, as well as in the North. It is greatly to be desired that its increase may be far more rapid; for the influence which is to overthrow slavery must come *from within* those States, not *from without*. The people of the North cannot liberate the slaves of the South. Of course, the people of other lands cannot. We may grow indignant, and blaspheme, and even curse, if we will; but it will not hasten,—it will only retard the work. The people of the South, who alone have control of the subject, cannot be driven. They may be persuaded, and the cause can be greatly aided by proper means; but those means are not denunciation and malediction, come from what quarter they may.

I have spoken to you my honest sentiments—as God is my witness. I have never held any other, because my reason will not permit it. If I am wrong in these views, I am *conscientiously* so. I am not aware that in holding them I am influenced by sinister or corrupt motives. I have never had but one opinion of slavery itself, however much I may respect many of those who are implicated in it, both masters and slaves; I sincerely pity them. I never made any extraordinary profession or enunciation of my abhorrence of this dreadful evil—this direful curse, which the Old World has bequeathed to my country,—either in England or elsewhere, to secure the favour or friendship of any man, nor shall I.

There are some things about which I cannot entertain a doubt. Whatever may be my opinion about the wisdom of some other measures for overthrowing slavery in the Southern States, I cannot despair of the influence of the Gospel as the grand means of its ultimate removal. I know of no slave-holding State in the Union where we cannot preach the Gospel to slaves, and where they are not allowed to hear, believe and be saved. In several States, not all, laws were made twenty-five years ago, forbidding to teach the slaves to read. This was done solely through fear, lest incendiary publications might be, as was madly attempted, circulated among them, to excite them to rise and destroy their masters. That these most unjust laws are disregarded by some masters is affirmed, and reasonably enough, as well as by slaves who can read. But no law has been made to prevent the preaching of the Gospel. For this we may well be thankful. I have devoted a great deal of my time, from first to last, to teaching persons of the coloured race, bond and free, to read. I have had in the classes I have taught, and in the Sabbath schools I have superintended, at least three hundred of them, in my younger years, before I entered the ministry. I am not indifferent to the importance of reading the Word of God, and I sincerely wish that all, bond and free, black and white, might be able to do it, and have a Bible to read. But so long as the Gospel can be preached to the slaves, I shall not despair of their salvation; for I know that it is emphatically by the preaching of the Gospel that men always have been, and always will be saved. Besides, I cannot but believe the laws to which I have referred must be temporary. In the mean while, those means of religious instruction which can be employed ought to be greatly augmented. And this is perfectly practicable; nor is the subject wholly neglected; as the missionary and other efforts of the Presbyterians, Methodists, and other religious bodies in the South attest. Indeed the interest in it is increasing from year to year. May it increase a hundredfold!

I am not ignorant of the evils of slavery in America. I feel sad when I think of them. The system injures, deeply injures both parties. Where there are none of the meliorating influences of religion, these evils are often horrible. Nothing, in my opinion, but the influence of the Gospel, can mitigate those evils, and finally and completely overthrow the system. The very slave-holders themselves, with us, are the only men who must be induced to overthrow it. Can we hope ever to see them do it, but through the influence of the Gospel upon their own hearts?

But the question is often asked: Can religion make progress in such a population? God has Himself answered that question. He pours out His Spirit and renders His word effective to the salvation of both masters and slaves. No man can deny this, who has any accurate knowledge of the slave-holding States. I have preached the Gospel too often to both masters and slaves, and conversed with both too much, to have a doubt on this subject. Indeed, if I did not feel confident on this subject, I should have no hope for the peaceable overthrow of slavery at all. And if I did not believe that the Spirit of God can renew the hearts of both masters and slaves in America, I should have little hope in regard to the debased and polluted heathen nations of the world. But where is the heart that the Spirit of God cannot change? Here, then, is *my* hope. And I think that the first and greatest duty of Christians in our Northern States is to say to their Southern brethren: "Slavery is a great evil to you, to the slave, to the country at large; we earnestly desire its abolishment; but it is a subject in which you must take the lead; for with you is the power, by the Constitution, to act effectively in it; the South is jealous of the Northern interference;—very well, do you take the lead in this movement, and we will follow and aid you; begin with what is practicable, and let every thing be done which can be done to cause the Gospel to be preached faithfully to masters and slaves; we will help you with our money and our prayers; where the slaves and free coloured people can be taught to read, let there be no want of schools; where they cannot be taught in schools, let it be done privately, if that be allowed; if that be not possible, let them be taught the Scriptures orally, and assembled regularly morning and evening for this purpose, as is done by some excellent masters in Georgia and South Carolina; where you have slaves who are capable of taking care of themselves, set them free, and if they may not remain in the State where you are, send them to the North, send them to the West, or send them to Liberia if they prefer; if they cannot take care of themselves, beside clothing and feeding them well, begin to give them reasonable wages, that they may lay up something for the day when they may set up for themselves; in a word, do all you can to hasten the coming of freedom, and we will stand by you and help you to the uttermost of our power; we will even bear, if a loss can be proved, our full share of the expense of a reasonable compensation for your slaves,—for the whole of them, in order that you may not be impoverished."

Something like this is the course which I would have our Northern Christians, and indeed all classes, pursue towards the people of the South. Alas, this course has not been pursued as it should have been. It is quite too old-fashioned to suit the views of those among us and abroad, who claim *par excellence* and exclusively to be the friends of the slave. But to something like this we shall have to come, I apprehend, before all is over, if ever slavery be abolished in a peaceable manner; nor do I doubt that this course will one day be pursued. In the meanwhile, the area of slavery has been limited by the providential arrangements of our Heavenly Father, rather than any efforts of man, in the results of the late Mexican war; California and Oregon can have no slaves; it is very certain that neither New Mexico nor Utah will have any; a portion of Texas has been saved from the evil; the slave-trade is abolished in the district of Columbia; the conviction is growing that slavery is a dreadful hindrance to the temporal prosperity of the States where it exists; the constantly increasing superiority of the free States;—all these things, and many more, are conspiring with moral causes to bring on the day when this dreadful evil must cease for ever among us. May God hasten it!

Source:
Robert Baird, *The Progress and Prospects of
Christianity in the United States of America*
(London: Partridge & Oakey, [1851]),
pp. 30–36.

33

Christian Nurture

BY HORACE BUSHNELL

Horace Bushnell (1802–1876), a prolific writer on religion, was pastor of the North Congregational Church in Hartford, Connecticut. In Christian Nurture *(1861)—first published in rudimentary form as* Views of Christian Nurture *(1847)—Bushnell mingles science and religion in asserting the beneficial effects of Christian indoctrination through "antenatal and post-natal nurture." Analogously, he criticizes the Jews for flaws of character that have been inbred as a result of generations of prejudice.*

CONSIDER A VERY IMPORTANT FACT in human physiology which goes far to explain, or take away the strangeness and seeming extravagance of the truth I am endeavoring to establish, viz., that qualities of education, habit, feeling, and character, have a tendency always to grow in, by long continuance, and become thoroughly inbred in the stock. We meet humble analogies of this fact in the domestic animals. The operations to which they are trained, and in which they become naturalized by habit, become predispositions, in a degree, in their offspring; and they, in their turn, are as much more easily trained on that account. The next generation are trained still more easily, till what was first made habitual, finally becomes functional in the stock, and almost no training is wanted. That which was inculcated by practice passes into a tendency, and descends as a natural gift, or endowment. The same thing is observable, on a large scale, in the families of mankind. A savage race is a race bred into low living, and a faithless, bloody character. The instinct of law, society, and order is substituted, finally, by the overgrown instinct of prey, and the race is lost to any real capacity of social regeneration; unless they can somehow be kept in ward, and a process of training, long enough to breed in what has been lost. A race of slaves becomes a physiologically servile race in the same way. And so it is, in part, that civilization descends from one generation to another. It is not merely that laws, social modes, and instrumentalities of education descend, and that so the new sprung generations are fashioned after birth, by the forms and principles and causes into which they have been set, but it is that the very type of the inborn quality is a civilized type. The civilization is, in great part, an inbred civility. There is a something functional in them, which is itself configured to the state of art, order, law, and property.

The Jewish race are a striking and sad proof of the manner in which any given mode of life may, or rather must, become a functional property in the offspring. The old Jewish stock of the Scripture times, whatever faults they may have had, certainly were not marked by any such miserable, sordid, usurious, garbage-vending propensity, as now distinguishes the race. But the cruelties they have suffered under Christian governments, shut up in the Jews' quarter of the great cities, dealing in old clothes and other mean articles for their gains, hiding these in the shape of gold and jewels in the crevices of their cellars, to prevent seizure by the emissaries of the governments, and disguising their prosperity itself by the squalid dress of their persons—these, continued from age to age, have finally bred in the character we so commonly speak of with contempt. Our children, treated as they have been for so many generations, would finally reveal the marks of their wrongs in the same sordid, miserly instincts.

Now if it be true that what gets power in any race, by a habit or a process of culture, tends by a fixed law of nature to become a propagated quality, and pass by descent as a property inbred in the stock; if in this way whole races of men are cultivated into properties that are peculiar— off into a savage character, down into a servile or a mercenary, up into civilization or a high social state—what is to be the effect of a thoroughly Christian fatherhood and motherhood, continued for a long time in the successive generations of a family? What can it be but a general mitigation of the bad points of the stock, and a more and more completely inbred piety. The children of such a stock are born, not of the flesh only, or the mere natural life of their parentage, but they are born, in a sense most emphatic, of the Spirit also; for this parentage is differed, as we are supposing, age by age, from its own mere nature in Adam, by the inhabiting grace of a supernatural salvation. Physiologically speaking, they are tempered by this grace, and it is all the while tending to become, in some sense, an inbred quality. Hence the very frequent remark—"How great a privilege and order of nobility to be descended of a pious ancestry!" It is the blessing that is to descend to the thousandth generation of them that love God and keep his commandments.

In this view it is to be expected, as the life of Christian piety becomes more extended in the earth, and the Spirit of God obtains a living power, in the successive generations, more and more complete, that finally the race itself will be so thoroughly regenerated as to have a genuinely populating power in faith and godliness. By a kind of ante-natal and post-natal nurture combined, the new-born generations will be started into Christian piety, and the world itself over-populated and taken possession of by a truly sanctified stock. This I conceive to be the expectation of Christianity. Not that the bad heritage of depravity will cease, but that the second Adam will get into power *with* the first, and be entered seminally into the same great process of propagated life. And this fulfills that primal desire of the world's Creator and Father, of which the prophet speaks—"That he might have a godly seed."

And let no one be offended by this, as if it supposed a possible in-growth and propagation of piety, by mere natural laws and conditions. What higher ground of supernaturalism can be taken, than that which supposes a capacity in the Incarnate Word, and Sanctifying Spirit, to penetrate our fallen nature, at a point so deep as to cover the whole spread of the fall, and be a grace of life, traveling outward from the earliest, most latent germs of our human development. It is only saying, with a meaning—"My substance was not hid from Thee, when I was made in secret, and curiously wrought in the lowest parts of the earth." Or, in still another view, it is only conceiving that those sporadic cases of sanctification from the womb, of which the Scripture speaks, such as that of Samuel, Jeremiah, and John, are to finally become the ordinary and common fact of family development.

In such cases, the faith or piety of a single pair, or possibly of the mother alone, begets a heavenly mold in the predispositions of the offspring, so that, as it is born of sin, it is also born of a heavenly grace. If then we suppose the heavenly grace to have such power, in the long continuing process of ages, as to finally work the general stock of parentage into its own heavenly mold, far enough to prepare a sanctified offspring for the world, what higher, grander fact of Christian supernaturalism could be asserted? Nor is it any thing more of a novelty than to say, that "where sin abounded, grace did much more abound." The conception is one that simply fulfills what Baxter, Hopkins, and others, were apparently struggling after, when contriving how to let the grace of God in our salvation, match itself by the hereditary damage, or depravation, that descends upon us from our parentage, and the organic unity of our nature as a race. And probably enough they were put upon this mode of thought, by the familiar passage of Paul just referred to.

Christianity then has a power, as we discover, to prepare a godly seed. It not only takes hold of the world by its converting efficacy, but it has a silent force that is much stronger and more reliable; it moves, by a kind of destiny, in causes back of all the eccentric and casual operations of mere individual choice, preparing, by a gradual growing in of grace, to become the great populating motherhood of the world.

Source:
Horace Bushnell, *Christian Nurture*
(New York: Scribner, 1861), pp. 202–7.

Our Country

BY JOSIAH STRONG

Josiah Strong (1847–1916) was a prolific writer on society and religion. A Congregational minister and general secretary of the Evangelical Alliance for the United States, Strong was a central figure in the "Social Gospel" movement and a leader in the fight against economic injustice. At the same time he evolved into an advocate of Anglo-Saxon supremacy and imperialism. Our Country *(1885) is one of the most exhaustive statements of his views.*

EVERY RACE WHICH HAS DEEPLY impressed itself on the human family has been the representative of some great idea—one or more—which has given direction to the nation's life and form to its civilization. Among the Egyptians this seminal idea was life, among the Persians it was light, among the Hebrews it was purity, among the Greeks it was beauty, among the Romans it was law. The Anglo-Saxon is the representative of two great ideas, which are closely related. One of them is that of civil liberty. Nearly all of the civil liberty of the world is enjoyed by Anglo-Saxons: the English, the British colonists, and the people of the United States. To some, like the Swiss, it is permitted by the sufferance of their neighbors; others, like the French, have experimented with it; but, in modern times, the peoples whose love of liberty has won it, and whose genius for self-government has preserved it, have been Anglo-Saxons. The noblest races have always been lovers of liberty. The love ran strong in early German blood, and has profoundly influenced the institutions of all the branches of the great German family; but it was left for the Anglo-Saxon branch fully to recognize the right of the individual to himself, and formally to declare it the foundation stone of government.

The other great idea of which the Anglo-Saxon is the exponent is that of a pure *spiritual* Christianity. It was no accident that the great reformation of the sixteenth century originated among a Teutonic, rather than a Latin people. It was the fire of liberty burning in the Saxon heart that flamed up against the absolutism of the Pope. Speaking roughly, the peoples of Europe which are Celtic are Roman Catholic, and those which are Teutonic are Protestant; and where the Teutonic race was purest, there Protestantism spread with the greatest rapidity. But, with beautiful exceptions, Protestantism on the continent has degenerated into mere formalism. By confirmation at a certain age, the state churches are filled with members who generally know nothing of a personal spiritual experience. In obedience to a military order, a regiment of German soldiers files into church and partakes of the sacrament, just as it would shoulder arms or obey any other word of command. It is said that, in Berlin and Leipsic, only a little over one per cent of the Protestant population are found in church. Protestantism on the Continent seems to be about as poor in spiritual life and power as Romanism. That means that most of the spiritual Christianity in the world is found among Anglo-Saxons and their converts; for this is the great missionary race. If we take all of the German missionary societies together, we find that, in the number of workers and amount of contributions, they do not equal the smallest of the three great English missionary societies. The year that the Congregationalists in the United States gave one dollar and thirty-seven cents per caput to foreign missions, the members of the great German State Church gave only three-quarters of a cent per caput to the same cause. Evidently it is chiefly to the English and American peoples that we must look for the evangelization of the world.

It is not necessary to argue to those for whom I write that the two great needs of mankind, that all men may be lifted up into the light of the highest Christian civilization, are, first, a pure, spiritual Christianity, and second, civil liberty. Without controversy, these are the forces which, in the past, have contributed most to the elevation of the human race, and they must continue to be, in the future, the most efficient ministers to its progress. It follows, then, that the Anglo-Saxon, as the great representative of these two ideas, the depositary of these two greatest blessings, sustains peculiar relations to the world's future, is divinely commissioned to be, in a peculiar sense, his brother's keeper. Add to this the fact of his rapidly increasing strength in modern times, and we have well-nigh a demonstration of his destiny. In 1700 this race numbered less than 6,000,000 souls. In 1800, Anglo-Saxons (I use the term somewhat broadly to include all English-speaking peoples) had increased to about 20,500,000, and now, in 1890, they number more than 120,000,000, having multiplied almost six-fold in ninety years. At the end of the reign of Charles II. the English colonists in America numbered 200,000. During these two hundred years, our population has increased two hundred and fifty-fold. And the expansion of this race has been no less remarkable than its multiplication. In one century the United States has increased its territory ten-fold, while the enormous acquisition of foreign territory by Great Britain—and chiefly within the last hundred years—is wholly unparalleled in history. This mighty Anglo-Saxon race, though comprising only one-thirteenth part of mankind, now rules more than one-third of the earth's surface, and more than one-fourth of its people. And if this race, while growing from 6,000,000 to 120,000,000, thus gained possession of a third portion of the earth, is it to be supposed that when it numbers 1,000,000,000, it will lose the disposition, or lack the power to extend its sway?. . .

There can be no reasonable doubt that North America is to be the great home of the Anglo-Saxon, the principal seat of his power, the center of his life and influence. Not only does it constitute seven-elevenths of his possessions, but here his empire is unsevered, while the remaining four-elevenths are fragmentary and scattered over the earth. Australia will have a great population; but its disadvantages, as compared with North America, are too manifest to need mention. Our continent has room and resources and climate, it lies in the pathway of the nations, it belongs to the zone of power, and already, among Anglo-Saxons, do we lead in population and wealth. Of England, Franklin once wrote: "That pretty island which, compared to America, is but a stepping-stone in a brook, scarce enough of it above water to keep one's shoes dry." England can hardly hope to maintain her relative importance among Anglo-Saxon peoples when her "pretty island" is the home of only one-twentieth part of that race. With the wider distribution of wealth, and increasing facilities of intercourse, intelligence and influence are less centralized, and peoples become more homogeneous; and the more nearly homogeneous peoples are, the more do *numbers tell*. . . .

And we are to have not only the larger portion of the Anglo-Saxon race, but we may reasonably expect to develop the highest type of Anglo-Saxon civilization. If human progress follows a law of development, if

"Time's noblest offspring is the last,"

our civilization should be the noblest; for we are

"The heirs of all the ages in the foremost files of time,"

and not only do we occupy the latitude of power, but *our land is the last to be occupied in that latitude*. There is no other virgin soil in the North

Temperate Zone. If the consummation of human progress is not to be looked for here, if there is yet to flower a higher civilization, where is the soil that is to produce it? Whipple says: "There has never been a great migration that did not result in a new form of national genius." Our national genius is Anglo-Saxon, but not English, its distinctive type is the result of a finer nervous organization, which is certainly being developed in this country. "The history of the world's progress from savagery to barbarism, from barbarism to civilization, and, in civilization, from the lower degrees toward the higher, is the history of increase in average longevity, corresponding to, and accompanied by, increase of nervousness. Mankind has grown to be at once more delicate and more enduring, more sensitive to weariness and yet more patient of toil, impressible, but capable of bearing powerful irritation; we are woven of finer fiber, which, though apparently frail, yet outlasts the coarser, as rich and costly garments oftentimes wear better than those of rougher workmanship."[1] The roots of civilization are the nerves; and other things being equal, the finest nervous organization will produce the highest civilization. Heretofore, war has been almost the chief occupation of strong races. The mission of the Anglo-Saxon has been largely that of the soldier; but the world is making progress, we are leaving behind the barbarism of war; as civilization advances, it will learn less of war, and concern itself more with the arts of peace, and for these the massive battle-ax must be wrought into tools of finer temper. The physical changes accompanied by mental, which are taking place in the people of the United States, are apparently to adapt men to the demands of a higher civilization. But the objection is here interposed that the "physical degeneracy of America" is inconsistent with the supposition of our advancing to a higher civilization. Professor Huxley, when at Buffalo he addressed the American Association for the Advancement of Science, said he had heard of the degeneration of the original American stock, but during his visit to the states he had failed to perceive it. We are not, however, in this matter, dependent on the opinion of even the best observers. During the War of the Confederacy, the Medical Department of the Provost Marshal General's Bureau gathered statistics from the examination of over half a million of men, native and foreign, young and old, sick and sound, drawn from every rank and condition of life, and, hence, fairly representing the whole people. Dr. Baxter's Official Report shows that our native whites were over an inch taller than the English, and nearly two-thirds of an inch taller than the Scotch, who, in height, were superior to all other foreigners. At the age of completed growth, the Irish, who were the stoutest of the foreigners, surpassed the native whites, in girth of chest, less than a quarter of an inch. Statistics as to weight are meager, but Dr. Baxter remarks that it is perhaps not too much to say that the war statistics show "that the mean weight of the white native of the United States is not disproportionate to his stature." Americans were found to be superior to Englishmen not only in height, but also in chest measurement and weight. "Dealers in ready-made clothing in the United States assert that they have been obliged to adopt a larger scale of sizes, in width as well as length, to meet the demands of the average American man, than were required ten years ago."[2] Such facts afford more than a hint that the higher civilization of the future will not lack an adequate physical basis in the people of the United States.

Mr. Darwin is not only disposed to see, in the superior vigor of our people, an illustration of his favorite theory of natural selection, but even intimates that the world's history thus far has been simply preparatory for our future, and tributary to it. He says: "There is apparently much truth in the belief that the wonderful progress of the United States, as well as the character of the people, are the results of natural selection; for the more energetic, restless, and courageous men from all parts of Europe have emigrated during the last ten or twelve generations to that great country, and have there succeeded best. Looking at the distant future, I do not think that the Rev. Mr. Zincke takes an exaggerated view when he says: 'All other series of events—as that which resulted in the culture of mind in Greece, and that which resulted in the Empire of Rome—only appear to have purpose and value when viewed in connection with, or rather as subsidiary to, the great stream of Anglo-Saxon emigration to the West.'"[3]

There is abundant reason to believe that the Anglo-Saxon race is to be, is, indeed, already becoming, more effective here than in the mother country. The marked superiority of this race is due, in large measure, to its highly mixed origin. Says Rawlinson: "It is a general rule, now almost universally admitted by ethnologists, that the mixed races of mankind are superior to the pure ones"; and adds: "Even the Jews, who are so often cited as an example of a race at once pure and strong, may, with more reason, be adduced on the opposite side of the argument."[4] The ancient Egyptians, the Greeks, and the Romans, were all mixed races. Among modern races, the most conspicuous example is afforded by the Anglo-Saxons. Mr. Green's studies show that Mr. Tennyson's poetic line,

"Saxon and Norman and Dane are we,"

must be supplemented with Celt and Gaul, Welshman and Irishman, Frisian and Flamand, French Huguenot and German Palatine. What took place a thousand years ago and more in England again transpires to-day in the United States. "History repeats itself"; but, as the wheels of history are the chariot wheels of the Almighty, there is, with every revolution, an on-ward movement toward the goal of His eternal purposes. There is here a new commingling of races; and, while the largest injections of foreign blood are substantially the same elements that constituted the original Anglo-Saxon admixture, so that we may infer the general type will be pre-served, there are strains of other bloods being added, which, if Mr. Emerson's remark is true, that "the best nations are those most widely re-lated," may be expected to improve the stock, and aid it to a higher des-tiny. If the dangers of immigration, which have been pointed out, can be successfully met for the next few years, until it has passed its climax, it may be expected to add value to the amalgam which will constitute the new Anglo-Saxon race of the New World. Concerning our future, Herbert Spencer says: "One great result is, I think, tolerably clear. From biological truths it is to be inferred that the eventual mixture of the allied varieties of the Aryan race, forming the population, will produce a more powerful type of man than has hitherto existed, and a type of man more plastic, more adaptable, more capable of undergoing the modifications needful for complete social life. I think, whatever difficulties they may have to sur-mount, and whatever tribulations they may have to pass through, the Americans may reasonably look forward to a time when they will have pro-duced a civilization grander than any the world has known."

It may be easily shown, and is of no small significance, that the two great ideas of which the Anglo-Saxon is the exponent are having a fuller development in the United States than in Great Britain. There the union of Church and State tends strongly to paralyze some of the members of the body of Christ. Here there is no such influence to destroy spiritual life and power. Here, also, has been evolved the form of government consistent with the largest possible civil liberty. Furthermore, it is signif-icant that the marked characteristics of this race are being here empha-sized most. Among the most striking features of the Anglo-Saxon is his money-making power—a power of increasing importance in the widen-ing commerce of the world's future. We have seen, in a preceding chap-ter, that, although England is by far the richest nation of Europe, we have already outstripped her in the race after wealth, and we have only begun the development of our vast resources.

Again, another marked characteristic of the Anglo-Saxon is what may be called an instinct or genius for colonizing. His unequaled energy, his indomitable perseverance, and his personal independence, made him a pioneer. He excels all others in pushing his way into new countries. It was those in whom this tendency was strongest that came to America, and this inherited tendency has been further developed by the westward sweep of successive generations across the continent. So noticeable has this characteristic become that English visitors remark it. Charles Dickens once said that the typical American would hesitate to enter heaven unless assured that he could go farther west.

Again, nothing more manifestly distinguishes the Anglo-Saxon than his intense and persistent energy, and he is developing in the United States an energy which, in eager activity and effectiveness, is peculiarly American.

This is due partly to the fact that Americans are much better fed than Europeans, and partly to the undeveloped resources of a new country, but more largely to our climate, which acts as a constant stimulus. Ten years after the landing of the Pilgrims, the Rev. Francis Higginson, a good observer, wrote: "A sup of New England air is better than a whole flagon of English ale." Thus early had the stimulating effect of our climate been noted. Moreover, our social institutions are stimulating. In Europe the various ranks of society are, like the strata of the earth, fixed and fossilized. There can be no great change without a terrible upheaval, a social earthquake. Here society is like the waters of the sea, mobile; as General Garfield said, and so signally illustrated in his own experience, that which is at the bottom to-day may one day flash on the crest of the highest wave. Every one is free to become whatever he can make of himself; free to transform himself from a rail-splitter or a tanner or a canal-boy, into the nation's President. Our aristocracy, unlike that of Europe, is open to all comers. Wealth, position, influence are prizes offered for energy; and every farmer's boy, every apprentice and clerk, every friendless and penniless immigrant, is free to enter the list. Thus many causes co-operate to produce here the most forceful and tremendous energy in the world.

What is the significance of such facts? These tendencies infold the future; they are the mighty alphabet with which God writes his prophecies. May we not, by a careful laying together of the letters, spell out something of his meaning? It seems to me that God, with infinite wisdom and skill, is training the Anglo-Saxon race for an hour sure to come in the world's future. Heretofore there has always been in the history of the world a comparatively unoccupied land westward, into which the crowded countries of the East have poured their surplus populations. But the widening waves of migration, which millenniums ago rolled east and west from the valley of the Euphrates, meet to-day on our Pacific coast. There are no more new worlds. The unoccupied arable lands of the earth are limited, and will soon be taken. The time is coming when the pressure of population on the means of subsistence will be felt here as it is now felt in Europe and Asia. Then will the world enter upon a new stage of its history—*the final competition of races, for which the Anglo-Saxon is being schooled.* Long before the thousand millions are here, the mighty *centrifugal* tendency, inherent in this stock and strengthened in the United States, will assert itself. Then this race of unequaled energy, with all the majesty of numbers and the might of wealth behind it—the representative, let us hope, of the largest liberty, the purest Christianity, the highest civilization—having developed peculiarly aggressive traits calculated to impress its institutions upon mankind, will spread itself over the earth. If I read not amiss, this powerful race will move down upon Mexico, down upon Central and South America, out upon the islands of the sea, over upon Africa and beyond. And can any one doubt that the result of this competition of races will be the "survival of the fittest"? "Any people," says Dr. Bushnell, "that is physiologically advanced in culture, though it be only in a degree beyond another which is mingled with it on strictly equal terms, is sure to live down and finally live out its inferior. Nothing can save the inferior race but a ready and pliant assimilation. Whether the feebler and more abject races are going to be regenerated and raised up, is already very much of a question. What if it should be God's plan to people the world with better and finer material?

"Certain it is, whatever expectations we may indulge, that there is a tremendous overbearing surge of power in the Christian nations, which, if the others are not speedily raised to some vastly higher capacity, will inevitably submerge and bury them forever. These great populations of Christendom—what are they doing, but throwing out their colonies on every side, and populating themselves, if I may so speak, into the possession of all countries and climes?"[5] To this result no war of extermination is needful; the contest is not one of arms, but of vitality and of civilization. "At the present day," says Mr. Darwin, "civilized nations are everywhere supplanting barbarous nations, excepting where the climate opposes a deadly barrier; and they succeed mainly, though not exclusively, through their arts, which are the products of the intellect."[6] Thus the Finns were supplanted by the Aryan races in Europe and Asia, the Tartars by the Russians, and thus the aborigines of North America, Australia and New Zealand are now disappearing before the all-conquering Anglo-Saxons. It seems as if these inferior tribes were only precursors of a superior race, voices in the wilderness crying: "Prepare ye the way of the Lord!" The savage is a hunter; by the incoming of civilization the game is driven away and disappears before the hunter becomes a herder or an agriculturist. The savage is ignorant of many diseases of civilization which, when he is exposed to them, attack him before he learns how to treat them. Civilization also has its vices, of which the uninitiated savage is innocent. He proves an apt learner of vice, but dull enough in the school of morals.

Every civilization has its destructive and preservative elements. The Anglo-Saxon race would speedily decay but for the salt of Christianity.

Bring savages into contact with our civilization, and its destructive forces become operative at once, while years are necessary to render effective the saving influences of Christian instruction. Moreover, the pioneer wave of our civilization carries with it more scum than salt. Where there is one missionary, there are hundreds of miners or traders or adventurers ready to debauch the native.

Whether the extinction of inferior races before the advancing Anglo-Saxon seems to the reader sad or otherwise, it certainly appears probable. I know of nothing except climatic conditions to prevent this race from populating Africa as it has peopled North America. And those portions of Africa which are unfavorable to Anglo-Saxon life are less extensive than was once supposed. The Dutch Boers, after two centuries of life there, are as hardy as any race on earth. The Anglo-Saxon has established himself in climates totally diverse—Canada, South Africa, and India— and, through several generations, has preserved his essential race characteristics. He is not, of course, superior to climatic influences; but even in warm climates, he is likely to retain his aggressive vigor long enough to supplant races already enfeebled. Thus, in what Dr. Bushnell calls "the out-populating power of the Christian stock," may be found God's final and complete solution of the dark problem of heathenism among many inferior peoples.

Some of the stronger races, doubtless, may be able to preserve their integrity; but, in order to compete with the Anglo-Saxon, they will probably be forced to adopt his methods and instruments, his civilization and his religion. Significant movements are now in progress among them. While the Christian religion was never more vital, or its hold upon the Anglo-Saxon mind stronger, there is taking place among the nations a widespread intellectual revolt against traditional beliefs. "In every corner of the world," says Mr. Froude, "there is the same phenomenon of the decay of established religions. . . . Among the Mohammedans, Jews, Buddhists, Brahmins, traditionary creeds are losing their hold. An intellectual revolution is sweeping over the world, breaking down established opinions, dissolving foundations on which historical faiths have been built up."[7] The contact of Christian with heathen nations is awakening the latter to new life. Old superstitions are loosening their grasp. The dead crust of fossil faiths is being shattered by the movements of life underneath. In Catholic countries, Catholicism is losing its influence over educated minds, and in some cases the masses have already lost all faith in it. Thus, while on this continent God is training the Anglo-Saxon race for its mission, a complemental work has been in progress in the great world beyond. God has two hands. Not only is he preparing in our civilization the die with which to stamp the nations, but, by what Southey called the "timing of Providence," he is preparing mankind to receive our impress.

Is there room for reasonable doubt that this race, unless devitalized by alcohol and tobacco, is destined to dispossess many weaker races, assimilate others, and mold the remainder, until, in a very true and important sense, it has Anglo-Saxonized mankind? Already "the English language, saturated with Christian ideas, gathering up into itself the best thought of all the ages, is the great agent of Christian civilization throughout the world; at this moment affecting the destinies and molding the character of half the human race."[8] Jacob Grimm, the German philologist, said of this language: "It seems chosen, like its people, to rule in future times in a still greater degree in all the corners of the earth." He predicted, indeed, that the language of Shakespeare would eventually become the language of mankind. Is not Tennyson's noble prophecy to find its fulfillment in Anglo-Saxondom's extending its dominion and influence—

"Till the war-drum throbs no longer, and the battle-flags are furl'd
  In the Parliament of man, the Federation of the world."[9]

In my own mind, there is no doubt that the Anglo-Saxon is to exercise the commanding influence in the world's future; but the exact nature of that influence is, as yet, undetermined. How far his civilization will be materialistic and atheistic, and how long it will take thoroughly to Christianize and sweeten it, how rapidly he will hasten the coming of the kingdom wherein dwelleth righteousness, or how many ages he may retard it, is still uncertain; but *is now being swiftly determined*. Let us weld together in a chain the various links of our logic which we have endeavored to forge. Is it manifest that the Anglo-Saxon holds in his hands the destinies of mankind for ages to come? Is it evident that the United States is to be the home of this race, the principal seat of his power, the great center of his influence? Is it true that the great West is to dominate the nation's future? Has it been shown that this generation is to determine the character, and hence the destiny of the West? Then may God open the eyes of this generation! When Napoleon drew up his troops before the Mamelukes, under the shadow of the Pyramids, pointing to the latter, he said to his soldiers: "Remember that from yonder heights forty centuries look down on you." Men of this generation, from the pyramid top of opportunity on which God has set us, *we look down on forty centuries!* We stretch our hand into the future with power to mold the destinies of unborn millions.

"We are living, we are dwelling,
  In a grand and awful time,

In an age on ages telling—
To be living is sublime!"

Notwithstanding the great perils which threaten it, I cannot think our civilization will perish; but I believe it is fully in the hands of the Christians of the United States, during the next ten or fifteen years, to hasten or retard the coming of Christ's kingdom in the world by hundreds, and perhaps thousands, of years. We of this generation and nation occupy the Gibraltar of the ages which commands the world's future.

Source:
Josiah Strong, *Our Country* (New York:
Baker & Taylor/American Home Missionary
Society, 1885; rev. ed. 1891), pp. 159–62,
165–66, 168–80.

PART SEVEN

Native Americans

CHRONOLOGICALLY, THE FIRST "ALIEN" race the American colonists encountered was the Native American. For nearly three centuries, from 1622 until the end of the nineteenth century, warfare with various Native American tribes was a constant feature of American life across the continent. The end result can scarcely be termed anything but a genocide. Whether one accepts a low figure of one million people or an upper figure of twelve million in North America north of Mexico, there is no debate that as of 1890 only 228,000 Native Americans were left in the United States.

Aside from racial prejudice, political maneuvering played a significant role in arousing the settlers' hatred of Native Americans. Thanksgiving at Plymouth rapidly passed into American legend, but this proved to be an isolated instance of harmony that was overshadowed by vicious bloodletting on both sides. The French alliance with the Native Americans in various unsuccessful wars during the first half of the eighteenth century, culminating in the French and Indian War (1754–63), proved disastrous for the aboriginal tribes. The Native Americans also made the tactical error of siding with the British during the Revolution, perceiving (correctly) that they had far more to worry about from the colonists than from the British government. After the war was over, the British made no attempt to negotiate for property or other rights for the Native Americans, and the result was that the tribes became obstacles in the relentless American march across the continent.

Prejudice against Native Americans was at once racial (they were "coppery," "bronze," or otherwise non-white), religious (they were heathens who actively resisted Christian indoctrination), cultural (they were "savages" who refused to be "educated" into proper Western customs), and economic (they occupied valuable land that could be put to "better" use by Americans). Perhaps it is not surprising that Mary Rowlandson, author of the first of the "Indian captivity" narratives, could liken the Native Americans to devils after undergoing an eight-week captivity. Still less surprising is Increase Mather's attribution of the colonists' victory over the Native Americans during King Philip's War (1675–76) to the sword of God, aided somewhat "by Famine and by Sickness."

The Native Americans did not lack friends, however. One of their most fervent supporters was Jedidiah Morse, whose *Report to the Secretary of War of the United States, on Indian Affairs* (1822) is a poignant plea for the salvation of the Native Americans through education and intermarriage. But the temper of the times was opposed to him. By 1825 the government had decreed that all Native Americans should be moved to reservations west of the Mississippi. This action precipitated a series of bitter wars in Georgia with the Cherokees and in Illinois with the Sac and Fox Indians. By 1846 all the tribes had been transferred either into the Indian Territory (later Oklahoma) or elsewhere in the Plains states. It was at this time that Lewis H. Morgan wrote his *League of the Iroquois* (1851) in which he pondered the fate of that tribe and of all Native Americans, now that they had fallen definitively within the jurisdiction of the United States. His answer, like Morse's, was education and Christianization—the only way the Native American could be "reclaimed and civilized." With friends like this, one scarcely needed enemies.

By this time Native Americans had begun to enter into American myth and, hence, literature. The chief figure in this transition was James Fenimore Cooper, whose favorable portrayals of Native American characters in his novels were themselves based on stereotypes. Cooper addressed the Native American tribes briefly in his travel book, *Notions of the Americans* (1828), in the course of which he declares that "the red man disappears before the superior moral and physical influence of the white" and that "neither the United States, nor any individual State, has ever taken possession of any land that, by usage or construction, might be decreed the property of the Indians, without a treaty and a purchase."[1] Perhaps a truer friend of the Native Americans was Herman Melville, whose satirical chapter 26 ("Containing the Metaphysics of Indian-Hating") of *The Confidence-Man* (1857) may be the last word on the subject.

The Indian wars prior to the Civil War were only a foretaste of the much bloodier conflicts to follow; accordingly, opinions of the Native Americans deteriorated even further. George Armstrong Custer's *My Life on the Plains* (1874), an account of his "personal experiences" with the Native Americans published two years before his extremely personal experience with Sitting Bull at Little Big Horn, ridicules Cooper's benevolent portrayal of the Native American as a "noble savage." The stage was set for Helen Hunt Jackson's fiery *A Century of Dishonor* (1881), the most exhaustive arraignment of American treachery toward the Native Americans ever written. But by this time the whole "Indian question" was a foregone conclusion: the massacre at Wounded Knee (1890) virtually ended the "Indian wars," and the reservation system (begun by the British colonists as early as 1653) was fully in place.

35

The History of King Philip's War

BY INCREASE MATHER

Increase Mather (1639–1723), clergyman, author, and father of the prolific theological writer Cotton Mather, officiated for most of his life at the North Church in Boston. He also served as president of Harvard (1685–1701). In his voluminous writings Mather attempted to incorporate science as an adjunct to religion, and he also devoted much attention to the history of the British colonies in New England. In A Brief History of the War with the Indians in New-England *(1676; later published as* The History of King Philip's War), *Mather expresses satisfaction at the ruthless massacre of Native Americans in King Philip's War (1675–76) but attributes a large part of the victory to the hand of God.*

To CONCLUDE THIS HISTORY, IT IS EVIDENT by the things which have been expressed, that our deliverance is not as yet perfected; for the *Nipmuck Indians* are not yet wholly subdued: Moreover, it will be a difficult thing, either to subdue, or to come at the *River Indians,* who have many of them withdrawn themselves and are gone far westward, and whilst they and others that have been in hostility against us, remain unconquered, we cannot enjoy such perfect peace as in the years which are past. And there seems to be a dark Cloud rising from the East, in respect of *Indians* in those parts, yea a Cloud which streameth forth blood. But that which is the saddest thought of all, is, that of late some unhappy scandals have been, which are enough to stop the current of mercy, which hath been flowing in upon us, and to provoke the Lord to

226

let loose more Enemies upon us, so as that the second error shall be worse than the first. Only God doth deliver his own Names sake: the Lord will not forsake his people for his great Names sake; because it hath pleased the Lord to make us his people. And we have reason to conclude that *Salvation is begun,* and in a gracious measure carried on towards us. For since last *March* there are two or 3000 *Indians* who have been either killed, or taken, or submitted themselves to the *English*. And those *Indians* which have been taken Captive & others also, inform that the *Narragansets* are in a manner ruined, there being (as they say) not above a hundred men left of them, who the last year were the greatest body of *Indians* in *New-England,* and the most formidable Enemy which hath appeared against us. But God hath consumed them by the Sword, and by Famine and by Sickness, it being no unusual thing for those that traverse the woods to find dead *Indians* up and down, whom either Famine, or sickness, hath caused to dy, and there hath been none to bury them. And *Philip* who was the *Sheba,* that began and headed the Rebellion, his head is thrown over the wall, therefore have we good reason to hope that this *Day of Trouble,* is near to an end, if our sins do not undoe all that hath been wrought for us. And indeed there is one sad consideration which may cause humble tremblings to think of it, namely, in that the *Reformation* which God expects from us is not so hearty and so perfect as it ought to be. Divines observe, that whereas upon *Samuels Exhortation,* the people did make but imperfect work of it, as to the *Reformation* of provoking evils, therefore God did only begin their de-liverance by *Samuel,* but left scattered *Philistines* unsubdued, who after-wards made head and proved a sore scourge to the Children of Israel, untill *Davids* time, in whose Reign there was a full Reformation, and then did the Lord give unto his people full deliverance. Nevertheless a sad *Catastrophe* will attend those that shall magnifie themselves against the people, of the Lord of Hosts. It hath been observed by many, that never any (whether *Indians* or others) did set themselves to do hurt to *New-England,* but they have come to lamentable ends at last. *New-England* hath been a burthensome stone, all that have burthened them-selves with it, have been cut in pieces. The experience of the present day, doth greatly confirm that observation, and give us ground to hope, that as for remaining enemies, they shall fare as others that have gone before them, have done. Yet this further must needs be acknowledged, that as to *Victoryes* obtained, we have no cause to glory in any thing that we have done, but rather to be ashamed and confounded for our own wayes. The Lord hath thus far been our Saviour for his Names sake, that it might not be profaned among the Heathen whither he hath brought us.

And God hath let us see that he could easily have destroyed us, by such a contemptible enemy as the Indians have been in our eyes, yea, he hath convinced us that we our selves could not subdue them. They have advantages that we have not, knowing where to find us, but we know not where to find them, who nevertheless are always at home, and have in a manner nothing but their lives and souls (which they think not of) to loose, every Swamp is a Castle to them, and they can live comfortably on that which would starve *English-men*. So that *we have no cause to glory,* for it is God which hath thus saved us, and not we our selves. If we consider the time when the enemy hath fallen, we must needs own that the Lord hath done it. For we expected (and could in reason expect no other) that when the Summer was come on, and the bushes and leaves of trees come forth, the enemy would do ten times more mischief than in the winter season; whereas since that, the Lord hath appeared against them, that they have done but little hurt comparatively. Had there not been a divine hand beyond all expectation manifested, we had been in a state most miserable this day. Also if we keep in mind the means and way whereby our deliverance hath thus been accomplished, we must needs own the Lord in all. For it hath not been brought to pass by our numbers, or skill, or valour, *we have not got the Lord in possession by our own Sword, neither did our own arm save us.* But God hath wasted the Heathen, by sending the destroying Angell amongst them, since this War began; and (which should alwayes be an humbling consideration unto us) much hath been done towards the subduing of the enemy, by the *Indians* who have fought for us, sometimes more than by the *English*. And no doubt but that a great reason why many of them have, of late been desirous to submit themselves to the *English*, hath been because they were afraid of the *Mohawgs* who have a long time been a Terror to the other *Indians*. I have received it from one who was returned out of Captivity this Summer, that the *Indians* where he was, would not suffer any fires to be made in the night, for fear lest the *Mohawgs* should thereby discern where they were, and cut them off.

Source:
Increase Mather, *A Brief History of the War
with the Indians in New-England* (1676);
reprinted as *The History of King Philip's War,*
edited by Samuel G. Drake (Albany:
J. Munsell, 1862), pp. 204–8.

36

A Narrative of the Captivity and Restauration of Mrs. Mary Rowlandson

BY MARY ROWLANDSON

Mary Rowlandson (c. 1635–c. 1678) was the wife of a minister at Lancaster, Massachusetts. She was captured by a Native American tribe on February 10, 1675, during King Philip's War and held for almost eight weeks; her daughter Sarah died during her captivity, and she was finally released by ransom. Her Narrative, *published in 1682, was the first and perhaps the best of the many "Indian captivity" narratives written in the late seventeenth and eighteenth centuries. Such narratives—many of which mingled fact and fiction or were entirely fictitious although purporting to be true—enjoyed tremendous popularity among readers thirsting for adventurous accounts of frontier life. They were also used by the Church as examples of Christian fortitude. At the same time they subtly prejudiced many colonists' views against the Native Americans, who were depicted as savage and violent. Given Rowlandson's manifest religiosity, it is no surprise that she speaks of her captors as barbarians and devils.*

N OW AWAY WE MUST GO with those barbarous creatures, with our bodies wounded and bleeding and our hearts no less than our bodies. About a mile we went that night, up upon a hill within sight of the town, where we intended to lodge. There was hard by a vacant house, (deserted by the English before, for fear of the Indians,) I asked them whether I might not lodge in the house that night? to which they answered, What, will you love Englishmen still? This was the dolefulest night that ever my eyes saw. Oh the roaring, and singing, and dancing, and yelling of those black creatures in the night, which made the place a lively resemblance of hell: And miserable was the waste that was there made, of horses, cattle, sheep, swine, calves, lambs, roasting pigs and fowls (which they had plundered in the town) some roasting, some lying and burning, and some boiling, to feed our merciless enemies: who were joyful enough, though we were disconsolate. To add to the dolefulness of the former day, and the dismalness of the present night, my thoughts ran upon my losses and sad bereaved condition. All was gone, my husband gone, (at least separated from me, he being in the Bay: and to add to my grief, the Indians told me they would kill him as he came homeward,) my children gone, my relations and friends gone, our house and home, and all our comforts within door and without, all was gone (except my life) and I knew not but the next moment that might go too.

There remained nothing to me but one poor wounded babe, and it seemed at present worse than death, that it was in such a pitiful condition, bespeaking compassion, and I had no refreshing for it, nor suitable things to revive it. Little do many think, what is the savageness and brutishness of this barbarous enemy, those even that seem to profess more than others among them, when the English have fallen into their hands.

Source:
Mary Rowlandson, *The Soveraignty &*
Goodness of God, Together with the Faithfulness
of His Promises Displayed: Being a Narrative of
the Captivity and Restauration of Mrs. Mary
Rowlandson (Cambridge, MA: Samuel Green,
1682), pp. 11–13.

37

A Report to the Secretary of War of the United States, on Indian Affairs

BY JEDIDIAH MORSE

Clergyman and author Jedidiah Morse (1761–1826), the father of the inventor of the telegraph, Samuel F. B. Morse, is perhaps best known for pioneering the study of geography on this continent. His Geography Made Easy *(1784) was the first book on the subject published in the United States, and his* American Geography *(1789) is a landmark. In 1820 he visited many Native American tribes and published a report for the Secretary of War in 1822. In this significant treatise Morse speaks of the threatened extinction of the Native American people and urges a variety of remedies to preserve their population.*

Increase of Indians Within the Extended Limits of the United States, and Their Peculiar Condition

By the treaty with Spain, of 1819, the Territory of the United States is extended from the Atlantic, to the Pacific Ocean; and a host of Indian tribes, in consequence, has been brought within our national limits. Many of these tribes, in point of numbers, rank among the largest in our country. These tribes are shut up within their present continually narrowing limits. They can migrate neither to the north, nor to the south; neither to the east, nor to the west. The cold and barren region, spreading from our northern boundary, in lat. 49 north to the Frozen Ocean, has already a population, as large as its scanty productions can support. Other tribes possess the narrow strip of territory, between our southern borders, west of the Mississippi, and the Spanish settlements. The rapid advance of the white population presses them on the east; and the great Pacific Ocean hems them in on the west.

"Where the white man puts down his foot, he never takes it up again," is a shrewd and correct remark of an Indian Chief. The hunting grounds of the Indians on our frontiers are explored in all directions, by enterprizing white people. Their best lands are selected, settled, and at length, by treaty purchased. Their game is either wholly destroyed, or so diminished, as not to yield an adequate support. The poor Indians, thus deprived of their accustomed means of subsistence, and of what, in their own view, can alone render them respectable, as well as comfortable, are constrained to leave their homes, their goodly lands, and the sepulchres of their fathers, and either to go back into new and less valuable wildernesses, and to mingle with other tribes, dependant on their hospitality for a meagre support; or, without the common aids of education, to change at once all their habits and modes of life; to remain on a pittance of the lands they once owned, which they know not how to cultivate, and to which they have not a complete title: In these circumstances they become insulated among those who despise them as an inferior race, fit companions of those only, who have the capacity and the disposition to corrupt them. In this degraded, most disconsolate, and heart sinking of all situations in which man can be placed, they are left miserably to waste away for a few generations, and then to become extinct forever! This is no fancied picture. In a few years it will be sad reality, unless we change our policy towards them; unless effectual measures be taken to bring them over this awful gulf, to the solid and safe ground of civilization. How many tribes, once numerous and respectable, have in succession perished, in the manner described, from the fair and productive territories, now possessed by, and giving support to TEN MILLIONS OF PEOPLE!. . .

The Education of Indian Females and Intermarriages Between Indians and White People

I connect these subjects, because, in contemplating the latter, the former should be kept in view. While Indians remain in their present state, the minds of civilized people must revolt at the idea of intermarrying with them. It is natural, and decent, that it should be so. Intermarriages, however, in the present state of the Indians, or, that which amounts to the same thing have taken place to a great extent, and this too by many men of respectable talents and standing in society. More than half the Cherokee nation, a large part of the Choctaws and Chickasaws, and I may add indeed, of all other tribes with whom the whites have had intercourse, are of mixed blood. The offspring of this intercourse, a numerous body, are of promising talents and appearance. Their complexion is nearly that of the white population. They require only *education,* and the enjoyment of our privileges, to make them a valuable portion of our citizens. Let this education then be given them, particularly to the female Indians.

It is essential to the success of the project of the Government, that the female character among our native tribes, be raised from its present degraded state, to its proper rank and influence. This should be a *primary* object with the instructors of Indians. By educating female children, they will become prepared, in turn, to educate their own children, to manage their domestic concerns with intelligence and propriety, and, in this way, they will gradually attain their proper standing and influence in society. Many examples exist, to shew that all this is practicable. Thus educated, and the marriage institution, in its purity, introduced, the principal obstacles to intermarriage with them would be removed. Let the Indians, therefore, be taught all branches of knowledge pertaining to civilized man; *then* let intermarriage with them become general, and the end which the Government has in view will be completely attained. They would then be literally of one blood with us, be merged in the nation, and saved from extinction. . . .

The Claims of the Indians on the Government and People of the United States, and the Way to Satisfy These Claims

In the existing state of the Indians, and of our connections with them, what do we owe them? What are the duties, in reference to them, of the civil, and of the religious community? The duties of each are different, but connected. Neither, alone, can do all that seems necessary to be done. There is enough for both to do; and a necessity that there should be mutual co-operation.

The Government, according to the law of nations, having jurisdiction over the Indian territory, and the exclusive right to dispose of its soil, the whole Indian population is reduced, of necessary consequence, to a *dependent* situation. They are without the privileges of self-government, except in a limited degree; and without any *transferable* property. They are ignorant of nearly all the useful branches of human knowledge, of the Bible, and of the only Savior of men, therein revealed. They are weak, and ready to perish; we are strong, and with the help of God, able to support, to comfort and to save them. In these circumstances, the Indians have claims on us of high importance to them, and to our own character and reputation, as an enlightened, just and christian nation. In return for what they *virtually* yield, they are undoubtedly entitled to expect from our honor and justice, protection in all the rights which they are permitted to retain. They are entitled, as *"children"* of the government, for so we call them, *peculiarly* related to it, to kind, paternal treatment, to justice in all our dealings with them, to education in the useful arts and sciences, and in the principles and duties of our religion. In a word, they have a right to expect and to receive from our civil and religious communities combined, that sort of education, in all its branches, which we are accustomed to give to the *minority* of our own population, and thus to be raised gradually and ultimately, to the rank, and to the enjoyment of all the rights and privileges of freemen, and citizens of the United States. This I conceive to be the precise object of the Government. If we fulfil not these duties, which grow naturally out of our relation to Indians, we cannot avoid the imputation of injustice, unkindness, and unfaithfulness to them,—our national character must suffer in the estimation of all good men. If we refuse to do the things we have mentioned for the Indians, let us be consistent, and cease to call them *"children"*—and let them cease to address our President, as their "great Father." Let us leave to them the unmolested enjoyment of the territories they now possess, and give back to them those which we have taken away from them.

But the Government, and it is honorable to their character, have not forgotten their obligations. In fulfilment of them, in part, the Congress of the United States have placed at the disposal of their President, the annual sum of ten thousand dollars, which will doubtless be increased, as the plans of the government shall be extended, and require it, to be expended by him in ways which he may judge the most suitable, for the civilization and happiness of the Indians. The regulations adopted to guide in the expenditure of this fund, and the account rendered by the Secretary of War, of the manner in which it has been expended, will exhibit this paternal and benevolent effort of the Government, both in principle and operation.

Objections to Civilizing the Indians

When we look back in the pages of history four or five hundred years, and see what then was the state of our own Ancestors, and whence sprung the most polished and scientific nations of Europe, we should scarcely have supposed, that any man, acquainted with history, or making any pretensions to candor, would be found among the objectors to attempts to civilize our Indians, and thus to save them from perishing. Yet, painful as is the fact, objections have been made to the present course of procedure with Indians, and from men too, whose standing and office in society are such, as it would be deemed disrespectful to pass unnoticed. "The project," it has been said, "is visionary and impracticable. Indians can never be tamed; they are incapable of receiving, or of enjoying, the blessings proposed to be offered to them." Some, I will hope, for the honor of our country, that the number is small, have proceeded farther, and said, "Indians are not worth saving. They are perishing—let them perish. The sooner they are gone, the better." And to hasten such a catastrophe, *a formal project has been actually devised, and put on paper,* and the projector has had the effrontery to offer his infernal project for the adoption of the government!!!

A sufficient answer to such of these objections, as require notice (for truly some of them are so shocking, that one can hardly *think* of them, much less undertake to *answer* them) will be found, I conceive, in the *facts* collected into the Appendix of this work. It is too late to say that Indians cannot be civilized. The facts referred to, beyond all question, prove the contrary. The evidence of actual experiment in every case, is paramount to all objections founded in mere *theory,* or, as in the present case, in naked and unsupported *assertions.* The specimens of composition, and the account given, on unquestionable authority, of the acquisitions of Indian youths, of other kinds of knowledge, in the Cornwall, and other Indian schools, can hardly fail to convince all, who are willing to be convinced, that it *is* practicable to civilize, educate and save Indians. Without fear of contradiction, then, we assume this point as established. Indians are of the same nature and original, and of one blood, with ourselves; of intellectual powers as strong, and capable of cultivation, as ours. They, as well as ourselves, are made to be immortal. To look down upon them, therefore, as an inferior race, as untameable, and to profit by their ignorance and weakness; to take their property from them for a small part of its real value, and in other ways to oppress them; is undoubtedly wrong, and highly displeasing to our common Creator, Lawgiver and final Judge.

Plan for Civilizing the Indians

The *general* plan, embracing all its ramifications, which I would respectfully submit to the consideration and adoption of the government, with the improvements hereafter mentioned, is that, *substantially,* which has been devised by the American Board of Commissioners for Foreign Missions, and is now in successful operation under the direction of this Board, and of other similar associations of different denominations, and has already received the sanction and patronage of the Government. This plan, "in the full tide of successful experiment," is now in a course of exhibition before the public, and is looked at with joy and admiration, by philanthropists on both sides of the Atlantic.

Removal and Colonization of the Indians, Now Living Within the Settlements of the White People

On the subject of the removal of the Indians, who now dwell within our settlements, there are different opinions among wise and good men. The point on which they divide is, whether it be best to let these Indians quietly remain on their present Reservations, and to use our endeavors to civilize them where they are; or for the Government to take their Reservations, and give them an equivalent in lands to be purchased of other tribes beyond our present settlements. The Indians themselves too, are divided in opinion on this subject; a part are for removing, and a part for remaining, as in the case of the Cherokees, Delawares, Senecas, Oneidas, Shawanees, and indeed most of the other tribes living among us. Difficulties in deciding this question present themselves, on which side soever it be viewed. To remove these Indians far away from their present homes, from "the bones of their fathers," into a wilderness, among strangers, possibly hostile, to live as their new neighbors live, by hunting, a state to which they have not lately been accustomed, and which is incompatible with civilization, can hardly be reconciled with the professed views and objects of the Government in civilizing them. This would not be deemed by the world a wise course, nor one which would very probably lead to the desired end. Should that part of the tribes only, remove, who are willing to go, and the remainder be permitted to stay— this division of already enfeebled *remnants* of tribes, would but still more weaken their strength, diminish their influence, and hasten their destruction. Nor would this partial removal satisfy those who are for removing the whole; nor those either, who are for retaining the whole. The latter wish them to remain for the benevolent purpose of educating them all where they now are, urging, that they are now among us, in view of examples of civilized life; and where necessary instruction can be conveniently, and with little expense, imparted to them. On the other hand there is much to be said in favor of the removal of the *smaller* tribes, and remnants of tribes—not, however, into the wilderness, to return again to the savage life, but to some suitable, *prepared* portion of our country, where, collected in one body, they may be made comfortable, and with advantage be educated together, as has already been mentioned, in the manner in which we educate our own children. Some such course as this, I apprehend, will satisfy a great majority of the reflecting part of those who interest themselves at all in this subject, and is, in my belief, the only practicable course which can be pursued, consistently with the professed object of the Government.

Source:
Jedidiah Morse, *A Report to the Secretary of War of the United States, on Indian Affairs* (New Haven, CT: S. Converse, 1822), pp. 65–66, 73–75, 79–83.

38

First Annual Message

BY ANDREW JACKSON

Andrew Jackson (1767–1845), seventh president of the United States (1829–37), was confronted with a complex and potentially violent situation as he entered office. During the 1820s the Cherokee tribe in Georgia, facing hostility and encroachment from American settlers, had repeatedly refused to cede their land and move to the Arkansas Territory, claiming that a variety of treaties with the U.S. government granted them the right to occupy the lands they had settled. In his first annual message to Congress, delivered on December 8, 1829, Jackson overlooked these treatises and asserted the nation's right to remove the Cherokees. In 1830 he proposed an Indian Removal Bill to resettle (by force if necessary) any Native American tribe without consideration of any previous treaties signed by the government.

THE CONDITION AND ULTERIOR DESTINY of the Indian tribes within the limits of some of our States have become objects of much interest and importance. It has long been the policy of Government to introduce among them the arts of civilization, in the hope of gradually reclaiming them from a wandering life. This policy has, however, been coupled with another wholly incompatible with its success. Professing a desire to civilize and settle them, we have at the same time lost no opportunity to purchase their lands and thrust them farther into the wilderness. By this means they have not only been kept in a wandering state, but been led to look upon us as unjust and indifferent to their fate. Thus, though lavish in its expenditures upon the subject, Government has constantly defeated its own policy, and the Indians in general, receding farther and farther to the west, have retained their savage habits. A portion, however, of the Southern tribes, having mingled much with the whites and made some progress in the arts of civilized life, have lately attempted to erect an independent government within the limits of Georgia and Alabama. These States, claiming to be the only sovereigns within their territories, extended their laws over the Indians, which induced the latter to call upon the United States for protection.

Under these circumstances the question presented was whether the General Government had a right to sustain those people in their pretensions. The Constitution declares that "no new State shall be formed or erected within the jurisdiction of any other State" without the consent of its legislature. If the General Government is not permitted to tolerate the erection of a confederate State within the territory of one of the members of this Union against her consent, much less could it allow a foreign and independent government to establish itself there. Georgia became a member of the Confederacy which eventuated in our Federal Union as a sovereign State, always asserting her claim to certain limits, which, having been originally defined in her colonial charter and subsequently recognized in the treaty of peace, she has ever since continued to enjoy, except as they have been circumscribed by her own voluntary transfer of a portion of her territory to the United States in the articles of cession of 1802. Alabama was admitted into the Union on the same footing with the original States, with boundaries which were prescribed by Congress. There is no constitutional, conventional, or legal provision which allows them less power over the Indians within their borders than is possessed by Maine or New York. Would the people of Maine permit the Penobscot tribe to erect an independent government within their State? And unless they did would it not be the duty of the General Government to support them in resisting such a measure? Would the people of New York permit each remnant of the Six Nations within her borders to declare itself an independent people under the protection of the United States? Could the Indians establish a separate republic on each of their reservations in Ohio? And if they were so disposed would it be the duty of this Government to protect them in the attempt? If the principle involved in the obvious answer to these questions be abandoned, it will follow that the objects of this Government are reversed, and that it has become a part of its duty to aid in destroying the States which it was established to protect.

Actuated by this view of the subject, I informed the Indians inhabiting parts of Georgia and Alabama that their attempt to establish an independent government would not be countenanced by the Executive of the United States, and advised them to emigrate beyond the Mississippi or submit to the laws of those States.

Our conduct toward these people is deeply interesting to our national character. Their present condition, contrasted with what they once were, makes a most powerful appeal to our sympathies. Our ancestors found them the uncontrolled possessors of these vast regions. By persuasion and force they have been made to retire from river to river and from mountain to mountain, until some of the tribes have become extinct and others have left but remnants to preserve for awhile their once terrible names. Surrounded by the whites with their arts of civilization, which by destroying the resources of the savage doom him to weakness and decay, the fate of the Mohegan, the Narragansett, and the Delaware is fast overtaking the Choctaw, the Cherokee, and the Creek. That this fate surely awaits them if they remain within the limits of the States does not admit of a doubt. Humanity and national honor demand that every effort should be made to avert so great a calamity. It is too late to inquire whether it was just in the United States to include them and their territory within the bounds of new States, whose limits they could control. That step can not be retraced. A State can not be dismembered by Congress or restricted in the exercise of her constitutional power. But the people of those States and of every State, actuated by feelings of justice and a regard for our national honor, submit to you the interesting question whether something can not be done, consistently with the rights of the States, to preserve this much-injured race.

As a means of effecting this end I suggest for your consideration the propriety of setting apart an ample district west of the Mississippi, and without the limits of any State or Territory now formed, to be guaranteed to the Indian tribes as long as they shall occupy it, each tribe having a distinct control over the portion designated for its use. There they may be secured in the enjoyment of governments of their own choice, subject to no other control from the United States than such as may be necessary to preserve peace on the frontier and between the several tribes. There the benevolent may endeavor to teach them the arts of civilization, and, by promoting union and harmony among them, to raise up an interesting commonwealth, destined to perpetuate the race and to attest the humanity and justice of this Government.

This emigration should be voluntary, for it would be as cruel as unjust to compel the aborigines to abandon the graves of their fathers and seek a home in a distant land. But they should be distinctly informed that if they remain within the limits of the States they must be subject to their laws. In return for their obedience as individuals they will without doubt be protected in the enjoyment of those possessions which they have improved by their industry. But it seems to me visionary to suppose that in this state of things claims can be allowed on tracts of country on which they have neither dwelt nor made improvements, merely because they have seen them from the mountain or passed them in the chase. Submitting to the laws of the States, and receiving, like other citizens, protection in their persons and property, they will ere long become merged in the mass of our population.

Source:
Andrew Jackson, "First Annual Message"
(1829), in *A Compilation of the Messages and
Papers of the Presidents* (New York: Bureau of
National Literature, 1897), vol. 3,
pp. 1019–22.

39

Crania Americana

BY SAMUEL GEORGE MORTON

Samuel George Morton (1799–1851) was president of the Academy of Natural Sciences in Philadelphia. He collected hundreds of skulls from around the world and thereby pioneered the "science" of craniological analysis. In his celebrated work Crania Americana *(1839), he studied the skulls of various Native American tribes in North and South America. He also indulged in a multitude of generalizations about the "aboriginals."*

CAUTIOUSNESS AND CUNNING are among the most prominent features in the character of these people. A studied vigilance marks every action. If an Indian speaks, it is in a slow and studied manner, and to avoid committing himself he often resorts to metaphorical phrases which have no precise meaning. If he seeks an enemy, it is through unfrequented paths, in the dead of night, and with every device for concealment and surprise. When he meets his victim, the same instinctive feeling governs all his movements. His motive is to destroy without being destroyed, and he avails himself of every subterfuge that can protect his own person while he seeks the life of his antagonist. It is by a refinement of cautious cunning that they have so often circumvented Europeans, and they pride themselves on this faculty more than on any other. Thus also when provoked they can mask their resentment under an unruffled exterior; but the mind which thus conceals its emotions, devises at the same moment a sleepless and bloody revenge. Their very politeness is a part of their cautiousness; for in conversation they seldom contradict or deny the remarks that are made to them, so that a stranger is unable to decide whether they are pleased or displeased, convinced or the contrary.

"The missionaries who have attempted to convert them to Christianity, all complain of this as one of the great difficulties of their mission. The Indians hear with patience the truths of the gospel explained to them, and give their usual tokens of assent and approbation; but this by no means implies conviction—it is mere civility."[1] For the same reason an Indian seldom expresses himself with surprise. If an object interests him on account of its novelty, he shows his gratification in a few subdued remarks, or by a significant gesture; but it is difficult to betray him into enthusiasm. That taciturnity which is also linked with their cautiousness, is fostered by all their usages. It is seen even in the marriage ceremony, which is often joyless and even melancholy, as if it were rather the harbinger of sorrow than of happiness. It is indeed seldom that their pastimes excite enthusiasm or hilarity, unless the performers are stimulated by intoxicating drinks; in which case, as among more civilised men, a temporary madness unmasks the darkest passions, and the natural reserve of the Indian gives place to extravagant mirth and brutal ferocity. . . .

As a result of habitual indolence, the Indians are remarkably improvident. What a missionary writer says of a few nations, is applicable to many, and indeed to most. "They live reckless of the past, little curious about the present, and very seldom anxious about the future."[2] When the cold pinches him he commences building a hut; but should the weather soften and invite to repose, he abandons his task until again stimulated by necessity. And so it is with his other domestic concerns. He will often suffer with want before he engages in the chase; and a successful hunting expedition is followed by a protracted season of indolence and gluttony.

It is usual to charge the Indians with treachery: but in most instances it will be found that they have only retorted the perfidiousness that has been heaped upon them by others. The annals of Indian history are ample evidence of this fact. A system of encroachment and oppression has been practised upon them since the first landing of Europeans on the shores of America: their lands have been seized upon the most frivolous pretences, and they have had no redress at the hand of the white man: wars have been fomented among them to procure their mutual destruction; and when they have been weakened by the conflict, the common enemy has stepped in and seized upon their possessions. They have been taken in their villages, or inveigled on ship-board, to be sold into slavery; and in fact every art that cupidity could devise has been put in practice to deprive them of liberty and life. Is it surprising that a people thus oppressed should retaliate on their oppressors? Or shall we stigmatise them as treacherous when they have received so much treachery at our hands?

It must in truth be confessed that the Indian is least to be admired at home; for in him the domestic virtues are but partially expanded. War and the chase, on the other hand, call forth all his energies. Hunger, fatigue and toil, are encountered without a murmur, and the mind, goaded on by the powerful impulse of ambition or revenge, becomes untiring and indomitable. The firmness of purpose, its attendant privations, and the final contest with a courageous adversary, give a seductive exaltation to the character of the American savage. He returns to his home, he is greeted by the applauding shouts of his countrymen, and the bloody deeds of a crafty and destroying spirit are recounted, even in civilised communities, as acts of heroism and greatness. How transient is this seeming glory! The excitement of the moment has passed away, and where is the warrior now? For him domestic life has no charms, and tranquillity resolves itself into the most grovelling pastimes. Behold him lounging under the shade of a tree, the victim of apathy and sloth, too vain to cultivate his fields, or to raise a hand for his own support, while he looks with complacency on the toils of a mother, a wife, or a daughter, whom the barbarous usages of Indian thraldom have condemned to perpetual slavery. To such an extent is this servitude carried, that mothers not unfrequently destroy their female children, alleging as a reason that it is better they should die than live to lead a life so miserable as that to which they are doomed; while among some tribes grief and jealousy drive the women to suicide. The Indian is habitually cold in his manner to the gentler sex, and stern to his children, considering it unmanly to show much tenderness to either. This exterior reserve, however, is by no means indicative of their real character; for after all that has been said to the contrary, these people are not remarkable for the purity of their morals. The very reverse, indeed, is true; for when they throw off the mask of reserve which they habitually assume in the presence of strangers, they are observed to be as much depraved by vice and sensuality as most other barbarous nations.

The Americans are, perhaps, less swayed by superstitious fears than most other savages; and their religion, if it merits the name, is more remarkable for its poverty than its grossness. It is chiefly a simple theism which acknowledges a good and an evil spirit; the former of course exerting a benign influence on the destinies of men, while the latter is looked upon as the author of all their misfortunes. Yet there is, for the most part, no regularity in the time or manner of their worship, which appears to be the mere result of occasion or impulse. The Indian hears God in the winds, and in the cataract, and acknowledges his presence in all the phenomena of the elements; yet these are always attributed to the same spirit, and not, as with most barbarous people, to a multiplicity of spiritual agents. Again, the Americans are little prone to idolatry; for it is rare to find any community among them paying homage to an image of their own making. So far as inquiry has been extended to this subject, it appears that all the American nations believe in the immortality of the soul, which is to enjoy in a future state the most exciting temporal pleasures without fatigue or alloy: of these pastimes hunting and fishing are the most esteemed, and hence the implements used in both are buried with the dead.

The Indians have an extraordinary veneration for their dead, which sometimes induces them, on removing from one section of the country to another, to disinter the remains of their deceased relatives, and bear them to the new home of the tribe. Heckewelder says, that when at Bethlehem, in Pennsylvania, about the middle of the last century, he saw a removing party of the Nanticokes pass through that town, loaded with the bones of their dead friends, some of which were in so recent a state as to taint the air as they passed.

The intellectual faculties of this great family appear to be of a decidedly inferior cast when compared with those of the Caucasian or Mongolian races. They are not only averse to the restraints of education, but for the most part incapable of a continued process of reasoning on abstract subjects. Their minds seize with avidity on simple truths, while they at once reject whatever requires investigation and analysis. Their proximity, for more than two centuries, to European institutions, has made scarcely any appreciable change in their mode of thinking or their manner of life; and as to their own social condition, they are probably in most respects what they were at the primitive epoch of their existence. They have made few or no improvements in building their houses or their boats; their inventive and imitative faculties appear to be of a very humble grade, nor have they the smallest predilection for the arts or sciences. The long annals of missionary labor and private benefaction bestowed upon them, offer but very few exceptions to the preceding statement, which, on the contrary, is sustained by the combined testimony of almost all practical observers. Even in cases where they have received an ample education, and have remained for many years in civilised society, they lose none of their innate love of their own national usages, which they have almost invariably resumed when chance has left them to choose for themselves. Such has been the experience of the Spanish and Portuguese missionaries in South America, and of the English and their descendants in the northern portion of the continent.

However much the benevolent mind may regret the inaptitude of the Indian for civilisation, the affirmative of this question seems to be established beyond a doubt. His moral and physical nature are alike adapted to his position among the races of men, and it is as reasonable to expect the one to be changed as the other. The structure of his mind appears to be different from that of the white man, nor can the two harmonise in their social relations except on the most limited scale. Every one knows, however, that the mind expands by culture; nor can we yet tell how near the Indian would approach the Caucasian after education had been bestowed on a single family through several successive generations.

Source:
Samuel George Morton, *Crania Americana;
or, A Comparative View of the Skulls of Various
Aboriginal Nations of North and South
America* (Philadelphia: J. Dobson; London:
Simpkin, Marshall & Co., 1839), pp. 76–82.

40

League of the Iroquois

BY LEWIS H. MORGAN

The lawyer Lewis Henry Morgan (1818–1881) wrote many works on anthropology, Native Americans, and other subjects, including Ancient Society; or, Researches in the Lines of Human Progress from Savagery, Through Barbarism to Civilization *(1877). He is frequently termed the "Father of American Anthropology." In the 1840s he joined a secret society that allowed him to make a detailed study of the Iroquois tribe. His 1851 treatise on the tribe, while expressing sympathy with their fate, nevertheless recommends education and Christian indoctrination in order to "reclaim" the Native Americans.*

T HE FUTURE DESTINY OF THE INDIAN upon this continent, is a subject of no ordinary interest. If the fact, that he cannot be saved in his native state, needed any proof beyond the experience of the past, it could be demonstrated from the nature of things. Our primitive inhabitants are environed with civilized life, the baleful and disastrous influence of which, when brought in contact with Indian life, is wholly irresistible. Civilization is aggressive, as well as progressive—a positive state of society, attacking every obstacle, overwhelming every lesser agency, and searching out and filling up every crevice, both in the moral and physical world; while Indian life is an unarmed condition, a negative state, without inherent vitality, and without powers of resistance. The institutions of the red man fix him to the soil with a fragile and precarious tenure; while those of civilized man, in his highest estate, enable him to seize it with a grasp which defies displacement. To uproot a race at the meridian of its intellectual power, is next to impossible; but the expulsion of a contiguous one, in a state of primitive rudeness, is comparatively easy, if not an absolute necessity.

The manifest destiny of the Indian, if left to himself, calls up the question of his reclamation, certainly, in itself, a more interesting, and far more important subject than any which have before been considered. All the Indian races now dwelling within the Republic have fallen under its jurisdiction; thus casting upon the government a vast responsibility, as the administrator of their affairs, and a solemn trust, as the guardian of their future welfare. Should the system of tutelage and supervision, adopted by the national government, find its highest aim and ultimate object in the adjustment of their present difficulties from day to day; or should it look beyond and above these temporary considerations, towards their final elevation to the rights and privileges of American citizens? This is certainly a grave question, and if the latter enterprise itself be feasible, it should be prosecuted with a zeal and energy as earnest and untiring as its importance demands. During the period within which this question will be solved, the American people cannot remain indifferent and passive spectators, and avoid responsibility; for while the government is chiefly accountable for the administration of their civil affairs, those of a moral and religious character, which, at least, are not less important, appeal to the enlightened benevolence of the public at large.

Whether a portion of the Indian family may yet be reclaimed and civilized, and thus saved eventually from the fate which has already befallen so many of our aboriginal races, will furnish the theme of a few concluding reflections. What is true of the Iroquois, in a general sense, can be predicated of any other portion of our primitive inhabitants. For this reason the facts relied upon to establish the hypothesis that the Indian can be permanently reclaimed and civilized, will be drawn exclusively from the social history of the former. . . .

There are but two means of rescuing the Indian from his impending destiny; and these are education and Christianity. If he will receive into his mind the light of knowledge, and the spirit of civilization, he will possess, not only the means of self-defence, but the power with which to emancipate himself from the thraldom in which he is held. The frequent attempts which have been made to educate the Indian, and the numerous failures in which these attempts have eventuated, have, to some extent, created a belief in the public mind, that his education and reclamation are both impossible. This enterprise may still, perhaps, be considered an experiment, and of uncertain issue; but experience has not yet shown that it is hopeless. There is now, in each Indian community in the State, a large and respectable class who have become habitual cultivators of the soil; many of whom have adopted our mode of life, have become members of the missionary churches, speak our language, and are in every respect, discreet and sensible men. In this particular class there is a strong desire for the adoption of the customs of civilized life, and more especially for the education of their children, upon which subject they often express the strongest solicitude. Among the youth who are brought up under such influences, there exists the same desire for knowledge, and the same readiness to improve educational advantages. Out of this class Indian youth may be selected for a higher education, with every prospect of success, since to a better preparation for superior advantages, there is superadded a stronger security against a relapse into Indian life. In the attempted education of their young men, the prime difficulty has been to render their attainments permanent, and useful to themselves. To draw an untutored Indian from his forest home, and, when carefully educated, to dismiss him again to the wilderness, a solitary scholar, would be an idle experiment; because his attainments would not only be unappreciated by his former associates, but he would incur the hazard of being despised because of them. The education of the Indian youth should be general, and chiefly in schools at home. . . .

It is, indeed, a great undertaking to work off the Indian temper of mind, and infuse that of another race. It is necessary, to its accomplishment, to commence in infancy, and at the missionary school, where our language is substituted for the Indian language, our religion for the Indian mythology, and our amusements and mode of life for theirs. When this has been effected, and upon a mind thus prepared has been shed the light of a higher knowledge, there is not even then a firm assurance that the Indian nature is forever subdued and submerged in that superior one which civilization creates. In the depths of Indian society there is a spirit and a sentiment to which their minds are attuned by nature; and great must be the power, and constant the influence which can overcome the one, or eradicate the other.

Source:
Lewis H. Morgan, *League of the Ho-de'-no-sau-nee, Iroquois* (Rochester, NY: Sage & Brother, 1851), pp. 444–50.

41

My Life on the Plains

BY GENERAL G. A. CUSTER

George Armstrong Custer (1839–1876) served with distinction in the Union cavalry during the Civil War, capturing General Robert E. Lee's army as it fled from Richmond on April 9, 1865, and effectively ending the war. His subsequent career in battling the Native Americans in the Plains states was checkered, and at one point he was court-martialed and sentenced to a year's suspension from the army. He was responsible for the discovery of gold in the Black Hills during an exploratory mission in the mid-1870s. His autobiography, My Life on the Plains *(1874), speaks harshly of the "Indian character." Custer died on June 25, 1876, when he led a small company of troops into battle against an overwhelmingly larger force of Sioux and Cheyenne Indians, led by Sitting Bull, at Little Big Horn.*

IF THE CHARACTER GIVEN TO THE INDIAN by Cooper and other novelists, as well as by well-meaning but mistaken philanthropists of a later day, were the true one; if the Indian were the innocent, simple-minded being he is represented, more the creature of romance than reality, imbued only with a deep veneration for the works of nature, freed from the passions and vices which must accompany a savage nature; if, in other words, he possessed all the virtues which his admirers and works of fiction ascribe to him, and were free from all the vices which those best qualified to judge assign to him, he would be just the character to complete the picture which is presented by the country embracing the Wichita mountains. Cooper, to whose writings more than to those of any other author are the people speaking the English language indebted for a false and ill-judged estimate of the Indian character, might well have laid the scenes of his fictitious stories in this beautiful and romantic country.

It is to be regretted that the character of the Indian as described in Cooper's interesting novels is not the true one. But as, in emerging from childhood into the years of a maturer age, we are often compelled to cast aside many of our earlier illusions and replace them by beliefs less inviting but more real, so we, as a people, with opportunities enlarged and facilities for obtaining knowledge increased, have been forced by a multiplicity of causes to study and endeavor to comprehend thoroughly the character of the red man. So intimately has he become associated with the Government as ward of the nation, and so prominent a place among the questions of national policy does the much mooted "Indian question" occupy, that it behooves us no longer to study this problem from works of fiction, but to deal with it as it exists in reality. Stripped of the beautiful romance with which we have been so long willing to envelop him, transferred from the inviting pages of the novelist to the localities where we are compelled to meet with him, in his native village, on the war path, and when raiding upon our frontier settlements and lines of travel, the Indian forfeits his claim to the appellation of the "*noble* red man." We see him as he is, and, so far as all knowledge goes, as he ever has been, a *savage* in every sense of the word; not worse, perhaps, than his white brother would be similarly born and bred, but one whose cruel and ferocious nature far exceeds that of any wild beast of the desert. That this is true no one who has been brought into intimate contact with the wild tribes will deny. Perhaps there are some who, as members of peace commissions or as wandering agents of some benevolent society, may have visited these tribes or attended with them at councils held for some pacific purpose, and who, by passing through the villages of the Indian while *at peace*, may imagine their opportunities for judging of the Indian nature all that could be desired. But the Indian, while he can seldom be accused of indulging in a great variety of wardrobe, can be said to have a character capable of adapting itself to almost every occasion. He has one character, perhaps his most serviceable one, which he preserves carefully, and only airs it when making his appeal to the Government or its agents for arms, ammunition, and license to employ them. This character is invariably paraded, and often with telling effect, when the motive is a peaceful one. Prominent chiefs invited to visit Washington invariably don this character, and in their "talks" with the "Great Father" and other less prominent personages they successfully contrive to exhibit but this one phase. Seeing them under these or similar circumstances only, it is not surprising that by many the Indian is looked upon as a simple-minded "son of nature," desiring nothing beyond the privilege of roaming and hunting over the vast unsettled wilds of the West, inheriting and asserting but few native rights, and never trespassing upon the rights of others. This view is equally erroneous with that which regards the Indian as a creature possessing the human form but divested of all other attributes of humanity, and whose traits of character, habits, modes of life, disposition, and savage customs disqualify him from the exercise of all rights and privileges, even those pertaining to life itself. Taking him as we find him, at peace or at war, at home or abroad, waiving all prejudices, and laying aside all partiality, we will discover in the Indian a subject for thoughtful study and investigation. In him we will find the representative of a race whose origin is, and promises to be, a subject forever wrapped in mystery; a race incapable of being judged by the rules or laws applicable to any other known race of men; one between which and civilization there seems to have existed from time immemorial a determined and unceasing warfare—a hostility so deep-seated and inbred with the Indian character, that in the exceptional instances where the modes and habits of civilization have been reluctantly adopted, it has been at the sacrifice of power and influence as a tribe, and the more serious loss of health, vigor, and courage as individuals. . . .

Inseparable from the Indian character, wherever he is to be met with, is his remarkable taciturnity, his deep dissimulation, the perseverance with which he follows his plans of revenge or conquest, his concealment and apparent lack of curiosity, his stoical courage when in the power of his enemies, his cunning, his caution, and last, but not least, the wonderful power and subtlety of his senses. Of this last I have had most interesting proof, one instance of which will be noted when describing the Washita campaign. In studying the Indian character, while shocked and disgusted by many of his traits and customs, I find much to be admired, and still more of deep and unvarying interest. To me Indian life, with its attendant ceremonies, mysteries, and forms, is a book of unceasing interest. Grant that some of its pages are frightful, and, if possible, to be avoided, yet the attraction is none the weaker. Study him, fight him, civilize him if you can, he remains still the object of your curiosity, a type of man peculiar and undefined, subjecting himself to no known law of civilization, contending determinedly against all efforts to win him from his chosen mode of life. He stands in the group of nations solitary and reserved, seeking alliance with none, mistrusting and opposing the advances of all. Civilization may and should do much for him, but it can never civilize him. A few instances to the contrary may be quoted, but these are susceptible of explanation. No tribe enjoying its accustomed freedom has ever been induced to adopt a civilized mode of life, or, as they express it, to follow the white man's road. At various times certain tribes have forsaken the pleasures of the chase and the excitement of the war-path for the more quiet life to be found on the "reservation." Was this course adopted voluntarily and from preference? Was it because the Indian chose the ways of his white brother rather than those in which he had been born and bred?

In no single instance has this been true. What then, it may be asked, have been the reasons which influenced certain tribes to abandon their predatory, nomadic life, and to-day to influence others to pursue a similar course? The answer is clear, and as undeniable as it is clear. The gradual and steady decrease in numbers, strength, and influence, occasioned by wars both with other tribes and with the white man, as well as losses brought about by diseases partly attributable to contact with civilization, have so lowered the standing and diminished the available fighting force of the tribe as to render it unable to cope with more powerful neighboring tribes with any prospect of success. The stronger tribes always assume an overbearing and dominant manner toward their weaker neighbors, forcing them to join in costly and bloody wars or themselves to be considered enemies. When a tribe falls from the position of a leading one, it is at the mercy of every tribe that chooses to make war, being forced to take sides, and at the termination of the war is generally sacrificed to the interests of the more powerful. To avoid these sacrifices, to avail itself of the protection of civilization and its armed forces, to escape from the ruining influences of its more warlike and powerful neighbors, it reluctantly accepts the situation, gives up its accustomed haunts, its wild mode of life, and nestles down under the protecting arm of its former enemy, the white man, and tries, however feebly, to adopt his manner of life. In making this change the Indian has to sacrifice all that is dear to his heart; he abandons the only mode of life in which he can be a warrior and win triumphs and honors worthy to be sought after; and in taking up the pursuits of the white man he does that which he has always been taught from his earliest infancy to regard as degrading to his manhood— to labor, to work for his daily bread, an avocation suitable only for squaws.

To those who advocate the application of the laws of civilization to the Indian, it might be a profitable study to investigate the effect which such application produces upon the strength of the tribe as expressed in numbers. Looking at him as the fearless hunter, the matchless horseman and warrior of the Plains, where Nature placed him, and contrasting him with the reservation Indian, who is supposed to be revelling in the delightful comforts and luxuries of an enlightened condition, but who in reality is grovelling in beggary, bereft of many of the qualities which in his wild state tended to render him noble, and heir to a combination of vices partly his own, partly bequeathed to him from the pale-face, one is forced, even against desire, to conclude that there is unending antagonism between the Indian nature and that with which his well-meaning white brother would endow him. Nature intended him for a savage state; every instinct, every impulse of his soul inclines him to it. The white race might fall into a barbarous state, and afterwards, subjected to the influence of civilization, be reclaimed and prosper. Not so the Indian. He cannot be himself and be civilized; he fades away and dies. Cultivation such as the white man would give him deprives him of his identity. Education, strange as it may appear, seems to weaken rather than strengthen his intellect. Where do we find any specimens of educated Indian eloquence comparing with that of such native, untutored orators as Tecumseh, Osceola, Red Jacket, and Logan; or, to select from those of more recent fame, Red Cloud of the Sioux, or Sa-tan-ta of the Kiowas? Unfortunately for the last-named chief, whose name has been such a terror to our frontier settlements, he will have to be judged for other qualities than that of eloquence. Attention has more recently been directed to him by his arrest by the military authorities near Fort Sill, Indian Territory, and his transportation to Texas for trial by civil court for various murders and depredations, alleged to have been committed by him near the Texas frontier. He has since had his trial, and, if public rumor is to be credited, has been sentenced to death. Reference will be made to this noted chief in succeeding pages. His eloquence and able arguments upon the Indian question in various councils to which he was called won for him the deserved title of "Orator of the Plains." In his boasting harangue before the General of the Army, which furnished the evidence of his connection with the murders for which he has been tried and sentenced, he stated as a justification for such outrages, or rather as the occasion of them, that they were in retaliation for his arrest and imprisonment by me some three years ago. As there are two sides to most questions, even if one be wrong, when the proper time arrives a brief account of Sa-tan-ta's arrest and imprisonment, with the causes leading thereto, will be given in these sketches. One of the favorite remarks of Sa-tan-ta in his orations, and one too which other chiefs often indulge in being thrown out as a "glittering generality," meaning much or little as they may desire, but most often the latter, was that he was tired of making war and desired now "to follow the white man's road." It is scarcely to be presumed that he found the gratification of this oft-expressed desire in recently following the "white man's road" to Texas, under strong guard and heavily manacled, with hanging, to the Indian the most dreaded of all deaths, plainly in the perspective. Aside, however, from his character for restless barbarity, and activity in conducting merciless forays against our exposed frontiers, Sa-tan-ta is a remarkable man—remarkable for his powers of oratory, his determined warfare against the advances of civilization, and his opposition to the abandonment of his accustomed mode of life, and its exchange for the quiet, unexciting, uneventful life of a reservation Indian. If I were an Indian, I often think that I would greatly prefer to cast my lot among those of my people who adhered to the free open plains, rather than submit to the confined limits of a reservation, there to be the recipient of the blessed benefits of civilization, with its vices thrown in without stint or measure. The Indian can never be permitted to view the question in this deliberate way. He is neither a luxury nor necessary of life. He can hunt, roam, and camp when and wheresoever he pleases, provided always that in so doing he does not run contrary to the requirements of civilization in its advancing tread. When the soil which he has claimed and hunted over for so long a time is demanded by this to him insatiable monster, there is no appeal; he must yield, or, like the car of Juggernaut, it will roll mercilessly over him, destroying as it advances. Destiny seems to have so willed it, and the world looks on and nods its approval. At best the history of our Indian tribes, no matter from what standpoint it is regarded, affords a melancholy picture of loss of life. Two hundred years ago it required millions to express in numbers the Indian population, while at the present time less than half the number of thousands will suffice for the purpose. Where and why have they gone? Ask the Saxon race, since whose introduction into and occupation of the country these vast changes have been effected.

Source:
General G. A. Custer, *My Life on the Plains;
or, Personal Experiences with Indians*
(New York: Sheldon & Co., 1874),
pp. 11–12, 16–18.

42

A Century of Dishonor

BY HELEN HUNT JACKSON

The poet and novelist Helen Hunt Jackson (1830–1885) spent the last ten years of her life at Colorado Springs, where she developed a sympathy for the Native Americans there. As a result, she wrote the treatise A Century of Dishonor *(1881) and sent it at her own expense to every member of Congress. In this work she recounts the repeated violations by the U.S. government of treaty agreements with the Native Americans and pleads that steps be taken to render them justice. Jackson's novel* Ramona *(1884) is a fictional plea for the Native American.*

THERE ARE WITHIN THE LIMITS of the United States between two hundred and fifty and three hundred thousand Indians, exclusive of those in Alaska. The names of the different tribes and bands, as entered in the statistical tables of the Indian Office Reports, number nearly three hundred. One of the most careful estimates which has been made of their numbers and localities gives them as follows: "In Minnesota and States east of the Mississippi, about 32,500; in Nebraska, Kansas, and the Indian Territory, 70,650; in the Territories of Dakota, Montana, Wyoming, and Idaho, 65,000; in Nevada and the Territories of Colorado, New Mexico, Utah, and Arizona, 84,000; and on the Pacific slope, 48,000."

Of these, 130,000 are self-supporting on their own reservations, "receiving nothing from the Government except interest on their own moneys, or annuities granted them in consideration of the cession of their lands to the United States."[1]

This fact alone would seem sufficient to dispose forever of the accusation, so persistently brought against the Indian, that he will not work.

256

Of the remainder, 84,000 are partially supported by the Government—the interest money due them and their annuities, as provided by treaty, being inadequate to their subsistence on the reservations where they are confined. In many cases, however, these Indians furnish a large part of their support—the White River Utes, for instance, who are reported by the Indian Bureau as getting sixty-six per cent. of their living by "root-digging, hunting, and fishing;" the Squaxin band, in Washington Territory, as earning seventy-five per cent, and the Chippewas of Lake Superior as earning fifty per cent. in the same way. These facts also would seem to dispose of the accusation that the Indian will not work.

There are about 55,000 who never visit an agency, over whom the Government does not pretend to have either control or care. These 55,000 "subsist by hunting, fishing, on roots, nuts, berries, etc., and by begging and stealing;" and this also seems to dispose of the accusation that the Indian will not "work for a living." There remains a small portion, about 31,000, that are entirely subsisted by the Government.

There is not among these three hundred bands of Indians one which has not suffered cruelly at the hands either of the Government or of white settlers. The poorer, the more insignificant, the more helpless the band, the more certain the cruelty and outrage to which they have been subjected. This is especially true of the bands on the Pacific slope. These Indians found themselves of a sudden surrounded by and caught up in the great influx of gold-seeking settlers, as helpless creatures on a shore are caught up in a tidal wave. There was not time for the Government to make treaties; not even time for communities to make laws. The tale of the wrongs, the oppressions, the murders of the Pacific-slope Indians in the last thirty years would be a volume by itself, and is too monstrous to be believed.

It makes little difference, however, where one opens the record of the history of the Indians; every page and every year has its dark stain. The story of one tribe is the story of all, varied only by differences of time and place; but neither time nor place makes any difference in the main facts. Colorado is as greedy and unjust in 1880 as was Georgia in 1830, and Ohio in 1795; and the United States Government breaks promises now as deftly as then, and with an added ingenuity from long practice.

One of its strongest supports in so doing is the wide-spread sentiment among the people of dislike to the Indian, of impatience with his presence as a "barrier to civilization," and distrust of it as a possible danger. The old tales of the frontier life, with its horrors of Indian warfare, have gradually, by two or three generations' telling, produced in the average mind something like an hereditary instinct of unquestioning and unreasoning aversion which it is almost impossible to dislodge or soften.

There are hundreds of pages of unimpeachable testimony on the side of the Indian; but it goes for nothing, is set down as sentimentalism or partisanship, tossed aside and forgotten.

President after president has appointed commission after commission to inquire into and report upon Indian affairs, and to make suggestions as to the best methods of managing them. The reports are filled with eloquent statements of wrongs done to the Indians, of perfidies on the part of the Government; they counsel, as earnestly as words can, a trial of the simple and unperplexing expedients of telling truth, keeping promises, making fair bargains, dealing justly in all ways and all things. These reports are bound up with the Government's Annual Reports, and that is the end of them. It would probably be no exaggeration to say that not one American citizen out of ten thousand ever sees them or knows that they exist, and yet any one of them, circulated throughout the country, read by the right-thinking, right-feeling men and women of this land, would be of itself a "campaign document" that would initiate a revolution which would not subside until the Indians' wrongs were, so far as is now left possible, righted.

In 1869 President Grant appointed a commission of nine men, representing the influence and philanthropy of six leading States, to visit the different Indian reservations, and to "examine all matters appertaining to Indian affairs."

In the report of this commission are such paragraphs as the following: "To assert that 'the Indian will not work' is as true as it would be to say that the white man will not work.

"Why should the Indian be expected to plant corn, fence lands, build houses, or do anything but get food from day to day, when experience has taught him that the product of his labor will be seized by the white man to-morrow? The most industrious white man would become a drone under similar circumstances. Nevertheless, many of the Indians" (the commissioners might more forcibly have said 130,000 of the Indians) "are already at work, and furnish ample refutation of the assertion that 'the Indian will not work.' There is no escape from the inexorable logic of facts.

"The history of the Government connections with the Indians is a shameful record of broken treaties and unfulfilled promises. The history of the border white man's connection with the Indians is a sickening record of murder, outrage, robbery, and wrongs committed by the former, as the rule, and occasional savage outbreaks and unspeakably barbarous deeds of retaliation by the latter, as the exception.

"Taught by the Government that they had rights entitled to respect, when those rights have been assailed by the rapacity of the white man, the arm which should have been raised to protect them has ever been ready to sustain the aggressor.

"The testimony of some of the highest military officers of the United States is on record to the effect that, in our Indian wars, almost without exception, the first aggressions have been made by the white man; and the assertion is supported by every civilian of reputation who has studied the subject. In addition to the class of robbers and outlaws who find impunity in their nefarious pursuits on the frontiers, there is a large class of professedly reputable men who use every means in their power to bring on Indian wars for the sake of the profit to be realized from the presence of troops and the expenditure of Government funds in their midst. They proclaim death to the Indians at all times in words and publications, making no distinction between the innocent and the guilty. They irate the lowest class of men to the perpetration of the darkest deeds against their victims, and as judges and jurymen shield them from the justice due to their crimes. Every crime committed by a white man against an Indian is concealed or palliated. Every offence committed by an Indian against a white man is borne on the wings of the post or the telegraph to the remotest corner of the land, clothed with all the horrors which the reality or imagination can throw around it. Against such influences as these the people of the United States need to be warned."

To assume that it would be easy, or by any one sudden stroke of legislative policy possible, to undo the mischief and hurt of the long past, set the Indian policy of the country right for the future, and make the Indians at once safe and happy, is the blunder of a hasty and uninformed judgment. The notion which seems to be growing more prevalent, that simply to make all Indians at once citizens of the United States would be a sovereign and instantaneous panacea for all their ills and all the Government's perplexities, is a very inconsiderate one. To administer complete citizenship of a sudden, all round, to all Indians, barbarous and civilized alike, would be as grotesque a blunder as to dose them all round with any one medicine, irrespective of the symptoms and needs of their diseases. It would kill more than it would cure. Nevertheless, it is true, as was well stated by one of the superintendents of Indian Affairs in 1857, that, "so long as they are not citizens of the United States, their rights of property must remain insecure against invasion. The doors of the federal tribunals being barred against them while wards and dependents, they can only partially exercise the rights of free government, or give to those who make, execute, and construe the few laws they are allowed to enact, dignity sufficient to make them respectable. While they continue individually to gather the crumbs that fall from the table of the United States, idleness, improvidence, and indebtedness will be the rule, and industry, thrift, and freedom from debt the exception. The utter absence of individual title to particular lands deprives every one among them of the chief incentive to labor and exertion—the very mainspring on which the prosperity of a people depends."

All judicious plans and measures for their safety and salvation must embody provisions for their becoming citizens as fast as they are fit, and must protect them till then in every right and particular in which our laws protect other "persons" who are not citizens.

There is a disposition in a certain class of minds to be impatient with any protestation against wrong which is unaccompanied or unprepared with a quick and exact scheme of remedy. This is illogical. When pioneers in a new country find a tract of poisonous and swampy wilderness to be reclaimed, they do not withhold their hands from fire and axe till they see clearly which way roads should run, where good water will spring, and what crops will best grow on the redeemed land. They first clear the swamp. So with this poisonous and baffling part of the domain of our national affairs—let us first "clear the swamp."

However great perplexity and difficulty there may be in the details of any and every plan possible for doing at this late day anything like justice to the Indian, however hard it may be for good statesmen and good men to agree upon the things that ought to be done, there certainly is, or ought to be, no perplexity whatever, no difficulty whatever, in agreeing upon certain things that ought not to be done, and which must cease to be done before the first steps can be taken toward righting the wrongs, curing the ills, and wiping out the disgrace to us of the present condition of our Indians.

Cheating, robbing, breaking promises—these three are clearly things which must cease to be done. One more thing, also, and that is the refusal of the protection of the law to the Indian's rights of property, "of life, liberty, and the pursuit of happiness."

When these four things have ceased to be done, time, statesmanship, philanthropy, and Christianity can slowly and surely do the rest. Till these four things have ceased to be done, statesmanship and philanthropy alike must work in vain, and even Christianity can reap but small harvest.

Source:
Helen Hunt Jackson, *A Century of Dishonor:
A Sketch of the United States Government's
Dealings with Some of the Indian Tribes* (New
York: Harper & Brothers, 1881), pp. 336–42.

PART EIGHT

African Americans

THE EXPERIENCES OF AFRICAN AMERICANS within American society since the introduction of slavery in 1619 can scarcely be treated in detail here. As with Native Americans, African Americans faced prejudice on all fronts, from skin color (which the physician Benjamin Rush, in a learned paper of 1799, seriously asserted was caused by leprosy) to their servile status (which, in a supreme bit of circular reasoning, was then claimed to be their "natural" condition) to their apparent ignorance (the slave owners' violent opposition to educating more than a small percentage of slaves was not taken into consideration). Jefferson, at any rate, partially recanted his harsh view of African Americans in a letter written two decades after his *Notes on the State of Virginia*, but he was unusual in keeping even a partially open mind on the subject.

By the 1830s, with the onset of abolitionist sentiment in the North, it became evident to southerners that an active defense of slavery was necessary to preserve the institution; a mere appeal to "states' rights" or even to the Constitution would not be sufficient. William Gilmore Simms and George Fitzhugh were only two of many noted southern writers who marshaled an array of prejudicial arguments to justify slavery. African Americans were, in their view, temperamentally incapable of governing themselves; slavery was a positive good for them, since they were well treated, well fed, and exempt from the cutthroat competition of a rapidly expanding capitalist economy. (What was left unspoken in this formulation was that African Americans thereby could not intrude upon the white economy by taking the place of white workers.) In fact, it was the abolitionists themselves—whom even a northerner like Oliver Wendell Holmes

261

would brand as "ultra melanophiles" (a neo-Greek coinage meaning simply "black-lover")—who were creating all the trouble.

Given the bitterness of the tensions between North and South, it seems incredible that Abraham Lincoln was elected president at all in 1860—incredible until one sees that throughout his career he steered a course on the slavery question that was moderate to the point of virtual capitulation to the South on a variety of issues. Even so, Lincoln failed to win a single vote in ten southern states in the election of 1860.

Both during and after the Civil War, southerners continued to defend the principle of slavery and to lament its fall; but the most unrestrained polemic came from a northerner, John H. Van Evrie, the very title of whose *White Supremacy and Negro Subordination* (1868) tells the whole story. His comment that "the Negro *is* a different being from the white man, and therefore, of necessity, was designed by the Almighty Creator to live a different life" could virtually serve as the synopsis of one of the most peculiar works in all American history, Charles Carroll's *The Negro a Beast* (1900), which establishes (at least to its author's satisfaction) that the theory of evolution is false and that the African American is really not human at all but merely an advanced ape.

Van Evrie's screed seems almost tame in comparison with some of the writing of the later nineteenth and early twentieth centuries. Whether it be the patronizing recollections of Henry Woodfin Grady ("I want no sweeter music than the crooning of my old 'mammy,' now dead and gone to rest") or the purportedly sober economic theorizing of Frederick L. Hoffman ("All the facts . . . prove that the colored population is gradually parting with the virtues and the moderate degree of economic efficiency developed under the regime of slavery") or the unabashed polemicizing of Robert Shufeldt ("the Negro is too grossly and hopelessly ignorant to recognize the ruin his very presence entails among us"), the tirade of antiblack prejudice continued on all sides, with few contradicting voices.

What most agitated racists, especially southerners who now had large numbers of freed African Americans in their midst, was the specter of intermarriage. Senator John T. Morgan bluntly declared: "It is the abhorrence that every white woman in our country feels toward the marriage of her son or daughter with a Negro, that gives the final and conclusive answer to this question." Another politician, the Georgia senator Thomas E. Watson, expressed outrage (emphasized by italics and all-capitals) at the very suggestion that white women accused black men of rape "*TO HIDE THE SHAME OF CONSENT!*" The later nineteenth and early twentieth centuries were of course the heyday of lynching; and yet, contrary to the opinion of Thomas Nelson Page (*The Negro: The Southerner's Problem,*

1904), who maintained that the lynching problem would simply go away if blacks merely stopped assaulting white women, African Americans who were even accused of rape accounted for less than 17 percent of all lynching cases between 1889 and 1941.[1]

The stage was set for Thomas Dixon's *The Clansman* (1905). In a singular case of art having a direct influence on politics and society, there is good reason to believe that this novel, along with its predecessor, *The Leopard's Spots* (1902), and D. W. Griffith's film adaptation of both of them in *The Birth of a Nation* (1914), were instrumental in the revival of the Ku Klux Klan in 1915. The Klan claimed three million members by the 1920s, and their prejudice extended to Jews and Catholics as well.

But as African Americans slowly combated prejudice and strove for social and legal equality, unregenerate racists were not silent. Had one been in the U.S. Senate on February 7, 1930, one could have heard the thundering tones of Alabama's J. Thomas Heflin reciting a letter he had written to a journalist bemoaning the legalization of interracial marriage in New York. The issue exercised Theodore G. Bilbo (governor and later senator from Mississippi) as well; his *Take Your Choice: Separation or Mongrelization* was written in 1947. Laws against interracial marriage remained legal in many states for some years thereafter.

The onset of the Civil Rights movement was rightly perceived by racists as perhaps their last stand against the "social equality" they so feared. Georgia governor George Wallace became notorious in the 1960s for his opposition to desegregation. In some ways more interesting is the obscure journalist Earl Lively, Jr., who deemed the sending of federal troops to quell race riots in Mississippi as *The Invasion of Mississippi* (1963). Lively resurrects old pro-slavery arguments about the benevolence of white slave owners and the evils of abolitionists; but his contemporary targets are the "liberals" and the "Comsymps" (Communist sympathizers) who are luring African Americans into collectivism, lawbreaking, and actual oppression of whites.

No one can deny that African Americans have progressed far along the path of social, political, and legal equality in the 130 years since the freeing of the slaves. Some scholars, like Dinesh D'Souza, can even speak blithely of the "end of racism," but how far we really are from unity in the matter of race can be highlighted by two of the most dramatic racial events of recent years: the Rodney King incident of 1991 and the trial of O. J. Simpson. Are these incidents linked, aside from the fact that they both took place in Los Angeles? What do we make of the fact that an all-white jury acquitted four white police officers of beating and kicking the African American motorist King while he was on the ground, while a largely black jury acquitted Simpson of the murder of his white wife and another white man? The Simpson case in particular exhibited deep fissures along both racial and gender lines. Can we account for its continuing fascination (there are already more than sixty books on the subject) merely by Simpson's celebrity? Is it not the case that whites are the more appalled at Simpson not merely because a preponderance of evidence appears to point to his guilt, but because he was a rare instance of the "good" African American, the black who played by white rules and became a kind of honorary white by his unthreatening persona?

43

Observations . . .

BY BENJAMIN RUSH

Benjamin Rush (1745–1813), physician, chemist, and signer of the Declaration of Independence, was a leading scientific authority in the early days of the American republic. His Medical Inquiries and Observations upon the Diseases of the Mind *(1812) helped to found modern psychiatry. Rush believed in the equality of all human beings, and in the following paper—read at a special meeting of the American Philosophical Society on July 14, 1792, and published in the society's* Transactions *in 1799—he puts forward a theory that black skin color is the result of leprosy. This conclusion, he maintains, would allow whites to regard African Americans with compassion and would also lead scientists to search for a "cure" for black skin color.*

D R. SMITH IN HIS ELEGANT and ingenious Essay upon the Variety of Color and Figure in the Human Species has derived it from four causes, viz. climate, diet, state of society, and diseases. I admit the Doctor's facts and reasonings as far as he has extended them, in the fullest manner. I shall only add to them a few observations which are intended to prove that the color and figure of that part of our fellow creatures who are known by the epithet of negroes, are derived from a modification of that disease, which is known by the name of Leprosy.

Many facts recorded by historians, as well as physicians show the influence of unwholesome diet in having produced the leprosy in the middle and northern parts of Europe in the 13th and 14th centuries. The same cause, combined with greater heat, more savage manners, and bilious fevers, probably produced this disease in the skin among the natives of Africa. But I will not rest the proofs of the color and figure of the negroes being a leprosy simply upon its causes. Other circumstances make it much more probable. I shall briefly enumerate them.

1. The leprosy is accompanied in some instances with a black color of the skin. Of this I have met with a satisfactory proof in Dr. Theiry's account of the diseases of Asturia in Spain. I shall insert a translation of his own words upon this subject. "There are (says this excellent physician) above twenty hospitals for lepers in this province, and I have observed six species of the disorder. One of them, viz. the second, is called the *black albaras* of the Arabians. The skin becomes black, thick and greasy.—There are neither pustules, nor tubercules, nor scales, nor any thing out of the way on the skin. The body is not in the least emaciated. The breathing is a little difficult, and the countenance has some fierceness in it. They exhale perpetually a peculiar and disagreeable smell, which I can compare to nothing but the smell of a mortified limb."[1] This smell mentioned by Dr. Theiry continues with a small modification in the native African to this day.

2. The leprosy is described in the Old Testament and by many ancient writers as imparting a preternatural whiteness to the skin. Persons thus marked have lately received the name of *albanos*. Solitary instances of this disease are often met with upon the Alps, but travellers tell us that it is one of the endemics of Java, Guinea and Panama where it is perpetuated through many generations. Mr. Hawkins in his travels into the interior parts of Africa has described the persons afflicted with this disease in the following words. "They go entirely naked; their skin is white, but has not that animated appearance so perceptible in Europeans. It has a dull deathlike whitish cast that conveys an idea more of sickness, than of health. Their hair is red, or ashes-coloured, yellowish wool, and their eyes are uniformly white, in that part by which others are distinguished into the black, grey and blue eyes. They are set deep in the head, and very commonly squint, for as their skin is deprived of the black mucous web, so their eyes are destitute of that black matter resembling a pigment, so universally found in people of all countries, and so useful in preventing the eye from being injured in cases of exposure to strong light." This artless traveller does not stop here. The idea of this peculiarity in the color and features of these people being a disease, and even its specific nature did not escape him, hence he adds: "These people rendered unfortunate by the prejudices of their countrymen, are born of black parents; they have all the features of other inhabitants, but differ from them only in the above circumstances. The difference of color cannot arise from the intercourse of whites and blacks, for the whites are very rarely among them, and the result of this union is well known to be the yellow color, or mulatto. Many of the natives assert that they are produced by the women being debauched in the woods by the large baboon, ourang-outang, and by that species in particular called the guaga mooroos. No sat-

isfactory discovery has been made to account for such singular, but not infrequent phænomena in the species. It may perhaps be ascribed to *disease,* and that of the *leprous* kind, with more reason than to any other cause that has been yet assigned." Mr. Bernadin concurs with Mr. Hawkins in ascribing this morbid whiteness in the skins of the Africans wholly to the leprosy[2]. However opposed it may be to their morbid blackness, it is in strict conformity to the operations of nature in other diseases. The same state of malignant fever is often marked by opposite colors in the stools, by an opposite temperature of the skin, and by opposite states of the alimentary canal.

The original connection of the black color of the negroes with the leprosy is further suggested by the following fact taken from Bougainville's voyage round the world. He tells us that on an island in the Pacific Ocean which he visited, the inhabitants were composed of negroes and mulattoes. They had thick lips, woolly hair, and were sometimes of a yellowish color. They were short, ugly, ill proportioned, and most of them infected with the leprosy, a circumstance from which he called the island they inhabited, the Isle of Lepers.

3. The leprosy sometimes appears with white and black spots blended together in every part of the body. A picture of a negro man in Virginia in whom this mixture of white and black has taken place, has been happily preserved by Mr. Peale in his museum.

4. The leprosy induces a morbid insensibility in the nerves. In countries where the disease prevails, it is common to say that a person devoid of sensibility, has no more feeling than a leper. This insensibility belongs in a peculiar manner to the negroes. Dr. Moseley says, "they are void of sensibility to a surprizing degree. They sleep sound in every disease, nor does any mental disturbance ever keep them awake. They bear surgical operations much better than white people, and what would be a cause of insupportable pain to a white man, a negro would almost disregard. I have amputated the legs of many negroes, who have held the upper part of the limb themselves."[3] This morbid insensibility in the negroes discovers itself further in the apathy with which they expose themselves to great heat, and the indifference with which they handle coals of fire.

5. Lepers are remarkable for having strong venereal desires. This is universal among the negroes, hence their uncommon fruitfulness when they are not depressed by slavery; but even slavery in its worst state does not always subdue the venereal appetite, for after whole days, spent in hard labor in a hot sun in the West Indies, the black men often walk five or six miles to comply with a venereal assignation.

6. The big lip, and flat nose so universal among the negroes, are symptoms of the leprosy. I have more than once seen them in the Pennsylvania hospital.

7. The woolly heads of the negroes cannot be accounted for from climate, diet, state of society, or bilious diseases, for all those circumstances, when combined have not produced it in the natives of Asia and America who inhabit similar latitudes. Wool is peculiar to the negro. Here the proofs of similarity in the symptoms of leprosy, and in the peculiarities of the negro body appear to fail, but there is a fact in the history of the leprosy which will probably throw some light upon this part of our subject. The Trichoma, or Plica Polonica of the Poles is a symptom of leprosy. This is evident not only from the causes which originally produced it, but from its symptoms as described in a late publication by F. L. De La Fontaine.[4] From this fact it would seem that the leprosy had found its way to the covering of the head, and from the variety of its effects upon the skin, I see no difficulty in admitting that it may as readily have produced wool upon the head of a negro, as matted hair upon the head of the Poles.

But how shall we account for the long duration of this color of the skin through so many generations and even ages?—I answer—1. That the leprosy is the most durable in its descent to posterity, and the most indestructible in its nature of any disease we are acquainted with. In Iceland Dr. Van Troil tells us, it often disappears in the second and third, and appears in the fourth generation.[5] 2dly. No more happens here than what happens to many nations who are distinguished by a peculiarity of figure, in any part of the body. Many of the inhabitants of the highlands of Scotland, have the same red hair, and the same high cheek bones which are ascribed to their ancestors by Tacitus after the invasion of Britain. Even the tumors in the throat in the Cretins who inhabit the Alps, are transmitted from father to son, through a long succession of generations. Madness, and consumption in like manner are hereditary in many families, both of which occupy parts of the body, much more liable to change in successive generations, than the skin.

Should it be objected to this theory that the leprosy is an infectious disorder, but that no infectious quality exists in the skin of the negro, I would reply to such objection by remarking in the first place, that the leprosy has in a great degree ceased to be infectious, more especially from contact, and secondly that there are instances in which something like an infectious quality has appeared in the skin of a negro. A white woman in North Carolina not only acquired a dark color, but several of the features of a negro, by marrying and living with a black husband. A similar instance of a change in the color and features of a woman in Buck's county in Pennsylvania has been observed and from a similar cause. In both these cases, the women bore children by their black husbands.

It is no objection to the theory I have attempted to establish, that the negroes are as healthy, and long lived as the white people. Local diseases of the skin seldom affect the general health of the body, or the duration of human life. Dr. Theiry remarks that the itch, and even the leprosy, did not impair longevity in those people who lived near the sea-shore in the healthy climate of Galicia.

The facts and principles which I have delivered, lead to the following reflections.

1. That all the claims of superiority of the whites over the blacks, on account of their color, are founded alike in ignorance and inhumanity. If the color of the negroes be the effect of a disease, instead of inviting us to tyrannise over them, it should entitle them to a double portion of our humanity, for disease all over the world has always been the signal for immediate and universal compassion.

2. The facts and principles which have been delivered should teach white people the necessity of keeping up that prejudice against such connections with them, as would tend to infect posterity with any portion of their disorder. This may be done upon the ground I have mentioned without offering violence to humanity, or calling in question the sameness of descent, or natural equality of mankind.

3. Is the color of the negroes a disease? Then let science and humanity combine their efforts, and endeavour to discover a remedy for it. Nature has lately unfurled a banner upon this subject. She has begun spontaneous cures of this disease in several black people in this country. In a certain Henry Moss who lately travelled through this city, and was exhibited as a show for money, the cure was nearly complete. The change from black to a natural white flesh color began about five years ago at the ends of his fingers, and has extended gradually over the greatest part of his body. The wool which formerly perforated the cuticle has been changed into hair. No change in the diet, drinks, dress, employments, or situation of this man had taken place previously to this change in his skin. But this fact does not militate against artificial attempts to dislodge the color in negroes, any more than the spontaneous cures of many other diseases militate against the use of medicine in the practice of physic.

To direct our experiments upon this subject I shall throw out the following facts.

1. In Henry Moss the color was first discharged from the skin in those places, on which there was most pressure from cloathing, and most attrition from labor, as on the trunk of his body, and on his fingers. The destruction of the black color was probably occasioned by the absorption of the coloring matter of the rete mucosum, or perhaps of the rete mucosum itself, for pressure and friction it is well known aid the absorbing action of the lymphatics in every part of the body. It is from the latter cause, that the palms of the hands of negro women who spend their lives

at a washing tub, are generally as fair as the palms of the hands in labouring white people.

2. Depletion, whether by bleeding, purging, or abstinence has been often observed to lessen the black color in negroes. The effects of the above remedies in curing the common leprosy, satisfy me that they might be used with advantage in that state of leprosy which I conceive to exist in the skin of the negroes.

3. A similar change in the color of the negroes, though of a more temporary nature, has often been oberved in them from the influence of fear.

4. Dr. Beddoes tells us that he has discharged the color in the black wool of a negro by infusing it in the oxygenated muriatic acid, and lessened it by the same means in the hand of a negro man. The land-cloud of Africa called by the Portuguese Ferrino Mr. Hawkins tells us has a peculiar action upon the negroes in changing the black color of their skins to a dusky grey. Its action is accompanied, he says, with an itching and prickling sensation upon every part of the body which increases with the length of exposure to it so as to be almost intolerable. It is probably air of the carbonic kind, for it uniformly extinguishes fire.

5. A citizen of Philadelphia upon whose veracity I have perfect reliance,[6] assured me that he had once seen the skin of one side of the cheek inclining to the chin, and of part of the hand in a negro boy, changed to a white color by the juice of unripe peaches (of which he ate a large quantity every year) falling, and resting frequently upon those parts of the body.

To encourage attempts to cure this disease of the skin in negroes, let us recollect that by succeeding in them, we shall produce a large portion of happiness in the world. We shall in the first place destroy one of the arguments in favor of enslaving the negroes, for their color has been supposed by the ignorant to mark them as objects of divine judgments, and by the learned to qualify them for labor in hot, and unwholesome climates.

Secondly, We shall add greatly to *their* happiness, for however well they appear to be satisfied with their color, there are many proofs of their preferring that of the white people.

Thirdly, We shall render the belief of the whole human race being descended from one pair, easy, and universal, and thereby not only add weight to the Christian revelation, but remove a material obstacle to the exercise of that universal benevolence which is inculcated by it.

Source:
Benjamin Rush, "Observations Intended to
Favour a Supposition That the Black Color (as
It Is Called) of the Negroes Is Derived from
the Leprosy," *Transactions of the American
Philosophical Society* 4 (1799): 289–97.

44

Letter to Henri Grégoire

BY THOMAS JEFFERSON

More than twenty years after writing his harsh remarks on African Americans in Notes on the State of Virginia *(1785), Jefferson had occasion to modify his views. In the following letter he admits that his opinions had derived from a limited perspective.*

Sir—I HAVE RECEIVED THE FAVOR of your letter of August 17th, and with it the volume you were so kind as to send me on the "Literature of Negroes." Be assured that no person living wishes more sincerely than I do, to see a complete refutation of the doubts I have myself entertained and expressed on the grade of understanding allotted to them by nature, and to find that in this respect they are on a par with ourselves. My doubts were the result of personal observation on the limited sphere of my own State, where the opportunities for the development of their genius were not favorable, and those of exercising it still less so. I expressed them therefore with great hesitation; but whatever be their degree of talent it is no measure of their rights. Because Sir Isaac Newton was superior to others in understanding, he was not therefore lord of the person or property of others. On this subject they are gaining daily in the opinions of nations, and hopeful advances are making towards their re-establishment on an equal footing with the other colors of the human family. I pray you therefore to accept my thanks for the many instances you have enabled me to observe of respectable intelligence in that race of men, which cannot fail to have effect in hastening the day of their relief; and to be assured of the sentiments of high and just esteem and consideration which I tender to yourself with all sincerity.

Source:
Thomas Jefferson, Letter to Henri Grégoire
(February 25, 1809), in *The Writings of
Thomas Jefferson*, edited by Albert Ellery
Bergh (Washington, DC: Thomas Jefferson
Memorial Association, 1907), vol. 12,
pp. 254–55.

45

Slavery in America

BY WILLIAM GILMORE SIMMS

William Gilmore Simms (1806–1870) was a prominent southern writer in the two decades prior to the Civil War. Residing for most of his life in Charleston, he was a voluminous poet and author of novels and romances in the tradition of Sir Walter Scott and James Fenimore Cooper. Simms was a vigorous supporter of the institution of slavery. In Slavery in America—*first published as a review of Harriet Martineau's* Society in America *in the* Southern Literary Messenger *for November 1837 and issued the next year as a pamphlet—Simms maintains that slavery is a positive good for African Americans, since in his view they lack the capacity for self-government.*

O UR GENERAL VIEWS, IN MODERN TIMES, on the subject of slaves and slavery, are distressingly narrow. Our forefathers were less pre-cipitate but, more certain in their philosophy. They did not scruple to go forward, but they were first sure that they were right in doing so. We do not resemble them in this. We are too ready to follow multitudes to do evil. Having commenced our political career by a grand innovation upon the existing condition of things, we would still innovate; and, like any other good principle suffering abuse, the zeal which released us from a foreign yoke would also release us from our allegiance to higher influences than kings. We are losing our veneration fast. We are overthrowing all sacred and hallowing associations and authorities. Marriage is now a bond which we may rend at pleasure. The Sabbath is a wrong and a superstition. Such is the progress of opinion and doctrine among those very classes which show themselves hospitable to Southern slavery. The cry is "On!" and we do not see the beginning of the end. Never was fanaticism more mad than on the subject of slavery; which was a very good thing enough when "England and the North" sold slaves, and the South bought them; and it is a good thing now, if we would only reason rightly, and find out what slavery is. We make no distinction between those restraints which impose labor upon the body—improving its health, bringing out its symmetry and strength, and fulfilling a destiny, which the analogies of all history, not less than the faith which we profess, teach us is the decree of the Universal Parent—and that bondage of the mind, and that denial of its exercise, which are always the aim of tyrannies, and which, as in the case of some of the *unlaboring* people of Europe, must result in the utter enervation, sluggishness, and shame of body and mind alike. Pity it is, that the lousy and lounging lazzaroni of Italy, cannot be made to labor in the fields, under the whip of a severe task-master! They would then be a much freer—certainly a much nobler animal—than we can possibly esteem them now;—and far better had it been for our native North American savage, could he have been reduced to servitude, and, by a labor imposed upon him, within his strength and moderately accommodated to his habits, have been preserved from that painful and eating decay, which has left but a raw and naked skeleton of what was once a numerous and various people—a people, that needed nothing but an Egyptian bondage of four hundred years to have been saved for the future, and lifted into a greatness to which Grecian and Roman celebrity might have been a faint and failing music.

This clamor about liberty and slavery, is, after all, unless we get some certain definitions to begin with, the most arrant nonsense. "License they mean when they cry liberty!"—and we may add, "license they mean when they cry slavery!" The extremes are near kindred, and in all these clamors they are sure to meet. The Russian boor is called a slave, and the German subject of Austria is called a slave, and the Italian is called a slave, and the negro in the Southern States is called a slave,—and yet, how unlike to one another is the condition of all these slaves! The right of ruling themselves, at pleasure, is that which is assumed to be the test of freedom. The native African has that right, and what is the rule of Africa? A sufficient commentary upon it will be found in the naked, unmarked outlines, hanging upon the walls of our houses, and dignified with the title of maps of Africa. Murder awaits the missionary and the traveller who penetrate the country; and civilization seems to be as far remote as ever from their attainment. And how should it be otherwise? And how should they improve, having never taken the first step in such a progress? They cannot improve until they learn to labor,—they will not learn to labor until they become stationary; and the wandering savage has seldom yet become stationary, unless by the coercion of a superior people. But the right to govern themselves requires, first, a capacity for such government. The right can only result from a compliance with the laws of their creation; and the capacity requires long ages of preparation, of great trial, hardship, severe labor and perilous enterprise. The responsibilities and the duties of self-government, demand a wonderful and wide-spread knowledge and practice of morals, before such a capacity can arise; and it would be an awkward and difficult inquiry at this moment to discover any one of the leading nations of the globe where such a capacity exists. *I will not even believe it to exist in the United States, until I see the people willing to tax themselves directly for their own protection. I will not believe it, so long as they need to be deceived by indirect and circuitous taxation, into the expenditures which are necessary for their own good. They are not yet willing to look in the face the cost of their own liberties.* The practice of the English government denies the existence of any such capacity among its people; and France!—what have all her bloody days, through successive ages, effected for her liberties, but cries for more blood, an increasing discontent, and the fever and phrensy which continually defy and defeat her own laws, in the appetite which calls for fresher uproar? Perhaps, the very homogeneousness of a people is adverse to the most wholesome forms of liberty. It may make of a selfish people (which has succeeded by the aid of other nations in the attainment of a certain degree of moral enlargement) a *successful* people—in the merely worldly sense of the word—but it can never make them, morally, a great one. For that most perfect form of liberty, which prompts us to love justice for its own sake, it requires strange admixtures of differing races—the combination and comparison of the knowledge which each has separately arrived at—the long trials and conflicts which precede their coming together; and their perfect union in the end, after that subjection on the part of the inferior class, which compels them to a knowledge of what is possessed by the superior. This was the history of the Saxon boors under the Norman conquest—a combination, which has resulted in the production of one of the most perfect specimens of physical organization and moral susceptibilities, which the world has ever known. And where this amalgamation cannot be effected—as in the case of the Israelites—who are too homogeneous for commixture or even communion with other people, —the slave, in the progress of events, acquires the knowledge of the master. When Moses could emulate the Egyptian priesthood, he was able to embody and to represent his people, and to lead them forth from bondage; for then they had acquired all the knowledge which was possessed by the Egyptian; and as they could derive nothing further from the instruction of their masters, the period had naturally arrived for their emancipation. Upon this susceptibility of acquisition, on the part of the slave, depends the whole secret of his release from bondage. It is his mental and moral inferiority which has enslaved, or subjected him to a superior. It is his rise, morally and intellectually, into the same form with his master, which alone can emancipate him. It is possible that a time will come, when, taught by our schools, and made strong by our training, the negroes of the Southern States may arrive at freedom; then, at least, his condition may be such as would entitle him to go forth out of bondage. It may be, when that time comes, that, like Pharaoh, we too shall prove unwilling to give up our bondmen. But that that time is very far remote, is sufficiently evident from the condition of the free negroes in the Northern States, and elsewhere—the British West Indies, for example. There, in both regions, without restraints of any kind, they rather decline to a worse brutality, with every increase of privilege. In the former region, after a fifty years' enjoyment of their own rule, they have yet founded no city to themselves, raised no community of their own; but are willing to remain the boot-cleaners and the bottle-washers of the whites, in a state of degrading inferiority, which they are too obtuse to feel; and are only made conscious of their degradation, by the occasional kicks and cuffs which they are made to endure, at the humor of the whites, and without any prospect of redress. They have not that moral courage—the true source of independence—which would prompt them, like the poor white pioneer, to sally forth into the wilderness, hew out their homes, and earn their rights by a compliance with their duties. They feel their inferiority to the whites, even when nominally freemen; and sink into the condition of serviles, in fact, if not in name, in compliance with their natural dependence, and unquestionable moral deficiencies. What they show themselves now, with every example around them stimulating them to freedom and ambition, taken in connection with what they have been shown to be from the earliest known periods of history, ought to be conclusive, with every person of common sense, not only that they have no capacity for an individual independent existence, but that they were always designed for a subordinate one. And why should we assume for the Deity, that he has set out with a design, in the creation and government of men, differing from those laws which he has prescribed in the case of all his other creatures. Why should there not be as many races of men, differing in degree, in strength, capacity, art, endowment, as we find them differing in shape, stature, color, organization? Why, indeed, should there not be differing organizations among men, which shall distinctly shadow forth the several duties, and the assigned stations, which they are to fulfil and occupy in life. This would seem to be a necessity, analogous to what is apparent every where in all the other works of God's creation. Nay, is it not absolutely consistent with all that we learn from history of the uses of men and nations? As we note their progress, we detect their mission; and, this done, they themselves disappear. The African seems to have his mission. He does *not* disappear, but he still remains a slave or a savage! I do not believe that he ever will be other than a slave, or that he was made to be otherwise; but that he is designed as an implement in the hands of civilization always. You may eradicate him from place, but not from life. If he ceases to exist in Virginia or Carolina, Georgia, or Louisiana, it is only because he is doing the allotted tasks of his master in regions farther South. I look upon Negro Slavery as the destined agent for the civilization of all the states of Mexico, and all the American states beyond.

The circumstance which, more than anything beside—apart from his original genius—prepared the Anglo-American for the comparative condition of freedom which he enjoys, was the desperate adventure, the trying necessity, and the thousand toils through which he had to go, in contending with the sterility of an unfriendly soil, and the continual and thwarting hostility of surrounding and savage men. The very sterility of New-England, by imposing upon all classes the necessity of labor, gave strength and energy to her sons, and stability to her institutions. Her severe austerity arose even more from her own toils and trials, than from her puritan ancestry; and, bating the bigotry and miserable exclusiveness which, among the vast majority of her people, can find no greatness and little worth beyond her own borders, she confessedly stands among the most successful, in worldly affairs, of any people on the face of the earth. The fertility of the soil in the South, by readily yielding to the hands of Labor, is, without any paradox, the true source of our enervation, and of the doubtful prosperity of our country—as a country merely. Individuals are successful and prosperous, but not the face of the country; and however much this may be the subject of regret on the one hand, like the trumpet of Miss Martineau, it is not without its advantages. It results, we may state, in individuality of character among its people; who never, in consequence, devolve upon societies, combinations, or their neighbors, their several duties of charity, hospitality and friendship; and who sufficiently esteem their own morals, their sense of honor and humanity, to think they can do justice to the claims of their dependants, without the interference or tuition of any gratuitous philanthropy.

The chapter which Miss Martineau devotes to the "Morals of Slavery," should rather be styled the morals of the community. The excesses to which she refers, and in some respects particularizes, are excesses not confined to the slave States, and which do not, in any State, result from slavery. We contend for the morality of slavery among us, as we assert that the institution has wrought, and still continues to work, the improvement of the negro himself; and we confidently challenge a comparison between the slave of Carolina, and the natives of the region from which his ancestors have been brought. No other comparison, with any other people, can properly be made. We challenge comparison between the negro slave in the streets of Charleston, and the negro freeman—so called—in the streets of New-York. Compare either of these with the native Indian, and, so far as the civilized arts, and the ideas of civilization are involved in the comparison, you will find that the negro who has been taught by the white man, is always deferred to, in matters of counsel, by his own Indian master. The negro slave of a Muscoghee warrior, to my knowledge, in frequent instances, is commonly his best counsellor; and the primitive savage follows the direction of him, who, having been forced to obey the laws of his creation, has become wiser, in consequence, than the creature who wilfully refuses. This subjection to the superior mind is the process through which every inferior nation has gone, and the price which the inferior people must always pay, for that knowledge of, and compliance with, their duties, which alone can bring them to the possession of their rights, and to the due attainment of their liberties—these liberties always growing in value and number with the improving tastes and capacities for their appreciation. Show me any people, which, complying with this inevitable condition, has not improved! Show me one, refusing to comply, which has not perished! Look at the history of man throughout the world, with the eye of a calm, unselfish, deliberate judgment, and say if this be not so. Regard the slave of Carolina, with a proper reference to the condition of the cannibal African from whom he has been rescued, and say if his bondage has not increased his value to himself, not less than to his master. We contend that it found him a cannibal, destined in his own country to eat his fellow, or to be eaten by him; —that it brought him to a land in which he suffers no risk of life or limb, other than that to which his owner is equally subjected; —that it increases his fecundity infinitely beyond that of the people from whom he has been taken—that it increases his health and strength, improves his physical symmetry and animal organization—that it elevates his mind and morals—that it extends his term of life—that it gives him better and more certain food, better clothing, and more kind and valuable attendance when he is sick. These clearly establish the morality of the slave institutions in the South; and, though they may not prove them to be as perfect as they may be made, as clearly show their propriety and the necessity of preserving them. Indeed, the slaveholders of the South, having the moral and physical guardianship of an ignorant and irresponsible people under their control, are the great moral conservators, in one powerful interest, of the entire world. Assuming slavery to be a denial of justice to the negro, there is no sort of propriety in the application of the name of slave to the servile of the South. He is under no despotic power. There are laws which protect him, *in his place,* as inflexible as those which his proprietor is required to obey, *in his place. Providence has placed him in our hands, for his good, and has paid us from his labor for our guardianship.* The question with us is, simply, as to the manner in which we have fulfilled our trust. How have we employed the talents which were given us—how have we discharged the duties of our guardianship? What is the condition of the dependant? Have we been careful to graduate his labors to his capacities? Have we bestowed upon him a fair proportion of the fruits of his industry? Have we sought to improve his mind in correspondence with his condition? Have we raised his condition to the level of his improved mind? Have we duly taught him his moral duties—his duties to God and man? And have we, in obedience to a scrutinizing conscience, been careful to punish only in compliance with his deserts, and never in brutality or wantonness? These are the grand questions for the tribunal of each slaveholder's conscience. He must answer them to his God. These are the only questions, and they apply equally to all his other relations in society. Let him carefully put them to himself, and shape his conduct, as a just man, in compliance with what he should consider a sacred duty, undertaken to God and man alike.

Source:
William Gilmore Simms, *Slavery in America*
(Richmond, VA: Thomas W. White, 1838);
reprinted as "The Morals of Slavery" in *The
Pro-Slavery Argument* (Charleston, SC:
Walker, Richards & Co., 1852), pp. 264–75.

46

Sociology for the South

BY GEORGE FITZHUGH

The Virginia lawyer George Fitzhugh (1806–1881) was the author of numerous pro-slavery treatises, including Slavery Justified *(1850),* What Shall Be Done with the Free Negroes *(1851), and* Cannibals All! or, Slaves Without Masters *(1857). In* Sociology for the South *(1854) Fitzhugh asserts that slavery in America is less harsh than slavery elsewhere and that rabid abolitionists are actually hindering the gradual amelioration of the slaves' condition.*

W E HAVE ALREADY STATED that we should not attempt to introduce any new theories of government and of society, but merely try to justify old ones, so far as we could deduce such theories from ancient and almost universal practices. Now it has been the practice in all countries and in all ages, in some degree, to accommodate the amount and character of government control to the wants, intelligence, and moral capacities of the nations or individuals to be governed. A highly moral and intellectual people, like the free citizens of ancient Athens, are best governed by a democracy. For a less moral and intellectual one, a limited and constitutional monarchy will answer. For a people either very ignorant or very wicked, nothing short of military despotism will suffice. So among individuals, the most moral and well-informed members of society require no other government than law. They are capable of reading and understanding the law, and have sufficient self-control and virtuous disposition to obey it. Children cannot be governed by mere law; first, because they do not understand it, and secondly, because they are so much under the influence of impulse, passion and appetite, that they want suf-

ficient self-control to be deterred or governed by the distant and doubtful penalties of the law. They must be constantly controlled by parents or
guardians, whose will and orders shall stand in the place of law for them.
Very wicked men must be put into penitentiaries; lunatics into asylums,
and the most wild of them into strait-jackets, just as the most wicked of
the sane are manacled with irons; and idiots must have committees to
govern and take care of them. Now, it is clear the Athenian democracy
would not suit a negro nation, nor will the government of mere law suffice for the individual negro. He is but a grown up child, and must be
governed as a child, not as a lunatic or criminal. The master occupies towards him the place of parent or guardian. We shall not dwell on this
view, for no one will differ with us who thinks as we do of the negro's capacity, and we might argue till dooms-day, in vain, with those who have
a high opinion of the negro's moral and intellectual capacity.

Secondly. The negro is improvident; will not lay up in summer for the
wants of winter; will not accumulate in youth for the exigencies of age.
He would become an insufferable burden to society. Society has the right
to prevent this, and can only do so by subjecting him to domestic slavery. In the last place, the negro race is inferior to the white race, and living in their midst, they would be far outstripped or outwitted in the
chase of free competition. Gradual but certain extermination would be
their fate. We presume the maddest abolitionist does not think the negro's providence of habits and money-making capacity at all to compare
to those of the whites. This defect of character would alone justify enslaving him, if he is to remain here. In Africa or the West Indies, he
would become idolatrous, savage and cannibal, or be devoured by savages and cannibals. At the North he would freeze or starve.

We would remind those who deprecate and sympathize with negro
slavery, that his slavery here relieves him from a far more cruel slavery in
Africa, or from idolatry and cannibalism, and every brutal vice and crime
that can disgrace humanity; and that it christianizes, protects, supports
and civilizes him; that it governs him far better than free laborers at the
North are governed. There, wife-murder has become a mere holiday pas-
time; and where so many wives are murdered, almost all must be brutally
treated. Nay, more: men who kill their wives or treat them brutally, must
be ready for all kinds of crime, and the calendar of crime at the North
proves the inference to be correct. Negroes never kill their wives. If it be
objected that legally they have no wives, then we reply, that in an experience of more than forty years, we never yet heard of a negro man
killing a negro woman. Our negroes are not only better off as to physical comfort than free laborers, but their moral condition is better.

But abolish negro slavery, and how much of slavery still remains. Soldiers and sailors in Europe enlist for life; here, for five years. Are they not slaves who have not only sold their liberties, but their lives also? And they are worse treated than domestic slaves. No domestic affection and self-interest extend their ægis over them. No kind mistress, like a guardian angel, provides for them in health, tends them in sickness, and soothes their dying pillow. Wellington at Waterloo was a slave. He was bound to obey, or would, like admiral Byng, have been shot for gross misconduct, and might not, like a common laborer, quit his work at any moment. He had sold his liberty, and might not resign without the consent of his master, the king. The common laborer may quit his work at any moment, whatever his contract; declare that liberty is an alienable right, and leave his employer to redress by a useless suit for damages. The highest and most honorable position on earth was that of the slave Wellington; the lowest, that of the free man who cleaned his boots and fed his hounds. The African cannibal, caught, christianized and enslaved, is as much elevated by slavery as was Wellington. The kind of slavery is adapted to the men enslaved. Wives and apprentices are slaves; not in theory only, but often in fact. Children are slaves to their parents, guardians and teachers. Imprisoned culprits are slaves. Lunatics and idiots are slaves also. Three-fourths of free society are slaves, no better treated, when their wants and capacities are estimated, than Negro slaves. The masters in free society, or slave society, if they perform properly their duties, have more cares and less liberty than the slaves themselves. "In the sweat of thy face shalt thou earn thy bread!" made all men slaves, and such all *good men* continue to be.

Negro slavery would be changed immediately to some form of peonage, serfdom or villienage, if the negroes were sufficiently intelligent and provident to manage a farm. No one would have the labor and trouble of management, if his negroes would pay in hires and rents one-half what free tenants pay in rent in Europe. Every negro in the South would be soon liberated, if he would take liberty on the terms that white tenants hold it. The fact that he cannot enjoy liberty on such terms, seems conclusive that he is only fit to be a slave.

But for the assaults of the abolitionists, much would have been done ere this to regulate and improve Southern slavery. Our negro mechanics do not work so hard, have many more privileges and holidays, and are better fed and clothed than field hands, and are yet more valuable to their masters. The slaves of the South are cheated of their rights by the purchase of Northern manufactures which they could produce. Besides, if we would employ our slaves in the coarser processes of the mechanic arts and manufacturers, such as brick making, getting and hewing timber for ships and houses, iron mining and smelting, coal mining, grading railroads and plank roads, in the manufacture of cotton, tobacco, &c., we would find a vent in new employments for their increase, more humane and more profitable than the vent afforded by new states and territories. The nice and finishing processes of manufactures and mechanics should be reserved for the whites, who only are fitted for them, and thus, by diversifying pursuits and cutting off dependence on the North, we might benefit and advance the interests of our whole population. Exclusive agriculture has depressed and impoverished the South. We will not here dilate on this topic, because we intend to make it the subject of a separate essay. Free trade doctrines, not slavery, have made the South agricultural and dependent, given her a sparse and ignorant population, ruined her cities, and expelled her people.

Would the abolitionists approve of a system of society that set white children free, and remitted them at the age of fourteen, males and females, to all the rights, both as to person and property, which belong to adults? Would it be criminal or praiseworthy to do so? Criminal, of course. Now, are the average of negroes equal in formation, in native intelligence, in prudence or providence, to well-informed white children of fourteen? We who have lived with them for forty years, think not. The competition of the world would be too much for the children. They would be cheated out of their property and debased in their morals. Yet they would meet every where with sympathizing friends of their own color, ready to aid, advise and assist them. The negro would be exposed to the same competition and greater temptations, with no greater ability to contend with them, with these additional difficulties. He would be welcome nowhere; meet with thousands of enemies and no friends. If he went North, the white laborers would kick him and cuff him, and drive him out of employment. If he went to Africa, the savages would cook him and eat him. If he went to the West Indies, they would not let him in, or if they did, they would soon make of him a savage and idolater.

We have a further question to ask. If it be right and incumbent to subject children to the authority of parents and guardians, and idiots and lunatics to committees, would it not be equally right and incumbent to give the free negroes masters, until at least they arrive at years of discretion, which very few ever did or will attain? What is the difference between the authority of a parent and of a master? Neither pay wages, and each is entitled to the services of those subject to him. The father may not sell his child forever, but may hire him out till he is twenty-one. The free negro's master may also be restrained from selling. Let him stand *in loco parentis,* and call him papa instead of master. Look closely into slavery, and you will see nothing so hideous in it; or if you do, you will find plenty of it at home in its most hideous form. . . .

We need never have white slaves in the South, because we have black ones. Our citizens, like those of Rome and Athens, are a privileged class. We should train and educate them to deserve the privileges and to perform the duties which society confers on them. Instead of, by a low demagoguism, depressing their self-respect by discourses on the equality of man, we had better excite their pride by reminding them that they do not fulfil the menial offices which white men do in other countries. Society does not feel the burden of providing for the few helpless paupers in the South. And we should recollect that here we have but half the people to educate, for half are negroes; whilst at the North they profess to educate all. It is in our power to spike this last gun of the abolitionists. We should educate all the poor. The abolitionists say that it is one of the necessary consequences of slavery that the poor are neglected. It was not so in Athens, and in Rome, and should not be so in the South. If we had less trade with and less dependence on the North, all our poor might be profitably and honorably employed in trades, professions and manufactures. Then we should have a rich and denser population. Yet we but marshal her in the way that she was going. The South is already aware of the necessity of a new policy, and has begun to act on it. Every day more and more is done for education, the mechanic arts, manufactures and internal improvements. We will soon be independent of the North.

We deem this peculiar question of negro slavery of very little importance. The issue is made throughout the world on the general subject of slavery in the abstract. The argument has commenced. One set of ideas will govern and control after awhile the civilized world. Slavery will every where be abolished, or every where be re-instituted. We think the opponents of practical, existing slavery, are stopped by their own admission; nay, that unconsciously, as socialists, they are the defenders and propagandists of slavery, and have furnished the only sound arguments on which its defence and justification can be rested. We have introduced the subject of negro slavery to afford us a better opportunity to disclaim the purpose of reducing the white man any where to the condition of negro slaves here. It would be very unwise and unscientific to govern white men as you would negroes. Every shade and variety of slavery has existed in the world. In some cases there has been much of legal regulation, much restraint of the master's authority; in others, none at all. The character of slavery necessary to protect the whites in Europe should be much milder than negro slavery, for slavery is only needed to protect the white man, whilst it is more necessary for the government of the negro even than for his protection. But even negro slavery should not be outlawed. We might and should have laws in Virginia, as in Louisiana, to make the master subject to presentment by the grand jury and to punishment, for any inhuman or improper treatment or neglect of his slave.

We abhor the doctrine of the "Types of Mankind;" first, because it is at war with scripture, which teaches us that the whole human race is descended from a common parentage; and, secondly, because it encourages and incites brutal masters to treat negroes, not as weak, ignorant and dependent brethren, but as wicked beasts, without the pale of humanity. This Southerner is the negro's friend, his only friend. Let no intermeddling abolitionist, no refined philosophy, dissolve this friendship.

Source:
George Fitzhugh, *Sociology for the South; or,
The Failure of Free Society* (Richmond, VA:
A. Morris, 1854), pp. 82–89, 93–95.

$\widehat{}$ *47* $\widehat{}$

Fourth Lincoln-Douglas Debate

BY ABRAHAM LINCOLN

Abraham Lincoln (1809–1865) was the sixteenth president of the United States (1861–65). His views on slavery have understandably been minutely analyzed, as he was the central figure in its abolition in this country. As early as 1837, when he was serving in the Illinois state legislature, he asserted that slavery is "founded in both injustice and bad policy," but he maintained his distance from abolitionists. This moderate course persisted throughout his political career. In 1849, as a U.S. Representative, he proposed the abolition of slavery in Washington, D.C., but with several modifying conditions. In 1856 he joined the newly formed Republican Party and quickly rose to prominence in it. He won the Republican nomination for the U.S. Senate in 1858, and in that year he engaged in seven celebrated debates with his Democratic rival, Stephen Douglas. In the following excerpt from the fourth of these debates, Lincoln makes clear his stance: he does not believe in social equality between African Americans and whites and maintains that the white race is superior; he also asserts that slavery should be kept out of any states that subsequently join the nation but that it remain "forever" in the southern states.

As president, Lincoln would adhere to all these policies except the last. He continued to seek accommodation with the South until war became inevitable. Lincoln is now celebrated for the issuance of the Emancipation Proclamation on January 1, 1863; but in July 1862, Congress had already passed most of the measures in the proclamation, and in any event the proclamation was largely empty of practical effect, since its decree freeing African-American slaves applied only to those "rebellious" southern states where it could not be enforced.

Lincoln was reelected president in the wartime election of 1864. Confederate general Robert E. Lee surrendered on April 9, 1865, ending the Civil War. On April 14, Lincoln was shot in Washington by John Wilkes Booth, dying the next day. The Thirteenth Amendment, declaring slavery illegal, was ratified on December 18, 1865, under the presidency of Lincoln's successor, Andrew Johnson.

WHILE I WAS AT THE HOTEL TO-DAY an elderly gentleman called upon me to know whether I was really in favor of producing a perfect equality between the negroes and white people. [Great laughter.] While I had not proposed to myself on this occasion to say much on that subject, yet as the question was asked me I thought I would occupy perhaps five minutes in saying something in regard to it. I will say then that I am not, nor ever have been in favor of bringing about in any way the social and political equality of the white and black races, [applause]—that I am not nor ever have been in favor of making voters or jurors of negroes, nor of qualifying them to hold office, nor to intermarry with white people; and I will say in addition to this that there is a physical difference between the white and black races which I believe will for ever forbid the two races living together on terms of social and political equality. And inasmuch as they cannot so live, while they do remain together there must be the position of superior and inferior, and I as much as any other man am in favor of having the superior position assigned to the white race. I say upon this occasion I do not perceive that because the white man is to have the superior position the negro should be denied everything. I do not understand that because I do not want a negro woman for a slave I must necessarily want her for a wife. [Cheers and laughter.] My understanding is that I can just let her alone. I am now in my fiftieth year, and I certainly never have had a black woman for either a slave or a wife. So it seems to me quite possible for us to get along without making either slaves or wives of negroes. I will add to this that I have never seen to my knowledge a man, woman or child who was in favor of producing a perfect equality, social and political, between negroes and white men. I recollect of but one distinguished instance that I ever heard of so frequently as to be entirely satisfied of its correctness—and that is the case of Judge Douglas' old friend Col. Richard M. Johnson. [Laughter.] I will also add to the remarks I have made, (for I am not going to enter at large upon this subject,) that I have never had the least apprehension that I or my friends would marry negroes if there was no law to keep them from it, [laughter] but as Judge Douglas and his friends seem to be in great apprehension that they might, if there were no law to keep them from it, [roars of laughter] I give him the most solemn pledge that I will to the very last stand by the law of this State, which forbids the marrying of white people with negroes. [Continued laughter and applause.] I will add one further word, which is this, that I do not understand there is any place where an alteration of the social and political relations of the negro and the white man can be made except in the State Legislature—not in the Congress of the United States—and as I do not really apprehend the approach of any such thing myself, and as Judge Douglas seems to be in constant horror that some such danger is rapidly approaching, I propose as the best means to prevent it that the Judge be kept at home and placed in the State Legislature to fight the measure. [Uproarious laughter and applause.] I do not propose dwelling longer at this time on this subject. . . .

Judge Douglas has said to you that he has not been able to get from me an answer to the question whether I am in favor of negro-citizenship. So far as I know, the Judge never asked me the question before. [Applause.] He shall have no occasion to ever ask it again, for I tell him very frankly that I am not in favor of negro citizenship. [Renewed applause.] This furnishes me an occasion for saying a few words upon the subject. I mentioned in a certain speech of mine which has been printed, that the Supreme Court had decided that a negro could not possibly be made a citizen, and without saying what was my ground of complaint in regard to that, or whether I had any ground of complaint, Judge Douglas has from that thing manufactured nearly every thing that he ever says about my disposition to produce an equality between the negroes and the white people. [Laughter and applause.] If any one will read my speech, he will find I mentioned that as one of the points decided in the course of the Supreme Court opinions, but I did not state what objection I had to it. But Judge Douglas tells the people what my objection was when I did not tell them myself. [Loud applause and laughter.] Now my opinion is that the different States have the power to make a negro a citizen under the Constitution of the United States if they choose. The Dred Scott decision decides that they have not that power. If the State of Illinois had that power I should be opposed to the exercise of it. [Cries of "good," "good," and applause.] That is all I have to say about it.

Judge Douglas has told me that he heard my speeches north and my speeches south—that he had heard me at Ottawa and at Freeport in the north, and recently at Jonesboro in the south, and there was a very different cast of sentiment in the speeches made at the different points. I will not charge upon Judge Douglas that he wilfully misrepresents me, but I call upon every fair-minded man to take these speeches and read them, *and I dare him to point out any difference between my printed speeches north and south.* [Great cheering.] While I am here perhaps I ought to say a word, if I have the time, in regard to the latter portion of the Judge's speech, which was a sort of declamation in reference to my having said I entertained the belief that this government would not endure, half slave and half free. I have said so and I did not say it without what seemed to me to be good reasons. It perhaps would require more time than I have now to set forth these reasons in detail; but let me ask you a few questions. Have we ever had any peace on this slavery question? [No, no.] When are we to have peace upon it if it is kept in the position it now occupies? [Never.] How are we ever to have peace upon it? That is an important question. To be sure if we will all stop and allow Judge Douglas and his friends to march on in their present career until they plant the institution all over the nation, here and wherever else our flag waves, and we acquiesce in it, there will be peace. But let me ask Judge Douglas how he is going to get the people to do that? [Applause.] They have been wrangling over this question for at least forty years. This was the cause of the agitation resulting in the Missouri Compromise— this produced the troubles at the annexation of Texas, in the acquisition of the territory acquired in the Mexican war. Again, this was the trouble which was quieted by the Compromise of 1850, when it was settled *"forever,"* as both the great political parties declared in their National Conventions. That "forever" turned out to be just four years, [laughter] *when Judge Douglas himself re-opened it.* [Immense applause, cries of "hit him again," &c.] When is it likely to come to an end? He introduced the Nebraska bill in 1854 to put *another end* to the slavery agitation. He promised that it would finish it all up immediately, and he has never made a speech since until he got into a quarrel with the President about the Lecompton Constitution, in which he has not declared that we are *just at the end* of the slavery agitation. But in one speech, I think last winter, he did say that he didn't quite see when the end of the slavery agitation would come. [Laughter and cheers.] Now he tells us again that it is all over, and the people of Kansas have voted down the Lecompton Constitution. How is it over? That was only one of the attempts at putting an end to the slavery agitation—one of these "final settlements." [Renewed laughter.] Is Kansas in the Union? Has she formed a Constitution that she is likely to come in under? Is not the slavery agitation still an open question in that Territory? Has the voting down of that Constitution put an end to all the trouble? Is that more likely to settle it than every one of these previous attempts to settle the slavery agitation? [Cries of "No," "No."] Now, at this day in the history of the world we can no more foretell where the end of this slavery agitation will be than we can see the end of the world itself. The Nebraska-Kansas bill was introduced four years and a half ago, and if the agitation is ever to come to an end, we may say we are four years and a half nearer the end. So, too, we can say we are four years and a half nearer the end of the world; and we can just as clearly see the end of the world as we can see the end of this agitation. [Applause.] The Kansas settlement did not conclude it. If Kansas should sink to-day, and leave a great vacant space in the earth's surface, this vexed question would still be among us. I say, then, there is no way of putting an end to the slavery agitation amongst us but to put it back upon the basis where our fathers placed it, [applause] no way but to keep it out of our new Territories [renewed applause]—to restrict it forever to the old States where it now exists. [Tremendous and prolonged cheering; cries of "That's the doctrine," "Good," "Good," &c.] Then the public mind *will* rest in the belief that it is in the course of ultimate extinction. That is one way of putting an end to the slavery agitation. [Applause.]

Source:
Abraham Lincoln, "Fourth Lincoln-Douglas
Debate, Charleston, Illinois" (September 18,
1858), in *Speeches and Writings 1832–1858*
(New York: Library of America, 1989),
pp. 636–37, 675–77.

48

White Supremacy and Negro Subordination

BY J. H. VAN EVRIE

John H. Van Evrie (1814–1896) was a physician in New York and part owner of a firm that published a magazine, The Old Guard *(1862–70), defending the South and the institution of slavery. He wrote* Negroes and Negro "Slavery" *(1853) and* Subgenation: The Theory of the Normal Relation of the Races *(1864). In* White Supremacy and Negro Subordination *(1868), his most unrestrained treatise, Van Evrie appeals to religion in proclaiming the radical difference, and inferiority, of African Americans to whites.*

THE NEGRO *IS* A DIFFERENT BEING from the white man, and therefore, of necessity, was designed by the Almighty Creator to live a different life, and to disregard this—to shut our eyes and blindly beat our brains against the decree—the eternal purpose of God himself, and force this negro to live *our life,* necessarily destroys him, for surely human forces can not dominate or set aside those of Omnipotence. Nor is the negro the sole sufferer from this blind impiety, this audacious attempt to disregard the distinctions and to depart from the purposes of the Almighty Creator. The large "free" negro populations of Maryland and Virginia are the great drawbacks on their prosperity, and if the hundred thousand or so of these people were supplanted by the same number of white laborers, or, indeed, the same number of "slave" negroes, a wide and beneficent change would rapidly follow. Furthermore, they are vicious as well as idle and non-productive, and every one of them a disturbing force—a dangerous element—which, in conjunction with those hideous wretches maddened with a monstrous theory like those miscreants at Harper's Ferry, are always liable to be made instruments of fearful mischief. The consequences of the fifty thousand "free" negroes in juxtaposition with the three millions of white people in New York are barely perceptible, but as scarcely one in fifty of these people are engaged in productive labor, they are a considerable burden upon the laboring and producing citizens. True, they do not see it or feel it—and multitudes of honest and laborious citizens in the rural districts are profoundly interested in the "cause of freedom," while thus contributing a certain portion of each day's labor for the support of some fifty thousand nonproductive negroes. Again, in the cities and larger towns, the vices and immoralities of the whites have an extended association with this free negro element.

The negro in his normal condition has attractive qualities. He is not degraded, for none of God's creatures are naturally degraded, and his fidelity and affection for his master and his master's family, sometimes reach a dignity that would reflect honor on the white man. Nor is there any prejudice or hatred between the races when they are in true relation to each other. One may travel for months, perhaps years, in the South, and never witness a collision or the slightest disturbance between them; but, on the contrary, they will often see a kindly feeling displayed even when the negro is not owned by those who exhibit it. The negro is in a social position and relation that accords with his nature, his wants, the purposes that God has adapted him to, in short, lives out his own life, and therefore, all that is good, that is healthy in his moral nature as in his physical nature, is duly manifested. But at the North, where he is thrust from his natural sphere and forced to live out the life of a different being, he exhibits the same moral defects that he does in his physical nature. He is a social monstrosity—and though his subordinate nature renders him less likely to commit great crimes than the superior white man, the tendencies to petty immoralities are almost universal. Some, indeed, bred up in well-regulated families, and others who are nearly white, escape the general demoralization of this people, but the instances are probably few—the moral defects march hand in hand with the physical, and, as they tend continually to disease and death, so, too, do they tend to universal immorality. And as it would be strange, indeed, if Providence visited the sins of the dominant race on these poor creatures alone, they are extensively associated, as has been observed, with the vices of the whites. With feeble perceptions of moral obligations, with strong tendencies to animal indulgences of every kind, and an utter repugnance to productive labor, they congregate in the cities; and the social exclusion to which they are exposed, as well as the absence of moral sentiment among them, renders them, to a wide extent, the instruments of the vices and corruptions of the whites.

Thus, it is not alone the negro's non-productiveness—the burden, the absolute tax imposed on the laboring classes—but the demoralization of this abnormal element, of this social monstrosity, that is inflicted on society as the legitimate and unavoidable punishment for having placed the negro in an abnormal condition. God created him a negro—a different and inferior being, and, therefore, designed him for a different and inferior social position. Society, or the State, has ignored the work of the Almighty, and declared that he should occupy the same position and live out the life of the white man; and the result is, the laboring and producing classes are burdened with his support, and society, to a certain extent, poisoned by his presence. To the negro it is death—necessarily death, as it always must be to all creatures, human or animal, forbidden to live the life God has blessed them with, or to live in accord with the conditions He has imposed on them. The ultimate doom of the poor creatures, therefore, is only a question of time. The great "anti-slavery" imposture of our times, which has rested on popular ignorance of a few fundamental truths in ethnology and political economy, has at last culminated, and few, if any more of these people will ever be turned loose, or manumitted as it has been called. Whether they will be restored to society and to usefulness at the North may be doubted, but necessity as well as humanity will doubtless prompt such a policy at the South; but, in any event, it is absolutely certain that, as a class, they will become extinct, and a hundred years hence it is reasonable to suppose that no such social monstrosity as a "free negro" will be found in America.

But another and far more embarrassing question is presented by free negroism outside of the American Union, and that now confronts us in Cuba, Jamaica, Hayti, Mexico, and on the whole line of our Southern border. This is the danger, the sole danger of the so-called slavery question, and it involves possibilities that are fearful to think of, though scarcely dangerous at all if our own people were truly enlightened on the general subject.

In a previous chapter it has been shown how climatic and industrial laws govern our mixed populations, and, without the slightest interference of government, the negro element goes just where its own welfare as well as that of the white citizenship and the general interests of civilization demand its presence. This law of industrial adaptation has carried it from northern ports into the Central States, from the latter to the

Border States, and is now, with even increased activity, carrying it from Virginia, etc., into the Gulf States, and thus permitted to go on, with all obstacles removed from the path of its progress, a time will come when the negro population of the New World will be within the centre of existence where it was created, and where the Almighty Creator has provided for its well-being. A sectional party in the North, taking advantage of popular ignorance, and actually enacting a law prohibiting it to exist anywhere where white labor is best adapted, could not by that sole act do any practical injury to the social order of the South. Such an act would indeed be a violation of the spirit of the federal compact, and, as an adjunct of the hostile policy of the foreign enemies of republican institutions, its moral bearings would be full of mischief; but, disconnected or disunited what is called slavery rather involves pecuniary considerations than a question of races.

The social condition, therefore, or so-called slavery may be overthrown any day in Brazil or Cuba, for, resting on a basis of property instead of the distinctions of nature common with us, there is no permanent security for the social safety, and in view of the policy of England on this subject and its influence in Brazil, we should not be surprised at any moment to hear that a revolution had broken out, and that slavery was overthrown in every portion of the Brazilian empire. This result which may happen at any moment, and which circumstances alone may protract for an indefinite period, would seem to be ultimately inevitable—for the white element is every day becoming more deteriorated and feeble; and, without the mental and moral power, without the healthy instinct of the race to buoy it up amid such corrupt and corrupting tendencies, without that high sense of manhood which makes the American "slaveholder" the perfect type and complete embodiment of the strength and power of the great master race of mankind, without, in short, the natural superiority of the white man to restrain this negro and mongrel population, it is certain sooner or later to escape from all legal restraint, and any hour the whole social fabric may collapse into utter and hopeless ruin. It will be well for Americans who desire to preserve American institutions and American civilization to heed this and ponder well on the uncertain and rotten foundations of social order in Brazil and Cuba, and which, already fatally undermined, may at any moment, as has been said, collapse into a huge mass of free negroism, and thus become a portion of that diseased, monstrous, and nameless condition which ignorance, and folly, and imposture, and hatred to American democracy have combined to pervert language as well as stultify reason and call freedom.

Elsewhere it has been shown that the negro isolated in Africa is in a natural condition, for he multiplies himself, but that he is in his normal, healthy, educated or civilized condition at the South, for he then multiplies with vastly greater rapidity than in a state of isolation, and consequently, *must* be more in harmony with those fixed and eternal decrees that God has ordained for the government of all His creatures. It has also been shown that the negro abandoned and left to himself in Virginia, etc., dies out, but, of course, less rapidly than at the North where the notion prevails that he is the same being as themselves, and therefore, in their efforts to make him manifest the same qualities, or, in other words, to force on him the same "rights," he rapidly tends to extinction. But there is still another phase of free negroism vastly more extended and more dangerous to republican institutions and the future civilization of America.

The negro is a creature of the tropics, and his labor is essential to the cultivation of tropical and tropicoid products, which, in turn, are essential to the happiness and well-being of all mankind. But, as has been shown, his *mental* organism renders him incapable—as absolutely and inevitably as the *physical* organism of the white man renders *him* incapable of tropical production. In the brief space allowed in this work to the consideration of this vital and most momentous truth, the author could only present a few leading facts in its support, but these *facts* are so overwhelming that no rational or honest mind in Christendom will venture to dispute the truth in question. Furthermore it may be stated without chance or possibility of historical contradiction, that in the entire experience of mankind no single instance has ever been known when the isolated negro or the labor of the white man has cultivated the soil or grown the products of the tropics. The mind of the white man and the body of the negro—the intellect of the most elevated and the industrial capacities of the most subordinate of all the known human races, therefore, constitute the elements and motive forces of tropical civilization. Every mind capable of reasoning at all will know that civilization is impossible without production, and production in the great tropical centre of our continent being forever absolutely and necessarily impossible without negro labor guided, controlled, and managed by the higher intelligence of the white man—it is therefore absolutely certain that the social relation which English writers have taught the world to regard as a condition of slavery, is simply that social adaptation of the industrial forces of the subordinate race, essential, not alone to their own welfare but to the welfare of all mankind, and without which there can no more exist what we call civilization in a large portion of America than there can be life without food or light without the sun. This is obvious, and indeed unavoidable to those who are in actual juxtaposition with negroes. But in Europe where there are white men only, and where negroes, Indians, Malays, etc., are in the popular imagination beings like themselves except in the complexion, and only need to be civilized, as they suppose, to be like others, it was an easy matter to excite a public feeling hostile to the prosperity of the people of the tropics. The theory, or rather dogma of a single race, that all mankind was a unit, and negroes, Indians, etc., had a common origin and common nature, and therefore common rights, had been set up by English writers during the conflict with the American colonies; and Dr. Johnson, with his usual coarseness of expression, had declared that "the Virginia slaveholders were the loudest yelpers for liberty"—thus, in utter unconsciousness, paying them a compliment when he believed he was inflicting a sarcasm of peculiar virulence.

Source:
J. H. Van Evrie, M.D., *White Supremacy and Negro Subordination* (New York: Van Evrie, Horton & Co., 1868), pp. 312–20.

49

The South and Her Problems

BY HENRY WOODFIN GRADY

The journalist and orator Henry Woodfin Grady (1850–1889) created a sensation with a speech before the New England Society of New York in 1886 entitled "The New South," which urged the South to industrialize and thereby achieve economic equality with the North. In "The South and Her Problems" (1887) Grady bluntly claims that "the white race is the superior race" but that it can and will produce an alliance with the "best" elements of the African-American population in order to preserve white political supremacy.

WHAT OF THE NEGRO? This of him. I want no better friend than the black boy who was raised by my side, and who is now trudging patiently with downcast eyes and shambling figure through his lowly way in life. I want no sweeter music than the crooning of my old "mammy," now dead and gone to rest, as I heard it when she held me in her loving arms, and bending her old black face above me stole the cares from my brain, and led me smiling into sleep. I want no truer soul than that which moved the trusty slave, who for four years while my father fought with the armies that barred his freedom, slept every night at my mother's chamber door, holding her and her children as safe as if her husband stood guard, and ready to lay down his humble life on her threshold.

History has no parallel to the faith kept by the negro in the South during the war. Often five hundred negroes to a single white man, and yet through these dusky throngs the women and children walked in safety, and the unprotected homes rested in peace. Unmarshaled the black bat-

297

talions moved patiently to the fields in the morning to feed the armies their idleness would have starved, and at night gathered anxiously at the big house to "hear the news from marster," though conscious that his victory made their chains enduring. Everywhere humble and kindly; the bodyguard of the helpless; the rough companion of the little ones; the observant friend; the silent sentry in his lowly cabin; the shrewd counselor. And when the dead came home, a mourner at the open grave. A thousand torches would have disbanded every Southern army, but not one was lighted. When the master going to a war in which slavery was involved said to his slave, "I leave my home and loved ones in your charge," the tenderness between man and master stood disclosed. And when the slave held that charge sacred through storm and temptation, he gave new meaning to faith and loyalty. I rejoice that when freedom came to him after years of waiting, it was all the sweeter because the black hands from which the shackles fell were stainless of a single crime against the helpless ones confided to his care.

From this root, imbedded in a century of kind and constant companionship, has sprung some foliage. As no race had ever lived in such unresisting bondage, none was ever hurried with such swiftness through freedom into power. Into hands still trembling from the blow that broke the shackles, was thrust the ballot. In less than twelve months from the day he walked down the furrow a slave, a negro dictated in legislative halls from which Davis and Calhoun had gone forth, the policy of twelve commonwealths. When his late master protested against his misrule, the federal drum-beat rolled around his strongholds, and from a hedge of federal bayonets he grinned in good-natured insolence. From the proven incapacity of that day has he far advanced? Simple, credulous, impulsive—easily led and too often easily bought, is he a safer, more intelligent citizen now than then? Is this mass of votes, loosed from old restraints, inviting alliance or awaiting opportunity, less menacing than when its purpose was plain and its way direct?

My countrymen, right here the South must make a decision on which very much depends. Many wise men hold that the white vote of the South should divide, the color line be beaten down, and the Southern States ranged on economic or moral questions as interest or belief demands. I am compelled to dissent from this view. The worst thing, in my opinion, that could happen is that the white people of the South should stand in opposing factions, with the vast mass of ignorant or purchasable negro votes between. Consider such a status. If the negroes were skilfully led—and leaders would not be lacking—it would give them the balance of power—a thing not to be considered. If their vote was not compacted, it would invite the debauching bid of factions, and drift surely to that which was the most corrupt and cunning. With the shiftless habit and ir-resolution of slavery days still possessing him, the negro voter will not in this generation, adrift from war issues, become a steadfast partisan through conscience or conviction. In every community there are colored men who redeem their race from this reproach, and who vote under rea-son. Perhaps in time the bulk of this race may thus adjust itself. But, through what long and monstrous periods of political debauchery this status would be reached, no tongue can tell.

The clear and unmistakable domination of the white race, dominating not through violence, not through party alliance, but through the in-tegrity of its own vote and the largeness of its sympathy and justice through which it shall compel the support of the better classes of the col-ored race—that is the hope and assurance of the South. Otherwise, the negro would be bandied from one faction to another. His credulity would be played upon, his cupidity tempted, his impulses misdirected, his passions inflamed. He would be forever in alliance with that faction which was most desperate and unscrupulous. Such a state would be worse than reconstruction, for then intelligence was banded, and its speedy triumph assured. But with intelligence and property divided—bidding and overbidding for place and patronage—irritation increasing with each conflict—the bitterness and desperation seizing every heart—political debauchery deepening, as each faction staked its all in the mis-erable game—there would be no end to this, until our suffrage was hopelessly sullied, our people forever divided, and our most sacred rights surrendered.

One thing further should be said in perfect frankness. Up to this point we have dealt with ignorance and corruption—but beyond this point a deeper issue confronts us. Ignorance may struggle to enlightenment, out of corruption may come the incorruptible. God speed the day when—every true man will work and pray for its coming—the negro must be led to know and through sympathy to confess that his interests and the in-terests of the people of the South are identical. The men who, from afar off, view this subject through the cold eye of speculation or see it dis-torted through partisan glasses insist that directly or indirectly the negro race shall be in control of the affairs of the South. We have no fears of this; already we are attracting to us the best elements of the race, and as we proceed our alliance will broaden; external pressure but irritates and impedes. Those who would put the negro race in supremacy would work against infallible decree, for the white race can never submit to its dom-ination, because the white race is the superior race. But the supremacy of the white race of the South must be maintained forever, and the domination of the negro race resisted at all points and at all hazards—because the white race is the superior race. This is the declaration of no new truth. It has abided forever in the marrow of our bones, and shall run forever with the blood that feeds Anglo-Saxon hearts.

In political compliance the South has evaded the truth, and men have drifted from their convictions. But we can not escape this issue. It faces us wherever we turn. It is an issue that has been, and will be. The races and tribes of earth are of divine origin. Behind the laws of man and the decrees of war, stands the law of God. What God hath separated let no man join together. The Indian, the Malay, the Negro, the Caucasian, these types stand as markers of God's will. Let no man tinker with the work of the Almighty. Unity of civilization, no more than unity of faith, will never be witnessed on earth. No race has risen, or will rise, above its ordained place. Here is the pivotal fact of this great matter—two races are made equal in law, and in political rights, between whom the caste of race has set an impassable gulf. This gulf is bridged by a statute, and the races are urged to cross thereon. This cannot be. The fiat of the Almighty has gone forth, and in eighteen centuries of history it is written.

Source:
Henry Woodfin Grady, "The South and Her Problems" (1887), in Grady's *The New South and Other Addresses,* edited by Edna Henry Lee Turpin (New York: Maynard, Merrill & Co., 1904), pp. 48–54.

50

The Race Question in the United States

BY SENATOR JOHN T. MORGAN

John Tyler Morgan (1824–1907) served in the Civil War on the Confederate side and later served as U.S. Senator (Democrat) from Alabama from 1876 to the end of his life. In "The Race Question in the United States" (1890) Morgan asserts the obvious inferiority of the "negro race" and holds that radical segregation of the races is the only remedy to the race problem, since white women will never countenance the marriage of their sons or daughters to an African American.

ALL THE OTHER NATIONS HAVE, with good cause, regarded the negroes as an inferior race, aside from all the physical distinctions by which they are separated from all other races of men. It was this estimate of their condition that led the great powers of Europe to enter into the Berlin Conference, which fixed the boundaries of the Congo Free State—a vast and beautiful country abounding in natural resources—and secure to the negro race immunity from foreign invasion, that they might become a civilized people. The negro race, in their native land, have never made a voluntary and concerted effort to rise above the plane of slavery; they have not contributed a thought, or a labor, except by compulsion, to aid the progress of civilization. Nothing has emanated from the negroes of Africa, in art, science, or enterprise that has been of the least service to mankind. Their own history, at home, demonstrates their inferiority when compared with that of other peoples.

They have been, for ages, the possessors of a fertile country, where they have bred in myriads, and no foreign power has attempted to subjugate them. The result of their contributions to the wealth of the world is limited to slaves, and the natural productions of the forests. They have no agricultural implement, except a rude, iron hoe; no ships for the seas and no beasts of burden. Their social development has never risen so high as to repress human sacrifices and cannibalism; while their religion is a witchcraft that is attended with every brutal crime.

The inferiority of the negro race, as compared with the white race, is so essentially true, and so obvious that, to assume it in argument, cannot be justly attributed to prejudice. If it is prejudice, it is rare prejudice, which affects nearly all of the white race, and proves the existence of a deep-seated race aversion. This aversion is not a result of slavery. If it were, we could not take pride in the race of English and Saxon masters and slaves from whom we are descended. Whether the law that created this aversion is natural, or contrary to nature; whether it is of human or divine origin; whether it is wicked, or good,—it equally affects and controls both races in all their relations, and it is immutable,—grounded in convictions and sentiments that neither race can yield. . . .

What is the cause of this condition of the negro race in the United States, which their power and political influence has not been able to remove, but has only aggravated? The answer is recorded in the home history of every white family in the United States. The negro race cannot be made homogeneous with the white race. It is the abhorrence that every white woman in our country feels towards the marriage of her son or daughter with a negro, that gives the final and conclusive answer to this question. Wealth, character, abilities, accomplishments and position, have no effect to modify this aversion of the white woman to a negro-marital alliance. Men may yield to such considerations, or to others of a baser sort; but the snows will fall from heaven in sooty blackness, sooner than the white women of the United States will consent to the maternity of negro families. It will become more and more the pride of the men of our race to resist any movement, social or political, that will promote the unwelcome intrusion of the negro race into the white family circle.

This is the central and vital point in the race question. If the negroes, being our equals in political privileges, could be absorbed into our race, as equals, there would be no obstacle to our harmonious and beneficent association, in this free country, but neither laws, nor any form of constraint, can force the doors to our homes and seat them at our firesides. . . .

The practical phase of the question is, whether the white race can be made to include the negro race in a free and honest welcome into their families, as "men and brethren." There are some enthusiasts, claiming to be exalted humanitarians, who advocate the solution of this difficulty by raising the negro race to the social level of the white race through legislative expedients that look to the mingling of the blood of the races; but this is far from being the sentiment of the great body of the people of the United States. They understand the impossibility of such a result. The full-blooded negroes also understand it, and hesitate, if they do not refuse, to make this effort. "The Afro-Americans," as the mulattoes describe themselves, believe that a precedent has been set, by their foremost man, which they can follow, with the aid of the politicians, that will secure their incorporation, by marriage, into the white families of the country. These vain expectations will be followed with the chagrin of utter disappointment, and will increase their discontent.

Every day the distance increases between these races, and they are becoming more jealous and intolerant of each other. This condition is disclosed in the schools, churches, and in every industrial pursuit. The field for negro labor, except in the heaviest drudgery and in menial occupations, is constantly narrowing, until their presence is not tolerated in the higher commercial pursuits, or in the use of important corporate franchises. This is more distinctly the result of race aversion than is the exclusion of the Chinese from our country. The political power given to the negro race, no matter how they may use it, only increases race antagonism. That power has, so far, greatly aggravated the opposition to them. It can never make their presence in this country, which has always been a cause of dissension, welcome to the white people.

The separation of the races under different governments will alone cure this flagrant evil, by giving to the negro race an opportunity for self government; and to the white race an unobstructed course in the accomplishment of their high destiny. The feeling of unrest among the negroes, which has made them homeless, and sweeps them in revolving eddies from one State to another, is a plain indication that they are preparing for a general exodus.

As soon as they have determined the way they would go, and have, in their own free will, concluded to depart to some other country, justice to them and ourselves, and the behests of peace and prosperity to both races, will call forth freely the financial aid of our people and government, for their deliverance.

For a great deliverance it will be!

Source:
Senator John T. Morgan, "The Race Question in the United States," *Arena* no. 10 (September 1890): 389–90, 395–98.

Race Traits and Tendencies of the American Negro

BY FREDERICK L. HOFFMAN

Frederick Ludwig Hoffman (1865–1946) was a statistician for the Prudential Life Insurance Company in New York. He was the author of many articles and monographs on insurance. In Race Traits and Tendencies of the American Negro *(1896), written under the auspices of the American Economic Association, Hoffman contrasts the pleasant, hardworking life of African Americans under slavery with their unhappy lot after the Civil War, and attributes the decline of the race to their own immorality and economic inefficiency.*

T HE CENTRAL FACT DEDUCIBLE from the results of this investigation into the traits and tendencies of the colored population of this country, is plainly and emphatically the powerful influence of *race* in the struggle for life. In marked contrast with the frequent assertions, such as that of Mill, that race is not important and that environment or the conditions of life are the most important factors in the final result of the struggle for life, individual as well as social, we have here abundant evidence that we find in race and heredity the determining factors in the upward or downward course of mankind.

In the field of statistical research, sentiment, prejudice, or the influence of pre-conceived ideas have no place. The data which have been here brought together in a convenient form speak for themselves. From the standpoint of the impartial investigator, no difference of interpretation of their meaning seems possible. The decrease in the rate of increase in the colored population has been traced first to the excessive mortality, which in turn has been traced to an inferior vital capacity. The mixture of the African with the white race has been shown to have seriously affected the longevity of the former and left as a heritage to future generations the poison of scrofula, tuberculosis and most of all of, syphilis. This racial inferiority, has in turn brought about a moral deterioration such as is rarely met with in civilized countries at the present time. Already subject to an inordinate rate of mortality, especially from all of the most destructive diseases, the sexual immorality prevailing between colored females and white males of a lower type, as well as between colored males and colored females, has also brought about a diminished power of vital resistance among the young, as is to be expected from the recognized fact that the death rate for illegitimate children is about twice that of children born in wedlock. As a general result there is diminished social and economic efficiency, which in the course of years must prove not only a most destructive factor in the progress of the colored race, but also in the progress, social as well as economic, of the white race brought under its influence.

Racial inferiority was the keynote of the pro-slavery argument. On the other hand, racial differences were explained away by those who saw in freedom the sure prospect of speedy amelioration of the lot of the southern slave; yet thirty years of freedom in this country and nearly sixty in the West Indies have failed to accomplish the original purpose of the abolition of slavery, that is, the elevation of the colored race to the moral, mental and economic level of the white race.

Nothing is more clearly shown from this investigation than that the southern black man at the time of emancipation was healthy in body and cheerful in mind. He neither suffered inordinately from disease nor from impaired bodily vigor. His industrial capacities as a laborer were not of a low order, nor was the condition of servitude such as to produce in him morbid conditions favorable to mental disease, suicide, or intemperance. What are the conditions thirty years after? The pages of this work give but one answer, an answer which is a most severe condemnation of modern attempts of superior races to lift inferior races to their own elevated position, an answer so full of meaning that it would seem criminal indifference on the part of a civilized people to ignore it. In the plain language of the facts brought together the colored race is shown to be on the downward grade, tending toward a condition in which matters will be worse than they are now, when diseases will be more destructive, vital resistance still lower, when the number of births will fall below the deaths, and gradual extinction of the race take place. Neither religion nor education nor a higher degree of economic well-being have been able to raise the race from a low and anti-social condition, a condition really fostered by the very influences which it was asserted would soon raise the race to a place even more elevated than that of the whites. . . .

A study of the race traits and tendencies of the negro in America makes plain the failure of modern education and other means in encouraging or permitting the development of these most important factors, without which no race has ever yet been able to gain a permanent civilization. Easy conditions of life, a liberal construction of the doctrine of the forgiveness of sins and an unwarranted extension of the principle of state or private interference in the conduct of individual life, have never yet raised a race or individual from a lower to a higher plane. On the contrary, the world's failures are largely those of races and individuals in whose existence the struggle for a higher life had practically come to an end. "For carrying on the chief objects of our life on earth, very little of what is now called civilization is really wanted;"[1] and, unfortunately, it is just the useless adjuncts to civilization that the lower races in their contact with the higher races first acquire.

The downward tendencies of the colored race, therefore, can only be arrested by radical and far-reaching changes in their moral nature. Instead of clamoring for aid and assistance from the white race the negro himself should sternly refuse every offer of direct interference in his own evolution. The more difficult his upward struggle, the more enduring will be the qualities developed. Most of all there must be a more general recognition of the institution of monogamic marriage and unqualified reprobation of those who violate the law of sexual morality. Intercourse with the white race must absolutely cease and race purity must be insisted upon in marriage as well as outside of it. Together with a higher morality will come a greater degree of economic efficiency, and the predominating trait of the white race, the virtue of thrift, will follow as a natural consequence of the mastery by the colored race of its own conditions of life. The compensation of such an independent struggle will be a race of people who will gain a place among civilized mankind and will increase and multiply instead of dying out with loathsome diseases.

The day is not far distant when, in the words of Mr. Kidd, "The last thing our civilization is likely to permanently tolerate is the wasting of the resources of the richest regions of the earth through the lack of the elementary qualities of social efficiency in the races possessing them." When the ever increasing white population has reached a stage where new conquests are necessary, it will not hesitate to make war upon those races who prove themselves useless factors in the progress of mankind. A race may be interesting, gentle and hospitable; but if it is not a useful race in the common acceptation of that term, it is only a question of time when a downward course must take place. All the facts brought together in this work prove that the colored population is gradually parting with the virtues and the moderate degree of economic efficiency developed under the regime of slavery. All the facts prove that a low standard of sexual morality is the main and underlying cause of the low and anti-social condition of the race at the present time. All the facts prove that education, philanthropy and religion have failed to develop a higher appreciation of the stern and uncompromising virtues of the Aryan race. The conclusion is warranted that it is merely a question of time when the actual downward course, that is, a decrease in the population, will take place. In the meantime, however, the presence of the colored population is a serious hindrance to the economic progress of the white race.

Instead of making the race more independent, modern educational and philanthropic efforts have succeeded in making it even more dependent on the white race at the present time than it was previous to emancipation. It remains to be seen how far a knowledge of the facts about its own diminishing vitality, low state of morality and economic efficiency will stimulate the race in adopting a higher standard. Unless a change takes place, a change that will strike at the fundamental errors that underlie the conduct of the higher races towards the lower, gradual extinction is only a question of time.

Source:
Frederick L. Hoffman, *Race Traits and
Tendencies of the American Negro* (New York:
American Economic Association/Macmillan,
1896), pp. 310–12, 327–29.

52

The Negro a Beast

BY CHARLES CARROLL

Little is known about Charles Carroll (1849-?), the author of two polemics against African Americans, The Negro a Beast *(1900) and* The Tempter of Eve *(1902), the latter a warning against miscegenation with blacks. In the former work, Carroll denies the theory of evolution and appeals to the Bible in maintaining that African Americans are a separate species from all other human races; since they lack a soul, they really belong to the species of apes.*

THE GREAT INTELLECTUAL QUALITIES which the men of this and preceding ages have displayed, are the result of inheritance from Adam, upon whom they were a Divine bestowal. Hence, they are transmittible. The low order of the Negro's mentality—his lack of inventive skill—is demonstrated by his meager accomplishments in his undomesticated state, which, as has been shown, are confined to the fashioning of a few rude weapons of stone; while the greater achievements of the domesticated Negro are due solely to the influence of man. Hence, if from any cause he is relieved of this influence and is thrown upon his own resources in the forest, he soon relapses into savagery and descends to the use of stones for weapons.

Among the older naturalists the opinion prevailed that the apes were quadrumana, or four-handed animals. But this delusion has long since been dispelled. There is no four-handed animal.

But for the existence of the lower apes we, at this late day, would have no alternative than to decide that the Negro is the sole representative of his species or that he is a man. But with this family, shading up from the Lemur to the Negro, we are enabled, with the aids of Scripture and the sciences, to determine that the Negro is a member of it. Thus this interesting family of animals, though unfit for general domestic purposes, are invaluable to man in that they enable him to determine the Negro's proper position in the universe—that he is simply an ape.

But, says the Enlightened Christian, the Negro possesses the moral faculty. Is not this the most positive evidence that he is a man—that he has a soul? Not the least evidence! In discussing this question it is essential that we bear in mind that there were just three Creations—Matter, Mind and Soul, and that these made their appearance in the Universe in the order stated. When we accept the teachings of the Bible, we must admit that everything belongs to, and is a part of one or the other of these three creations and necessarily made its appearance in the material universe simultaneously with the Creation of which it is a part. Hence, the question is, which of these three creations is the moral faculty a part of?

Evidently it is not a part of matter, since it does not exist in the plant. Hence, it belongs either to the mind creation, or to the spiritual creation. If it is a part of the latter creation it is peculiar to man. If it is a part of the former creation it is common to man and the animals. It is this faculty—the moral faculty—which enables man to distinguish between right and wrong; and that it is right to obey, and wrong to disobey God. But for the existence of this faculty in man, he could not in justice, be held responsible to God for his acts. This leads us to realize that it is the moral faculty in the animals which makes it possible for man to teach them that it is right to obey, and wrong to disobey their master. But for their possession of this faculty the animals would be unfit for domestic purposes. Hence, inasmuch as the moral faculty does not exist in the plant, in which the matter creation is alone represented, and inasmuch as it is not peculiar to man, in whom the soul creation is alone represented, we have no alternative than to decide that it is a part of the mind creation. Further evidence of this is found in the fact that this faculty, like any physical or mental character, is subject to accident or disease. If from accident or from disease, the mind creation of man, or woman is impaired, the moral faculty is correspondingly impaired. If, as in the case of an insane person, the mind is so impaired as to temporarily, or permanently, destroy the reasoning faculty, the moral faculty is temporarily or permanently destroyed as the case may be. The soul creation of the individual cannot be impaired, and the matter creation as presented in the physical structure may not be impaired by its combination with mind that has been injured or become diseased. The individual may live long after his reasoning faculties have been destroyed. But the very moment he ceases to be a rational being, he ceases to be a moral being. Then, if his mind is restored his moral faculty is restored. The same argument holds good with the animals. The moral, like any faculty of the mind, may be cultivated and developed, or it may be neglected and dwarfed. This can be demonstrated by comparing the cultivated with the uncultivated man; the domesticated with the undomesticated Negro; or our domesticated quadrupeds with the same class of animals in their undomesticated state. When the world of mankind is freed from the thralldom of atheism, and its great intellects are turned upon the Mosaic Record, and the characters peculiar to each of the three Creations are already ascertained (as they will be), our present opinions as to the characters peculiar to man will be very materially modified. Under the influence of The Theory of Natural Development, the Negro has been taken into the family of man; the result is, that we have been led to believe that mind, with its intellectual and moral faculties, articulate speech, the erect posture, a well developed hand and foot, the ability to fashion and handle implements, are characters peculiar to man. This is a sad mistake. It will yet be ascertained that man has just two characters peculiar to him. (1.) His flesh is a different kind of flesh from that of the lower animals. (2.) Man possesses immortality, while the animals are mere creatures of time.

"But," says the enlightened Christian, "If a man is married to a negress, will not their offspring have a soul?" No; it is simply the product resulting from God's violated law, and inherits none of the Divine nature of the man, but, like its parent, the ape, it is merely a combination of matter and mind. "Then, if the half-breed marries a man, will not their offspring have a soul?" No! "Then if the three-quarter white marries a man will not their offspring have a soul?" No. "If the offspring of man and the Negro was mated with pure whites for generations, would not their ultimate offspring have a soul?" No! In discussing this question we must bear in mind that there were just three Creations—matter, mind and soul. That these three creations made their appearance in the order stated. That matter is the basis of all formations in the material universe; whether it exists alone as in the plant, or in combination with mind as in the animal, and with soul as in man. Let us also bear in mind that, the reproduction of these Creations as they exist in the plants, in the animals, and in man, was not left to chance, but is governed by laws which God established in the Creation, and which are unerring and positive in their operations and results.

In order to acquaint ourselves with the operations and results of these laws, let us first discuss the reproduction of plants, in which the matter creation is alone represented; and, since the manner of their reproduction is more generally understood, let us take as an illustration, the flowering plants, in which the sexes are represented in the male, and in the female flower. As is well known reproduction results from the union of the pollen, or fecundating dust, of the stamen of the male flower with the pollen of the pistil of the female flower. This indicates that one side or part of the matter creation, exists in the male flower; and that its corresponding side or part exists in the female flower. These opposite sides or parts, each act as a magnet which attracts its corresponding side or part in the opposite sex; and, when united, the matter creation is perfected and reproduced in the young plant. But if, from any cause, the matter creation, as it exists in its imperfect state in the respective germs of the male and the female flowers, are not united and perfected in the female flower, these vital elements are wasted, and the reproduction of the matter creation in the young plant is not accomplished. The same law holds good with the animal, in which the two Creations—Matter and Mind, exist in the respective germs of the male, and the female. One side or part of the Matter Creation, and one side or part of the Mind Creation, exists in an imperfect state in the male germ; the corresponding sides or parts of these imperfect Creations exists in the female germ. By uniting these imperfect creations in the female, they are perfected and reproduced in the young animal. This indicates that each of these creations maintains its individuality in their respective male and female germs; and that each side or part of these creations, act as a magnet, which attracts its corresponding side or part in the opposite sex. When sexual union takes place, each side or part of these two creations—Matter and Mind—are united and perfected in the female, conception and birth ensues, and the combination of matter and mind is reproduced in the offspring.

But, if from any cause these imperfect matter and mind creations, as they exist in the respective germs of the male and the female animal, are not united and perfected in the female, these vital elements are wasted, conception does not ensue, and the reproduction of these two creations in a young animal is not accomplished. The strength of our position on this subject is demonstrated by the actions of our domestic fowls; it frequently occurs that the female fowl, when not associated with the male fowl, will lay eggs. But only one part of the two creations—matter and mind—as they existed in an imperfect state in the germ of the female were represented in the egg; their corresponding side or part in the male, which was necessary to perfect the creations, was absent. The result of the effort of the female to reproduce these two creations without their corresponding side or part in the male, was abortion—the egg would not "hatch."

The same law holds good with man, in whom the three creations—matter, mind and soul—exist. As in the plant and in the animal, so it must be in man; one side or part of the matter creation, and one side or part of the mind creation, and one side or part of the soul creation exists in the male germ; the corresponding side or part of each of these creations exists in the female germ. Each side or part of these three creations maintains its individuality in their respective male and female germs; and each side or part of these three creations acts as a magnet which attracts its corresponding side or part in the opposite sex. When sexual union takes place, each side or part of these three creations unite and are perfected in the female germ; conception ensues and the three creations—matter, mind and soul—are reproduced in the offspring. But when no corresponding side or part of one of these creations exists in the opposite sex, this creation finds no attraction and is passive. Hence, if the sexual act results in conception, this passive creation is not perfected and forms no part of the offspring. For example: In the Negro, as in any other animal, but two creations—matter and mind—are combined. One side or part of each of these creations exists in the male germ; their corresponding side or part exists in the female germ, as mutually dependent sides or parts of the life system of the animal. In the sexual act each of these creations acts as a magnet, which attracts its corresponding side or part in the opposite sex, and, if united, these two creations are perfected; conception ensues and the combination of matter and mind is transmitted to the offspring.

Thus, while but two creations—matter and mind—combine to perfect the Negro, three creations—matter, mind and soul—combine to perfect man. While these two creations—matter and mind—exist in an imperfect state in the germs of the male and female Negro, as mutually dependent sides or parts of the life system of the animal, three creations—matter, mind and spiritual life—exist in an imperfect state in the germs of the male and female man, as mutually dependent sides or parts of the life system of man; and such is the attraction between matter and mind as they exist in their imperfect state in the germs of man and the Negro that sexual intercourse between the two will unite and perfect these two creations. But the soul creation in its imperfect and dependent state in the germ of the man, finds no corresponding side or part in the negress. Hence, this creation having no attraction remains passive, and if conception ensues from the union of the germs and the consequent perfecting of the matter and mind creations of man and the Negro, this passive creation forms no part of the offspring of this unnatural union. Thus, it is impossible for either side or part of the life system of man—the male or the female—to transmit these three creations—matter, mind and soul to their offspring by the Negro, in whom matter and mind alone exists.

In other words, the male and the female can only transmit to their off-spring such creations as are common to both.

Let us bear in mind that prior to the creation of man there was no connecting link—no tie of kinship between the Creator and His creatures. All things in the material universe were material, there was nothing spiritual; all was mortal, there was no immortality; but when the Lord God formed man out of "the dust of the ground," this "dust of the ground" being a part of the original creation—matter—"and breathed into his nostrils the breath of life," spiritual, immortal life, "man became a living soul." This spiritual, immortal life, "this living soul," was a part of the substance of God. Hence, its combination with matter and with mind, as presented in man's physical, mental and spiritual organisms, formed the connecting link—the link of kinship—between the Creator and creature. Thus, man became "the Son of God." His failure to form this link of kinship between Himself and the fish, or fowl, or beast, clearly demonstrates the design of God that no kinship should exist between them. Hence, when man becomes so degenerated as to associate himself carnally with the Negro, the very act brings into operation the law which governs the reproduction of the creations, which makes it impossible for man to transmit to his offspring by the beast the slightest vestige of kinship with God.

This law becomes active and operates with the same result when man associates himself carnally with the mixed breeds; without reference to what their proportions of white and black blood may be. The immediate offspring of man and the Negro—the half breed—like the Negro, is merely a combination of two creations—matter and mind. Hence, but two—matter and mind—of the three creatures—matter, mind and soul—as they exist in their imperfect state in the germ of the man find their corresponding sides or portion in the opposite sex of the half breed. The result is, that the one side or part of the soul creation, as it exists in its imperfect state in the germ of the man, finding no corresponding side or part in the opposite sex of the half breed, with which it may be united and perfected, is not attracted and remains passive. Hence, if the matter creation and the mind creation as they exist in their imperfect state in the respective germs of man and the half breed, are united and perfected, and conception ensues, this passive creation forms no part of the offspring. This unvarying law would hold good through millions of generations. Man, in associating himself carnally with the mixed-breeds, would continually oppose three creations—matter, mind and soul—as they exist in their imperfect state in his germ, to only two creations—matter and mind—as they exist in their imperfect state in the germ of the mixed bloods. As a result it could only be possible to unite and perfect the matter and mind creations as they exist in their imperfect state in the respective germs of man and the mixed bloods, and thus reproduce and transmit them to the offspring. But the soul creation as it exists in its imperfect state in the germ of man, finding no corresponding side or part in the opposite sex of the mixed bloods with which it might be united and perfected, is not affected in the sexual act and remains passive, hence it is not represented in the offspring.

Source:
Charles Carroll, *The Negro a Beast; or, In the Image of God* (St. Louis, MO: American Book & Bible House, 1900), pp. 125–36.

53

The Negro:
The Southerner's
Problem

BY THOMAS NELSON PAGE

Thomas Nelson Page (1853–1922) practiced law in Richmond, Virginia, before turning to the writing of novels and stories. His novel Red Rock *(1898) deals with the South's violent protest against Reconstruction. In* The Negro: The Southerner's Problem *(1904), Page addresses the issue of the lynching of African Americans, claiming that the problem would be solved if blacks refrained from sexual attacks on white women.*

N<small>OW, HOW IS THIS CRIME OF ASSAULT</small> to be stopped? For stopped it must be, and stopped it will be, whatever the cost. One proposition is that separation of the races, complete separation by the deportation of the Negroes, is the only remedy. The theory, though sustained by many thoughtful men, appears Utopian. Colonization has been the dream of certain philanthropists for a hundred years. And, meantime, the Negroes have increased from less than a million to nine millions. They will never be deported; not because we have not the money, for an amount equal to that spent in pensions during three years would pay the expenses of such deportation, and an amount equal to that paid in six years would set them up in a new country. But the Negroes have rights; many of them are estimable citizens; and even the great body of them, when well regulated, are valuable laborers. It might, therefore, as well be assumed that this plan will never be carried out, unless the occasion becomes so imperative that all other rights give way to the supreme right of necessity.

It is plain, then, that we must deal with the matter in a more practicable manner, accepting conditions as they are, and applying to them legal methods which will be effective. Lynching does not end ravishing, and that is the prime necessity. Most right-thinking men are agreed as to this. Indeed, lynching, through lacking the supreme principle of law, the deliberateness from which is supposed to come the certainty of identification, fails utterly to meet the necessity of the case even as a deterrent, though it must be admitted that there are a respectable number of thoughtful men who dissent from this view. The growth of a sentiment which, at least, condones lynching as a punishment for assaults on women is a significant and distressing fact. Not only have assaults occurred again and again in the same neighborhood where lynching has followed such crime; but, a few years ago, it was publicly stated that a Negro who had just witnessed a lynching for this crime actually committed an assault on his way home. However this may be, lynching as a remedy is a ghastly failure; and its brutalizing effect on the community is incalculable.

The charge that is often made, that the innocent are sometimes lynched, has little foundation. The rage of a mob is not directed against the innocent, but against the guilty; and its fury would not be satisfied with any other sacrifice than the death of the real criminal. Nor does the criminal merit any consideration, however terrible the punishment. The real injury is to the perpetrators of the crime of destroying the law, and to the community in which the law is slain.

It is pretty generally conceded that the "law's delay" is partly responsible for the "wild justice" of mob vengeance, and this has undoubtedly been the cause of many mobs. But it is far from certain if any change in the methods of administration of law will effect the stopping of lynching; while to remedy this evil we may bring about a greater peril. Trial by jury is the bed-rock of our liberties, and the inherent principle of such trial is its deliberateness. It has been said that the whole purpose of the Constitution of Great Britain is that twelve men may sit in the jury-box. The methods of the law may well be reformed; but any movement should be jealously scanned which touches the chief bulwark of all liberty.

The first step, then, would appear to be the establishment of a system securing a reasonably prompt trial and speedy execution by law, rather than a wholesale revolution of the existing system.

Many expedients have been suggested; some of the most drastic by Northern men. One of them proposed, not long since, that to meet the mob-spirit, a trial somewhat in the nature of a drum-head court-martial might be established by law, by which the accused may be tried and, if found guilty, executed immediately. Others have proposed as a remedy emasculation by law; while a Justice of the Supreme Court has recently given the weight of his personal opinion in favor of prompt trial and the abolishment of appeals in such cases. Even the terrible suggestion has been made that burning at the stake might again be legalized!

These suggestions testify how grave the matter is considered to be by those who make them.

But none of these, unless it be the one relating to emasculation, is more than an expedient. The trouble lies deeper. The crime of lynching is not likely to cease until the crime of ravishing and murdering women and children is less frequent than it has been of late. And this crime, which is well-nigh wholly confined to the Negro race, will not greatly diminish until the Negroes themselves take it in hand and stamp it out.

From recent developments, it may be properly inferred that the absence of this crime during the later period of slavery was due more to the feeling among the Negroes themselves than to any repressive measures on the part of the whites. The Negro had the same animal instincts in slavery that he exhibits now; the punishment that follows the crime now is quite as certain, as terrible, and as swift as it could have been then. So, to what is due the alarming increase of this terrible brutality?

To the writer it appears plain that it is due to two things: first, to racial antagonism and to the talk of social equality that inflames the ignorant Negro, who has grown up unregulated and undisciplined; and, secondly, to the absence of a strong restraining public opinion among the Negroes of any class, which alone can extirpate the crime. In the first place, the Negro does not generally believe in the virtue of women. It is beyond his experience. He does not generally believe in the existence of actual assault. It is beyond his comprehension. In the next place, his passion, always his controlling force, is now, since the new teaching, for the white women.

That there are many Negroes who are law-abiding and whose influence is for good, no one who knows the worthy members of the race—those who represent the better element—will deny. But while there are, of course, notable exceptions, they are not often of the "New Issue," nor, unhappily, even generally among the prominent leaders: those who publish papers and control conventions.

As the crime of rape of late years had its baleful renascence in the teaching of equality and the placing of power in the ignorant Negroes' hands, so its perpetuation and increase have undoubtedly been due in large part to the same teaching. The intelligent Negro may understand what social equality truly means, but to the ignorant and brutal young Negro, it signifies but one thing: the opportunity to enjoy, equally with white men, the privilege of cohabiting with white women. This the whites of the South understand; and if it were understood abroad, it would serve to explain some things which have not been understood hitherto. It will explain, in part, the universal and furious hostility of the South to even the least suggestion of social equality.

A close following of the instances of rape and lynching, and the public discussion consequent thereon, have led the writer to the painful realization that even the leaders of the Negro race—at least, those who are prominent enough to hold conventions and write papers on the subject—have rarely, by act or word, shown a true appreciation of the enormity of the crime of ravishing and murdering women. Their discussion and denunciation have been almost invariably and exclusively devoted to the crime of lynching. Underlying most of their protests is the suggestion that the victim of the mob is innocent and a martyr. Now and then, there is a mild generalization on the evil of lawbreaking and the violation of women; but, for one stern word of protest against violating women and cutting their throats, the records of Negro meetings will show many resolutions against the attack of the mob on the criminal. And, as to any serious and determined effort to take hold of and stamp out the crime that is blackening the good name of the entire Negro race to-day, and arousing against them the fatal and possibly the undying enmity of the stronger race, there is, with the exception of the utterances of a few score individuals like Booker T. Washington, who always speaks for the right, Hannibal Thomas, and Bishop Turner, hardly a trace of such a thing. A crusade has been preached against lynching, even as far as England; but none has been attempted against the ravishing and tearing to pieces of white women and children.

Happily, there is an element of sound-minded, law-abiding Negroes, representative of the old Negro, who without parade stand for good order, and do what they can to repress lawlessness among their people. Except for this class and for the kindly relations which are preserved between them and the whites, the situation in the South would long since have become unbearable. These, however, are not generally among the leaders, and, unfortunately, their influence is not sufficiently extended to counteract the evil influences which are at work with such fatal results.

Source:
Thomas Nelson Page, *The Negro:
The Southerner's Problem* (New York:
Scribner's, 1904), pp. 107–15.

54

The Clansman

BY THOMAS DIXON, JR.

The Baptist minister and lawyer Thomas Dixon, Jr. (1864–1936), was the author of The Leopard's Spots *(1902), a novel that claims to show what would happen if the African American were raised above his "station," and* The Clansman *(1905), about the formation of the Ku Klux Klan following the Civil War. These two novels were adapted by D. W. Griffith in his controversial film* The Birth of a Nation *(1914). Dixon subsequently wrote a sequel to the film,* The Fall of a Nation *(1916). In this excerpt from* The Clansman, *Dixon describes how the Klan captures an African American accused of raping and murdering a white woman and lynches him.*

The Ku Klux Klan was founded in 1866 but was taken over in 1867 by Confederate veterans under the leadership of Gen. Nathaniel Bedford Forrest and turned into an organ for maintaining white supremacy in the South. After a reign of terror lasting several years, the Klan was wiped out by the federal government in 1872. It was reestablished in Georgia in 1915, apparently much influenced by Dixon's novels and Griffith's film.

THE MEN, WHO GATHERED IN THE WOODS, dismounted, removed their saddles, and from the folds of the blankets took a white disguise for horse and man. In a moment it was fitted on each horse, with buckles at the throat, breast, and tail, and the saddles replaced. The white robe for the man was made in the form of an ulster overcoat with cape, the skirt extending to the top of the shoes. From the red belt at the waist were swung two revolvers which had been concealed in their pockets. On each man's breast was a scarlet circle within which shone a white cross. The same scarlet circle and cross appeared on the horse's breast,

319

while on his flanks flamed the three red mystic letters, K. K. K. Each man wore a white cap, from the edges of which fell a piece of cloth extending to the shoulders. Beneath the visor was an opening for the eyes and lower down one for the mouth. On the front of the caps of two of the men appeared the red wings of a hawk as the ensign of rank. From the top of each cap rose eighteen inches high a single spike held erect by a twisted wire. The disguises for man and horse were made of cheap unbleached domestic and weighed less than three pounds. They were easily folded within a blanket and kept under the saddle in a crowd without discovery. It required less than two minutes to remove the saddles, place the disguises, and remount.

At the signal of a whistle, the men and horses arrayed in white and scarlet swung into double-file cavalry formation and stood awaiting orders. The moon was now shining brightly, and its light shimmering on the silent horses and men with their tall spiked caps made a picture such as the world had not seen since the Knights of the Middle Ages rode on their Holy Crusades.

As the train neared the flag-station, which was dark and unattended, the conductor approached Gus, leaned over, and said: "I've just gotten a message from the sheriff telling me to warn you to get off at this station and slip into town. There's a crowd at the depot there waiting for you and they mean trouble."

Gus trembled, and whispered:

"Den fur Gawd's sake lemme off here."

The two men who got on at the station below stepped out before the negro, and, as he alighted from the car, seized, tripped, and threw him to the ground. The engineer blew a sharp signal, and the train pulled on.

In a minute Gus was bound and gagged.

One of the men drew a whistle and blew twice. A single tremulous call like the cry of an owl answered. The swift beat of horses' feet followed, and four white-and-scarlet clansmen swept in a circle around the group.

One of the strangers turned to the horseman with red-winged ensign on his cap, saluted, and said:

"Here's your man, Night Hawk."

"Thanks, gentlemen," was the answer. "Let us know when we can be of service to your county."

The strangers sprang into their buggy and disappeared toward the North Carolina line.

The clansmen blindfolded the negro, placed him on a horse, tied his legs securely, and his arms behind him to the ring in the saddle.

The Night Hawk blew his whistle four sharp blasts, and his pickets galloped from their positions and joined him.

Again the signal rang, and his men wheeled with the precision of trained cavalrymen into column formation three abreast, and rode toward Piedmont, the single black figure tied and gagged in the centre of the white-and-scarlet squadron.

The clansmen with their prisoner skirted the village and halted in the woods on the river bank. The Night Hawk signalled for single file, and in a few minutes they stood against the cliff under Lover's Leap and saluted the chief, who sat his horse, awaiting their arrival.

Pickets were placed in each direction on the narrow path by which the spot was approached, and one was sent to stand guard on the shelving rock above.

Through the narrow crooked entrance they led Gus into the cave which had been the rendezvous of the Piedmont Den of the Klan since its formation. The meeting-place was a grand hall eighty feet deep, fifty feet wide, and more than forty feet in height, which had been carved out of the stone by the swift current of the river in ages past when its waters stood at a higher level.

To-night it was lighted by candles placed on the ledges of the walls. In the centre, on a fallen boulder, sat the Grand Cyclops of the Den, the presiding officer of the township, his rank marked by scarlet stripes on the white-cloth spike of his cap. Around him stood twenty or more clansmen in their uniform, completely disguised. One among them wore a yellow sash, trimmed in gold, about his waist, and on his breast two yellow circles with red crosses interlapping, denoting his rank to be the Grand Dragon of the Realm, or Commander-in-Chief of the State.

The Cyclops rose from his seat:

"Let the Grand Turk remove his prisoner for a moment and place him in charge of the Grand Sentinel at the door, until summoned."

The officer disappeared with Gus, and the Cyclops continued:

"The Chaplain will open our Council with prayer."

Solemnly every white-shrouded figure knelt on the ground, and the voice of the Rev. Hugh McAlpin, trembling with feeling, echoed through the cave:

"Lord God of our Fathers, as in times past thy children, fleeing from the oppressor, found refuge beneath the earth until once more the sun of righteousness rose, so are we met to-night. As we wrestle with the powers of darkness now strangling our life, give to our souls to endure as seeing the invisible, and to our right arms the strength of the martyred dead of our people. Have mercy on the poor, the weak, the innocent and defenseless, and deliver us from the body of the Black Death. In a land of light and beauty and love our women are prisoners of danger and fear. While the heathen walks his native heath unharmed and unafraid, in this fair Christian Southland, our sisters, wives, and daughters dare not stroll at twilight through the streets, or step beyond the highway at noon. The terror of the twilight deepens with the darkness, and the stoutest heart grows sick with fear for the red message the morning bringeth. Forgive our sins—they are many, but hide not thy face from us, O God, for thou art our refuge!"

As the last echoes of the prayer lingered and died in the vaulted roof, the clansmen rose and stood a moment in silence.

Again the voice of the Cyclops broke the stillness:

"Brethren, we are met to-night at the request of the Grand Dragon of the Realm, who has honoured us with his presence, to constitute a High Court for the trial of a case involving life. Are the Night Hawks ready to submit their evidence?"

"We are ready," came the answer.

"Then let the Grand Scribe read the objects of the Order on which your authority rests."

The Scribe opened his Book of Record, *"The Prescript of the Order of the Invisible Empire,"* and solemnly read:

"To the lovers of law and order, peace and justice, and to the shades of the venerated dead, greeting:

"This is an institution of Chivalry, Humanity, Mercy, and Patriotism: embodying in its genius and principles all that is chivalric in conduct, noble in sentiment, generous in manhood, and patriotic in purpose: its peculiar objects being,

"First: To protect the weak, the innocent, and the defenseless from the indignities, wrongs and outrages of the lawless, the violent, and the brutal; to relieve the injured and the oppressed: to succour the suffering and unfortunate, and especially the widows and the orphans of Confederate Soldiers.

"Second: To protect and defend the Constitution of the United States, and all the laws passed in conformity thereto, and to protect the states and the people thereof from all invasion from any source whatever.

"Third: To aid and assist in the execution of all Constitutional laws, and to protect the people from unlawful seizure, and from trial except by their peers in conformity to the laws of the land."

"The Night Hawks will produce their evidence," said the Cyclops, "and the Grand Monk will conduct the case of the people against the negro Augustus Caesar, the former slave of Dr. Richard Cameron."

Dr. Cameron advanced and removed his cap. His snow-white hair and beard, ruddy face and dark-brown brilliant eyes made a strange picture in its weird surroundings, like an ancient alchemist ready to conduct some daring experiment in the problem of life.

"I am here, brethren," he said, "to accuse the black brute about to appear of the crime of assault on a daughter of the South—"

A murmur of thrilling surprise and horror swept the crowd of white and scarlet figures as with one common impulse they moved closer.

"His feet have been measured and they exactly tally with the negro tracks found under the window of the Lenoir cottage. His flight to Columbia and return on the publication of their deaths as an accident is a confirmation of our case. I will not relate to you the scientific experiment which first fixed my suspicion of this man's guilt. My witness could not confirm it, and it might not be to you credible. But this negro is peculiarly sensitive to hypnotic influence. I propose to put him under this power to-night before you, and, if he is guilty, I can make him tell his confederates, describe and rehearse the crime itself."

The Night Hawks led Gus before Doctor Cameron, untied his hands, removed the gag, and slipped the blindfold from his head.

Under the doctor's rigid gaze the negro's knees struck together, and he collapsed into complete hypnosis, merely lifting his huge paws lamely as if to ward a blow.

They seated him on the boulder from which the Cyclops rose, and Gus stared about the cave and grinned as if in a dream seeing nothing.

The doctor recalled to him the day of the crime, and he began to talk to his three confederates, describing his plot in detail, now and then pausing and breaking into a fiendish laugh.

Old McAllister, who had three lovely daughters at home, threw off his cap, sank to his knees, and buried his face in his hands, while a dozen of the white figures crowded closer, nervously gripping the revolvers which hung from their red belts.

Doctor Cameron pushed them back and lifted his hand in warning.

The negro began to live the crime with fearful realism—the journey past the hotel to make sure the victims had gone to their home; the visit to Aunt Cindy's cabin to find her there; lying in the field waiting for the last light of the village to go out; gloating with vulgar exultation over their plot, and planning other crimes to follow its success— how they crept along the shadows of the hedgerow of the lawn to avoid the moonlight, stood under the cedar, and through the open windows watched the mother and daughter laughing and talking within—

"Min' what I tells you now— Tie de ole one, when I gib you de rope," said Gus in a whisper.

"My God!" cried the agonised voice of the figure with the double cross—"that's what the piece of burnt rope in the fireplace meant!"

Doctor Cameron again lifted his hand for silence.

Now they burst into the room, and with the light of hell in his beady, yellow-splotched eyes, Gus gripped his imaginary revolver and growled:

"Scream, an' I blow yer brains out!"

In spite of Doctor Cameron's warning, the white-robed figures jostled and pressed closer—

Gus rose to his feet and started across the cave as if to spring on the shivering figure of the girl, the clansmen with muttered groans, sobs and curses falling back as he advanced. He still wore his full Captain's uniform, its heavy epaulets flashing their gold in the unearthly light, his beastly jaws half covering the gold braid on the collar. His thick lips were drawn upward in an ugly leer and his sinister bead-eyes gleamed like a gorilla's. A single fierce leap and the black claws clutched the air slowly as if sinking into the soft white throat.

Strong men began to cry like children.

"Stop him! Stop him!" screamed a clansman, springing on the negro and grinding his heel into his big thick neck. A dozen more were on him in a moment, kicking, stamping, cursing, and crying like madmen.

Doctor Cameron leaped forward and beat them off:

"Men! Men! You must not kill him in this condition!"

Some of the white figures had fallen prostrate on the ground, sobbing in a frenzy of uncontrollable emotion. Some were leaning against the walls, their faces buried in their arms.

Again old McAllister was on his knees crying over and over again:

"God have mercy on my people!"

When at length quiet was restored, the negro was revived, and again bound, blindfolded, gagged, and thrown to the ground before the Grand Cyclops.

A sudden inspiration flashed in Doctor Cameron's eyes. Turning to the figure with yellow sash and double cross he said:

"Issue your orders and despatch your courier to-night with the old Scottish rite of the Fiery Cross. It will send a thrill of inspiration to every clansman in the hills."

"Good—prepare it quickly," was the answer.

Doctor Cameron opened his medicine case, drew the silver drinking-cover from a flask, and passed out of the cave to the dark circle of blood still shining in the sand by the water's edge. He knelt and filled the cup half full of the crimson grains, and dipped it into the river. From a saddle he took the lightwood torch, returned within, and placed the cup on the boulder on which the Grand Cyclops had sat. He loosed the bundle of lightwood, took two pieces, tied them into the form of a cross, and laid it beside a lighted candle near the silver cup.

The silent figures watched his every movement. He lifted the cup and said:

"Brethren, I hold in my hand the water of your river bearing the red stain of the life of a Southern woman, a priceless sacrifice on the altar of outraged civilisation. Hear the message of your chief."

The tall figure with the yellow sash and double cross stepped before the strange altar, while the white forms of the clansmen gathered about him in a circle. He lifted his cap, and laid it on the boulder, and his men gazed on the flushed face of Ben Cameron, the Grand Dragon of the Realm.

He stood for a moment silent, erect, a smouldering fierceness in his eyes, something cruel and yet magnetic in his alert bearing.

He looked on the prostrate negro lying in his uniform at his feet, seized the cross, lighted the three upper ends and held it blazing in his hand, while, in a voice full of the fires of feeling, he said:

"Men of the South, the time for words has passed, the hour for action has struck. The Grand Turk will execute this negro to-night and fling his body on the lawn of the black Lieutenant-Governor of the state."

The Grand Turk bowed.

"I ask for the swiftest messenger of this Den who can ride till dawn."

The man whom Doctor Cameron had already chosen stepped forward:

"Carry my summons to the Grand Titan of the adjoining province in North Carolina whom you will find at Hambright. Tell him the story of this crime and what you have seen and heard. Ask him to report to me here the second night from this, at eleven o'clock, with six Grand Giants from his adjoining counties, each accompanied by two hundred picked men. In olden times when the Chieftain of our people summoned the clan on an errand of life and death, the Fiery Cross, extinguished in sacrificial blood, was sent by swift courier from village to village. This call was never made in vain, nor will it be to-night in the new world. Here, on this spot made holy ground by the blood of those we hold dearer than life, I raise the ancient symbol of an unconquered race of men—"

High above his head in the darkness of the cave he lifted the blazing emblem—

"The Fiery Cross of old Scotland's hills! I quench its flames in the sweetest blood that ever stained the sands of Time."

He dipped its ends in the silver cup, extinguished the fire, and handed the charred symbol to the courier, who quickly disappeared.

Source:
Thomas Dixon, Jr., *The Clansman: An Historical
Romance of the Ku Klux Klan* (New York:
Doubleday, Page & Co., 1905), pp. 315–26.

55

The Negro:
A Menace to
American Civilization

BY R. W. SHUFELDT

Robert Wilson Shufeldt (1850–1934) was a biologist and ornithologist who served in the Civil War and later married the granddaughter of the celebrated ornithologist John James Audubon. He served in the medical department of the U.S. Army for most of his life. He wrote two volumes on African Americans, The Negro: A Menace to American Civilization *(1907) and* America's Greatest Problem: The Negro *(1915). In the former, Shufeldt excoriates the ineducability, criminality, and moral obtuseness of the Negro.*

Dating the days of slavery, untold thousands of hybrids were produced, due to a crossing of the black and the white races, and this took place principally in the South, though by no means altogether confined to that region. When they gained their liberty, after the Civil War, much was brought to bear, from a great variety of sources and diverse influences that profoundly affected their history. In the forty years that followed, however, it has been amply proven that hybridization with a certain class of the Indo-Europeans of the United States is still actively going on; that the typical negro remains very much the same kind of a being that he was on his having been brought here from Africa; that the dozen and odd who have risen to prominence in the black race of this country are not typical negroes, but have from sixty to eighty per cent. of white blood in their composition, and that blood probably derived from the best class of educated

Americans. It has further been shown, both physiologically and anatomi-cally, that the bulk of them derive no benefit from educational measures of any kind, and as for the matter of that they have, even when crossed with the best of the white race, produced no man or woman in any way entitled to be recognized as a profound thinker or as one possessing skill in any of the crafts of sciences above the plane of mediocrity. And, as has been pointed out, this has been the case only when the individual exhibiting such prominence had a very large proportion of white blood in his com-position. On the other hand, there is a very considerable amount of proof available toward establishing the fact that in a very large proportion of cases modern education has been downright harmful to the negro, and had the sole effect of improving his opportunities for criminal practices of various kinds; of having him entertain entirely false notions of his worth, ability and real social status; and of furnishing thoroughly untrustworthy evidence of his value as a factor in modern civilization, which baseless tes-timony has been employed by the short-sighted, narrow-minded and une-ducated supporters of this race in the United States to continue their attempts to force these savage and semi-simian creatures upon a long-suf-fering and civilized community.

It is equally clear that the criminality and savagery of the negro in this country has, in the case of the more criminally disposed whites, begotten both savagery and crime, as well as lawlessness. It is the presence of the negro among us that is responsible for lynch-law, and not the tastes of our people for such brutal horrors. Among a progressive race, such as the Indo-European in the United States is, it is the effect of their own higher and elevating civilization that as time goes on eliminates crime, bestiality, brutality and all else that is ethically and morally undesirable in man's composition; but when a cultured, advancing, highly plastic and superior race of this kind has introduced among it another race in large numbers characterized by its lack of truthfulness, its bestial sensuality, its morbid criminal characteristics, its mental density and its religious and other su-perstitions, and its physical repulsiveness, the influence of such an intro-duction is bound to be felt. The case is precisely the same as though we were to introduce into a large boarding-school composed of refined, moral, educated, progressive and mentally and physically healthy boys and girls, a lot of new pupils largely given to lying, to thieving, to mas-turbating and other varieties of sexual looseness, to criminal propensities of various kinds, and other human frailties. It would be clearly due to that blindness which is the outcome of pseudo-philanthropy which would induce any one to state candidly that the effect of such an intro-duction would be anything but a beneficial one. Many a barrel of sound and sweet apples has been rendered rotten and worthless by disregarding the few unsound ones injudiciously left among them, or thoughtlessly thrown among them, as the narrow-minded, greedy and short-sighted slave-trader of three centuries ago unloaded upon our shores the black men of Africa, with a similar result.

Owing to his ever-present desire to ravish the white women of the dominant race, be their social position what it may, he, the negro demonstrates to us every year that now goes by, by scores of successful assaults upon our womankind, often associated with their murder and mutilation, that, in spite of fire, hanging and lead, in spite of any kind of suasion, he intends, if possible, in any number of individual cases, to gratify this heinous lust of his, be the consequences what they may. This seething mass of black sensual bestiality, ever ready to erupt in hundreds of isolated instances and in localities of every conceivable kind, has at last had the effect of terrorizing white women throughout very large sections of the country, to the detriment of the sex, both individually as well as collectively, and thus fostering a factor, at once disadvantageous to the community, and inimical to the progress of a true and advanced civilization.

Of himself, either as an individual or a class, the negro is too grossly and hopelessly ignorant to recognize the ruin his very presence entails among us; too dastardly and too much of a moral coward to inaugurate as a race any general movement along the lines of segregation that would relieve the people which has taken so many years to arrive at the state of perfection that it now enjoys, and which for humanity's sake it is so important and essential it should at all hazards preserve. The negro is not that much of a practical and self-sacrificing humanitarian. These negroes would see the entire Indo-European race rot in its tracks before they would take a single step to prevent it, even if they recognized that they were the cause of the danger of the putridity. Many of them know enough to realize the fact that the potential elements of a successful growth and a clean civilization is not inherent in them, as a race; and that if with all their boasted improvements since they were liberated in this country, they were transported to any other country to work out their own destiny, a lapse back to savagery would be the inevitable result,—a result, I may say, that would be of the most far-reaching advantage to the real civilizers of the world, and of the most superlative import to the world at large and to posterity.

Plenty of uninformed people among us there are to say, "Oh, but give this race a chance, an opportunity for its uplifting" (its uplifting is a favorite expression of such people), "and you will soon see the wonders it will effect." To such people it may be plainly said, that the black or

Ethiopian race is probably many, many centuries older than our own, that is, older than the Indo-European stock, and yet what has it done for civilization? Nothing, except in the case of a corporal's guard of hybrids, some dead and a few living, who have made a noise in the world, owing to the fact that the black mammies along the line of their ancestry, at various periods of its evolvement, lay to a white man, and the progeny at different times inherited its modicum of brains, and a certain degree of expansibility of the cranial sutures. That's all, and that's all there is to it.

Nowhere in all history has such a state of affairs, as the one here presented, fallen to the lot of mankind. At no time have two such distinct races, each numbered by its millions, the one representing the highest stage of civilization and advancement, the other practically but a day removed from savagery and cannibalism and all that that means, been thrown together in the same geographical region and not separated by any natural barriers. As a matter of fact, we have no examples in the history of man to guide us in our action or to point the way for us toward any effective and rational solution. The state of affairs preëminently requires some very independent thinking, and the exercise of more than usual judgment. Mixed races, we know from experience, however, rarely if ever succeed in the world's history and in mankind's career. The blacks, for a long time past, have interbred with the Indo-Europeans along the shores of the Mediterranean Sea, and although those blacks are of an infinitely better race than the stock we have with us in this country, it has been to the decided detriment of the whites, and resulted in distinctly retarding their progress. There is no reason whatever why we have any right to hope for any better results in the United States, and every reason to believe that they will be at all as good.

The great question now is, What will the eventual outcome of it all be? That is not so difficult to see. Possibly in a few places in the present volume I may have termed the state of affairs under consideration—a problem, while, as a matter of fact, there really is no problem, and to my mind the outcome of it all can hardly even be considered problematical. From mice to monkeys, and from monkeys to men, the mixing of a low and undesirable stock with a high and cultured stock is sure to produce a mixed stock, which is almost invariably not as good as either of the others that produced it. As I have before remarked, many times, there is but one remedy available, inasmuch as we cannot utterly destroy all the inferior race, and that is complete and thorough separation. Will this ever be done in the case of the negroes and their hybrids in the United States? No, I think not. I fear matters have now gone altogether too far to have any hope of such a thing's happening. Of course, *we could do it,* because we have the power, but it simply will not be done. Neither the government or those in power, as a whole, possess the necessary foresight and intelligence to perceive the danger. Some few do, but the vast majority do not; and, therefore, there can be no consensus of opinion in the premises, and certainly no accord in the action. As a race, the negroes themselves are altogether too pusillanimous by nature to dream of doing anything of the kind, nor have they the qualifications of mind, character, ability or organization to effect any such common movement. They are only great when sustained by a high civilization; remove this from them and they would all soon return to savagery and the practices of their forefathers,—their black forefathers.

What then? Just what I have said in print a dozen times during the last dozen years or more. Hybridization, mixing of the two races, and all the horrors, all the set-backs, all the assaults and consequent lynchings, all the increase of crime and rot of every imaginable nature which that entails.

The placing of the race in this country has been and still is a most supreme piece of stupidity,—no one's particular fault, in fact, perfectly natural, though none the less a glaring ethnological fiasco. Practically we exterminated the Indians occupying the country; we for years imported all the scum we could from Europe, Asia and Africa; we flooded the territory with black savages and cannibals; and we declared the Chinese could not land upon our soil. A combination of orders and exploits, apart from the natural migratory instincts of the human race, that has had its influence, which will surely bear its fruit some day, but it will be so gradual that the race will never realize it at any period of its evolution and development.

Source:
R. W. Shufeldt, *The Negro: A Menace to American Civilization* (Boston: Richard G. Badger, 1907), pp. 175–82.

56

Letter to
Sam H. Reading

BY SENATOR J. THOMAS HEFLIN

James Thomas Heflin (1869–1951) was a longtime U.S. representative (1905–20) and senator (1920–31) from Alabama. A white supremacist who was supported by the Ku Klux Klan in the 1920s while delivering anti-Catholic speeches throughout the country, Heflin joined with Klansmen and fundamentalist Protestants in a futile attempt to oppose the nomination of Alfred E. Smith as the Democratic candidate for president in 1928. In a letter written to a journalist, Sam H. Reading, on October 15, 1929, and read in the Senate on February 7, 1930, Heflin expresses violent opposition to the prospect of intermarriage between whites and African Americans.

MY DEAR SIR: In reply to your request I will say that I have read with a feeling of sadness and indignation the newspaper account of the humiliated and grief-stricken white father and mother in New York City who could get no assistance from either Governor Roosevelt or Mayor Walker or anyone else in authority in their effort to prevent the marriage of their daughter to a negro. The press reports tell us that the white father and mother wept freely when interviewed by the newspaper men and made no attempt to hide their tears and humiliation when New York officials issued a marriage license to a negro to marry their daughter. And this terrible thing has happened here in what we used to call the land of Anglo-Saxon rule and white supremacy. Shame on those in authority who will permit such a humiliating, disgraceful, and dangerous thing to happen in the United States. Where are the white men of self-respect, of

331

race pride, and love of the white man's country in America whose brave forbears long ago decreed that there should be no pollution of the blood of the white race by permitting marriage between whites and negroes? What has become of the brave knights of the white race who once boasted of their proud Caucasian lineage? For many generations they stood guard on the dividing line between the Caucasian race and the Negro race.

The far-reaching harm and danger of marriage between whites and negroes to the great white race that God intended should rule the world is apparent to all intelligent students of history; such mixtures have always resulted in weakening, degrading, and dragging down the superior to the level of the inferior race. God had a purpose in making four separate and distinct races. The white, the red, the yellow, and the black. God intended that each of the four races should preserve its blood free from mixture with other races and preserve race integrity and prove itself true to the purpose that God had in mind for each of them when He brought them into being. The great white race is the climax and crowning glory of God's creation. God in His infinite wisdom has clothed the white man with the elements and the fitness of dominion and rulership, and the history of the human race shows that wherever he has planted his foot and unfurled the flag of his authority he has continued to rule. No true member of the great white race in America is going to approve or permit, if he can prevent it, the marriage between whites and negroes.

This desire and purpose on the part of the great white race in America to keep its blood strain pure and to prevent marriage between whites and negroes can better be designed as the "call of the blood." It has come down to us through the centuries. White women, rather than become the wives of the black man, whenever the issue was presented, fought and died, if necessary, to remain true to the "call of the blood." But it seems that in New York, under alien influence, that the line of demarcation between the great white race and the Negro race, the "great divide," that once constituted the "dead line" in America on questions of social equality and marriage between whites and negroes, have been repudiated by those of the Roman-Tammany régime now in charge of New York City and New York State. These officials owe it to the great white race in the State of New York and in the whole United States to protect, safeguard, and preserve in their integrity these principles and ideals so dear to the great white race in America.

The time has come for all true Americans of the Caucasian race to wake up to the dangers that threaten us. There can be no yielding on this great question in order to serve the program and purpose of the Roman-

Tammany political machine. We must stand steadfast, and we will stand steadfast, in our purpose and determination to preserve in its integrity race pride and purity and white man's government in the United States. I regret to say that the present disgusting and deplorable situation in New York State, which permitted a white father and mother to be subjected to the humiliating and shameful ordeal of having to submit to the marriage of their daughter to a negro, is not new under the modern Roman-Tammany system in New York City and State. Scores of negroes in Harlem, New York, members of the so-called Democratic Tammany organization, have been permitted to marry white wives with license granted by and with the hearty approval of the State and city government presided over by Governor Smith and Jimmie Walker and now by Gov. Franklin Roosevelt and Jimmie Walker. These things are shocking, disgusting, and sickening not only to the Democrats but to the true representatives of the great white race in all parties the country over.

The fact that the Roman Catholic Church permits negroes and whites to belong to the same Catholic Church and to go to the same Catholic schools and permits and sanctions the marriage between whites and negroes in the United States is largely responsible for the loose, dangerous, and sickening conditions that exist in New York City and State to-day and the all-important question of preserving the integrity of our race and white supremacy in the United States.

My knowledge of this open and notorious social equality policy, this terrible system in New York State, permitted and approved by Governor Smith, was one of the things that made it impossible for me to support him for President in 1928. Many States in the Union have laws which forbid marriage between whites and negroes; all of the States should have, and some day will have, such laws. I understand that New York would have had such a law but for the opposition of Governor Smith and his Tammany friends in the legislature. Alabama has such a law, and I helped to put it in the constitution of that State in 1901.

Very truly,

J. Thos. Heflin.

Source:
Senator J. Thomas Heflin, Letter to Sam H.
Reading (October 15, 1929), *Congressional
Record* 72, no. 3 (February 7, 1930):
3234–35.

57

Take Your Choice: Separation or Mongrelization

BY THEODORE G. BILBO

Theodore Gilmore Bilbo (1877–1947) was a Democratic governor of Mississippi (1916–20, 1928–32) and U. S. senator (1935–47). Although initially a supporter of the New Deal, Bilbo became preoccupied with the issue of race in the later 1930s. He advocated the resettlement of blacks in Africa and attacked a law passed in the District of Columbia allowing racial intermarriage. In Take Your Choice: Separation or Mongrelization *(1947) Bilbo looks with horror at the idea of intermarriage, especially in the South.*

WHENEVER THE MINGLING of the races on terms of social equality is permitted, then the possibility of intermarriage must be admitted. If the social segregation of the white and black races is destroyed, then intermarriage becomes a question of the personal preference of the individual. The possible might then become the actual. There are all sorts of people, and there is no explanation for the actions or tastes of some individuals; for example, note the recent marriage of the twenty-one year old white girl from Canada to the corpulent, fraudulent, pot-bellied, coal-black, seventy year old Negro who calls himself Father Divine.

If social equality should be granted and intermarriage should become a matter of individual taste, then the pride of race and the sense of blood superiority which has heretofore protected the Southern whites would be destroyed. Racial self-respect has been the rock of salvation of the

334

South. Because the otherwise proud Spaniard in South America did not possess this characteristic, he amalgamated with the colored races around him, and the results are evident for all the world to view. Anyone who would destroy racial pride and break down segregation of the races in the South by implanting the infamous doctrine of social equality must realize that such efforts would plunge Dixie into hopeless depths of mongrelism.

The white Southerner firmly, absolutely, and irrevocably denies the contention of the social equality advocates that mongrelization would not degrade the South. Any one who is familiar with the pages of history and the doctrines of biology must know the dangerous results of the amalgamation of the white and black races. That the Negro is inferior to the Caucasian has been proved by six thousand years of world wide experimentation as well as craniologically, and that the mingling of the superior with the inferior will result in the lowering of the higher is just as certain as the fact that half the sum of six and two is only four.

Even if only the lower strata of whites mingled with the upper strata of Negroes, the result would be the same. Not only would the other circles be broken within the foreseeable future, but it is wholly erroneous to contend that a child is born of its immediate parents only. Every child is a child of its race, and there is no escape from the almightiness of heredity. However weak the white man, his ancestors produced the greatness of Europe; however strong the black, his ancestors never lifted themselves from the darkness of Africa.

Should the social barriers in the South be broken down, the mongrel poison would spread far and wide, and there would be no power sufficient to stop it. Once the blood has been corrupted, neither fame nor fortune, neither culture nor science, not even religion itself can ever restore its purity. If the blood of the white and black races mixed freely within her borders, the South, like the white race, would be forever doomed. Pure blood may flow in some veins, but who could prove it? And no power on earth can redeem the vitiated blood of a race.

At this point, the advocates of social equality are quick to point to the miscegenation which has already occurred in the South. Those who advance this argument must either advocate widespread miscegenation or admit that the South should strengthen her racial barriers instead of removing the ones which exist. We deplore the conditions which have poured a broad stream of white blood into black veins, but we deny that any appreciable amount of black blood has entered white veins. As disgraceful as the sins of some white men may have been, they have not in any way impaired the purity of Southern Caucasian blood. Southern white women have preserved the integrity of their race, and there is no one who can today point the finger of suspicion in any manner whatsoever at the blood which flows in the veins of the white sons and daughters of the South.

The South stands for blood, for the preservation of the blood of the white race. We shall not relax in any way whatsoever the social barriers which have been erected to maintain the purity of that blood. The South will not grant to the Negro race social equality with the whites. There may be individual cases which claim our sympathy and appeal to our sense of fair play, but it is no more a case of individual justice than of individual morality. It is a question of preserving for ourselves and for our posterity the blood, heritage, and culture of the white race.

If the racial instinct of the white race is so strong, then wherein does the danger lie? There is, of course, no real danger when the instinct is aroused and on guard. Without a doubt, this has been the salvation of the South. But today a constant warfare is being waged against this instinct, and every conceivable effort is being made to destroy it altogether or to drug it to sleep in the name of science, of democracy, or of religion. Time and time again the white South is scorned and ridiculed; her people are called "unenlightened" and "prejudiced"; her customs and institutions are insulted and attacked. Agencies of the Federal Government, men and women in high office, powerful political organizations, pressure groups, various associations and individuals are throwing the weight of their power and influence to destroy racial segregation. When those who are preaching social equality are advocating a policy which would be ruinous to the South, can they expect the Southern people to sit idly by?

Let no one doubt but that the fighting South will defend her position. In our section the Negro problem is neither academic nor hypothetical; we live in the midst of it. The South will pledge her strength, wealth, and sacred honor to maintain racial segregation and the color line. Mr. Ethridge was right. There is not enough power in all the world, not in all the mechanized armies of the Allies and the Axis, including the atomic bomb, which could now force white Southerners to abandon the policy of the social segregation of the white and black races.

But let us be realistic. What about the next generation and the next and the next? The Southern whites are in the minority when it comes to determining the policy of the Federal Government; the Negro problem increases yearly; and there are centuries ahead of us. The South needs help, and for the sake of generations yet unborn the South pleads for that help before it is too late. Alone and unaided, Southerners may maintain a white South for many decades yet, and we shall do so in spite of all outside attacks even those coming from members of our own race whose battles we are also fighting. But the South can hope for no permanent victory over the Negro problem without the aid of the North, East, and West. We must have the help of the entire Nation to bring about the physical separation of the races. This is a problem which the Nation created and which only the Nation as a whole can adequately and permanently solve.

Source:
Theodore G. Bilbo, *Take Your Choice:
Separation or Mongrelization* (Poplarville, MS:
Dream House Publishing Co., 1947),
pp. 56–59.

58

The Invasion of Mississippi

BY EARL LIVELY, JR.

Opposition to desegregation was widespread in the South in the 1950s and 1960s. One of the most striking incidents occurred at Oxford, Mississippi, when James H. Meredith attempted to enroll at the University of Mississippi. Although the Fifth Circuit Court of Appeals maintained in June 1962 that Meredith had been denied enrollment "solely because he was a Negro," Governor Ross R. Barnett continued to oppose Meredith's entrance into the university. On September 30, 1962, Meredith was escorted by U.S. marshals into the university. Rioting subsequently broke out in which two people were killed and 375 injured. Three thousand federal soldiers were brought in to quell the tumult.

The journalist Earl Lively, Jr., subsequently produced a monograph, The Invasion of Mississippi *(1963), in which he protested the actions of the government, maintaining that many African Americans have been indoctrinated into communism and that whites are now the oppressed party in the South.*

NEITHER THE NEGRO NOR THE WHITE MAN in the South deserve the trouble that is being agitated by outsiders. The southern white man *lived* with the near-savages dumped into the slave markets by Yankee traders; with rare exception he treated the Negro kindly and sheltered him through early encounters with the fears, frustrations and complexities of civilization. The Negro often took his white master's name and the two shared a genuine affection.

Much of the racial discord in the South since those early days can be traced to interference by northern radicals—the rabid abolitionists, Reconstruction congressmen, carpetbaggers and today's do-gooders and Comsymps. True, the Negro does have some legitimate complaints, and deep prejudices exist. But these prejudices have been carved deeper by outside interference. And—Warren's "modern scientific authority" to the contrary—prejudice is a natural thing which can exist within man's rights. Illegal and immoral discrimination, however, should be eliminated; but the Negro is being led along the wrong path to this goal.

The objective observer should ponder the circumstance of the Negro's alliance with the Communists. The Negro did not seek out the Communist. (Most Negroes are still unaware that he is in their camp.) The Communist *exploited* the Negro's propaganda potential. The Reds capitalized (if they will pardon the expression) on the relative social status of the Negro. Communism was always the highly-*vocal* "champion" of the "downtrodden masses." The Negro offered an even greater potential for propaganda, disruption and eventual revolution than did the "workers of the world" at whom the party pitch had always been aimed.

For decades, the party's inoculation of the Negro would not "take." This failure resulted from the *nature* of the Negro in America—he was a *spiritual* being. Patriotism to the Negro for many years was as natural as his complete faith in and fear of God. But after several decades of "liberal" education in colleges well-stocked with Communist-front "educators," and after years of the altruist-collectivist ethics preached from the pulpit, the Negro is changing from a spiritual being to a socially oriented *political* being.

Identified as a "have-not" by the Communists, drooled-over, fawned-on and fondled by "altruistic," integrationist white "intellectuals," the Negro has gradually accepted his martyred status and has come to believe that all the economic and social *privileges* they accord him are his by *right*.

The Negro's inflated "civil rights" have now become the concern of do-gooders and collectivists of all stripes, crowding completely out of the picture those who would help him in his legitimate endeavors. As a means of achieving these "rights" the liberals advocate disobedience. In other words, the Negro is urged to gain what he believes to be *lawful* by the *breaking* of laws! Such schizophrenia is commonplace in the altruist mentality. . . .

The tremendous external pressures applied to the political atmosphere of the South have forced an inversion in which the Negro has risen to the political top. He is still outvoted locally, but he no longer has to deal with the white man on the local level; the Justice Department does the

Negro's bargaining there, and he can expect *more than justice* when he deals on the national level. The Southern Negro is no longer in the minority; his alliance with radical northern voting blocs—and with the Kennedy Administration—has forced the southern white man into the minority role.

If anyone is oppressed in the South today, it is the white man. His laws are violated and struck down by edicts of a judicial oligarchy, his rights are trampled, and his land is repeatedly invaded by the brute force of a tyrannical federal Administration.

Southern whites are now feeling the pressures which seek to extend the new political advantage of the Negro to the social and economic spheres. This can not be accomplished, of course, without far worse erosion of the property rights of whites than has already occurred. The whites are, by and large, the producers; and collectivist "sharing" will have to be at their expense.

This thrusting of the Negro into the driver's seat in the South can only result in chaos. This was tried during the Reconstruction period with tragic results that have not yet been overcome.

Differences between the races in the South were gradually disappearing until the Supreme Court's desegregation decision of 1954. Then the Warren Court drove a wedge between Negroes and, whites that has been hammered deeper by the blows at Little Rock, Oxford, Greenwood, Birmingham, Jackson and elsewhere. Now the evolution toward racial harmony has stalled just short of its goal and revolution has been substituted as the means to Negro achievement.

Revolution will achieve only bloodshed, chaos and a victory for communism. Southern whites and Negroes alike will be heavy losers; so will the nation.

Source:
Earl Lively, Jr., *The Invasion of Mississippi*
(Belmont, MA: American Opinion, 1963),
pp. 115–17.

59

Public Record of George C. Wallace

BY ANONYMOUS

The political career of George Corley Wallace (1919–1998) was changed forever when he lost the 1958 Georgia gubernatorial election to a rabid segregationist; Wallace subsequently vowed never to be "out-niggered" again. Wallace served four terms as governor of Georgia (1963–67, 1971–79, 1983–87). He ran as a third-party candidate for president in 1968 and 1972; in the former election he won ten million votes, and in the latter he was secretly supported by operatives for President Richard M. Nixon who hoped to divide the Democratic vote. On May 15, 1972, one day before he won the Maryland and Michigan primaries, Wallace was shot and seriously wounded by a mentally disturbed white man, Arthur Bremner. The following article in the Congressional Quarterly *summarizes Wallace's stands on civil rights. In later years Wallace renounced many of his racist views. Wallace died September 13, 1998.*

BIRMINGHAM. On April 3, 1963, Negroes seeking greater civil rights began mass demonstrations in Birmingham. A temporary truce between the demonstrators and white businessmen was finally arranged on May 8, and on May 10 it was announced that public accommodations would be desegregated within 90 days, that greater job opportunities would be made available to Negroes, and that formal means of communication would be set up between the white and Negro communities.

Violence, however, broke out the next day when bombs were thrown at a motel room occupied by the Rev. Martin Luther King Jr., president

341

of the Southern Christian Leadership Conference and an organizer of the demonstrations, and at the home of his brother, the Rev. A. D. King. President Kennedy May 12 announced that he had instructed the Defense Department to "alert" military units specially trained in riot control and dispatch them to Birmingham. The following day the President sent a telegram to Wallace saying that federal troops would be sent to Birmingham if necessary. Wallace immediately filed a court appeal protesting the use of federal troops. The appeal was rejected by the U.S. Supreme Court May 27 in a one paragraph *per curiam* opinion. The troops were never sent.

University of Alabama. On June 11, 1963, Wallace fulfilled his campaign pledge to "stand in the school house door" to prevent integration of Alabama's schools. The door was to Foster Hall, where two Negro students, Vivian Malone and James Hood, were to register to enter the University of Alabama at Tuscaloosa. Wallace was under a federal court injunction not to bar their entry, but he was waiting in the doorway when Deputy Attorney General Nicholas deB. Katzenbach and other federal officials arrived to aid the admittance of the Negroes. When Katzenbach told Wallace that he had a proclamation from the President directing the Governor to end his defiant stand, Wallace replied by reading a long statement charging that the federal action was "a frightful example of the oppression of the rights, privileges and sovereignty of this state by officers of the Federal Government," and claiming that "the operation of the public school system is a power reserved to the state of Alabama- under the Constitution of the United States and the 10th Amendment."

Katzenbach withdrew to return a few hours later with an order from President Kennedy federalizing the Alabama National Guard. At the second confrontation, Wallace declared, "The trend toward military dictatorship continues. But this is a constitutional fight and we are winning." He then stepped away from the door and the two students were successfully registered. By the fall of 1966, 396 Negro students were enrolled in the entire University of Alabama.

School Integration. In September 1963, Wallace again attempted to prevent integration of Alabama's schools, this time in elementary and secondary public schools in Birmingham, Tuskegee, Mobile and Huntsville. President Kennedy Sept. 10 once again issued an Executive order federalizing the Alabama National Guard. However, the troops were never called into action.

At the same time, riots broke out in Birmingham, culminating in the Sept. 15 bombing of a church and the deaths of four Negro girls attending Sunday school there. In a statement expressing the nation's sympathy to the families of the children, President Kennedy Sept. 16 said, "It is regrettable that public disparagement of law and order had encouraged violence which has fallen on the innocent." The statement was widely interpreted as a reference to Wallace's defiance of court orders effecting desegregation.

Selma. In January 1965, Martin Luther King chose Selma, Ala., as the site of a campaign to "dramatize" to the nation the existing bars to Negro voting in several Southern states. Throughout the next two and a half months demonstrators from across the nation met in Selma to protest voting discrimination. On March 7, state troopers, under orders from Wallace to stop a march from Selma to Montgomery, used tear gas, night sticks and whips, seriously injuring about 40 persons. Civil rights workers immediately filed petitions with the U.S. district court in Montgomery for a temporary restraining order against Wallace and the state troopers. On March 17, Judge Johnson, Wallace's longtime foe, issued the requested injunction, while denying Wallace's petition for an injunction forbidding the march. The demonstrators completed their march to Montgomery March 25 under the protection of the Alabama National Guard which had been federalized by President Johnson. . . .

School Desegregation. Wallace is bitterly critical of the school busing laws aimed at creating a racial balance among children, and tells his campaign audiences that "when I am President not one dime of federal money will be spent for busing one single student." He adds that, "If you people want to take your children and send them all the way to Montreal, Canada, to go to school, it's all right by me. You do whatever you want to do."

Asked about his views on desegregation on a June 30 Meet the Press program (NBC-TV), Wallace said: "Many people think the idea of a separate school system in the South meant separation of the races. There has been more mingling association and togetherness among the people of opposite races in our part of the country than exist in places throughout the entire world. So we are not talking about separation of the races; we are talking about local democratic institutions."

Appearing on Face the Nation (CBS-TV) July 21, Wallace said "we did have a social separation in the school system because the school systems of the rural South were the social center. So we just quite candidly and honestly said we will have a separate school system. And we were honest about it." Wallace said if he were President, "I wouldn't advocate segregation," but would only say, "you run your schools yourselves." As to what he would do about the laws on desegregation, Wallace said the guidelines set forth by the Department of Health, Education and Welfare "transcend even the Civil Rights law," particularly on school busing, "and I would stop that." Wallace said "we have more togetherness in Alabama than you have in Washington, D.C. This is a segregated city here, because of the hypocrites that have moved out."

Wallace has said in the past, however, that he favored federal aid to education.

In an Aug. 18 speech in Hammond, Ind., Wallace told the audience that he was not a racist. "They say it is racist to oppose those federal guidelines that would tell us how to run lives. Well, when you can't talk about upholding the Constitution without being called a racist, this country has come to a sad day. They say it's racist what I say, but they're really using this as an excuse to get control of your heart and mind."

On a campaign flight to Montgomery Sept. 20, Wallace told reporters that he expected "the people" to "physically take over the schools through the police power" of the states if he loses the 1968 Presidential election. "It's within the law and nobody can do anything about it," he said. Wallace said this revolution would have two steps. First, he predicted, there would be huge rallies and demonstrations throughout the United States. Then, he said, states would begin to assert their police powers to protect the health and safety of the populace. He flatly predicted this revolution would occur in Alabama. Referring to an Orlando, Fla., rally he had just left, Wallace said, "Did you see those women in there? They were hysterical—about their children . . . folks are mad about law and order . . . and about schools. . . . Race mixing doesn't work. Show me a place where it's worked." Wallace Sept. 22 said he meant a political and not a violent takeover of the schools. Wallace stressed that such a takeover would remain within the law and be brought about through the police powers of individual states. "The people are going to rise up, but rise up at the ballot box," Wallace said, to demand a return of local control of school districts.

Source:
Anonymous, "Public Record of George C. Wallace," *Congressional Quarterly Weekly Report* 26, no. 39 (September 27, 1968): 2559–60, 2564–65.

60

Presumed Guilty

BY SERGEANT
STACEY C. KOON, L.A.P.D.

Stacey C. Koon (b. 1950) was one of four Los Angeles police officers who pursued African-American motorist Rodney King in the early morning hours of March 3, 1991, and (as revealed by an amateur videotape) beat and kicked King in an attempt to subdue him. In a subsequent state trial for police brutality, Koon and two other officers were found not guilty of all charges; the all-white jury split on charges for the fourth officer, Laurence Powell, with eight out of twelve jurors voting for acquittal. Days of rioting followed the verdict. The four officers were subsequently brought to trial on federal charges of violating King's civil rights. Koon and Powell were convicted on April 17, 1993, and later sentenced to two and a half years in prison; the other two officers were acquitted. King was awarded $3.8 million in a subsequent civil suit against the city.

In Presumed Guilty *(1992), written by Koon (with the assistance of journalist Robert Deitz) after his acquittal in the first trial but before the commencement of the second, Koon condemns the media's treatment of the incident and defends his and his colleagues' conduct.*

T HE ULTIMATE MEDIA ESTABLISHMENT voice, the *New York Times,* made its judgment on May 1, two days after the verdict. Of course, this meant the editorial was written within twenty-four hours of the Simi Valley decision, since the *Times'* deadline schedule cannot accommodate instant response. And, again, that judgment was based on the videotape—to their minds, the only evidence—and not on the evi-

345

dence presented during the trial, which the nation's newspaper of record had presumably covered.

On Friday, May 1, the *Times* said that the George Holliday videotape "made the verdict rendered Wednesday by the Rodney King jury doubly shocking. It found the four defendant policemen to be not guilty of brutality that millions of Americans, the other jury, thought was indisputable. And far from discouraging uncontrolled police brutality, the trial jury's actions seemed to *validate* it" (emphasis in original).

The only hero during the riots, suggested *Newsweek* competitor *Time* magazine, was Rodney King.

"For more than a year he had been a writhing body twisting on the ground under kicks and nightstick blows in what may be the most endlessly replayed videotape ever made," *Time* said. "Then on Friday afternoon TV finally gave Rodney King a face and a voice—a hesitant, almost sobbing voice that yet was more eloquent than any other that spoke during the terrible week. 'Stop making it horrible,' King pleaded with the rioters who had been doing just that in Los Angeles—and, to a lesser degree in San Francisco, Atlanta, Seattle, Pittsburgh and other cities."

It is necessary here to dwell on Rodney King's "writhing" on the ground under "kicks and nightstick blows." The evidence clearly shows that the "writhing" was repeated attempts to get up in order to assault a police officer. He wasn't feeling pain. Nor did he suffer major injuries. All of the proof presented at the trial validated that point. Even the prosecution's proof conceded that point.

Was he being kicked? Yes, at least once. For the rest, they weren't kicks so much as efforts to keep a dangerous felony suspect down on the ground, to keep his hands out of pockets we hadn't yet had an opportunity to search. Did the kicks hurt Rodney King? No. Did they keep him from assaulting an officer again? We'll never know. All we know is that he didn't have another chance to attack an officer.

Was he being beaten? Absolutely. That's because we had exhausted every tool we had available short of shooting the suspect. And we didn't want to shoot him, we didn't want to kill him.

It is not frivolous, I think, to dwell for a short time on the "eloquence" that *Time* ascribed to Rodney King. It is worth a moment to question whether a dangerous drunken driver, parole violator, and aggressively violent felony offender has earned noble, even heroic, status for repeatedly violating the law and resisting arrest. And it is worth another to observe that Rodney King's "hesitant, almost sobbing" eloquence referred to by *Time* magazine might have been, as *Vanity Fair* later suggested, due more to being tranquilized by modern drugs and the prospect of collecting on a $56 million lawsuit than a result of any other factor.

The reason for mentioning these matters is that of all the victims of the violence, Rodney King was not one of them. Indeed, he and his attorneys may be the only winners in the entire affair. Rodney King stands to collect millions of dollars in ransom from the city of Los Angeles because he got drunk and violently resisted arrest on March 3, 1991. He also may get millions of dollars more by selling T-shirts and other collectibles bearing his name. As evidence can demonstrate, in today's society, the criminal can extract ransoms and make the law enforcement community the bad guy. Rodney King and his promoters reportedly are peddling a life story and a movie script lionizing him as a courageous champion of civil rights somewhere in the midst of the passive resistance of Martin Luther King, the militant activism of Malcolm X, and the political savvy of Nelson Mandela. . . .

But even if you regard him as the first victim, Rodney King was the least victimized of all. That's certainly true when you compare the profits he stands to reap from his actions on March 3, 1991, with the price paid by the people who died and were hurt in the riots, those storekeepers who lost their shops and livelihood, the workers whose jobs vanished in the smoke of flames from the riots.

But let's begin with the Simi Valley jurors. They are most certainly victims. According to press reports, since the trial some have been menaced by death threats from anonymous callers. All have suffered abusive criticism from the media for their verdicts of not guilty. They have become outcasts in their own communities. Some have had children threatened. Others have lost friendships. The media have reported that one woman juror fears for her job. All of the jurors were deeply affronted by communications from the Ku Klux Klan, notifying them that they had been made members of the KKK and that the right-wing lunatic fringe "stands ready to defend you at a moment's notice."

This dubious compliment from the KKK right-wing wackos is in sharp contrast to the absence of support from the court system for the bravery of the jurors' actions and verdict, their willingness to judge a case on facts, evidence, and law and not on the emotional politics of media-fed passions. After the trial, the jurors were abandoned by the court without even the customary expression of appreciation for their service. According to *Los Angeles Magazine,* the jurors suffer many of the same symptoms of stress and tension experienced by war veterans. Not surprisingly, they have formed a mutual support group that meets occasionally to offer comfort to one another.

And what about the cops who were found innocent? Even before the spurious charges of violating Rodney King's civil rights that a federal grand jury returned on August 5, 1992, it was disturbing to see what had happened to the officers who were doing their duty on March 3, 1991. This is especially true when you compare their experience with Rodney King's apparent reprieve from parole violations that would have returned him to prison, and his efforts to gouge millions of dollars from the city of Los Angeles.

Tim Wind, Ted Briseno, and Larry Powell have been doing odd jobs since going on unpaid suspension in April 1991. These three trained, dedicated police officers have had to spend most of their time preparing for the defense of a criminal trial, a federal trial, and subsequent internal administrative hearings that have yet to be scheduled. The three have been able to pick up some cash by helping the police league move its offices, working as part-time security guards, and doing other routine blue collar work. But none has been able to find a full-time job. No employer is going to hire somebody whose time is being taken up defending against criminal charges, even if an employer could ignore the massive publicity attending those charges.

Even after the federal civil rights suit and LAPD trial boards are concluded, their careers on the Los Angeles Police Department are effectively over. However unjust it might be, Wind, Briseno, and Powell will always bear the stigma of having been involved in the Rodney King affair.

Source:
Sergeant Stacey C. Koon, L.A.P.D., with
Robert Deitz, *Presumed Guilty: The Tragedy of
the Rodney King Affair* (Washington, DC:
Regnery Gateway, 1992), pp. 193–97.

61

Reasonable Doubts

BY ALAN M. DERSHOWITZ

Few events in recent years have highlighted racial tensions in the United States more keenly than the case of O. J. Simpson. Orenthal James Simpson (b. 1947) is an African American who achieved high distinction as a football player at both the collegiate and the professional levels; he subsequently became a widely popular television personality. On June 13, 1994, his white wife, Nicole Brown Simpson, and a white man, Ronald Goldman, were found murdered outside her condominium in the Brentwood section of Los Angeles. A few days later Simpson was charged with the murder; after a car chase along the highways of southern California viewed by millions on television, Simpson was apprehended. The trial began on September 26, 1994. One of Simpson's defense team's central tactics was to broach the possibility that Simpson had been framed by the Los Angeles Police Department, a charge made more plausible by the revelation of sloppy police work and also by tapes revealing police detective Mark Fuhrman to be highly prejudiced against African Americans. On October 3, 1995, the largely black jury's decision was read: Simpson was found not guilty of both murders. A majority of whites continue to believe that Simpson is guilty, while a majority of African Americans believe he is innocent. It is also widely believed that the jury's verdict was a kind of retribution for the Los Angeles Police Department's handling of the Rodney King case.

In a subsequent civil trial brought against Simpson by the Goldman family, a largely white jury found Simpson guilty of wrongful death and awarded the Goldmans $8.5 million in compensatory damages and $25 million in punitive damages.

Alan M. Dershowitz (b. 1938), a civil liberties lawyer and professor of law at Harvard, has written several books on legal matters, including The

Best Defense *(1982), a lively summary of several of his previous cases, and* Reversal of Fortune *(1986), an account of his successful defense of Claus von Bulow for the attempted murder of his wife.* Chutzpah *(1991) is his autobiography. In* Reasonable Doubts *(1996), Dershowitz, who served as part of O. J. Simpson's defense team, ponders the influence of race in the Simpson criminal trial and the verdict, pointing out that African Americans and whites frequently view the same incidents from different perspectives because of their differing backgrounds, especially in regard to their treatment by the police.*

I HAVE ALWAYS BELIEVED THAT RACE is a salient characteristic in our criminal justice system. Race matters in how one is treated from the initial encounter with the police to the gubernatorial decision whether to commute the death sentence. For more than a quarter of a century, race has been a central concern in my first-year criminal law course at Harvard Law School. I tell my students that to study criminal justice in America while omitting the impact of race is to blink at reality. Many criminal law teachers deliberately omit controversial issues, such as race and gender, from their courses. Especially if they are white and male, they regard classroom discussions of these hot-button issues as no-win situations. Most of those who do allow discussion of these issues stay above the fray, allowing the students to "vent" their frustrations but rarely expressing their own views. I take the opposite tack. Since many students are reluctant to express views in class which may be "politically incorrect," I go out of my way to play the devil's advocate whenever controversial issues are discussed.

Most of my students are aware of my strong personal views on race, especially as relevant to the death penalty, since I began writing about that issue even before I became a professor. When I was a law clerk for Justice Arthur Goldberg on the Supreme Court, I was responsible for a memorandum which raised the first challenge to the constitutionality of capital punishment as racially discriminatory. That memorandum eventuated in a dissenting opinion by three justices—Goldberg, Brennan and Douglas—that for the first time in American judicial history raised questions about the constitutionality of the death penalty and invited the bar to begin to challenge it, especially in racially discriminatory contexts.

Over the next quarter of a century, I have fought against the disparate application of the death penalty based on the race of the perpetrator and assailant. In a *Nightline* debate on the eve of the Supreme Court's most important decision on this subject, I took the position that the death penalty, as administered, violates the "equal protection" clause of the

Constitution because a black man who kills a white is far more likely to be executed than a white man who kills a black.

The attorney general of Georgia, Michael Bowers, responded that it "so happens that the highly aggravated cases will generally involve, or to a higher degree involve, white victims, while those with more mitigating circumstances, or more highly mitigated, will more likely involve black victims." I replied that this did not just "so happen"—it was "not a coincidence." Instead, "it reflects a kind of racist ideology. It says that when a white person is killed, we perceive the circumstances as more aggravated than when a black person is killed. . . . [W]e look at cases through the lens of our own perspectives."

It is interesting that some conservatives who are now confident that the Simpson verdict was based on black racial bias are the same conservatives who argue against blaming disparate death penalty verdicts on white racial bias. The statistical evidence is clear: Predominantly white juries impose the death penalty far more frequently on blacks who kill whites than on whites who kill blacks. When our equal protection challenge was brought to the Supreme Court on the basis of these statistics, many conservatives were quick to argue that we cannot know *for certain* that race was the determining factor in these sentences. In my *Nightline* debate with Attorney General Bowers, he discounted the statistical proof and demanded proof that each particular juror "intended" to discriminate on the basis of race. I responded as follows:

> The [Attorney] General says that it doesn't matter what the statistics show, unless you can show in a particular case that the jurors sat there and said, "We're going to consider race." Well, we can't get into the jury box; we can't get into the jury mind. The only way we can figure out what juries and prosecutors and judges are using—whether intentionally or unintentionally—is to look at a mass of cases. If, for example, some employer has a pattern of never, never hiring a black—always preferring the white—we can't know in any particular case that the white wasn't more qualified than the black, but nonetheless, the courts around the country say, "That's enough for us."

All people—white, black, Hispanic, Asian, Jewish, male, female, gay, heterosexual—view the world through the prism of their experiences. I am even prepared to believe that the original twelve jurors from Simi Valley who voted to acquit the Los Angeles policemen caught on videotape beating Rodney King honestly saw that videotape differently than did the twelve Los Angeles jurors who subsequently convicted the same cops of essentially the same crime on the basis of the same evidence.

The social science research supports this conclusion, *both* for white jurors *and* for black jurors. Darnell Hunt, a sociology professor at University of Southern California, set up separate black and white focus groups to test their perceptions of the same evidence in the Simpson case. His preliminary conclusion was that "based on their respective life experiences in our still largely segregated society, blacks and whites often perceive the same event or individual in different ways." Vanderbilt University law professor Nancy J. King, in her review of the effect of race on jury verdicts, concluded that, "studies . . . confirm that juror race affects jury decisions in some cases." Two frequent findings are (1) that blacks are more likely to acquit than whites, and (2) that both blacks and whites are more likely to acquit defendants of their own race than those of other races.

A significant number of studies have found that white jurors are more likely than black jurors to convict black defendants and that they are also more likely to acquit defendants charged with crimes against black victims.

One mock-juror study found that black jurors were more likely to acquit defendants of either race, and white jurors were especially resistant to developing reasonable doubts about black defendants during deliberation. Other such studies have found that both black and white jurors favor defendants of their own race. White subjects in these studies were more likely to find a minority-race defendant guilty than they were to find an identically situated white defendant guilty. . . .

The consensus seems to be that race is more likely to affect juror verdicts indirectly, through perceptions of the evidence, than directly, through explicit racial favoritism. This way of looking at the impact of race on jury verdicts explains a common finding in several juror research studies. In some mock-juror studies, researchers systematically vary the strength of the evidence in the simulated trials. The results reveal that race strongly affects verdicts only when the evidence is inconclusive, neither very strong nor very weak.

This suggests that, contrary to the views of prosecutor Marcia Clark and others, jurors do not necessarily "vote their race" by disregarding strong evidence. Instead, their life experiences condition their view of the evidence, and that view in turn influences their verdict.

One particular element of the life experience of many blacks, likely to affect their views of criminal evidence, was central to the Simpson case. Many black jurors did not need to hear the Fuhrman tapes in order to accept the possibility that the police would lie and tamper with evidence in order to set up a black man. Many blacks, in Los Angeles and elsewhere, experience racist police harassment regularly. They also encounter more subtle discrimination from white-dominated authorities on a daily basis.

Rare is the African American who cannot relate a tale of having been stopped by police in an affluent neighborhood or followed closely at the heels around a clothing store. As [black Harvard law professor Charles Ogletree] recently put it, "If I'm dressed in a knit cap and hooded jacket, I'm probable cause." One consequence of such treatment is that the attitudes of blacks and whites toward police diverge markedly.[1]

This difference was recently confirmed, in a way directly relevant to the Simpson case, by a study of eight hundred former jurors. This study found that "forty-two percent of whites believed that, given a conflict between a law enforcement officer and a defendant, the police officer should be credited. Only twenty-five percent of African-American jurors interviewed felt that the police officer's testimony should be believed."[2]

Evidence of the misdeeds of detectives Vannatter and Fuhrman directly implicated these attitudes and beliefs of black jurors. According to many researchers and scholars, the most important verdict-affecting belief that black citizens bring to the jury box is an appreciation that the police may lie, tamper with evidence, and violate constitutional rights in order to investigate and prosecute a defendant—especially a black defendant. For whites, on the other hand, police perjury is a concept largely outside their realm of experience. "For whites, such a situation could only be imagined."

It may well be the case that in some instances minority jurors have a fuller, more realistic picture of the criminal justice system and its vagaries than do members of the white mainstream. Given their disparate experiences of law enforcement, middle-class white jurors are more inclined than African Americans to believe that police officers always tell the truth, act with integrity, and protect the innocent.

Much of the white United States had a very difficult time believing the possibility that the O.J. blood evidence in the trial was suspect. . . . Most of black America did not. That's because most of us know, or know of, somebody who has been through some kind of funky business with the police trying to make their arrests air-tight. Mark Fuhrman was not nearly the shock for black people as he seemed to be for whites.[3]

As *The New York Times* asked rhetorically in an editorial about "police thuggery" in cities ranging from Los Angeles to New Orleans and Philadelphia:

What must it be like to grow up in a neighborhood where the only difference between police and out-and-out criminals is that the police wear uniforms? More and more Americans are finding out. The effect on communities, and on the attitudes of jurors, is corrosive. . . . The children who witness police lawlessness will one day grow up to be jurors. No one should be surprised when they take a jaundiced view of police testimony. . . .

Immediately after the swift verdict, Marcia Clark provided a simple-minded racial explanation that was echoed by many commentators and observers: "Liberals don't want to admit it, but a majority black jury won't convict in a case like this. They won't bring justice." Vincent Bugliosi, who prosecuted the Charles Manson gang, gave a similar assessment: "I've never seen a more obvious case of guilt. . . . Yet this jury apparently gave no weight to the mountain of incriminating evidence and instead bought into the defense argument that this was a case about race." Apparently this view is widely shared in some quarters:

> Since the Simpson verdict was announced, more than a few people seem to think that the jury system needs to be revamped, that black people cannot discern fact from fiction and that a predominantly black jury will acquit a black defendant regardless of the facts.
> The prosecution's defenders say the race issue blinded the jurors to the evidence.
> Incited by Johnnie Cochran—good lawyer, bad citizen—to turn the trial into a political caucus, the jurors did that instead of doing their banal duty of rendering a just verdict concerning two extremely violent deaths. The jurors abused their position in order to send a message about racism, police corruption or whatever.[4]

The extremity of some of these simpleminded views has produced equally extreme and simpleminded claims from some that race played no role in this case. The truth is more complex and multilayered. Though we will never be able to get into the minds of the jurors—even those who give (understandably self-justifying) accounts of their votes—it is clear that race alone cannot account for this verdict, especially since it was joined by three nonblacks, one of whom had previously turned around a jury that had originally voted eleven to one for acquittal. This is not to say that the verdict necessarily would have been the same if the case had been presented to an all-white or predominantly white jury. Race matters, in all kinds of subtle and overt ways.

For example, one middle-class black juror said that he experienced racism directly for the first time while on this jury, at the hands of court deputies. This experience "colored his view" of some of the police testimony. Although he thinks Simpson may have committed the murders, he is convinced that the police may have "attempted to frame a murderer."

This juror may have become open to considering this possibility as a result of his treatment by deputies in this very case. If this is true, it certainly illustrates the unpredictable ways in which race can influence a juror. (Interestingly, the defense team was hearing reports of possible racism by deputies, and we were of two minds about how to react: On the one hand, no one wanted to tolerate any form of discrimination, but on the other hand, we suspected that any perceived racism on the part of uniformed deputies might redound to the disadvantage of the prosecution. As defense attorneys, we had to place the interests of our client first.) . . .

We certainly also hoped and expected that some of the black jurors would be open to the possibility that white police officers might lie about a black defendant. *We* believed that Vannatter and Fuhrman were not telling the truth. We hoped the jury would agree with us. We were pleased that we had a largely black jury, which might be more open to arguments about police perjury, evidence tampering, and so on—arguments we believed were correct. If that is playing the race card, then the race card *should* be played—because the fact is that police do routinely lie and do sometimes tamper with evidence, and it is good that juries include people whose life experiences make them receptive to these possibilities.

It is possible, of course, that a largely black jury could be wrong in a particular case and find police perjury where none occurred. It is equally possible that a largely white jury could also be wrong in a particular case and find no police perjury where it did occur. Which is the worse type of error? I submit that under our system of justice, it is far better for a jury to err on the side of finding perjury where it did not occur than in failing to find it where it did occur. This is precisely how one juror—a white woman—put it after the verdict. In describing why she voted for acquittal even though she was uncertain whether the police had tampered with evidence, Anise Aschenbach said: "If we made a mistake, I would rather it be a mistake on the side of a person's innocence than the other way." This is the correct approach under our law because of the strong presumption of innocence, based on the judgment that it is better that ten guilty defendants go free than that one innocent be wrongly condemned. I believe it is also good policy, because most *judges* refuse to find perjury by the police even when it is obvious to everyone. The jury is our only realistic protection against police perjury, and if black jurors are more likely than whites to be open to finding police perjury, then that is a racial "bias" that promotes justice.

Indeed, it is fair to ask why so much more criticism has been directed against black jurors (and blacks in general) for "closing their minds" to the possibility that Simpson might be guilty, than against whites for closing *their* minds to the possibility that the police might have planted evidence against him. Lorraine Adams, a white reporter for *The Washington Post*, found that African-Americans were much more open-minded about the case than were whites. "The whites . . . are more implacable and [are] hearing less. . . . I find an unwillingness on the part of whites to hear, to actually listen and absorb and give credit to the black experience [with] the criminal justice system." Adams was especially critical of the white media, whose reporting in any "conspiracy" claim "always . . . says it's implausible." She found blacks "much more able to come up with reasons why [Simpson] could be guilty." This observation led *Los Angeles Times* reporter Andrea Ford to ask why the media did not do stories "trying to explain why whites were so overwhelmingly certain of his guilt? Why were blacks, rather than whites, cast as the people whose position needed explaining?"

In fact, the black suspicion of police—even if sometimes exaggerated—is generally more accurate than the white trust of police, which is also exaggerated. According to a *Los Angeles Times* poll, 67 percent of whites believe that "false testimony" by police is "uncommon," while only 21 percent of blacks believe it is uncommon. Notwithstanding the vagueness of the operative terms, the empirical evidence suggests that the black respondents' position is closer to the truth.

Ford continued: "There's an underlying tone of, 'These [black] people are irrational. They're ignoring the evidence.' Well, what was so rational about those white people in these early polls deciding [Simpson] was guilty before they learned a scintilla of evidence? I have seen no stories on that." Several white journalists were "equally outraged" at the implicit assumption that black open-mindedness was more "rational" than white closed-mindedness.

If we consider the matter in a larger perspective, we can all agree, I hope, that racially diverse juries—in particular cases and in the range of cases—are essential for justice in America. For generations, there were no blacks on juries, even on juries that were trying black defendants. Those all-white juries made many mistakes, because they viewed the evidence through the prism of their white life experiences. All-black juries would make similar mistakes. In many parts of the country, even today, juries are still predominantly white, with only a few blacks. These juries, too, make mistakes based on a dominant white bias (although we hope that this bias is ameliorated somewhat by the presence of even a small number of blacks). We rarely hear complaints from the majority community or media about these mistakes.

Those who believe that *this* predominantly black jury may have made a mistake because of its dominant black bias, and that this bias was not ameliorated by the presence of three nonblacks on the jury, should consider that possible mistake in the context of our hundreds of years of jury mistakes on the other side. This is not an argument for some kind of "affirmative action" in jury trials. It is an attempt to explain that some degree of bias in assessing the evidence, based on race and gender, is inherent in the jury system. Sometimes the bias falls on one side. Sometimes it falls on the other. Yet the criticism of *this* verdict, on the ground of racial bias, has been louder, angrier, and more sustained than in any other case, with the possible exception of the first Rodney King verdict. Moreover, words were used to describe the Simpson verdict that have not been used to criticize other verdicts. Characterizing the Simpson jury as "dominated and controlled by highly emotional, racist blacks" and the verdict as a "racially motivated and racist verdict," "charade," "simply unbelievable," and "one of the biggest travesties in the history of American jurisprudence," suggest something beyond mere disagreement. They suggest a double standard in evaluating the "erroneous" verdicts of predominantly white and black juries.

Several weeks after the verdict, Christopher Darden offered an assessment of the Simpson verdict dramatically different from the one offered by Marcia Clark. He was not prepared to characterize the verdict as "race-based," since, in his view, "a whole lot of other things" went into it. Paramount among those factors, he said, was the sorry history of the Los Angeles Police Department's abuses, which made the predominantly black jury more likely to acquit Simpson when considering the standard of reasonable doubt. If a juror's "experience has always been negative, if it involves contact with the police and courts, then what kind of a jury verdict can we expect?" Darden asked. He then reported that virtually any African-American man, himself included, could tell a personal story of injustice at the hands of the police. Darden thus confirmed the soundness of the defense approach of challenging the credibility of certain Los Angeles police officers in the expectation that the Simpson jury would be more open to such challenges than would be jurors to whom police abuses are a distant abstraction. As to those—including, presumably, some of his fellow prosecutors—who characterize this verdict as entirely race-based, Darden remarked that "It is easy to wave that flag."

The jurors in this case—three quarters of whom were black women—viewed the case more through the prism of race than through that of gender because on its facts, it turned more on race-related than on gender-related life experiences. Even for the sole white woman on the jury, this case turned more on the racial bias of the police than on the spousal abuse of the defendant.

Source:
Alan M. Dershowitz, *Reasonable Doubts: The O. J. Simpson Case and the Criminal Justice System* (New York: Simon & Schuster, 1996), pp. 109–15, 121–27.

PART NINE

Jews

ANTI-SEMITISM REPRESENTS A DIFFERENT brand of racism from that affecting African Americans: lacking a different skin color and stereotyped as being skillful in finance, Jews have often elicited a grudging respect and envy rather than scorn and contempt. Jews were present in small numbers in the early colonial period, and Roger Williams—a champion of the Native Americans and promoter of religious liberty, who welcomed Jews into his new colony of Rhode Island—nevertheless encapsulated, as early as 1652, two of the principal justifications for anti-Semitism: the Jews are not Christians (they had killed Jesus) and they are good at making money, particularly through usury. These accusations would resound with mechanical sameness throughout the length and breadth of American history. Hannah Adams, America's first professional woman author, whose *History of the Jews* (1812) is a strange mixture of praise and censure, finds it perplexing that the Jews, "notwithstanding the calamities they have so long endured, still look down upon all nations, and continue to claim the partial kindness and protection of heaven." How can they be the "chosen people" if they are scorned by all and sundry?

Anti-Semitism has been endemic in all Western civilization, and indeed a kind of genteel prejudice against Jews was long fashionable among the British and American upper classes, as the examples of John Hay, John Jay Chapman, T. S. Eliot, and others attest. William Lloyd Garrison and Lydia Maria Child, ardent abolitionists that they were, could not see the contradiction in deprecating prejudice against African Americans and adhering to prejudice against Jews. One of the most vicious polemics was written by the obscure novelist Telemachus Thomas Timayenis, who in *The Original*

359

Mr. Jacobs (1888) and *Judas Iscariot* (1889) urged nothing less than an uprising on the part of working-class people to overthrow the Jews: "The Jew does not earn his living, he does not produce. He thrives only through usury and exploitation. His life is a continued plot; he is a thief."

One of the flashpoints for anti-Semitic sentiment was the Leo Frank case. On April 26, 1913, a thirteen-year-old Irish girl, Mary Phagan, was raped and murdered at the pencil factory in Marietta, Georgia, where she worked. Leo M. Frank, superintendent of the factory, was subsequently tried and on August 25, 1913, found guilty of the murder; he was sentenced to death. The evidence on which his conviction was based was highly suspect, and there is good reason to believe that Frank was framed. Governor John M. Slaton, aware of the uncertainties surrounding Frank's conviction, evoked tremendous outrage when, on June 21, 1915, he commuted Frank's sentence to life imprisonment. On August 16, 1915, a mob broke into Frank's prison in Milledgeville, took him to Cobb County, and lynched him the next day. The case itself, however, refused to die. On March 11, 1986, after a three-year investigation, the State Board of Pardons and Paroles issued a statement in which it did not find "conclusive evidence proving beyond any doubt that Frank was innocent" but nonetheless granted him a posthumous pardon.

All this did not, of course, stop the racist Thomas E. Watson—later a U.S. senator—from being incensed at the many Jewish individuals and organizations that aided Frank's defense, interpreting it as an instance of big Jewish money attempting to overturn the truth. Watson quotes with approval E. A. Ross's remark (although one suspects that the italics and capitals are Watson's) that "pleasure-loving Jewish businessmen *spare Jewesses, but PURSUE GENTILE GIRLS*," adding his own comment that the case clearly demonstrates *"a lustful eagerness enhanced by the racial novelty of the girls of the uncircumcised!"* Absurd as this may sound, it nevertheless created an atmosphere that led to the death of a man who was probably innocent.

Anglo-American anti-Semitism received a momentary boost in 1920 by the translation into English of a work called *Protocols of the Wise Men of Zion*. The *Protocols* had first appeared in Russian in Sergei Aleksandrovich Nilus's *Tsarkoye Selo* (1905) and claimed to be a Jewish work outlining a conspiracy for political and economic domination of the world. Although quickly revealed as a hoax, it continued to be reprinted by anti-Semites and was hailed as the proof of the Jews' nefarious intentions. At any rate, it convinced Henry Ford; when asked in a 1921 interview whether he believed the *Protocols* to be genuine, he stated blandly: "The only statement I care to make about the protocols is that they fit in with what is going on. They are sixteen years old, and they have fitted the world situation up to this time. They fit it now." Ford's *Dearborn Independent* was then launching vicious attacks on Jews, which would be collected in four volumes under the title *The International Jew* (1922). One wonders whether the Ford Motor Company's sponsoring of the television broadcast of Steven Spielberg's *Schindler's List* was an attempt to make amends for its founder's embarrassing views or an attempt to brush them under the rug.

Three of the most notorious anti-Semites, who raised their share of turbulence from the 1930s to the 1950s, were William Dudley Pelley, Charles E. Coughlin, and Gerald L. K. Smith. Pelley's Silver Shirts was only one of several neofascist groups of the 1930s, always remaining on the fringe of American political life but potentially dangerous in at least a limited capacity. Pelley's development of the idea of a Christian commonwealth can only be likened, in the present day, to a hypothetical union of Christian fundamentalists with paramilitary groups. In "How I Would Treat the Jews" (1936) he proposes an ingenious plan for rounding up all the Jews in the country and depositing them in one designated city in each state, where they would be obliged to remain, doing business only with themselves. Charitably, Pelley did not plan to separate Jewish families as his compatriot across the ocean in Germany would later do. Coughlin masked his anti-Semitism under the guise of social justice, while Smith—appalled as both Pelley and Coughlin were at the fancied infiltration of Jews into government during the Roosevelt administration and the apparent leniency in cracking down on communism—fulminated from the pages of his magazine, *The Cross and the Flag*, and preached "Christian Nationalism." Can anyone wonder at the emergence of Senator Joseph McCarthy shortly thereafter?

While it can be said that anti-Semitism, as with most other forms of prejudice, is no longer tolerated in mainstream culture, it would be naive to imagine that it has disappeared altogether. Laura Z. Hobson's trenchant novel *Gentleman's Agreement* (1947) highlighted the degree to which prejudice against Jews continued to function in the business world even after World War II, and evidence suggests that many colleges and universities up to a very recent time had a tacit quota system for Jews in order to restrict their numbers. Barefaced anti-Semitism is perhaps now only the prerogative of the Black Muslims or of fringe groups venting their hatred on the Internet; but that covert prejudice continues to exist in a variety of forms—as perhaps in some historians' denial of the severity of the Jewish Holocaust in the interest of historical "accuracy"—can scarcely be denied.

62

A Testimony . . .

BY ROGER WILLIAMS

Roger Williams (c. 1603–1683) was a Puritan pastor in Salem and Plymouth who was sentenced to exile in 1635 by the Massachusetts General Court for his opposition to religious authoritarianism; he fled south and founded the city of Providence in what later became Rhode Island. Williams became renowned for his tolerance of all creeds and his benevolent treatment of Native Americans; he also allowed Jews into the colony, but the following passage from a treatise of 1652 suggests that he was not without prejudice against them.

LASTLY, I HUMBLY CRAVE LEAVE to say, That I am not without thoughts of many *Objections*, and cannot without *horror* think of the *Jews* killing of the *Lord Jesus*, of their *cursing* themselves and their *posterity*; of the *wrath* of *God* upon them; of their denying the *Fundamentals* of all our *Christian Worship*; of some *crimes* alleged for which they have been so afflicted by this *Nation*; of their known Industry of inriching themselves in all places where they come. But I dare not prejudice the high *wisdom* and *experience* of the *State*, abundantly rich and able to provide answerable *Expedients*, if once it please the most *High* to affect their Honorable breasts with the *piety* and *equity*, the *duty* and *necessity* of so great a Work.

Source:
Roger Williams, "A Testimony to the 4th Paper Presented by Major Butler to the Honorable Committee for Propagating the Gospel" (1652), in *The Complete Writings of Roger Williams*, edited by Perry Miller (New York: Russell & Russell, 1963), vol. 7, p. 137.

63

The History of the Jews

BY HANNAH ADAMS

Hannah Adams (1755–1831) was the first professional woman writer in the United States. She was the author of many volumes of history, among them The History of the Jews *(1812). In this work, Adams asserts that "the history of the Jews exhibits a melancholy picture of human wretchedness and depravity."*

THE JEWS, NOTWITHSTANDING THE CALAMITIES they have so long endured, still look down upon all nations, and continue to claim the partial kindness and protection of heaven. The miracles, performed in favour of the first Hebrews, inspired their descendants with a contempt for those nations which the Deity never honoured in the same manner. They are more elated with the advantages granted to their ancestors, than humiliated by the calamities which they have endured since their dispersion.

We may number among the most striking traits which designate the Jewish character, the wonderful uniformity of views that appear to have influenced the actions of this extraordinary people through the course of so many ages. The Rabbinists, which form the bulk of the nation in different countries, agree in their dogmas, rites, and religious habits; because no religion establishes such an uniformity in doctrine as the Mosaic, which, joined to the traditions of the doctors, regulates with the utmost minuteness every thing which respects life. These people, wherever dispersed, have carried with them their language and religion, and abandoned none of the customs but those which they could not preserve. Even climate has had scarcely any effect upon them, because their manner of life counteracts and weakens its influence. Difference of periods and countries has, therefore, strengthened their character, instead of altering its original traits.

The Jews, since their final expulsion from Palestine, have universally attached themselves to traffic for a subsistence. Being generally prohibited from acquiring and cultivating land, and interdicted from following trades and professions, the objects of their industry have been limited, and they compelled to confine themselves to commerce. The political state of the European powers in the middle ages furnished them with many and even lawful means, of enriching themselves. Buying and selling were occupations confined exclusively to them; and they conducted the whole retail trade in Europe, especially in Germany. They improved the opportunities afforded them of acquiring wealth; and their opulence having awakened the avarice and jealousy of their enemies, interest conspired with superstition to endeavour their destruction. Being continually persecuted and stript of their riches, they found it essential to their existence to oppose oppression by fraud. These acquired habits were continued from age to age, and all the energy of their minds directed to the pursuit of gain. In consequence of which their usurious practices increased the public hatred, and excited fresh persecutions.

"It would, however," says a celebrated author, "be highly unjust to imagine, that the whole Hebrew nation are a people destitute of principles and good morals. We find a number of striking exceptions among the Jews of Portugal, Italy, France, and above all Holland, where, for two centuries, not one of them has been condemned to death; among the Jews of Germany, Amsterdam, Berlin, and even in Lorrain; among those in the English colonies, where many of them, by their good conduct, have attracted the notice of government; and if we attend to the general prejudice entertained against them, we must allow, that the Jews who meet with esteem are undoubtedly worthy of it."[1]

Another late author remarks, that "the Jews on many accounts are entitled to a very high degree of esteem, from their general character and deportment. Their charities to the poor of their own communion are immense; and their peculiar isolated situation through the world, in the midst of strangers, has drawn the bonds of affection towards one another more close. Their care to adjust their differences in civil concerns amicably among themselves is edifying; and let it not be forgotten, that, if on any account they are justly censurable, our unworthy treatment of them may have forced them into the very acts which we condemn."[2]

In the midst of their calamities and depression, the Jews have all along paid some attention to their language and religion; but dispersed as they are, and without a country of their own, they cannot be expected to have such national establishments as universities; yet in almost every considerable town on the continent, where they reside in any great numbers, schools are formed under the auspices of their presiding or dominant rabbies, who confer titles on their scholars, or on others who deserve them. They appear to have two degrees, analogous to, and most probably taken from the usages at universities; the one rabbi, nearly equivalent to A. B. and the other Morenu Rab, answering to doctor. These appear to be of modern institution, and to have commenced about the year 1420; previous to which the latter term is not found; and the distinction is supposed to have become necessary, in order to prevent the irregular conducting of marriages and divorces, which every one presumed to do, in consequence of the title of rabbi, although not sufficiently informed, or qualified for the office. The origin of these schools was evidently the sanhedrim in the temple; by whose determination the laws were explained, and all the Mosaic institutions were reduced to minute and actual practice. The form, period, and manner of all ceremonies and observances were by them established, and handed down to successive sanhedrims, who, as intricate circumstances and questions arose, gradually enlarged the code, and provided for both extraordinary and ordinary situations.

An ingenious author, who is said to be of Jewish origin,[3] has, however, observed, that "the entire system of Hebrew education is inimical to the progress of the human mind. Dark and stationary in ignorance, or bewildered with intricate superstition, their modes of life are little favourable to forming a taste for the productions of nature and art; and the sole occupation permitted them, the art of acquiring wealth, extinguishes their bolder and prominent passions. Men of learning among the Jews are obliged to encounter numerous obstacles; and their most malignant and powerful enemies are found among their domestic associates. If a literary Christian is matured at thirty, a literary Jew can scarcely be matured at forty. They have, therefore, addicted themselves to those studies which have little connexion with the manners of men. They have had severe metaphysicians, and industrious naturalists; and have excelled in the practice of medicine. But in polite letters they have had few literary characters of eminence. Sensible that they do not at present bear chains under tyrants, they feel grateful that they exist under men; but the energies of glory die in inertion, and honour is strangled by the silken cord of commerce.". . .

The history of the Jews exhibits a melancholy picture of human wretchedness and depravity. On one hand we contemplate the lineal descendants of the chosen people of God, forfeiting their inestimable privileges by rejecting the glory of Israel, and involving themselves in the most terrible calamities; condemned to behold the destruction of their city and temple; expelled [from] their native country; dispersed through the world; by turns persecuted by Pagans, Christians, and Mahometans; continually duped by impostors, yet still rejecting the true Messiah.

On the other hand, we see the Christian world enveloped in darkness and ignorance; and the professed disciples of the benevolent Redeemer violating the fundamental precepts of the Gospel; assuming a shew of piety as a mask for avarice, and a pretence for pillaging an unhappy people. If from the west we turn to the east, we shudder over similar scenes of horror; wherever the Mahometan banner is erected, contempt and misery await the Jews. In short, their history exhibits all the wild fury of fanaticism; the stern cruelty of avarice; a succession of massacres; a repetition of plunders; shade without light; a dreary wilderness, unenlivened with one spot of verdure.

Still, however, in traversing the desert, a wonderful object arrests our attention, and the feelings of indignation and compassion are suspended by astonishment while we contemplate the "bush burning with fire, and not consumed,"—a helpless race of men, whom all nations have endeavoured to exterminate, subsisting during ages of unrelenting persecution; and though dispersed in all nations, still in all countries preserving their own customs and religious rites; connected with each other by a community of sentiments, of antipathies, and pursuits, yet separated by a wonderful destination from the general mass of mankind.

Source:
Hannah Adams, *The History of the Jews from the Destruction of Jerusalem to the Present Time* (Boston: J. Eliot, Jr., 1812; reprinted London: A. Macintosh, 1818), pp. 543–51.

64

Letters from New York

BY LYDIA MARIA CHILD

*Lydia Maria Child (1802–1880) was a novelist and polemicist who wrote
the first antislavery tract,* Appeal in Favor of That Class of Americans
Called Africans *(1833). She was an advocate of woman's suffrage and sex
education, and the author of* A History of the Condition of Women in
Various Ages and Nations *(1835). In* Letters from New York *(1844),
Child acknowledges Judaism's role in giving rise to Christianity but dwells
at length on Jewish economic domination.*

T HERE IS SOMETHING DEEPLY IMPRESSIVE in this remnant of a
scattered people, coming down to us in continuous links through the
long vista of recorded time; preserving themselves carefully unmixed by
intermarriage with people of other nations and other faith, and keeping
up the ceremonial forms of Abraham, Isaac, and Jacob, through all the
manifold changes of revolving generations. Moreover, our religions are
connected, though separated; they are shadow and substance, type and
fulfilment. To the Jews only, with all their blindness and waywardness,
was given the idea of one God, spiritual and invisible; and, therefore,
among them only could such a one as Jesus have appeared. To us they
have been the medium of glorious truths; and if the murky shadow of
their Old dispensation rests too heavily on the mild beauty of the New,
it is because the Present can never quite unmoor itself from the Past; and
well for the world's safety that it is so. . . .

The proverbial worldliness of the Jews, their unpoetic avocations, their
modern costume, and mechanical mode of perpetuating ancient forms,
cannot divest them of a sacred and even romantic interest. The religious

idea transmitted by this remarkable people, has given them a more abiding and extended influence on the world's history, than Greece attained by her classic beauty, or Rome by her triumphant arms. Mohammedism and Christianity, the two forms of theology which include nearly all the civilized world, both grew from the stock planted by Abraham's children. On them lingers the long-reflected light of prophecy; and we, as well as they, are watching for its fulfilment. And verily, all things seem tending toward it. Through all their wanderings, they have followed the direction of Moses, to be *lenders* and not *borrowers*. The sovereigns of Europe and Asia, and the republics of America, are their debtors, to an immense amount. The Rothschilds are Jews; and they have wealth enough to purchase all Palestine if they choose; a large part of Jerusalem is in fact mortgaged to them. The oppressions of the Turkish government, and the incursions of hostile tribes, have hitherto rendered Syria an unsafe residence; but the Sultan has erected it into an independent power, and issued orders throughout his empire, that the Jews shall be as perfectly protected in their religious and civil rights, as any other class of his subjects; moreover, the present controversy between European nations and the East seems likely to result in placing Syria under the protection of Christian nations. It is reported that Prince Metternich, Premier of Austria, has determined, if possible, to constitute a Christian kingdom out of Palestine, of which Jerusalem is to be the seat of government. The Russian Jews, who number about 2,000,000 have been reduced to the most abject condition by contempt and tyranny; but there, too, government is now commencing a movement in their favour, without requiring them to renounce their faith. As long ago as 1817 important privileges were conferred by law on those Jews who consented to embrace Christianity. Land was gratuitously bestowed upon them, where they settled, under the name of The Society of Israelitish Christians.

These signs of the times cannot, of course, escape the observation, or elude the active zeal of Christians of the present day. England has established many missions for the conversion of the Jews. The Presbyterian Church of Scotland have lately addressed a letter of sympathy and expostulation to the scattered children of Israel, which has been printed in a great variety of Oriental and Occidental languages. In Upper Canada, a Society of Jews, converted to Christianity, have been organized to facilitate the return of the wandering tribes to the Holy Land.

The Rev. Solomon Michael Alexander, a learned Rabbi, of the tribe of Judah, has been proselyted to Christianity, and sent to Palestine by the Church of England; being consecrated the first Bishop of Jerusalem.

Moreover the spirit of schism appears among them. A numerous and influential body in England have seceded, under the name of Reformed Jews. They denounce the Talmud as a mass of absurdities, and adhere exclusively to the authority of Moses; whereas, orthodox Jews consider the rabbinical writings of equal authority with the Pentateuch. They have sent a Hebrew circular to the Jews of this country, warning them against the seceders. A General Convention is likewise proposed, to enable them to draw closer the bonds of union.

What a busy, restless age is this in which we are cast! What a difficult task for Israel to walk through its midst, with mantles untouched by the Gentiles.

'And hath she wandered thus in vain,
A pilgrim of the past!
No! long deferred her hope hath been,
But it shall come at last;
For in her wastes a voice I hear,
As from some prophet's urn,
It bids the nations build not there,
For Jacob shall return.'

Source:
Lydia Maria Child, *Letters from New York*
(New York: C. S. Francis & Co., 1844),
pp. 45–47.

65

The Original Mr. Jacobs

BY TELEMACHUS THOMAS TIMAYENIS

Telemachus Thomas Timayenis (1853–?) was a novelist and classical scholar who wrote two vicious polemics against Jews, The Original Mr. Jacobs *(1888) and* Judas Iscariot: An Old Type in a New Form *(1889). In the former work, Timayenis urges the working classes to rise up against Jews.*

THROUGHOUT THE WORLD THOSE who disgrace the profession of law, those who are ready to espouse any side for pay, those who have monopolized the lowest and dirtiest practice of the lawyer's profession, and who have acquired that narrow and confined mode of thinking that a liberal mind would so greatly despise as to be unable to acquire it, are all Jews. Lawyers of infamous character, blasted with imputations of the most atrocious kinds, in the walks of private and domestic life, are Jews.

There is no order in the community more contemptible than that of those Jew practitioners of the law, who, without one liberal principle of justice or of equity, possess skill in little else than quibbles, and are strong in those points only by which villainy is taught to proceed with impunity, cunning enabled to elude legal enactments, and truth perplexed, obscured, and lost in the mazes of chicanery.

Should such men preside as judges where life and death, liberty and property are at stake? What justice, for instance, can a Gentile obtain if he has a case against a Jew, and the case is tried before a Jew judge! See the Talmud. "If a Christian and an Israelite come before you to decide any difference whatsoever, see that the Israelite wins the case. . . . If you cannot openly do so, have the Israelite win the case in any way, through craft and deceit."

What security, we repeat, can a person have if judicial positions fall into the hands of Jews? Our country would be thrust into a darkness as dark as Rome's in her decadence.

Workingmen, never cease, with your votes and your influence, to oppose the Jew—the Jew who has no character, who is steeped in libertinism, in infidelity, in every kind of profligacy which tends to harden the heart and to deaden the feelings of humanity—no less than to stifle the sentiments of true honor. Do not listen to them, workingmen, when they preach to you the German doctrines of socialism, which are those of the German Jew, Karl Marx. The Jew was not, is not, and never will be your friend. Do not let him deceive you. The strike is a system of warfare that belongs to the Jew. The strike is the outcome of the preaching of Karl Marx; it is an idea peculiarly Jewish, an idea of death. It is the death of work under pretext of a struggle against the capitalist. We repeat it to you, workingmen, the strike comes of the teachings of the German Jew, a thing fostered by anarchists, by violators of law, by men who seek to use you as instruments of their private designs; in a word, by the Jews.

Workingmen, if you suffer evils, enlighten yourselves with regard to the nature and the origin of these evils before you surrender yourselves, body and soul, to socialism. Trust not the foreigner who whispers in your ears un-American doctrines, and, above all, do not trust the Jew. It is he who has invented, in order to seduce you, aggressive and insolent liberalism. One cannot compass anything by this course, unless it be to provoke disorders and mutual resistance, evils which stop production, kill the industries of the country and ruin its prosperity.

Workingmen, as soon as you study the manœuvres of the Jew, you will declare him a criminal. His work among you is revolution and disorder. His pretended love for you is the love of the fox for the geese. He is like the swimmer who makes a great ado in the water, but makes no headway. The Jew is a false brother. He is constantly occupied in concealing his designs, the designs of the socialist and the enemy of good order. The hatred of the Jew for the Gentile is a historic fact which the Jew writers themselves are unable to deny. Formerly they bought Gentile prisoners from the Romans solely to torment them and to put them to death. Do not be deceived by smiles, for the smiles of the fiend are dangerous.

Workingmen, you, like us, come from generations that have lived in this country. Our ancestors fashioned our heritage, successively improved it, aggrandized it in honor and dignity. They have given us a history in accordance with our character, our hopes, our ambitions. These ancestors are our own, our dead, just as the fallen leaves of autumn are the ancestors, so to speak, of the leaves of the following spring. The Jew can have no love for this country of yours, for it is not his.

To preserve the honor and dignity of this country, workingmen, to keep its reputation untarnished, is a duty which you must discharge with the same watchful care as that with which you would protect the lives and the honor of your wives and daughters. No one of you would allow his daughter or wife to associate with libertines, with men of low and bad character. How much more earnest and watchful you ought to be of your country! This country cannot tolerate the Jew. She sees him sowing poison everywhere, and she implores you to defend her against the Jew before it is too late.

The men who made both France and Spain so great in the past were neither malefactors nor imbeciles. The measures they adopted against the Jews were not the whims of tyrants, but were forced upon them by existing perils. The workingmen of old refused to endure the oppression of the Semite, refused to listen to his anarchical doctrines, and were unanimous in boycotting everything sold by a Jew. They knew that the furniture, for instance, the Jew sold was of poor workmanship; they knew that the provisions he sold were of bad quality and that he gave false weight. They knew that to secure their own advancement it was necessary to transact no business with the Jews. An association of individuals thinking alike, a community representing certain sentiments, beliefs, aspirations, aptitudes and traditions, defended itself properly against a race that represented sentiments, beliefs, aspirations, aptitudes and traditions absolutely hostile to its own.

The faith of Abraham definitely puts the Jew beyond our law, because the law that the Jews obey in their homes is the negation of ours. The Jew has never done anything that entitles him to be called "the chosen." If our space permitted us to analyze the characters of many of their most prominent men, we should have no difficulty in showing that the best among them were imitators and arrant plagiarists. The strength of the Jew is the strength of the weak—deceitfulness. In the past he was a sorcerer, because as a sorcerer he had no difficulty in deceiving the people. Some people claim that the destiny of the Jew is sad and humiliating, and that consequently he is entitled to our sympathy. Sympathy bestowed upon a Jew is misplaced sympathy.

One does not pity the criminal who does not wish to be pitied. If the Jew is without the pale of law, it is his own fault. He does not change his course. He asserts that he wishes to follow our laws, yet he adheres to his own. Can be ever conform to our usages and really obey our laws? He does not work, he does not produce, he lives by exploitation and dishonest transactions. He proclaims himself a cosmopolitan, a layman, and employs against us violence and exaction, which are the essence of his law—a religious law. He seeks to share the advantages and comforts of our homes, while he aims to deprive us of them. He says he is hungry; we give him free access to our tables, while he moves Heaven and earth to deprive us of our daily bread. He is cold, and asks an asylum in our house; he enters, and it is not long before the house is his. He proposes to engage in commercial affairs with us, that he may sell us trash or stolen goods.

The Jew reminds us of the words of Mirabeau: "There are only two kinds of men, those who work and those who do not work; those who earn their living and those who steal."

The Jew does not earn his living, he does not produce. He thrives only through usury and exploitation. His life is a continued plot; he is a thief.

In a word, hypocrisy and lying are the salient features in the Jew.

"Send your children to the public schools," said Crémieux to his co-religionists, "but be sure and bring them up at home in the law of Moses."

If the Jew is not engaged in blackmailing the rich, the aristocrat, he plots to keep down the poor. The children of the poor whose lives promise to be the hardest, and who most of all need a hope, an ideal, are deprived of all religious teaching in the public schools. Reared without a God, living without a God, they will die without a God.

Source:
[Telemachus Thomas Timayenis],
The Original Mr. Jacobs: A Startling Exposé
(New York: Minerva Publishing Co., 1888),
pp. 295–99.

66

Concerning the Jews

BY MARK TWAIN

Samuel Langhorne Clemens (1835–1910), who wrote under the pseudonym Mark Twain, has come under scrutiny for his racial views, as some African-American scholars believe that his portrayal of Jim in Adventures of Huckleberry Finn *(1884) is racist. Twain's views on Jews are also of interest. In an article, "Stirring Times in Austria," published in the March 1898 issue of* Harper's, *Twain mentioned in passing some attacks on Jews in Austria. Asked by a lawyer to clarify his remarks, Twain responded with "Concerning the Jews" (1899), which caused much discussion in the Jewish press around the world. While Twain's writing is not virulently anti-Semitic, he seems guilty of adopting stereotypes even when he means to praise Jews. In his article he quotes the lawyer's letter and finds six points made in it; he then seeks to answer them one by one.*

IN THE ABOVE LETTER ONE NOTES THESE POINTS:

1. The Jew is a well-behaved citizen.
2. Can ignorance and fanaticism *alone* account for his unjust treatment?
3. Can Jews do anything to improve the situation?
4. The Jews have no party; they are non-participants.
5. Will the persecution ever come to an end?
6. What has become of the golden rule?

Point No. 1.—We must grant proposition No. 1, for several sufficient reasons. The Jew is not a disturber of the peace of any country. Even his enemies will concede that. He is not a loafer, he is not a sot, he is not noisy, he is not a brawler nor a rioter, he is not quarrelsome. In the statistics of crime his presence is conspicuously rare—in all countries. With murder and other crimes of violence he has but little to do: he is a stranger to the hangman. In the police court's daily long roll of "assaults" and "drunk and disorderlies" his name seldom appears. That the Jewish home is a home in the truest sense is a fact which no one will dispute. The family is knitted together by the strongest affections; its members show each other every due respect; and reverence for the elders is an inviolate law of the house. The Jew is not a burden on the charities of the state nor of the city; these could cease from their functions without affecting him. When he is well enough, he works; when he is incapacitated, his own people take care of him. And not in a poor and stingy way, but with a fine and large benevolence. His race is entitled to be called the most benevolent of all the races of men. A Jewish beggar is not impossible, perhaps; such a thing may exist, but there are few men that can say they have seen that spectacle. The Jew has been staged in many uncomplimentary forms, but, so far as I know, no dramatist has done him the injustice to stage him as a beggar. Whenever a Jew has real need to beg, his people save him from the necessity of doing it. The charitable institutions of the Jews are supported by Jewish money, and amply. The Jews make no noise about it; it is done quietly; they do not nag and pester and harass us for contributions; they give us peace, and set us an example—an example which we have not found ourselves able to follow; for by nature we are not free givers, and have to be patiently and persistently hunted down in the interest of the unfortunate.

These facts are all on the credit side of the proposition that the Jew is a good and orderly citizen. Summed up, they certify that he is quiet, peaceable, industrious, unaddicted to high crimes and brutal dispositions; that his family life is commendable; that he is not a burden upon public charities; that he is not a beggar; that in benevolence he is above the reach of competition. These are the very quintessentials of good citizenship. If you can add that he is as honest as the average of his neighbors—But I think that question is affirmatively answered by the fact that he is a successful business man. The basis of successful business is honesty; a business cannot thrive where the parties to it cannot trust each other. In the matter of numbers the Jew counts for little in the overwhelming population of New York; but that his honesty counts for much is guaranteed by the fact that the immense wholesale business of Broadway, from the Battery to Union Square, is substantially in his hands.

I suppose that the most picturesque example in history of a trader's trust in his fellow-trader was one where it was not Christian trusting Christian, but Christian trusting Jew. That Hessian Duke who used to sell his subjects to George III. to fight George Washington with got rich at it; and by-and-by, when the wars engendered by the French Revolution made his throne too warm for him, he was obliged to fly the country. He was in a hurry, and had to leave his earnings behind—$9,000,000. He had to risk the money with some one without security. He did not select a Christian, but a Jew—a Jew of only modest means, but of high character; a character so high that it left him lonesome—Rothschild of Frankfort. Thirty years a later, when Europe had become quiet and safe again, the Duke came back from overseas, and the Jew returned the loan, with interest added.

The Jew has his other side. He has some discreditable ways, though he has not a monopoly of them, because he cannot get entirely rid of vexatious Christian competition. We have seen that he seldom transgresses the laws against crimes of violence. Indeed, his dealings with courts are almost restricted to matters connected with commerce. He has a reputation for various small forms of cheating, and for practising oppressive usury, and for burning himself out to get the insurance, and for arranging cunning contracts which leave him an exit but lock the other man in, and for smart evasions which find him safe and comfortable just within the strict letter of the law, when court and jury know very well that he has violated the spirit of it. He is a frequent and faithful and capable officer in the civil service, but he is charged with an unpatriotic disinclination to stand by the flag as a soldier—like the Christian Quaker.

Now if you offset these discreditable features by the creditable ones summarized in a preceding paragraph beginning with the words, "These facts are all on the credit side," and strike a balance, what must the verdict be? This, I think: that, the merits and demerits being fairly weighed and measured on both sides, the Christian can claim no superiority over the Jew in the matter of good citizenship.

Yet in all countries, from the dawn of history, the Jew has been persistently and implacably hated, and with frequency persecuted.

Point No. 2.—"Can fanaticism *alone* account for this?"

Years ago I used to think that it was responsible for nearly all of it, but latterly I have come to think that this was an error. Indeed, it is now my conviction that it is responsible for hardly any of it.

In this connection I call to mind Genesis, chapter xlvii.

We have all thoughtfully—or unthoughtfully—read the pathetic story of the years of plenty and the years of famine in Egypt, and how Joseph, with that opportunity, made a corner in broken hearts, and the crusts of the poor, and human liberty—a corner whereby he took a nation's money all away, to the last penny; took a nation's live-stock all away, to the last hoof; took a nation's land away, to the last acre; then took the nation itself, buying it for bread, man by man, woman by woman, child by child, till all were slaves; a corner which took everything, left nothing; a corner so stupendous that, by comparison with it, the most gigantic corners in subsequent history are but baby things, for it dealt in hundreds of millions of bushels, and its profits were reckonable by hundreds of millions of dollars, and it was a disaster so crushing that its effects have not wholly, disappeared from Egypt to-day, more than three thousand years after the event.

Is it presumable that the eye of Egypt was upon Joseph the foreign Jew all this time? I think it likely. Was it friendly? We must doubt it. Was Joseph establishing a character for his race which would survive long in Egypt? and in time would his name come to be familiarly used to express that character—like Shylock's? It is hardly to be doubted. Let us remember that this was *centuries before the crucifixion.*

I wish to come down eighteen hundred years later and refer to a remark made by one of the Latin historians. I read it in a translation many years ago, and it comes back to me now with force. It was alluding to a time when people were still living who could have seen the Saviour in the flesh. Christianity was so new that the people of Rome had hardly heard of it, and had but confused notions of what it was. The substance of the remark was this: Some Christians were persecuted in Rome through error, they being *"mistaken for Jews."*

The meaning seems plain. These pagans had nothing against Christians, but they were quite ready to persecute Jews. For some reason or other they hated a Jew before they even knew what a Christian was. May I not assume, then, that the persecution of Jews is a thing which *antedates* Christianity and was not born of Christianity? I think so. What was the origin of the feeling?

When I was a boy, in the back settlements of the Mississippi Valley, where a gracious and beautiful Sunday-school simplicity and unpracticality prevailed, the "Yankee" (citizen of the New England States) was hated with a splendid energy. But religion had nothing to do with it. In a trade, the Yankee was held to be about five times the match of the Westerner. His shrewdness, his insight, his judgment, his knowledge, his enterprise, and his formidable cleverness in applying these forces were frankly confessed, and most competently cursed.

In the cotton States, after the war, the simple and ignorant negroes made the crops for the white planter on shares. The Jew came down in force, set up shop on the plantation, supplied all the negro's wants on credit, and at the end of the season was proprietor of the negro's share of the present crop and of part of his share of the next one. Before long, the whites detested the Jew, and it is doubtful if the negro loved him. . . .

I feel convinced that the Crucifixion has not much to do with the world's attitude toward the Jew; that the reasons for it are older than that event, as suggested by Egypt's experience and by Rome's regret for having persecuted an unknown quantity called a Christian, under the mistaken impression that she was merely persecuting a Jew. *Merely* a Jew—a skinned eel who was used to it, presumably. I am persuaded that in Russia, Austria, and Germany nine-tenths of the hostility to the Jew comes from the average Christian's inability to compete successfully with the average Jew in business—in either straight business or the questionable sort.

In Berlin, a few years ago, I read a speech which frankly urged the expulsion of the Jews from Germany; and the agitator's *reason* was as frank as his proposition. It was this: *that eighty-five per cent.* of the successful lawyers of Berlin were Jews, and that about the same percentage of the great and lucrative businesses of all sorts in Germany were in the hands of the Jewish race! Isn't it an amazing confession? It was but another way of saying that in a population of 48,000,000, of whom only 500,000 were registered as Jews, eighty-five per cent. of the brains and honesty of the whole was lodged in the Jews. I must insist upon the honesty—it is an essential of successful business, taken by and large. Of course it does not rule out rascals entirely, even among Christians, but it is a good working rule, nevertheless. The speaker's figures may have been inexact, but *the motive of persecution* stands out as clear as day.

The man claimed that in Berlin the banks, the newspapers, the theatres, the great mercantile, shipping, mining, and manufacturing interests, the big army and city contracts, the tramways, and pretty much all other properties of high value, and *also* the small businesses—were in the hands of the Jews. He said the Jew was pushing the Christian to the wall all along the line; that it was all a Christian could do to scrape together a living; and that the Jew *must* be banished, and soon—there was no other way of saving the Christian. Here in Vienna, last autumn, an agitator said that all these disastrous details were true of Austria-Hungary also; and in fierce language he demanded the expulsion of the Jews. When politicians come out without a blush and read the baby act in this frank way, *unrebuked,* it is a very good indication that they have a market back of them, and know where to fish for votes.

You note the crucial point of the mentioned agitation; the argument is that the Christian cannot *compete* with the Jew, and that hence his very bread is in peril. To human beings this is a much more hate-inspiring thing than is any detail connected with religion. With most people, of a necessity, bread and meat take first rank, religion second. I am convinced that the persecution of the Jew is not due in any large degree to religious prejudice.

No, the Jew is a money-getter; and in getting his money he is a very serious obstruction to less capable neighbors who are on the same quest. I think that that is the trouble. In estimating worldly values the Jew is not shallow, but deep. With precocious wisdom he found out in the morning of time that some men worship rank, some worship heroes, some worship power, some worship God, and that over these ideals they dispute and cannot unite—but that they all worship money; so he made it the end and aim of his life to get it. He was at it in Egypt thirty-six centuries ago; he was at it in Rome when that Christian got persecuted by mistake for him; he has been at it ever since. The cost to him has been heavy; his success has made the whole human race his enemy—but it has paid, for it has brought him envy, and that is the only thing which men will sell both soul and body to get. He long ago observed that a millionaire commands respect, a two-millionaire homage, a multi-millionaire the deepest deeps of adoration. We all know that feeling: we have seen it express itself. We have noticed that when the average man mentions the name of a multi-millionaire he does it with that mixture in his voice of awe and reverence and lust which burns in a Frenchman's eye when it falls on another man's centime.[1]

Point No. 4.—"The Jews have no party; they are non-participants."

Perhaps you have let the secret out and given yourself away. It seems hardly a credit to the race that it is able to say that; or to you, sir, that you can say it without remorse; more, that you should offer it as a plea against maltreatment, injustice, and oppression. Who gives the Jew the right, who gives any race the right, to sit still, in a free country, and let somebody else look after its safety? The oppressed Jew was entitled to all pity in the former times under brutal autocracies, for he was weak and friendless, and had no way to help his case. But he has ways now, and he has had them for a century, but I do not see that he has tried to make serious use of them. When the Revolution set him free in France it was an act of grace—the grace of other people; he does not appear in it as a helper. I do not know that he helped when England set him free. Among the Twelve Sane Men of France who have stepped forward with great Zola at their head, to fight (and win, I hope and believe) the battle for the most infamously misused Jew of modern times, do you find a great or rich or illustrious Jew helping? In the United States he was created free in the beginning—he did not need to help, of course. In Austria and Germany and France he has a vote, but of what considerable use is it to him? He doesn't seem to know how to apply it to the best effect. With all his splendid capacities and all his fat wealth he is to-day not politically important in any country. In America, as early as 1854, the ignorant Irish hod-carrier, who had a spirit of his own and a way of exposing it to the weather, made it apparent to all that he must be politically reckoned with; yet fifteen years before that we hardly knew what an Irishman looked like. As an intelligent force, and numerically, he has always been away down, but he has governed the country just the same. It was because he was *organized*. It made his vote valuable—in fact, essential.

You will say the Jew is everywhere numerically feeble. That is nothing to the point—with the Irishman's history for an object-lesson. But I am coming to your numerical feebleness presently. In all parliamentary countries you could no doubt elect Jews to the legislatures—and even *one* member in such a body is sometimes a force which counts. How deeply have you concerned yourselves about this in Austria, France, and Germany? Or even in America, for that matter? You remark that the Jews were not to blame for the riots in this Reichsrath here, and you add with satisfaction that there wasn't one in that body. That is not strictly correct; if it were, would it not be in order for you to explain it and apologize for it, not try to make a merit of it? But I think that the Jew was by no means in as large force there as he ought to have been, with his chances. Austria opens the suffrage to him on fairly liberal terms, and it must surely be his own fault that he is so much in the background politically. . . .

Point No. 3.—"Can Jews do anything to improve the situation?"

I think so. If I may make a suggestion without seeming to be trying to teach my grandmother how to suck eggs, I will offer it. In our days we have learned the value of combination. We apply it everywhere—in railway systems, in trusts, in trade unions, in Salvation Armies, in minor politics, in major politics, in European Concerts. Whatever our strength may be, big or little, we *organize* it. We have found out that that is the only way to get the most out of it that is in it. We know the weakness of individual sticks, and the strength of the concentrated fagot. Suppose you try a scheme like this, for instance. In England and America put every Jew on the census-book *as* a Jew (in case you have not been doing that). Get up volunteer regiments composed of Jews solely, and, when the drum beats, fall in and go to the front, so as to remove the reproach that you have few Massénas among you, and that you feed on a country but don't like to fight for it. Next, in politics, organize your strength, band together, and deliver the casting vote where you can and where you can't, compel as good terms as possible. You huddle to yourselves already in all countries, but you huddle to no sufficient purpose, politically speaking. You do not seem to be organized, except for your charities. There you are omnipotent; there you compel your due of recognition— you do not have to beg for it. It shows what you can do when you band together for a definite purpose.

And then from America and England you can encourage your race in Austria, France, and Germany, and materially help it. It was a pathetic tale that was told by a poor Jew in Galicia a fortnight ago during the riots, after he had been raided by the Christian peasantry and despoiled of everything he had. He said his vote was of no value to him, and he wished he could be excused from casting it, for indeed casting it was a sure *damage* to him, since no matter which party he voted for, the other party would come straight and take its revenge out of him. Nine per cent. of the population of the empire, these Jews, and apparently they cannot put a plank into any candidate's platform! If you will send our Irish lads over here I think they will organize your race and change the aspect of the Reichsrath.

You seem to think that the Jews take no hand in politics here, that they are "absolutely non-participants." I am assured by men competent to speak that this is a very large error, that the Jews are exceedingly active in politics all over the empire, but that they scatter their work and their votes among the numerous parties, and thus lose the advantages to be had by concentration. I think that in America they scatter too, but you know more about that than I do.

Speaking of concentration, Dr. Herzl has a clear insight into the value of that. Have you heard of his plan? He wishes to gather the Jews of the world together in Palestine, with a government of their own—under the suzerainty of the Sultan, I suppose. At the convention of Berne, last year, there were delegates from everywhere, and the proposal was received with decided favor. I am not the Sultan, and I am not objecting; but if that concentration of the cunningest brains in the world was going to be made in a free country (bar Scotland), I think it would be politic to stop it. It will not be well to let that race find out its strength. If the horses knew theirs, we should not ride any more.

Point No. 5.—"Will the persecution of the Jews ever come to an end?"

On the score of religion, I think it has already come to an end. On the score of race prejudice and trade, I have the idea that it will continue. That is, here and there in spots about the world, where a barbarous ignorance and a sort of mere animal civilization prevail; but I do not think that elsewhere the Jew need now stand in any fear of being robbed and raided. Among the high civilizations he seems to be very comfortably situated indeed, and to have more than his proportionate share of the prosperities going. It has that look in Vienna. I suppose the race prejudice cannot be removed; but he can stand that; it is no particular matter. By his make and ways he is substantially a foreigner wherever he may be, and even the angels dislike a foreigner. I am using this word foreigner in the German sense—*stranger*. Nearly all of us have an antipathy to a stranger, even of our own nationality. We pile gripsacks in a vacant seat to keep him from getting it; and a dog goes further, and does as a savage would—challenges him on the spot. The German dictionary seems to make no distinction between a stranger and a foreigner; in its view a stranger *is* a foreigner—a sound position, I think. You will always be by ways and habits and predilections substantially strangers—foreigners—wherever you are, and that will probably keep the race prejudice against you alive.

But you were the favorites of Heaven originally, and your manifold and unfair prosperities convince me that you have crowded back into that snug place again. Here is an incident that is significant. Last week in Vienna a hailstorm struck the prodigious Central Cemetery and made wasteful destruction there. In the Christian part of it, according to the official figures, 621 windowpanes were broken; more than 900 singing-birds were killed; five great trees and many small ones were torn to shreds and the shreds scattered far and wide by the wind; the ornamental plants and other decorations of the graves were ruined, and more than a hundred tomb lanterns shattered; and it took the cemetery's whole force of 300 laborers more than three days to clear away the storm's wreckage. In the report occurs this remark—and in its italics you can hear it grit its Christian teeth: ". . . lediglich die *israelitische* Abtheilung des Friedhofes vom Hagelwetter *gänzlich verschont* worden war." Not a hailstone hit the Jewish reservation! Such nepotism makes me tired.

Point No. 6.—"What has become of the golden rule?"

It exists, it continues to sparkle, and is well taken care of. It is Exhibit A in the Church's assets, and we pull it out every Sunday and give it an airing. But you are not permitted to try to smuggle it into this discussion, where it is irrelevant and would not feel at home. It is strictly religious furniture, like an acolyte, or a contribution-plate, or any of those things. It has never been intruded into business; and Jewish persecution is not a religious passion, it is a business passion.

To conclude.—If the statistics are right, the Jews constitute but *one per cent.* of the human race. It suggests a nebulous dim puff of star dust lost in the blaze of the Milky Way. Properly the Jew ought hardly to be heard of; but he is heard of, has always been heard of. He is as prominent on the planet as any other people, and his commercial importance is extravagantly out of proportion to the smallness of his bulk. His contributions to the world's list of great names in literature, science, art, music, finance, medicine, and abstruse learning are also away out of proportion to the weakness of his numbers. He has made a marvellous fight in this world, in all the ages; and has done it with his hands tied behind him. He could be vain of himself, and be excused for it. The Egyptian, the Babylonian, and the Persian rose, filled the planet with sound and splendor, then faded to dream-stuff and passed away; the Greek and the Roman followed, and made a vast noise, and they are gone; other peoples have sprung up and held their torch high for a time, but it burned out, and they sit in twilight now, or have vanished. The Jew saw them all, beat them all, and is now what he always was, exhibiting no decadence, no infirmities of age, no weakening of his parts, no slowing of his energies, no dulling of his alert and aggressive mind. All things are mortal but the Jew; all other forces pass, but he remains. What is the secret of his immortality?

Source:
Mark Twain, "Concerning the Jews,"
Harper's New Monthly Magazine 99, no. 4
(September 1899): 528–35.

67

The Leo Frank Case

BY THOMAS E. WATSON

Thomas E. Watson (1856–1922) was a Georgia politician and writer who declared himself a Populist and a supporter of agrarian causes in opposition to Henry W. Grady's "New South." He was the author of several volumes of history and biography and the founder of Watson's Magazine *(1905–17). He was the Populist candidate for president in 1904 and was elected to the U.S. Senate in 1920, dying in office.*

By the turn of the century Watson had become violently prejudiced against African Americans and Jews. His hatred of the latter was fueled by the Leo Frank case of 1913–15. In "The Leo Frank Case" (1915) Watson expresses outrage at the wealthy Jews who are supporting Frank and condemning Jewish men's lust for Gentile women.

LET ME QUOTE ONE SENTENCE from a masterful book which has recently been published, and which has been widely read. Its author is Edward A. Ross, Professor of *Sociology* in the University of Wisconsin: the name of the book is, "The Old World and the New."

This expert in Sociology makes a study of Immigration, the changes brought about by it, the diseases, crimes and vices incident to this foreign flood, &c.

On page 150, he says—"The fact that the pleasure-loving Jewish business men *spare Jewesses, but PURSUE GENTILE GIRLS* excites bitter comment."

This bitter comment is made by *the city authorities,* who have had to deal with these pleasure-loving Jewish business men who spare the Jewish girls, and run down the Gentile girls!

If Professor Ross had had the Frank case in his mind, he could not have hit it harder.

Here we have the pleasure-loving Jewish business man.

Here we have the Gentile girl.

Here we have the typical young libertine Jew who is dreaded and detested by the city authorities of the North, for the very reason that Jews of this type have an utter contempt for law, and a ravenous appetite for the forbidden fruit—*a lustful eagerness enhanced by the racial novelty of the girls of the uncircumcised!* . . .

What do rich Jews care for Jews who are poor?

Suppose Leo Frank had been a moneyless Hebrew immigrant, recently arrived from Poland, and peddling about from house to house to get a few dollars for the wife and child he left behind in the war-zone, *would the wealthy Jews,* of Athens, Atlanta, Baltimore, Brooklyn, Philadelphia and New York *be spending half-a-million dollars to save him from the legal consequences of premeditated and horrible crime?*

Or suppose Mary Phagan had been Jacob Schiff's daughter, or Belmont's daughter, or Pulitzer's daughter, or Och's daughter, or Collier's daughter, would Leo Frank be the subject of a propaganda of libellous misrepresentations of the people of Georgia?

It hasn't been so long ago, since *Collier's* published the slander on Southern white women, in which the editor alleged that *the white women accused negro men of rape, TO HIDE THE SHAME OF CONSENT!*

Having championed the negro rapist against the Southern white woman, *Collier's* now champions an abnormal Sodomite, who comes as near *carrying it on his face,* as any lascivious degenerate ever did. . . .

All over this great Republic lawlessness is raging like the wild waves of a stormy sea. All over this Christian land the crimes against women are taking wider range, vaster proportions, and types more fiendish. The white-slaver stands almost openly in crowded streets, in waiting rooms, and at factory doors, with his net in his hands, ready to cast it over some innocent, unsuspecting girl. The lascivious employer—from the highest to the lowest, from the lawyer and politician who advertise for type-writers and stenographers, down to the department stores, the small factories, the laundries and the sweat-shops—are on the lookout for poor girls and young women who will exchange virtue for "a good time."

Do not we all know it?

Where the girl is of the age of consent, and consents, it is bad enough, God knows!

But where the girl is good, and wants to stay so, and she is pursued, and importuned, and entrapped, and is not permitted to keep the one jewel that her poverty allows her, but is forcibly robbed of it, and then killed to hush her mouth—O what shall we say of that?

And what are we to think of the men, *and the women,* who can forget the poor, weak, lonely little heroine *who died, for her honor*—amid this magnificent people who rear monuments to regiments of *strong men* who have died for principle?

The Creator that made me, best knows how I revere brave and good men that stand the storm, resist temptation, keep to the right path, and go to their graves—martyrs to Faith, and Duty, and Honor—rather than surrender the glorious crown of Manhood.

But the words have never been coined which can express what a true man feels for the woman who is so great, in the divine simplicity of unconquerable innocence, that she, like the snow-white ermine of the frozen Arctic, *will die, rather than soil the vestment that God gave her.*

In this day of fading ideals and disappearing landmarks, little Mary Phagan's heroism is an heirloom, than which there is nothing more precious among the old red hills of Georgia.

Sleep, little girl! Sleep in your humble grave! but if the angels are good to you, in the realms beyond the troubled sunset and the clouded stars, they will let you know that many an aching heart in Georgia beats for you, and many a tear, from eyes unused to weep, has paid you a tribute too sacred for words.

Source:
Thomas E. Watson, "The Leo Frank Case,"
Watson's Magazine 20, no. 3 (January 1915):
160–63.

68

"Peace" Object, Says Ford, in an Attempt to Justify His Anti-Semitic Attitude

BY JOSEPH JEFFERSON O'NEIL

Henry Ford (1863–1947), the developer of the automobile, became notorious in the 1920s for his anti-Semitism. Taking over the Dearborn Independent *in 1919, he turned the weekly paper into an organ for the expression of violent antipathy against Jews. The articles published in the* Independent *were collected in four volumes between 1920 and 1922 under the title* The International Jew *and were translated into German, Spanish, Portuguese, and Italian. In 1941 they were reprinted by the Ku Klux Klan. Although Ford publicly repudiated* The International Jew *in 1927, he apparently continued to believe in its major tenets; he later maintained that World War II was caused by Jewish financiers. In the following interview, published in the* New York World *on February 17, 1921, Ford gives a detailed account of his beliefs.*

DETROIT, FEB. 16.—HENRY FORD holds the belief that "international Jewry with its racial programme of domination" is an evil influence in America and the world.

He believes with equal sinerity that this "international Jewry" has been responsible for the world's greatest disasters—its wars. He believes he can convert—or "wake up" as he puts it—both the Jews and non-Jews of the world to this idea and so make a beginning of the end of war.

It is for these reasons that the *Dearborn Independent,* the Ford weekly paper, is printing the series of articles which are commonly accepted as attacks on the Jews, but which he, however, says are not intended as attacks but as "lessons" that the American public should learn.

New York, the stronghold of American Jewry, is soon to be treated of in the Ford paper. The activities of the Jews in finance, in politics, in the law and in other fields are to be studied and described. Some highly interesting reading is promised.

All this—and more—came to me this afternoon in the course of a two-hour talk with Mr. Ford. It was the first time, he said, he had ever discussed his views freely and frankly with any newspaper writer. Hundreds have sought him. Fragmentary talks with him have been printed. Quotations from him, given through his secretary and others, have been published. But this is the first real interview in which he has been outspoken and unreticent. . . .

At the beginning of our talk Mr. Ford took pains to say, "We do not hate the Jews; we do not hate anybody. There is no good in hating anybody. That never accomplishes anything. There is no campaign against the Jews. What everybody needs is clear understanding of the facts of the Jewish question, then every one can co-operate for the general good."

It is an idiosyncrasy of Mr. Ford to say "We" instead of "I." He tries to avoid the personal pronoun and then again he does not want to appear as individually conducting the present articles.

"How long have you had the idea that there was anything about the so-called international Jewish system which should be placed before the American public?" I asked.

"I have been thinking about this matter for many years," said Mr. Ford, "but not until about five years ago, on the peace ship, did the full importance of the subject come into view. That voyage gave me an insight into the responsibility for the war and who profited by it. It is surprising how frequently you come upon the same groups of influences.

"You know, back in 1915, I said I was going to devote my life and fortune to bring about an end to war. That was not just talk. I meant it then and I mean it more than ever now. In studying the possibilities of permanent world peace from every angle, I studied also the causes of war, and I am convinced that nearly all wars were caused so that some one would profit, and those who have profited and are profiting now are the international financiers—the Jews, with possibly among them a few Gentiles with Jewish connections. They are what is called the International Jew, German Jews, French Jews, English Jews and American Jews.

"I believe that in all these countries except our own the Jewish financier is supreme. He is not on top here because there has always been a strong group of Gentiles in this country awake to the situation. But the Gentiles of America must be kept informed of what the International Jews here are trying to do. They would control America, as they control the Old World countries, if they could. Therefore, it is a duty to open the eyes of the American people to the danger they are in."

"How do you think the International Jew started the World War?" was the next question the inquirer asked.

Mr. Ford replied: "By arousing national passions, that is, by propaganda which set one people against another people. These dangerous groups profit before a war by making munitions of war, during a war by national loans and after a war, as they are doing now in the free-for-all grab which goes on. All nations that fight have to use materials that are controlled by the Jews—copper, for instance.

"Some of this has already been explained in the *Dearborn Independent*," he added, "and the rest of the facts will be given in good time. When names are needed they will be given. My life is devoted to peace. Peace is the real purpose behind this educational campaign."

I asked Mr. Ford if he did not feel that it was dangerous to America to cause feelings to be aroused between Gentiles and Jews such as might be aroused by the articles which his paper is publishing.

"The answer to that question is that no such thing has happened," Mr. Ford replied. "I have not heard of any conflict between Jews and Gentiles started by those articles, and there is no reason why there should be any conflict. To set class against class is not the way to accomplish anything. If the *Dearborn Independent*'s articles were based on class prejudice they would stop. No, there will be no difficulties on that score. The Jews themselves will be educated to the evils into which their leaders have taken them. And so will the Gentiles."

"Is your belief that the Jews are endeavoring to control the world based in any degree upon the so-called protocols—these alleged secret documents said to have been formulated by the Elders of Zion? You know of course that these have been denounced as forgeries or inventions. Do you believe they are genuine?"

"The only statement I care to make about the protocols is that they fit in with what is going on. They are sixteen years old, and they have fitted the world situation up to this time. They fit it now.

"The purpose of this campaign is not anti-Semitic. It is not a persecution. It is really not a campaign. It is an investigation. It is an open case before the people of the world, who will act as a jury. There have always been whispers about the Jew and his seeking of world control, but never has there been an outspoken discussion of the Jewish question without rancor or contempt. It is a good thing to let the sunshine and air into a problem that has always been kept in the dark. Sunshine, you know, is a good germicide."

"But what tangible result is sought by these publications?" I asked. "What solution is offered the American people? The articles in the *Independent* talk of the solidarity of the Jews. Do you advocate a similar solidarity of non-Jews?"

"Oh, no," was the reply of the motor manufacturer. "I do not believe in correcting one mistake by making another. Theirs is a solidarity that is anti-social. We want social unity, but not clannishness."

"What then do you hope for? What do you want the American people to do about the so-called Jewish question? What do you think they will do? Anything?"

"I feel that if we let enough light in on this matter the evil of the International Jew will cure itself."

Mr. Ford obviously has no specific remedy for what he designates as the Jewish evil. He believes—as he believes about many other things— that it will work out its own solution.

There is not the slightest question about the man's belief that there is a Jewish evil; that there is an attempt on foot by the Jews to dominate the world. No matter what others may think or say, he holds to his idea. . . .

Whatever statements he issues to anybody for publication are gone over carefully before they are released. In fact, all the direct quotations from him which appear in this article were read and formally O.K.'d by him with some extensive deletions. That was one of the stipulations he made in consenting to talk without reserve for the first time. . . .

The current issue of the paper, which is due to appear Saturday, contains an article headed "Jewish Supremacy in the Motion Picture World," and dates the career of such well known film magnates as Adolph Zukor, Oliver Morosco, William Fox, Marcus Loew, Lewis J. Selznick, Carl Laemmle and Jesse Lansky. . . .

Mr. Ford is said to believe that New York is now not only the American centre of Jewry, but also the world centre—that it has "taken the place Warsaw occupied before the war." Therefore it is certain that a lot of attention will be paid to the Jews of the metropolis in the forthcoming articles.

All the indications are that Mr. Ford's "Educational Campaign" will go on and become more vigorous rather than halt or cease.

Source:
Joseph Jefferson O'Neil, "'Peace' Object, Says Ford,
in an Attempt to Justify His Anti-Semitic Attitude,"
New York World (February 17, 1921): 1, 5.

69

The Jews in America

BY BURTON J. HENDRICK

Burton J. Hendrick (1871–1949), a biographer, historian, and journalist who won three Pulitzer prizes, wrote one of the most vicious works of anti-Semitism in The Jews in America *(1922). In the following extract, Hendrick voices skepticism regarding the* Protocols of the Elders of Zion, *but does so for a peculiar reason: the Jews' intense individualism could not possibly allow them to unite into a world conspiracy.*

THE PROGRESS WHICH THE JEWS are making in the economic life of the United States is generally regarded as one of the most conspicuous portents of the times. The phrases that are not infrequently used to describe this progress—the "menace" of the Jew, the "Jewish peril," the "Judaization" of America—best portray the emotions which it arouses in certain quarters. It is the ambition of the Jewish race, we are told, to "dominate" the United States. This is the ultimate achievement in a widespread Jewish plot to conquer modern civilization, to destroy its Christian quality, to heap up its accumulated riches all to the glory of Israel. Probably there is no more astounding fact in modern life than the seriousness with which certain people have accepted a curious document which has been widely circulated in all European countries and the United States in the last four or five years. This is known as "The Protocols of the Elders of Zion." It purports to describe a campaign waged by the Jews with diabolical persistence for the destruction of modern civilization and the erection of a universal Jewish state on the ruins. If one accepts this document as authentic, he must believe that the Jews, for several centuries, have been working with supreme ability and supreme malevolence to wreck all

Christian nations, to set them at cross purposes with one another, to start wars, revolutions, riots, strikes, financial panics—to create disorder everywhere, all for the purpose of overturning the present system of society. They started the French Revolution, all the wars of the Nineteenth Century, the recently ended World War; their supreme accomplishment, a foretaste of the chaos and the ruin that they plan to precipitate in every civilized country, is the Bolshevist régime in Russia. Naturally in this plan of mighty conquest the United States represents an ultimate goal. The fact that there are 3,000,000 Jews in this country, that they "control" or "dominate" so many departments of American life, is hailed as proof that this century-old conspiracy is rapidly achieving success.

Certainly this is a scheme so magnificent in its iniquity that it is in itself almost a compliment to any racial group to which it is attributed, especially one so numerically inferior and so generally ostracized as the Jews; not less astonishing than the plot itself is the fact that so many normally level-headed people believe it. That Henry Ford should base his anti-Jewish campaign upon these "Protocols" is perhaps not surprising; but that such organs of public opinion as the London *Morning Post* and the London *Spectator* should take them seriously is much more significant. What, then, is the truth, so far as the United States is concerned? Are the American people being "Judaized"? First of all, are American business and finance rapidly passing into the hands of the sons of Abraham?

This conspiracy of the "Elders of Zion" is the most startling discovery of the Anti-Semite, yet its conception involves a quality which the anti-Semitic writers themselves have always denied the Jews. "The Jew," says the historian Mommsen, "unlike the Occidental, has not received the gift of political organization"; and it is not only in matters national and political that this same failing is apparent. If there is one thing that the Jews have proved in their age-long wandering over the face of the earth, it is that they lack the power of coöperation. They occupy their present isolated position, not because they have been persecuted by the Christians, but because they lack that aptitude for coherence and organization whose ultimate expression is nationality. This nomadic tendency of Israel is nothing new. It is not even modern. It does not date from the fall of Jerusalem in 70 A.D., as most people suppose; the Jewish proclivity for circulating among other unfriendly peoples was as much a feature of the ancient world as it is of the present one. The city of Rome, in the mixture of its peoples, filled a place in ancient times not unlike that occupied by the New York of the present day; and Jews were proportionately almost as common along the Tiber in the days of Julius Cæsar as they are along the Hudson in the days of Warren G. Harding. "This remarkable people"—I am again quoting Mommsen—"yielding and yet tenacious, was in the ancient as in the modern world everywhere and nowhere at home, and everywhere and nowhere powerful. The successors of David and Solomon were of hardly more significance for the Jews of that age than Jerusalem for those of the present day; the nation furnished doubtless for its religious and intellectual unity a visible rally-point in the petty kingdom of Jerusalem, but the nation itself consisted not merely of the subjects of the Hasmonæans, but of the innumerable bodies of Jews scattered through the whole Parthian and Roman empire. . . . How numerous even in Rome the Jewish population was already before Cæsar's time, and how closely the Jews even then kept together as fellow countrymen, is shown by the remark of an author of this period, that it was dangerous for a governor to offend the Jews in his province, because he might then certainly reckon on being hissed after his return by the populace of the capital." And the great historian adds another important detail. The usual explanation for the trading and commercial propensities of the Jew and his aversion to agriculture, is that the laws of the Christian world have prevented him from owning land and thus have forced him into business activities. Yet, according to Mommsen, the Jew of Rome in the day of Julius Cæsar was precisely like the Jew of modern times; he was scattered in all parts of the Roman world, and, as today, he was a city dweller and a trader. The individualistic trading instinct of the Jew is not the result of fortuitous circumstances; it is inherent in the very germ-plasm of the race.

Evidently this absence of national organization, this inability to coöperate for the achievement of a unified purpose, is a deep-lying racial trait. It explains why the Jews lost their standing as a nation and why they have never regained it. Read the story of the fall of Jerusalem, as painted by the great English historian of the Jews, Dean Milman. Why did Jerusalem succumb? Not necessarily because Titus had greater military strength, but because the Jews themselves were divided. While the siege was going on, and all the resources of the Jews were needed to resist the exterior enemy, three factions within the city were engaged in brawls and riots, massacring one another in most horrible fashion. Though this is an extreme illustration, the fact remains that the most conspicuous trait of the Jew is an intense individualism. Each man is an entity in himself; the faculty of association, even in matters that concern his own race and religion, does not appear to be an Hebraic quality.

The million and a half Jews who comprise the Jewish population of New York City are standing illustrations of this truth. Their intense individualism regulates practically every phase of their daily existence. From this point of view there is no sight more significant than that of Fifth Avenue, south of Thirty-Second Street, at the noon hour, when the Jewish workers in the clothing factories, many thousands strong, pour into this great thoroughfare. It is one of the New York sights that most astonishes the visitor. New York has plenty of other crowds, but this one differs from the others. The aggregation moves differently from most human groups; it advances more slowly; there is a conspicuous lack of order; the pavement seems full of obstructions; little assemblages stand frequently in the middle of the throng, forcing the pedestrian to make detours around them. Most American crowds divide into two files, going in opposite directions, an instinctive arrangement that produces order and comfort; but this is not invariably the case with these throngs of Jewish clothing workers. Each person seems to be for himself; he takes the right side, the left side, or the middle, irrespective of any rules of the road; he frequently travels in the street; the result is an impression of a slow-moving, rather aimless horde, without precision and without the slightest regard for coöperation. The scene is typical of the Jewish community as a whole. It really consists of a mass of incoherent human particles, each revolving in his own orbit.

This complaint constantly runs through all the Jewish literature produced in New York. The difficulty of making their people coöperate for Jewish ends, even in so inspiring a cause as Zionism, is the perpetual despair of the leaders of their race. The disregard with which the mass of New York Jews treat their own religion is the unending complaint of the rabbis. The problem of the unchurched is one of the pressing issues of Protestantism, and, to a lesser degree, of Catholicism, but even more acute is the Jewish problem of the unsynagogued. The synagogue itself is perhaps the most outstanding illustration of Jewish individualism. There are 700 or 800 synagogues in Greater New York, but each one is a separate group, having absolutely no relation with the others. The Jewish religion is the only one in the United States which exists without an organization; there are no Jewish bishops, or presbyters, or conferences, or convocations; all attempts to create a Grand Rabbi, a functionary who would have a kind of pope-like supervision over all the Jewish congregations, have failed. In politics the same condition prevails. There is no such thing as the "Jewish vote"; Jews notoriously vote independently—be it said to their credit; a Jewish district that goes Republican this year may go Democratic the next. If the Jews of New York acted as a political unit, they could easily control the city and capture many of the offices; yet that trait which the politicians regard as their "instability" all but robs them of political influence. Though the Jews are far more numerous than the Irish, there are only five or six Jewish district leaders out of thirty-two in Tammany Hall; the Irish still control this organization. The Jews cannot be depended on to vote even for members of their own race; they could easily have elected Morris Hillquit mayor in 1917, and, had they manifested that clannishness in politics which their critics regard as a Jewish quality, they would certainly have done so; instead, the masses threw their support to the Irish candidate of Tammany Hall, John F. Hylan. . . .

The Jewish labour leaders are always complaining of the unresponsiveness of their people. The fact that almost every barrel orator operating in New York streets is a recent importation from Russia, creates the impression that the Jews are enthusiastic devotees of trade unionism; yet the truth is quite the other way. That they are persistent "joiners" and that, at times of crisis, they do engage in great and tumultuous strikes, is true; yet it is also true that they hold their allegiance lightly, that they backslide as soon as the particular strike is over, and that they are most undependable as dues payers. The explanation is that trade unionism demands organization, and that the power of organization is not a characteristic of this individualistic race. It is just as significant that stocks and bonds are difficult to sell in the New York Jewish quarter. The Russian immigrant cannot understand that a piece of paper can possibly be property. Stocks and bonds imply joint ownership, coöperation, organization, whereas the Jewish conception of property is individualistic. Diamonds that he can carry in his pocket, a tenement house that he can own and manage himself, a pushcart that his arms can propel through the streets, a small shop that he can operate to his own personal profit, even a great bank in which the system of control is either individual or a select partnership—these are the forms of business enterprise in which the Jewish genius best expresses itself. But the mere possession of a scrap of paper that makes the Jew a partner with several thousand others, and this in a form of property—such as a railroad, a steel mill, a great factory—which he never sees, and which he cannot manage exclusively himself, fails to arouse his interest. In business, as in politics, in religion, and in social activities, the Jew is thus primarily an individualist. It is the one clear and unfailing quality of an otherwise complex character. Perhaps the Jew's constitutional restlessness under restraint, his determination to strike out for himself, his unwillingness to accept the station in which circumstances have placed him, explain this independence; at any rate, the quality is an active one and is of the utmost importance in considering the place which the Jew occupies in American life. In itself it shows that the idea that the Jew is organized in a mighty secret plot having ramifications in all parts of the world for the undermining of Christian civilization, is about the most grotesque manifestation of that hysteria which is part of the psychosis which we owe to the World War.

Source:
Burton J. Hendrick, *The Jews in America*
(New York: Doubleday, Page & Co., 1922),
pp. 44–55.

70

How I Would
Treat the Jews

BY WILLIAM DUDLEY PELLEY

William Dudley Pelley (1890–1965), a widely published novelist and Hollywood screenwriter, was inspired by Adolf Hitler to found a paramilitary organization, the Silver Legion (later the Silver Shirts), in 1933; by 1934 it claimed to have fifteen thousand members. Uniting mystical Christianity with a ferocious anti-Semitism, Pelley developed the theories in The International Jew *and evolved the notion of a Christian Commonwealth. Many of his views were expressed in* Pelley's: The Silvershirt Weekly *(1934–36). As the 1930s progressed Pelley violently attacked the Roosevelt administration, claiming it was infiltrated by Jews. The Silver Shirts disbanded in 1941, and the next year Pelley was sentenced to fifteen years in prison for violating the Espionage Act of 1917. In the following essay, Pelley asserts that the only solution to the Jewish problem would be to gather up all American Jews and assign them to one city in each state.*

WHAT ARE YOU GOING TO DO with the Jews, assuming The Christian Commonwealth becomes triumphant in revitalized America?" is the major query now being addressed to Chief Pelley. "Certainly no true Christian wants to see violence done to them. There are too many millions of them that have found their way into the United States, for general deportation to be practical. Taking away their rights of citizenship might be done if the American populace could be convinced of the need for it. But how would you stop them being a constantly disruptive factor in the practical working of the Commonwealth?"

To which The Chief has replied: "People who are in Councils of Safety are not asking such questions because they have had the solution fully revealed to them in the Council Address 'Abraham's Seed'. Nevertheless, The Commonwealth is fully prepared with a statesmanlike gesture for treating with the Jews. I propose the wholesale and drastic segregation of Jews from Gentiles. Jews are going to be restricted to Beth-Avens, or Cities of Safety, and so long as this peculiar people stay in their own cities they will be accorded full personal safety and economic security!

"It is true that no real Christian wants to see violence done to American Jews. But violence is going to be done to American Jews, and in appalling fashion, if the present megalomania of Jews maintains and Jewry in the United States continues to increase as a problem for statesmen and sociologists.

"Young Gudstadt, in his speech defaming me in Seattle last week, called attention to the fact that there were now 55 organized anti-Semitic movements in the United States. Personally I think the Jew is exaggerating, as he exaggerates everything that makes it appear that his plight is much worse than it is. But assuming for the sake of argument that his figures are true, the existence of 55 organizations working for the destruction of Jewry in what up to 1929 was a free country, presents a shocking picture of the resentment which has grown up against the Israelites in the past half-dozen years and particularly since the installation of the current Administration.

"This resentment has not been professionally promoted for profit, as Jews like Gudstadt persist in telling their fellow Hebrews. Such libels for the moment may serve to arouse Jews to give money into organizations for their 'defense' and keep men like Gudstadt in jobs. The grim truth of the matter is, that the whole American people are arising spontaneously against the arrogance and non-social aggressiveness of Jews, and the Jew is faced with all the perils of mass violence in the United States as in every country.

"I say swift and drastic segregation is the only answer. I say further that segregation can be executed rationally, constructively, without the slightest loss of embarrassment to any Hebrew. I say that segregation can be rendered not only practical but to the better profit and certainly the permanent safety of the Jew.

"The Jew, because of his peculiar racial and religious insanity, must be protected against himself. If he is not protected against himself, America will see pogroms over the next decade that, as Ambassador Girard first said, 'will make those of the Tzar appear as small parades.' I propose to protect the Jew against himself, but more than all else, I propose to protect the Christian from the Israelite. My plans for dealing with Jewry are as cleanly-cut, and sharply defined, as any of the economic stipulations so minutely set forth in 'No More Hunger'. . . .

"The first thing I shall demand in treating with the Jewish question in my country shall be an accurate and drastic census of every person of Jewish blood or Jewish extraction now found within the public domain of the United States. I do not mean how many Jews attend the synagogue. The Jews are not fooling me for a moment that they are religionists. Jews are a political nation and an economic and ethical unit. I have the attestment of no less a personage than Supreme Court Justice Brandeis that such consideration of Jews is the only correct one.

"I want to know every Jew in the country, no matter how many Christian surnames cover up his quasi-asiatic blood. I want to know how and when he got into the United States, whether he has entangled himself or herself with a Christian wife or husband, where the Jews are congregated, whether they are locally known as 'good Jews' or 'bad Jews' . . . certainly I shall demand a full dossier on every Jew's communistic and subversive activities. I am especially interested too in whether or not each male Jew is a member of B'nai B'rith, since I have my own ideas as to what B'nai B'rith is, why it was formed, and what it was intended to accomplish against the Gentiles.

"With such an accurate census of American Jews before me I shall conduct the immediate deportation of every Jew who can be shown to be in this country in defiance of the recent immigration laws and for the specific purpose of carrying on unsocial and subversive activity against the American form of government. Those Jews are going OUT. They have violated every vestige of hospitality which my Christian brethren have extended to them. They have no claims on American citizenship or Christian chivalry. If they won't assent to deportation, or escape it, wherever they are discovered, they will be JAILED. No greasy son of the bolshevist satan is going to tell me that I can't stop Communism as a certain stripe of Israelite is instigating and promoting it. It is a foregone conclusion, of course, that a Christian-Commonwealth government will immediately repudiate any previous recognitions of Red Russia, and the whole breed of Third International weasles, official, ambassadorial, or otherwise, will be packed off home.

"Whereupon I shall study the concentrations of Jews that remain, throughout the Commonwealth, and shall say to the Christian Party men: 'There is but one sensible way to treat with this people and their irrational ethics as applied by them to neighboring races. They must be segregated and isolated. But such segregation must be wholesome, humane, and constructively administered. It would be a constant blot upon the American scene to allow the United States to revert to any such social conditions as formerly maintained in the ghettos of Europe.'

"Instead of designating certain districts of our cities and cooping the Jews therein as animals, I would designate one city in each of the 48 States where Jews may reside, have their own form of religious government under the rabbis, carry on trade and social activities among themselves, have their synagogues, their cahillas, and their B'nai B'riths to their hearts' content. In such cities Jews would be allowed to hold homestead property, and be assured full personal safety and economic security. But nowhere else! I would designate such municipalities as Beth-Havens. 'Beth' is the Hebrew word meaning 'house of, or abode of'. Everybody knows the meaning of the word 'haven'. It is a well-known fact that among all ancient peoples the term Beth-haven, or Beth-Aven, was translated 'Abode of Wickedness,' but if the Jews even in ancient times so deported themselves as to win such appellation from their neighbors, that's not my fault in the present. These American Beth-Havens would be 'abodes of safety or refuge' for the Jews. But Christians in their own towns and cities henceforth and thereafter would enjoy exemption from contact with Israelites. They would know exactly where Jews were to be found and be enabled to remain away from such places. Furthermore, with the example of such localities forever before the future non-Jewish school child, he would have a constant object-lesson in the true character of Jewry and forever be forewarned and forearmed against it. . . .

"It is not the proposal of The Christ Men to work domestic hardship on any citizen of the United States, Jew or Gentile. Therefore no families shall be broken up by this alteration.

"It is proposed that wherever a Gentile woman has married a Jewish man, she must accompany her husband to the Beth-Haven, since she is thereby listed on the Commonwealth roster as a Jewess to all intents and purposes.

"If, however, a Jewess has married a Gentile man, no such stipulation is enforced. She is not required to reside in the Beth-Haven but may enjoy all the privileges of citizenship under her Christian marriage. BUT, in order that tens of thousands of Jewesses do not begin the practice of marrying Gentiles merely to percolate through Christian society anew and produce a race of mongrels, every Jewess so married to an Aryan must be registered and known for what she is, and all Christians throughout the whole United States be warned of her nationality by the peculiar cover of her cheque-book. . . .

"The aim of The Christ Men is to deal absolutely fair with the Jew, insofar as his unbalanced social psychology permits. He cannot have legislative political privileges among the Christians because he has shown his absolute unfitness to exercise such during the past quarter-century. Neither can he longer have control of Gentile instruments of publicity.

He must confine himself and his social activities strictly to his own people. If he breeds promiscuously and strives to overcome his segregation by numbers of his progeny, it will effect him little, since such progeny under the new Commonwealth arrangement shall not be entitled to political representation. . . .

"Unless The Christ Men 'take the bull by the horns' and administer such an arrangement for the solution of the Jewish problem, terrible scenes are soon to be realized in these United States. Since the beginning of human civilization there has been but two solutions or alternatives to the Hebrew enigma: segregation or pogroms.

"In whatever land Jews have resided, even far far back before the time of Christ, this people have so deported themselves as to earn the swift and terrible reprisals of their neighbors. They have never been able to govern themselves, their one kingdom of Israel under Solomon lasting only forty years, and then all sections went into one grand fight among themselves. Whenever Jews have essayed to govern Gentiles, history has repeated itself with grisly results. Always after the Jewish coup has been executed, there has come a period of sufferance, that has ended in Gentile revolt and the extermination of their oppressors. It is a peculiarity of the race that such a thing happens which we are called upon neither to explain nor treat with. . . .

"The Christ Men are quite capable of coping with this Jewish menace in the United States, and the Jews themselves know it. They know among themselves that I am NOT a racketeer, that I am quite enlightened in every phase of their strategizing against Christian institutions, that I am quite capable of treating effectively with them if it comes to a showdown and I have the moral backing of a thoroughly enlightened people.

"Defaming me for being the victim of their infamous North Carolina frame-up, and thinking to dismiss me from the picture by vilifying me for a little hour, is pretty poor protection for themselves in the final sum up. They are frenzied to get rid of me because they have tried everything against me but attempted murder, and they have not prevailed against me.

"It is the American masses themselves, however, that are slowly and fearfully raising the Jewish question. Mayhap before the climax is reached, good and bad Jews may be thankful that I am in the American scene and have the agencies ready for solving the quandary of their jeopardy."

Source:
William Dudley Pelley, "How I Would
Treat the Jews," *Pelley's Weekly* 1, no. 25
(May 6, 1936): 1–2.

71

Why Leave Our Own?

BY CHARLES E. COUGHLIN

Father Charles E. Coughlin (1891–1979) was a Catholic priest who in 1930 began a popular radio broadcast, The Golden Hour of the Little Flower, *from a church in Royal Oak, Michigan. Attacking capitalism and initially supporting Franklin Delano Roosevelt, he expressed impatience with the slowness of New Deal reforms and became increasingly radical. In 1934 he founded the National Union for Social Justice and in 1936 supported William Lemke as a third-party candidate. He continued to attack the New Deal as a Communist conspiracy and by 1938 had become openly anti-Semitic, expressing sympathy with Hitler and Mussolini. His radicalism led to the cessation of his radio broadcasts in 1940, and his influence waned considerably thereafter. In "Why Leave Our Own?" (a transcript of a broadcast on January 29, 1939), Coughlin shows disdain for those Jews urging American opposition to Hitler.*

IT WAS NOVEMBER 20, 1938 when I broadcast the proposal to American Jews to take sides with American Christians in liquidating all persecution. It was only then that I observed that the atrocities committed by the Communists against Christians were exceedingly more serious than those suffered by the Jews at the hands of the Nazis. At that time—less than three months ago—I also had occasion to observe that the well publicized persecution of Jews in Germany was remarkable in that not one Jew was put to death officially for his race or religion. In comparison with this, more than 20-million Christians had been done to death under the Trotskys and Bela Kuns of Communism, both of whom are Jews.

Six months before I made this appeal to the religious Jews of America, I was only one of many Christians who were disturbed by an article which appeared in the American Hebrew Magazine, one of the most important Jewish publications in America.

Precisely on June 3, 1938, an article in this magazine determined the necessity for our bringing into the open not the question of anti-Semitism but the question of sound Semitism—a Semitism which is perfectly legitimate for all Jews to uphold and perfectly reasonable for all non-Jews to respect.

On that date I was shocked to learn how far-reaching and international in scope the unsound Semitism of certain Jews extended. It was a Semitism which confused race and nationality. Because their co-racials in Germany were suffering from the persecutions of the Nazi Government—co-racials and co-religionists who were not co-nationals of the Jews in the United States—I was shocked when certain American Jews entertained the idea that the resources of this and other nations should be employed against the Hitler Government on the principle that the entire world should go to war on behalf of German Jews to settle an internal problem in Germany.

I asked myself the abstract question: "If Irish Roman Catholics were persecuted by the Irish Government, would it not be unpatriotic, unsound and unjust for the Irish Catholics of this nation to propagandize the United States into war against Ireland?"

While persecution itself must be condemned, the Irish Catholics of America have no right to expect the Protestants and Jews and other racial Catholics of America and the resources of this entire nation to be placed at the disposal of the Irish Catholics in Ireland; for I believe they understand the difference between race and nationality.

Then there was the concrete case in Mexico where Catholics actually were persecuted. There was also the concrete case in Germany where Protestants actually were persecuted. Neither Catholic nor Protestant groups in America sought to throw this nation's men, munitions and money against Mexico or Germany; for we, as Americans, do not subscribe to such policies. Sound racialism admits that the allegiance of a man is owing to his nation in preference to his race. . . .

Since last November two phases of our discussion on these subjects have been under consideration. I refer to the persecution phase of Jews and of Christians, and to the lifting of the Spanish embargo. Neither has been terminated as we enter upon the third and the most important. The third phase deals with the question: "Shall the United States become embroiled in a world war on the side of either Naziism or Communism?" The answer to the question is of such vast importance to the youth of this nation, to their parents, to the future of our country and to the rise or fall of civilization itself that no effort may be spared to answer it according to American principles. Therefore, we not only welcome the cooperation of the religious Jews of America. We plead for it in order to keep America out of a war in which it has no good reason to enter other than a trumped up commercial reason, or a fictitious diplomatic reason. The real reason—that of becoming the policeman of the world to protect race minorities whenever they find themselves in disagreement with their national government—is never disclosed.

The burden of my theme has been and will continue to be the leaguing together of all Americans, be they Jew or Gentile, against all persecution wherever it exists. But in doing so, I do not support the theory that this nation should risk its future and destroy its democracy by permitting itself to fight the battles of any persecuted religious or race minority outside our nation, or of entering as a partisan into the internal struggle of any foreign power.

Ladies and gentlemen, we have a multitude of tasks to perform at home and little time to expend on problems abroad, particularly when meddling with these problems begets ill-will and ill-feeling for the United States. . . .

The appearance of anti-Semitism in America is to be deprecated now and forever more. Every American must work towards the liquidation of all anti-racialism. But we should remember that we are Americans though we be Catholic or Protestant or Jew, of Irish, of English, of Hebraic or of any other racial descent. We should remember that our American nationality takes precedence over our racial origin. We should remember that in this country where freedom of conscience and of religion is guaranteed to every citizen, that freedom may not be exploited by any racial group to the end that all Americans will become embroiled in a world war either to destroy Hitler or Stalin, either to defend Catholic or Protestant or Jew as such in any other country of the world outside the United States of America.

"Why leave our own?" asked George Washington.

Or, may I ask, "Is this our own; is this country, this nation, a private domain of any race and we, its citizens, their subjects?" . . .

Let hatred be the only object of boycott in this fair land of ours. If we must hate, let us hate hate. In doing so, let us distinguish between radical policies upheld by the governments abroad and the patient populations thereof.

As much as we are out of tune and tempo with the program of Stalin and his commissars, we American Christians look behind the veil of his Government and visualize the 160-million Russians who are neither

Roman Catholics nor Protestants, but Greek Catholic Christians. We recognize that these would be the ultimate sufferers of boycott. Therefore, in conscience, we may not favor any pagan policy of boycotting the innocent victims of Stalin's rule in Russia.

And so with the Jews of America. If they are intelligent and religious—and I believe great numbers of them are—they may not permit themselves to be regimented by factional, injudicious, super-racial leaders who are attempting to inflict the lash of economic persecution upon the backs of 68-million German Protestants and Catholics, and thereby add to the sufferings which already this victimized people experience.

Source:
Charles E. Coughlin, "Why Leave Our Own?" in Coughlin's *Why Leave Our Own? 13 Addresses on Christianity and Americanism* (Detroit, MI: Inland Press, 1939), pp. 48–50, 54, 57–58.

72

Adam and Cain

BY WILLIAM H. MURRAY

William Henry David Murray (1869–1956) was a Democratic politician with Populist leanings; he gained the nickname "Alfalfa Bill" for his own success with that crop as a farmer. He was one of the first U.S. representatives from the newly formed state of Oklahoma and was governor of Oklahoma from 1931 to 1935. Late in life he became a white supremacist and Christian fundamentalist. In Adam and Cain *(1951) Murray attacks the Anti-Defamation League of B'nai B'rith (an organization founded in 1913 to combat anti-Semitism and to foster civil rights) as covertly communist.*

M ANY PEOPLE HAVE PROBABLY HEARD of the Anti-Defamation League (A.D.L.), and left it at that. It is important that we should know a little more about this oddly-named organisation, which provides a Jewish Secret Police for the United States, because a similar body—probably an offshoot of the parent League—functions in our own land, and is employed to intimidate and besmirch the reputations of any citizens who offend League tenets.

The A.D.L. of B'nai B'rith was founded in Chicago in 1913. This date is important, because it shows that Anti-Semitism was anticipated as a result of World War I, which was just about to be launched. The League is richly endowed, heavily staffed, and extends its tentacles all through the United States. Its professed aims are to combat racial and religious intolerance, specifically against Jews. In actual practice it operates against all those who oppose Communism, although the victims are usually accused of Anti-Semitism, which is an ugly term, of which Americans fight shy. In addition to a propaganda programme of great scope and power, the organisation maintains a censorship over public speech, radio, lectures, movies and schools. Naturally, the more important the individual under suspicion the greater attention paid to him. As in our land, the surveillance extends to clubs and drawing-rooms. In fact, the League conducts a nationwide espionage service, and endeavours to stop any objectionable activities by threats or foul defamation in some form or another; if a victim has an otherwise clean conduct sheet, he is assailed by innuendo or other offensive method, at which the Jews are adepts. The methods employed against the Press or Hollywood are similar in aim but differ in execution. Does anybody remember how the *Morning Post* was run out of business for the crime of publishing the Protocols of the Learned Elders?

The B'nai B'rith (Children of the Covenant) is the oldest and largest Masonic lodge in the United States: it was founded in 1843, and only Jews can belong. The League's files were used by the American Government in the recent war to help in discovering persons likely to possess Nazi sympathies. A deplorable practice, which was duplicated throughout the British Empire by means of the various Defence Regulations 18B. Nobody in his right mind would credit these Jewish reports if he had read the Protocols of Zion and the Kol Nidre prayer. The League is not particular about the character of the agents it employs. One of their ex-employees visited this country recently, travelling as Charles L. Morey, of the Homestead Farm Appliances, Inc. This beauty is an Armenian born in Greece, whose real name, if such a person can be said to own a real name, is Avedis Boghos Derounian, alias John Roy Carlson, amongst a string of fifteen aliases. Three Federal Courts have found him guilty of libel, and Federal Judge Barnes of Chicago said in regard to his book *Undercover:* "I find this book 500 pages of twaddle . . . mere twaddle. . . . I would not believe this author if he were on oath. . . . I believe he would do anything for a dollar. . . ." Derounian is publishing shortly a book on *Post-war Fascism in Europe and America,* which, I have no doubt, will be given wide publicity by his brother smearers, who will conveniently forget that this supposed representative of Farm Appliances has probably never got nearer the land than his own literary "twaddle," for which a stronger word might be used.

The important point to remember is that when our Government makes use of this Jewish intelligence service for prosecuting its own countrymen it is, wittingly or unwittingly, supporting the world Communist offensive, which it professes to abhor. Communism and Zionism are both products of Jewry. Those who honestly fight

Communism, and are not merely engaged in shadow-boxing, like the British Government, are promptly branded by the A.D.L. as anti-Semitic. If action is taken against these persons by the Government in deference to the wishes or command of the Jewish fraternity, such action undoubtedly strikes a blow for Communism. Let me give one or two quotations to support my argument. Dr. Louis Reynolds, writing in the *California Jewish Voice* of 5 July 1946:

"I cannot conceive of any Jew in the role of an enemy of the Soviet Union. To me, such a Jew is an unnatural monstrosity, a travesty of everything that is decent and right."

J. L. Fishbein, editor of *The Sentinel,* on 20 January 1946:

"The Fascist-minded scum and Naziphiles of this country are threatening Russia with everything, from atom bombs to 'democratic elections.' . . . We recognise that in this country the 'Hate-Russia' element is also the 'Hate-the-Jews' element. . . . Did you ever hear of any anti-Semites anywhere in the world who were not also anti-Soviet? . . . We recognise our foes. Let us recognise our friends, the Soviet people."

Both Britain and the United States have swallowed the Jewish lie that the Sovereign State of Israel will be a buffer against Communism. Simple souls—or are they? We have soiled our national honour by recognising the existence of this State, and have struck a resounding blow for Communism in doing so. It would require a surgical operation to separate the Siamese twins of Zionism and Communism, but such is the power of Jewry in the so-called democratic lands that we have dispensed with the operation and enthroned the sinister twins safely in the Holy Land. By doing so, we have done more to destroy our prestige in the Middle East than any other single act could have accomplished. Unless we call a halt to the demands of International Jewry we are doomed. Once we adopt a firm attitude, the opposition will crumble away far more easily than our timid rulers venture to believe, in spite of all the efforts of the Anti-Defamation League to keep us in subjection.

Source:
William H. Murray, *Adam and Cain*
(Boston: Meador Press, 1951), pp. 460–62.

73

Jews in Government

BY GERALD L. K. SMITH

Gerald Lyman Kenneth Smith (1898–1976) joined the Disciples of Christ early in life and preached in Illinois, Indiana, and Louisiana, where he became an ardent supporter of Senator Huey P. Long and adopted Long's views on a redistribution of wealth to ensure social harmony. In the later 1930s he became increasingly radical and was branded a fascist. Nevertheless, he developed a large following in Detroit and continued his advocacy of social reform. During World War II he revealed himself as virulently anti-communist and hostile to organized labor. Around this time he became friends with Henry Ford and read The International Jew. *His anti-Semitism was fueled by his anti-communism, as is revealed in "Jews in Government," an article published in his monthly magazine,* The Cross and the Flag, *founded in 1942. Smith continued writing into the 1970s. His autobiography,* Besieged Patriot, *appeared in 1978.*

JEWS IN OUR GOVERNMENT and organized Jew pressure upon our Government constitute the most powerful factor in determining the foreign and domestic policy of America. Even among the so-called right wing statesmen in our Government, there is a dreadful fear of Jew-power and Jew pressure. Men who command respect fear the accusation of anti-Semitism more than they hate Communism itself.

On December 15, 1938, the largest daily newspaper in America from the point of circulation, the New York Daily News, carried on page 2 an article by John O'Donnell and Doris Fleeson dealing with an attack that had been made on the New Deal Administration because of the high percentage of Jew personalities that were directing the New Deal machine.

The article by Fleeson and O'Donnell summarized the accusations by list-ing the names of 500 Jews who had been planted in strategic positions of power and control in the Government of the United States. These men and women gave America the Roosevelt New Deal. Many of them since that time have been exposed as out-and-out Communists or underground agents. Space in this brief manuscript does not permit the listing of these 500 and their thousands of Jew subordinates; neither does it permit even a listing of Jews in key positions in the Government today. Suffice it to say, there are many thousands more (many of whom cannot even speak the American language clearly) in the Government now than when the list was supplied by the New York Daily News. Although the article by O'Donnell and Fleeson was so written as to attack anti-Semitism, the Daily News, and Mr. O'Donnell especially, have never been forgiven for allowing these names to appear in print even associated with criticism.

The Key to Understanding

No person can understand the world crisis and no person can make a ra-tional interpretation of events unless he understands what the organized Jew is up to.

Mature-minded people recognize the following facts as keys to an in-telligent understanding of world problems.

Key No. 1: The Original Plot

The Jew Zionist machine, which is the most powerfully financed politi-cal organization on earth, is after world power and world control. This plot was uncovered by the London Daily Post in the early part of this century when it published "The Protocols of the Learned Elders of Zion," a secret document which the international board of directors of the Zionist organization never intended for the public to read. More than half of what these Zionists planned on the occasion that these min-utes were written has already been fulfilled.

The Zionists have long since given up explaining the Protocols. Their strategy now is to so persecute writers and publishers that they will be afraid to print this deadly volume.

A sample paragraph appearing in Protocol No. 1 is sufficient to indi-cate the trend of the Zionists' ambition:

"Our countersign is—Force and Make-believe. Only force conquers in political affairs, especially if it be concealed in the talents essential to statesmen. Violence must be the principle, and cunning make-believe the rule for governments which do not want to lay down their crowns at the feet of agents of some new power. This evil is the one and only means to attain the end, the good. Therefore we must not stop at bribery, deceit, and treachery when they should serve towards the attainment of our end. In politics one must know how to seize the property of others without hesitation if by it we secure submission and sovereignty."

A paragraph from Protocol No. 2 will help the reader to understand how realistically ruthless the plot for Jew-Zionist power is:

"The administrators, whom we shall choose from among the public, with strict regard to their capacities for servile obedience, will not be persons trained in the arts of government, and will therefore easily become pawns in our game in the hands of men of learning and genius who will be their advisers, specialists bred and reared from early childhood to rule the affairs of the whole world."

Key No. 2: Jew Money Behind Russian Revolution

Jew banking houses in the United States and Germany and England and France cooperated with both Lenin and Trotsky in the precipitation of the original Russian Revolution. Millions of dollars were supplied, and when Lenin came to power at least 290 of the 300 commissars were Jews. A study of this situation is a book in itself. An effective outline of this has been prepared, the title of which is, "Is Communism Jewish?"

Key No. 3: Jew Power Gained in First and Second World Wars

David Lloyd George in a speech before Parliament revealed that England owed a debt of gratitude to the World Zionist Organization for bringing the United States into the war on the side of England, because of commitments that had been made to the Zionist organization in harmony with their political ambitions. The second World War, in spite of its so-called self-righteous claims, resulted in a Marxist-Socialist government for Britain and the virtual enslavement of one billion additional human beings under the Christ-hating lash of Jew-Russian-Zionist power.

Key No. 4: Jew Control Behind the Iron Curtain

Honest observers who have been behind the Iron Curtain admit freely and without any tinge of prejudice that the deadly secret police organizations in the Iron Curtain countries are Jew-controlled and Jew-directed. Even in front of the Iron Curtain we find Jews rationing the food in Britain, determining policy in West Germany, and ruling with an iron hand in France and Italy. . . .

Key No. 5: Jew Power Behind Oriental Crisis

The background of the Oriental crisis lies in the doublecrossing of Chiang Kai-shek and the anti-Communist forces in China and elsewhere. It has been a State Department policy, influenced and virtually controlled by the Jew Felix Frankfurter and the Jew David Niles. Even Drew Pearson, the tool of Zionism and the obedient character assassin who never fails to fulfill the desires of the Jew Anti-Defamation League has admitted in numerous columns that Dean Acheson (Secretary of State) walks to work every morning with Felix Frankfurter, the dominant personality in the Supreme Court and mentor for numerous Marxist personalities in the Government. (More later.) . . .

Key No. 6:. Jew Opposition to Chiang Kai-Shek

Every important Jew organization has been opposed to Chiang Kai-shek, the Christian General who has fought Communism in the Orient. They have also been anxious and willing to smear and belittle General MacArthur, who was handcuffed and bound in leg irons, figuratively speaking, while waiting for the Jew manipulators in the United Nations to give them authority to proceed effectively against the Communists. He never received that full authority and even the authority he received came strategically late.

Key No. 7: Jew Control in FDR's Administration

The Roosevelt Administration cannot be understood unless it is admitted at the outset that the dominant positions in the New Deal machine were held by Jews. The chief advisor concerning personnel was Felix Frankfurter. It is estimated that he and his agents brought at least 1,000 key personalities in the Government who were either Jews or Marxists, subject to his will.

Key No. 8: Jew Power in the Press

Jews may not own a majority of the newspapers, but they own a majority of the big department stores. These big local department stores are the biggest purchasers of advertising in these newspapers. Their power is so great that the Jew gestapo organization, known as the Anti-Defamation League, has boasted in writing of its quarantine policy as it pertains to Gerald L. K. Smith. This policy requires that my name not be mentioned favorably or unfavorably in connection with any of my activities on the grounds that any publicity favorable or unfavorable aids the Christian Nationalist Crusade.

The editor of one important daily newspaper defined the quarantine policy when he said: *"We shall print Gerald Smith's name in our paper only when we print his obituary."* The reader might say, *"Why this quarantine of Smith and his associates when we see enough of all other controversial figures, such as Stalin, Harry Bridges, Henry Wallace, leading Democrats, leading Republicans, and Communist personalities?"* It is because the Jew machine knows that anything that attracts the eye of the public to their activities endangers their stronghold upon our people.

A sensational note: A quiet, secret survey, which was not even understood by the members of Congress, revealed that whereas most of the members of Congress will flatter the Jews in public, over 300 of them are at heart anti-Semitic. This was discovered by individuals who took the time to casually visit with members of Congress and get their frank opinion when they were confident that no one else was listening. The same backlog of frustration exists in the hearts of the American people. They have learned to misrepresent their actual feelings for public consumption, but behind closed doors and when the Jew ear is not present, they express their great apprehension and fear of Jew power. A recent poll which the Jews were afraid to publicize, taken by themselves, revealed that 41 million Americans are obviously and openly anti-Semitic.

Key No. 9: Jew Power in Movies, Television and Radio

The movies, the radio and television are controlled by the Jews. The authority of Louis B. Mayer, the Warner Bros., the Paleys, and the Saronoffs is too obvious to require more space in this brief pamphlet. Future tracts, however, will deal with these subjects in detail.

Key No. 10: Jews in the Present Administration

This tenth key becomes the subject of the body of this manuscript. In discussing the Jews in Government, I shall discuss also the Jews behind the Government and near the Government and influential over the Government. This, too, is a book in itself, and I only regret that time and space and limited funds do not permit a more thorough treatment of this vital phase of our discussion.

Any patriot interested in truth who thinks he can grasp an understanding of the world crisis without recognizing the above enumerated keys to understanding will find himself buried in the marsh lands of confusion and propaganda and deceit. . . .[1]

The individuals thus far listed, represent only a microscopic fraction of the Jew personalities involved in the manipulation of our social, political and religious life. They have reached into every field of endeavor, and the long arm of their gestapo machine can be felt in the remotest community. A humble preacher in a little Texas city merely announced that he was going to preach a sermon dealing with the Zionist controversy. As soon as the announcement appeared rich and powerful Zionist Jews moved in on the school board and forced the cancellation of the use of the schoolhouse.

It is the theory of the writer that although all Communists are not Zionists and all Zionists are not Communists, there is an alarming fraternization between the two organized groups, enough to convince the writer that the Zionist machine and the Communist machine and the coercive power exerted even in the old political parties by organized Jews is all a part of the aggressive campaign for world power as outlined in the original secret minutes by the Zionist Jews as recorded in the "Protocols of the Learned Elders of Zion." Every reader of this manuscript should have a copy of this sensational volume.

What Shall We Do About It?

Victories cannot be won on negatives alone. America cannot be saved by just being against something. We must be alert to evil, but we must be intelligent concerning what is right. We appeal to every reader of this manuscript to join the Christian Nationalist Crusade, committed to the following ten high principles.

Christian Nationalism, What Is It?

Christian Nationalism, the most rapidly growing people's movement in America, is building its activities on the following 10 high principles:

1. Preserve America as a Christian Nation, being conscious of the fact that there is a highly organized campaign to substitute Jewish tradition for Christian tradition.

2. Expose, fight and outlaw Communism.
3. Safeguard American liberty against the menace of bureaucratic Fascism.
4. Maintain a government set up by the majority which abuses no minority and is abused by no minority. Fight mongrelization and all attempts being made to force the intermixture of the black and white races.
5. Protect and earmark national resources for our citizenry first.
6. Maintain the George Washington Foreign Policy of Friendship with all nations, trade with all nations, entangling alliances with none.
7. Oppose a world government and a super-state.
8. Prove that the Worker, the Farmer, the Businessman, the Veteran, the Unemployed, the Aged, and the Infirm can enjoy more abundance under the true American system than any alien system now being proposed by foreign propagandists.
9. Stop immigration in order that American jobs and American houses may be safeguarded for American citizens.
10. Enforce the Constitution as it pertains to our monetary system. . . .

Join this increasing throng of awakened Americans who recognize that the rich tradition of our Republic lies in its Christian heritage, its representative government, and its Constitutional provision that no underground force or outside force or pressure minority shall rule us, but under God we shall be ruled as a Republic whose officials are chosen by the majority rather than any minority and who shall fulfill their oath by acting on their own initiative in harmony with the will of the people.

Source:
Gerald L. K. Smith, "Jews in Government and Related Positions of Power," *The Cross and the Flag* 9, no. 10 (February 1951): 5–7, 25, 30–31.

74

The Holocaust Controversy: The Case for Open Debate

BY BRADLEY R. SMITH

In recent years a variety of historians have questioned the extent of the atrocities committed by Nazis against Jews in World War II. Many of these individuals pursue their inquiries under the guise of revisionist scholarship, but occasionally their own anti-Semitic prejudices rise close to the surface, and they themselves become guilty of oversimplification, special pleading, and outright error. (For refutations of their views, see the volumes by Deborah E. Lipstadt and Pierre Vidal-Nacquet cited in the Bibliography.) In the following essay, written in 1991 and revised on several occasions thereafter, Bradley R. Smith (b. 1931), author of a pamphlet, Confessions of a Holocaust Revisionist *(1987), offers his views of the subject.*

The Contemporary Issue

No subject enrages campus thought police more than holocaust revisionism. We debate every other great historical controversy as a matter of course, but influential pressure groups with private agendas have made the Jewish holocaust an exception. Elitist dogma manipulated by special interest groups has no place in academia. Students should be encouraged to investigate the holocaust story the same way they are encouraged to investigate every other historical event. This isn't a radical point of view. The premises for it were worked out some time ago during a little something called the Enlightenment.

The Historical Issue

Revisionists agree with orthodox historians that the German National Socialist State singled out the Jewish people for special and cruel treatment. In addition to viewing Jews in the framework of traditional anti-Semitism, the Nazis also saw them as being an influential force behind international communism. During the Second World War, Jews were considered to be enemies of the State and a potential danger to the war effort, much like the Japanese were viewed in this country. Consequently, Jews were stripped of their rights, forced to live in ghettos, conscripted for labor, deprived of their property, deported from the countries of their birth and otherwise mistreated. Many tragically perished in the maelstrom.

Revisionists part company with orthodox historians in that revisionists deny that the German State had a policy to exterminate the Jewish people (or anyone else) by putting them to death in gas chambers or by killing them through abuse or neglect. Revisionists also maintain that the figure of 6 million Jewish deaths is an irresponsible exaggeration, and that no execution gas chambers existed in any camp in Europe which was under German control. Fumigation gas chambers did exist to delouse clothing and equipment to prevent disease at the camps. Most likely it is from this lifesaving procedure that the myth of extermination gas chambers emerged.

Revisionists generally hold that the Allied governments decided to carry their wartime "black propaganda" of unique German monstrosity over into the postwar period. This was done for essentially three reasons. First, they felt it necessary to continue to justify the great sacrifices that were made in fighting two world wars. A second reason was that they wanted to divert attention from and to justify their own particularly brutal crimes against humanity which, apart from Soviet atrocities, involved massive incendiary bombings of the civilian populations of German and Japanese cities. The third and perhaps most important reason was that they needed justification for the postwar arrangements which, among other things, involved the annexation of large parts of Germany into Poland. These territories were not disputed borderlands but included huge parts of Germany proper. The millions of Germans living in these regions were to be dispossessed of their property and brutally expelled from their homelands. Many hundreds of thousands were to perish in the process. A similar fate was to befall the Sudeten Germans.

During the war, and in the postwar era as well, Zionist organizations were deeply involved in creating and promulgating anti-German hate propaganda. There is little doubt that their purpose was to drum up world sympathy and political and financial support for Jewish causes, especially for the formation of the State of Israel. Today, while the political benefits of the holocaust story have largely dissipated, the story still plays an important role in the ambitions of Zionists and others in the Jewish community. It is the leaders of these political and propaganda organizations who continue to work to sustain the holocaust legend and the myth of unique German monstrosity during the Second World War.

For those who believe that the Nuremberg Trials revealed the truth about German war crimes, it is a bracing shock to discover that the then Chief Justice of the U.S. Supreme Court, Harlan Fiske Stone, described the Nuremberg court as "a high-class lynching party for Germans."

The "Photographs"

We've all seen "The Photographs." Endlessly. Newsreel photos taken by U.S. and British photographers at the liberation of the German camps, especially the awful scenes at Dachau, Buchenwald and Bergen-Belsen. These films are typically presented in a way in which it is either stated or implied that the scenes resulted from deliberate policies on the part of the Germans. The photographs are real. The uses to which they have been put are base.

There was no German policy at any of those camps to deliberately kill the internees. In the last months of the war, while Soviet armies were advancing on Germany from the east, the British and U.S. air arms were destroying every major city in Germany with saturation bombing. Transportation, the food distribution system and medical and sanitation services all broke down. That was the purpose of the Allied bombing, which has been described as the most barbarous form of warfare in Europe since the Mongol invasions.

Millions of refugees fleeing the Soviet armies were pouring into Germany. The camps still under German control were overwhelmed with internees from the east. By early 1945 the inmate population was swept by malnutrition and by epidemics of typhus, typhoid, dysentery and chronic diarrhea. Even the mortuary systems broke down. When the press entered the camps with British and U.S. soldiers, they found the results of all that. They took—"The Photographs."

Still, at camps such as Buchenwald, Dachau and Bergen-Belsen tens of thousands of relatively healthy internees were liberated. They were there in the camps when "The Photographs" were taken. There are newsreels of these internees walking through the camp streets laughing and talking. Others picture exuberant internees throwing their caps in the air and cheering their liberators. It is only natural to ask why you haven't seen those particular films and photos while you've seen the others scores and even hundreds of times.

Documents. Spokespersons for the Holocaust Lobby assure us that there are "tons" of captured German documents which prove the Jewish genocide. When challenged on this, however, they produce only a handful of documents, the authenticity or interpretation of which is always highly questionable. If pressed for reliable documentation, the Lobby will then reverse itself and claim that the Germans destroyed all the relevant documents to hide their evil deeds, or it will make the absurd claim that the Germans used a simplistic code language, or whispered verbal orders for mass murder into each others' ears.

The truth appears to be, with regard to the alleged extermination of the European Jews, that there was no order, no plan, no budget, no weapon (that is, no so-called execution gas chamber) and no victim (that is, not a single autopsied body at any camp has been shown to have been gassed).

Eyewitness Testimony. As documentary "proofs" for the mass-murder of the European Jews fall by the wayside, Holocaust historians depend increasingly on "eyewitness" testimonies (and censorship) to support their theories. Many such testimonies are ludicrously unreliable. History is filled with stories of masses of people claiming to be eyewitnesses to everything from witchcraft to flying saucers.

During and after the war there were "eyewitnesses" to mass murder in gassing chambers at Buchenwald, Bergen-Belsen, Dachau and other camps in Germany proper. Today, virtually all recognized scholars dismiss this eyewitness testimony as false, and agree that there were no extermination gas chambers in any camp in Germany proper.

Establishment historians, however, still claim that extermination gas chambers existed at Auschwitz and at other camps in Poland. The eyewitness testimony and the evidence for this claim is, in reality, qualitatively no different than the false testimony and evidence for the alleged gas chambers at the camps in Germany proper.

During the war crimes trials many "eyewitnesses" testified that Germans made soap out of human fat and lamp shades from human skin. Allied prosecutors even produced evidence to support those charges. Today, most scholars agree that the testimony was false and the evidence to support it was manufactured.

With regard to confessions by Germans at war crimes trials, it is now well documented that many were obtained through coercion, intimidation and even physical torture.

Auschwitz. British historian David Irving, perhaps the most widely read historian writing in English, has called the Auschwitz death-camp story a "sinking ship" and states that there were "no gas chambers at Auschwitz."

The Auschwitz State Museum has recently revised its half-century-old claim that "4 million" humans were murdered there. The Museum now says maybe it was "1 million." But what documentary proof does the Museum provide to document the 1 million figure? None. Revisionists want to know where those 3 million souls have been the last 45 years. Were they not part of the fabled Six Million? One might ask why, when some 3 million Auschwitz dead were brought back to life (by the stroke of a pen, as it were, much like they "died" in the first place) that no one in the Holocaust Lobby thought a celebration to be in order.

Those who are most dedicated to promoting the Holocaust story complain that "the whole world" was indifferent to the genocide which allegedly was occurring in German occupied Europe. When asked why this was the case the promoters usually respond by saying that it was due to some great moral flaw in the nature of Western Man. At other times they made the absurd claim that people did not realize the enormity of what was happening. It is true that the world responded with indifference. How else should people have responded to that which they did not believe, and which for them was a non-event?

For it is certain that if there had been "killing factories" in Poland murdering millions of civilians, the Red Cross, the Pope, humanitarian agencies, the Allied governments, neutral governments, and prominent figures such as Roosevelt, Truman, Churchill, Eisenhower and many others would have known about it and would have often and unambiguously mentioned it, and condemned it. They didn't. The promoters admit that only a tiny group of individuals believed the story at the time—many of whom were connected with Jewish propaganda agencies. The rise of the Holocaust story reads more like the success story of a PR campaign than anything else.

Winston Churchill wrote the six volumes of his monumental work, The Second World War, without mentioning a program of mass-murder and genocide. Maybe it slipped his mind. Dwight D. Eisenhower, in his memoir Crusade in Europe, also failed to mention gas chambers. Was the weapon used to murder millions of Jews unworthy of a passing reference? Was our future president being insensitive to Jews?

Political Correctness and Holocaust Revisionism

Many people, when they first hear holocaust revisionist arguments, find themselves bewildered. The arguments appear to make sense but, they reason, "How is it possible?" The whole world believes the holocaust story. It's just not plausible that so great a conspiracy to suppress the truth could have functioned for 50 years.

To understand how it could very well have happened, one needs only to reflect on the intellectual and political orthodoxies of medieval Europe, or those of Nazi Germany or the Communist-bloc countries. In all of these societies the great majority of scholars were caught up in the existing political culture. Committed to a prevailing ideology and its interpretation of reality, these scholars and intellectuals felt it was their right, and even their duty, to protect every aspect of that ideology. They did so by oppressing the evil dissidents who expressed "offensive" or "dangerous" ideas. In every one of those societies, scholars became Thought Police.

In our own society, in the debate over the question of political correctness, there are those who deliberately attempt to trivialize the issues. They claim there is no real problem with freedom of speech on our campuses, and that all that is involved with PC are a few rules which would defend minorities from those who would hurt their feelings. There is, of course, a deeper and more serious aspect to the problem. On American campuses today there is a wide range of ideas and viewpoints that are forbidden to be discussed openly. Even obvious facts and realities, when they are politically unacceptable, are denied and suppressed. One can learn much about the psychology and methodology of thought police by watching how they react when just one of their taboos is broken and holocaust revisionism is given a public forum.

First they express outrage that such offensive and dangerous ideas were allowed to be expressed publicly. They avoid answering or debating these ideas, claiming that to do so would give them a forum and legitimacy. Then they make vicious personal attacks against the revisionist heretic, calling him dirty political names such as "anti-Semite," "racist" or "neo-Nazi," and they even suggest that he is a potential mass murderer. They publicly accuse the revisionist of lying, but they don't allow the heretic to hear the specific charge or to face his accusers so that he can answer this slander.

The Holocausters accuse revisionists of being hate filled people who are promoting a doctrine of hatred. But revisionism is a scholarly process, not a doctrine or an ideology. If the holocaust promoters want to expose hatred, they should take a second look at their own doctrines, and a long look at themselves in the mirror.

Anyone on campus who invites a revisionist to speak is himself attacked as being insensitive. When a revisionist does speak on campus he is oftentimes shouted down and threatened. If he has books or other printed materials with him they might be "confiscated." All this goes on while the majority of faculty and university administrators sit dumbly by, allowing campus totalitarians to determine what can be said and what can be read on their campus.

Next, the thought police set out to destroy the transgressor professionally and financially by "getting" him at his job or concocting a lawsuit against him. The courts are sometimes used to attack Revisionism. The holocausters often deceptively claim that revisionist scholarship has been proven false during a trial. The fact is, revisionist arguments have never been evaluated or judged by the courts in an atmosphere of intellectual freedom.

Finally, the thought police try to "straighten out" that segment of academia or the media that allowed the revisionists a forum in the first place.

It can be an instructive intellectual exercise to identify taboo subjects, other than holocaust revisionism, which would evoke comparable responses from thought police on our campuses.

Recently, some administrators in academia have held that university administrations should take actions to rid the campus of ideas which are disruptive to the university. This is a very dangerous position for administrators to take. It is an open invitation to tyranny. It means that any militant group with "troops at the ready" can rid the campus of ideas it opposes, then impose its own orthodoxy. The cowardly administrator finds it much easier and safer to rid the campus of controversial ideas than to face down a group of screaming and snarling militants. But it is the duty of university administrators to insure that the university remains a free marketplace of ideas. When ideas are used as an excuse to disrupt the campus, it is the disrupters who must be subdued, not the ideas.

Conclusion

The influence of holocaust revisionism is growing steadily both here and abroad. Those who become involved in the controversy created by revisionist theory represent a wide spectrum of political and philosophical positions. They are certainly not the scoundrels, liars and demons the Holocaust Lobby makes them out to be.

Nevertheless, there are those who use revisionist scholarship as a weapon to attack Jews with. The Holocaust Lobby has chosen to demonize and attempt to censor all revisionists for what a minority do and say. We choose a different path. We will use revisionism as a tool to remove from the holocaust story all that is false, after which it will be useless as a weapon with which to attack Jews or any other ethnic group.

The fact is, there are no demons in the real world. We are at our worst when we see those who do not believe what we believe to be an embodiment of evil, and then begin to demonize them. Such people are preparing to do something simply awful to their opponents. Their logic is that you can say or do anything you want—to a demon!

The demonizers are going to fail. Growing numbers of revisionist sympathizers and supporters assure us that the political forces that promote the Jewish holocaust story as it stands today are going to have to accept the role that revisionist scholarship plays in promoting open debate on the controversy in our universities and media. The effect will be to broaden intellectual freedom for all of us, no matter what any one of us believes or doubts. That's what academics are supposed to do. Until they begin to do it with respect to the holocaust controversy, others will have to do it for them.

Source:
Bradley R. Smith, "The Holocaust
Controversy: The Case for Open Debate,"
http://www.codoh.com (1991).

PART TEN

Asian Americans

PREJUDICE AGAINST ASIAN AMERICANS has on the whole been less virulent only because they have constituted such a relatively small proportion of the population and because they tended to congregate in restricted regions of the country. When that prejudice did emerge, it manifested itself in customary ways, as Asians were criticized on the basis of appearance, culture, religion, and language. The first instance of significant prejudice occurred in California in the middle of the nineteenth century, since this is where Asians first settled in large numbers.

By 1852 there were already twenty-five thousand Chinese in California, and many more would arrive as the railroad companies required hardworking cheap labor for the mammoth transcontinental railroad, which reached completion in a quaint ceremony in Utah in May 1869. A year before, the Burlingame treaty facilitated Chinese immigration by allowing citizens of China the same right to enter the country as that granted to people of other nations. The treaty later came under heavy criticism from nativists; Denis Kearney, rabble-rousing leader of California's short-lived Workingmen's Party, staged many protests against the "coolies" throughout the state, and he was joined by voices one would have thought more responsible. The first Chinese Exclusion Act was passed by Congress in 1882, and it was augmented by further measures in 1888 and 1892; the latter law (the Geary Act) stipulated, among other things, that all Chinese immigrants possess certificates of registration or face deportation. But by the fall of 1893, when it was learned that the cost of deporting the eighty-five thousand Chinese who had failed to register would be in excess of $10,000,000, the government repealed the requirement for deportation. Nevertheless, the three laws radically reduced Asian immigration for decades.

As early as 1869, Henry George—the political thinker whose *Progress and Poverty* (1879), inspired by his horror at the increasing gap between rich and poor (white) Americans, became an instant classic—was speaking harshly of Asians. Not merely did they, in his opinion, bring down wages for other workers, but their morals were supposedly inferior: "They practice all the unnamable vices of the East, and are as cruel as they are cowardly." The fiery satirist Ambrose Bierce was, from the 1870s onward, one of the lone voices speaking out against anti-Asian prejudice.

Is it a surprise that Samuel Gompers, founder of the American Federation of Labor, should oppose the Chinese? Hardly; for organized labor was among the chief opponents of foreign immigration. To the degree that labor's hostility was principally economic—a question of maintaining livable wages for the working class—it was perhaps only secondarily racist; but when Gompers quoted with approval the words of well-known politician James G. Blaine (Republican candidate for president in 1884 and secretary of state under Benjamin Harrison), "Either the Anglo-Saxon race will possess the Pacific slope or the Mongolians will possess it," he crossed the line.

By the turn of the century, with the onset of the Boxer Rebellion in China (1900) and the Russo-Japanese War (1904–5), increasing fears of a "yellow peril" emerged. What would the hundreds of millions of Chinese do if they ever wakened from their long political sleep and exercised their power of numbers in the Western world? Would it one day be necessary to battle the millions in Japan, increasingly crowded on a small chain of islands and evidently intent on imperialist aggression? Jack London devoted attention to this issue in one of the last of his reports from Japan in 1904, concluding that the "yellow peril" would arise only if the Japanese (the "brown" peril) overwhelmed the Chinese and then used them to further their conquests.

One of the most shameful episodes in American racial history was the internment of more than one hundred thousand Japanese immigrants, many of them U.S. citizens, in 1942–45, in several concentration camps in California. It is the more shameful because one of its leaders was then Attorney General Earl Warren, later to gain deserved fame as chief justice of the Supreme Court when it overturned segregation laws in 1954. To be sure, a certain level of war hysteria should have been expected after the Pearl Harbor attack, the first foreign military attack on soil controlled by the United States since the War of 1812. But when the "Intelligence Officer" who in late 1942 recommended in a *Harper's* article that Japanese Americans on the West Coast be regarded as "guilty until proven innocent" of potential sabotage activities, one wonders when he had last read the Constitution.

75

The Chinese in California

BY HENRY GEORGE

Henry George (1839–1897) grew up in Philadelphia but spent most of his adult life in California, working for several newspapers in San Francisco and Oakland. Enduring a life of poverty in early manhood and appalled by the inequities of wealth between rich and poor in New York and elsewhere, George wrote the landmark treatise Progress and Poverty *(1879), which gave birth to the "single tax" movement whereby the taxation of land values would be the only tax exacted by the government. Early in his career, however, George exhibited hostility and prejudice against the many Asian immigrants who had entered California, blaming them for lowering wages for other workers and accusing them of moral deficiencies.*

Character of the Asiatic Immigration— the Problem of the Pacific Coast

Opposite our Western front, on the other shore of the Pacific, is a people whose numbers are variously estimated at from four to five hundred millions—more than the population of Europe, America, Africa, and Oceanica combined. A people who possessed the mariner's compass, gunpowder, and the art of printing when our ancestors were yet barbarians, ere the walls of Rome had been traced or Greek civilization had begun to dawn.

Had it not been for the strange petrifaction, which, as though by the fiat of the Almighty, fell upon this people ages ago—had they made but a few steps forward in their utilization of the powers of nature, made of the junk a good sea boat, of gunpowder an effective instrument of destruction as well as a toy, universal history would have taken another direction, and America, if not the world, would to-day be Mongolian.

We have now gone by them far enough. In knowledge, power, and wealth, we surpass them more than two thousand years ago they surpassed the painted savages of the British Isles, yet they still retain their preëminence of numbers.

And now that the barriers that for ages have isolated these people from the rest of the world are being broken down, their mere numbers, if nothing else, make them a force of vast importance to the future of the rest of mankind. Four or five hundred millions of people are coming into the line of our attractions and repulsions, like some new Saturn taking up its place to circle round the sun.

Now that the race which started from the plains of Central Asia has completed in its march the circuit of the globe, China may wake from her sleep of ages, and learn from Western civilization; she may pass into the hands of intelligent conquerors, or be broken up into fragmentary provinces; but whether welded into a vast power, or to remain the political cypher she now is, the Chinese people, by the mere force of their numbers, must exercise an immense influence upon the rest of the world.

Look at the swarming that is possible from this vast human hive! Consider that if all humanity were marshaled, every third man in the line would wear the queue and the blouse of a Chinaman; that this half billion people could throw off annually six, ten, twenty millions of emigrants, and this not merely without feeling the loss, but without there being any loss, for over-population keeps reproduction down, and new Chinamen would spring into the vacancies created by those who left as air into a vacuum.

According to the count of the six great Chinese Companies—to one or the other of which all, or nearly all of the Chinese upon the Pacific Coast belong—there are some 65,000 Chinamen in California and adjacent States and Territories. Knowing the jealousy with which they are regarded, the Chinese are disposed to understate their numbers, and it is probable that the true figures are nearer 100,000 than those given. Speaking roughly, they may be said to constitute at least one-fourth of the adult male population.

From San Diego to Sitka, and back into Montana, Idaho, Nevada, and Arizona, throughout the enormous stretch of country of which San Francisco is the commercial center, they are everywhere to be found. Every town and hamlet has its "Chinatown"—its poorest, meanest, and filthiest quarter, and wherever the restless prospectors open a new district, there, singly or in squads, appears the inevitable Chinaman. . . .

Capacity

The great characteristics of the Chinese as laborers are patience and economy—the first makes them efficient laborers, the second cheap laborers. As a rule they have not the physical strength of Europeans, but their steadiness makes up for this. They take less earth at a spadefull than an Irishman, but in a day's work take up more spadesfull. This patient steadiness peculiarly adapts the Chinese for tending machinery and for manufacturing. The tendency of modern production is to a greater and greater subdivision of labor—to confine the operative to one part of the process, and to require of him close attention, patience, and manual dexterity, rather than knowledge, judgment, and skill. It is in these qualities that the Chinese excel. The superintendents of the cotton and woolen mills on the Pacific prefer the Chinese to other operators and in the same terms the railroad people speak of their Chinese graders, saying they are steadier, work longer, require less watching, and do not go on strikes or go on drunks. And one of them is reported as boasting that he would yet have Chinamen building and running his locomotives.

Cheapness of Chinese Labor

But the great recommendation of Chinese labor is its cheapness. There are no people in the world who are such close economists as the Chinese. They will live, and live well, according to their notions, where an American or Englishman would starve. A little rice suffices them for food, a little piece of pork cooked with it constitutes high living, an occasional chicken makes it luxurious. Their clothes cost but little and last for a long while. Go into a Chinese habitation and you will see that every inch of space is utilized. A room ten by twelve will bunk a dozen besides affording workshop, kitchen, and dining-room. Pass through their quarters in the towns, and you will see that nothing that can possibly be used is thrown away, unless it be human labor. Chinamen, of course, as other people, like luxuries, and indulge in them as far as they can, but their standard of comfort is very much lower than that of our own people—very much lower than that of any European immigrants who come among us. This fact enables them to underbid all competitors in the labor market. Reduce wages to the starvation point for our mechanics, and the Chinaman will not merely be able to work for less, but to live better than at home, and to save money from his earnings. And thus in every case in which Chinese comes into fair competition with white labor, the whites must either retire from the field or come down to the Chinese standard of living. . . .

Hostility to the Chinese—
Unequal Taxation

That the Chinese population of our Pacific Coast is not now much larger, is due to the feeling that has existed against them. This feeling has been very strong, but at the present time is weakening, or rather is being counteracted. The early Chinese immigrants did not come into competition with any class or settled interest, great or small. As washermen, cooks, and servants they supplied the need of female labor, did not displace it, for there was comparatively none in the country to displace. Nor in the diggings did they struggle with the white miners for the rich claims, for such a struggle could have had only one result; but followed them as the jackal follows the lion, contented with diggings which the whites did not consider remunerative or had abandoned, but from which their economy and industry enabled them to extort large returns. After a placer mining district has been utterly exhausted and abandoned by whites, it will, for a long time, be worked by Chinamen, and with apparently satisfactory results, though, for obvious reasons, they endeavor to conceal their earnings as much as possible.

But though the Chinamen were thus contented with the white man's leavings, their presence from the first developed a strong adverse feeling, which found expression not only in legal enactments, but in many acts of oppression, violence, injustice, and imposition. A "Foreign Miners' License Law" was early passed, which compelled Chinamen engaged in mining to pay a monthly tax of $4 a head. Ostensibly the law applies to all foreign miners; but no one ever dreams of collecting it of any one but Chinamen. But it must be said, in justice to the white miners, that the sentiment which dictated this and kindred legislation, and which condoned, if it did not justify, the numerous extra legal exactions and outrages to which Chinamen have been subjected, was not merely a blind race-hatred or a dog-in-the-manger feeling, provoked by seeing other people enjoy that which they could not use themselves. Their reasoning ran thus: "though we do not want the poorer diggings, which the Chinamen are working out, we should have a care for those of our own race who will follow us. The day will come when wages in California will sink to an Eastern level, and when white men—white men with families depending on them—will be glad to find and work these poor diggings; and for these men we should see that they are reserved, and not permit them to be despoiled by the long-tailed barbarians, who have no interest in the country, and whose earnings do not add to its wealth." . . .

But taxation, comparatively heavy as it is on them, is the least burden which the Chinese in California have to bear. They are subject to all sorts of exactions and impositions beside. For rent, etc., they must always pay more than the whites. They are fair game for all sorts of rascals, from highwaymen and camp-robbers to those who go round with revolvers in their hands personating tax collectors. To rob these timid people, who, even in their own defense, will seldom fight, unless in overpowering numbers, is comparatively safe; nor, unless a white man happens to witness the operation, is there any danger of subsequent punishment, for in the courts of California the testimony of a Chinaman cannot be received against a white. A strong effort was made at the last session of the California Legislature to get through a law permitting Chinamen to testify against whites in cases of outrage upon them; but, though the bill passed the Senate, it failed in the Assembly, the real cause of the defeat being the anti-Chinese feeling, though the opposition was ostensibly based upon the ground that the Chinese have no regard for the sanctity of an oath, which indeed is the case. In any matter in which they are interested, they can bring up a cloud of witnesses on either or both sides.

But though the Chinese in many parts of the Pacific coast have been treated badly enough, a most exaggerated idea upon this subject prevails in the East. It is not true, as is sometimes asserted, that a Chinaman cannot walk the streets of a Pacific town without being insulted or assailed. One cannot walk half a block in these towns without meeting a Chinaman, and in any part of San Francisco, at any time, day or night, Chinamen (though boys occasionally shy stones at them) are much safer than are strangers in New-York.

As the competition of Chinese labor with white labor has become more general and threatening, the feeling against them has become correspondingly intense. But a counteracting feeling in their favor has also been developed. While making enemies of the workmen with whom they come into competition, they have made friends of the employers, who found a profit in their labor, and as they have become massed in the employ of great corporations, and in the cities, they are more easily protected.

There is now more reason for an anti-Chinese feeling in California than at any time before; and that feeling, though less general, may be more intense, but it certainly is not as powerful as it has been, and it is doubtful if it could at present secure the prohibition of Chinese immigration, even were there no Constitutional obstacles in the way; though should such an issue come fairly before the people, the prohibitionists would have a clear majority. There are too many interests becoming involved in the employment of Chinese labor to make this feasible, unless by some sudden awakening to their danger the working classes should be led to such thorough union as should make numbers count for more than capital. From the great corporations, like the Central Pacific Railroad and Pacific Mail Steamship Company, or the large manufacturing establishments, like the Mission Woolen Mills or San Francisco Rope Works, to the families of moderate incomes who employ a Chinese servant, or the journeymen harness maker, who takes his work home, and teaches four or five Chinamen to help him there, a very large and powerful class, rapidly becoming larger and more powerful, is directly interested in maintaining their right to avail themselves of Chinese labor; and this class is further reënforced by those who will prospectively profit by the cheapening of wages, and those whom political sentiment has led to an acceptance in all its fullness of the doctrine of the equality of races. And further still, the prejudices of race and religion are, strange as it may seem, to a certain extent themselves enlisted in "John's" defense and there are not a few stanch supporters of Chinese immigration and employment who base, or at least defend, their views by the assertion that "a Chinaman is as good as an Irishman," with the implication that he is a good deal better. . . .

The Wages Question

That a reduction of wages through the employment of Chinese labor will increase the aggregate of production there is no doubt, and thus far its advocates are right. Capital would be made more efficient, and new capital be attracted from abroad. But whether home capital would continue to increase at its former rate may well be doubted. The savings of employers would be more as their profits would be more; but the savings of the laborers (which, through the medium of loan societies, &c., become as much part of the active capital or "wages fund" of the community as the savings of any manufacturer) would be less, and, in the case of the Chinese, would be sent abroad and lost to the country. Whether the increase of production thus brought about is to be considered a benefit to the community depends upon our idea of "what constitutes a State." For this increase of production we must pay a high price, one of the smallest items of which, in my opinion, will be (if the substitution of Mongolians for Anglo-Saxons goes far enough) the utter subversion of Republicanism upon the Pacific, perhaps upon the continent. . . .

Character of the Chinese

The population of our country has been drawn from many different sources; but hitherto, with but one exception, these accessions have been of the same race, and though widely differing in language, customs, and national characteristics have been capable of being welded into a homogenous people. The Mongolians, who are now coming among us on the other side of the continent, differ from our own race by as strongly marked characteristics as do the negroes, while they will not as readily fall into our ways as the negroes. The difference between the two races in this respect is as the difference between an ignorant but docile child, and a grown man, sharp but narrow-minded, opinionated and set in character. The negro when brought to this country was a simple barbarian with nothing to unlearn; the Chinese have a civilization and history of their own; a vanity which causes them to look down on all other races, habits of thought rendered permanent by being stamped upon countless generations. From present appearances we shall have a permanent Chinese population; but a population whose individual components will be constantly changing, at least for a long time to come. A population born in China, reared in China, expecting to return to China, living while here in a little China of its own, and without the slightest attachment to the country—utter heathens, treacherous, sensual, cowardly, and cruel. They bring no women with them (and probably will not for a little while yet) except those intended for purposes of prostitution, and the children of these, of whom there are some hundreds in California, will exercise upon the whole mass but little perceptible influence, while they will be in all respects as essentially Chinese as though born and reared in China.

To a certain extent the Chinese become quickly Americanized; but this Americanization is only superficial. They learn to buy and sell, to labor, according to American modes, just as they discard the umbrella-shaped hat, wide drawers, and thick paper shoes, for the felt hat, pantaloons, and boots; but they retain all their essential habits and modes of thought just as they retain their queues. The Chinaman running a sewing machine, driving a sand cart, or firing an engine in California, is just as essentially a Chinaman as his brother who, on the other side of the Pacific, is working in the same way, and with the same implements as his fathers worked a thousand years ago.

Immorality

Their moral standard is as low as their standard of comfort, and though honest in the payment of debts to each other, lying, stealing, and false swearing are with the Chinamen venial sins—if sins at all. They practice all the unnameable vices of the East, and are as cruel as they are cowardly. Infanticide is common among them; so is abduction and assassination. Their bravos may be hired to take a life for a sum proportionate to the risk, to be paid to their relatives in case of death. In person the Chinese are generally apparently cleanly, but filthy in their habits. Their quarters reek with noisome odors, and are fit breeding-places for pestilence. They have a great capacity for secret organizations, forming a State within a State, governed by their own laws; and there is little doubt that our Courts are frequently used by them to punish their own countrymen, though more summary methods are oftentimes resorted to. The administration of justice among them is attended with great difficulty. No plan for making them tell the truth seems to be effective. That of compelling them behead a cock and burn yellow paper is generally resorted to in the Courts.

A great many good people doubtless fancy that they see in this migration to our shores a providential opportunity for the conversion of Asia to Christianity; but a more intimate acquaintance with the Chinese in California would probably induce a modification of this sanguine expectation. Though here and there may be an individual exception, the Chinese among us will, as a rule, remain the heathens they are. If any progress is made in their conversion, it will be in China, not in America.

The Chinese seem to be incapable of understanding our religion; but still less are they capable of understanding our political institutions. To confer the franchise upon them would be to put the balance of power on the Pacific into the hands of a people who have no conception of the trust involved, and who would have no wish to use it rightly if they had—would be to give so many additional votes to the employers of Chinese, or put them up for sale by the Chinese head centers in San Francisco. At least one Chinaman has already been naturalized, and though none of them have any intention of remaining here permanently, if it would pay them to acquire votes and they could be protected in voting, there are none of them who would object to being naturalized every hour in the day. The swearing required is nothing to them, and as for identification, all Chinamen look alike to the unpracticed eye. At present, law or no law, the Chinese on the Pacific coast could not vote, unless between lines of bayonets; but this does not prove they will never vote. Who could have dreamed ten years ago that the slaves of the South would now be the voters?

Source:
Henry George, "The Chinese in California," *New-York Daily Tribune* (May 1, 1869): 1–2.

76

Prattle

BY AMBROSE BIERCE

Although Ambrose Bierce (1842–1914?) is today best known for his short stories of the Civil War (in which he served with distinction on the Union side) and his tales of the supernatural, in his day he was renowned as a prolific journalist and fearless satirist. Spending most of his adult life in or around San Francisco, Bierce became notorious for his outspoken opinions. Although he exhibited prejudice against Native Americans and African Americans, he courageously defended the Asian-American "coolies" in spite of the unpopularity of the stance among white Californians. In the following excerpt from his column, "Prattle," in the Argonaut, *a San Francisco weekly paper, Bierce uses both logic and satire in defending the coolies and attacking their opponents.*

MR. PICKERING OF THE *Call* says he has "always claimed that, as the Chinese population in this city and state increased in numbers, they would become more exacting and aggressive." In proof of his prescience, he states that "now Chinese demand common-school advantages, which means that they wish to learn the English language, so as to obtain larger wages and work their way into all the avenues of trade—so as to more completely compete with our own citizens." A wise enemy is a joy to the mind, but a foolish ally wrings the heart; and people who are honorably and intelligently working to restrict Chinese immigration will regard Mr. Pickering as a protagonist who puts weapons into the hands of the adversary and delivers battle with his back.

> *John Chinaman, your race I hate,*
> *Because you "won't assimilate."*

You say you will? I know you will,
And so, my lad, I'll hate you still.
For what you will, or will not, do,
I hate you, and for t'other too.
Severely hold yourself aloof,
Or eat of salt beneath my roof.
A beggar be, or earn your bread
By thieving, or by work instead.
Bring Mrs. John and make a home;
Or mateless o'er the country roam;
Or, if your taste incline you, bring
That other woman—horrid thing!—
To learn our language and compete
With ladies of the larger feet.
Eat rat unspiced, or mutton spiced,
And worship Joss, or Jesus Christ.
(Man's creed depends, and much beside,
On what he eats, and if it's fried;
And heathen merely are a folk
Their pig that purchase in a poke
And cook it like John Rogers, one
Or Persecution's overdone.)
Our laws examine, with intent
To guilty plead, or innocent,
When haled before the magistrate
To justify your broken pate;
Or don't examine. All is one—
I'll hate you from the rise of the sun
Until (also because) the seas
Allay his flame—until you please
To stand aside and make a ring
For Paddy when he's brandishing
His fair and lordy length of ear
In this contracted hemisphere.

I fear the foregoing lines are not as frigidly and rigidly anti-coolie in the sentiment as they ought to be to make them suitable for this paper and agreeable to Mr. Pickering; but, like the wife (with nine small children and one at breast) of the martyr John Rogers, whom, incidentally, they roast afresh, or at least warm over, I hate to see anything overdone; and it will reappear at his mouth as a prejudice. Of ten men who write or speak against Chinese immigration, eight do the cause incalculable harm, for the unwisdom of their method makes it obvious to the observant that they are merely echoing local mobgabble, or voicing the reasonless antipathies of race. Of the other two, half the energies are wasted refuting the arguments provoked by the zeal and strengthened by the errors of these asses, who, flat on their sides in the arena, each with an Eastern editor sitting on his head disputing with the rest of us, can only bray into the dust and raise a cloud to darken counsel.

By the way, there is one argument which, aside from its weakness, suggesting as it does an analogy that makes against us, we would do well to "abandon at sea," for we shall be "all at sea" as long as we trust it. I mean the mistake of assuming that we are better qualified to speak on the subject than the people of the East are. Now the evils of Chinese competition in the labor market, like all other evils of which that intricate and difficult science, political economy, makes account, are of so general a character, and are so modified by advantages in special directions—the mischiefs and benefits are so intertwined, overlapped, and trajected—that only omniscience could ravel the tangled web. They are not capable of demonstration, and must remain matters of opinion. Writers and speakers of the Atlantic States being better educated and less provincial than ours are better qualified in judgment. Having no present concern in the matter, they are impartial. It is a proverbial, and all history proves it a political, truth that the looker-on sees most of the game. But, over and above, though inclusive of, these considerations, actual contact with an alien and dissimilar civilization has not affected them with that horrible Race Antipathy—that mother of darkness, whose hideous touch lays upon the eyes of men's minds a blindness so black that not even clay and spittle could let in the miracle of light.

I said our favorite argument suggested a hostile analogy. Let me inquire of any man of observation and understanding, northern or southern: Who were right about the social and industrial phases of negro slavery?—those who had, or those who had not, the "light of experience?"—those whose interests were, or those whose interests were not, most affected by it?—those who knew the negro through life-long association and by observation, or those who had but a literary acquaintance with him?—the practical insiders or the sentimental outsiders?—the players or the onlookers? The parallel, so far as I have drawn it, is perfect. The moral is, that it is better to show wherein the eastern Chinophile is wrong than to protest his inability to be right. The rascal has been so very right so exceedingly often that the fertility of the inner consciousness in which he grows his opinions ought to command our admiration and engage our civility.

Source:
Ambrose Bierce, "Prattle," *Argonaut* 2,
no. 9 (March 9, 1878): 9.

77

Meat vs. Rice: American Manhood Against Asiatic Coolieism

BY SAMUEL GOMPERS AND HERMAN GUTSTADT

Samuel Gompers (1850–1924), born into a Jewish working-class family in London, came to the United States in 1863. He became involved in the labor union movement and in 1886 organized the American Federation of Labor. By 1904 the AFL had enrolled 10 percent of all non-agricultural wage earners in its membership. Gompers, however, frequently revealed prejudice against African Americans and immigrants, and this trait along with his single-minded emphasis on the unionization of skilled craftsmen impeded the broadening of the AFL and hindered industrial unionism. In Meat vs. Rice, *a monograph first published in 1902 by the AFL, Gompers and his collaborator Herman Gutstadt not only opposes Chinese immigrant workers but quotes other local and national politicians who express hostility toward them.*

Much has been said recently, as in the past, of the necessity of having more Asiatics for the purpose of tilling the lands and harvesting the crops of California and at the last convention of the fruitgrowers that great champion of Asiatic immigration, Mr. John P. Irish, railroaded a memorial calling for a letting down of the exclusion bars. The earlier declarations of Mr. Irish upon this important question has estopped him from being a competent witness on behalf of his clients and his utterances, at this late day when placed in comparison with those of gentlemen who were already eminent in California public life when Mr. Irish was a country editor in Iowa, exposes the fact that his conscience has been quieted by his interests.

The late Morris M. Estee in an address before the State Agricultural Society at Sacramento said:

> "I am satisfied that if in our orchards, vineyards, hopfields and grainfields our farmers, instead of hiring the thieving, irresponsible Chinaman, [what would he say of the Japanese?] who like the locusts of Egypt, are eating out our substance, would give some encouragement to our boys, and by hiring them instead, that in a few years we would be rid in California of that curse to farmers and ranchmen, the irresponsible character of farm labor and have in its stead a far more valuable and intelligent class of farm laborers. If this were done, then the question, 'what shall we do with our boys' would be answered."

Had the honorable and learned judge lived he would have been gratified to know that the ranchers and fruitgrowers are now exerting themselves to obtain white laborers, having become heartily tired of their experience with the much-lauded Asiatics.

Though much more could be said upon each phase of this great and burning question we have tried to touch upon all of them sufficiently to enable our readers to obtain reliable information on a subject that is yet barely understood east of the Rocky Mountains. It must be clear to every thinking man and woman that while there is hardly a single reason for the admission of Asiatics, there are hundreds of good and strong reasons for their absolute exclusion.

In view of those reasons we ask, nay, we expect, the undivided support of Americans, and those of American sentiment, in the great effort being made to save our nation from a similar fate that has befallen the islands of the Pacific now overrun with Asiatics.

As a fitting close to this document we submit the remarks made by one of the greatest of American statesmen, Hon. James G. Blaine, February 14, 1879, when a bill for restriction of Chinese immigration was before the United States Senate. Mr. Blaine said:

> "Either the Anglo-Saxon race will possess the Pacific slope or the Mongolians will possess it. You give them the start today, with the keen

thrust of necessity behind them, and with the inducements to come, while we are filling up the other portions of the Continent, and it is inevitable, if not demonstrable, that they will occupy that space of the country between the Sierras and the Pacific.

"The immigrants that come to us from the Pacific isles, and from all parts of Europe, come here with the idea of the family as much engraven on their minds and hearts, and in customs and habits, as we ourselves have. The Asiatic can not go on with our population and make a homogeneous element.

"I am opposed to the Chinese coming here. I am opposed to making them citizens. I am unalterably opposed to making them voters. There is not a peasant cottage inhabited by a Chinaman. There is not a hearthstone, in the sense we understand it, of an American home, or an English home, or an Irish, or German, or French home. There is not a domestic fireside in that sense; and yet you say it is entirely safe to sit down and permit them to fill up our country, or any part of it.

"Treat them like Christians say those who favor their immigration; yet I believe the Christian testimony is that the conversion of Chinese on that basis is a fearful failure; and that the demoralization of the white race is much more rapid by reason of the contact than is the salvation of the Chinese race. You cannot work a man who must have beef and bread, alongside of a man who can live on rice. In all such conflicts, and in all such struggles, the result is not to bring up the man who lives on rice to the beef-and-bread standard, but it is to bring down the beef-and-bread man to the rice standard.

"Slave labor degraded free labor. It took out its respectability, and put an odious cast upon it. It throttled the prosperity of a fine and fair portion of the United States in the South; and this Chinese, which is worse than slave labor, will throttle and impair the prosperity of a still finer and fairer section of the Union on the Pacific coast.

"We have this day to choose whether we will have for the Pacific coast the civilization of Christ or the civilization of Confucius."

Source:
Samuel Gompers and Herman Gutstadt,
*Meat vs. Rice: American Manhood Against
Asiatic Coolieism* (1902; reprinted San
Francisco: Asiatic Exclusion League, 1908),
pp. 21–23.

The Yellow Peril

BY JACK LONDON

Jack London (1876–1916), an immensely prolific short story writer and novelist, lived for much of his life in and around San Francisco. Suffering an impoverished childhood in which he had to work long hours at various menial jobs, London became a socialist as a teenager and persisted in the belief for the whole of his life. In much of his fiction, however, he stresses the virtues of primitivism and Anglo-Saxon courage. In 1904 he spent six months as a war correspondent covering the Russo-Japanese war for the Hearst papers. Just prior to his return he wrote "The Yellow Peril," first published in the San Francisco Examiner *for September 25, 1904, and reprinted in* Revolution and Other Essays *(1910). In it London warns that if the Japanese were to conquer China, they would be a dangerous menace to white civilization.*

HERE WE HAVE THE CHINESE, four hundred million of him, occupying a vast land of immense natural resources—resources of a twentieth century age, of a machine age; resources of coal and iron, which are the backbone of commercial civilization. He is an indefatigable worker. He is not dead to new ideas, new methods, new systems. Under a capable management he can be made to do anything. Truly would he of himself constitute the much-heralded Yellow Peril were it not for his present management. This management, his government, is set, crystallized. It is what binds him down to building as his fathers built. The governing class, entrenched by the precedent and power of centuries and by the stamp it has put upon his mind, will never free him. It would be the suicide of the governing class, and the governing class knows it.

Comes now the Japanese. On the streets of Antung, of Feng-Wang-Chang, or of any other Manchurian city, the following is a familiar scene: One is hurrying home through the dark of the unlighted streets when he comes upon a paper lantern resting on the ground. On one side squats a Chinese civilian on his hams, on the other side squats a Japanese soldier. One dips his forefinger in the dust and writes strange, monstrous characters. The other nods understanding, sweeps the dust slate level with his hand, and with his forefinger inscribes similar characters. They are talking. They cannot speak to each other, but they can write. Long ago one borrowed the other's written language, and long before that, untold generations ago, they diverged from a common root, the ancient Mongol stock.

There have been changes, differentiations brought about by diverse conditions and infusions of other blood; but down at the bottom of their being, twisted into the fibres of them, is a heritage in common—a sameness in kind which time has not obliterated. The infusion of other blood, Malay, perhaps, has made the Japanese a race of mastery and power, a fighting race through all its history, a race which has always despised commerce and exalted fighting.

To-day, equipped with the finest machines and systems of destruction the Caucasian mind has devised, handling machines and systems with remarkable and deadly accuracy, this rejuvenescent Japanese race has embarked on a course of conquest, the goal of which no man knows. The head men of Japan are dreaming ambitiously, and the people are dreaming blindly, a Napoleonic dream. And to this dream the Japanese clings and will cling with bull-dog tenacity. The soldier shouting "Nippon, Banzai!" on the walls of Wiju, the widow at home in her paper house committing suicide so that her only son, her sole support, may go to the front, are both expressing the unanimity of the dream.

The late disturbance in the Far East marked the clashing of the dreams, for the Slav, too, is dreaming greatly. Granting that the Japanese can hurl back the Slav and that the two great branches of the Anglo-Saxon race do not despoil him of his spoils, the Japanese dream takes on substantiality. Japan's population is no larger because her people have continually pressed against the means of subsistence. But given poor, empty Korea for a breeding colony and Manchuria for a granary, and at once the Japanese begins to increase by leaps and bounds.

Even so, he would not of himself constitute a Brown Peril. He has not the time in which to grow and realize the dream. He is only forty-five millions, and so fast does the economic exploitation of the planet hurry on the planet's partition amongst the Western peoples that, before he could attain the stature requisite to menace, he would see the Western giants in possession of the very stuff of his dream.

The menace to the Western world lies, not in the little brown man, but in the four hundred millions of yellow men should the little brown man undertake their management. The Chinese is not dead to new ideas; he is an efficient worker; makes a good soldier, and is wealthy in the essential materials of a machine age. Under a capable management he will go far. The Japanese is prepared and fit to undertake this management. Not only has he proved himself an apt imitator of Western material progress, a sturdy worker, and a capable organizer, but he is far more fit to manage the Chinese than are we. The baffling enigma of the Chinese character is no baffling enigma to him. He understands as we could never school ourselves nor hope to understand. Their mental processes are largely the same. He thinks with the same thought-symbols as does the Chinese, and he thinks in the same peculiar grooves. He goes on where we are balked by the obstacles of incomprehension. He takes the turning which we cannot perceive, twists around the obstacle, and, presto! is out of sight in the ramifications of the Chinese mind where we cannot follow.

The Chinese has been called the type of permanence, and well he has merited it, dozing as he has through the ages. And as truly was the Japanese the type of permanence up to a generation ago, when he suddenly awoke and startled the world with a rejuvenescence the like of which the world had never seen before. The ideas of the West were the leaven which quickened the Japanese; and the ideas of the West, transmitted by the Japanese mind into ideas Japanese, may well make the leaven powerful enough to quicken the Chinese.

We have had Africa for the Africander, and at no distant day we shall hear "Asia for the Asiatic!" Four hundred million indefatigable workers (deft, intelligent, and unafraid to die), aroused and rejuvenescent, managed and guided by forty-five million additional human beings who are splendid fighting animals, scientific and modern, constitute that menace to the Western world which has been well named the "Yellow Peril." The possibility of race adventure has not passed away. We are in the midst of our own. The Slav is just girding himself up to begin. Why may not the yellow and the brown start out on an adventure as tremendous as our own and more strikingly unique?

The ultimate success of such an adventure the Western mind refuses to consider. It is not the nature of life to believe itself weak. There is such a thing as race egotism as well as creature egotism, and a very good thing it is. In the first place, the Western world will not permit the rise of the yellow peril. It is firmly convinced that it will not permit the yellow and the brown to wax strong and menace its peace and comfort. It advances this idea with persistency, and delivers itself of long arguments showing how and why this menace will not be permitted to arise. To-day, far more voices are engaged in denying the yellow peril than in prophesying it. The Western world is warned, if not armed, against the possibility of it.

In the second place, there is a weakness inherent in the brown man which will bring his adventure to naught. From the West he has borrowed all our material achievement and passed our ethical achievement by. Our engines of production and destruction he has made his. What was once solely ours he now duplicates, rivalling our merchants in the commerce of the East, thrashing the Russian on sea and land. A marvellous imitator truly, but imitating us only in things material. Things spiritual cannot be imitated; they must be felt and lived, woven into the very fabric of life, and here the Japanese fails.

It required no revolution of his nature to learn to calculate the range and fire a field-gun or to march the goose-step. It was a mere matter of training. Our material achievement is the product of our intellect. It is knowledge, and knowledge, like coin, is interchangeable. It is not wrapped up in the heredity of the new-born child, but is something to be acquired afterward. Not so with our soul stuff, which is the product of an evolution which goes back to the raw beginnings of the race. Our soul stuff is not a coin to be pocketed by the first chance comer. The Japanese cannot pocket it any more than he can thrill to short Saxon words or we can thrill to Chinese hieroglyphics. The leopard cannot change its spots, nor can the Japanese, nor can we. We are thumbed by the ages into what we are, and by no conscious inward effort can we in a day rethumb ourselves. Nor can the Japanese in a day, or a generation, rethumb himself in our image.

Back of our own great race adventure, back of our robberies by sea and land, our lusts and violences and all the evil things we have done, there is a certain integrity, a sternness of conscience, a melancholy responsibility of life, a sympathy and comradeship and warm human feel, which is ours, indubitably ours, and which we cannot teach to the Oriental as we would teach logarithms or the trajectory of projectiles. That we have groped for the way of right conduct and agonized over the soul betokens our spiritual endowment. Though we have strayed often and far from righteousness, the voices of the seers have always been raised, and we have harked back to the bidding of conscience. The colossal fact of our history is that we have made the religion of Jesus Christ our religion. No matter how dark in error and deed, ours has been a history of spiritual struggle and endeavor. We are preëminently a religious race, which is another way of saying that we are a right-seeking race.

"What do you think of the Japanese?" was asked an American woman after she had lived some time in Japan. "It seems to me that they have no soul," was her answer.

This must not be taken to mean that the Japanese is without soul. But it serves to illustrate the enormous difference between their souls and this woman's soul. There was no feel, no speech, no recognition. This Western soul did not dream that the Eastern soul existed, it was so different, so totally different. . . .

The religion of Japan is practically a worship of the State itself. Patriotism is the expression of this worship. The Japanese mind does not split hairs as to whether the Emperor is Heaven incarnate or the State incarnate. So far as the Japanese are concerned, the Emperor lives, is himself deity. The Emperor is the object to live for and to die for. The Japanese is not an individualist. He has developed national consciousness instead of moral consciousness. He is not interested in his own moral welfare except in so far as it is the welfare of the State. The honor of the individual, per se, does not exist. Only exists the honor of the State, which is his honor. He does not look upon himself as a free agent, working out his own personal salvation. Spiritual agonizing is unknown to him. He has a "sense of calm trust in fate, a quiet submission to the inevitable, a stoic composure in sight of danger or calamity, a disdain of life and friendliness with death." He relates himself to the State as, amongst bees, the worker is related to the hive; himself nothing, the State everything; his reasons for existence the exaltation and glorification of the State.

The most admired quality to-day of the Japanese is his patriotism. The Western world is in rhapsodies over it, unwittingly measuring the Japanese patriotism by its own conceptions of patriotism. "For God, my country, and the Czar!" cries the Russian patriot; but in the Japanese mind there is no differentiation between the three. The Emperor is the Emperor, and God and country as well. The patriotism of the Japanese is blind and unswerving loyalty to what is practically an absolutism. The Emperor can do no wrong, nor can the five ambitious great men who have his ear and control the destiny of Japan.

No great race adventure can go far nor endure long which has no deeper foundation than material success, no higher prompting than conquest for conquest's sake and mere race glorification. To go far and to endure, it must have behind it an ethical impulse, a sincerely conceived righteousness. But it must be taken into consideration that the above postulate is itself a product of Western race-egotism, urged by our belief in our own righteousness and fostered by a faith in ourselves which may be as erroneous as are most fond race fancies. So be it. The world is whirling faster to-day than ever before. It has gained impetus. Affairs rush to conclusion. The Far East is the point of contact of the adventuring Western people as well as of the Asiatic. We shall not have to wait for our children's time nor our children's children. We shall ourselves see and largely determine the adventure of the Yellow and the Brown.

Source:
Jack London, "The Yellow Peril" (1904),
in London's *Revolution and Other Essays*
(New York: Macmillan, 1910), pp. 277–89.

79

Testimony of the Honorable Earl Warren

BY EARL WARREN

Earl Warren (1891–1974) was attorney general of California from 1939 to 1943 and a central figure in the internment of Japanese Americans in California during World War II. In testimony given before the Select Committee Investigating National Defense Migration on February 21, 1942 (two days after Franklin Delano Roosevelt issued the executive order that initiated the internments), Warren displayed hostility to both foreign-born and American-born Japanese in spite of a complete lack of evidence of any sabotage activities on their part.

As governor of California (1943–53), Warren made partial amends by helping to prevent violence against the returning Japanese Americans in 1945. Appointed chief justice of the Supreme Court in 1953 (a position he held until his retirement in 1969), Warren oversaw the unanimous Brown vs. Board of Education of Topeka *ruling of 1954 that led to racial desegregation of public schools. In his autobiography,* The Memoirs of Earl Warren *(1977), Warren briefly discusses his role in the Japanese internments.*

Alien Enemies as Problem for the Military

For some time I have been of the opinion that the solution of our alien enemy problem with all its ramifications, which include the descendants of aliens, is not only a Federal problem but is a military problem. We believe that all of the decisions in that regard must be made by the military command that is charged with the security of this area. I am convinced that the fifth-column activities of our enemy call for the participation of people who are in fact American citizens, and that if we are to deal realistically with the problem we must realize that we will be obliged in time of stress to deal with subversive elements of our own citizenry.

If that be true, it creates almost an impossible situation for the civil authorities because the civil authorities cannot take protective measures against people of that character. We may suspect their loyalty. We may even have some evidence or, perhaps, substantial evidence of their disloyalty. But until we have the whole pattern of the enemy plan, until we are able to go into court and beyond the exclusion of a reasonable doubt establish the guilt of those elements among our American citizens, there is no way that civil government can cope with the situation.

On the other hand, we believe that in an area, such as in California, which has been designated as a combat zone, when things have happened such as have happened here on the coast, something should be done and done immediately. We believe that any delay in the adoption of the necessary protective measures is to invite disaster. It means that we, too, will have in California a Pearl Harbor incident.

I believe that up to the present and perhaps for a long time to come the greatest danger to continental United States is that from well organized sabotage and fifth-column activity.

Opportunities for Sabotage

California presents, perhaps, the most likely objective in the Nation for such activities. There are many reasons why that is true. First, the size and number of our naval and military establishments in California would make it attractive to our enemies as a field of sabotage. Our geographical position with relation to our enemy and to the war in the Pacific is also a tremendous factor. The number and the diversification of our war industries is extremely vital. The fire hazards due to our climate, our forest areas, and the type of building construction make us very susceptible to fire sabotage. Then the tremendous number of aliens that we have resident here makes it almost an impossible problem from the standpoint of law enforcement.

A wave of organized sabotage in California accompanied by an actual air raid or even by a prolonged black-out could not only be more destructive to life and property but could result in retarding the entire war effort of this Nation far more than the treacherous bombing of Pearl Harbor.

I hesitate to think what the result would be of the destruction of any of our big airplane factories in this State. It will interest you to know that some of our airplane factories in this State are entirely surrounded by Japanese land ownership or occupancy. It is a situation that is fraught with the greatest danger and under no circumstances should it ever be permitted to exist.

I have some maps here that will show the specific instances of that character. In order to advise the committee more accurately on this subject I have asked the various district attorneys throughout the State to submit maps to me showing every Japanese ownership and occupancy in the State. Those maps tell a story, a story that is not very heartening to anyone who has the responsibility of protecting life and property either in time of peace or in war.

To assume that the enemy has not planned fifth column activities for us in a wave of sabotage is simply to live in a fool's paradise. These activities, whether you call them "fifth column activities" or "sabotage" or "war behind the lines upon civilians," or whatever you may call it, are just as much an integral part of Axis warfare as any of their military and naval operations. When I say that I refer to all of the Axis powers with which we are at war.

It has developed into a science and a technique that has been used most effectively against every nation with which the Axis powers are at war. It has been developed to a degree almost beyond the belief of our American citizens. That is one of the reasons it is so difficult for our people to become aroused and appreciate the danger of such activities. Those activities are now being used actively in the war in the Pacific, in every field of operations about which I have read. They have unquestionably, gentlemen, planned such activities for California. For us to believe to the contrary is just not realistic.

Unfortunately, however, many of our people and some of our authorities and, I am afraid, many of our people in other parts of the country are of the opinion that because we have had no sabotage and no fifth column activities in this State since the beginning of the war, that means that none have been planned for us. But I take the view that that is the most ominous sign in our whole situation. It convinces me more than perhaps any other factor that the sabotage that we are to get, the fifth column activities that we are to get, are timed just like Pearl Harbor was timed and just like the invasion of France, and of Denmark, and of Norway, and all of those other countries. . . .

Invisible Deadline for Sabotage

Approaching an invisible deadline as we do, it seems to me that no time can be wasted in making the protective measures that are essential to the security of this State. And when I say "this State" I mean all of the coast, of course. I believe that Oregon and Washington are entitled to the same sort of consideration as the zone of danger as California. Perhaps our danger is intensified by the number of our industries and the number of our aliens, but it is much the same.

Gentlemen, it has become no longer a simple question of protecting life and property in this State, because people can't fight in the dark and you can't protect against things about which you don't know. We have all been good soldiers out here and we played the game. We have cooperated with the Federal authorities in every respect, and individual agencies have cooperated with us. As Chief Dullea told you, we work in complete harmony with the Federal authorities and I think that we have accomplished something, but we haven't scratched the surface and because of certain fundamental things.

In our civilian defense we are supposed as State and local officers to protect the lives and the property of our people whether it is in normal times or whether it is in times of great emergency. But when this emergency comes along we are going to have to deal with enemy aliens and those who are acting in concert with them.

Civilian Authorities Instructed Not to Investigate Subversive Activities

We don't know in this State who the enemy aliens are and it is not permitted for us to know. In the first place, the directive of the President (and I think wisely) at the outset of this situation placed the internal security in the hands of a Federal agency, the F.B.I. All local and State officers were instructed not to investigate subversive activities, but immediately upon the receipt of any information to turn it over to the F.B.I.

We have played the game in California. We have followed that directive, and everything we have had we have turned over to them. We have not made independent investigations concerning subversive activities or espionage matters or things of that kind. As a result, we don't have as local officers the pattern of the Axis plans for fifth column activities and sabotage.

In addition to that, we are not permitted to have the names, even, of the alien enemies in our midst. And at the present time every police station in this State, every sheriff's office, every law-enforcement agency can be flanked by aliens with weapons that we know absolutely nothing about.

Potential Danger from American-Born Japanese

I want to say that the consensus of opinion among the law-enforcement officers of this State is that there is more potential danger among the group of Japanese who are born in this country than from the alien Japanese who were born in Japan. That might seem an anomaly to some people, but the fact is that, in the first place, there are twice as many of them. There are 33,000 aliens and there are 66,000 born in this country.

In the second place, most of the Japanese who were born in Japan are over 55 years of age. There has been practically no migration to this country since 1924. But in some instances the children of those people have been sent to Japan for their education, either in whole or in part, and while they are over there they are indoctrinated with the idea of Japanese imperialism. They receive their religious instruction which ties up their religion with their Emperor, and they come back here imbued with the ideas and the policies of Imperial Japan.

While I do not cast a reflection on every Japanese who is born in this country—of course we will have loyal ones—I do say that the consensus of opinion is that taking the groups by and large there is more potential danger to this State from the group that is born here than from the group that is born in Japan.

Mr. Arnold. Let me ask you a question at this point.

Attorney General Warren. Yes, Congressman.

Mr. Arnold. Do you have any way of knowing whether any one of this group that you mention is loyal to this country or loyal to Japan?

Many American-Born Japanese Educated in Japan

Attorney General Warren. Congressman, there is no way that we can establish that fact. We believe that when we are dealing with the Caucasian race we have methods that will test the loyalty of them, and we believe that we can, in dealing with the Germans and the Italians, arrive at some fairly sound conclusions because of our knowledge of the way they live in the community and have lived for many years. But when we deal with the Japanese we are in an entirely different field and we cannot form any opinion that we believe to be sound. Their method of living, their language, make for this difficulty. Many of them who show you a birth certificate stating that they were born in this State, perhaps, or born in Honolulu, can hardly speak the English language because, although they were born here, when they were 4 or 5 years of age they were sent over to Japan to be educated and they stayed over there through their adolescent period at least, and then they came back here thoroughly Japanese.

The Chairman. There are certain Japanese schools here, are there not?

Attorney General Warren. Then we have the Japanese school system here. There is no way that we know of of determining that fact.

I had together about 10 days ago about 40 district attorneys and about 40 sheriffs in the State to discuss this alien problem. I asked all of them collectively at that time if in their experience any Japanese, whether California-born or Japan-born, had ever given them any information on subversive activities or any disloyalty to this country. The answer was unanimously that no such information had ever been given to them.

Now, that is almost unbelievable. You see, when we deal with the German aliens, when we deal with the Italian aliens, we have many informants who are most anxious to help the local authorities and the State and Federal authorities to solve this alien problem. They come in voluntarily and give us information. We get none from the other source.

Does that answer your question, Congressman?

Mr. Arnold. That answers it fully.

Attorney General Warren. There is one thing that concerns us at the present time. As I say, we are very happy over the order of the President yesterday. We believe that is the thing that should be done, but that is only one-half of the problem, as we see it. It is one thing to take these people out of the area and it is another thing to do something with them after they get out. Even from the small areas that they have left up to the present time there are many, many Japanese who are now roaming around the State and roaming around the Western States in a condition that will unquestionably bring about race riots and prejudice and hysteria and excesses of all kind.

I hate to say it, but we have had some evidence of it in our State in just the last 2 or 3 days. People do not want these Japanese just loaded from one community to another, and as a practical matter it might be a very bad thing to do because we might just be transposing the danger from one place to another.

So it seems to me that the next thing the Government has to do is to find a way of handling these aliens who are removed from any vital zone.

In the county of Tulare at the present time and in the county of San Benito and in other counties there are large numbers of the Japanese moving in and sometimes the suggestion has come from the place that they leave, that they ought to go to this other community. But when they go there they find a hostile situation. We are very much afraid that it will cause trouble unless there is a very prompt solution of this problem.

Source:
Earl Warren, "Testimony of the Hon. Earl Warren," in U.S. House of Representatives, 77th Congress, Second Session, *Hearings Before the Select Committee Investigating Defense Migration* (Washington, DC: Government Printing Office, 1942), Part 29 (San Francisco Hearings, February 21 and 23, 1942), pp. 11010–16.

80

The Japanese in America

BY AN INTELLIGENCE OFFICER

"The Japanese in America," published in Harper's *in October 1942, was almost certainly written by Lieutenant Commander Kenneth D. Ringle, an authority on Japanese Americans in the Office of Naval Intelligence (ONI). Ringle prepared two papers, "Report on Japanese Question" (January 26, 1942) for the ONI and "The Japanese Question in the United States" (June 15, 1942) for the War Relocation Committee. These two reports are the basis of the* Harper's *article. Although Ringle, in his first report, stressed that the "'Japanese Problem' has been magnified out of its true proportion ... [and] should be handled on the basis of the* individual, *regardless of citizenship, and not on a racial basis," he expresses the view in "The Japanese in America" that certain segments of the Japanese-American population should be regarded as "guilty until proven innocent" and segregated from the rest of the population.*

WITHIN THE PAST EIGHT OR TEN YEARS the entire "Japanese question" in the United States has reversed itself. The alien menace is no longer paramount, and is becoming less important every day as the original alien immigrants grow older and die, and as more and more of their American-born children reach maturity.

Three words are commonly used in identifying the Japanese in the United States:

> *Issei* (pronounced ee-say) meaning "first generation." The word refers to those who were born in Japan—hence, alien Japanese in the United States.

Nisei (pronounced nee-say) meaning "second generation." The word identifies the children, born in the United States, of *Issei*.

Kibei (pronounced kee-bay) meaning "returned to America." The word refers to those *Nisei* who spent all or a large portion of their lives in Japan and who have now returned to the United States.

The primary present and future problem is that of dealing with the American born United States citizens of Japanese ancestry. I consider that at least seventy-five per cent of them are loyal to the United States. . . .

Of the *Japanese-born alien* residents [the *Issei*],[1] the large majority are at least passively loyal to the United States.

There are among the Japanese, both aliens and United States citizens, certain individuals, either deliberately placed by the Japanese government or actuated by a fanatical loyalty to that country, who would act as saboteurs or enemy agents. This number is estimated to be less than three per cent of the total, or about 3,500 in the entire United States.

The most potentially dangerous element of all are the *Kibei*—those American citizens of Japanese ancestry who have spent the formative years of their lives, between ten and twenty, in Japan and have returned to the United States to claim their legal American citizenship within the past few years. These people are essentially and inherently Japanese and may have been deliberately sent back to the United States by the Japanese government to act as agents. In spite of their legal citizenship and the protection afforded them by the Bill of Rights they should be looked upon as enemy aliens. . . .

It is my belief that the identity of the *Kibei* can be readily ascertained from United States government records.

Such persons must be considered guilty until proven innocent beyond a reasonable doubt. *They should be segregated from those not in that classification.* [At the moment all West Coast Japanese—*Issei, Nisei,* and *Kibei*—except those who are definitely known to be dangerous and who are in custody, are together in the assembly centers.] They should not be allowed their liberty and should really be treated almost as alien internees. Furthermore, the parents or guardians who sent them back to Japan must have done so for a reason. It appears to me that they are equally suspect.

There is another reason for such segregation. There are a number of people, both alien and citizen, who, if given an opportunity and assurance that such an admission would not result in bodily harm, would frankly state their desire to be considered as Japanese nationals and would like to return to Japan either in exchange for American nationals or after the war. Such people should be given the opportunity to announce their choice, and be interned, have their American citizenship revoked, and be returned to Japan as soon as possible, with no opportunity of ever re-entering this country as citizens. The country would be well rid of them.

In the operation of such a classification some injustice would probably result. Some perfectly honest and loyal persons would fall into this category. They could well be given opportunity to make application for a change of status. On the basis of information submitted, a thorough investigation as to background, reputation, employment, associates could be made to determine—not loyalty entirely, but degree of probable menace. I would recommend that groups or committees of *Nisei* of known loyalty and integrity also pass on the applicant, and that such group or committee state in writing whether or not they would be willing to sponsor the applicant. If the investigation showed beyond a reasonable doubt that the applicant was trustworthy, he could be released and take his place in the non-suspect group.

Similar tests could be made among the *Issei*, the older ones who were born in Japan. Determining factors could be the age when each one came to America; the number and lengths of trips made back to Japan; whether or not he is a member of any nationalistic Japanese society; the strength of ties with Japan, including the degree of kinship with any relatives there; whether or not contributions were made in the past to the Japanese war funds; his reputation among his Caucasian-American friends; above all, he should likewise be passed upon by the same committee of loyal *Nisei* as in the *Kibei* procedure outlined above.

In this manner I firmly believe that the potentially dangerous could be readily sifted out, leaving a balance of about three-fourths of the total Japanese population which could be safely accepted as American citizens.

A forcible argument in favor of separation of the *Kibei* and potentially dangerous aliens from the other Japanese is the effect such a segregation would have on the American populace as a whole. If other American citizens could be assured [through strong and vigorous advertisement and publicity by the government] that some step of this nature had been taken, and that those persons permitted to accept private employment or to be members of the War Relocation Authority work corps were only those who were not considered to be dangerous by the Authority, I believe that much of the hysterical resentment against these people would disappear. [Employers] would have far less hesitancy about accepting such people for harvesting crops or even doing war production work. Such action would permit a very appreciable saving in government funds and effort. . . .

The Christian religion as practiced in the United States is a powerful influence toward Americanization. In order to persist, the Buddhist religion is conforming to the American way of life and now includes Young Men's and Young Women's Buddhist Associations, modeled on the Y.M.C.A. and Y.W.C.A. That many of the priests are alien importations who have deliberately used their influence in favor of Japan, and who may have been planted here by the Japanese government for that very purpose, is freely admitted and must always be borne in mind. Most of the pro-Japanese *Issei* are members of the Buddhist faith. Nevertheless, the tenets of the faith are perfectly acceptable and cannot be classed as anti-American. . . .

To sum up: The entire "Japanese Problem" has been magnified out of its true proportion, largely because of the physical characteristics of the people. It should be handled on the basis of the *individual*, regardless of citizenship, and *not* on a racial basis.

Source:
An Intelligence Officer, "The Japanese in America: The Problem and the Solution," *Harper's Magazine* 185, no. 5 (October 1942): 490–93, 495, 497.

81

The Rise in Hate Crime

BY DEVAL L. PATRICK

The continuing prejudice against, and violence directed toward, Asian Americans is the subject of the following speech delivered at the Organization of Chinese Americans in Los Angeles on July 8, 1994, by Deval L. Patrick, who at the time was assistant attorney general of the Civil Rights Division of the U.S. Department of Justice. Patrick urges Asian Americans to join with other minorities in putting up a united front against discrimination.

I HAVE BEEN TROUBLED by the rise in hate crime over the past several years, including anti-Asian violence. The latest figures from the FBI, under the Hate Crimes Statistics Act, showed 236 incidents of anti-Asian violence in 1993, against 293 victims. The National Asian Pacific American Legal Consortium reported 335 incidents in 1993. According to the Consortium, at least 30 of these incidents resulted in death. Imagine: 30 homicides just last year in which Asian Pacific Americans were killed simply because they were Asian Pacific Americans.

And that's 30 *reported* homicides, 335 *reported* incidents. No doubt these statistics represent only a fraction of the incidents of anti-Asian violence in this country. Language barriers, mistrust of police by recent immigrants, ignorance of hate crimes protections and civil rights laws, a reluctance of law enforcement to identify hate crimes as such—all can and often do suppress the figures reported.

The Civil Rights Division has prosecuted a number of anti-Asian violence cases in the past, most notably the Vincent Chin case in Detroit. But we can do better. To develop a more coordinated response, the Civil

Rights Division has been working with the FBI and the Criminal Division of the Department of Justice to develop a joint Hate Crimes Task Force. Our objective is to identify particular problem areas and patterns of violence—including those involving the growing numbers of organized hate groups—and to pounce on problems as we learn of them. We will need your help to get the information, to find the cases appropriate for federal prosecution. And we will vigorously pursue these cases where we have the information and the evidence. Personal safety, freedom from violence based on status, is a central concern of President Clinton. In the Civil Rights Division, we will do our part by bringing the federal prosecutions that demonstrate that such violence has no place in this society today.

Voting issues also appear to be uniquely serious in Asian American communities. My starting point is simple: the right to vote is at the heart of a meaningful democracy. That principle was a driving force behind the civil rights gains in the south in the 1960s, and that movement helped us all appreciate that a seat at the table has not only symbolic significance, but improves in important ways the whole business of governing.

We have the tools to advance that national interest. For example, the 1992 Amendments to the Voting Rights Act strengthened the minority language provisions of the Act, to allow persons who do not read or speak English well to have effective access to voting materials and the voting process. The Act now has a more responsive formula for covering jurisdictions, which has resulted in nearly 80 more jurisdictions being covered, in 24 states.

In the Civil Rights Division we have targeted jurisdictions with minority language populations to provide more effective assistance. For example, in New York City recently, we objected when the jurisdiction refused to translate the names of candidates into Chinese. That produced a change. Now, New Yorkers more comfortable in Chinese than in English can join in the political process. There is much more we can do, and we are working to develop an aggressive enforcement plan for minority language issues. . . .

I have to note a personal concern, too; perhaps a little outside of my official role and duties. I have been very troubled by the rash of anti-immigrant politics sweeping certain parts of the nation. This attitude has unfortunately spread to Washington, as we have seen a multitude of anti-immigrant amendments and bills. But more troubling than anything we have seen in Washington is the so-called "Save Our State" (SOS) initiative on the ballot here in California this November. If passed, among other things, SOS would:

—Limit public education to children who can prove citizenship or legal residency;
—Require school districts to verify the legal residency of *all* students, as well as the status of their parent or guardian, under threat of expulsion;
—Deny publicly-funded health services to non-citizens; and
—Require government officials to report "suspected" undocumented persons to INS, nullifying any sanctuary ordinance already passed by local governments in the state.

"SOS" raises serious constitutional problems. Some of its provisions run right up against *Plyler V. Doe,* decided by the Supreme Court in 1982. According to *Plyler,* it is a denial of equal protection to deny public schooling to illegal alien children. And there are chilling incidents we can envision for Hispanic Americans and Asian Americans in particular, who will get reported to and hassled by immigration officials because they "look" like undocumented aliens, whatever that means. As a response to immigration problems, "SOS" is like swatting a flea with a sledge hammer. As a symbolic matter, this initiative will simply permit the narrow-minded to deny that we are a multi-cultural society—as we always have been. It is wrong for politicians to stir up and exploit anti-immigrant sentiment, passing it off as a comprehensive immigration and border control policy, rather than the rank, political maneuver it is. . . .

On many issues the Chinese-American community has joined with Japanese-Americans, Korean-Americans, Vietnamese-Americans, Cambodian-Americans and Filipino-Americans—and found strength. But we must learn to cross even these broad group boundaries and invest in our *common* struggle. The struggle that your community wages against anti-immigrant sentiment, hate crimes, unfairness in employment, and language discrimination is a struggle shared by Hispanic-Americans and Jewish-Americans and African-Americans as well. Of course there are differences—large and small. And there are differences in histories, which we must learn to appreciate and respect. But we must keep in our minds and our hearts that the indignity of discrimination is just as profound whether it comes because you speak accented English, or have dark skin, or worship a different God than your neighbor does. Discrimination is wrong. And there is both comfort and strength that comes when we commit to each other's struggle.

At the most basic level, I think Americans understand this. Summoned to think about what makes us proud of this country Americans understand at some level that we have a national creed, one deeply rooted in the concepts of equality, opportunity and fair play. At some level we understand that civil rights progress—however sometimes wrenching or resisted—is ultimately the measure of the progress of our civilization. And it is up to us as members of the civil rights community to remind our fellow citizens of that creed and to help them see that the American community as a whole is ultimately the real civil rights community.

We are a great nation, it seems to me, not just because of what we have accomplished, but because of what we have committed ourselves to become. And it is that sense of hope, that sense of looking forward, that I believe has made not only our civil rights movement, but ourselves as a nation, an inspiration to the world.

Now, it's up to us. Neither this administration as a whole nor its Civil Rights Division may have all the answers. God knows, I don't. And it would be absurd to believe that we will always be beyond your criticism or someone else's. But we are here with you, looking forward, committed to *earning* the hope so many place in us.

Source:
Deval L. Patrick, "The Rise in Hate
Crime," *Vital Speeches of the Day* 61, no. 1
(October 15, 1994): 13–15.

PART ELEVEN

Latinos

Prejudice against Latinos was initially manifested, in American history, principally on two occasions—the Mexican War and the Spanish-American War. It was exactly at these moments when American thirst for land encountered the obstacle of a "foreign" (that is, non-English-speaking) population that had been established for more than a century. Unlike the Native Americans, the Spanish who had settled in California and the Southwest could hardly be said to lack a recognizable "civilization"; so other excuses had to be devised to explain why they did not deserve the land they occupied. In California the Spanish were content to control the region with a light hand by the mission system, along with a smattering of military garrisons and pueblos. The mission system predictably gave birth to prejudice based upon anti-Catholic sentiment. Lansford W. Hastings, who led a group of settlers from Ohio to California in 1842–44, lambasted the Spaniards for allowing themselves to be dominated by their priests, "the most dissolute and abandoned characters of the whole community." With the onset of war, prejudice became rampant; but it is still sad to see the young Walt Whitman succumbing to imperialist rhetoric and declaring: "What has miserable, inefficient Mexico—with her superstition, her burlesque upon freedom, her actual tyranny by the few over the many—what has she to do with the great mission of peopling the New World with a noble race?"

The Spanish-American War led to further rhetoric of this kind, focusing on the inherent inability of the Cubans, the Puerto Ricans, and especially the Filipinos to govern themselves, thereby requiring the ostensibly beneficent American annexation. Political commentator Edmond Wood de-

461

clared in 1901 that Congress's declaration that "the people of the island of Cuba are, and of right ought to be, free and independent" would result in an "opera bouffe government."

As the new century dawned and the former Spanish colonies became thoroughly integrated into the nation, nativists began to worry increasingly about the dangerously close proximity of Mexico. They were not concerned about an actual invasion from the weak and divided country, let alone from the principalities to the south; rather, they pondered the specter of illegal immigration of "peons." John Box of Texas delivered a speech in the House of Representatives in 1928 that concisely enunciated the racists' objections to any kind of Mexican immigration, legal or otherwise. To Box the mere presence of Mexicans in American communities would "destroy schools, churches, and all good community life." And as for intermarriage with the Mexicans, since they clearly had "different and lower social and political ideals," any such union would be a disaster.

Latinos now make up large minorities in many localities, notably New York, Los Angeles, and several cities in Texas. Prejudice against them now seems to be exhibited in anger over their failure or refusal to learn English, a sentiment that frequently masks an intolerance of their attempts to preserve their own culture. Similarly, opponents of illegal immigration from Mexico put forth seemingly rational arguments, especially in regard to fears that such immigrants are merely seeking to capitalize on the more abundant social and economic opportunities to be found in the United States; but the level of hostility some of these opponents exhibit makes one wonder whether racist considerations can be very far under the surface of their opposition.

82

The Emigrants' Guide to Oregon and California

BY LANSFORD W. HASTINGS

Lansford Warren Hastings (1819–c. 1870) grew up in Mount Vernon, Ohio. In 1842, at the age of twenty-three, he joined a group of 160 people, under the leadership of Dr. Elijah White, who were determined to cross the continent and settle in the West. Hastings quickly superseded White as leader of the expedition, which first settled in Oregon and then, in 1844, in California. Hastings returned east and wrote a book, The Emigrants' Guide to Oregon and California *(1845), to encourage further settlement of California. In a chapter describing the peoples he encountered there, Hastings criticizes the Mexicans for their ignorance and their domination by priests. In a later section of the chapter, Hastings speaks of the military dictatorship of the last Mexican governor, Manuel Micheltorena, who was driven out by the Californians in 1844–45.*

THE ENTIRE POPULATION OF UPPER CALIFORNIA, including foreigners, Mexicans and Indians, may be estimated at about thirty-one thousand human souls, of whom, about one thousand are foreigners, ten thousand are Mexicans, and the residue are Indians. By the term foreigners, I include all those who are not native citizens of Mexico, whether they have become citizens by naturalization, or whether they remain in a state of alienage. They consist, chiefly, of Americans, Englishmen, Frenchmen, Germans and Spaniards, but there is a very

463

large majority of the former. The foreigners are principally settled at the various towns, and upon the Sacramento; those of whom who, are located at the latter place, consist almost entirely of our own citizens. The foreigners of this country are, generally, very intelligent; many of them have received all the advantages of an education; and they all possess an unusual degree of industry and enterprise. . . .

The Mexicans differ, in every particular, from the foreigners; ignorance and its concomitant, superstition, together with suspicion and superciliousness, constitute the chief ingredients, of the Mexican character. More indomitable ignorance does not prevail, among any people who make the least pretentions to civilization; in truth, they are scarcely a visible grade, in the scale of intelligence, above the barbarous tribes by whom they are surrounded; but this is not surprising, especially when we consider the relation, which these people occupy to their barbarous neighbors, in other particulars. Many of the lower order of them, have intermarried with the various tribes, and have resided with them so long, and lived in a manner so entirely similar, that it has become almost impossible, to trace the least distinctions between them, either in reference to intelligence, or complexion. There is another class, which is, if possible, of a lower order still, than those just alluded to, and which consists of the aborigines themselves, who have been slightly civilized, or rather *domesticated*. These two classes constitute almost the entire Mexican population, of California, and among them almost every variety and shade of complexion may be found, from the African black, to the tawny brown of our southern Indians. Although there is a great variety, and dissimilarity among them, in reference to their complexions, yet in their beastly habits and an entire want of all moral principle, as well as a perfect destitution of all intelligence, there appears to be a perfect similarity. A more full description of these classes, will be found, in what is said, in reference to the Indians, for as most of the lower order of Mexicans, are Indians in fact, whatever is said in reference to the one, will also be applicable to the other. The higher order of the Mexicans, in point of intelligence, are perhaps about equal, to the lower order of our citizens, throughout our western states; but among these even, are very few, who are, to any extent, learned or even intelligent. Learning and intelligence appear to be confined, almost entirely, to the priests, who are, generally, both learned and intelligent. The priests are not only the sole proprietors, of the learning and intelligence, but also, of the liberty and happiness of the people, all of which they parcel out to their blind votaries, with a very sparing hand; and thus it is, that all the Mexican people are kept, in this state of degrading ignorance, and humiliating vassalage. The priests here, not only have the possession of the keys of the understanding, and the door of liberty, but they also, have both the present and ultimate happiness, of these ignorant people, entirely at their disposal. Such at least, is the belief of the people, and such are the doctrines there taught by the priests. At times, I sympathize with these unfortunate beings, but again, I frequently think, that, perhaps, it is fortunate for the residue of mankind, that these semi-barbarians, are thus *ridden* and restrained, and if they are to be thus priest ridden, it is, no doubt, preferable, that they should retain their present *riders.*

Notwithstanding the general learning of the priests, they are the most dissolute and abandoned characters of the whole community. They indulge, without restraint, in all the vices common to those people, and, especially, in those of drunkenness and gambling. To such an extent do they indulge in the former of these vices, that it is not unusual, to see them so much intoxicated, as to prevent the discharge of their ordinary religious duties. . . .

The Judiciary of this government, is extremely simple; it is divested of all that complexity, peculiar to our judiciary system. The judicial officers consist simply of a few alcaldes, or justices of the peace, who are appointed for each town, and settlement, throughout the country, and who have unlimited jurisdiction, in the precinct for which they are appointed. The chief duties of these alcaldes, are merely to adjudge all trivial difficulties, which arise among the people, and to issue passports for those who wish to pass from one precinct to another, and prohibit their passing without them. A passport, issued by the alcalde, is a mere written authority, given you, to pass to and from, such places as are designated, without limiting you to any particular time, though they always contain the words, valid for the time necessary, or words of similar import, and a request, of the alcalde, to the civil and military authorities, to permit you to pass unmolested. The officers are latterly, very inattentive to that branch of their duty, for it is very seldom now, that a foreigner is interrogated in reference to his passport; perhaps it is never the case, unless the foreigner is an entire stranger, and the officers have some good reason, to apprehend some improper conduct. In passing from place to place, no Mexican even spoke of my passport, unless it was, when I applied for its renewal, which I sometimes did, as I passed from one precinct to another, although it was not strictly necessary. Upon one occasion, when I applied for a passport, I remember to have spoken to the "commandante," in reference to the propriety of being thus required, like slaves, to obtain a permission, to pass from place to place, when he remarked, that the authorities were not as strict, with foreigners, in that respect, as they had formerly been, for instance, he remarked, that if I should pass throughout the entire country, the question would never be asked, whether I had obtained a passport. The reason of this great difference, in this respect, he said, was that from the long residence of foreigners among them, they were satisfied, that they were not as evilly disposed, as they had formerly been supposed to be; but the true reason is, that they have not the balance of power, in their favor, as they formerly had, which if they had, all their former hostility and barbarity, would be renewed, with infinite pleasure. The foreigners are annually increasing in numbers and power, the inevitable tendency of which, is clearly seen and understood, even by the Mexicans, hence it is, that foreigners are now treated with the utmost respect, kindness and hospitality. The bombardment of Vera Cruz, the triumph of Texas, and the impromptu conquest of California, by Com. Jones, have long since, taught them the propriety, of respecting the rights of foreigners.

Now, instead of that inhuman oppression, which was formerly inflicted upon foreigners, without measure and without mercy, they are treated with all the deceptive kindness imaginable, and instead of that hostile opposition, which formerly existed to the emigration of foreigners to that country, every inducement is held out, to encourage foreign imigration. Large grants of land are given to each emigrant, averaging from one to eleven square leagues, the quantity depending upon the number of members, composing the applicant's family, and his means of improving, by building, fencing or otherwise. In order to obtain a grant of land, it becomes necessary for a foreigner, first to make an application for naturalization, then to present a petition addressed to the governor, praying for a grant of the land which he may have selected, and of which, he, at the same time, presents a general map, representing its extent and surface. This being done, he is entitled to the possession of his land, and when the process of his naturalization is accomplished, he is entitled to his deed, which is made by the government, of California, under the hand and seal of the governor. Although the quantity of land usually granted is from one to eleven square leagues, yet it is seldom that either extreme is taken, perhaps there are no instances of any individuals' having obtained but one league, though there are some instances, of their having obtained eleven square leagues. There are also several grants of twenty or thirty square leagues; among these extensive grants, is Captain Sutter's, which contains thirty square leagues, or two hundred and seventy square miles. Grants of this extent, are given only upon the condition that the grantee settle a certain number of families upon it, within a certain number of years, according to the provisions of the colonization law, which law, however, it is said, has recently been repealed. Any person arriving in that country, is at liberty to take any lands which are not taken, or which have not been applied for, even without making any application for that purpose, but in such case, he is liable to be dispossessed at any time, by the lands being regularly applied for, by another. All those who emigrated to that country, with me, settled in that manner, and made some extensive improvements, without having made an application for a title, yet they all designed to make their applications, in due time. The reason of their not making their application, immediately, upon their arrival, was, that it was, at that time, rumored, that foreigners would be enabled to obtain their titles, without becoming citizens, which they all very much preferred, if it could be accomplished. I am aware that a certain high functionary, at Washington city, who represents the government of Mexico, insists that foreigners can not obtain lands, in California, merely by becoming citizens, but that their obtaining lands, depends entirely, upon the option of the governor of California. Now how this may be, I do not pretend to say, but I do say, that the only prerequisites, required, are those just stated, and in reference to this matter, I speak from my own personal knowledge, as I called upon the governor, with a view of applying for the grant of a certain tract of land, when he informed me, as above stated. But as I did not think proper to become a Mexican citizen, I did not obtain my title, and as I am fully determined *never* to become a Mexican citizen, the presumption is, that I shall *never* obtain a title to the lands for which I applied, especially if it is the destiny of Mexico *forever* to retain possession of the Californias. In reference to the option of the governor to grant lands or not, as contended by the Mexican functionary alluded to, it is not at all material, more specially, as it happens to be his *preference,* or at least his *practice,* to grant lands to all foreigners, who make application in conformity with the requisitions before stated. And should his preference suggest a different course, I am inclined to the opinion, that his excellency would still find it much more conducive, both to public policy and peace, to grant lands upon the same terms, to all who make application for that purpose; and thus, avoid creating distinctions and prejudices, between native and naturalized citizens.

Source:
Lansford W. Hastings, *The Emigrants'*
Guide to Oregon and California (Cincinnati:
G. Conclin, 1845), pp. 112–14, 122–24.

83

Editorials for the *Brooklyn Daily Eagle*

BY WALT WHITMAN

The poet Walt Whitman (1819–1892) became associated with newspapers and magazines in New York and Brooklyn from at least the age of thirteen, when he served as a printer's apprentice. From 1846 to 1848 he was editor of the Brooklyn Daily Eagle, *the leading newspaper in Brooklyn. Editorials written during 1846 display how Whitman became caught up in the imperialistic jingoism of the period, urging annexation of Texas and California and vilifying Mexico. Whitman, however, lost his position at the* Eagle *for criticizing the Democratic Party's failure to face up to the issue of slavery in the new states that wished to join the union.*

Annexation

The more we reflect on the matter of annexation as involving a part of Mexico, or even the main bulk of that republic, the more do doubts and obstacles resolve themselves away, and the more plausible appears that, at first blush, most difficult consummation. The scope of our government, (like the most sublime principles of Nature), is such that it can readily fit itself, and extend itself, to almost any extent, and to interests and circumstances the most widely different.

It is affirmed, and with great probability, that in several of the departments of Mexico—the large, fertile and beautiful one of Yucatan, in particular—there is a wide popular disposition to come under the wings of our eagle. The Yucatecos are the best and most industrious citizens in Mexico. They have for years been on bad terms with the central power,

468

and have repeatedly reached open ruptures with the executive and the federal government. The new Congress, which the last accounts mention as having just assembled at Merida, the capital, is acting at the present moment in a manner entirely independent of Mexico—passing tariff laws for itself, and so on. Rumor also states that a mission had been, or is to be, despatched to the United States, with the probable object of treating for annexation or something like it.

Then there is California, in the way to which lovely tract lies Santa Fé; how long a time will elapse before *they* shine as two new stars in our mighty firmament?

—Speculations of this sort may seem idle to some folks. So do they not, we are assured, to many who look deep into the future. Nor is it the much condemned lust of power and territory that makes the popular heart respond to the idea of these new acquisitions. Such greediness might very properly be the motive of widening a less liberal form of government; but such greediness is not ours. We pant to see our country and its rule far-reaching, only inasmuch as it will take off the shackles that prevent men the even chance of being happy and good—as most governments are now so constituted that the tendency is very much the other way. We have no ambition for the mere physical grandeur of this Republic. Such grandeur is idle and deceptive enough. Or at least it is only desirable as an aid to reach the truer good, the good of the whole body of the people.

Our Territory on the Pacific

However soon the passage-at-arms between this Republic and Mexico, be closed, we hope—since things have resolved themselves into the state they now hold—that the United States will, (in some way,) fix their mark of ownership on the American coast of the Pacific, down a bit below our old boundary. California, or rather Upper California, stretches between the 32d and 42d degrees of latitude on this coast: and here is the proposed field of Colonel Stevenson's expedition. That stretch is irrigated by two great rivers, the Buenaventara and Timpanogos, between which lie St. Francisco, (on the latter river), and Monterey. Even at this moment, the Star Spangled Banner may be floating from those towns.

We love to indulge in thoughts of the future extent and power of this Republic—because with its increase is the increase of human happiness and liberty.—Therefore hope we that the United States will keep a fast grip on California. What has miserable, inefficient Mexico—with her superstition, her burlesque upon freedom, her actual tyranny by the few over the many—what has she to do with the great mission of peopling the New World with a noble race? Be it ours, to achieve that mission! Be it ours to roll down all of the upstart leaven of old despotism, that comes our way!

Source:
Walt Whitman, "Annexation" (June 6,
1846) and "Our Territory on the Pacific"
(July 7, 1846), in Whitman's *The Gathering of
the Forces,* edited by Cleveland Rodgers and
John Black (New York: Putnam's, 1920),
vol. 1, pp. 242–44, 246–47.

⁓ *84* ⁓

California Pastoral

BY HUBERT HOWE BANCROFT

Hubert Howe Bancroft (1832–1918) was a publisher and prolific historian, especially of the western states and of Mexico. Many of his works, however, were apparently researched and in part written by a large but unnamed staff of assistants. Bancroft was the author of a five-volume work, Native Races of the Pacific States *(1874). Bancroft describes "pastoral" California prior to the days of the gold rush, speaking with disdain of both the Native American and Spanish inhabitants who were destined to fall to the conquering Anglo-Saxon. Bancroft also reveals severe prejudice against African Americans in his memoir* Retrospection *(1912).*

IN AMERICA, WHEREVER THE EUROPEAN plants himself, the native is overshadowed. And the lower in the scale of humanity he is, the quicker he dies. No people have longer endured the intimate contact of Europeans than the Nahuas of the Mexican table-land. The Tasmanians have gone, and the Australians, the New Zealanders, and the Hawaiians are fast going. Our food, our drink, our clothes, our shelter, our piety, our cruelty, our diseases—all tend to waste them away. Being intellectually weak and inferior, they sink into the earth beside their neighbor of ranker individuality.

Take from the mountains or prairies hardy wild cattle; confine, feed, and fatten them, and they are the first to fall before some rinderpest. Wild beasts never can be made to work beside domesticated animals. A civilized horse would kill a dozen of the untamed kind at ploughing, whereas, free, the wild horse would soon run the tame one to death on the prairies. Our present civilization tends to toughen men; it does not

471

enervate and degrade, like that of ancient Greece and Rome. In Spain, in Sicily, and in Gual, the barbarian with the Roman endured. The contact was beneficial rather than prejudicial to both barbarian and Roman. But then, these barbarians were not exactly savages, nor were the Romans then the hardy, warlike people they once were. . . .

Natural advantages exercise a powerful influence upon a people, particularly where they are indigenous. But those countries possessing the greatest advantages of soil and climate do not always produce the greatest people. Of energy there was enough among the Spanish colonists, but it was of that spasmodic kind which aroused by passion subsides before beneficial results are secured. It was the very opposite of that tenacious and stubborn principle which governed the Anglo-Saxons in America, whose patient and self-denying industry laid the foundations of superior political institutions.

Both Indian and Spaniard were alike in natural indolence, love of luxury, fondness for amusement, and hatred of menial occupations. Both would undergo the greatest hardships without a murmur; but when the passion had cooled, or when the exigency which called forth these spasms of energy had passed, there came a reaction in which indulgence was in as great excess as the discipline had been severe. For the continuous application of those faculties of body and mind which alone achieve permanent greatness, the Latin races were children beside the Anglo-Saxon. . . .

The blood of Spain, already somewhat mixed with that of the people of Montezuma, was still further reduced by the occasional union of the Mexican and Indian. When in 1835 the government began to make grants of land, and the missions were secularized and sold and the troops disbanded, many of the common soldiers wived with Indians. Hence came the baser stock of Hispano-Californians, such as, in the time of gold discoveries, were yclept greasers.

Thus there were two distinct classes—that which sprang from the admixture of Mexican and Indian, and that of Mexican blood alone.

Whiteness was the badge of respectability, and the white Anglo-American mated with her he chose from among the rich dusky daughters of Mexican descent. This claim is to this day rather a sensitive point, not only with the Mexico-Californians themselves, but with the Americans and Englishmen who married here. A too close scrutiny of the blood with which they allied themselves is not always palatable to the fathers of dark-complexioned children, especially if the fathers be rich and respectable and the sons and daughters educated and accomplished. . . .

In conclusion, we may sum up our Lotos-land society in this wise: ignorant, lazy, religious, the religion being more for women, children, and Indians than for European men—though Coronel speaks of pausing in the midst of a fandango or rodeo to pray; and all went to church, though they gambled freely afterwards. It was common for heads of families and all circumspect persons to wear sanctimonious faces in the presence of the young, refraining from the mention of wickedness lest they should be contaminated. Morals at first were quite pure; later they became very bad, syphilis being quite common among all classes and both sexes.

They were a frank, amiable, social, hospitable people, and honest enough where it did not require too great an exertion to pay their debts. No obligations of any kind weighed very heavily upon them. They were an emotional race; their qualities of mind and heart floated on the surface; they not only possessed feeling but they showed it.

They were not a strong community in any sense, either morally, physically, or politically; hence it was that as the savages faded before the superior Mexicans, so faded the Mexicans before the superior Americans. Great was their opportunity, exceedingly great at first if they had chosen to build up a large and prosperous commonwealth; and later no less marvelous, had they possessed the ability to make avail of the progress and performance of others. Many were defrauded of their stock and lands; many quickly squandered the money realized from a sudden increase in values. They were foolish, improvident, incapable; at the same time they were grossly sinned against by the people of the United States. There was a class of lawyers, the vilest of human kind, whose lives were devoted to a study of the cunning and duplicity necessary to defraud these simple-minded patriarchs. Nevertheless, as I have said, it would be difficult to find in any age or place, a community that got more out of life, and with less trouble, with less wear and wickedness, than the people of Pastoral California.

Source:
Hubert Howe Bancroft, *California Pastoral
1769–1848* (The Works of Hubert Howe
Bancroft, Volume XXXIV) (San Francisco:
The History Co., 1888), pp. 267, 269–70,
278–79, 292–93.

85

Can Cubans
Govern Cuba?

BY EDMOND WOOD

*The liberation of Cuba from Spanish control in 1898 led to much discussion
as to the fate of the island and its people and to the precise degree of
American involvement, ranging from outright annexation to a complete
"hands-off" policy. In the end Cuba was declared a U.S. protectorate. In
"Can Cubans Govern Cuba?" the political commentator Edmond Wood
ponders the question of whether the Cubans are even capable of self-government.*

A JOINT RESOLUTION PASSED BY the United States Congress declaring that "the people of the island of Cuba are, and of right ought to
be, free and independent," is responsible for what will prove to be an
opera bouffe government in that island, unless Cubans have learned from
the mistakes of other Spanish-Americans, and are able to develop character and capacity never yet displayed by any nation of Spanish descent.

No one can detract from the bravery and daring of Spanish character
as demonstrated by the deeds and discoveries of the new world pioneers
in their explorations and conquests. Unsailed oceans, unmapped coasts,
mighty mountains, tangled forests, and the hostility of native tribes
could not stay their venturesome progress. Early in the sixteenth century
they had overrun America from the Arkansas to Cape Horn, and had
added an empire larger than all Europe to the dominions of their royal
master. This was accomplished by a ridiculously small force. A little
group of men, no more in number than the police of a second-class city,

conquered for Spain her territories in North and Central America, and an even smaller number planted her banner on the ruins of the Inca Empire. No braver or more daring men ever girded sword on thigh or followed a leader to battle.

During both the ten years' war and the later one in Cuba, which resulted in the overthrow of Spanish sovereignty, as well as during the Philippine insurrections, many deeds of daring were performed, and much suffering was patiently endured, worthy of being enshrined in song and story. Admiral Cervera's dash out of the harbor of Santiago de Cuba in the face of the loaded muzzles of the American fleet, in obedience to superior authority, and to save the honor of Spain, when his judgment told him that the effort would meet with certain defeat, was as brave a deed as any recorded in the annals of naval heroism.

But the architects of states need more than bravery in order to build for generations yet to come. Neither Spanish colonists nor their descendants, whether of pure or mixed blood, have ever developed the constructive faculty and executive capacity that are necessary in order to establish a stable government. The evolution of constitutional liberty, the sanctity of the ballot, the purity of courts of justice, and the ability to administer national finances are matters of slow growth and development. They cannot be secured by imitation, and they have never been successfully exercised by people of Spanish origin or training. With the exception of Benito Juarez, a pure Indian, by the way, it is difficult to recall the name of a single person in Spanish-American history eminent for those qualities of mind which can plan with careful forethought institutions fit to endure the test of time.

Spain destroyed in America two civilizations, those of Mexico and Peru, each superior in some respects to that planted by the conquerors. The vice-regal domination of the mother country in both America and the Philippines has a history of centuries of misrule, violence, injustice, and oppression. The gentle natives of the West Indies, who had received the first comers as guests, were utterly destroyed in less than fifty years after the discovery; and it has been estimated that during this period not less than 12,000,000 native Americans perished under the mailed hand of the soldiers of Spain. When one of the last native casiques of Cuba, the heroic Hatuey, was urged to embrace Christianity in order to be saved, he frankly said that if there were Spaniards in heaven he did not want to go there. Aztecs and Incas were slaughtered or enslaved. The rich treasures of America corrupted rather than strengthened the Peninsular government, and the provinces of Ultra Mar became the spoil of those who had friends at court. Weyler was a legitimate descendant of such men as

Cortés, Pizarro, Tacón, and Balmaceda, and followed the historical examples established by a long list of predecessors. It is a sad story from beginning to end, with here and there a ray of light from noble churchmen like Bartolomé de Las Cases and Junípero Serra, who struggled in vain against the abuses of the secular arm of the government.

Columbus was a victim of Spanish injustice, and fretted out his last years in futile attempts to secure a small portion of the honors and emoluments which the Throne had solemnly covenanted to bestow upon him. Cortés murdered Montezuma, and his followers tortured Guatomozin. Then, in turn, the conqueror became the victim of conspiracies, and was discredited at court; and a little later his son Martín was put to the torture by avaricious rascals, devoid alike of mercy, fear, and shame. In Peru, Pizarro slaughtered with scant ceremony both the natives and those of his own race who conspired against him. He, too, met with a violent death, as did his brother Gonzalo, who succeeded him as a leader of the Spanish troops in Peru. It is a painful record, conceived in avarice, born of blood, and cradled in gross injustice—growing a little better, perhaps, after the conquest, but so full of wrong that in the early years of the nineteenth century it gave rise to the revolutions by which Spain lost all her colonial possessions except Cuba, Porto Rico, and the Philippines.

It was thought that independence would be the panacea for all the ills of the body politic. The wrongs under which the colonies labored had been charged to the representatives of the Crown; and with the achievement of independence it was fondly hoped and believed that the reign of justice had begun. The condition of things, however, instead of improving became worse. The injustice of Spanish government was succeeded by other evils of domestic origin.

As a rule the Constitution of the United States was taken by the blood-born republics of Spanish America as the model by which to shape and fashion their forms of government. The application of its provisions became, however, a travesty on justice. Force, intrigue, and violence were in effect substituted for the legislative, executive, and judicial powers of government. In Mexico, Iturbide was proclaimed emperor, was then deposed and banished, and upon his return to the country was shot with but little attention to the forms of law. Then was inaugurated a series of revolutions which continued almost without interruption until Porfirio Diaz, raised in an atmosphere of revolution, seized by means of a revolution the reins of power, which he has held for more than twenty years, to the material benefit of his country rather than to the evolution of true democratic ideals. The history of Mexico is but a replica of the history of Peru, Venezuela, and most of the other Latin republics of America. The wars which have so retarded the development of these fertile lands grew, in almost every instance, out of personal ambition, and were not occasioned by the advocacy of great principles of government or in defence of human rights. The interpretation of a constitution never reddened a Spanish battle-field or changed the course of history. These conflicts were the mad struggles of ambitious and strong men for supreme power. One of their own poets has described the condition which usually obtained by saying of his land:

"Cada año un gobernante,
Cada mes un motín."

This may be freely rendered:

"Each year a constitution,
Each month a revolution."

All these republics, owing to their Spanish training, have been of one mind as to customs tariffs, and have made commerce bear all the burdens it could possibly carry, both for the purpose of producing revenue and for the advantages this system gave to those who had an opportunity to evade the exactions of the customs collector. An honest and efficient customs administration cannot be found in any Spanish country on earth. "Entre los amigos no hay ley"—among friends there is no law—is one of the proverbs of the Spanish people, and it would not be a bad inscription to place over the portals of their custom houses.

Not only are customs assessed upon goods entering the country, but there are also state or provincial tariffs, as well as municipal tariffs; so that a shipment of merchandise to an interior city must pay a federal tariff, a state tariff, and a municipal tariff. This, of course, calls for a large civil force, and the expense of collection is by no means small. The new Cuban constitution has no provision for the free interchange of commerce between the provinces of the island; and should they follow the lead of other countries of like origin, an effort will be made to secure funds for provincial and municipal expenses by means of local tariffs, which will operate against the development of the island, and add enormously to the cost of the administration of government.

Unlettered people have never been successful in guarding their liberties, but have become the prey of ambitious leaders who have ruled by passion or force. The masses of the Spanish-speaking people of America are not educated, and their high percentage of illiteracy is a sad comment on the lack of interest taken by the respective governments in the education of the people. This was originally an inheritance from Spain, where illiterates are in the majority. Cuba, having been so long under the rule of Spain, has about the same record, which is not very different from the condition of other Spanish-American countries. In the republics already established the difficulty was originally chargeable to the mother country; but now, after they have been independent for almost a century, with no marked advance in the direction of general education, the conclusion is that a true conception of the importance of education has not been grasped by the rulers of these lands. The truth is that these countries are making a ghastly play at government. General education is not necessary in a despotism, whether royal or military. By these people any general scheme of public instruction is looked upon as an ornamental adjunct of government, rather than a necessary part of it.

While prolific of constitutions the Latin republics of America allow none of them to endure long enough to acquire a respectable age. In the adoption of the fundamental laws of other lands they are inclined to seize upon what is superficial and spectacular rather than upon those principles which lie at the basis of liberty, security, and order. The desire to rule makes the brave Latin-American follow many a Don Quixote, as did Sancho Panza, upon the promise of an island to govern. The very bravery and daring of the Spanish character, prone to act without counting the cost or foreseeing results, are breeders of revolutions. . . .

There is grave danger that the experiment of the independent government of Cuba by Cubans will have the following results: The revenues will decrease and expenses will increase; projected improvements, absolutely necessary for the development of the country, will languish; schools will be neglected; sanitary measures will not be intelligently prosecuted; and the country will retrograde. These things may now be predicted with some degree of confidence without assuming that rival parties will raise the standard of revolution, as has so often happened in every Spanish country in America. The latter possibility has been scarcely mentioned in treating of the Cuban question, as it is a matter which time alone can develop; but as every one of the fifteen Latin-American republics has had many domestic revolutions, the conclusion is reasonable that Cuba is not free from the same tendency, and may in the near future appeal to the bayonet rather than the ballot to decide presidential contests. The President, under the Cuban constitution, will have almost supreme power in the distribution of patronage, even in the provinces. The government will be a central one, and the provinces for governmental purposes will have a nominal rather than a real existence. Conservative Cubans, with large interests in the island, urge the speedy establishment of independence, not because they have confidence in its permanency, but because they see that the trial must be made; and they look upon it simply as a necessary step to final annexation or control by the United States.

The joint resolution of Congress will withdraw the American forces from Cuba, but the Platt amendment will sooner or later send them back with more serious problems to solve and a large debt to provide for. It is the custom among nations for the conqueror to impose an indemnity upon the conquered, as was done recently by the Western Powers in the case of China; but the United States, the conqueror in the late war, paid an indemnity to Spain, returned her soldiers to their native land, clothed the naked, nursed the sick, and assumed the payment of the losses of her own citizens which arose from the war, asking no money indemnity from either Spain or Cuba for the enormous cost of the Cuban campaign. Neither has Cuba expressed any sense of financial indebtedness to the United States for the expense incurred in driving the saffron flag of Spain from American soil and American waters. The end is not yet.

Source:
Edmond Wood, "Can Cubans Govern
Cuba?" *Forum* 32, no. 1 (September 1901):
66–70, 73.

～ *86* ～

Restriction of Mexican Immigration

BY JOHN BOX

John Box (1871–1941) was a Methodist minister and longtime U.S. representative from Texas (1919–31). In a speech delivered in the House of Representatives on February 9, 1928, Box recited a litany of reasons that Mexican immigration ought to be severely curtailed: they will adversely affect the lives of American laborers and degrade American "racial stock" by intermixture; they are illiterate and ignorant, and bring disease and crime in their wake.

THE PEOPLE OF THE UNITED STATES have so definitely determined that immigration shall be rigidly held in check that many who would oppose this settled policy dare not openly attack it. The opposition declares itself in sympathy with the policy and then seeks to break down essential parts of the law and opposes any consistent completion of it making it serve the Nation's purpose to maintain its distinguishing character and institutions. Declaring that they do not believe that paupers and serfs and peons, the ignorant, the diseased, and the criminal of the world should pour by tens and hundreds of thousands into the United States as the decades pass, they nevertheless oppose the stopping of that very class from coming out of Mexico and the West Indies into the country at the rate of 75,000, more or less, per year.

Every reason which calls for the exclusion of the most wretched, ignorant, dirty, diseased, and degraded people of Europe or Asia demands that the illiterate, unclean, peonized masses moving this way from

Mexico be stopped at the border. Few will seriously propose the repeal of the immigration laws during the present Congress, but the efforts of those who understand and support the spirit and purpose of these laws to complete them and make them more effective by the application of their quota provisions to Mexico and the West Indies, will be insidiously and strenuously opposed.

The admission of a large and increasing number of Mexican peons to engage in all kinds of work is at variance with the American purpose to protect the wages of its working people and maintain their standard of living. Mexican labor is not free; it is not well paid; its standard of living is low. The yearly admission of several scores of thousands from just across the Mexican border tends constantly to lower the wages and conditions of men and women of America who labor with their hands in industry, in transportation, and in agriculture. One who has been in Mexico or in Mexican sections of cities and towns of southwestern United States enough to make general observation needs no evidence or argument to convince him of the truth of the statement that Mexican peon labor is poorly paid and lives miserably in the midst of want, dirt, and disease.

In industry and transportation they displace great numbers of Americans who are left without employment and drift into poverty, even vagrancy, being unable to maintain families or to help sustain American communities. Volumes of data could be presented by way of support and illustration of this proposition. It is said that farmers need them. On the contrary, American farmers, including those of Texas and the Southwest, as a class do not need them or want them. I state the rule as of country-wide application, without denying that a small percentage of farmers want them, and that in some restricted regions this percentage is considerable. I doubt if a majority of the bona fide farmers of any State want or need them. I have given much attention to the question and am convinced that as a state-wide or nation-wide proposition they are not only not needed and not wanted, but the admission of great numbers of them to engage in agricultural work would be seriously hurtful to the interests of farmers, farm workers, and country communities. They take the places of white Americans in communities and often thereby destroy schools, churches, and all good community life. . . .

Another purpose of the immigration laws is the protection of American racial stock from further degradation or change through mongrelization. The Mexican peon is a mixture of Mediterranean-blooded Spanish peasant with low-grade Indians who did not fight to extinction but submitted and multiplied as serfs. Into that was fused much negro slave blood. This blend of low-grade Spaniard, peonized Indian, and negro slave mixes with negroes, mulatoes, and other mongrels, and some sorry whites, already here. The prevention of such mongrelization and the degradation it causes is one of the purposes of our laws which the admission of these people will tend to defeat.

Every incoming race causes blood mixture, but if this were not true, a mixture of blocs of peoples of different races has a bad effect upon citizenship, creating more race conflicts and weakening national character. This is worse when the newcomers have different and lower social and political ideals. Mexico's Government has always been an expression of Mexican impulses and traditions. Rather, it is an exhibition of the lack of better traditions and the want of intelligence and stamina among the mass of its people. One purpose of our immigration laws is to prevent the lowering of the ideals and the average of our citizenship, the creation of race friction and the weakening of the Nation's powers of cohesion, resulting from the intermixing of differing races. The admission of 75,000 Mexican peons annually tends to the aggravation of this, another evil which the laws are designed to prevent or cure.

To keep out the illiterate and the diseased is another essential part of the Nation's immigration policy. The Mexican peons are illiterate and ignorant. Because of their unsanitary habits and living conditions and their vices they are especially subject to smallpox, venereal diseases, tuberculosis, and other dangerous contagions. Their admission is inconsistent with this phase of our policy.

The protection of American society against the importation of crime and pauperism is yet another object of these laws. Few, if any, other immigrants have brought us so large a proportion of criminals and papers as have the Mexican peons. . . .

The volume of Mexican immigration, the attending circumstances, and the prospects for its continuance and enlargement are such as to make this an important part of one of the Nation's greatest problems. Mexico has nearly 15,000,000 people who are prolific breeders, capable of producing millions of new inhabitants every year.

Their economic condition will continue worse than ours for an indefinite time and cause their laborers to want to migrate to the United States. Under a well-known law of population, the gaps left at home by those who come from year to year will be rapidly refilled by a natural increase. Thus Mexico will become an inexhaustible source of this low-grade immigration.

Immigrants who have poured upon our shores from Europe and Old World countries have had to pay the expense of land travel in reaching foreign seaports, after which the heavy expense of ocean transportation had to be paid. Mexico's masses have only to tramp to the border. The expense of their transportation, whether paid by them or others, is trifling compared to the cost of crossing the ocean from Europe or Asia to America. The methods by which labor importers reach them and induce them to come are inexpensive and easy. The building of barriers against the flood flowing in from elsewhere must increase the inpouring from Mexico. Unless it is checked it will continue with increasing volume.

The most dangerous mass immigration now menacing us is that from Mexico.

Source:
John Box, "Restriction of Mexican
Immigration," *Congressional Record* 69, no. 3
(February 9, 1928): 2817–18.

87

Alien Workers in America

BY RAYMOND G. CARROLL

In 1936 the journalist Raymond G. Carroll wrote a study of "Alien Workers in America" for the Saturday Evening Post. *In one section of his essay he devotes attention both to Mexican immigrants and to illegal Mexican aliens.*

MEXICANS DO ABOUT ALL the outdoor hard labor of the Southwest. An eye flash of one class of work that they perform came when the Golden State Limited of the Southern Pacific Railroad halted less than 100 miles west of El Paso, where there had been an overflow of the Rio Grande. The 300 odd men who had repaired the tracks, who were revealed doffing their hats as the train slowly went over the newly made patch of roadway, were Mexicans. When there are railroads to be built in this country of cactus and sand, they build them.

Where the Mexicans excel is as vegetable laborers in the onion and lettuce fields, growers of cantaloupe and the citrus fruits, berry gatherers, cotton pickers and coal, copper and silver miners in Texas. I rode for an entire day in an automobile through the cantaloupe country near Brownsville, skirting the new oil region along the Gulf, and entering the onion-growing, winter-garden district south of San Antonio without seeing a single native-born white at work.

Although termed the most unassimilable of aliens, Mexicans have leap-frogged from the Rio Grande into the sugar-beet fields of Colorado, and on beyond into Illinois, Indiana and Michigan, where they are active in the meat-packing plants of Chicago, the steel industry of Gary and the copper mines of the Calumet region.

Others than Mexicans come out of Mexico. Not long ago two foreign-looking men were picked up by the Immigration Border Patrol near El Paso, Texas. They were standing in a puzzled mood on the El Paso and Southwestern Railroad tracks when apprehended. Under pressure of sharp questioning which necessitated the employment of an Italian inter-preter, one of the men broke down and confessed that each had paid an immigrant agent back in Italy $300 to land them in Chicago. They were Italians who had come to Mexico, and an alien smuggler had waded them across the Rio Grande below Juarez, brought them to the railroad tracks, and, pointing in two directions, said: "That way is Chicago and this way is Los Angeles. Take your choice and keep walking." The two Italians were deported to Italy, but nothing further was developed con-cerning this undoubted underground route for shipping Italians to America via Mexico.

The immigration patrolmen of the El Paso district, embracing Arizona, New Mexico and West Texas, are expected to guard a border line of about 1100 miles. The present authorized personnel for that pur-pose consists of eighty-three patrol inspectors and twenty-seven senior patrol inspectors, a total force of 110 men. Apparently this would give each officer a distance of ten miles to patrol. But at least two officers must work together as a measure of self-protection, so that in theory, the border has one man—or one team—patrolling twenty miles of territory twenty-four hours of every day, which is a physical impossibility. The work is accordingly apportioned in shifts of eight hours each, which in effect places upon each man or team the responsibility of patrolling ap-proximately sixty miles of frontier. But being human beings they are sub-ject to illness and need time off to rest, and when there is a criminal prosecution they must attend court to testify, a procedure requiring three appearances, one each before the United States Commissioner, the Federal grand jury and the trial jury, in addition to which is the time lost in the general turnover resulting from deaths, transfers, resignations and dismissals. It is estimated that the loss of manpower from purely patrol work attributable to these several causes is about 25 per cent, so that in-stead of ten miles, each man or team must account for a border line of not less than seventy-five miles.

The entire frontier of the United States is some 10,000 miles, about half land and half water. There are 172 ports of entry and sixteen airports designated as ports for aliens. To cover the intervening space between ports of entry with the total present border patrol of 900 men on the yardstick of the assignments of the El Paso district is an apparent farce—almost 700 miles of additional Mexican border and 3898 miles of Canadian border. Is it not possible that thousands of aliens from Europe have flocked to Mexico and Canada also, to use those countries as bases from which to walk into the United States, legally if possible, illegally if not? What is to prevent the bulk of them getting in?

The Mexican peon cannot understand the reason for any border line between his native land and the United States. In either case, when he works, so far as Southern Texas, New Mexico, Arizona and California are concerned, he is among other Mexicans. There is this difference: In Mexico he is always paid starvation wages, and only when he works, but in America, upon his standard of living, he is bountifully fed and housed, whether he works or not. So, whenever the Border Patrol is not looking, he gathers his family together and they wade across the river into the land of plenty during both good times and hard times, and there need be no record of his impromptu migration when the border patrolmen are sixty miles or more apart.

Source:
Raymond G. Carroll, "Alien Workers in
America," *Saturday Evening Post* 208, no. 30
(January 25, 1936): 86, 89.

88

New York: Confidential!

BY JACK LAIT
AND LEE MORTIMER

Jack Lait (1882–1954) was the author of several novelizations of films along with four volumes cowritten with Lee Mortimer discussing social conditions in key American cities or in the nation at large. In the first of these, New York: Confidential! *(1948), Lait and Mortimer include a chapter addressing the large numbers of Puerto Ricans then entering New York. Lait and Mortimer went on to write* Chicago: Confidential! *(1950),* Washington Confidential *(1951), and* U.S.A. Confidential *(1952).*

DURING THE LAST TEN YEARS and growing every year, there has descended on Manhattan Island like a locust plague an influx of Puerto Ricans.

They arrive now frequently at the rate of 2,000 a month and there are today more than 600,000 natives of the island (one authority calculates 710,000) cramped, some 30 in one cold-water flat, mostly in one section of this great island, the whole of which is much smaller than theirs in area.

One of every four persons born in this generation in Puerto Rico is in New York; one of every 13 New Yorkers is a Puerto Rican.

Referring to these Caribbean wards of the nation as a plague is not prompted by prejudice, anger or careless use of phraseology.

Puerto Ricans were not born to be New Yorkers. They are mostly crude farmers, subject to congenital tropical diseases, physically unfitted for the northern climate, unskilled, uneducated, non-English-speaking and almost impossible to assimilate and condition for healthful and useful existence in an active city of stone and steel.

It would be tragic enough if the sorry results were the consequences only of desperate displaced persons fleeing to a haven of hope from the circumscribed possibilities of their birthplace.

But the story is far more sordid. A majority of these people were lured here deliberately, because, as American citizens, they can vote. They are a power behind Congressman Vito Marcantonio, until recently the only American Labor Party member of the House, who rules the wretched section into which a majority of the 600,000 have poured from leaky ships and from miserable chartered planes which are almost beyond description.

The Puerto Ricans at this moment are costing New York City $12,000,000 a year in relief. There is no residence-period requirement, that having been knocked out during the LaGuardia administration, when Marcantonio's word could wipe out law.

Not only are many of these Puerto Ricans on relief within an hour after their feet land on a dock or a secondary airport, but some are already booked on the dole in advance, while they are in the air or on the water.

Marcantonio maintains a full-time representative in the office of the Welfare Department, whose business it is to get his constituents not only registered on the rolls but also provided with fat and flowing allowances, using broadly every channel created for emergency cases.

For voting, the law requires one year in the state, four months in the county, one month in the district. But it is impossible to check, even if the holdover handout officials would want to. The Puerto Ricans all look alike, their names all sound alike and if an inspector calls in one of the swarming flats in the teeming tenements, nobody speaks English.

Travel agencies whip up the movement through agents in Puerto Rico. The newspapers and the billboards and even signs stuck beside the dirt roads of the remote regions shout with bargain rates as low as $20 for a flight to New York; ship transportation is sometimes even cheaper than that.

Very few Puerto Ricans at home have or ever have had $20. But the money seems to come from somewhere.

Privately, these poverty-numbed, naïve natives are sold a bill, of the tremendous possibilities in the great New York which they have seen in the movies and in the patent insides of their local sheets. They are told that here fortunes await many and the rest can quickly go on relief for sums undreamt-of by them or their fathers' fathers.

The result is a sullen, disappointed, disillusioned mass of people, alien to everything that spells New York. The children quickly learn to resent the fact that, though they are Americans, they are foreigners who cannot speak the language and are thus teased and humiliated in schools and on the streets.

Because they are dark of complexion, they are commonly classified as Negroes and share a large portion of the unfortunate prejudice which still bedevils non-Caucasians, even in a community as broad-minded as New York.

Few can obtain employment, though Marcantonio and a few other politicians place them, to a conspicuous disproportion, in minor public jobs, in hospitals, prisons, public works and other institutions where no skills and no English are required.

The youths of both sections run wild. They take on the vilest habits of their surroundings, and the description elsewhere in this book of conditions in Harlem apply very generally to the sections where the Puerto Ricans have swarmed.

As in the case of Harlem, the Puerto Ricans are concentrated in a small area but do not entirely make that their pleasure ground.

During the last two years there has been a steady flow toward Broadway, until the corners in the lower 50's are crowded day and night with zoot-suited men who hang around the riffraff of the amusement centers and so behave that it has long been necessary to post extra police south of Columbus Circle, around the clock.

They soon become marijuana addicts, throng into cheap and crowded dives which cater to their trade, and many become violent criminals with gun and knife.

In their own district the children are natural cop-haters, throw stones at prowl cars and drop bricks from the roofs on uniformed policemen.

There are no tougher saloons in Marseilles, Shanghai, Port Said or Panama City than those which seethe with these island immigrants.

The crime rate is stupendous and it is increasing and spreading.

One General Sessions judge who had just finished a six-week trial calendar of criminal cases covering the entire boroughs of Manhattan and the Bronx reported to one of your authors that more than 40 per cent of convictions during that term had been of Puerto Ricans, of whom 2 per cent were born on the United States mainland.

The disease statistics are even more shocking.

Not a few of the natives are cursed with tuberculosis and syphilis before they arrive; a Puerto Rican leper was discovered not long ago. But once they are here, the venereal incidence is marked with a rapid rise, due to association with low prostitutes, with the result that a random health inspection of 1,000 Puerto Rican males between the ages of 15 and 40 revealed 80 per cent infected.

The conditions which cause these frightful statistics are largely parallel to those which afflict the Negroes, but the Puerto Ricans are harmed even more by these conditions because they are strangers, because they have not come of their own free will, like adventurers of courage and enterprise from other lands, who brave regions beyond their horizon to fight for their opportunities.

Most of these are not only outmatched in every battle of life in the fastest and biggest city in the world, but they were far behind in their own unhappy land before they left, and that was why they left.

The callous exploitation of these weaklings is one of the dirtiest crimes in the long and shameful record of practical American politics. None knows better than those who have primed and prompted and financed the exodus, what they are doing to these victims and what they are doing to the city where they bring them in gutted one-motor planes, sitting on bucket seats, sometimes so crowded that many stand all the way, airsick and already homesick.

The sight of one of these outmoded flying cattle boats, long since discarded by the government services and regular transport lines, is horrifying and nauseating.

The pilgrims are dropped off at Newark or small private landing places, carrying bundles and babies and the weight of fear and sorrow, through which the gleam of new hope cannot penetrate.

They are marched in and carried in dilapidated buses directly to the filthy, shrieking, miserable rookeries where housing has long been exhausted. This means that each new arrival will be shoe-horned into already jammed, unsanitary, indecent lodgings, to sleep on the floor or even in a hallway.

The relief figures look good and they should, because they are designedly excessive. But prices are high and before these strangers arrive the sharks are waiting and smacking their lips.

And so they constitute not only a horde unfitted for the new habitat, but they quickly become resentful under the hostile conditions, so different from the utopia which smooth-tongued agents painted to people who had never been off the island on which they were born.

Not only that frame of mind, but public support, with a tremendous factor of idleness, proximity to the regions of lowest vice and highest crime, easy opportunity to mingle in the swirl of the unwashed underworld, rapidly perverts them.

They pick up the bad habits of those with whom they are forced to associate, and these they amplify with the enthusiasm of untutored islanders for illegitimate revelry and dissipation.

Merchants of every form of dope, vice and alcohol await them eagerly with merchandise within their means.

Finding themselves unable physically, mentally or financially to compete, they turn to guile and wile and the steel blade, the traditional weapon of the sugar-cane cutter, mark of their blood and heritage.

New York, of course, is not easily pushed around and turns on them, which makes them more bitter and more belligerent, which brings upon them heavier punishment, which makes them uglier, and thus a constant and increasing spiral of hatred spins around these hundreds of thousands.

Some manage to straggle back. But it is an established fact that the city holds and fascinates and imprisons those who have once felt the magic of its embrace.

Columbia University is now busily making a survey of the situation. The governor of Puerto Rico has put through an appropriation for the island legislature to run down the facts. The Welfare Department of the city and state have thrown up their hands in helpless surrender to this modern scandal, entirely unforeseen only a few years ago, though Puerto Ricans have had free access without passport to the United States since 1898.

The City Welfare Council, in a sympathetic report glossing over much of the situation, nevertheless described *"back yards piled high with garbage,"* also one block so *infested with drunks, marijuana smokers, brawlers, holdup men and insulters of women that decent citizens and even the police deliberately avoid it.*

So, this chapter is not merely an observation about a portion of Manhattan Island. It is an exposition of a situation which will echo in the halls of Congress and will write its own pages in the history of the nation, because, as has been pointed out, it is far from static; in every phase it is growing and the sorry end is nowhere in sight.

Source:
Jack Lait and Lee Mortimer, *New York: Confidential!* (Chicago: Ziff-Davis Publishing Co., 1948), pp. 126–33.

89

Roll Down
Your Window

BY JUAN GONZALEZ

Juan Gonzalez is a reporter for the New York Daily News *and the author of a pamphlet,* The Other America: True Stories of the Latino Experience *(1991), and a full-length treatise,* Roll Down Your Window: Stories of a Forgotten America *(1995). In an extract from the latter work, Gonzalez focuses on a case of prejudice by members of the New York police force against Latinos and sees it as emblematic of the hostility of suburban whites against urban immigrants.*

Iᴛ ᴡᴀs sᴜᴘᴘᴏsᴇᴅ ᴛᴏ ʙᴇ just another police shooting in this new era of law and order. The official account in the newspapers the next day seemed fairly open and shut: two Hispanic men forced their way into a South Bronx tenement apartment on the night of January 11, 1995, robbed a young couple, then threatened to return the next night. But when the men knocked on the door of the apartment with a third man the following night, two police detectives responding to the couple's frightened call were waiting inside. The detectives burst from the kitchen and ordered the intruders, each of whom had a gun hidden on him, to put their hands in the air and drop to the floor. The men resisted. A shoot-out erupted. When the smoke cleared, two of the robbers were dead. Multiple gunshot wounds to the front, side and back, reported the city medical examiner. As if to put the final exclamation point to this official story, a police spokesman told the press all three men had criminal records.

Case closed.

Well, not quite. Something didn't make sense as I read the account. Why would robbers warn their victims they were coming back? I decided to look a little closer, especially since one of the detectives in the case had been involved a few years earlier in the vicious, off-duty beating of a fellow black detective.

The official story, I soon discovered, was riddled with more holes than the two dead men. During the next few months I kept peeling away at the layers of confusion and deceit that enveloped the incident. First, police clarified that none of the "robbers" had fired their guns, while the two detectives had unleashed a fusillade of twenty-six shots, hitting the dead men twenty-two times. The "shoot-out" suddenly became a "shoot-in."

The surviving intruder, an 18-year-old named Fred Bonilla, claimed that he and his friends had already surrendered and were on the ground when police opened fire. Still, I was not about to believe the word of a teenager caught in a robbery against two hero detectives. But then the families of the dead men secured their own pathologist, who concluded that the city medical examiner's report was wrong: all the bullets—fourteen in one man and eight in the other—had pierced their bodies from the rear or side, none from the front. After I reported that new revelation, the city medical examiner hastily changed his conclusion. A doctor had misread a wound chart, the examiner's office admitted.

I followed with a report that the alleged robbery had not even been a robbery! In fact, the couple in the apartment were running an illegal marriage ring, where they paid citizens to marry undocumented immigrants so they could be naturalized. The young men who came to the door, two of whom had only a previous juvenile conviction for disorderly conduct, were friends of a young disgruntled woman to whom the couple in the apartment owed money from one of those illegal marriages. The men had come to collect the money owed to the young woman.

Before long, I started getting phone calls and letters from anonymous detectives. The tipsters insisted the shooting was being covered up because the two detectives were former bodyguards of Mayor Rudy Giuliani, and one was a boyhood friend of the mayor's.

In the midst of these revelations, and after a Bronx grand jury voted to absolve the officers of wrongdoing, one of the jurors contacted me. The vote in the secret proceeding had been very close, the juror said, even though the prosecutor had steered the jury toward no indictment. I decided to keep digging for facts. In a subsequent column I reported that investigators for the city's Civilian Complaint Review Board (CCRB), the agency charged with probing police abuse complaints, concluded that both dead men were shot numerous times while lying on the floor on their stomachs. Another column revealed that police from the local precinct improperly helped move the couple who lived in the apartment to new housing, hid the couple's whereabouts from the CCRB investigators, and tried to prevent investigators from subpoenaing the pair to give testimony. I reported further that the mayor's office had shown uncommon interest in the case. In late July, the CCRB concluded that the two dead men had not drawn guns against the police. Instead, the agency ruled that detectives had used "unnecessary force" in arresting them. By this time, the public uproar in the Hispanic community over the case had prompted the US Justice Department to begin a probe of possible civil rights violations.

Instead of carefully reviewing the results of the review board's investigation, the city's police commissioner immediately blasted the agency as unprofessional. The mayor's own Department of Investigations suddenly opened a wide-ranging probe of the agency's work. Police sources began leaking information to friendly reporters to make the agency appear out of control.

Thus, the watchdog agency legally charged with monitoring police abuse itself became the target of investigation. As of this writing, the federal probe into the police shooting of Anthony Rosario and Hilton Vega is not concluded. But the case has already revealed in chilling fashion how far some guardians of law and order will go to obstruct a search for the truth.

The case confirms my belief that the criminal justice industry, both in its public and private forms, is the fastest growing, least monitored and potentially most dangerous force in American society today. Mushrooming construction of prisons. Increased production of high-tech surveillance and control systems for the public. Skyrocketing budgets for law enforcement and court personnel while other parts of government spending shrink. Tougher sentencing laws creating record prison populations. The steady erosion of individual rights and the presumption of innocence by the courts and legislators. All of these trends are inching our nation closer to a police state. The streets of Santo Domingo, after all, were never safer than under Trujillo, Moscow's never freer of violent crime than under Stalin, and Berlin's never more orderly than under Hitler. Meanwhile, we in the mass media, by nurturing the public frenzy with one lurid tale of violent crime after another, by failing too often to investigate diligently and report the most horrific examples of police and government abuse of citizens' rights, are unwittingly preparing the soil for such a police state, one where blacks, Hispanics and immigrants will undoubtedly become the main target of its wrath.

With minorities and immigrants now a majority in most of the nation's big cities, it is no surprise that the rise of law-and-order politicians parallels the coming to power, in both the Democratic and Republican parties, of anti-urban interests based in suburbia. In this, the media are no exception. The dominance of television news, where the stark image is always preferred to nuanced analysis, over big-city newspapers signals the eclipsing of the complex information needs of a diverse urban population in favor of the homogenized needs of suburbia. Television stations, after all, reach further and deeper into the population than do newspapers. They broadcast beyond the urban center to the wealthier suburban fringes, spreading images of crime and chaos from the city core far beyond its borders. Gradually, in the consciousness of the manicured lawns and picture-perfect living rooms of suburbia, the vision takes root of an inner-city hell, of urban areas teeming with all that is evil and wasteful in American life.

Any balanced appreciation that our cities remain the nexus of wealth, social vibrancy and cohesion for America's regions becomes lost. The cities, lest we forget, provide police protection not just to their own residents but to the legions of suburbanites who stream in each day on urban public transportation systems and highways, to office buildings, theaters, restaurants, medical centers and universities, institutions which provide jobs and modern amenities for everyone in the region, not just the city residents. At night, the suburbanites retire to sleepy townships and rural communities which boast none of these things.

The city of Trenton, for instance, has long been considered one of New Jersey's urban eyesores. Located in the middle of the state, it was once a blue-collar manufacturing center and, for years, as visitors entered town they could see a large sign spanning one of its bridges: "Trenton Makes: The World Takes." Today in America, it is the suburbs which constantly milk the wealth that our cities provide them—the best jobs, the transportation, the culture.

Meanwhile, back in the inner city, blacks and Hispanics, who are now the majority in virtually all the great metropolises of America, are relatively powerless to stop the nation's disinvestment in its urban infrastructure. Whether it be roads, bridges, parks, hospitals, public schools, libraries or community centers, our inner cities are decaying at a frightening rate. Government refuses basic maintenance precisely because the cities are now so black and brown that the wealthy downtown enclaves and well-to-do suburban areas simply will not allow it.

Nearly half of all New York City's 37,000 police officers, for example, live in the suburbs. If the city wanted to reduce its unemployment and increase its tax base, it could simply require all future cops to be city residents. But suburban politicians in the state capital have repeatedly thwarted efforts by several mayors to change residency laws for cops. Even the move to privatize government has become a means to cannibalize many urban city services and contract them out to low-wage companies where, in the name of efficiency, government-subsidized profits go to suburban entrepreneurs. Anti-urban interests know the political deck is stacked in their favor, especially at the national level, where under our federal system rural states with small populations, such as South Dakota, Idaho and Utah, have as many votes in the US Senate as giant, highly urbanized states like New York, California and Illinois. . . .

Urban America is fed up with those conservative demagogues who seized the national spotlight the past twenty years in the name of law and order and diverted public attention to racial squabbling between everyday Americans, while their corporate friends fled abroad in search of cheap labor, prodded government to ignore the decay of the cities, gutted trade unions, eroded the living standards of American workers, and amassed unparalleled wealth.

In the neighborhoods of forgotten urban America, rage gathers in the shadows. Quadruple the jail cells and you will not lock it up. Break all the unions and you will not chase it away. Urban America wants decent jobs, not part-time work at lower hourly wages than ten years ago. Its people want to know that a single illness will not drive them into poverty. They want clean parks and the kinds of schools that give their children a chance at success, just like those kids from the suburbs. They are tired of suburban white America regarding the black and brown cities with dread instead of hope, as enemies instead of partners, as alien instead of family.

We either heed the rage or wait for it to spring from the shadows.

Source:
Juan Gonzalez, *Roll Down Your Window:
Stories of a Forgotten America* (London &
New York: Verso, 1995), pp. 197–201,
203–4.

PART TWELVE

The Debate over Immigration

IN MANY WAYS THE DEBATE over immigration fuses all the manifold strains of racist thought, or, rather, provides a focal issue whereby every racist argument can be applied. The course of immigration in this country is well known. Of the four million people (exclusive of approximately 750,000 African-American slaves) registered in this country in the first census of 1790, the overwhelming majority came from England, Wales, Scotland, Ireland, and Germany. From 1815 to 1860, five million people entered the country, half from England and close to 40 percent from Ireland (as a result of the potato famine of the 1840s). This large infusion of Irish immigrants provoked what was probably the first anti-immigrationist sentiment, as nativist Protestants fought with Irish Catholics and the Know-Nothing Party enjoyed its brief popularity. Already by 1865 the Irish-American journalist E. L. Godkin was chastising conservative thinkers for blaming the nation's troubles on immigrants. Godkin was convinced that the overwhelming majority of immigrants sought to harmonize with the social and political culture in which they found themselves; and it was this widespread belief, held by the immigrants themselves, that they ought to "assimilate" that gave birth to the notion of the "melting pot," enunciated by Anglo-Jewish writer Israel Zangwill in his 1908 play of that title.

Immigration at the time of the Civil War and up to 1890 followed familiar patterns: ten million immigrants arrived, largely from England, Ireland, Wales, Germany, and Scandinavia. The shift came in the next twenty-five years: from 1890 to 1914 fifteen million immigrants entered the United States, but now they were drawn largely from eastern and southern Europe. It was this shift in population that led to furious opposition. In the poem "Unguarded Gates" (1892), Thomas Bailey Aldrich viciously jeered at the newcomers, ridiculing their "featureless faces" and their "unknown gods and rites."

What actually disturbed the nativists is now hard to say. Certainly, the unprecedented numbers of "foreigners" was manifestly altering the social milieu, as Henry James discovered to his dismay when he returned to his native land after decades spent in England and spoke in *The American Scene* (1907) of "the inconceivable alien." Was it a concern over the loss of jobs that were somehow thought to "belong" to Americans? Was it the foreign customs they brought with them ("Their habits of life . . . are of the most revolting kind," stated General Francis A. Walker in 1896)? It was all this, but it was more.

Many nativists adopted the question-begging fallacy that American civilization would cease to be "American" if too many foreigners entered. But what *is* the character of American civilization except that which is established by the people who were either here originally (Native Americans) or by those who came here from somewhere else? What the nativists feared was not the collapse of American civilization but the collapse of their conception of American civilization, based chiefly on the Anglo-American heritage of the colonial period. This is why anti-immigration sentiment was strongest in New England, which gave birth in 1894 to the Immigration Restriction League and elected as its first president John Fiske, Harvard instructor and popular historian.

"I look at these things, you know, from a Darwinian point of view," Fiske wrote in defense of his views on immigration. What he meant was that his Social Darwinism led him to believe that many of these immigrants were "unfit" for the struggle of life and should therefore be barred. Science and pseudo-science were brought into play by John R. Commons, noted labor historian who strove to gauge the relative industrial capacity of immigrants: "It is not conceivable that the immigrants of the present day from Southern Europe and from Asia could have succeeded as frontiersmen and pioneers in the settlement of the country." It becomes very easy to say that, since disproof of the proposition is impossible: the country has already been settled, so there is no way to test whether any other nationality could have done so. It was this Anglo-Saxon prejudice that gave rise to one of the most vicious of racist tracts, Lothrop Stoddard's *The Rising Tide of Color Against White World-Supremacy* (1920).

One curious argument of the anti-immigrationists focused on the obvious fact that most immigrants crowded into large cities, frequently dwelling in shabby quarters until they could establish themselves economically; but this very endurance of harsh conditions was paradoxically held against them, as if immigrants were somehow "naturally" predisposed to live in filth and squalor. It did not seem to occur to many that improvements in housing and social services might be of long-term benefit to the whole of American civilization.

The onslaught of anti-immigration tracts had by this time reached epic proportions: Frank Julian Warne's *The Immigrant Invasion* (1913), Edward Alsworth Ross's *The Old World and the New* (1914), Clinton Stoddard Burr's *America's Race Heritage* (1922), Charles W. Gould's *America: A Family Matter* (1922), Kenneth L. Roberts's *Why Europe Leaves Home* (1922), to name only a few. Is it any surprise that in 1924, during the presidency of Calvin Coolidge (who had himself written an essay against immigration, "Whose Country Is This?" [1921], while waiting to take office as vice president under Harding), the most restrictive immigration law in the nation's history was passed? Not only did it establish minuscule quotas for most nations (immigrants comprising 2 percent of that country's population in the United States would be allowed every year), but it decreed that the 1890 census would be the basis of the quotas, thereby giving preference to immigrants from northern Europe rather than southern or eastern Europe or Asia. By 1929, when the National Origins Act was passed, annual immigration levels had been reduced to 150,000.

After World War II, immigration increased briefly under the Displaced Persons Act of 1948, which allowed four hundred thousand Europeans uprooted by the war to enter the country. Even this provoked opposition: Eddie Rickenbacker, president of Eastern Airlines, argued in a 1947 speech that many of these new immigrants may be communists.

By the 1960s it became evident that the immigration restriction laws of the 1920s had gone too far, and in the face of predictable opposition the Immigration Act of 1965 was passed. The former quotas were abolished; and although the total number of immigrants was set at less than three hundred thousand per year, this figure did not include close relatives of individuals already in the country. The flow of illegal aliens, mostly from Mexico, in the 1980s led to the Immigration Reform Act of 1986, which stipulated heavy penalties for employers who hired such aliens. Moreover, many recent attacks on affirmative action (such as Proposition 209 in California, which passed by a wide margin in the election of 1996) appear to have racial fears at their foundation—the threat of immigrants overrunning the country or gaining excessive economic or political power, and the possibility that white people could actually become a minority in this country (as Patrick J. Buchanan noted in a October 31, 1994, editorial in the *Washington Times*).

In spite of the success of recent laws restricting immigrants, the doomsayers are still with us. The journalist Lawrence Auster, in the brief monograph *The Path to National Suicide* (published in 1990 by the American Immigration Control Foundation), warns that the whole of American civilization is endangered by immigration, multiculturalism, and many other recent tendencies. Without realizing it, Auster gets to the heart of the matter when he paints a depressing portrait of "the present American people" who "see their civilization disappearing piece by piece, city by city, state by state, from before their eyes"; later "there will be the repressed knowledge that America is becoming an utterly different country from what it had been, and that this means the end of their world." It may be the end of their world, but it does not seem to occur to Auster that it may be the beginning of someone else's.

90

Aristocratic Opinions of Democracy

BY E. L. GODKIN

Edwin Lawrence Godkin (1831–1902) was an Irish-born journalist who was the first editor of the Nation *(1865–81) and then the editor of the* New York Evening Post *(1883–1900). In "Aristocratic Opinions of Democracy" (1865), a review-essay of a translation of Tocqueville's* Democracy in America, *Godkin criticizes the attitude of conservatives in attributing all social troubles to immigrants.*

W̲HEN WE COME TO INQUIRE to what extent the social or political condition of the Northern States has been influenced or modified by foreign immigration, we find ourselves dealing with a subject on which all those writers whose opinions are largely affected by their taste are agreed; and most of those who in America venture on political speculation belong to this class. If we take up the hundred laments over the degeneracy of our political condition, which issue from them every year in books, newspapers, speeches, and sermons, we shall find that in nine cases out of ten it is ascribed to the great influx of ignorant foreigners which has been going on for the last thirty years. In many, perhaps most, of the controversies which are carried on with European critics touching the state and prospects of the republic, this argument is put very prominently forward. Any coarseness, corruption, or recklessness, either of conduct or language, which shows itself in the management of our public affairs, and attracts the attention of foreign critics, is apt to be ascribed by the native advocate to the malign influence of the human drift which the convulsions and misfortunes of European society have cast on our shores.

We suspect that much of the prevalence of this theory is due to the fact, that those who most frequently put it forward in print live in the great cities, where foreigners are most numerous, where they are in the habit of acting in masses, and where their influence is most easily seen and felt. It is there that the evils which flow from their presence are most palpable; and those who have under their eyes its effects on the local government are apt to draw from the spectacle the most lugubrious inferences as to the condition of the rest of the country. But the estimate of the weight and extent of foreign influence upon polities and society, based on the impressions thus formed, is not confirmed by a careful consideration of the facts.

The whole number of foreigners who have entered the country between 1790 and 1860 is 5,296,414; and of these, 5,062,000 entered since the year 1820, or an average of 126,500 a year during forty years, being of course a mere driblet when compared to the native population. The immigration since 1860 has been very large; and the number actually resident in the whole of the United States in that year was about 4,000,000, or less than one seventh of the entire population. But it is not since 1860 that the political or social deterioration which we are discussing has shown itself. One might imagine, on listening to some of the accounts one hears of the extent to which foreigners are responsible for the vices of American polities, that at least half the inhabitants of the Free States had for many years been persons of European birth, and that the intelligent and educated natives of the country had had a severe struggle, under universal suffrage, to retain any share in the government, and had been long threatened with seeing the management of a political system, which requires a large amount of virtue and knowledge on the part of those who live under it to enable it to work successfully, pass into the hands of a class of men bred in ignorance and degraded by oppression. But when it is taken into account that the foreign immigration has flowed slowly during a great number of years, that a large proportion of it has, of course, been composed of women and children, and that the small number of voters which it in any one year has contributed to the electoral body have been scattered over the Union from Maine to California, and have been divided into different camps by difference of language, religion, and nationality, and have been generally too ignorant and helpless to devise or pursue a common policy, it is easy to see that the current notion of the extent of their influence on national politics and on political life has been greatly exaggerated.

The only instance, we believe, in which the foreigners can be said to have combined to make their influence felt at the elections, occurred during the "Know Nothing" movement; but this was the result of a direct attack on their own privileges and standing. On all other occasions, we find them serving under American leaders, and assailing or defending purely American ideas; and so far from seeking position or influence by banding together, their great aim and desire are, as is well known, to efface all marks of their foreign origin, and secure complete absorption in the American population. And how do they accomplish this? Not by imposing their ideas on the natives, or dragging them down to their level, but by adopting native ideas and manners and customs, educating their children in American habits, or, in other words, raising themselves to the American level. In fact, there is nothing they resent so keenly as any attempt to place them in a different category, or ascribe to them different interests or motives, from those of Americans. If they were conscious of the power of making themselves felt as a separate body, this would hardly be the case. So far from seeking to obliterate the distinction between themselves and Americans, they would endeavor to maintain and perpetuate it.

It may be said, however, that, although the foreign element in the population may not influence American polities in a way sufficient to account for the political changes of the last half-century directly by its votes, it does influence them indirectly by the modifications it effects in the national character through intermarriage and social intercourse. The effect upon temperament of intermixture of blood is very much too obscure a subject, in our opinion, to be safely made the basis of any theory of national progress or decline, even by those who attach most importance to it, and profess to know most about it. But even if we accord it all the force they claim for it, time enough has not yet elapsed to enable us to judge of its effects in this country. This much is certain, that the great features of the American character do not seem to have undergone any sensible change since the Revolution. The American of to-day, as an individual, presents very much the same great traits, moral and intellectual, which his father and grandfather presented before him; the main difference between the three generations being, that the present one displays its idiosyncrasies on a very much wider field. A chemical analysis (as it has been termed) of natural character is, however, something from which no sound thinker will ever hope to arrive at conclusions of much value for any purposes not purely speculative.

As regards the influence exercised on American life by foreigners through the medium of social intercourse, we doubt very much if anybody has ever attached much importance to it who has given the matter any serious consideration. All that seems necessary to remove the idea that it has been instrumental in modifying either American opinions or manners, is to call attention to the class of society from which the immigrants are generally drawn, and to the social position which they occupy in this country. If we except a few lawyers, a few doctors, a few professors and teachers, and a few merchants in the large cities, eager to make money enough to enable them to return with fortunes to their native country, it may be said that ninety-nine out of every hundred foreigners who come to the United States with the intention of settling here are drawn from the ranks of the European peasantry;—Germans, entirely ignorant of the English language; and Irish, who, as well as the Germans, are separated from even the poorest of the native population by an entirely different standard of living, and a wide difference of habits and of religion. There is between them and even the lower grades of American society a barrier, which is none the less formidable for not being recognized by law. They fill, all but exclusively, the menial callings, and intermarriage between them and pure-blooded Americans is very rare. And, as we have said, so far from acting as propagators of foreign opinions or manners, the whole energy of the newcomers is spent, for years after their arrival, not in diffusing their own ways of thinking and feeling, but in strenuous and generally successful efforts to get rid of them, and adopt those of their American neighbors.

Source:
E. L. Godkin, "Aristocratic Opinions of
Democracy," *North American Review* 100,
no. 1 (January 1865): 202–5.

91

Political Mission of the United States

BY CHAUNCEY DEPEW

Chauncey Mitchell Depew (1834–1928) was one of the most prominent Republican political figures in the later nineteenth century. He served as the president of the New York Central and Hudson River Railroad (1885–98), was U.S. senator from New York (1899–1911), and declined several other prestigious posts, including secretary of state under Benjamin Harrison. He delivered an oration at the unveiling of the Statue of Liberty in 1886. In "Political Mission of the United States," an oration delivered on February 22, 1888, Depew asserts that immigrants should be allowed into the country only if they fully adopt Americanism.

THE TEACHERS OF DISINTEGRATION, destruction, and infidelity possess the activity of propagandists and the self-sacrificing spirit of martyrs. Their field is ignorance, their recruiting sergeant is distress. Only faith grounded in knowledge can meet these dangerous, ceaseless, and corrupting influences. In the midst of the perils, the sheet-anchor of the Ship of State is the common school. Before the era of great cities and crowded populations, when it was easy both to earn a living and to gain a competence, when the best influences of every settlement reached every part of it, the State met every requirement in furnishing, free, a fair business education. But now by far the larger part of our people have no common ancestry in the Revolutionary War, and a generation has come to its majority which knows little of the Rebellion and its results. Colonists from Europe form communities, both in city and country, where they retain the language, customs, and traditions of the Fatherland, and live and die in the belief that the Government is their enemy. To meet these conditions the State provides an education which does not educate, and the prison and the poorhouse.

Ignorance judges the invisible by the visible. Turn on the lights. Teach, first and last, Americanism. Let no youth leave the school without being thoroughly grounded in the history, the principles, and the incalculable blessings of American liberty. Let the boys be the trained soldiers of constitutional freedom, the girls the intelligent mothers of freemen, and the sons of the anarchists will become the bulwarks of the law. American liberty must be protected against hostile invasion.

We welcome the fugitives from oppression, civil or religious, who seek our asylum with the honest purpose of making it their homes. We have room and hospitality for emigrants who come to our shores to better their condition by the adoption of our citizenship, with all its duties and responsibilities. But we have no place for imported criminals, paupers, and pests. The revolutionist who wants to destroy the power of the majority with the same dynamite with which he failed to assassinate the Emperor or the Czar is a public enemy, and must be so treated. We are no longer in need of the surplus population of the Old World, and must carefully examine our guests. The priceless gift of citizenship should never be conferred until by years of probation the applicant has proved himself worthy, and then a rigid examination in open court should test his knowledge of its limitations as well as its privileges, and his cordial acceptance of both. It is monstrous that the time of our courts and the patience of our juries should be occupied and tried in the repeated prosecution of persistent disturbers of the peace who refuse to become citizens. On the first conviction by a jury they should be expelled from the country.

Source:
Chauncey Depew, "Political Mission of United States" (1888), in Depew's *Orations, Addresses and Speeches,* edited by John Denison Champlin (New York: Privately printed, 1910), vol. 1, pp. 33–34.

92

Unguarded Gates

BY THOMAS BAILEY ALDRICH

Thomas Bailey Aldrich (1836–1907) was once a highly regarded poet and novelist and the editor of the Atlantic Monthly *(1881–90). Much of his poetry is marred by racism. In "Unguarded Gates," Aldrich has written a direct response to such works as Emma Lazarus's "The New Colossus" (1883), the poem inscribed on the pedestal of the Statue of Liberty.*

> *Wide open and unguarded stand our gates,*
> *Named of the four winds, North, South, East, and West;*
> *Portals that lead to an enchanted land*
> *Of cities, forests, fields of living gold,*
> *Vast prairies, lordly summits touched with snow,*
> *Majestic rivers sweeping proudly past*
> *The Arab's date-palm and the Norseman's pine—*
> *A realm wherein are fruits of every zone,*
> *Airs of all climes, for lo! throughout the year*
> *The red rose blossoms somewhere—a rich land,*
> *A later Eden planted in the wilds,*
> *With not an inch of earth within its bound*
> *But if a slave's foot press it sets him free!*
> *Here, it is written, Toil shall have its wage,*
> *And Honor honor, and the humblest man*
> *Stand level with the highest in the law.*
> *Of such a land have men in dungeons dreamed,*
> *And with the vision brightening in their eyes*
> *Gone smiling to the fagot and the sword.*

Wide open and unguarded stand our gates,
And through them presses a wild motley throng—
Men from the Volga and the Tartar steppes,
Featureless figures of the Hoang-Ho,
Malayan, Scythian, Teuton, Kelt, and Slav,
Flying the Old World's poverty and scorn;
These bringing with them unknown gods and rites,
Those, tiger passions, here to stretch their claws.
In street and alley what strange tongues are these,
Accents of menace alien to our air,
Voices that once the Tower of Babel knew!
O Liberty, white Goddess! is it well
To leave the gates unguarded? On thy breast
Fold Sorrow's children, soothe the hurts of fate,
Lift the down-trodden, but with hand of steel
Stay those who to thy sacred portals come
To waste the gifts of freedom. Have a care
Lest from thy brow the clustered stars be torn
And trampled in the dust. For so of old
The thronging Goth and Vandal trampled Rome,
And where the temples of the Cæsars stood
The lean wolf unmolested made her lair.

Source:
Thomas Bailey Aldrich, "Unguarded
Gates," *Atlantic Monthly* 70, no. 1
(July 1892): 57.

93

Restriction of Immigration

BY FRANCIS A. WALKER

General Francis Amasa Walker (1840–1897) served in the Union army during the Civil War and later became superintendent of the census for 1870 and 1880 and U.S. commissioner of Indian Affairs in 1871–72. He was professor of political economy at Yale and was later president of the Massachusetts Institute of Technology. A widely published economist and historian, he produced one of the most exhaustive attacks on immigrants in "Restriction of Immigration" (1896), maintaining that many recent immigrants from southern Europe were degraded peasants with "revolting" habits and were potential subversives.

F IFTY, EVEN THIRTY YEARS AGO, there was a rightful presumption regarding the average immigrant that he was among the most enterprising, thrifty, alert, adventurous, and courageous of the community from which he came. It required no small energy, prudence, forethought, and pains to conduct the inquiries relating to his migration, to accumulate the necessary means, and to find his way across the Atlantic. To-day the presumption is completely reversed. So thoroughly has the continent of Europe been crossed by railways, so effectively has the business of emigration there been exploited, so much have the rates of railroad fares and ocean passage been reduced, that it is now among the least thrifty and prosperous members of any European community that the emigration agent finds his best recruiting-ground. The care and pains required have been reduced to a minimum; while the agent of the Red Star Line or the

White Star Line is everywhere at hand, to suggest migration to those who are not getting on well at home. The intending emigrants are looked after from the moment they are locked into the cars in their native villages until they stretch themselves upon the floors of the buildings on Ellis Island, in New York. Illustrations of the ease and facility with which this Pipe Line Immigration is now carried on might be given in profusion. So broad and smooth is the channel, there is no reason why every foul and stagnant pool of population in Europe, which no breath of intellectual or industrial life has stirred for ages, should not be decanted upon our soil. Hard times here may momentarily check the flow; but it will not be permanently stopped so long as *any difference of economic level* exists between our population and that of the most degraded communities abroad.

But it is not alone that the presumption regarding the immigrant of to-day is so widely different from that which existed regarding the immigrant of thirty or fifty years ago. The immigrant of the former time came almost exclusively from western and northern Europe. We have now tapped great reservoirs of population then almost unknown to the passenger lists of our arriving vessels. Only a short time ago, the immigrants from southern Italy, Hungary, Austria, and Russia together made up hardly more than one per cent of our immigration. To-day the proportion has risen to something like forty per cent, and threatens soon to become fifty or sixty per cent, or even more. The entrance into our political, social, and industrial life of such vast masses of peasantry, degraded below our utmost conceptions, is a matter which no intelligent patriot can look upon without the gravest apprehension and alarm. These people have no history behind them which is of a nature to give encouragement. They have none of the inherited instincts and tendencies which made it comparatively easy to deal with the immigration of the olden time. They are beaten men from beaten races; representing the worst failures in the struggle for existence. Centuries are against them, as centuries were on the side of those who formerly came to us. They have none of the ideas and aptitudes which fit men to take up readily and easily the problem of self-care and self-government, such as belong to those who are descended from the tribes that met under the oak-trees of old Germany to make laws and choose chieftains.

Their habits of life, again, are of the most revolting kind. Read the description given by Mr. Riis of the police driving from the garbage dumps the miserable beings who try to burrow in those depths of unutterable filth and slime in order that they may eat and sleep there! Was it in cement like this that the foundations of our republic were laid? What effects must be produced upon our social standards, and upon the ambitions and aspirations of our people, by a contact so foul and loathsome? The influence upon the American rate of wages of a competition like this cannot fail to be injurious and even disastrous. Already it has been seriously felt in the tobacco manufacture, in the clothing trade, and in many forms of mining industry; and unless this access of vast numbers of unskilled workmen of the lowest type, in a market already fully supplied with labor, shall be checked, it cannot fail to go on from bad to worse, in breaking down the standard which has been maintained with so much care and at so much cost. The competition of paupers is far more telling and more killing than the competition of pauper-made goods. Degraded labor in the slums of foreign cities may be prejudicial to intelligent, ambitious, self-respecting labor here; but it does not threaten half so much evil as does degraded labor in the garrets of our native cities.

Finally, the present situation is most menacing to our peace and political safety. In all the social and industrial disorders of this country since 1877, the foreign elements have proved themselves the ready tools of demagogues in defying the law, in destroying property, and in working violence. A learned clergyman who mingled with the socialistic mob which, two years ago, threatened the State House and the governor of Massachusetts, told me that during the entire disturbance he heard no word spoken in any language which he knew,—either in English, in German, or in French. There may be those who can contemplate the addition to our population of vast numbers of persons having no inherited instincts of self-government and respect for law; knowing no restraint upon their own passions but the club of the policeman or the bayonet of the soldier; forming communities, by the tens of thousands, in which only foreign tongues are spoken, and into which can steal no influence from our free institutions and from popular discussion. But I confess to being far less optimistic. I have conversed with one of the highest officers of the United States army and with one of the highest officers of the civil government regarding the state of affairs which existed during the summer of 1894; and the revelations they made of facts not generally known, going to show how the ship of state grazed along its whole side upon the rocks, were enough to appall the most sanguine American, the most hearty believer in free government. Have we the right to expose the republic to any increase of the dangers from this source which now so manifestly threaten our peace and safety?

For it is never to be forgotten that self-defense is the first law of nature and of nations. If that man who careth not for his own household is worse than an infidel, the nation which permits its institutions to be endangered by any cause which can fairly be removed is guilty not less in Christian than in natural law. Charity begins at home; and while the people of the United States have gladly offered an asylum to millions upon millions of the distressed and unfortunate of other lands and climes, they have no right to carry their hospitality one step beyond the line where American institutions, the American rate of wages, the American standard of living, are brought into serious peril. All the good the United States could do by offering indiscriminate hospitality to a few millions more of European peasants, whose places at home will, within another generation, be filled by others as miserable as themselves, would not compensate for any permanent injury done to our republic. Our highest duty to charity and to humanity is to make this great experiment, here, of free laws and educated labor, the most triumphant success that can possibly be attained. In this way we shall do far more for Europe than by allowing its city slums and its vast stagnant reservoirs of degraded peasantry to be drained off upon our soil. Within the decade between 1880 and 1890 five and a quarter millions of foreigners entered our ports! No nation in human history ever undertook to deal with such masses of alien population. That man must be a sentimentalist and an optimist beyond all bounds of reason who believes that we can take such a load upon the national stomach without a failure of assimilation, and without great danger to the health and life of the nation. For one, I believe it is time that we should take a rest, and give our social, political, and industrial system some chance to recuperate. The problems which so sternly confront us to-day are serious enough without being complicated and aggravated by the addition of some millions of Hungarians, Bohemians, Poles, south Italians, and Russian Jews.

Source:
Francis A. Walker, "Restriction of
Immigration," *Atlantic Monthly* 77, no. 6
(June 1896): 827–29.

94

Letter to
William Lloyd Garrison

BY JOHN FISKE

John Fiske (1842–1901) was a widely published historian and philosopher. An ardent advocate of the theory of evolution, he wrote Myths and Myth-Makers *(1872), a treatise on anthropology, along with a variety of important works on American history. He taught for many years at Harvard, although he was never given a professorship. In 1894, Fiske became the first president of the Immigration Restriction League of Boston. In the following excerpts from a letter to William Lloyd Garrison (son of the abolitionist), he claims that immigration should be restricted to individuals "of good quality." Elsewhere in the letter he praises his friend Francis A. Walker's "Restriction of Immigration": "I can say truly that every sentence in it expresses my own convictions."*

DEAR SIR:

My attention has been called to a letter addressed by you to me as President of the Immigration Restriction League, in which you enter a protest against the position which the League has taken. In the course of this letter, you express the opinion that I ought not to be connected with such a movement. I therefore feel called upon to say a few words in explanation of my own attitude in the matter. The perusal of your letter leads me to think that you and I start from widely different premises in forming our opinions on the subject. It appears to me that it is a question with which inalienable rights have very little to do. . . .

It appears to me that the theory of the equal right of all human beings to the use of the earth is one which can only be accepted with such qualifications as largely to destroy it. If I can, by dint of my labour, or my contributions to social welfare, for which I receive an equivalent in money, buy an estate and build a fence about it and keep off intruders, I have a perfect right to do so. It is a right without the exercise of which I believe civilized society would cease to exist and the world would relapse into barbarism. So, too, with regard to an island or a continent. If a community of people can take possession of such a territory and make such use of its resources as favours the general welfare of mankind, it appears to me that they have a perfect right to build a wall around it and exclude such people as they do not wish to have among them. It will be generally admitted, I think, that our government has a right to refuse to admit shiploads of criminals. It appears to me that the same right extends to shiploads of lepers or persons inflicted with any incurable and contagious disease. It appears to me that the same principle applies to shiploads of paupers; and now I go a little further and state as my own view—one in which I expect to find few sympathizers—that I think we have a perfect right to exclude persons whom we think for any reason would be undesirable citizens, such as for example the Chinese; in other words, I do not admit for any other people in the world any inalienable right to come to this country. It appears to me that there are no inalienable rights in the matter but that it is purely a question of public policy, the only ground I think on which the question admits of rational discussion.

Now when we leave on one side all generalizations about rights and come to speak of public policy, there can be no doubt that as a general rule the policy of exclusion of foreigners is illiberal and unwise. I look at these things, you know, from a Darwinian point of view. Nothing is more conducive to the strength of a nation than the free play of individuality which comes from admitting varieties of people, varieties in race, and therefore in inherited and acquired experience. As a rule, Chinese exclusiveness is bad. One source of the weakness of Spain and of her decline in modern times has been the expulsion of Moors and Jews. One cause of the superabundant strength of England is the readiness with which she has welcomed immigrants from all quarters and of all ways of thinking. We Americans have continued in our broad country the policy which we inherited from England, and throughout a considerable portion of our history the influx of immigrants from various parts of Europe has been a source of strength to us. It does not, however, necessarily follow that all immigration under all circumstances should be encouraged. If it is undeniable that variety is a source of national strength, it is equally undeniable that no nation can pursue a worthy career unless it is made up of individuals of good quality. It is impossible for the character of any nation to be better than the average character of its units. No ingenuity of legislation or of constitution making can evolve good political results out of base human material. Circumstances, therefore, may arise in which it is necessary for a nation to change, or at least qualify, its policy. I am told that a proposal to restrict foreign immigration is in violation of the nation's noblest traditions. To this I answer in the words of an old assemblyman in Virginia in the days of Bacon's Rebellion; "If we have any bad customs among us, it is time we should mend them." Now I think the time has come. Let us look at the history of the subject for a moment. The immigration to this country in our Colonial period was mostly of a very superior quality. In many cases, it consisted of persons who had left their country for reasons of political or religious dissent. We all know that such persons are of picked quality. Five hundred Huguenots or Scotch-Irish, such as came here in the Eighteenth Century, would be of more value as members of the community than one thousand persons taken at random. It was fortunate for us that we collected so many such fine people in this country. There was another kind of immigration, mostly involuntary, consisting of criminals sent from England, mostly to the Middle and Southern colonies. Did those Colonies welcome such immigration? They did not, but protested against it with all the vigour of which they were capable, sometimes using rather hard language on the subject. Were they right in thus objecting to receive criminals? I think they were. There was also a very large immigration, also involuntary, of black men from Africa. Protests were sometimes uttered against the rapid increase of such population. Were these protests justifiable? I think there was much that was sound in them. These poor black men came through no fault of their own. No doubt their descendants are far better off than if the race had remained in Africa. No doubt we have conferred good upon part of the African race by bringing them to this country, an argument which both you and I used in old times to hear used to justify the iniquities of slavery. But the question arises—has not the injury inflicted upon the white race been more than equivalent to the benefit conferred upon the black? I do not care to try to answer this question; it is enough to suggest that the question is a real one.

Source:
John Fiske, Letter to William Lloyd
Garrison (February 1, 1898), in *The Letters of
John Fiske,* edited by Ethel F. Fisk (New York:
Macmillan, 1940), pp. 666–68.

95

Races and
Immigrants in America

BY JOHN R. COMMONS

John R. Commons (1862–1945) taught economics at several universities, including the University of Wisconsin. A widely respected scholar of the labor movement, he was the coauthor of History of Labour in the United States *(1918–35) and chief editor of* A Documentary History of American Industrial Society *(1910–11). He was one of the intellectual forces behind the Social Security Act of 1935. Early in his career he prepared a report on immigration for the United States Industrial Commission and subsequently wrote a treatise,* Races and Immigrants in America *(1907). Here, Commons attempts to gauge the relative worth of various immigrants in terms of their industrial capacity.*

T HE MENTAL AND MORAL QUALITIES suited to make productive workers depend upon the character of the industry. It is not conceivable that the immigrants of the present day from Southern Europe and from Asia could have succeeded as frontiersmen and pioneers in the settlement of the country. In all Europe, Asia, and Africa there was but one race in the seventeenth and eighteenth centuries that had the preliminary training necessary to plunge into the wilderness, and in the face of the Indian to establish homes and agriculture. This was the English and the Scotch-Irish. The Spaniards and the French were pioneers and adventurers, but they established only trading stations. Accustomed to a paternal government they had not, as a people, the self-reliance and capacity for sustained exertion required to push forward as individuals, and to cut themselves off from the support of a government across the ocean. They shrank from the herculean task of clearing the forests, planting crops among the stumps, and living miles away from their neighbors. True, the pioneers had among their number several of German, French, and Dutch descent, but these belonged to the second and third generations descended from the immigrants and thrown from the time of childhood among their English-Scotch neighbors. The French trappers and explorers are famous, and have left their names on our map. But it was the English race that established itself in America, not because it was first to come, not because of its armies and navies, but because of its agriculture. Every farm newly carved out of the wilderness became a permanent foothold, and soon again sent out a continuous colony of sons and daughters to occupy the fertile land. Based on this self-reliant, democratic, industrial conquest of the new world the military conquest naturally, inevitably followed.

But at the present day the character of industry has entirely changed. The last quarter of the nineteenth century saw the vacant lands finally occupied and the tribe of frontiersmen coming to an end. Population now began to recoil upon the East and the cities. This afforded to manufactures and to the mining industries the surplus labor-market so necessary for the continuance of large establishments which to-day need thousands of workmen and to-morrow hundreds. Moreover, among the American-born workmen, as well as the English and Scotch, are not found that docility, obedience to orders, and patient toil which employers desire where hundreds and thousands are brought like an army under the direction of foremen, superintendents, and managers. Employers now turn for their labor supply to those eastern and southern sections of Europe which have not hitherto contributed to immigration. The first to draw upon these sources in large numbers were the anthracite coal operators of Pennsylvania. In these fields the English, Scotch, Welsh, and Irish miners, during and following the period of the Civil War, had effected an organization for the control of wages, and the outrages of a secret society known as the Molly Maguires gave occasion for the importation of new races unaccustomed to unionism, and incapable, on account of language, of coöperation with English-speaking miners. Once introduced in the mining industry, these races rapidly found their way into the unskilled parts of manufactures, into the service of railroads and large contractors. On the construction of the Erie Canal in 1898, of 16,000 workmen, 15,000 were unnaturalized Italians. The census of 1900 showed that while the foreign-born males were one-fourteenth of the laborers in agriculture, they were three-fourths of the tailors, more than one-half of the cabinet makers, nearly one-half of the miners and quarrymen, tannery workers, marble and stonecutters, more than two-fifths of the boot and shoe-makers and textile workers, one-third of the coopers, iron and steel workers, wood-workers and miscellaneous laborers, one-fourth of the carpenters, painters, and plasterers, and one-fifth of the sawmill workers. The foreign-born females numbered nearly two-fifths of the female cotton-mill operatives and tailors, one-third of the woollen-mill operatives, one-fourth of the tobacco and silk-mill operatives.

On the Pacific slope the Chinese and Japanese immigrants have filled the place occupied by the southeast European in the East and the negro in the South. They were the workmen who built the Pacific railroads, and without them it is said that these railroads could not have been constructed until several years after their actual completion.

The immigration of the Chinese reached its highest figures prior to the exclusion laws of 1882, and since that time has been but an insignificant contribution. In their place have come the Japanese, a race whose native land, in proportion to its cultivable area, is more densely populated than any other country in the world. The Chinese and Japanese are perhaps the most industrious of all races, while the Chinese are the most docile. The Japanese excel in imitativeness, but are not as reliable as the Chinese. Neither race, so far as their immigrant representatives are concerned, possesses the originality and ingenuity which characterize the competent American and British mechanic. In the Hawaiian Islands, where they have enjoyed greater opportunities than elsewhere, they are found to be capable workmen of the skilled trades, provided they are under the direction of white mechanics. But their largest field of work in Hawaii is in the unskilled cultivation of the great sugar plantations. Here they have been likened to "a sort of agricultural automaton," and it becomes possible to place them in large numbers under skilled direction, and thus to secure the best results from their docility and industry.

In the United States itself the plantation form of agriculture, as distinguished from the domestic form, has always been based on a supply of labor from backward or un-Americanized races. This fact has a bearing on the alleged tendency of agriculture toward large farms. Ten years ago it seemed that the great "bonanza" farms were destined to displace the small farms, just as the trust displaces the small manufacturer. But it is now recognized that the reverse movement is in progress, and that the small farmer can compete successfully with the great farmer. It has not, however, been pointed out that the question is not merely an economic one and that it depends upon the industrial character of the races engaged in agriculture. The thrifty, hard-working and intelligent American or Teutonic farmer is able to economize and purchase his own small farm and compete successfully with the large undertaking. He is even beginning to do this in Hawaii since the compulsory labor of his large competitors was abolished. But the backward, thriftless, and unintelligent races succeed best when employed in gangs on large estates. The cotton and sugar fields of the South with their negro workers have their counterpart in the plantations of Hawaii with their Chinese and Japanese, and in the newly developed sugar-beet fields of Nebraska, Colorado, and California, with their Russians, Bohemians, Japanese, and Mexicans. In the domestic or small form of agriculture the bulk of immigrants from Southern and Eastern Europe are not greatly desired as wage-earners, and they do not succeed as proprietors and tenants because they lack oversight and business ability. Where they are located in colonies under favorable auspices the Italians have achieved notable success, and in the course of Americanization they will doubtless rival older nationalities. But in the immigrant stage they are helpless, and it is the immigrants from Northwestern Europe, the Germans and Scandinavians, whose thrift, self-reliance, and intensive agriculture have made them from the start the model farmers of America.

The Jewish immigrant, particularly, is unfitted for the life of a pioneer. Remarkably individualistic in character, his field of enterprise is society, and not the land. Of the thirty thousand families sent out from New York by industrial and agricultural removal societies, nine-tenths are located in industry and trade, and the bulk of the remainder, who are placed on farms, succeed by keeping summer boarders. Depending on boarders, they neglect agriculture and buy their food-stuff. Their largest colony of hoped-for agriculturists, Woodbine, New Jersey, has become a clothing factory. Yet the factory system, with its discipline and regular hours, is distasteful to the Jew's individualism. He prefers the sweatshop, with its going and coming. If possible, he rises through peddling and merchandising.

These are a few of the many illustrative facts which might be set forth to show that the changing character of immigration is made possible by the changing character of industry; and that races wholly incompetent as pioneers and independent proprietors are able to find a place when once manufactures, mines, and railroads have sprung into being, with their captains of industry to guide and supervise their semi-intelligent work.

Source:
John R. Commons, *Races and Immigrants
in America* (New York: Macmillan, 1907; rev.
ed. 1920), pp. 127–34.

96

The American Scene

BY HENRY JAMES

Distinguished novelist Henry James (1843–1916) spent a comfortable childhood in New York that involved frequent visits to Europe. Two trips to Europe, in 1869–70 and 1872–74, exercised a significant influence on his thought and writing, and James became fascinated with the richness and sophistication of European culture. He left the United States permanently in 1875, settling first in Paris and then in London. Aside from two brief journeys in the early 1880s, James did not return to the United States until 1904, when he spent ten months revisiting the scenes of his childhood. His travel book The American Scene *(1907) is the result. James criticizes many features of American political, social, and cultural institutions and in a section entitled "Ellis Island" he directs his attention to the large number of immigrants entering the country.*

I N THE BAY, the rest of the morning, the dense raw fog that delayed the big boat, allowing sight but of the immediate ice-masses through which it thumped its way, was not less of the essence. Anything blander, as a medium, would have seemed a mockery of the facts of the terrible little Ellis Island, the first harbour of refuge and stage of patience for the million or so of immigrants annually knocking at our official door. Before this door, which opens to them there only with a hundred forms and ceremonies, grindings and grumblings of the key, they stand appealing and waiting, marshalled, herded, divided, subdivided, sorted, sifted, searched, fumigated, for longer or shorter periods—the effect of all which prodigious process, an intendedly "scientific" feeding of the mill, is again to give the earnest observer a thousand more things to think of

520

than he can pretend to retail. The impression of Ellis Island, in fine, would be—as I was to find throughout that so many of my impressions would be—a chapter by itself; and with a particular page for recognition of the degree in which the liberal hospitality of the eminent Commissioner of this wonderful service, to whom I had been introduced, helped to make the interest of the whole watched drama poignant and unforgettable. It is a drama that goes on, without a pause, day by day and year by year, this visible act of ingurgitation on the part of our body politic and social, and constituting really an appeal to amazement beyond that of any sword-swallowing or fire-swallowing of the circus. The wonder that one couldn't keep down was the thought that these two or three hours of one's own chance vision of the business were but as a tick or two of the mighty clock, the clock that never, never stops— least of all when it strikes, for a sign of so much winding-up, some louder hour of our national fate than usual. I think indeed that the simplest account of the action of Ellis Island on the spirit of any sensitive citizen who may have happened to "look in" is that he comes back from his visit not at all the same person that he went. He has eaten of the tree of knowledge, and the taste will be for ever in his mouth. He had thought he knew before, thought he had the sense of the degree in which it is his American fate to share the sanctity of his American consciousness, the intimacy of his American patriotism, with the inconceivable alien; but the truth had never come home to him with any such force. In the lurid light projected upon it by those courts of dismay it shakes him—or I like at least to imagine it shakes him—to the depths of his being; I like to think of him, I positively *have* to think of him, as going about ever afterwards with a new look, for those who can see it, in his face, the outward sign of the new chill in his heart. So is stamped, for detection, the questionably privileged person who has had an apparition, seen a ghost in his supposedly safe old house. Let not the unwary, therefore, visit Ellis Island.

The after-sense of that acute experience, however, I myself found, was by no means to be brushed away; I felt it grow and grow, on the contrary, wherever I turned: other impressions might come and go, but this affirmed claim of the alien, however immeasurably alien, to share in one's supreme relation was everywhere the fixed element, the reminder not to be dodged. One's supreme relation, as one had always put it, was one's relation to one's country—a conception made up so largely of one's countrymen and one's countrywomen. Thus it was as if, all the while, with such a fond tradition of what these products predominantly were, the idea of the country itself underwent something of that profane overhauling through which it appears to suffer the indignity of change.

Is not our instinct in this matter, in general, essentially the safe one—that of keeping the idea simple and strong and continuous, so that it shall be perfectly sound? To touch it over-much, to pull it about, is to put it in peril of weakening; yet on this free assault upon it, this readjustment of it in *their* monstrous, presumptuous interest, the aliens, in New York, seemed perpetually to insist. The combination there of their quantity and their quality—that loud primary stage of alienism which New York most offers to sight—operates, for the native, as their note of settled possession, something they have nobody to thank for; so that *un*settled possession is what we, on our side, seem reduced to—the implication of which, in its turn, is that, to recover confidence and regain lost ground, we, not they, must make the surrender and accept the orientation. We must go, in other words, *more* than half-way to meet them; which is all the difference, for us, between possession and dispossession. This sense of dispossession, to be brief about it, haunted me so, I was to feel, in the New York streets and in the packed trajectiles to which one clingingly appeals from the streets, just as one tumbles back into the streets in appalled reaction from *them*, that the art of beguiling or duping it became an art to be cultivated—though the fond alternative vision was never long to be obscured, the imagination, exasperated to envy, of the ideal, in the order in question; of the luxury of some such close and sweet and *whole* national consciousness as that of the Switzer and the Scot.

Source:
Henry James, *The American Scene* (New York: Harper & Brothers, 1907), pp. 84–86.

~ *97* ~

The Old World
and the New

BY EDWARD ALSWORTH ROSS

Edward Alsworth Ross (1866–1951) taught sociology at Stanford, the University of Wisconsin, and elsewhere. He wrote several important works on sociology, including The Foundations of Sociology *(1905) and* Sin and Society *(1907), in the course of which he urged an increased governmental role in ameliorating social problems. In* The Old World and the New *(1914), a tract on immigration, Ross foresees the decline of American society through excessive and indiscriminate immigration. A later volume,* Standing Room Only *(1927), is another attack on immigrants.*

Insanity Among the Foreign-Born

Not only do the foreign-born appear to be more subject to insanity than the native-born, but when insane they are more likely to become a public charge. Of the asylum population they appear to constitute about a third. In New York during the year ending September 30, 1911, 4218 patients who were immigrants or of immigrant parents were admitted to the insane hospitals of the State. This is three-quarters of the melancholy intake for that year. Only one out of nine of the first admissions from New York City was of native stock. The New York State Hospital Commission declares that "the frequency of insanity in our foreign population is 2.19 times greater than in those of native birth." In New York City it "is 2.48 times that of the native-born."

Excessive insanity is probably a part of the price the foreign-born pay for the opportunities of a strange and stimulating environment, with greater strains than some of them are able to bear. America calls forth powerful reactions in these people. Here they feel themselves in the grasp of giant forces they can neither withstand nor comprehend. The passions and the exertions, the hopes and the fears, the exultations and the despairs, America excites in the immigrant are likely to be intenser than anything he would have experienced in his natal village.

In view of the fact that every year New York cares for 15,000 foreign-born insane at a cost of $3,500,000 and that the State's sad harvest of demented immigrants during the single year 1911 will cost about $8,000,000 before they die or are discharged, there is some offset to be made to the profits drawn from the immigrants by the transporting companies, landlords, real-estate men, employers, contractors, brewers, and liquor-dealers of the State. Besides, there is the cost of the paupers and the law-breakers of foreign origin. All such burdens, however, since they fall upon the public at large, do not detract from or qualify that private or business-man's prosperity which it is the office of the true modern statesman to promote.

Social Decline

"Our descendants," a social worker remarked to me, "will look back on the nineteenth century as our Golden Age, just as we look back on Greece." Thoughtful people whose work takes them into the slime at the bottom of our foreignized cities and industrial centers find decline actually upon us. A visiting nurse who has worked for seven years in the stock-yards district of Chicago reports that of late the drinking habit is taking hold of foreign women at an alarming rate. In the saloons there the dignified *stein* has given way to the beer pail. In the Range towns of Minnesota there are 356 saloons, of which eighty-one are run by native-born, the rest chiefly by recent immigrants. Into a Pennsylvania coal town of 1,800 people, mostly foreign-born, are shipped each week a car-load of beer and a barrel of whisky. Where the new foreign-born are numerous, women and children frequent the saloons as freely as the men. In the cities family desertion is growing at a great rate among foreign-born husbands. Facts are justifying the forecast made ten years ago by H. G. Wells: "If things go on as they are going, the great mass of them will remain a very low lower class—will remain largely illiterate, industrialized peasants."

The continuance of depressive immigration will lead to nothing catastrophic. Riots and labor strife will oftener break out, but the country will certainly not weaken nor collapse. Of patriotism of the military type there will be no lack. Scientific and technical advance will go on the same. The spread of business organization and efficiency will continue. The only thing that will happen will be a mysterious slackening in social progress. The mass will give signs of sluggishness, and the social procession will be strung out.

We are engaged in a generous rivalry with the West Europeans and the Australians to see which can do the most to lift the plane of life of the masses. Presently we shall be dismayed by the sense of falling behind. We shall be amazed to find the Swiss or the Danes or the New Zealanders making strides we cannot match. Stung with mortification at losing our erstwhile lead in the advancement of the common people, we shall cast about for someone to blame. Ultimate causes, of course, will be overlooked; only proximate causes will be noticed. There will be loud outcry that mothers, or teachers, or clergymen, or editors, or social workers are not doing their duty. Our public schools, solely responsible as they obviously are for the intellectual and moral characteristics of the people, will be roundly denounced; and it will be argued that church schools must take their place. There will be trying of this and trying of that, together with much ingenious legislation. As peasantism spreads and inertia proves unconquerable, the opinion will grow that the old American faith in the capacity and desire of the common people for improvement was a delusion, and that only the superior classes care for progress. Not until the twenty-first century will the philosophic historian be able to declare with scientific certitude that the cause of the mysterious decline that came upon the American people early in the twentieth century was the deterioration of popular intelligence by the admission of great numbers of backward immigrants.

Source:
Edward Alsworth Ross, *The Old World and the New: The Significance of Past and Present Immigration to the American People* (New York: Century Co., 1914), pp. 249–50, 254–56.

❧ 98 ❧

The Rising Tide of Color Against White World-Supremacy

BY LOTHROP STODDARD

The lawyer Theodore Lothrop Stoddard (1883–1950) wrote a variety of works discussing the role of race in national culture, including Racial Realities in Europe *(1924) and* Re-Forging America *(1927). The Rising Tide of Color Against White World-Supremacy *(1920) is his most unrestrained attack on non-white races and the supposed threat they pose to white civilization. Stoddard's work had the honor of being alluded to in a passage of F. Scott Fitzgerald's* The Great Gatsby *(1925) as "The Rise of the Colored Empires *by this man Goddard."*

OURS IS A SOLEMN MOMENT. We stand at a crisis—the supreme crisis of the ages. For unnumbered millenniums man has toiled upward from the dank jungles of savagery toward glorious heights which his mental and spiritual potentialities give promise that he shall attain. His path has been slow and wavering. Time and again he has lost his way and plunged into deep valleys. Man's trail is littered with the wrecks of dead civilizations and dotted with the graves of promising peoples stricken by an untimely end.

Humanity has thus suffered many a disaster. Yet none of these disasters were fatal, because they were merely local. Those wrecked civilizations and blighted peoples were only parts of a larger whole. Always some strong barbarians, endowed with rich, unspoiled heredities, caught the falling torch and bore it onward flaming high once more.

Out of the prehistoric shadows the white races pressed to the front and proved in a myriad ways their fitness for the hegemony of mankind. Gradually they forged a common civilization; then, when vouchsafed their unique opportunity of oceanic mastery four centuries ago, they spread over the earth, filling its empty spaces with their superior breeds and assuring to themselves an unparalleled paramountcy of numbers and dominion.

Three centuries later the whites took a fresh leap forward. The nineteenth century was a new age of discovery—this time into the realms of science. The hidden powers of nature were unveiled, incalculable energies were tamed to human use, terrestrial distance was abridged, and at last the planet was integrated under the hegemony of a single race with a common civilization.

The prospects were magnificent, the potentialities of progress apparently unlimited. Yet there were commensurate perils. Towering heights mean abysmal depths, while the very possibility of supreme success implies the possibility of supreme failure. All these marvellous achievements were due solely to superior heredity, and the mere maintenance of what had been won depended absolutely upon the prior maintenance of race-values. Civilization of itself means nothing. It is merely an effect, whose cause is the creative urge of superior germ-plasm. Civilization is the body; the race is the soul. Let the soul vanish, and the body moulders into the inanimate dust from which it came.

Two things are necessary for the continued existence of a race: it must remain itself, and it must breed its best. Every race is the result of ages of development which evolves specialized capacities that make the race what it is and render it capable of creative achievement. These specialized capacities (which particularly mark the superior races), being relatively recent developments, are highly unstable. They are what biologists call "recessive" characters; that is, they are not nearly so "dominant" as the older, generalized characters which races inherit from remote ages and which have therefore been more firmly stamped upon the germ-plasm. Hence, when a highly specialized stock interbreeds with a different stock, the newer, less stable, specialized characters are bred out, the variation, no matter how great its potential value to human evolution, being *irretrievably lost*. This occurs even in the mating of two superior stocks if these stocks are widely dissimilar in character. The valuable specializations of both breeds cancel out, and the mixed offspring tend strongly to revert to generalized mediocrity.

And, of course, the more primitive a type is, the more prepotent it is. This is why crossings with the negro are uniformly fatal. Whites, Amerindians, or Asiatics—all are alike vanquished by the invincible prepotency of the more primitive, generalized, and lower negro blood.

There is no immediate danger of the world being swamped by black blood. But there is a very imminent danger that the white stocks may be swamped by Asiatic blood.

The white man's very triumphs have evoked this danger. His virtual abolition of distance has destroyed the protection which nature once conferred. Formerly mankind dwelt in such dispersed isolation that wholesale contact of distant, diverse stocks was practically impossible. But with the development of cheap and rapid transportation, nature's barriers are down. Unless man erects and maintains artificial barriers the various races will increasingly mingle, and the inevitable result will be the supplanting or absorption of the higher by the lower types.

We can see this process working out in almost every phase of modern migration. The white immigration into Latin America is the exception which proves the rule. That particular migration is, of course, beneficent, since it means the influx of relatively high types into undeveloped lands, sparsely populated by types either no higher or much lower than the new arrivals. But almost everywhere else, whether we consider interwhite migrations or colored encroachments on white lands, the net result is an expansion of lower and a contraction of higher stocks, the process being thus a disgenic one. Even in Asia the evils of modern migration are beginning to show. The Japanese Government has been obliged to prohibit the influx of Chinese and Korean coolies who were undercutting Japanese labor and thus undermining the economic bases of Japanese life.

Furthermore, modern migration is itself only one aspect of a still more fundamental disgenic trend. The whole course of modern urban and industrial life is disgenic. Over and above immigration, the tendency is toward a replacement of the more valuable by the less valuable elements of the population. All over the civilized world racial values are diminishing, and the logical end of this disgenic process is racial bankruptcy and the collapse of civilization.

Now why is all this? It is primarily because we have not yet adjusted ourselves to the radically new environment into which our epochal scientific discoveries led us a century ago. Such adaptation as we have effected has been almost wholly on the material side. The no less sweeping idealistic adaptations which the situation calls for have not been made. Hence, modern civilization has been one-sided, abnormal, unhealthy—and nature is exacting penalties which will increase in severity until we either fully adapt or *finally perish.*

"Finally perish!" That is the exact alternative which confronts the white race. For white civilization is to-day conterminous with the white race. The civilizations of the past were local. They were confined to a particular people or group of peoples. If they failed, there were always some unspoiled, well-endowed barbarians to step forward and "carry on." But to-day *there are no more white barbarians.* The earth has grown small, and men are everywhere in close touch. If white civilization goes down, the white race is irretrievably ruined. It will be swamped by the triumphant colored races, who will obliterate the white man by elimination or absorption. What has taken place in Central Asia, once a white and now a brown or yellow land, will take place in Australasia, Europe, and America. Not to-day, nor yet to-morrow; perhaps not for generations; but surely in the end. If the present drift be not changed, we whites are all ultimately doomed. Unless we set our house in order, the doom will sooner or later overtake us all.

And that would mean that the race obviously endowed with the greatest creative ability, the race which had achieved most in the past and which gave the richer promise for the future, had passed away, carrying with it to the grave those potencies upon which the realization of man's highest hopes depends. A million years of human evolution might go uncrowned, and earth's supreme life-product, man, might never fulfil his potential destiny. This is why we to-day face "The Crisis of the Ages."

To many minds the mere possibility of such a catastrophe may seem unthinkable. Yet a dispassionate survey of the past shows that it is not only possible but probable if present conditions go on unchanged. The whole history of life, both human and subhuman, teaches us that nature will not condone disobedience; that, as I have already phrased it, "no living being stands above her law, and protozoön or demigod, if they transgress, alike must die."

Now we have transgressed; grievously transgressed—and we are suffering grievous penalties. But pain is really kind. Pain is the importunate tocsin which rouses to dangerous realities and spurs to the seeking of a cure.

As a matter of fact we are confusedly aware of our evil plight, and legion are the remedies to-day proposed. Some of these are mere quack nostrums. Others contain valuable remedial properties. To be sure, there is probably no *one* curative agent, since our troubles are complex and magic elixirs heal only in the realm of dreams. But one element should be fundamental to all the compoundings of the social pharmacopoeia. That element is *blood.*

It is clean, virile, genius-bearing blood, streaming down the ages through the unerring action of heredity, which, in anything like a favorable environment, will multiply itself, solve our problems, and sweep us on to higher and nobler destinies. What we to-day need above all else is a changed attitude of mind—a recognition of the supreme importance of heredity, not merely in scientific treatises but in the practical ordering of the world's affairs. We are where we are to-day primarily because we have neglected this vital principle; because we have concerned ourselves with dead things instead of with living beings.

This disregard of heredity is perhaps not strange. It is barely a generation since its fundamental importance was scientifically established, and the world's conversion to even the most vital truth takes time. In fact, we also have much to unlearn. A little while ago we were taught that all men were equal and that good conditions could, of themselves, quickly perfect mankind. The seductive charm of these dangerous fallacies lingers and makes us loath to put them resolutely aside.

Fortunately, we now know the truth. At last we have been vouchsafed clear insight into the laws of life. We now know that men are not, and never will be, equal. We know that environment and education can develop only what heredity brings. We know that the acquirements of individuals are either not inherited at all or are inherited in so slight a degree as to make no perceptible difference from generation to generation. In other words: we now know that heredity is paramount in human evolution, all other things being secondary factors.

This basic truth is already accepted by large numbers of thinking men and women all over the civilized world, and if it becomes firmly fixed in the popular consciousness it will work nothing short of a revolution in the ordering of the world's affairs.

For race-betterment is such an intensely *practical* matter! When peoples come to realize that the *quality* of the population is the source of all their prosperity, progress, security, and even existence; when they realize that a single genius may be worth more in actual dollars than a dozen gold-mines, while, conversely, racial decline spells material impoverishment and decay; when such things are really believed, we shall see much-abused "eugenics" actually moulding social programmes and political policies. Were the white world to-day really convinced of the supreme importance of race-values, how long would it take to stop debasing immigration, reform social abuses that are killing out the fittest strains, and put an end to the feuds which have just sent us through hell and threaten to send us promptly back again?

Well, perhaps our change of heart may come sooner than now appears. The horrors of the war, the disappointment of the peace, the terror of Bolshevism, and the rising tide of color have knocked a good deal of the nonsense out of us, and have given multitudes a hunger for realities who were before content with a diet of phrases. Said wise old Benjamin Franklin: "Dame Experience sets a dear school, but fools will have no other." Our course at the dame's school is already well under way and promises to be exceeding dear.

Only, it is to be hoped our education will be rapid, for time presses and the hour is grave. If certain lessons are not learned and acted upon shortly, we may be overwhelmed by irreparable disasters and all our dear schooling will go for naught.

What are the things we *must* do promptly if we would avert the worst? This "irreducible minimum" runs about as follows:

First and foremost, the wretched Versailles business will have to be thoroughly revised. As it stands, dragon's teeth have been sown over both Europe and Asia, and unless they be plucked up they will presently grow a crop of cataclysms which will seal the white world's doom.

Secondly, some sort of provisional understanding must be arrived at between the white world and renascent Asia. We whites will have to abandon our tacit assumption of permanent domination over Asia while Asiatics will have to forego their dreams of migration to white lands and penetration of Africa and Latin America. Unless some such understanding is arrived at, the world will drift into a gigantic race-war—and genuine race-war means war to the knife. Such a hideous catastrophe should be abhorrent to both sides. Nevertheless, Asia should be given clearly to understand that we cannot permit either migration to white lands or penetration of the non-Asiatic tropics, and that for these matters we prefer to fight to a finish rather than yield to a finish—because our "finish" is precisely what surrender on these points would mean.

Thirdly, even within the white world, migrations of lower human types like those which have worked such havoc in the United States must be rigorously curtailed. Such migrations upset standards, sterilize better stocks, increase low types, and compromise national futures more than war, revolutions, or native deterioration.

Such are the things which simply *must* be done if we are to get through the next few decades without convulsions which may render impossible the white world's recovery.

These things will not bring in the millennium. Far from it. Our ills are so deep-seated that in nearly every civilized country racial values would continue to depreciate even if all three were carried into effect. But they will at least give our wounds a chance to heal and they will give the new biological revelation time to permeate the popular consciousness and transfuse with a new idealism our materialistic age. As the years pass, the supreme importance of heredity and the supreme value of superior stocks will sink into our being, and we will acquire a true *race*-consciousness (as opposed to national or cultural consciousness) which will bridge political gulfs, remedy social abuses, and exorcise the lurking spectre of miscegenation.

Source:
Lothrop Stoddard, *The Rising Tide of Color
Against White World-Supremacy* (New York:
Scribner's, 1920), pp. 299–309.

99

Whose Country Is This?

BY CALVIN COOLIDGE

Calvin Coolidge (1872–1933), vice president under Warren G. Harding (1921–23) and thirtieth president of the United States (1923–29), was long known for his stance on immigrants. In "Whose Country Is This?" (1921), published in Good Housekeeping *a month before he took office as vice president, Coolidge insists that future immigrants must be "temperamentally keyed for our national background." He repeated his sentiments in his State of the Union address in 1923 and signed into law the restrictive Immigration Act of 1924.*

M EN AND WOMEN, IN AND of themselves, are desirable. There can not be too many inhabitants of the right kind, distributed in the right place. Great work there is for each and every one of them to perform. The country needs all the intelligence, and skill, and strength of mind and body it can get, whether we draw such from those within our gates, or from those without, seeking entrance.

But since we are confronted by the clamor of multitudes who desire the opportunity offered by American life, we must face the situation unflinchingly, determined to relinquish not one iota of our obligations to others, yet not so sentimental as to overlook our obligations to ourselves.

It is a self-evident truth that in a healthy community there is no place for the vicious, the weak of body, the shiftless, or the improvident. As Professor Sumner of Yale, asserts in his book, "The Forgotten Man," "Every part of capital which is wasted on the vicious, the idle, and the shiftless, is so much taken from the capital available to reward the independent and productive laborer." We are in agreement with him in his conviction that the laborer must be protected "against the burdens of the good-for-nothing."

We want no such additions to our population as those who prey upon our institutions or our property. America has, in the popular mind, been an asylum for those who have been driven from their homes in foreign countries because of various forms of political and religious oppression. But America can not afford to remain an asylum after such people have passed the portals and begun to share the privileges of our institutions.

These institutions have flourished by reason of a common background of experience; they have been perpetuated by a common faith in the righteousness of their purpose; they have been handed down undiminished in effectiveness from our forefathers who conceived their spirit and prepared the foundations. We have put into operation our faith in equal opportunity before the law in exchange for equal obligation of citizenship.

All native-born Americans, directly or indirectly, have the advantage of our schools, our colleges, and our religious bodies. It is our belief that America could not otherwise exist. Faith in mankind is in no wise inconsistent with a requirement for trained citizenship, both for men and women. No civilization can exist without a background—an active community of interest, a common aspiration—spiritual, social, and economic. It is a duty our country owes itself to require of all those aliens who come here that they have a background not inconsistent with American institutions.

Such a background might consist either of a racial tradition or a national experience. But in its lowest terms it must be characterized by a capacity for assimilation. While America is built on a broad faith in mankind, it likewise gains its strength by a recognition of a needed training for citizenship. The Pilgrims were not content merely to reach our shores in safety, that they might live according to a sort of daily opportunism. They were building on firmer ground than that. Sixteen years after they landed at Plymouth, they and their associates founded Harvard College. They institutionalized their faith in education; that was their offering for the common good. It would not be unjust to ask of every alien: What will you contribute to the common good, once you are admitted through the gates of liberty? Our history is full of answers of which we might be justly proud. But of late, the answers have not been so readily or so eloquently given. Our country must cease to be regarded as a dumping ground. Which does not mean that it must deny the value of rich accretions drawn from the right kind of immigration.

Any such restriction, except as a necessary and momentary expediency, would assuredly paralyze our national vitality. But measured practically, it would be suicidal for us to let down the bars for the inflowing of cheap manhood, just as, commercially, it-would be unsound for this country to allow her markets to be overflooded with cheap goods, the product of a cheap labor. There is no room either for the cheap man or the cheap goods. . . .

I do not fear the arrival of as many immigrants a year as shipping conditions or passport requirements can handle, provided they are of good character. But there is no room for the alien who turns toward America with the avowed intention of opposing government, with a set desire to teach destruction of government—which means not only enmity toward organized society, but toward every form of religion and so basic an institution as the home.

If we believe, as we do, in our political theory that the people are the guardians of government, we should not subject our government to the bitterness and hatred of those who have not been born of our tradition and are not willing to yield an increase to the strength inherent in our institutions. American liberty is dependent on quality in citizenship. Our obligation is to maintain that citizenship at its best. We must have nothing to do with those who would undermine it. The retroactive immigrant is a danger in our midst. His discontent gives him no time to seize a healthy opportunity to improve himself. His purpose is to tear down. There is no room for him here. He needs to be deported, not as a substitute for, but as a part of his punishment.

We might avoid this danger were we insistent that the immigrant, before he leaves foreign soil, is temperamentally keyed for our national background. There are racial considerations too grave to be brushed aside for any sentimental reasons. Biological laws tell us that certain divergent people will not mix or blend. The Nordics propagate themselves successfully. With other races, the outcome shows deterioration on both sides. Quality of mind and body suggests that observance of ethnic law is as great a necessity to a nation as immigration law. . . .

We must remember that we have not only the present but the future to safeguard; our obligations extend even to generations yet unborn. The unassimilated alien child menaces our children, as the alien industrial worker, who has destruction rather than production in mind, menaces our industry. It is only when the alien adds vigor to our stock that he is wanted. The dead weight of an alien accretion stifles national progress. But we have a hope that can not be crushed; we have a background that we will not allow to be obliterated. The only acceptable immigrant is the one who can justify our faith in man by a constant revelation of the divine purpose of the Creator.

Source:
Calvin Coolidge, "Whose Country Is
This?" *Good Housekeeping* 72, no. 2 (February
1921): 13–14, 109.

100

America's
Race Heritage

BY CLINTON STODDARD BURR

Little is known of Clinton Stoddard Burr, author of America's Race
Heritage *(1922). In this polemic against immigration—one of the many
such works that fueled a public groundswell leading to the restrictive
Immigration Act of 1924—Burr looks with foreboding at the increase in
women immigrants who will produce large numbers of foreign offspring.*

UPON THE COUNTRY'S PRESENT immigration policy depends the
future of the people of the United States. For it is the care we shall take in
selecting our immigrants that will determine what blood in future years
shall mingle with the blood of our descendants in generations to come.

Perhaps the two factors that stand out above all others are: (1) that if
two races be not of the same basic stock, according to the law of God
and nature the more numerous, or in the case of equally numerous, the
more primitive, or the more adapted race will breed out the other, but
only after an indefinite era of mongrelism which may disintegrate the
mixed element altogether; and (2) that our immigration includes in the
main, not the higher type intellectual classes from Southern and Eastern
Europe, but the mongrel submerged populations, the very dregs of
European humanity. . . .

It is to be expected that great migrations of restless peoples will take
place in the future. We have already restricted the Chinese and Hindus to
Asia; and we are about to restrict Japan to that continent also. The Slavs
have the vast undeveloped resources of Siberia to exploit. The Latins

have the Barbary coast and all of Latin America as an outlet. But what have the overcrowded people of Northwest Europe, if not North America and Australia, as lands to be saved for them alone? Even the Germans should be welcomed to North America and the British Colonies, lest they become embittered and swarm into the Russian Empire, where they may become a far greater menace than before as capable leaders of the Slavic myriads. But that is another story.

Today the United States can welcome the choice, the pick of the inhabitants of Northwest Europe, the farmers and others of a desirable nature. Yet we are discouraging such immigration by our present inadequately regulated laws that cheapen labor and frighten away the skilled workers of Europe.

The organization of the Jewish people in America exercises its influence by gaining priority of passage accommodations for the least self-reliant of the Eastern European Jews. Offices in Europe systematize Jewish immigration to America and encourage the same. It has been necessary to fit many ships with "kosher" kitchens to cater to the thousands of Jewish emigrants to America.

The hundreds of thousands of women arrived since the Armistice of 1918 point toward a large permanent inflow from Eastern and Southern Europe. Also, this offers various new complications in the problem of our immigration from those regions. Thus many Slav and Italian women are now coming over with their husbands, not as additions to the labor forces, but to keep house and, incidentally, rear large families. Many Greek, South Italian and other Southern European women now reach this country under the barbarous custom of "parental arrangement" to marry men they have never seen, a form of legalized prostitution that our immigration authorities are compelled to countenance for lack of laws against such procedure. . . .

But there is a far more significant phase in the gain of the female sex among our immigrants. It lies in the fact that in the past the rate of increase of the native stock has kept pace with the foreign stock only because of the disproportionate number of males, and the scarcity of women and children, among most of the elements of our immigration from Southern and Eastern Europe. The significance of the changes which have come to pass in this connection is very apparent. Incidentally, it may be added that hitherto the net results of the rate of increase of population has been actually in favor of the native Americans, in spite of the fecundity of the women of foreign stock; indeed every two or three native children lived to become adults, marry and raise children of their own, whereas the majority, perhaps, of the average five or six children of the immigrant mother were doomed to die before reaching maturity from lack of nutriment or of intelligent care, from disease, or owing to the dangers of city streets or unwholesome surroundings. Now, however, the institution of hygienic organizations in our great cities will actually accentuate the problem by saving infant lives at birth and in adolescence. Of course the decrease in the death rate may compensate, or more than compensate, for the drop in the birth rate among civilized folk; that is, the net crop of children may be greater in each generation. (Havelock Ellis.) But among the prolific and less civilized races sanitary methods may reduce the death rate long before the birth rate is reduced by natural conditions. We need not cast aside our sense of charity to comprehend the truth of this assertion.

The biological aspect of the immigration problem is by far the most important of all the questions involved. For, as explained in the previous chapter, we must not only share America with the immigrant of remote race stock, but we must allow his children and grandchildren ad infinitum to marry with ours. It may be a matter of centuries, but the futile character of the caste system in India is sufficient evidence of the injury that will be done the race in decades or centuries to come. Mixture of races of genius with races of mediocre character may somewhat uplift the lower stock, but will inevitably blot out the essential quality of the higher. "President Roosevelt was one of the first of our statesmen who looked steadily beyond his day and generation to the more distant future. He inaugurated, or at least gave impetus to, a great movement for the conservation of the natural resources of this country and he maintained that selective immigration was second only to conservation in its importance for the welfare of future generations."[1]

So must we all of us "look beyond" our own passing generation, prompted by unselfish and devoted patriotism and goodwill toward mankind.

Source:
Clinton Stoddard Burr, *America's Race
Heritage* (New York: National Historical
Society, 1922), pp. 177, 179–83.

101

America:
A Family Matter

BY CHARLES W. GOULD

Charles Winthrop Gould (1849–1931) was a lawyer who practiced in New York from 1872 to 1916. In America: A Family Matter *(1922) Gould urges not merely that immigrants be barred from entering the country but that they also be prohibited from naturalization.*

IF WE KNEW THAT NEARLY ONE man in every ten we casually meet on the street could not read or write English; if we knew that seven millions over ten years of age could not read or write at all; if we knew that 3,000,000 farmers could not read the government circulars urging them to increase food production during the war, nor read the Liberty Loan appeals; if we knew that a considerable percentage of our conscripts had to be taught the meaning of the simple words of military command, how to sign payrolls, which was the left foot, would we be pleased and content? Yet such are the dreadful facts. It seems incredible!

Fortunately for us, foreigners seem to be beginning to look upon American citizenship with indifference or scorn. The report from over a hundred business firms shows that two-thirds of their foreign-born laborers had not even taken out their so-called first papers; and still more fortunate for us is the disclosure of the fact that the more undesirable, the greater their aversion to becoming our fellow citizens. Nearly all the Mexicans and members of four other nationalities, lesser breeds without the law, refuse it.

Benighted Americans insist that these people should be forced into becoming citizens as one would drive sheep into a pen, or as the Alsatians were forced to become Germans. They insist that such people must be compelled to love America, for, of course, failing that love, the fundamental basis of patriotic citizenship is wanting, and if they cannot be compelled to love America, the alternative must be presented to them of deportation, that is to say, banishment. Now, banishment has from time immemorial always been one of the most terrible of all punishments—a worse punishment than temporary imprisonment. We who love our country and are proud that we are Americans are inclined to resent the suggestion that our citizenship shall be placed before an unwilling Mexican in a worse light than a State's prison sentence.

Nor can we stop here. We must also consider the claims advanced by sympathetic demagogues on behalf of the Filipino, who is picturesquely represented as already knocking at our door, he and his wife, or, in view of the large Mussulman population, his wives, each one eager to express political acumen by voting. At the time of the Spanish War the population of the Philippines was estimated to be nine millions. Since that time, under favoring conditions such as the suppression of head hunting and slavery, we are promised a large increase. Naturally the demagogue favors additions to our ignorant vote, whether it be Filipino, or Russian, or Pole, or any other, for it is easily manipulated. It may well be doubted, however, if the demagogue is in this matter the patriotic statesman he so loudly claims to be.

The statements just made are but a hint or suggestion of the vast mass of facts which a slight amount of consideration will array before each of us. Even this mere hint or suggestion may well give us pause—nay, more, for the moment we begin to consider the mess of pottage for which we are exchanging our birthright, it becomes revolting. Our whole theory and our whole practice in regard to naturalization betray the sacred privileges won for us and sealed to us by the lifelong devotion, the hopes and aspirations, the trials, toil and suffering of all of our beloved and honored dead.

The teachings of science, the records of history, the warnings of common sense, our own bitter present experience, cry out unto us. There is no ground on which utterly alien people, alien in race, in language, in customs, mature men, mature women, settled in their foreign ways should be admitted to our citizenship. There is no line of reasoning on which such procedure can be justified. It is monstrous. We despise the wretched individual who wantonly wastes his patrimony, and yet among their equals his children may redeem their fortune. We have robbed and are robbing our children of their heritage. We dissipate our fortune of American freedom and condemn the children to rub shoulders politically, not with their mates, but with strangers and foreigners whose sympathies are with each other and not with the American-born.

We know that our institutions depend on the intelligence of each citizen. We know that a republic is possible only to men of homogeneous race, determined and united in intelligent control of their own affairs. We know that the greater the common impulse, the greater the common intelligence, the more community of action and individual capacity are fostered, the better, the more splendid, the happier will be the result. We know that to sustain us in the effort we need every ounce of power we can derive from birth, breeding, the nurture and admonition of loved and honored tradition, the memory of patient self-sacrifice in upbuilding, of courageous persistence in calamity, of deliberate purpose in statesmanship; and we know that such things cannot be taught, they must come to us with the mother's milk, the baby's lisping questions, and grow with our nerves and thews and sinews until they become part and parcel of our very being.

No naturalization certificates can carry with them any part of this, our heritage, impalpable, intangible, and yet more worth on the great altar of our country than the suffrage of untold millions of the ignorant and debased. Already, seventy years ago, de Tocqueville noted that the whole country east of the Mississippi was settled up, was teeming with vigorous race life; forests and prairies were giving way to homesteads and farms, mines were worked, factories busy, railroads and steamboats pushing forward rapid communication, and every community permeated with full knowledge and understanding of self-government by free institutions. There were then seventeen millions of Americans busily engaged in developing our resources. Were we helpless that we needed to call in thirty or forty million strangers to do the work? Suppose we had imported two hundred million Russians, Poles, Syrians, South Italians, Greeks, Negroes, and had cut down every suitable tree for lumber, mined every ounce of coal and ore, and exploited the land down to its rock foundations, what would it have profited us? Lost in these foreign millions, America would be no more.

Americans, the Philistines are upon us. Burst the fetters of our unseemly thraldom. Bar out all intruders. Repeal our naturalization laws. Deafen your ears to the clamor of demagogues. Make strong your hearts against the appeals of emotional humanitarianism. Repel the beguiling approaches of the grasping, who in short-sighted greed would at once rob the children and the children's children of those natural resources which we should guard as their patrimony, and worse—far worse—their right to sway and control law and government which is their heritage. Already the plunderers, availing themselves of the importation of cheap labor, without thought of replanting, have recklessly swept away great forests, wantonly careless of provision for those who are to come after them, and thus leave, as their fitting memorial, vast reaches of barren acres and a diminished water supply. Already they have brought in hordes of the witless, so that now millions of our voters are mental children. Their dividends we pay in the children's resources, in the children's happiness, and in the children's minds and souls. Evil communications corrupt.

Arise—stand alert—trifle no more with Opportunity. She knocks but once. Repeal our naturalization laws; bar out the feeble-minded, the vicious, and the debased; secure our children and our children's children in their legitimate birthright.

Source:
Charles W. Gould, *America: A Family Matter* (New York: Scribner's, 1922), pp. 160–65.

102

Shall We Maintain Washington's Ideal of Americanism?

BY HENRY FAIRFIELD OSBORN

The paleontologist Henry Fairfield Osborn (1857–1935) taught at Princeton and Columbia, and was president of the New York Zoological Society. A prolific author, Osborn in his later years developed an antipathy toward immigrants. In the following essay, first published in Eugenics, Genetics and the Family *in 1923 and reprinted in Madison Grant's anthology* The Alien in Our Midst *(1930), Osborn asserts that immigrants are responsible for a decline in morals and standards of conduct.*

RACIAL PREFERENCES, RACIAL LOYALTY and racial pride are not bounded by the relatively brief six thousand year period of the history of man but extend infinitely further back into the aeons of human prehistory. While among the finest of human characteristics, while essential to racial preservation, they are often linked with almost equally profound religious prejudices and prepossessions so that in America we find ourselves confronted by two horns of a dilemma; if we are able to steer clear of racial pre-judgments, we are almost certain to run counter to religious prejudgments. This Scylla and Charybdis dilemma is the actual situation which confronts us today in all parts of the United States—namely, to maintain our own civilization despite these profound and unalterable instinctive sentiments which are often enhanced by contemporary social environment and religious education.

In New York, Boston and Chicago at the present moment there are accordingly three standards of right and wrong on almost every social and political question. It is not an exaggeration to say that there are three standards of integrity, of candour, of loyalty, of unselfishness, of individual liberty. Even among the highest and finest representatives of the Semitic race, there is a sense of cohesion and racial solidarity, which may or may not be strengthened by religious aloofness; which affects the judgment in the choice of educators as well as acceptance or rejection of distinctively Christian doctrines; which sets up almost insurmountable religious barriers; which influences the selection of representatives in Congress, of judges, of superintendents of schools; which gives a bias to the control of immigration, which is reflected in the attitude of the press, in the conduct of the stage, in many of the most essential features of our civilization. Similarly there is the religious bias of the fundamentalist, Catholic or Protestant, which also enters into the choice of superintendents of schools, into the selection of social and political leaders, into the municipal and national conduct of education, on the one hand in the exclusion from our public schools of certain forms or religions which were inculcated by the founders of the republic, on the other hand in the taking out of our public schools of a large element of our youthful population for purposes of religious control and education.

A house divided against itself shall fall. There are real dangers to a representative government like our own in these new definitions and conceptions of the ancient watchwords, liberty and equality, which were formulated in the minds of the founders of our republic to express the ideals of a relatively pure single race. Whenever a voice is raised against this *alienation* of the original American standards the speaker is at once charged with religious or racial prejudice and the attempt is made to blind our reason, to stifle our conscience, to alter the original concept of true Americanism by an appeal to emotion rather than by calm and rational vision of things as they really are. I love the ideals of our founders. I cling to the preservation of their interpretation of the magic watchwords of democracy. At the same time I recognize that splendid qualities may be found in other racial stocks and splendid contributions made by them to human progress, but I do not confuse this dispassionate admiration of the fine qualities of people of other races, other origins, other religions than my own, with the notions that true Americanism was derived from these other stocks or races, or that true Americanism can survive wherever its original principles are *alienated* by the influx of foreign elements which have different definitions for each of the great watchwords of human freedom.

In face of the increasing tide of Oriental and decadent European influence in current literature, in some sections of the daily and weekly press, in the "movies" and on the stage, we witness with alarm in all the smaller as well as the larger social centers in America the decline of original American standards of life, of conduct, of Sabbath observance, of the marriage relation. The entire control of the "movie" industry and the larger part of the control of the stage industry in the United States are now in the hands of people of near or remote Oriental origin. It is no exaggeration to say that there has been a complete revolution in the standards of the popular stage in fifty years. Ridiculing religion, modesty and chastity, substituting European for American ideals of love and marriage, grossly decadent and dissolute librettos saved only from obscenity by the occasional hand of the censor, ridiculed as Puritanism the original American standards are all insidiously tending toward moral decadence. A people must be judged by its press, by its literature and by its stage. Such judgment at the present time cannot be expressed in terms of optimism.

If we observe what is going on in our large cities in which the original American element has entirely lost control and the alien or foreign-born element is in absolute power, we note that every social and educational question which arises is judged from three different aspects rather than from a united American aspect. Apart from the spiritual, moral and political invasion of *alienism* the practical question of day by day competition between the original American and the alien element turns upon the struggle for existence between the Americans and the aliens whose actions are controlled by entirely different standards of living and of morals. In hundreds of small and large communities in all parts of this country the American is driven out of the smaller branches of business and trade and of property transactions because he will not adopt the mode of life or stoop to the illegal methods resorted to by the alien. It is only in the larger and more constructive affairs of business that the American element is maintaining its original supremacy and leadership.

Our right and duty to maintain the predominance of our own race through the regulation of immigration and the very careful selection of the new peoples entering our borders are not for a moment to be confused with racial prejudice, with narrow sectarianism or with religious and social bigotry. The American people, partly through sad experience, have become conscious of their own great heritage and determined to maintain the high standards of that heritage. We are avoiding the same insidious sources of national decadence and decline which undermined the great ancient republics of Greece and Rome. From their downfall we have learned what we now feel compelled to avoid despite the appeals of false humanitarianism and of false sentimentality.

Thus after more than a century of experience we see clearly the profound wisdom of George Washington in warning his countrymen against the influx of alien ideas and ideals. The benefits of this awakening of the national consciousness will not be instantly visible, but years hence we shall see the rebirth of America.

Source:
Henry Fairfield Osborn, "Shall We
Maintain Washington's Ideal of
Americanism?" (1923), in *The Alien in Our
Midst,* edited by Madison Grant and Charles
Stewart Davison (New York: Galton
Publishing Co., 1930), pp. 205–9.

103

The Melting-Pot Mistake

BY HENRY PRATT FAIRCHILD

Henry Pratt Fairchild (1880–1956) taught at Yale and New York University, and wrote several textbooks on economics and sociology. He was the special immigration agent in Europe for the U.S. Department of Labor. Immigration: A World Movement and Its American Significance *(1913) was his first treatise on immigration, and it was followed by* The Melting-Pot Mistake *(1926). Here Fairchild likens a nation to a tree and immigrants to parasites who sap its vitality.*

IT HAS BEEN REPEATEDLY STATED that the consequence of nonassimilation is the destruction of nationality. This is the central truth of the whole problem of immigration and it cannot be overemphasized. An immigration movement that did not involve nonassimilation might be tolerated, though it might have other evil consequences which would condemn it. But an immigration movement that does involve nonassimilation—like the movement to the United States during the last fifty years at least—is a blow at the very heart of nationality and can not be endured if nationality is conceived to have any value whatsoever. The American nationality has already been compared to a plant. There is, indeed, a striking parallelism between a nation and a noble tree—for instance, one of our own incomparable redwoods—which may be followed a little further, not with any expectation or desire of popularizing a new symbol, but merely for the clarification that it affords.

A nation, like a tree, is a living vital thing. Growth is one of its conditions of life, and when it ceases to grow there is good reason to fear that it is about to decay and die. Every nation, like every tree, belongs to a certain general type, but it is also uniquely individual within that type. Its peculiar form is determined by various forces, some of which are internal and some external. No nation need fear the changes which come as the result of the operation of natural, wholesome internal forces, that is to say, the ideas and activities of its own true members. These forces may, in the course of time, produce a form and character wholly different from the original, just as the mature plant may have an entirely different aspect from the seedling. This is nothing to be dreaded or opposed. No change that represents the natural evolution of internal forces need be dreaded. But there are other forces which originate without which threaten not only the form and character but also the vigor and perhaps the very life of the nation. Some of these are the forcible attacks of other nations, like the crowding of trees upon each other, or the unwholesome influence of alien ideas which may be compared with harsh and uncongenial winds which blow upon trees, dwarfing and distorting them.

Most dangerous of all however, are those foreign forces which, among trees, are represented by minute hostile organisms that make their way into the very tissue of the tree itself and feed upon its life substances, and among nations to alien individuals who are accepted as immigrants and by a process of "boring from within" (in something much more than a mere trade-union sense) sap the very vitality of their host. In so doing the immigrants may be merely following out their natural and defensible impulses without any hostility toward the receiving nation, any more than the parasites upon a tree may be considered to have any hostility to the tree. Nor can the immigrants, any more than the parasites, be expected to foresee that their activities will eventually destroy the very organism upon which they depend for their existence. The simple fact is that they are alien particles, not assimilated, and therefore wholly different from the foreign particles which the tree takes in the form of food, and transforms into cells of its own body. . . .

It actually seems as if each nation developed an immunity to certain ideas, just as the trees in a given locality develop a practical immunity to the pests of their own vicinity. Our own Department of Agriculture is constantly on the alert to prevent the introduction of foreign parasites against which our native plants have no effective protection. Numerous cases are on record—one of the most spectacular being the chestnut trees of New England—where a type of plant which from time immemorial had been able to hold its own in its native balance of nature has been devastated if not exterminated by the sudden introduction of a parasite against which it had not developed a means of protection. So in a nation, ideas are constantly circulating which are inherently destructive, but against which the natives have developed an adequate protection so that they produce no serious harm. But the sudden entrance of new ideas or of foreign varieties of old ideas may find the country unprepared to counteract them. The safest way to guard against such a calamity is to reduce to a small figure the number of those newcomers by which such alien ideas may be introduced. . . .

The central factor in the world organization of the present is nationalism. Strong, self-conscious nationalities are indispensable to the efficient ordering and peaceful promotion of international relations. Every well-developed nationality is a priceless product of social evolution. Each has its peculiar contribution to make to future progress. The destruction of any one would be an irreparable loss to mankind.

Among the nations of the world America stands out unique, and in many ways preëminent. Favored by Nature above all other nations in her physical endowment, favored by history in the character of her people and the type of her institutions, she has a rôle to play in the development of human affairs which no other nation can play. Foremost in this rôle is the development of true democracy. In America the stage is set more favorably than anywhere else for the great drama of the common man. Here if anywhere the conditions are auspicious for the upward movement of the masses. If democracy fails in America, where shall we look for it to succeed? Any program or policy which interferes in the slightest degree with the prosecution of this great enterprise must be condemned as treason to our high destiny. Any yielding to a specious and superficial humanitarianism which threatens the material, political, and social standards of the average American must be branded as a violation of our trust. The highest service of America to mankind is to point the way, to demonstrate the possibilities, to lead onward to the goal of human happiness. Any force that tends to impair our capacity for leadership is a menace to mankind and a flagrant violation of the spirit of liberalism.

Unrestricted immigration was such a force. It was slowly, insidiously, irresistibly eating away the very heart of the United States. What was being melted in the great Melting Pot, losing all form and symmetry, all beauty and character, all nobility and usefulness, was the American nationality itself. Let the justification for checking this force for all time be voiced in the words of two distinguished foreigners. First, Rabbi Joel Blau: "The chief duty that a people owes both itself and the world is reverence for its own soul, the mystic centre of its being." Then, Gustave LeBon: "A preponderating influence of foreigners is a sure solvent of the existence of States. It takes away from a people its most precious possession—its soul."

Source:
Henry Pratt Fairchild, *The Melting-Pot Mistake*
(Boston: Little, Brown, 1926), pp. 253–57, 259–61.

104

America, Nation or Confusion

BY EDWARD R. LEWIS

Even after the passage of the Immigration Act of 1924, polemicists contin-ued their attacks on immigrants. Edward Rieman Lewis (1886–?), author of several pamphlets for the Immigration Restriction Association of Chicago, wrote America, Nation or Confusion *(1928), in which he asserts that likemindedness is more likely to breed social and intellectual variety and that racial diversity will result in uniformity.*

LIKE-MINDEDNESS AND COMMON TRADITIONS will not entail a dull uniformity, the suppression of all variety and originality. The England of Elizabeth was coherent and yet it flowered with amazing beauty and diversity of expression. The England of Shakespeare, Ben Jonson, Beaumont and Fletcher and Marlowe, was not dull and uniform. The England of Victoria was coherent, but the country that produced Tennyson, Browning, Dickens, Thackeray, Kipling and Stevenson was not dull and uniform. The France of Louis Fourteenth was coherent but the country that produced Molière, Racine, La Fontaine, La Bruyère and La Rochefoucauld was not dull and uniform. In fact, racial diversity is more likely to breed uniformity than is like-mindedness, for when we are racially diverse it is only on a low level that we can understand each other. Diversity of standards and background, means, in politics, the newspaper. The movie, that we must appeal to the masses on a low common denominator. Like-mindedness gives genius a chance to be understood in the bigger and deeper things as well as the obvious. Like-mindedness gives originality and variety a chance. Racial diversity stifles them.

We may profit by moderate change. Small accretions will only enrich us. Mass increases may swamp us. We can afford to take small groups as England took the Huguenots and the Flemish. We cannot afford to take immigrants as Gaul took the Franks, or as Rome took the Teutonic hordes. We may take accretions as a river takes in the brooks and rivulets along its course. But if we take immigration as the Mississippi takes in the Missouri, we will become a different nation just as the Mississippi, clear and unified above St. Louis, is a different stream after it is joined by the muddy Missouri. Its name is the same, as our name would be the same, but it is a different river, and we would be a different nation.

The essential, the crucial fact, emphasized all through this book, then, has been not the inferiority of the new immigration to the old, or to the colonial stock, but their numbers and their difference. We do not criticize them for their difference. They cannot help it. But we can criticize a fatuous and cowardly politics which will not see the tragic effects of difference when multiplied by overwhelming numbers. After all, the blame for hyphenism is less on the hyphenates than on our mad immigration policy. Being different and coming in great masses, they have threatened our unity. Being different and continuing to come in great masses, they will in the end destroy our unity. The essential object we should have is to preserve our unity. All who realize that danger should agree on our object. When we are asked, therefore, by what right those who came first can exclude others, the reply can only be by the right that they have made a nation, and that the existence of that nation for them and for those who came later is threatened by disunion and diversity. The country will not be a haven or a beacon-light for native or immigrant if it is not maintained a country.

Source:
Edward R. Lewis, *America, Nation or Confusion: A Study of Our Immigration Problems* (New York: Harper & Brothers, 1928), pp. 406–8.

105

"America Must Return to Fundamentals"

BY CAPTAIN EDDIE RICKENBACKER

Edward Vernon Rickenbacker (1890–1973) was commander of the first American air force unit to operate on the Western front in World War I (1917–18). Rickenbacker was one of the most decorated soldiers in the U.S. Army, receiving the Distinguished Service Cross and the Congressional Medal of Honor. He was president of Eastern Airlines from 1938 to 1953 and chairman of the board from 1954 to 1963. In a speech delivered before the Executives' Club of Chicago on December 12, 1946, Rickenbacker opposed the reception of refugees following World War II, maintaining that many of them are communists.

... WE HAVE REACHED A POINT where it becomes essential to take some inventory of our country and reexamine the character and caliber of the immigrants who have accumulated in this country during the past twenty years, including the war years.

I mean specifically the kind of immigrants who do not call themselves immigrants, but call themselves refugees. Now according to Webster a refugee is one who flees to a refuge, especially one who flees from persecution or political danger to a foreign land.

By this label these refugees, as a class, would be entitled to our sympathy and our hospitality and I dare say without reservation that they have been the recipients of both. Many of them, in fact, large numbers of them have been entitled to the sanctuary they have found here, but on the other hand, under the guise of refugees, vast forces of dissension have established beachheads along our Eastern and Western Seaboards and now are driving their underground, undercover and un-American invasion clear across the country from both fronts.

It would be easy to resist this invasion if it had a single European national source, but the sinister agents within the refugee army come from many European countries, although they represent only one single cause—Communism.

They are here to destroy the very freedom that the immigrants of yesterday and of yesteryears came to enjoy; namely, freedom of politics, freedom of religion, freedom of opportunity, freedom from oppression, and freedom from poverty.

The prewar immigrants from way back came to build America, our canals, our highways, our cities, our industries, and our railroads. They came to dig mines, to cultivate the soil, to drill for oil, to cut timber, and build homes for themselves, their children and their children's children.

Most of them couldn't speak English, but they all knew one word and that word was "Gimme." It meant give me work, give me opportunity, give me a chance. Nowadays, to the new brand of immigrants it means, "Gimme what you got or else." . . .

It is time to stop the breach. It is time to plug the leak. It is time to take steps against undeserving aliens, and by those I mean hostile aliens who are now in this country, aliens who are horsemen of the modern Apocalypse of intolerance, division, hate, suspicion, and strife; aliens who are devoted agents of Old World dictators, and who fight not only against the Four Freedoms but any kind of human dignity.

Let us close our doors against these enemies of freedom. Let us send those who are here back to the land from which they came. Let us add a postscript to the Atlantic Charter in the form of a one-way passage back across the Atlantic for this motley crew.

Source:
Captain Eddie Rickenbacker, "'America
Must Return to Fundamentals,'"
Vital Speeches of the Day 13, no. 7
(January 15, 1947): 211.

106

Keeping
America American

BY POLITICUS

The American Mercury, founded by H. L. Mencken and George Jean Nathan in 1924, began as a distinguished monthly magazine discussing significant literary, political, and social issues. By the 1950s it had degenerated into a narrow and parochial organ of polemics. In "Keeping America American," a writer using the pseudonym "Politicus" criticizes the reception of "DPs" (displaced persons following World War II) and the flood of illegal aliens.

UNDER THE BLUDGEONING of the minority groups and their political allies, the immigration policies of the United States remain in continuous insecurity. So far, the immigration restrictionist sentiment of Congress has been an effective safeguard against the wrecking of our policies. This sentiment undoubtedly reflects the attitudes of the general population. However, with skilled propaganda by the minority groups continually increasing, the nation cannot depend upon the permanent continuance of these grassroots attitudes.

The most disquieting aspect of this continuous anti-restriction ballyhoo is that it discredits the conscientious efforts of immigration and visa officials to protect the United States against Communist infiltration. The screening procedures of the Immigration Service are continuously under fire. Under the guise of humanitarianism, the emphasis is upon haste rather than vigilance against Communism. Through the successive DP and refugee special provisions, thousands of Communists and

Communist sympathizers have slipped past our immigration safeguards. They are now in the United States—a dangerous and unpredictable element in any future American crisis. Any attempt to weed them out meets with the noisy and indignant outcry of the swarm of "Liberal" and minority group organizations now in the field. With the Cold War still unwon, the United States is recklessly admitting enemy agents to mingle purposefully with our foreign-born population.

The irresponsible administration of DP admissions takes on a more serious light when seen against the background of outright illegal immigration. It is estimated that aliens now illegally in the United States number between three and five million persons. These gatecrashers win admittance to the United States in various ways. Some smuggle themselves across the Mexico and Canadian borders. Some slip through the net by entering as seamen and jumping ship. Every year, 2,000,000 alien seamen visit the United States. In this number are enemy agents and flagrantly un-American elements. Another break in the dike results from the admission each year of 1,000,000 temporary visitors. Another means of ingress is to slip in among the 50,000 Puerto Rican immigrants who swarm in each year. As American citizens, Puerto Ricans are under no quota or exclusion provisions. How many of these unrecorded aliens in our midst are potential Red saboteurs is a sobering question for Americans. This grim underside of the picture is overlooked by those who fatuously center attention upon the weakening of our immigration safeguards.

Source:
Politicus, "Keeping America American,"
American Mercury 438 (July 1960): 19–20.

107

America's Scapegoats

BY CHANG-LIN TIEN

A variety of recent developments—including movements to enforce the use of English only in state and local governments, legislation depriving legal immigrants of social services, and repeated calls to limit immigration—testifies to continuing prejudice against immigrants in this country. In the following editorial published in Newsweek *for October 31, 1994, Chang-Lin Tien (b. 1935), A. Martin Berlin Professor of Mechanical Engineering and chancellor of the University of California at Berkeley, speaks of his own life as an immigrant and urges Americans not to blame immigrants for the racial problems that continue to beset the nation.*

MY LIFE HAS BEEN FAR MORE SATISFYING than I dreamed possible when I arrived in the United States, 38 years ago. I am privileged to head a world-class institution, the University of California, Berkeley. My former Ph.D. students are professors at major universities. My engineering research has contributed to America's space technology, nuclear-reactor safety and energy technology.

Yet no matter the scope of my accomplishments, when many Americans see my face and hear my Chinese accent, they think of me as an immigrant, first and foremost. In the eyes of many, that has come to mean a drain on public services, a competitor for jobs and a threat to a cohesive society.

I have watched the campaign to discourage immigration with growing concern. Whether we preside over universities or work the fields, immigrants are becoming the scapegoats for America's ills. I don't object to controlling the volume of immigration. Today, with unprecedented shifts in the global population, no nation can afford to throw its borders wide open. But we are in danger of forgetting that America was built by immigrants, and that our immigrant heritage is the wellspring of our nation's strength and vitality.

Even as a university chancellor, I am no stranger to the sharp sting of anti-immigrant hostility. Perhaps the most dramatic incident took place when I represented Berkeley a few years ago at a football rally after the Citrus Bowl. As I walked to the stage, a few people in the audience chanted, "Buy American, Buy American." This was profoundly disturbing. I am American and proud of it.

Just looking like an immigrant can make you the target of heckling. Any of us of Asian, Latin American and Middle Eastern heritage knows this. Several friends and family members have been subjected to taunts of "Go back to your own country." It's difficult for them to respond; like Bruce Springsteen, they were born in the U.S.A. This anti-immigrant mood is not new. Throughout our history, whenever the economy suffered, immigrants became easy targets. But today it is not only the immigrants who suffer. Ultimately, all Americans stand to lose, native and foreign born alike.

Now our nation faces the formidable challenge of forging a unified society from highly diverse constituencies. The population is undergoing a rapid transformation, and by the middle of the 21st century, the majority of Americans will trace their roots to Latin America, Africa, Asia, the Middle East and the Pacific Islands.

Evolving into a cohesive society based on respect and understanding is far from automatic. Throughout human history, racial and ethnic tensions have divided and destroyed peoples and countries. The ethnic strife that ripped apart Brooklyn's Crown Heights and South-Central Los Angeles is a sobering reminder of the challenge posed by rapid diversification.

Yet if there is a nation that promises to be a model for how to make diversity work, it is the United States. This is the nation with the strongest and deepest democratic roots. This is a nation with a living Constitution that guarantees rights to all its citizens. This is a nation that has taken pride not in its homogeneity, but in its immigrant heritage.

It was America's promise that drew me here in 1956. Even as a penniless graduate student from China, I believed I could make a contribution in this land of opportunity. Indeed, I am deeply grateful to America for offering opportunities difficult to find anywhere else in the world.

Today, however, in the headlong rush to restrict immigration, we are jeopardizing this promise. Hundreds of state and federal measures have been introduced to curb legal and illegal immigration. The backers of these proposals often rely on inflammatory anti-immigrant rhetoric to rivet the attention of Americans, ignite their rage and move them to action.

In the hoopla, the debate is now moving away from the legitimate question of how much immigration America can sustain. Instead, we're blaming immigrants for many of our most urgent problems and trying to convince ourselves that we'll solve them by simply restricting immigration.

Effective immigration policy must be grounded in reason, not emotion. Racial and cultural hostilities fanned by the present anti-immigration frenzy must cool down. Then I am confident we can make immigration work for America, just as it has from the time of our nation's infancy.

After all, in my 38 years here, I have seen this nation make amazing progress. When I came here to study in the South, I encountered Jim Crow segregation. Whites rode in the front of buses and blacks in the back. This racial system did not apply to Asian Americans and left us in an ugly limbo. It troubled me and left a lifelong impression. The rest of the country was not free from racial discrimination. When I joined the Berkeley faculty, in 1959, my wife and I could not live in certain Bay Area neighborhoods.

In less than four decades, I have seen the enactment of civil-rights legislation that has created opportunities for all Americans. I have seen universities open doors to students who reflect our diverse society. I have seen women and men of all backgrounds become leaders in government, business, science, arts and education. Now I look forward to seeing the promise of America fulfilled. We can turn our national motto of *e pluribus unum,* or "one out of many," into more than an expression in a dead language. What it will take is the same kind of unwavering commitment that forged one nation from highly diverse colonies more than two centuries ago.

Immigrants are not the cause of America's major problems. It's time America stopped putting all the blame on immigrants and started facing up to the difficult reality of a world in transition. Let's seize the opportunity to transform America into a model of diversity for the future.

Source:
Chang-Lin Tien, "America's Scapegoats,"
Newsweek, October 31, 1994, p. 19.

Notes

Foreword

1. Visiting Professor, New York University Law School. Bell is the author of several books on race, including *Faces at the Bottom of the Well: The Permanence of Racism*.

2. Beverly Daniel Tatum, *Why Are All the Black Kids Sitting Together in the Cafeteria?* (Basic Books, 1997).

3. *Race Traitor*, Noel Ignatiev, editor, P.O. Box 603, Cambridge, MA 02140-0005.

4. Pamela Burdman, "Scholars Gather in Berkeley to Talk About Whiteness in Three-Day Meeting on UC Campus," *The San Francisco Chronicle* April 12, 1997, p. A7

5. Howard Winant, "Racial Dualism at Century's End," in *The House That Race Built: Black Americans, U.S. Terrain*, ed. Wahneema Lubiano, (New York: Pantheon Books, 1997).

Introduction

1. Readers of this book will readily perceive my debt to Thomas F. Gossett's *Race: The History of an Idea in America* (1963), perhaps still the finest analysis of the evolution of American racial prejudice in all its forms and ramifications.

2. Kevin Sack, "Hate Groups in U.S. Are Growing, Report Says," *New York Times,* March 3, 1998, p. A10.

Chapter 1

1. The citation is from the work of Georges-Louis Leclerc, Comte de Buffon (1707–1788), against whom much of Jefferson's polemic is aimed.—S.T.J.

2. The reference is to the African-American poet Phillis Wheatley (c. 1753–1784).—S.T.J.

Chapter 3

1. Holmes refers to the "Maine Law" (1851), a highly restrictive law prohibiting the sale or consumption of alcoholic beverages in Maine.—S.T.J.

Chapter 4

1. The reference is to the *Germania* by the Roman historian Cornelius Tacitus (1st century C.E.)—S.T.J.

Part Two

1. François Bernier, "Nouvelle Division de la terre, par les differentes especes ou races d'hommes qui l'habitent, envoyée par un fameus voyageur à M. l'Abbé de la *** à peu près en ces termes," *Journal des Sçavans* (April 24, 1684), pp. 133–40.

2. For one of the best of these, see Richard C. Lewontin, "Race and Intelligence," *Bulletin of the Atomic Scientists* 26, no. 3 (March 1970): 2–8.

Chapter 17

1. See Walter Kaufmann, *Nietzsche: Philosopher, Psychologist, Antichrist* (Princeton: Princeton University Press, 1950; 4th ed. 1974), passim.

Part Four

1. Henry Clay, "Emancipation of the South American States" (March 24, 1818), in *The Speeches of Henry Clay,* ed. Calvin Colton (New York: A. S. Barnes & Co., 1857), vol. 1, p. 146.

Part Five

1. Theodore Roosevelt, "Race Decadence," *Outlook* (April 8, 1911), pp. 763–69.

Chapter 34

1. George M. Beard, *American Nervousness* (New York, 1881), p. 287.

2. David A. Wells, *Recent Economic Changes* (New York, 1889), pp. 348–349.

3. Charles Darwin, *The Descent of Man* (New York, 1888), p. 142.

4. George Rawlinson, "Duties of Higher Toward Lower Races," *Princeton Review* (November 1878), pp. 837, 840.

5. Horace Bushnell, *Christian Nurture* (New York, 1861), pp. 207, 213.

6. Charles Darwin, *The Descent of Man* (New York, 1871), p. 154.

7. James Anthony Froude, "Romanism and the Irish Race in the United States," *North American Review* 129 (December 1879), 535–536.

8. Rev. Nathaniel George Clark.

9. "Locksley Hall."

Part Seven

1. James Fenimore Cooper, *Notions of the Americans Picked Up by a Travelling Bachelor* (London: Henry Colburn, 1828), vol. 1, pp. 277, 282.

Chapter 39

1. Hist. of Amer. (Anon.), p. 77.
2. Dobrizhoffer, Abipones, II, p. 55.

Chapter 42

1. Annual Report of Indian Commissioner for 1872.

Part Eight

1. Thomas F. Gossett, *Race: The History of an Idea in America* (Dallas, TX: Southern Methodist University Press, 1963), p. 270.

Chapter 43

1. Observations de Physique et de Medicine faites en differens lieux de l'Espagne. vol. ii. p. 130.
2. Studies of Nature, vol. ii. p. 2.
3. Treatise upon Tropical Diseases, p. 475.
4. Surgical and medical treatises upon various subjects respecting Poland.
5. Letters on Iceland, p. 122.
6. Mr. Thomas Harrison.

Chapter 51

1. Max Mueller, "The Savage."

Chapter 61

1. Tanya E. Coke, Note: "Lady Justice May Be Blind, but Is She a Soul Sister? Race Neutrality and the Ideal of Representative Juries," 69 *N.Y.U.L. Rev.* 327, 354–55 (1994).
2. Ibid.
3. Ibid., p. 355; *Wilmington News Journal,* Oct. 5, 1995.
4. *St. Louis Post-Dispatch,* Oct. 8, 1995, p. 2B; *Providence Journal-Bulletin,* Oct. 10, 1995, p. 4B; *Chicago Sun-Times,* Oct. 5, 1995, p. 41.

Chapter 63

1. Gregoire on the Reformation of the Jews, p. 40.
2. Adam's Religious World Displayed, vol. i, p. 80.

3. M. Berr Isaac Berr, a celebrated literary Jew, in a letter addressed to his brethren, 1791, observes, "we have been in a manner compelled to abandon the pursuit of all moral and physical sciences, of all sciences in short, which tend to the improvement of the mind, in order to devote ourselves entirely to commerce, to be enabled to gather as much money as would ensure protection and satisfy the rapacity of our persecutors."—*Transactions of the Sanhedrim of Paris,* p. 14.

Chapter 66

1. Twain deliberately treats points 3 and 4 in reverse order.—S.T.J.

Chapter 73

1. Smith proceeds to make a long list of Jewish individuals in the government. —S.T.J.

Chapter 80

1. Words in brackets were added by the editors of *Harper's.*—S.T.J.

Chapter 100

1. Edwin Grant Conklin, "Some Biological Aspects of Immigration," Scribner's, 1921.

Bibliography

Some Overviews

Allport, Gordon W. *The Nature of Prejudice*. Cambridge, MA: Addison-Wesley, 1954.

Aptheker, Herbert. *Anti-Racism in U.S. History: The First Two Hundred Years*. Westport, CT: Greenwood Press, 1992.

Bar-Tal, Daniel, et al., eds. *Stereotyping and Prejudice: Changing Conceptions*. New York: Springer-Verlag, 1989.

Berry, Wendell. *The Great Wound*. Boston: Houghton Mifflin, 1970.

Brown, Rupert. *Prejudice: Its Social Psychology*. Oxford: Basil Blackwell, 1995.

Dijk, Teun A. Van. *Communicating Racism: Ethnic Prejudice in Thought and Talk*. Newbury Park, CA: Sage, 1987.

Duckitt, J. H. *The Social Psychology of Prejudice*. New York: Praeger, 1992.

Dyer, Thomas G. *Theodore Roosevelt and the Idea of Race*. Baton Rouge: Louisiana State University Press, 1980.

Feldstein, Stanley, ed. *The Poisoned Tongue: A Documentary History of American Racism and Prejudice*. New York: Morrow, 1972.

Field, Geoffrey C. *Evangelist of Race: The Germanic Vision of Houston Stewart Chamberlain*. New York: Columbia University Press, 1981.

Flynn, Kevin, and Gary Gerhardt. *The Silent Brotherhood: Inside America's Racist Underground*. New York: Free Press, 1989.

Frederickson, George M. *White Supremacy: A Comparative Study in American and South African History*. New York: Oxford University Press, 1981.

Gioseffi, Daniela, ed. *On Prejudice: A Global Perspective*. New York: Anchor, 1993.

Goldberg, David Theo, ed. *Anatomy of Racism*. Minneapolis: University of Minnesota Press, 1990.

Gossett, Thomas F. *Race: The History of an Idea in America*. Dallas, TX Southern Methodist University Press, 1963.

Handlin, Oscar. *Race and Nationality in American Life*. Boston: Little, Brown, 1957.

Hannaford, Ivan. *Race: The History of an Idea in the West*. Washington, DC: Woodrow Wilson Center Press, 1996.

Huckfeldt, R. Robert. *Race and the Decline of Class in American Politics.* Urbana: University of Illinois Press, 1989.

Jones, James M. *Prejudice and Racism.* New York: Random House, 1972.

Kleg, Milton. *Hate, Prejudice, and Racism.* Albany: State University of New York Press, 1993.

Kovel, Joel. *White Racism: A Psychohistory.* New York: Pantheon, 1970.

Levin, Jack, and William C. Levin. *The Functions of Discrimination and Prejudice.* 2nd ed. New York: Harper & Row, 1982.

Lyman, Stanford M. *Color, Culture, Civilization: Race and Minority Issues in American Society.* Urbana: University of Illinois Press, 1994.

McPhail, Mark Lawrence. *The Rhetoric of Racism.* Lanham, MD: University Press of America, 1994.

Malik, Kenan. *The Meaning of Race: Race, History and Culture in Western Society.* New York: New York University Press, 1996.

Miller, John Chester. *The Wolf by the Ears: Thomas Jefferson and Slavery.* New York: Free Press, 1977.

Perlmutter, Philip. *Divided We Fall: A History of Ethnic, Religious, and Racial Prejudice in America.* Ames: Iowa State University Press, 1992.

Pincus, Fred L., and Howard J. Ehrlich, eds. *Race and Ethnic Conflict: Contending Views on Prejudice, Discrimination, and Ethnoviolence.* Boulder, CO: Westview Press, 1994.

Roediger, David R. *The Wages of Whiteness: Race and the Making of the American Working Class.* London: Verso, 1991.

Rothenberg, Paula S., ed. *Race, Class, and Gender in the United States: An Integrated Study.* 3rd ed. New York: St. Martin's Press, 1995.

Rowan, Carl T. *The Coming Race War in America: A Wake-Up Call.* Boston: Little, Brown, 1996.

Sanders, Ronald. *Lost Tribes and Promised Lands: The Origins of American Racism.* Boston: Little, Brown, 1978.

Shepherd, George W., Jr., and David Penna, eds. *Racism and the Underclass: State Policy and Discrimination Against Minorities.* Westport, CT: Greenwood Press, 1991.

Simpson, George Eaton, and J. Milton Yinger. *Racial and Cultural Minorities: An Analysis of Prejudice and Discrimination.* 5th ed. New York: Plenum Press, 1985.

Smedley, Audrey. *Race in North America: Origin and Evolution of a Worldview.* Boulder, CO: Westview Press, 1993.

Snider, Paul M., and Thomas Piazza. *The Scar of Race.* Cambridge, MA: Harvard University Press, 1993.

Solomos, John, and Les Back. *Racism and Society.* New York: St. Martin's Press, 1996.

Sowell, Thomas. *Race and Culture: A World View.* New York: BasicBooks, 1994.

Taylor, Jared. *Paved with Good Intentions: The Failure of Race Relations in Contemporary America.* New York: Carroll & Graf, 1992.

Van Dyke, Vernon. *Human Rights, Ethnicity, and Discrimination.* Westport, CT: Greenwood Press, 1985.

Vaughan, Alden T. *The Roots of American Racism: Essays on the Colonial Experience.* New York: Oxford University Press, 1995.

Wellman, David T. *Portraits of White Racism.* Cambridge: Cambridge University Press, 1977.

West, Cornell. *Race Matters.* Boston: Beacon Press, 1993.

Wetherell, Margaret, and Jonathan Potter. *Mapping the Language of Racism: Discourse and the Legitimation of Exploitation.* New York: Columbia University Press, 1992.

Young-Bruehl, Elizabeth. *The Anatomy of Prejudices.* Cambridge, MA: Harvard University Press, 1996.

Science and Pseudo-Science

Banton, Michael P. *Racial Theories.* Cambridge: Cambridge University Press, 1987.

Barkan, Elazar. *Retreat of Scientific Racism: Changing Concepts of Race in Britain and the United States Between the World Wars.* Cambridge: Cambridge University Press, 1992.

Biddis, Michael D. *Father of Racist Ideology: The Social and Political Thought of Count Gobineau.* New York: Weybright & Talley, 1970.

Eckberg, Douglas Lee. *Intelligence and Race: The Origins and Dimensions of the IQ Controversy.* New York: Praeger, 1978.

Ehrlich, Paul R., and S. Shirley Feldman. *The Race Bomb: Skin Color, Prejudice, and Intelligence.* New York: Quadrangle/New York Times Book Co., 1977.

Fraser, Steven, ed. *The Bell Curve Wars: Race, Intelligence, and the Future of America.* New York: BasicBooks, 1995.

Gates, E. Nathaniel, ed. *Racial Classification and History.* New York: Garland, 1997.

Grover, Sonja C. *The Cognitive Basis of the Intellect: A Response to Jensen's Bias in Mental Testing.* Washington, DC: University Press of America, 1981.

Haller, John S. *Outcasts from Evolution: Scientific Attitudes of Racial Inferiority, 1859–1900.* Urbana: University of Illinois Press, 1971.

Jacoby, Russell, and Naomi Glauberman, eds. *The Bell Curve Debate: History, Documents, Opinions.* New York: Times Books, 1995.

Joseph, Andre. *Intelligence, IQ, and Race: When, How, and Why They Became Associated.* San Francis: R & E Research Associates, 1977.

Katz, Irwin, and Patricia Gurin, eds. *Race and the Social Sciences.* New York: BasicBooks, 1969.

Kincheloe, Joe L.; Shirley R. Steinberg; and Aaron D. Gresson III, eds. *Measured Lies: The Bell Curve Examined.* New York: St. Martin's Press, 1996.

King, James C. *The Biology of Race.* Berkeley: University of California Press, 1981.

Kohn, Marek. *The Race Gallery: The Return of Racial Science.* London: Jonathan Cape, 1995.

Lawler, James M. *IQ, Heritability, and Racism.* New York: International, 1978.

Loehlin, John C.; Gardner Lindzey; and J. N. Spuhler. *Race Differences in Intelligence*. San Francisco: W. H. Freeman, 1975.

Mead, Margaret, et al. *Science and the Concept of Race*. New York: Columbia University Press, 1968.

Mensh, Elaine. *The IQ Mythology: Class, Race, Gender, and Inequality*. Carbondale: Southern Illinois University Press, 1991.

Mogdil, Sohan, and Celia Mogdil, eds. *Arthur Jensen: Consensus and Controversy*. London: Falmer Press, 1987.

Montagu, Ashley, ed. *Race and IQ*. New York: Oxford University Press, 1975.

Shipman, Pat. *The Evolution of Racism: Human Differences and the Use and Abuse of Science*. New York: Simon & Schuster, 1994.

Stanton, William Ragan. *The Leopard's Spots: Scientific Attitudes Toward Race in America, 1815–59*. Chicago: University of Chicago Press, 1960.

Tobach, Ethel, and Harold M. Proshansky, eds. *Genetic Destiny: Race as a Scientific and Social Controversy*. New York: AMS Press, 1976.

Tucker, William H. *The Science and Politics of Racial Research*. Urbana: University of Illinois Press, 1994.

Williams, Vernon J. *Rethinking Racism: Franz Boas and His Contemporaries*. Lexington: University Press of Kentucky, 1996.

Wolpoff, Milford, and Rachel Caspari. *Race and Human Evolution*. New York: Simon & Schuster, 1997.

Aryans, Anglo-Saxons, and Teutons

Anderson, Stuart. *Race and Rapprochement: Anglo-Saxonism and Anglo-American Relations, 1895–1904*. Rutherford, NJ: Fairleigh Dickinson University Press, 1981.

Crapol, Edward P. *America for Americans: Economic Nationalism and Anglophobia in the Late Nineteenth Century*. Westport, CT: Greenwood Press, 1973.

Dangerfield, George. *The Awakening of American Nationalism, 1815–1828*. Prospect Heights, IL: Waveland Press, 1994.

Friedman, Lawrence J. *Inventors of the Promised Land*. New York: Knopf, 1975.

Gruver, Rebecca Brooks, ed. *American Nationalism, 1783–1830: A Self-Portrait*. New York: Putnam, 1970.

Kauffman, Bill. *America First!: Its History, Culture, and Politics*. Amherst, NY: Prometheus, 1995.

MacDougall, Hugh A. *Racial Myth in English History: Trojans, Teutons, and Anglo-Saxons*. Hanover, NH: University Press of New England, 1982.

Manifest Destiny and Imperialism

Beisner, Robert L. *Twelve Against Empire: The Anti-Imperialists, 1898–1900*. New York: McGraw-Hill, 1968.

Brack, Gene M. *Mexico Views Manifest Destiny, 1821–1846: An Essay on the Origins of the Mexican War.* Albuquerque: University of New Mexico Press, 1975.

Brown, Charles H. *Agents of Manifest Destiny: The Lives and Times of the Filibusters.* Chapel Hill: University of North Carolina Press, 1979.

Hietala, Thomas R. *Manifest Design: Anxious Aggrandizement in Late Jacksonian America.* Ithaca, NY: Cornell University Press, 1985.

Hitchens, Christopher. *Blood, Class, and Nostalgia: Anglo-American Ironies.* New York: Farrar, Straus & Giroux, 1990.

Horsman, Reginald. *Race and Manifest Destiny: The Origins of American Racial Anglo-Saxonism.* Cambridge, MA: Harvard University Press, 1981.

Kaplan, Amy, and Donald E. Pease, eds. *Cultures of United States Imperialism.* Durham, NC: Duke University Press, 1993.

Levine, Alan J. *Race Relations Within Western Expansion.* Westport, CT: Praeger, 1996.

Magdoff, Harry. *Imperialism: From the Colonial Age to the Present.* New York: Monthly Review Press, 1978.

Merk, Frederick, and Lois Bannister Merk. *Manifest Destiny and Mission in American History: A Reinterpretation.* New York: Knopf, 1963.

Pletcher, David M. *The Diplomacy of Annexation: Texas, Oregon, and the Mexican War.* Columbia: University of Missouri Press, 1973.

Stephanson, Anders. *Manifest Destiny: American Expansionism and the Empire of Right.* New York: Hill & Wang, 1995.

Tucker, Frank H. *The White Conscience.* New York: Ungar, 1969.

Weinberg, Albert K. *Manifest Destiny: A Study of Nationalist Expansionism in American History.* Baltimore, MD: Johns Hopkins Press, 1935.

Weston, Rubin Francis. *Racism in U.S. Imperialism: The Influence of Racial Assumptions on American Foreign Policy, 1893–1946.* Columbia: University of South Carolina Press, 1972.

Social Darwinism and Eugenics

Alexander, Richard D. *Darwinism and Human Affairs.* Seattle: University of Washington Press, 1979.

Bannister, Robert C. *Social Darwinism: Science and Myth in Anglo-American Social Thought.* Philadelphia: Temple University Press, 1979.

Chase, Allan. *The Legacy of Malthus: The Social Costs of the New Scientific Racism.* New York: Knopf, 1977.

Degler, Carl N. *In Search of Human Nature: The Decline and Revival of Darwinism in American Social Thought.* New York: Oxford University Press, 1991.

Duster, Troy. *Backdoor to Eugenics.* New York: Routledge, 1990.

Haller, Mark Hughlin. *Eugenics: Hereditarian Attitudes in American Thought.* New Brunswick, NJ: Rutgers University Press, 1963.

Hasian, Marouf Arif, Jr. *The Rhetoric of Eugenics in Anglo-American Thought.* Athens: University of Georgia Press, 1996.

Hofstadter, Richard. *Social Darwinism in American Thought.* Philadelphia: University of Pennsylvania Press, 1944.

Kevles, Daniel J. *In the Name of Eugenics: Genetics and the Uses of Human Heredity.* New York: Knopf, 1985.

Kuhl, Stefan. *The Nazi Connection: Eugenics, American Racism, and German National Socialism.* New York: Oxford University Press, 1994.

Larson, Edward J. *Sex, Race, and Science: Eugenics in the Deep South.* Baltimore, MD: Johns Hopkins University Press, 1995.

Packard, Vance. *The People Shapers.* Boston: Little, Brown, 1977.

Paul, Diane B. *Controlling Human Heredity: 1865 to the Present.* Atlantic Highlands, NJ: Humanities Press, 1995.

Pickens, Donald K. *Eugenics and the Progressives.* Nashville, TN: Vanderbilt University Press, 1968.

Shockley, William. *Shockley on Eugenics and Race: The Application of Science to the Solution of Human Problems.* Washington, DC: Scott-Townsend, 1992.

Prejudice and Religion

Aho, James A. *The Politics of Righteousness: Idaho Christian Patriotism.* Seattle: University of Washington Press, 1990.

Alvis, Joel L., Jr. *Religion and Race: Southern Presbyterians, 1946–1983.* Tuscaloosa: University of Alabama Press, 1994.

Barndt, Joseph R. *Dismantling Racism: The Continuing Challenge to White America.* Minneapolis, MN: Augsburg Fortress, 1991.

Davis, Lawrence B. *Immigrants, Baptists, and the Protestant Mind in America.* Urbana: University of Illinois Press, 1973.

Earl, Riggins R., Jr. *Dark Symbols, Obscure Signs: God, Self, and Community in the Slave Mind.* Maryknoll, NY: Orbis, 1993.

La Farge, John. *The Catholic Viewpoint on Race Relations.* Garden City, NY: Hanover House, 1956.

Lincoln, C. Eric. *Race, Religion, and the Continuing American Dilemma.* New York: Hill & Wang, 1984.

Luker, Ralph E. *The Social Gospel in Black and White: American Racial Reform, 1885–1912.* Chapel Hill: University of North Carolina Press, 1991.

McGreevy, John T. *Parish Boundaries: The Catholic Encounter with Race in the Twentieth-Century Urban North.* Chicago: University of Chicago Press, 1996.

Rausch, David A. *Fundamentalist-Evangelicals and Anti-Semitism.* Valley Forge, PA: Trinity Press International, 1993.

Smith, John David, ed. *The Biblical and "Scientific" Defense of Slavery.* New York: Garland, 1993.

Weatherford, Willis Duke. *American Churches and the Negro: An Historical Study from Early Slave Days to the Present.* Boston: Christopher Publishing House, 1957.

White, Ronald C., Jr. *Liberty and Justice for All: Racial Reform and the Social Gospel (1877–1925).* San Francisco: Harper & Row, 1990.

Wood, Forrest G. *The Arrogance of Faith: Christianity and Race in America from the Colonial Era to the Twentieth Century.* New York: Knopf, 1990.

Native Americans

Axtell, James. *The Invasion Within: The Contest of Cultures in Colonial America.* New York: Oxford University Press, 1985.

Berkhofer, Robert F., Jr. *The White Man's Indian: Images of the American Indian from Columbus to the Present.* New York: Knopf, 1978.

Beuf, Ann H. *Red Children in White Ameirca.* Philadelphia: University of Pennsylvania Press, 1977.

Bird, S. Elizabeth, ed. *Dressing in Feathers: The Construction of the Indian in American Popular Culture.* Boulder, CO: Westview Press, 1996.

Bordewich, Fergus M. *Killing the White Man's Indian: The Reinvention of Native Americans at the End of the 20th Century.* New York: Doubleday, 1996.

Bourne, Russell. *The Red King's Rebellion: Racial Politics in New England, 1675–1678.* New York: Atheneum, 1990.

Brandon, William. *The Last Americans: The Indian in American Culture.* New York: Hill & Wang, 1974.

Bray, Warwick, ed. *The Meeting of Two Worlds: Europe and the Americas, 1492–1650.* Oxford: British Academy/Oxford University Press, 1993.

Cook, Sherburne F. *The Conflict Between the California Indian and White Civilization.* Berkeley: University of California Press, 1976.

Crosby, Alfred W. *The Columbian Exchange: Biological and Cultural Consequences of 1492.* Westport, CT: Greenwood Press, 1972.

Daniel, Paul N., et al. *We Were Not the Savages: A Micmac Perspective on the Collision of European and Aboriginal Civilizations.* Halifax, NS: Nimbus, 1993.

Dowd, Gregory Evans. *A Spirited Resistance: The North American Indian Struggle for Unity, 1745–1815.* Baltimore, MD: Johns Hopkins University Press, 1992.

Drinnon, Richard. *Facing West: The Metaphysics of Indian-Hating and Empire Building.* Minneapolis: University of Minnesota Press, 1980.

Falkowski, James E. *Indian Law, Race Law: A Five-Hundred-Year History.* New York: Praeger, 1992.

French, Laurence Armand. *The Winds of Injustice: American Indians and the U.S. Government.* New York: Garland, 1994.

Harring, Sidney L. *Crow Dog's Case: American Indian Sovereignty, Tribal Law, and United States Law in the Nineteenth Century.* Cambridge: Cambridge University Press, 1994.

Heard, Joseph Norman. *White into Red: A Study of the Assimilation of White Persons Captured by Indians.* Metuchen, NJ: Scarecrow Press, 1973.

Heizer, Robert F., and Alan F. Almquist. *The Other Americans: Prejudice and Discrimination Under Spain, Mexico, and the United States to 1920.* Berkeley: University of California Press, 1971.

Highwater, Jamake. *Native Land: Sagas of the Indian Americas.* Boston: Little, Brown, 1986.

Hilger, Michael. *From Savage to Nobleman: Images of Native Americans in Film.* Metuchen, NJ: Scarecrow Press, 1995.

Horsman, Reginald. *Expansion and American Indian Policy, 1783–1812.* East Lansing: Michigan State University Press, 1967.

Hoxie, Frederick E. *A Final Promise: The Campaign to Assimilate the Indians, 1880–1920.* Lincoln: University of Nebraska Press, 1984.

Kehoe, Alice B. *North American Indians: A Comprehensive Account.* Englewood Cliffs, NJ: Prentice-Hall, 1981.

Koning, Hans. *The Conquest of America: How the Indian Nations Lost Their Continent.* New York: Monthly Review Press, 1993.

Larsen, Clark Spencer, and George R. Milner, eds. *In the Wake of Contact: Biological Responses to Conquest.* New York: Wiley-Liss, 1994.

Mander, Jerry. *In the Absence of the Sacred: The Failure of Technology and the Survival of the Indian Nations.* San Francisco: Sierra Club, 1991.

Mathes, Valerie Sherer. *Helen Hunt Jackson and Her Indian Reform Legacy.* Austin: University of Texas Press, 1990.

Monkman, Leslie. *A Native Heritage: Images of the Indian in English-Canadian Literature.* Toronto: University of Toronto Press 1981.

Ortiz, Roxanne Dunbar. *Indians of the Americas: Human Rights and Self-Determination.* New York: Praeger, 1984.

Oswalt, Wendell H. *This Land Was Theirs: A Study of the North American Indian.* New York: Wiley, 1966.

Pearce, Roy Harvey. *Savagism and Civilization: A Study of the Indian and the American Mind.* Berkeley: University of California Press, 1988.

Ramenofsky, Ann F. *Vectors of Death: The Archaeology of European Contact.* Albuquerque: University of New Mexico Press, 1987.

Rivera, Luis N. *A Violent Evangelism: The Political and Religious Conquest of the Americas.* Louisville, KY: Westminster/John Knox Press, 1992.

Rogin, Michael Paul. *Fathers and Children: Andrew Jackson and the Subjugation of the American Indian.* New York: Knopf, 1975.

Sandos, James A., and Larry E. Burgess. *The Hunt for Willie Boy: Indian-Hating and Popular Culture.* Norman: University of Oklahoma Press, 1994.

Saum, Lewis O. *The Fur Trader and the Indian.* Seattle: University of Washington Press, 1965.

Spicer, Edward Holland. *Cycles of Conquest: The Impact of Spain, Mexico, and the United States on the Indians of the Southwest, 1533–1960.* Tucson: University of Arizona Press, 1962.

Stannard, David E. *American Holocaust: Columbus and the Conquest of the New World.* New York: Oxford University Press, 1992.

Stedman, Raymond William. *Shadows of the Indian: Stereotypes in American Culture.* Norman: University of Oklahoma Press, 1982.

Steele, Ian K. *Warpaths: Invasions of North America.* Oxford: Oxford University Press, 1994.

Steiner, Stan. *The New Indians.* New York: Harper & Row, 1968.

Stern, Kenneth S. *Loud Hawk: The United States Versus the American Indian Movement.* Norman: University of Oklahoma Press, 1994.

Taylor, William B., and Franklin Pease, eds. *Violence, Resistance, and Survival in the Americas: Native Americans and the Legacy of Conquest.* Washington, DC: Smithsonian Institution Press, 1994.

Turner, Frederick. *Beyond Geography: The Western Spirit Against the Wilderness.* New Brunswick, NJ: Rutgers University Press, 1983.

Verano, John W., and Douglas H. Ubelaker, eds. *Disease and Demography in the Americas.* Washington, DC: Smithsonian Institution Press, 1992.

Williams, Robert A. *The American Indian in Western Legal Thought: The Discourses of Conquest.* New York: Oxford University Press, 1990.

Wright, Ronald. *Stolen Continents: The Americas Through Indian Eyes Since 1492.* Boston: Houghton Mifflin, 1992.

Wunder, John R. *"Retained by the People": A History of American Indians and the Bill of Rights.* New York: Oxford University Press, 1994.

African Americans

Ashmore, Harry S. *Hearts and Minds: The Anatomy of Racism from Roosevelt to Reagan.* New York: McGraw-Hill, 1982.

Baldwin, James. *Notes of a Native Son.* Boston: Beacon Press, 1955.

Belknap, Michael R. *Federal Law and Southern Order: Racial Violence and Constitutional Conflict in the Post-Brown South.* Athens: University of Georgia Press, 1987.

Bell, Derrick. *And We Are Not Saved: The Elusive Quest for Racial Justice.* New York: BasicBooks, 1987.

———. *Faces at the Bottom of the Well: The Permanence of Racism.* New York: BasicBooks, 1992.

Berger, Raoul. *The Fourteenth Amendment and the Bill of Rights.* Norman: University of Oklahoma Press, 1989.

Berry, Mary Frances. *Black Resistance, White Law: A History of Constitutional Racism in America.* New York: Alan Lane/Penguin Press, 1994.

Blauner, Bob. *Black Lives, White Lives: Three Decades of Race Relations in America.* Berkeley: University of California Press, 1989.

———. *Racial Oppression in America.* New York: Harper & Row, 1972.

Brink, William J., and Louis Harris. *Black and White: A Study of U.S. Racial Attitudes Today.* New York: Simon & Schuster, 1967.

Bunche, Ralph J. *The Political Status of the Negro in the Age of FDR.* Ed. Dewey W. Grantham. Chicago: University of Chicago Press, 1973.

Carnoy, Martin. *Faded Dreams: The Politics and Economics of Race in America.* New York: Cambridge University Press, 1994.

Carter, Stephen L. *Reflections of an Affirmative Action Baby*. New York: BasicBooks, 1991.

Cashman, Sean Dennis. *African-Americans and the Quest for Civil Rights, 1900–1990*. New York: New York University Press, 1991.

Dates, Jannette L., and William Barlow, eds. *Split Image: African Americans in the Mass Media*. Washington, DC: Howard University Press, 1990.

Dykstra, Robert R. *Bright Radical Star: Black Freedom and White Supremacy on the Hawkeye Frontier*. Cambridge, MA: Harvard University Press, 1993.

Eastland, Terry, and William J. Bennett. *Counting by Race: Equality from the Founding Fathers to Bakke*. New York: BasicBooks, 1979.

Ezekiel, Raphael S. *The Racist Mind: Portraits of Neo-Nazis and Klansmen*. New York: Viking, 1995.

Feagin, Joe R., and Melvin P. Sikes. *Living with Racism: The Black Middle-Class Experience*. Boston: Beacon Press, 1994.

Finkenstaedt, Rose L. H. *Face-to-Face: Blacks in America: White Perceptions and Black Realities*. New York: Morrow, 1994.

Franklin, John Hope. *Racial Equality in America*. Chicago: University of Chicago Press, 1976.

Frazier, E. Franklin. *Black Bourgeoisie*. Glencoe, IL: Free Press, 1957.

Frederickson, George M. *The Black Image in the White Mind: The Debate on Afro-American Character and Destiny, 1817–1914*. New York: Harper & Row, 1971.

Furnas, J. C. *Goodbye to Uncle Tom*. New York: William Sloane Associates, 1956.

Goldfield, David R. *Black, White, and Southern: Race Relations and Southern Culture, 1940 to the Present*. Baton Rouge: Louisiana State University Press, 1990.

Gordon, Lewis R. *Bad Faith and Antiblack Racism*. Atlantic Highlands, NJ: Humanities Press, 1995.

Gordon-Reed, Annette. *Thomas Jefferson and Sally Hemings*. Charlottesville: University Press of Virginia, 1997.

Gross, Samuel R., and Robert Mauro. *Death and Discrimination: Racial Disparities in Capital Sentencing*. Boston: Northeastern University Press, 1989.

Hacker, Andrew. *Two Nations: Black and White, Separate, Hostile, Unequal*. New York: Scribner's, 1992.

Harris, Trudier. *Exorcising Blackness: Historical and Literary Lynching and Burning Rituals*. Bloomington: Indiana University Press, 1984.

Higginbotham, A. Leon, Jr. *Shades of Freedom: Racial Politics and Presumptions of the American Legal Process*. New York: Oxford University Press, 1996.

Hill, Herbert, and James E. Jones, Jr., eds. *Race in America: The Struggle for Equality*. Madison: University of Wisconsin Press, 1993.

Hoberman, John. *Darwin's Athletes: How Sport Has Damaged Black America and Preserved the Myth of Race*. Boston: Houghton Mifflin, 1997.

Jacoway, Elizabeth, and David R. Colburn, eds. *Southern Businessmen and Desegregation*. Baton Rouge: Louisiana State University Press, 1982.

King, Desmond. *Separate but Unequal: Black Americans and the U.S. Federal Government*. New York: Oxford University Press, 1995.

Kull, Andrew. *The Color-Blind Constitution*. Cambridge, MA: Harvard University Press, 1992.

Lacy, Dan. *The White Use of Blacks in America*. New York: Atheneum, 1972.

Levine, Michael L. *African Americans and Civil Rights: From 1619 to the Present*. Phoenix, AZ: Oryx Press, 1996.

Lively, Donald E. *The Constitution and Race*. New York: Praeger, 1992.

Marable, Manning. *Beyond Black and White: Rethinking Race in American Politics and Society*. New York: Verso, 1995.

Martindale, Carolyn. *The White Press and Black America*. Westport, CT: Greenwood Press, 1986.

Middleton, Stpehen. *The Black Laws in the Old Northwest: A Documentary History*. Westport, CT: Greenwood Press, 1993.

Munford, Clarence J. *Race and Reparations: A Black Perspective for the 21st Century*. Trenton, NJ: Africa World Press, 1996.

Myrdal, Gunnar. *An American Dilemma: The Negro Problem and Modern Democracy*. New York: Harper & Brothers, 1944. 2 vols.

Newby, Idus A. *Jim Crow's Defense: Anti-Negro Thought in America, 1900–1930*. Baton Rouge: Louisiana State University Press, 1965.

Nolen, Claude H. *The Negro's Image in the South: The Anatomy of White Supremacy*. Lexington: University Press of Kentucky, 1967.

Pearson, Roger. *Race, Intelligence, and Bias in Academe*. Washington, DC: Scott-Townsend, 1991.

Rhines, Jesse Algernon. *Black Film, White Money*. New Brunswick, NJ: Rutgers University Press, 1996.

Shaprio, Herbert. *White Violence and Black Response: From Reconstruction to Montgomery*. Amherst: University of Massachusetts Press, 1988.

Snowden, Frank M., Jr. *Before Color Prejudice: The Ancient View of Blacks*. Cambridge, MA: Harvard University Press, 1983.

Swinney, Everette. *Suppressing the Ku Klux Klan: The Enforcement of the Reconstruction Amendments, 1870–1877*. New York: Garland, 1987.

Van Deburg, William L. *Slavery and Race in American Popular Culture*. Madison: University of Wisconsin Press, 1984.

Wade, Wyn Craig. *The Fiery Cross: The Ku Klux Klan in America*. New York: Simon & Schuster, 1987.

Washington, Joseph R., Jr. *Race and Religion in Mid-Nineteenth Century America, 1850–1877*. Lewiston, NY: Edwin Mellen Press, 1988. 2 vols.

Weisbrot, Robert. *Freedom Bound: A History of America's Civil Rights Movement*. New York: W. W. Norton, 1990.

Williams, Walter E. *The State Against Blacks*. New York: McGraw-Hill, 1982.

Williamson, Joel. *The Crucible of Race: Black/White Relations in the American South Since Emancipation*. New York: Oxford University Press, 1984.

Wilson, Midge, and Kathy Russell. *Divided Sisters: Bridging the Gap Between Black Women and White Women*. New York: Anchor, 1996.

Wilson, William Julius. *The Declining Significance of Race: Blacks and Changing American Institutions.* Chicago: University of Chicago Press, 1978.

Wood, Forrest G. *Black Scare: The Racist Response to Emancipation and Reconstruction.* Berkeley: University of California Press, 1968.

Woodward, C. Vann. *The Strange Career of Jim Crow.* 3rd ed. New York: Oxford University Press, 1974.

Jews

Buckley, William F., Jr. *In Search of Anti-Semitism.* New York: Continnum, 1992.

Carmichael, Joel. *The Satanizing of the Jews: Origin and Development of Mystical Anti-Semitism.* New York: Fromm International, 1992.

Dinnerstein, Leonard. *Antisemitism in America.* New York: Oxford University Press, 1994.

——. *Uneasy at Home: Antisemitism and the American Jewish Experience.* New York: Columbia University Press, 1987.

Dobkowski, Michael N. *The Tarnished Dream: The Basis of American Anti-Semitism.* Westport, CT: Greenwood Press, 1979.

Ferrarotti, Franco. *The Temptation to Forget: Racism, Anti-Semitism, Neo-Nazism.* Westport, CT: Greenwood Press, 1994.

Gould, Allan, ed. *What Did They Think of the Jews?* Northvale, NJ: Aronson, 1991.

Grosser, Paul E., and Edwin G. Halperin. *Anti-Semitism: Causes and Effects.* 2nd ed. New York: Philosophical Library, 1983.

Harrowitz, Nancy A., ed. *Tainted Greatness: Antisemitism and Cultural Heroes.* Philadelphia: Temple University Press, 1994.

Hertzberg, Arthur. *Being Jewish in America: The Modern Experience.* New York: Schocken, 1979.

Isaac, Jules. *The Teaching of Contempt: Christian Roots of Anti-Semitism.* Trans. Helen Weaver. New York: Holt, Rinehart & Winston, 1964.

Jaher, Frederic Cople. *A Scapegoat in the New Wilderness.* Cambridge, MA: Harvard University Press, 1994.

Katz, Jacob. *From Prejudice to Destruction: Anti-Semitism, 1700–1933.* Cambridge, MA: Harvard University Press, 1980.

Langmuir, Gavin I. *History, Religion, and Antisemitism.* Berkeley: University of California Press, 1990.

Levy, Richard S., ed. *Antisemitism in the Modern World: An Anthology of Texts.* Lexington, MA: D. C. Heath, 1991.

Lewis, Bernard. *Semites and Anti-Semites: An Inquiry into Conflict and Prejudice.* New York: W. W. Norton, 1986.

Lindemann, Albert S. *The Jew Accused: Three Anti-Semitic Affairs (Dreyfus, Beilis, Frank), 1894–1915.* Cambridge: Cambridge University Press, 1991.

Lipstadt, Deborah E. *Denying the Holocaust: The Growing Assault on Truth and Memory.* New York: Free Press, 1993.

Litvinoff, Barnet. *The Burning Bush: Anti-Semitism and World History.* New York: E. P. Dutton, 1988.

Mayo, Louise A. *The Ambivalent Image: Nineteenth-Century America's Perception of the Jew.* Rutherford, NJ: Fairleigh Dickinson University Press, 1988.

Nelson, Jack. *Terror in the Night: The Klan's Campaign Against the Jews.* New York: Simon & Schuster, 1993.

Prager, Dennis, and Joseph Telushkin. *Why the Jews? The Reason for Antisemitism.* New York: Simon & Schuster, 1983.

Quinley, Harold E., and Charles Y. Glock. *Anti-Semitism in America.* New York: Free Press, 1979.

Ribuffo, Leo. *The Old Christian Right: The Protestant Far Right from the Great Depression to the Cold War.* Philadelphia: Temple University Press, 1983.

Samuel, Maurice. *The Great Hatred.* New York: Knopf, 1940.

Segel, Binjamin W. *A Lie and a Libel: The History of the* Protocols of the Elders of Zion. Ed. and trans. Richard S. Levy. Lincoln: University of Nebraska Press, 1995.

Selznick, Gertrude J., and Stephen Steinberg. *The Tenacity of Prejudice: Anti-Semitism in Contemporary America.* New York: Harper & Row, 1969.

Stern, Kenneth S. *Holocaust Denial.* New York: American Jewish Committee, 1993.

Vidal-Nacquet, Pierre. *Assassins of Memory: Essays on the Denial of the Holocaust.* Trans. Jeffrey Nehlman. New York: Columbia University Press, 1992.

Weinberg, Meyer. *Because They Were Jews: A History of Antisemitism.* New York: Greenwood Press, 1986.

Asian Americans

Barringer, Herbert R.; Robert W. Gardner; and Michael J. Levin. *Asians and Pacific Islanders in the United States.* New York: Russell Sage Foundation, 1993.

Chang, Sucheng, ed. *Entry Denied: Exclusion and the Chinese Community in America, 1882–1943.* Philadelphia: Temple University Press, 1991.

Chen, Jack. *The Chinese of America.* San Francisco: Harper & Row, 1980.

Choy, Philip P.; Lorraine Dong; and Marlon K. Hom, eds. *Coming Man: 19th-Century American Perceptions of the Chinese.* Seattle: University of Washington Press, 1995.

Collins, Donald E. *Native American Aliens: Disloyalty and the Renunciation of Citizenship by Japanese Americans During World War II.* Westport, CT: Greenwood Press, 1985.

Daniels, Roger. *Asian America: Chinese and Japanese in the United States Since 1850.* Seattle: University of Washington Press, 1988.

———. *Concentration Camps USA: Japanese Americans and World War II.* New York: Holt, Rinehart & Winston, 1972.

———. *The Politics of Prejudice: The Anti-Japanese Movement in California and the Struggle for Japanese Exclusion.* Berkeley: University of California Press, 1972.

Dower, John W. *War Without Mercy: Race and Power in the Pacific War.* New York: Pantheon, 1986.

Drinnon, Richard. *Keeper of Concentration Camps: Dillon S. Myer and American Racism.* Berkeley: University of California Press, 1987.

Foner, Philip S, and Daniel Rosenberg, eds. *Racism, Dissent, and Asian Americans from 1850 to the Present: A Documentary History.* Westport, CT: Greenwood Press, 1993.

Hatamiya, Leslie T. *Righting a Wrong: Japanese Americans and the Passage of the Civil Liberties Act of 1988.* Stanford, CA: Stanford University Press, 1993.

Hing, Bill Ong. *Making and Remaking Asian America Through Immigration Policy, 1850–1990.* Stanford, CA: Stanford University Press, 1993.

Hohri, William Minoru. *Repairing America: An Account of the Movement for Japanese-American Redress.* Pullman: Washington State University Press, 1988.

Irons, Peter, ed. *Justice Delayed: The Record of the Japanese American Internment Cases.* Middletown, CT: Wesleyan University Press, 1988.

Kim, Hyung-Chan. *A Legal History of Asian Americans 1790–1990.* Westport, CT: Greenwood Press, 1994.

Knoll, Tricia. *Becoming Americans: Asian Sojourners, Immigrants, and Refugees in the Western United States.* Portland, OR: Coast to Coast Books, 1982.

Markus, Andrew. *Fear and Hatred: Purifying Australia and California, 1850–1901.* Sydney, Australia: Hale & Iremonger, 1979.

McClain, Charles J. *In Search of Equality: The Chinese Struggle Against Discrimination in Nineteenth-Century America.* Berkeley: University of California Press, 1994.

Okihiro, Gary Y. *Margins and Mainstreams: Asians in American History and Culture.* Seattle: University of Washington Press, 1994.

Sandmeyer, Elmer Clarence. *The Anti-Chinese Movement in California.* Urbana: University of Illinois Press, 1939.

Smith, Page. *Democracy on Trial: The Japanese-American Evacuation and Relocation in World War II.* New York: Simon & Schuster, 1995.

Takaki, Ronald. *Strangers from a Different Shore: A History of Asian Americans.* Boston: Little, Brown, 1989.

Wong, Eugene Franklin. *On Visual Media Racism: Asians in the American Motion Pictures.* New York: Arno Press, 1978.

Wu, Cheng-Tsu, ed. *"Chink!": A Documentary History of Anti-Chinese Prejudice in America.* New York: World Publishing Co., 1972.

Latinos

Browning, Harley L., and Rodolfo O. de la Garza, eds. *Mexican Immigrants and Mexican Americans: An Evolving Relation.* Austin: Center for Mexican American Studies, University of Texas, 1986.

Cockcroft, James D. *Outlaws in the Promised Land: Mexican Immigrant Workers and America's Future.* New York: Grove Press, 1986.

Gamio, Manuel. *Mexican Immigration to the United States: A Study of Human Migration and Adjustment.* Chicago: University of Chicago Press, 1930.

Garcia, Juan Ramon. *Operation Wetback: The Mass Deportation of Mexican Undocumented Workers in 1954.* Westport, CT: Greenwood Press, 1980.

Masud-Polito, Felix Roberto. *With Open Arms: Cuban Migration to the United States.* Totowa, NJ: Rowman & Littlefield, 1988.

Menchaca, Martha. *The Mexican Outsiders: A Community History of Marginalization and Discrimination in California.* Austin: University of Texas Press, 1995.

Monto, Alexander. *The Roots of Mexican Labor Migration.* Westport, CT: Praeger, 1994.

Rodriguez. Clara. *The Ethnic Queue in the U.S.: The Case of Puerto Ricans.* San Francisco: R & E Research Associates, 1974.

Senior, Clarence Ollson. *Strangers—Then Neighbors: From Pilgrims to Puerto Ricans.* New York: Freedom, 1961.

Urciuoli, Bonnie. *Exposing Prejudice: Puerto Rican Experiences of Language, Race, and Class.* Boulder, CO: Westview Press, 1996.

The Debate over Immigration

Beck, Roy. *The Case Against Immigration: The Moral, Economic, Social, and Environmental Reasons for Reducing U.S. Immigration Back to Traditional Levels.* New York: W. W. Norton, 1996.

Borjas, George L. *Friends or Strangers: The Impact of Immigrants on the U.S. Economy.* New York: BasicBooks, 1990.

Brimelow, Peter. *Alien Nation: Common Sense About America's Immigration Disaster.* New York: Random House, 1995.

Carlson, Robert A. *The Americanization Syndrome: A Quest for Conformity.* New York: St. Martin's Press, 1987.

Cose, Ellis. *A Nation of Strangers: Prejudice, Politics, and the Populating of America.* New York: Morrow, 1992.

Curran, Thomas J. *Xenophobia and Immigration 1820–1930.* Boston: Twayne, 1975.

Dinnerstein, Leonard. *Ethnic Americans: A History of Immigration.* New York: Harper & Row, 3rd ed., 1988.

Fitzgerald, Keith. *The Face of the Nation: Immigration, the State, and the National Identity.* Stanford, CA: Stanford University Press, 1996.

Hansen, Marcus Lee. *The Immigrant in American History.* Cambridge, MA: Harvard University Press, 1940.

Harwood, Edwin. *In Liberty's Shadow: Illegal Aliens and Immigration Law Enforcement.* Stanford, CA: Hoover Institution Press, 1986.

Higham, John. *Send These to Me: Jews and Other Immigrants in Urban America.* New York: Atheneum, 1975.

———. *Strangers in the Land: Patterns of American Nativism 1860–1925.* New Brunswick, NJ: Rutgers University Press, 1955.

Hull, Elizabeth. *Without Justice for All: The Constitutional Rights of Aliens.* Westport, CT: Greenwood Press, 1985.

Hutchinson, E. P. *Legislative History of American Immigration Policy, 1798–1965.* Philadelphia: Temple University Press, 1981.

Isbister, John. *The Immigration Debate: Remaking America.* West Hartford, CT: Kumarian Press, 1996.

Kraut, Alan M. *Silent Travelers: Germs, Genes, and the "Immigrant Menace."* New York: BasicBooks, 1994.

Maharidge, Dale. *The Coming White Minority: California's Eruptions and America's Future.* New York: Times Books, 1996.

Maidens, Melinda, ed. *Immigration: New Americans, Old Questions.* New York: Facts on File, 1981.

Mills, Nicolaus, ed. *Arguing Immigration: The Debate over the Changing Face of America.* New York: Simon & Schuster, 1994.

Neuman, Gerald L. *Strangers to the Constitution: Immigrants, Borders, and Fundamental Law.* Princeton, NJ: Princeton University Press, 1996.

Nugent, Walter T. K. *Crossing: The Great Transatlantic Migrations, 1870–1914.* Bloomington: Indiana University Press, 1992.

Perea, Juan F., ed. *Immigrants Out!: The New Nativism and the Anti-Immigrant Impulse in the United States.* New York: New York University Press, 1997.

Simon, Julian L. *The Economic Consequences of Immigration.* Oxford: Basil Blackwell, 1989.

Simon, Rita James. *Public Opinion and the Immigrant: Mass Media Coverage, 1880–1980.* Lexington, MA: Lexington Books/D. C. Heath, 1985.

Williamson, Chilton. *The Immigration Mystique: America's False Conscience.* New York: BasicBooks, 1996.

Yans-McLaughlin, Virginia, ed. *Immigration Reconsidered: History, Sociology, and Politics.* New York: Oxford University Press, 1990.

Acknowledgments

The editor and publisher are grateful to the following individuals and publishers for permission to reprint the following selections:

Dinesh D'Souza, *The End of Racism: Principles for a Multiracial Society,* © 1995 by Dinesh D'Souza. Reprinted by permission of The Free Press, a division of Simon & Schuster.

David Duke, "America at the Crossroads," http://www.duke.org/mission.htm, © 1997 by David Duke. Reprinted by permission of the author.

Arthur R. Jensen, "How Much Can We Boost IQ and Scholastic Achievement?" *Harvard Educational Review* 39, no. 1 (1969), © 1969 by the President and Fellows of Harvard College. Reprinted by permission of Harvard Educational Review.

Richard J. Herrnstein and Charles Murray, *The Bell Curve: Intelligence and Class Structure in American Life,* © 1994 by Richard J. Herrnstein and Charles Murray. Reprinted by permission of The Free Press, a division of Simon & Schuster.

"Is Quality of U.S. Population Declining?" *U.S. News & World Report* 59, no. 21 (November 22, 1965), © 1965 by U. S. News & World Report, Inc. Reprinted by permission of U.S. News & World Report.

"Public Record of George C. Wallace," *Congressional Quarterly Weekly Report* 26, no. 39 (September 27, 1968), © 1968 by Congressional Quarterly, Inc. Reprinted by permission of Congressional Quarterly.

Sgt. Stacey C. Koon, L.A.P.D., with Robert Deitz, *Presumed Guilty: The Tragedy of the Rodney King Affair,* © 1992 by Stacey C. Koon. Reprinted by special permission of Regnery Publishing, Inc., Washington, D.C.

Alan M. Dershowitz, *Reasonable Doubts: The O. J. Simpson Case and the Criminal Justice System,* © 1996 by Alan Dershowitz. Reprinted by permission of Simon & Schuster.

Bradley R. Smith, "The Holocaust Controversy: The Case for Open Debate," http://www.codoh.com, © 1991 by Bradley R. Smith. Reprinted by permission of the author.

An Intelligence Officer, "The Japanese in America: The Problem and the Solution," *Harper's Magazine* 185, no. 5 (October 1942), © 1942 by Harper & Brothers. Reprinted by special permission.

Deval L. Patrick, "The Rise in Hate Crime," *Vital Speeches of the Day* 61, no. 1 (October 15, 1994), © 1994 by City News Publishing Co., Inc. Reprinted by permission of the author.

Juan Gonzalez, *Roll Down Your Window: Stories of a Forgotten America,* © 1995 by Juan Gonzalez. Reprinted by permission of Verso.

Chang-Lin Tien, "America's Scapegoats," *Newsweek,* October 31, 1994, © 1994 by Newsweek, Inc. Reprinted by permission of Newsweek.

Index